AN INDIAN RURAL ECONOMY
1880–1955

The Tamilnad Countryside

AN INDIAN RURAL ECONOMY
1880–1955

The Tamilnad Countryside

CHRISTOPHER JOHN BAKER

CLARENDON PRESS · OXFORD
1984

Oxford University Press, Walton Street, Oxford OX2 6DP

London New York Toronto
Delhi Bombay Calcutta Madras Karachi
Kuala Lumpur Singapore Hong Kong Tokyo
Nairobi Dar es Salaam Cape Town
Melbourne Auckland

and associated companies in
Beirut Berlin Ibadan Mexico City Nicosia

Oxford is a trade mark of Oxford University Press

Published in the United States
by Oxford University Press, New York

British Library Cataloguing in Publication Data

Baker, Christopher John
An Indian rural economy 1880–1955
1. Tamil Nadu (State)—Economic conditions
—History
I. Title
330. 954'82   HC437. T/
ISBN 0–19–821572–X

Filmset by Sri Aurobindo Ashram Press, Pondicherry
Printed by All India Press, Pondicherry, India
Bound at the University Press, Oxford

For Tiew

Preface

Books need time and friends. Most of the important research for this one was carried out in Madras during trips in 1974–5, 1976 and 1977–8. I am particularly grateful to the staff and several commissioners (especially Chaturvedi Badrinath) at the Tamilnadu Archives, and to the librarians and assistants at the Madras University library, Madras Secretariat library, Marimalai Adigal library and Connemara library. I also thank the staffs of the National Archives, Sapru House, and Nehru Memorial Museum in Delhi; the university, economics, history, anthropology, geography, applied biology and South Asian studies libraries in Cambridge; Mary Thatcher at the Cambridge South Asian Archive; and the libraries of SOAS, the Indian High Commission, the Indian Institute in Oxford, and the University of Birmingham. I owe a special debt to Mr Aditya Nehru and Sandoz (India) agrochemicals division, especially Messrs Krishnamurthy, Ramamurthi, Shetty, Kumar, Tyagarajan and Rajaram; and would like to apologize to all those disturbed by the arrival of the 'anglaikaran-chinikatchi' in the baggage train of their friendly neighbourhood pesticide salesman. Mr P. Sunderraj provided an insider's account of Coimbatore's textile industry. My thanks also to OUP editorial and production staff in both Oxford and India. It is entirely appropriate that a book, among whose major themes is the rural dominance over the urban economy, should have been delayed in production by a drought in the region with which it deals.

The research was carried out while I held posts at the South Asian Studies Centre and Queen's College, Cambridge, and it could not have happened without a generous project grant from the Social Science Research Council. Never had patrons such a grateful client. For all sorts of encouragement and assistance I must thank Jack

Gallagher, Eric Stokes, Ben Farmer, the indispensable Mrs Brown, John and Barbara Harriss, Sudhir Wanmali, Norman Reynolds, Susan Kaufmann, Sunanda Sen, Robi and Ruchira Chatterji, Raj Chandarvarkar, Pamela Price, Susan Lewandowski, Debbie Swallow, Arup Banerji, David and Kathleen Ludden, Pat and Geoffrey of Nayland Secretarial Services, Polly Hill, Chris Bayly, Tom Tomlinson, Anil Seal and David Washbrook. None of it was their fault. From now on I shall stick to haikus.

Contents

Notes, Abbreviations, Conventions

Government Files

Unless specifically indicated otherwise, all citations of official files refer to the records of the Government of Madras held in the Tamilnadu Archives, Madras. References come in the form:

Department (or Proceedings)   File number   Date

The departments and proceedings are abbreviated as follows:

BP	Proceedings of the Board of Revenue
CoW	Proceedings of the Court of Wards
Dvt	Development Department
Home	Home Department
Jud	Judicial Department
LSG	Local Self Government Department
Pub	Public Department
PWL	Public Works and Labour Department
Rev	Revenue Department

Occasionally the references contain a subsidiary indication of, say, a sub-department. For instance, many of the PWL file numbers have a suffix '-I' of '-L', which indicate the Irrigation and Labour sub-departments respectively; and many of the wartime files have suffixes '(S)' or '(M)' which indicate they emanated from the sections of the secretariat which were hived off to Salem and Madurai respectively when Madras was threatened with attack. '(C)' indicates a confidential file. Generally speaking, these subsidiary indications are not important in locating a file, and I have omitted many subsidiary indications such as 'Ms' (= miscellaneous).

Other abbreviations in references

Authorities
  GB   Great Britain
  GOI   Government of India
  GOM   Government of Madras

Journals

  IESHR   *Indian Economic and Social History Review*
  IJE   *Indian Journal of Economics*
  JAS   *Journal of Asian Studies*
  JIH   *Journal of Indian History*
  JMGA   *Journal of the Madras Geographical Association*
  MAJ   *Madras Agricultural Journal*

Miscellaneous

  AERC   Agricultural Economics Research Centre, Univer-
             sity of Madras. References in the form 'AERC (30)
             Kaliyanapuram' refer to the series of village sur-
             veys conducted in the 1950s and 1960s.
  IIC Evidence III   *Minutes of Evidence taken before the Indian
             Industrial Commission 1916–1918. Volume III,
             Madras and Bangalore* (London, 1919)
  MELAC   *Report of the Madras Estates Land Act Committee*
             (Madras, 1938), various volumes (see bibliography).
  MPBC   *Madras Provincial Banking Enquiry Committee*
             (Madras, 1931), various volumes (see bibliography).
  SAS Archive   Collections of private papers held in the archive
             of the Centre of South Asian Studies, Cambridge.

Statistics

Figures drawn from standard statistical sources are not allotted
individual references. Unless otherwise indicated, data on population, trade and cropping come from the following sources:

  Data on population come from the Madras volumes of the *Census
  of India* from 1891 to 1961.
  Data on overseas trade come from the *Annual Statement of the
  Sea-Borne Trade and Navigation of British India* and the *Annual
  Statement of the Sea-Borne Trade and Navigation of the Madras
  Presidency.*

Data on land-use and cropping come from *Season and Crop Report of the Madras Presidency* and *Agricultural Statistics of British India*.

Tamil and place names

I have not tried to transliterate Tamil words. Those who know the language will have no difficulty identifying the original and those who do not need not be bamboozled by odd typography. For many place names there is no standard English rendering, and I have used a fairly arbitrary selection from the options available. For instance, the river sometimes written as Cauvery or Cauveri here appears as Kaveri, and among the towns and districts the forms I have chosen are Madurai (rather than Madura), Ramnad (Ramanathapuram), Tanjavur (Thanjavur, Tanjore), Tiruchi (Tiruchiripalli, Trichino-poly, Trichy), and Tirunelveli (Tinnevelly).

Miscellaneous

I have not used italics for those Indian words which are either so commonly used that they have been 'naturalized' within the subject (for instance, inam, mirasidar), or which appear so regularly in this book that the effect would be ugly (for instance, pannaiyal). The glossary does not include several Indian words which are used only once in the text and are explained adequately at that appearance.

Glossary

adumayal	slave, serf, labourer
amaram;	
amaranayak	a grant of land or discount of revenue in return for military service (lit., command of a thousand foot); holder of such a grant
amin	judicial clerk or process-server
amman	goddess
angavastram	upper cloth
anicut	dam
beedi	cheap cheroot
benami	an agent, often meaning an agent used for subterfuge
bhakti	devotional Hinduism
brahmadeya	a grant to Brahmins, especially a village settled on Brahmans
bund	bank, especially surrounding a field or reservoir
cadjan	a leaf traditionally used for writing on
candashara	form of military peonage
cheri	labourers' quarter in a village
chit	note or ticket
cholam	sorghum, jowar
crore	ten million
cumbu	bullrush or spiked millet, bajra
dacoit	bandit, in law one of a band of more than five persons
darkhast	contract or petition, word used in south Indian revenue terminology for the initial grant of the deeds for a piece of land
dewan	agent, minister, manager
dhoti	lower cloth
hundi	credit note, bill of exchange
inam	grant of land with total or partial discount of revenue, usually in return for some form of service

jaghir; jaghirdar	a military land grant; holder of such a grant
jajmani	north Indian term to describe local patron-client relations
jamabandi	annual settlement of village revenue accounts
kandu	hand-loan
kaniyatchi;	
kaniyatchidar	land control; land controller, particularly in valley tracts (a status conventionally referred to as mirasidar in the British period)
kapa	the boll of the cotton plant
karai	share, particularly in joint property
karnam	village accountant
karunganni	genus of cotton plant
kattubadi	fixed rent on lands granted to public servants, term used to describe land grants associated with military service
kaval; kavalgar	watch and ward, guardianship; a guard or protector
kist	land revenue payment
kottai	fort
kudimaramat	repair of irrigation works by their beneficiaries
lakh	hundred thousand
lungi	fancy lower cloth
maniam	allotment or inam
math, mutt	Hindu monastic institution
maund	measure of weight, usually reckoned as 82.28 lbs
mirasi; mirasidar	customary rights, particularly in land; a customary, privileged landholder, the conventional word in the British period for *kaniyatchidar*
mitta; mittadar	estate created in early nineteenth century; holder of such an estate
mofussil	upcountry
munsiff	subordinate magistrate, sometimes loosely used to refer to village headman
nad, nadu	territory, state
nadappu	current (rate of interest)
nanja	wet land
nayak	leader, general, Vijayanagar viceroy
nellu mandi	rice market
nidhi	mutual savings and loan bank (lit: treasure)
nirganti	village irrigation overseer
oppandam	compact, contract, association
padiyal	hired servant, roughly equivalent to pannaiyal
palaiyam	camp, military land grant

palaiyagar	holder of *palaiyam*, local military chieftain
panchayat	local court of arbitration or council of administration
pangu	share, particularly in wet land
pannai; pannaiyal	form of tied labour, especially in wet cultivation (lit: a field); tied labourer
parakudi, porakudi	'outsider' tenant
patta; pattadar	land deed; holder of land deed, especially under ryotwari revenue system
pattagar	hereditary title of leading families of the Gounder community
peshkash, peishcush	land revenue paid by a zamindar
pettai	market
poligar	conventional form of *palaiyagar*
poramboke	uncultivated common land in village including roads, house plots etc.
ragi	a dry grain (*eleusine coracana*)
ryot, raiyat	cultivator
ryotwari	land-revenue system based on principle of direct collection from each cultivator
samai	low grade of dry grain (*panicum miliare*)
sandai	local occasional market
shandy	conventional form of *sandai*
sivoijama	ancillary revenue charge, especially a charge for temporary occupation of land
sowcar, sahukar	banker, moneylender
taccavi	government loan
tahsildar	lowest rank of executive officer in the revenue department in the districts
talaiyari	village watchman
taluk	administrative subdivision of a district
tharagu mandi	brokerage market
thottam	a 'garden' or plot watered by a well
toddy	country liquor
tuppukuli	stealing and ransoming cattle
ulkudi	'insider' tenant
vakil	agent, especially a legal representative
varam	same as waram
waram; waramdar	share, share-cropping; share-cropper
zamin; zamindar; zamindari	an estate; holder of an estate, particularly under the Permanent Settlement of 1801; the Permanent Settlement system

Maps, Tables, Graphs

MAPS

TABLES

GRAPHS

Introduction

Over the past two decades economists, geographers and anthropologists have rediscovered the past. Historical geography is no longer curious but respectable; the resurgence of political economy has despatched economists into the archives; the demise of structural-functionalism has persuaded anthropologists that time matters. For historians this trend has provided stimulation and confusion. On the one hand, there has been a good deal of grumpy irredentism. Historians find that the tourists from the social sciences often seem rather careless in their looting of source material, daring in their faith in old statistics, flighty in the way they leap from historical narrative to analytic conclusions. Yet on the other hand there is a feeling that in their flashes of theoretical elegance, cybernetic wizardry, and philosophical speculation they have indicated some interesting exits from the prison-house of idealist historiography, the problem of 'intention', and the narrative method. This book is a result of both this stimulation and this confusion.

It is aimed at that part of the academic landscape where the interests of economists, geographers, historians, and other social scientists converge on the question of economic change in non-western societies. The specific field of enquiry is India's agrarian history, and it is a field which has been only very patchily cultivated. There are in fact just two areas which have been treated pretty intensively. The first consists of the several studies whose basic source materials are the British rulers' early attempts to understand rural India so that they might tax it and control it. The second is the ever-mounting literature on contemporary India's agrarian development, out of which some narrow statistical paths have been cut into the recent past. Between these two areas of work lies almost a century of virtually fallow territory. Students of this intervening period of India's economic history have, with some notable exceptions, tended to concentrate on the towns (and in particular on heavy industry) rather than the countryside. This is quite understandable; the massive expansion of the urban population, the growth of the big business houses, the colonial rulers' attempts to juggle imperial and local interests, the maverick potential of a new urban working class—such subjects have been rightly alluring. The countryside has been stuck in a curious historical limbo.

Moreover the two existing areas of study differ enormously in aim and method. The studies of the early and mid nineteenth century have dwelt chiefly on questions of tenure—the British land settlements with their tax demands, legal apparatuses and notions of property; the legacy of Baden-Powell has proved difficult to ignore. The development economists' probings into the recent past, meanwhile, have concentrated on agricultural production—particularly the stagnation or decline in per capita agricultural output. One curious result of this wide difference in aims and methods is that the intervening period is often subjected to feats of historical imagination which are designed to build a bridge across the gap betwen the two periods and two types of study; there are many attempts to locate the origins of agricultural decline in the impact of the British and their tenurial notions. In this historiography, various creations of the colonial regime have been identified as the agent of decline—the parasitic landlord, the rich peasant, the moneylender, the public works engineer, the finance member, the Lancashire M.P. The results have often been curious, not least because such studies often set off to answer the question of why something has *not* happened: that is, why the Indian economy did not develop and industrialize. There is, of course, an infinite range of possible answers to a question posed in this way.

This book is hurled with some trepidation into the gap between the elaboration of the colonial system on the one hand and the early years of independence and 'development' on the other. It tries to explain how things became as they did, not why they did not become something else. It traces the history of the countryside in Tamilnad, the south-eastern corner of peninsular India, from roughly the 1880s to the early 1950s by examining how labour was utilized on the land, how agrarian trade was organized, how internal and external trade were connected, how the market for capital functioned, what were the links between countryside and town, and what was the role played by the state in rural society and economy. Although the study is limited to a single region of India, it should not be thought that it qualifies as a 'micro' study. In 1950 Tamilnad covered some 48,500 square miles and contained a population of some 29 million. At that time only one country (or colonial territory) in Africa or Latin America—Brazil—could boast a larger population, and only ten other countries in the rest of the world.[1] Tamilnad today has a fertile and rapidly developing agriculture, side by side with an immense amount of rural poverty; and a large number of towns and cities which house a rather torpid urban economy. This book looks at the recent historical background of such a region.

The urban student is never very happy in the countryside. The wide open spaces and distant horizons of India's agrarian history have induced some tremulous and nervous reactions. The strangeness of the environment, the uncertainty over method, and the sparse state of historical research have conspired to create a peculiarly volatile academic milieu. In attempts to impose some sort of order on this arcane and complex environment, explanatory devices have been imported from all over the academic world—middle peasants, family farms, kulaks, involuted agricultures, peripheral capitalisms, semi-feudalisms, post-peasantries. Many of these imports have not acclimatized very well. In the last decade, studies of the countryside in the non-western world have thrown up three very distinct approaches. The first has attempted to understand the society and economy of the countryside through a model of the working of the individual farm. Works of this kind have multiplied since the translation and reinterpretation of Chayanov's work on early twentieth-century rural Russia.[2] In these studies the family farm plays an explanatory role remarkably like that of the Marshallian firm in marginalist economics; the farm-firm is isolated both from other parts of society and (with the help of notions of cyclical self-equilibration) from time. The second approach builds outwards from a similar view of the individual farm towards an interpretation of the cognitive universe of the peasant.[3] Such studies draw heavily on games theory and Parsonian social science in order to construct a model of what the farmer

wants and how he tries to get what he wants. Such studies deploy
behavioural evidence to adduce the subjective notions of morality,
justice, and rationality of the individual peasant, and then use
those notions to explain the behaviour. Most historians are left
quite speechless. Both these approaches seem difficult to accept
and impossible to apply. Any attempt to work out the logic of the
peasant's mental universe or his household economics must involve
an enormous amount of presumption. Moreover any attempt to
use such logic to explain the course of history makes the mistake of
ripping the peasant out of his political and economic environment
and making him the autonomous arbiter of his own fate. But
peasantries are, at best, only 'part-societies' and cannot really be
understood in isolation from the political context, demographic
pressures, marketing systems, and other social classes which hem
them in on all sides.[4] The third approach to the study of rural
society has emerged from under the creeping groundcover of the
dependency literature, and attempts by contrast to understand how
the political and economic environment of the extra-European
rustic has been altered out of all recognition in the past two
centuries. This study is aligned rather cantankerously with this
latter approach.

Theories of underdevelopment and dependency[5] have penetrated the Indian historiography more slowly than the parallel
historiographies of Latin America and Africa. There may be many
reasons for this. Indianists have formal colonialism to deal with;
they are heavily weighed down by source documents; they tend to
be too attached to old post-colonial delusions, Marxist theologies
or empiricist dogmas. Yet it is clear that it is no longer possible to
wall off the 'local study' from the outside world. The fundamental
proposition of the sprawling mass of dependency writings—namely
that the connections forged between the west and the rest, particularly over the last two centuries, have moulded the societies and
histories of non-western regions in a *structural* fashion—is now
undeniable; Latin American economists, French anthropologists
working in Africa, Marxist theoreticians in India, and an enthusiastic audience in various parts of the globe have made sure of
that.

Over the last decade there has been a number of largely
sympathetic criticisms levelled at the theories and approaches of
dependency writing. The first and most general set of criticisms

pointed out that a theory which argued that the active under-development of much of the non-western world has been merely the reverse side of the growth of the west seemed mechanical and depressingly irreversible. The second and slightly more specific set of criticisms pointed out that dependency writing had a tendency to colonize its subject matter. Often the only 'moving part' of the argument seemed to be the intrusive power of the west, sometimes reduced to the single concept of 'capitalism'. The description of the way in which the economic system based in the west invaded, hobbled, and reshaped non-European societies seemingly left little space for any appreciation of the specific character of the sub-jected society, or for any concession to the impetus of the sub-jected society's own history. The third and more theoretical set of criticisms concerned the precise mechanism which tipped the see-saw of development and underdevelopment. Some writers appeared to rely on visible levers of subjection which they found in colonial policies, latifundia and plantation economies, the tech-niques of multinational enterprise, the strategies of international organizations and aid-giving agencies. Others meanwhile made a direct appeal to historically based structures of dependence which resulted in an international division of labour; the world had become a unified marketplace which allotted roles to different regions just as the marketplace of the classical political economists allotted roles to different classes. Following on from this there have been a number of debates among Marxists about the theoretical respectability of many of the devices which have been used to explain dependency. In particular they have criticized much of the dependency writing for relying heavily on the explanatory power of unequal relations of exchange—how in effect the advanced nations skimmed off the economic surplus on a world scale—and for thus placing 'exchange' analytically prior to 'production' in a most un-Marxist fashion.

The attempt to add some theoretical rigour to the intuitive propositions about dependency opened up the way for a meeting between dependency writers, post-Althusserians interested in using the concept of a 'mode of production' to fill out the rather scant Marxist texts on pre-industrial societies, and students of non-European agrarian societies who wanted to escape from the Chayanovian equilibrium trap. All were interested in finding a way to characterize and explain the perverse mixture of change and decay which marked so many of the agrarian economies of the non-western world. In this context, a peripheral exchange of views over the meaning of certain Indian official survey data exploded into a fiercely contested debate about the mode of production in Indian agriculture in the post-colonial era.[6] The debate unfolded through the early and mid 1970s in parallel (and often in inter-relation) with an energetic *marxisant* literature about the history of rural societies in various parts of the world.[7] These writings have thrown up a number of important issues.

The Indian mode-of-production debate began with disputes over the interpretation of certain empirical data on Indian farming, progressed quickly to the question of whether Indian agriculture enjoyed a capitalist, feudal, semi-feudal, or colonial mode of production, and dissolved in a series of unresolved problems over what defined a mode of production in the first place. Despite its inconclusive result, the debate did raise important questions about approaches to the study of agrarian societies, and it did help to expose many of the difficulties which are shared by all those who use the writings of Marx, Lenin, and Kautsky on the peasantry as aids to interpretation of the recent rural history of the non-western world.

The participants in the Indian debate, and many of the writers in the parallel literature on other agrarian histories, proceeded by a similar sort of method, based largely on Lenin's study of Russian farming[8] and Kautsky's study of German farming[9] in the late nineteenth century. They looked for social and economic differentiation, the rise of wage labour, capital accumulation, and technological advance, as evidence that capitalism was taking over in agriculture. They concluded that capitalism and capitalists were certainly present, often in quite advanced forms, but that much of the finance, labour, and other resources used in agriculture was still being marshalled and deployed in ways which belied the aims of capitalist accumulation; as a result there seemed to be no sign that a dynamic transformation of the economy was imminent. This peculiar mixture of capitalist and pre-capitalist features created a 'theoretical' problem. It was argued that if elements of capitalism were present, then capitalism must soon sweep away all the detritus of more primitive forms of economic organization into the dustbin of agrarian history; yet this did not seem to be happening. The contributors to the mode-of-production debate were in general agreement about the evidence on the current circumstances and conditions of Indian agriculture; but they differed radically in the ways that they chose to characterize the peculiar mixture of advanced and backward elements, and to explain the 'blocked', 'transitional', or 'underdeveloped' state of Indian agriculture. One set of explanations relied on singling out a particular class of people who could be held responsible for maintaining the current, curious state of Indian agriculture for their own personal benefit; they pointed to established landlords able to exact an ever higher ground-rent, moneylenders able to extract an ever higher revenue from usury, merchants able to profit from selling goods produced by cheap peasant labour, or some beings who combined some or all of these attributes. Other arguments suggested that as capitalism had intruded into Indian agriculture from abroad, rather than being generated locally, it had not the same impetus to transform the existing local society and indeed often found it profitable to exploit the existing system more or less as it was found. A variety of terms were found to describe this state of affairs—the articulation of modes of production, the stage of 'formal' rather than 'real' subsumption under capitalism, 'conservation-dissolution', the 'blocked transition'.

There were several assumptions which were held by all the participants in the debate, and it is these common attitudes rather than their manifold differences which are of most interest. First, they shared a very similar and chronologically shallow view of India's history. They tended to accept that the combination of capitalist and pre-capitalist features in Indian agriculture was the achievement of the later years of the colonial period (although subsequently Jairus Banaji has pushed that event back to the early colonial period),[10] and that it was essentially the demands of colonial trade which expanded commodity production to a significant level, increased wage labour, differentiated the peasantry, and froze certain pre-capitalist economical and social forms. The situation which preceded the impact of colonial trade was presumed to be either self-evident or else unimportant. Now it is true that the debaters might not have got a lot of help in filling out their view of India's economic history even if they had sought long and hard in the historical literature, and thus it is not surprising that they resorted to theoretical works rather than empirical evidence to explain the evolution of Indian agriculture. However the point

is that the Marxist texts which have provided most of the theoretical underpinning for the mode-of-production debate and for
parallel writing on other agrarian economies suffer from the same
sort of chronological shallowness. Kautsky and Lenin both focused
specifically on the late nineteenth century, with Lenin explicitly
beginning at the emancipation of the serfs. The references which
Kautsky, Lenin, and the recent writers make to Marx himself
generally cite those parts of *Capital* which deal with the transition
to a capitalist society and economy.[11] In these writings (particularly Lenin) the references to the state of affairs before capitalism began to take root are sparse and vague. There is some
mention of a 'natural economy', and some of the 'feudal mode'.
The relationship between these two is never carefully specified.
We are left with a hazy picture of a simple agriculture practised by
roughly equal farmers with only a limited development of markets
and perhaps an over-arching structure of aristocratic control.

There are two points to be made here. The first is that the
difficulty which dependency writing had in accommodating any
view of the importance of the motive force of the dependent
society's own history is in fact corroborated in much of the
'peasant' and 'mode-of-production' writing by the readiness to
allot the only motive role to capitalism or colonialism. Moreover
this perspective finds assurance in the texts which are used as the
major source of vocabulary and theory. The past is reduced to a
conceptual fog in which loom some dark and amorphous shapes;
these shapes only take on more substantial and more definite form
by dint of their subsequent history, by vitrue of 'change'. The
second point is that despite the conceptual vagueness of some of
these analytic terms applied to the pre-capitalist past, writers on
Africa and Latin America have still found it useful to domesticate
and deploy them, yet this may be much more difficult in Asia. The
idea of a 'natural economy' has been transported to pre-colonial
Africa;[12] the idea of a 'feudal mode' finds enough resonance in
Latin American history to have provoked a debate which accepts
the descriptive utility of the term even if it involves disagreement
over its historical relevance.[13] In south Asia pre-colonial history
would seem to be too important, too *strong* to be ignored, and too
esoteric to be fitted into the bland descriptions of a 'natural
economy' or a 'feudal mode'. The long history of internal and
external trade, wage labour, and complex agrarian hierarchies

would seem to make any concept of a 'natural economy' misleading; while the existence of powerful state systems has long led
to doubts about the usefulness of the notion of feudalism. We shall
return to this point below.

A second problem in the recent literature is also immanent in
the works by Lenin and Kautsky. How far does the pattern of
capitalist transformation in agriculture as envisaged by Lenin and
Kautsky assume the existence of a considerable surplus, potentially or actually realized? Certainly the transformation of rural
society in late nineteenth-century Europe was accompanied by
considerable rises in productivity both per unit of labour and per
unit of land. The Kautsky-Lenin models of accumulation and
differentiation seem to rest on the notion that there is a considerable surplus and that it can be expanded. In Europe investment in
machinery did pay dividends, and labour could be despatched
from the land without loss of productive capacity. How far may we
transport these assumptions into the non-European world and
particularly into the highly developed agricultural system of India?
Certainly the size of farms and volume of produce which Lenin
cites from the *zemstvo* data are much larger than those in existence
in most parts of the non-western world by the early twentieth
century.

The third problem arises from the way in which the mode-of-
production debaters sought a mode of production *in agriculture*.
Marx himself was far from consistent in the use he made of the
term mode of production, but most commonly deployed it to
describe the stage of development of a whole society rather than
the techniques employed in a single sector. Yet the Indian debate
confined itself to agriculture, and within agriculture to the performance of certain factor markets—notably land, labour, and
credit. Among the many important elements which were thereby
thrust aside were the role of the urban side of the economy, and
the aims and activities of the state. Lenin and Kautsky both argued
that the towns were the source from which capitalism penetrated
into agriculture (though there is some confusion in both works on
the question of whether capitalism did or could develop unaided
within agriculture).The modern literature has substituted colonialism or world capitalism in this role and thus managed to push
the problem off to a respectable distance. On the matter of the
state, both Lenin and Kautsky were pretty reticent in their major

works on the agrarian transition. Yet in his (admittedly imprecise) writings on pre-capitalist modes of production, Marx attributed a very powerful role to political institutions, both in creating and maintaining classes and class relations, and in stimulating the transition from one mode to another.[14] Marx counted warfare and other forms of state aggrandizement among the most important motors of early history, and the bulk of mainstream historiography would seem to agree with him.

These three elements have been hoisted out of the mode-of-production debate because they illustrate one theme—the extent to which the writers in the debate share a view that India's history was either subsumed by colonialism, or was sufficiently similar to that of late nineteenth-century eastern Europe that the assumptions in analyses of that history can safely be translated into the Indian climate. It seems hardly surprising that one of the participants (Jairus Banaji), while joining energetically in the debate, seemed from the very beginning to have been trying to destroy the whole platform on which it was mounted; and has since himself retreated into historical research.[15] This book hopes to contribute to the understanding of Indian agriculture through some empirical research into the history of one agrarian region. The difficulties encountered in the recent debate suggest that it is necessary to pay more attention to the character of agriculture and rural society in pre-colonial times, to look in detail at social and institutional changes during the colonial period, and to attempt an understanding of the logic and impetus of the agrarian economy which the colonial rulers left behind. Such an enterprise should not be mistaken for a weird attempt to exculpate colonialism or to reintroduce some idea of the original sin of poverty. To prevent too much misunderstanding of the heavily empirical matter which follows, it might be useful to offer briefly in advance some of the tentative suggestions which emerged from the research and which have shaped the form of the book. These suggestions concern the nature of pre-colonial society, social change in the colonial period, and the relationship of state and agriculture in the aftermath.

India's pre-colonial history tends to suffer from the same fate as once did Europe's Dark Ages; it is too easy to smother and excuse our ignorance of the period by arguing that its history was torpid and changeless. Yet the literature on early and medieval south India, however sparse, conveys a picture of a rather breathless history of political and social change, with occasional glimpses of more arcane but no less energetic processes of economic transformation. There were elaborate state systems, overseas trading, flourishing networks of internal markets, as far back as the sources penetrate. Moreover, there appears to have been a substantial change, roughly in what would be called the early modern period in European terms, which was associated with Marx's favourite precapitalist dynamic — warfare. The result was that in the three to five hundred years which preceded the colonial intrusion, south Indian society developed in a special way. This was not 'the Asiatic mode' with a strong centralized state controlling irrigation works on the one hand, and isolated villages content in the sleep of ages on the other. Yet the relationship of state and rural society was very different to that which prevailed in Europe and it had very different consequences for the development of agriculture and rural society. The state was powerful but it was not centralized. There have been various attempts to analyse and label (with terms like 'segmentary state', 'galactic polity')[16] the dispersed state systems which prevailed in many regions of Asia in the pre-colonial period. Though the examples, and the characterizations, differ enormously in detail and emphasis, they concur in many general respects. The authority of the state was scattered through at least two levels of political management. At the top was the monarch (king, emperor) and below that a stratum of secondary authorities (provincial nobles, feudatories, upper gentry, princes, regional chiefs, warlords). There was no real concept of exclusive sovereignty, and monarchs and secondary authorities corroborated one another's position and shared in one another's power in a way which was radically different from the more antagonistic relationship of king and nobility in pre-modern Europe. The extent of this co-operation was probably especially marked in southern India because of the need to resist Muslim invaders.[17] From the later medieval period onwards, the state authorities conspired to push forward the frontiers of the agrarian economy in order to provide the resources required for warfare—namely food and other produce on the one hand, and manpower on the other. They encouraged more intensive use of established agricultural regions, and also urged colonization in new areas. Both intensification and extension entailed some state investment in irrigation. The effect of the pressure was to multiply the numbers of small-scale farmers, and to develop to a sophisticated level the practice of small-scale agriculture based on labour-intensive production with multiple strains of crops, intensive patterns of mixed and multiple-cropping, careful use of irrigation water, and extensive coercion of available labour. Commerce developed alongside the agrarian economy but along special lines. First there was a network of local exchange necessary to provision a complex agriculture. Secondly there were networks of trade, transport and finance involved in the conversion of agricultural surplus into the resources required by the state. Thirdly there was a growth of overseas trade which was looked on as an additional source of revenue and a necessary device for acquiring many strategic materials. This was not a society of lord, vassal, and weak kingship within which the free peasant, the free merchant, and absolutist royalty could emerge as the agents of transformation. Rather there was a powerful though dispersed state system, a mass of basically unfree rural labourers, and a commercial system which was not directly controlled by the state but which served a society in which the state played a powerful role.[18] As Pierre-Philippe Rey has argued, the experience of colonialism is not the only, nor perhaps even the major, thing which differentiates between the histories of the west on the one hand and the rest on the other.[19] There were good analytical and empirical reasons which led Marx to thrash around in search of an Asiatic mode of production, even if his findings were a bit threadbare. Colonial history did not appear in a vacuum but was predicated on what had gone before.

The developments of the pre-colonial period imposed many conditions and constraints on later history. The colonial regime, at least in its early stages, fitted snugly into the mould formed by its predecessors, and with a similar end of military strength in view continued to push forward the economy of small-scale agriculture.[20] The expansion in the scale of agrarian marketing, and the opportunities and dangers offered by the growing connection to international markets, tended to widen the gap between those capable of taking advantage of the market on the one hand, and those denied access or treated badly by the wheels of commercial fortune on the other. It has been unsurprisingly tempting to apply Lenin's model of differentiation to this period in south India and in other parts of the sub-continent. Kulaks, rich peasants, local bosses, and various other synonyms have been appearing in the literature for some time, and the inevitable reaction to their appearance is now well advanced. In southern India, these entre- preneurial farmers were very visible and are not just a product of imaginative theory; they did make profits and sink them in con- sumption, trade, and reinvestment. Yet the numbers of these 'rich peasants', and the scale of their operations, were pretty small in comparison to that of the accumulating capitalist farmers of late nineteenth-century eastern Europe. The prior development of small-scale agriculture had reduced the potential for future growth. The capital accumulated by the enterprising farmers was pretty small, and the opportunities for profitable investment in agriculture in the future were far from obvious. It is far from insignificant that virtually all the advances in productivity (per unit of land or labour) achieved since the early nineteenth century have depended on investments by the state rather than by the individual farmer.[21] Colonial irrigation works, the development of artificial fertilizers by western industry, and international research on the technology of seeds, have been the keys to progress. There was little incentive for the individual south Indian farmer to use agriculture as an engine of accumulation.

The legacy of the colonial period in southern India has perhaps been not so much the emergence of a dominating class in the countryside, as the development of a powerful and purposive state. The theories which portray the state apparatus in India as hostage of a rich rural stratum have perhaps misinterpreted the nature of the post-colonial state and to some extent got the two principal elements (the state and the rural interest) the wrong way round. Of course there was a powerful rural interest which began to flex its political muscles in the early twentieth century, which has dominated institutional politics since the 1930s, and which has attempted to influence and control the policies of government. But this was not the case of hefty, independent kulaks successfully taking the offices of authority by storm. On the one hand, the ranks of the rural rich were pretty thin, and their power vis-à-vis the government immensely qualified by their reliance on govern- mental assistance. They were bound to recognize that they needed a helping hand from the state to preserve their position and their privileges as a class, and to provide them with the means to go on making wealth in such a difficult and involuted agriculture. On the other hand, the colonial period, building on its own inheritance of an elevated and self-aggrandizing state system, had succeeded in creating (and willing to Independent India) a state which was unusually remote, unusually independent, and unusually self-regarding. In the first half of the twentieth century, the government in India was nudged towards a greater degree of economic management by the same sort of factors which nudged other extra-European governments—namely the attractiveness of ideas and techniques of economic management being developed in the more advanced economies of the world, and fiscal problems of an unavoidable nature. But in India there was, besides these pressures, an increasingly imposing problem over the supply of food, and an increasing awareness that government revenue and effective demand depended ultimately on the health of the agrarian economy. It was the state, rather than the individual cultivator, which needed to turn agriculture into an engine of accumulation and which also thought that it had the means to do so. Government, therefore, would assist the dominant class of the countryside very much on government's own terms. Government was anxious to increase the agricultural surplus and to that extent would provide them with facilities. But government was wary of setting in motion processes of social and economic change which would radically alter the foundations of its own authority. It would not, for instance, assist the dominant class of the countryside to follow the logic of individual enrichment and individual accumulation to the point where a society of small producers dissolved into a society of capitalists and proletarians. The logic of state intervention has not been to push through an aborted capitalist transformation begun by foreign firms, but rather to preserve and extend the society of small producers which provided the foundations of the region's economy and the region's history. In a period which straddled the coming of Independence the government started to provide the organization and technology which would enable the highly developed economy of small-scale agriculture to persist.

This short sketch is meant to be descriptive rather than properly analytic, suggestive rather than definite. Readers should not expect, or fear, that the rest of the book is organized as an exposition of these tentative notions. Historical research of this sort cannot aim so high. There were four main difficulties in the research which have helped to shape the rather curious treatment which follows and these need to be pointed out in advance. Firstly, the region is not a simple, unified, or small society. Rather it is ancient, complex, and fragmented. In pre-modern India, the main centres of population lay in the Gangetic plain and on the peninsula's coastal strip. The Tamils created perhaps the largest, most ancient, and wealthiest of the civilizations on the coastal strip. The area I call 'Tamilnad' consists of the ten Tamil-majority districts of the Madras Presidency in British India. It accords closely but by no means precisely with the state of Tamil Nadu in contemporary India.[22] Since this is predominantly a rural history, it deals only in passing with the history of the City of Madras which has served as capital both of the Presidency and of Tamil Nadu. Even after omitting this complex subject, we are still left with a large and unruly area. In an attempt to reduce the enormous variety of Tamilnad to some form of analytic order, I have divided it into three constituent regions and called these 'the valleys', 'the plains', and Kongunad. It is not a particularly good terminology — particularly since the description 'valleys' tends to suggest a verdant vale or otherwise a sharply-defined tract like the valley of the Nile. Except in the case of Kongunad, these regional divisions are not geographically exact, nor are the regions themselves neat and homogenous. Both analytically and geographically the regions overlap at the edges and merge into one another. The treatment of each region is necessarily stylized and paradigmatic. Each region contained a population of some 5 to 10 million (putting each in the same demographic league as Australia, Peru, Hungary, Algeria) and numberless internal varieties.

Secondly, this work is emphatically the view from the archival reading-rooms of Madras, and the research garret and computer terminal of a distant university, although the dry flatness of this technique was leavened by extensive travelling in the Tamilnad countryside. Most of the research was carried out in the governmental archives in Madras, though this was extensively supplemented by work on other written materials (biographies, contemporary research projects, political literature, newspapers, journals) and by some haphazard interviewing in the countryside. The files and reports compiled by the colonial administration provide us with a lot of material on the ideas and activities of the Indian farmer. The administrative files are stuffed with letters, petitions, confessions, statements of evidence in court, and personal documents as well as the appraisals of officials themselves. The run of official enquiries conducted in the late nineteenth and early twentieth centuries into agriculture, irrigation, money-lending, labour, forests, and many other subjects, trail huge volumes of evidence through which the rural population speak and write from the past. Of course such material contains certain biasses, but then the first technique a research historian has to learn is how to apply the question *cui bono* to a document. The main problem in conducting the research was not so much that it was difficult to attain a satisfying level of detail, but rather that it was almost impossible to impose proper limits on the ever-broadening scope of the project. A study of the twentieth century got pulled back into medieval history. A study of Tamilnad got lured into south-east Asia. A study of the countryside got transported into the town. A study of rural society got muddled up with manure. The existing literature on south India's rural history is good but sparse. Constantly I kept discovering new topics which would merit a full project of their own. Here many of these topics are briefly touched upon before the analysis hurries on to something else. In the arid and rather deserted plain of south India's agrarian history, it is often difficult to find the cart-tracks.

Thirdly, much of the research material on which this study is based is bitty and fallible. Many of the arguments depend on cobbling together snippets of information from different places and from different years in order to build up a composite picture. Other arguments depend on statistics of dubious accuracy. From the late nineteenth century the British rulers began counting things with extraordinary zeal and the resulting heap of statistical data is probably unequalled in the non-western world in this period. The quality is very variable. Some it has been prudent just to disregard; this would include most statistics on wage-rates, numbers of livestock, ownership of land, and internal trade. The very government which ordered the collection of these figures disbelieved the results. Other numerical data have been used only when the information they convey seems to accord with the picture gained from other sources; this category would include most of the figures on cropping, occupational divisions and money-lending. Finally there are statistics which can be considered pretty reliable; these would include the aggregated demographic data after 1871 and the records of overseas trade. Unfortunately, these sources also harbour difficulties. The trade figures refer to the Madras Presidency, a British Indian province which was twice as large as Tamilnad since it contained not only the Tamil districts but also some Telugu-, Kannada- and Malayalam- speaking regions. Moreover, the figures of foreign trade may be quite misleading in the absence of reliable data about trade between Madras and the rest of India. Similarly, the demographic (and many other) statistics are often inconvenient because of the geographic units employed. The district and taluk boundaries of British south India were administrative innovations which cut annoyingly across the regional divisions, based on geography and history, employed in this study. The three regions — plains, valleys, Kongunad — bear very little relation to these administrative boundaries. I often use the statistics of Coimbatore district to exhibit developments in Kongunad, even though Kongunad in fact excludes about a third of Coimbatore and includes small but important chunks of Salem, Tiruchi and Madurai districts. Similarly the (rough) line between valleys and plains succeeds in bisecting eight of Tamilnad's ten districts. At times I use figures from Tanjavur to mount arguments about the valleys, on the grounds that Tanjavur falls more completely than any other district inside the valleys zone. This is occasionally dangerous for the simple reason that by being the largest and oldest of the valleys tracts, Tanjavur differs in important respects from other parts. Salem provides the same perilous service for the plains.

These difficulties mean that this study is something of a tightrope act. They have also ensured that there are some questions which should not be asked and some questions which cannot be answered. Among the latter fall such important problems as: what was the distribution of productive assets in rural society; what was the level of private investment in agriculture and how did it vary; what were the margins of profit in trade; how unevenly was income distributed. As a consequence, a number of very basic questions turn up in the former category: what was the mode of production in south Indian agriculture; did rural society become more or less stratified; how far was the state responsible for agrarian stagnation. The aim of this study is to translate these grand and imponderable matters into more mundane questions which can be provided at least with partial and suggestive answers.

The research began as a project on the depression of the 1930s, but was pulled out of those narrow confines firstly by the conviction that both internationally and locally the period of the depression made no sense in isolation from the periods of the two world wars, and secondly because it seemed impossible to write such an intensive study when there was no wider context in which it might be placed. Yet this book still reflects the earlier emphasis and in many ways it pivots around the early 1930s. It does however try to adopt a long view of Tamilnad's history and thus begins in the deeper recesses of the pre-colonial period and ends with more recent developments. The density of the material increases as the story approaches the inter-war period and then declines away in the aftermath. After all, history does not start and stop.

1

Prologue: the history of rural Tamilnad

This book is about the south Indian countryside in the twentieth century. In this chapter the aim is to introduce the region under study. In order to understand the development of agriculture and of rural society in the twentieth century, we need to know something about the geographical setting, about the population, and about the principal social institutions. It would be possible to mount such an account through simple geographical description with some additional anthropological details. However, such a method tends, either implicitly or explicitly, to present a picture of a rather static 'baseline' from which the rest of the study must proceed. And such a suggestion would redound against one of the points which this chapter hopes to make: that south Indian rural society was not an unchanging 'traditional' thing. Therefore this introduction uses history as the framework of description. It traces how the peoples of south India have made a certain sort of society within the south Indian landscape.

The chapter does not set out to be a potted history of Tamilnad. It is highly selective in the subjects with which it deals. It takes the view that the rural society of the region has been shaped by the geographical constraints on agricultural and other production, by the process of population settlement, and by the development of certain institutions mounted on and interested in the production of agricultural and other goods—communal organization, state formation, warfare, religion and trade. Moreover, because of the absence of sources which deal very directly with the history of the

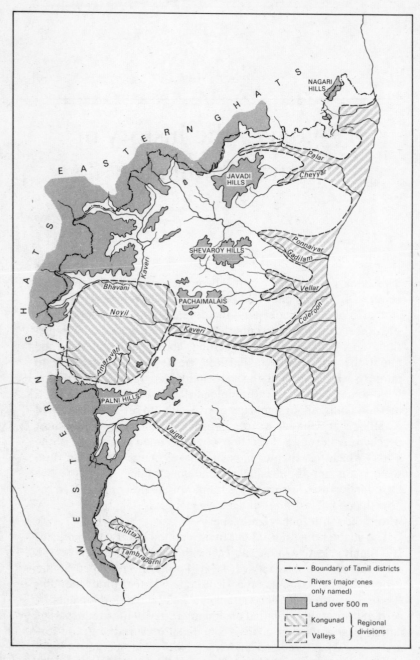

Map 1   Tamilnad: relief, rivers, and regions

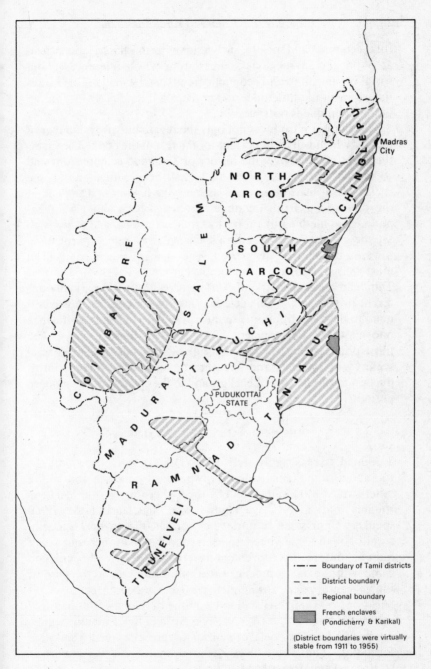

Map 2   Tamilnad: regions and British districts

Within the map:

NORTH ARCOT

SOUTH ARCOT

CHINGLEPUT

Madras City

SALEM

COIMBATORE

TIRUCHI

TANJAVUR

MADURAI

PUDUKOTTAI STATE

RAMNAD

TIRUNELVELI

Legend:
—·— Boundary of Tamil districts
— — — District boundary
— — Regional boundary
French enclaves (Pondicherry & Karikal)
(District boundaries were virtually stable from 1911 to 1955)

rural economy and society, such a survey as this has to look instead at political and religious sources from which inferences about social organization and economic trends can be made. This makes the exposition a little odd, and perhaps a little dangerous, but no other technique is possible.

The chapter introduces not only the region but also a number of themes which will be important for the rest of the book. The first is the point made above; the history of Tamilnad is quite short and somewhat breathless. While there had been settlements in the region for at least three times as long, the history of Tamilnad at the time of the British conquest stretched back about a millennium, or something like forty to fifty generations, and as we shall see below the rate of internal change was rapid, particularly towards the end of the period. The changes under colonialism must be set into this dynamic background. The second is that Tamilnad contains markedly different regions with markedly different populations, ecologies, and histories. These regions continued to develop differently in the colonial period and to influence one another's development in peculiarly important ways. The third point is that the relationship of the state to Tamil rural society was complex and idiosyncratic and we need some introduction to this by way of background to the changes of the modern period.

THE DOMINANCE OF THE VALLEYS

Tamilnad is reasonably well defined as a geographical unit,—a rhomboid shape demarcated on two sides by the sea and on the other two by mountains—and by the first century A.D. it had been roughly marked off as a cultural unit, the land of the Tamil speakers.[1] For some centuries before that, this tropical and sub-tropical region had been sparsely populated by herdsmen and hunters, but the first movement towards a more settled population came with the development of rice cultivation around the third or fourth century B.C. From then until the sixteenth century, the backbone of Tamil civilization lay in the development of irrigated rice agriculture in the river valleys. Around this agriculture grew up specific forms of social organization, religious practice and state formation. Thus the valleys nurtured one of the two important strains in Tamil society and culture.

Tamilnad's climate is dictated by its location, straddling the tropic of cancer and sitting in the path of the monsoons. In such a hot latitude, plant growth is spectacular if there are supplies of water, and virtually impossible if there are not. This has always made the pattern of the monsoons peculiarly important.

The south Indian monsoon arrives from the south-west in early June, meets the line of the Western Ghats (the hills which divide Tamilnad from Kerala), and drops most of its load into the jungles. It reaches the Tamil plain as a spent force, and deposits only some five to twenty inches as it passes over between mid-June and early September. This rain is very erratic and unreliable, and places only a few miles apart may be treated very differently. Around the end of September the monsoon curls back over the Bay of Bengal and approaches the Tamil country from the north-east. This time it is usually more abundant and reliable, and deposits between thirty and sixty inches over the north-eastern corner of the country. As it continues, however, it rapidly slackens, and the rainfall decreases steadily towards the south and towards the interior. Thus the pattern of rainfall over Tamilnad should be seen as a fan-shape, with the apex in the north-east corner, around the present site of Madras City, and the blades stretching out towards the south and the centre. On the more northerly part of the Tamil coast, annual rainfall is between forty and sixty inches, and it is moderately reliable: in only about one year in ten is there a serious deficit, and one year in twenty a damaging abundance. Moreover, this is the most temperate region, being (comparatively) northerly and maritime. Further down the coast, the rainfall is less heavy—thirty to forty inches being the usual range—and slightly less reliable: one year in every seven or eight is deficient, although there is rarely any embarrassment of water. It is rather hotter, but it still has the moderating influence of the sea. Towards the interior, however, the climate rapidly deteriorates. Within a hundred miles of Madras City, the annual delivery is reduced by about a third, and in the centre of the peninsula the annual average is in the range of fifteen to thirty inches. Here too it is much less reliable and one or two years in every five are expected to yield insufficient rainfall for even the most basic agriculture, and here too the continental effects create a hotter and drier atmosphere.[2]

Over most of the region, any serious agriculture depends on

storing rain water, both in order to concentrate its benefits and
also to extend the season in which it is available. In parts of the
coastal strip, the rainfall is enough and the geology suitable to
enable the direct collection of run-off in 'tanks', small (and occasionally big) reservoirs formed by the natural lie of the land and
some small-scale earth-works. A much better method, however, is
to tap the rainfall that falls heavily on the Western Ghats and is
carried by rivers across the south-easterly slopes of the Tamilnad
plain towards the Bay of Bengal.[3]

Naturally enough it was the river valleys which were the sites of
the earliest agricultural settlements, but even within the valleys the
locations were limited. The Tamil plain is crossed by many rivers
but few of them are of any great use for irrigation. Many of them
crash off the Ghats with considerable power, cutting deep gorges
in the rock and thus putting themselves out of the reach of the
farmer or irrigation engineer. When they reach the gentler slopes,
they slow up, meander, spread out, and evaporate with speed.
These lower reaches are dry for most of the year, and provide
facilities for irrigation only for a few months and only from those
middle reaches between the gorge and delta.

There are however three more substantial river systems, and
two rather lesser ones which are associated with these major
systems. The least of these is situated in the north of the region, on
the river Palar (and its tributary, the Cheyyar), and includes the
tract falling under the rivers Ponnaiyar and Gadilam to the south.
These rivers have a substantial catchment area on the Eastern
Ghats and the southern 'steps' of the Deccan. The second, and
largest, is found on the delta of the Kaveri which cuts across the
centre of Tamilnad. Its main catchment stretches far up into the
southern Deccan, and is supplemented by innumerable streams
and rivers running off three hundred miles of the Western Ghats,
between Coorg and the Palni hills. The third is the valley of the
river Tambraparni (and its tributary, the Chittar), just thirty
miles from the tip of India at Cape Comorin. The valley is short
but extremely fertile, for the river collects rain from both the
Western and Eastern Ghats, and washes down tons of alluvium.
Historically the Tambraparni has been associated with the upper
reaches of the river Vaigai, a smaller and more seasonal river,
which drains much of the Ghats between the Kaveri and Tambraparni.

It was soon found that the most favoured parts of these three valley regions could support a remarkably productive agricultural regime. They could grow two crops of rice, one in each phase of the monsoon, and sometimes even three or, alternatively, a long-period crop which needed a reasonably assured supply of water for most of the year. Such favoured areas were situated in the upper Vaigai, the middle reaches of the Tambraparni, and at the neck of the Kaveri delta. Elsewhere in these valleys the water-supply would generally support one crop of rice in most years, while on the fringes there were areas where agriculture depended on a combination of seasonal fortune and some investment in local water-storage.

The favoured reliable parts of the valleys were the sites of the early agrarian settlements. The movement into the valleys seems to have been associated, chronologically at least, with two other important developments—the gradual immigration of Aryan peoples from the north, and the development of sea-borne trade. The Aryans brought some of the ideals of the urban society of the north. The merchants of the classical Mediterranean, who discovered the direct route across the Arabian Sea in the first century A.D., sought the precious stones and the fine cloths of southern India and were happy to set up a lucrative trade in luxury goods. Abundant agriculture, urbane ideas and luxury trade helped to shape a civilization which saw its first remarkable climax in the Sangam period, roughly the first three centuries A.D.[4]

The poetry which survives from that age and gives it its name (from the 'sangams' or literary schools) has often been studied for its sheer elegance or for clues to dynastic and cultural history. What is less often noticed is that the effusive enthusiasm of the poetry expressed the delight of a fairly new civilization in its own material culture. Three things stand out in this enthusiasm. The first is a celebration of the agricultural economy on which the civilization was founded; one theme of the poems is a classification of ecological regions—mountain, forest, pasture, arable, littoral—with a firm stress on the superiority of the arable. The second is a celebration of the warriors whose personal bravery defended the valley civilizations against outside predators.[5] The poems are divided into two genres, *akam* (romantic) and *puram* (martial), and the latter is about the heroic deeds of kings, chiefs, and soldiers. One poem deploys an agrestic metaphor which graphically joins the bloodiness of warfare to the fecundity of valley agriculture:

Like [the farmer] reaping the ears of grain with his scythe, heaping them in stacks, spreading them on the floor and threshing them by driving the bulls to trample them on the floor and offering oblation to gods and giving away a portion to needy beggars and then enjoying the ceremonial meal with the kinsfolk, so the king mows down the enemy forces, piles up dead bodies on the battlefield, uses elephants instead of oxen to trample the corpses, gets this 'minced' corpses and carcass cooked by a virgin, who stirs it in a huge pot containing blood and fat. The thick gruel is offered as libation to the gods.[6]

The third is that the combination of fertile agriculture and martial prowess laid the basis for a proudly aristocratic culture. The society was strictly divided into two sections. On the one hand were those who had landed wealth and 'good stock' (*viluttinai*), who were thus fitted to win glory by military service, and who deserved thereafter to live at leisure and be celebrated in poetry. On the other hand were the hoi polloi of slaves, servants, and errandmen who clearly were not so privileged.[7]

One way in which this noble stratum could mark itself off culturally from the rest was by adopting some of the urbane notions of the immigrant Aryans. The immigrants brought with them a collection of philosophical ideas and rules of social conduct, and the noble southerners eagerly took over those ideas and rules which flattered their pretentions and buttressed their authority. In particular they welcomed the Aryan interdictions against alcohol and meat, for abstention clearly marked them off from the rude dwellers in the plains where the staple food was game and where the toddy-yielding palm grew wild. The immigrants who brought these useful notions formed the core of a new social group—the Brahmans—who gradually established themselves as the ritual overseers of valley society. The valley nobles adopted many of the Brahmans' gods, rules about marriage and conviviality, death rites, and age ceremonies.[8]

Eventually this noble stratum became known as the Vellala, a term which in its most probable derivation merely means the lord of the land. Certainly the twin props of the Vellalas' dominance were the control of the fecund valley lands, and the alliance with the ritually distinguished Brahmans.[9] At the centre of this noble culture of Brahman and Vellala was the king. From the beginning there were separate societies and separate kingdoms in the different valley centres, and thus the kingdoms were quite small. In the earliest period there seem to have been two: the Pandya kingdom on the Vaigai and Tambraparni rivers in the south, the Chola kingdom in the Kaveri delta. The main task of the king was to protect the prosperity of the valleys both by organizing defence, and by leading the nobility in sacrificial ceremonies which aimed to secure victory in war and abundance at the harvest.[10] The king also had a responsibility to extend the economic base of valley civilization. In this respect, the Chola kings were the most active. They pursued two strategies. First they built massive irrigation works, particularly the *Kallanai* or Grand Anicut at the neck of the Kaveri delta which helped to protect the lowland against flooding. This made possible a great expansion of agriculture in the lower delta, and also facilitated the second tactic, greater involvement in foreign trade.[11] The Cholas extended colonies into the lower delta, and also for a time moved their capital to a port on the coast. By the seventh century the delta was criss-crossed with irrigation canals. Secondly the Cholas sought to extend their culture by colonizing valleys outside the Kaveri. By defeating and domesticating the upland dwellers around the basin of the Palar river, and encouraging settlement by noble Kaveri Vellalas (and by migrants from the west coast) they transported the rice-based civilization into what later became known as Tondaimandalam, meaning possibly the country of the Chola colonizer, Adondai. Another, perhaps less credible story, talks of a similar movement of colonization back from Tondai region to the Tambraparni and other valleys of the far south.[12]

These early settlements and migrations helped to define the Vellala aristocracy. The myths and titles of the oldest and most prestigious Vellala groups to this day carry the memory of these early movements. In the northern valleys, for example, there are the Tondaimandalam Tuluva Vellalas who clearly appeal back to the original population of the valleys with settlers from Tulunad in the west coast; Kondaikottai Vellalas who may (at a guess) hark back to the indigenous people of the area; and a few Choliya Vellalas who clearly see their origin in the early settlers from the Kaveri (most of whom returned because, as they said and as is true, the region was nowhere near so fertile as the Kaveri—hence the relative fewness of Choliya Vellalas currently in Tondaimandalam). In the Vaigai area, there are still Pandya Vellalas and also some Choliyas—denoting the extraordinary enterprise of the Kaveri peoples in this important period—and also some settlements of Tondaimandala Vellalas who came south much later on because of civil disorder in the northern parts of the region.[13]

Thus by the third or fourth century A.D. there had emerged three centres of valley civilization marked by rice agriculture, a Vellala aristocracy, foreign trading, and sacrificial kingship. After this early climax, however, the development of valley civilization was seriously disrupted. Between the fifth and the seventh centuries there is a mysterious gap in the record. The disruption was probably caused by an invasion by uncouth uplands peoples—sometimes referred to as the 'kalabhras'—and a possibly associated upsurge of the Jain religion.[14] Whatever the exact nature of this disruption, by the eighth century valley civilization had revived and it moved into a new and climactic phase between the eighth and thirteenth centuries.

In this new phase, valley civilization was still founded upon its rich rice agriculture. However, rural society in this period seems to have become significantly more complex.[15] There is voluminous evidence of complex corporate management of agriculture, trade, and other aspects of village society. This complex institutionalization was almost certainly related to the demands of irrigated agriculture. Irrigation sources had to be maintained, disputes over water arbitrated, the organization of labour rationalized for mutual benefit, the product of agriculture distributed both for internal consumption and for foreign trade with the minimum of social disruption. Valley society was still dominated by the Vellalas, and the valley tracts were divided into *nads* which, as one analysis of the Kaveri in this period has suggested, were territories each focused on a specific irrigation source and each populated by a separate kin group.[16] There were assemblies to administer the affairs of the *nad*, but much more important were the institutions to manage individual villages. These assemblies transacted in land, invested in irrigation, raised taxes, provided social welfare, and helped to settle disputes. They also contributed to the management of religious places, and to the governance of trading centres where the exchange between local goods and imported goods could be controlled in such a way that it did not disrupt the local economy and society. These assemblies, in other words, were testament to the wealth, organizing ability and conscious independence of rural society.[17]

The natural corollary of the wealth, power, and ritual pretensions of the Brahman-Vellala elite was the poverty, subordination, and ritual degradation of their client labourers. Possibly from the Sangam period and certainly from medieval times, the elite of the valleys managed to distance themselves from cultivation. Those local residents and immigrants whom the elites managed to exclude from control of land were still attracted to live in the valleys where the fertility of the fields guaranteed a fairly secure food supply (the alternative was to risk an independent existence in the harsh climate of the plains). The Brahmans and Vellalas could thus delegate the work of cultivation to others while they themselves concentrated on more cultural pursuits. They also managed to emphasize the enormous social and cultural difference between those who controlled the land and those who worked it. As David Ludden notes in his study of Tirunelveli, 'labour itself became associated with low status in the economic subculture of the wet zone: the physical lowness (*paḷḷam*) of irrigated lands and irrigation channels (*paḷḷak-kal*) became identified with the physical labour of ritually low cultivators (*paḷḷakudi*).'[18] In much of the valleys, the specialist labourers in the wet-rice cultivation were the Pallans.

While the local organization of valley society thus became even stronger in this second phase of its growth, there were two important changes in politics and religion. Both most probably originated as a reaction to the disorderly 'kalabhra' period. Firstly, there was increasing attention to the question of defence against the outsiders. Secondly, there was a revival of Hinduism which resulted in a conclusive triumph over Jainism.

If the Sangam works give a proper impression, before the kalabhra interregnum the defence of the valleys required little more than heroic endeavour on the part of individual warriors and small groups.[19] After the kalabhra period, however, there appear more elaborate militia organizations. There was nothing like a centralized standing army, but village and *nad* assemblies, mercantile organizations and other corporate groups now raised and supported militia troops. These militias provided their own arms which were mostly sticks, swords and, especially, the long lance.[20] However there was a further factor encouraging changes in military organization. There was a continued attempt to expand the area of settled, cultivated territory and in this second phase of valley culture this entailed a move into the outskirts of the valleys. These were areas where agriculture was less secure; one crop of rice was the norm and in bad years even that would be threatened. The expansion often entailed considerable investment in irrigation, often in 'tanks' to store rain and river water outside the monsoon season. Moreover these colonising movements elongated the frontiers of the valley civilizations and brought them much closer to the less civilized peoples of the uplands and mountains. Thus as they pushed out into these areas, the valley-dwellers took new measures for defence. They built rings of forts along the new frontiers of the valleys, and tried to build up diplomatic alliances with some of the chiefs and chieftains so that the latter might not attack the valleys and, in certain cases, so that they might act as 'marcher lords' and help to defend the valleys. The requirements of irrigation and defence in these newly colonized areas affected their social and political structure. The colonizing movement was often undertaken by a noble who thus emerged as something of a power in his own right within the domain which he contrived to irrigate and defend.[21]

We should notice at this point that the largest of these defensive-cum-expansive movements of colonization helped to create a new and distinctive tract which we will consider as separate region throughout this book. This was Kongunad, which lay right in the centre of the southern peninsula and had long acted as a buffer between the Cholas, Pandyas, and Tondai rulers in Tamilnad and also the Chera rulers on the west coast. Kongunad's unique position, straddling north-south trade routes and also one of the few east-west routes over the Ghats, had made it important in trade and warfare from the earliest times. Its soil was especially fertile but irrigation from rivers and tanks meagre, and by the Sangam period only a few settlers had founded an arable cultivation based on wells. In the ninth and tenth centuries it remained a flattish plain, surrounded on nearly all sides by hills, mostly covered with forest, and with only a few islands of cultivation. It had been regularly raided by the valley kings, and had several local chiefs, but had until this time remained outside the mainstream of valley civilization. In the ninth and tenth centuries, the Chola kings tried to draw these chiefs into closer tributary and military relations and also en-couraged colonists from the Chola domain to settle in Kongunad. These Brahman and Vellala settlers spread into the Kongu region along the upper reaches of the Kaveri river, fanning out along the tributary streams of the Noyil, Amaravati, and Bhavani. Most of the settlements were in fortified, 'camp' or *palaiyam* villages.[22]

The revival of Hinduism was the work of the *bhakti* saints. These itinerant poets, singers and teachers, known as Alwars and Nayan-mars, trekked through the Tamil valleys preaching a warm, demo-cratic, and spiritual form of religion which had considerably more popular appeal than the architectonic metaphysics of priestly Brahmanism or Jainism. The *bhakti* preachers argued for a direct relationship of man to god and a direct role of god in the world. Through hymns, poems and stories written in the vernacular rather than sanskrit, the *bhakti* saints created a mythology and a religious literature which was accessible to a wide section of the population.[23] The followers of the original *bhakti* saints soon founded monaste-ries and schools of learning which gave institutional solidity to the movement and perpetuated the strategy of popular preaching.[24]

This new form of Hinduism was potentially quite damaging for some of the important institutions of the earlier phase of valley culture, namely kingship and the Brahmanical sense of hierarchy which underlined the social superiority of the noble Vellalas. Indeed in the early phase of *bhakti* expansion such sects as the Saivite Pasupatas and the 'southern' sect of Sri Vaishnavas opposed most forms of social and political hierarchy and suggested the abolition of Brahmanism.[25] But the levelling tendencies of these ideologies were soon brought under control, and in the end the force of *bhakti* revivalism was harnessed for the benefit of kingship and hierarchy.

It is probable, as we noted above, that in the Sangam period the Vellalas adopted some of the urbanity of the immigrant Brahmans to emphasize their status as the upper stratum of society in the valleys. In this medieval period, as Burton Stein has argued,[26] the alliance of Brahman and peasant was consolidated and extended. Indeed the roles of Brahman priest and Vellala landed gentleman became gradually interpenetrated. The Brahmans came to control tracts of land; the Vellalas adopted a Brahmanically 'clean' life-style and occasionally joined the privileged ranks of the literati, studied the sacred texts, and officiated as priests. Meanwhile in this period of agricultural expansion, probably accompanied by the immigration of new peoples and by religious ferment marked by strong levelling tendencies, the Vellalas found a particular use for the priestly Brahman. Since the latter stood marginally apart from valley society and claimed spiritual superiority over it, he had the distance and authority to give ritual confirmation to the Vellalas' wish to be distinguished from the common herd. In this medieval period, the

Hindu temple emerged as a vital local institution through which the Brahmans and Vellalas could enact this drama of superiority. To make the process easier, many of the local gods and goddesses were carefully and elegantly absorbed into the Brahmanical pantheon. Most notably, the favoured Tamil god, Murugan, was identified with the Brahmanical Subrahmanya. Thus paradoxically the wave of religious enthusiasms which began with the levelling *bhakti* cults ended with the building of temples which confirmed the rigid stratification of valley society between priests and gentlemen on one side, and all the rest on the other.

Temples were also the principal means whereby royalty took charge of the *bhakti* movement. In this medieval period, the development of masonry techniques made possible the construction of massive and permanent temples. The kings of the medieval period built such massive temples as striking visual metaphors of their claims to power and, by covering their walls with inscriptions and icons, made them into the hoardings of an ambitious royal culture. This temple-building helped to harness the force of *bhakti* spirituality for the glorification of monarchy. The major temples also served as the focus for the more widespread movement of temple construction in the villages and thus acted as a link between monarchy and the proud alliance of priest and country gentleman. Around these massive temples there grew up new royal and religious centres. Here were held ostentatious festivals which dramatized kingly power and at the same time replicated the village temples' role in confirming the political pre-eminence and social exclusiveness of the upper strata of valley society. Thus the central and village temples became the organizing points of a complex structure of ritual and material exchange. Through the hierarchy of temples the king channelled resources of men, money and livestock which could be used to assist and expand the agricultural base of the society. The king was no longer just the warrior-leader and sacrificial priest of the Sangam period, but a protector and a distributor—of both material and spiritual resources.[27]

Thus in the medieval period the role of the king in valley society significantly changed. He was no longer merely the protector, that is the leading warrior, of the whole region but he was also the protector of many of the individual temples, and that meant taking actions to provide for the upkeep of temples and to resolve their internal disputes. The king settled groups of Brahmans in villages known usually as *brahmadeyas*, and endowed other villages for temple upkeep. He affixed his royal imprimatur to the actions of others who similarly endowed and managed temples. He redistributed war-booty by giving it to the temples so that it would pass into village society.

Although this was a considerable change in the level of royal interference, it is important to keep it in perspective. The rural settlements were still largely and proudly autonomous. They managed their own affairs and, it seems, passed little in the way of tax on to the royal treasury. They called on the king to assist in their prosperity, back up their own authority, and arbitrate certain disputes, but there was no trend towards any properly centralized control. The power of the king was balanced by the independence of the village assemblies in the valley centres, and of the frontier chieftains at the fringes. The pre-eminence of the king lay in the way in which he underwrote the authority of these secondary levels of political power. He helped them by redistributing through them the material resources which he commanded and the political authority which he won by right of divinely-descended royalty. This political system has been described as a 'segmentary state'.[28]

But as a system it was inherently unstable. The vital redistributive role of the king depended on his abililty to amass material as well as spiritual resources, and since he had little ability to levy revenue from his own population this presented considerable difficulties. The medieval kings appear to have attempted to solve this dilemma by foreign trade and by military plunder, and by actions which contained a little of both. Duties and monopolies in foreign trade provided one source of revenue which did not interfere with local society. Kings patronized merchant groups and often brought merchants in from foreign regions rather than taking the risk of showing special favours to merchants from the local society. The Cholas of the Kaveri were particularly enthusiastic about this strategy. They followed up foreign trade with foreign conquest, plunder and even colonization in Ceylon and parts of southeast Asia.[29] They also sought booty closer to hand and this meant that through the medieval period the three Tamil valley kingdoms—the Pandyas in the south, Cholas in the Kaveri, Pallavas in Tondaimandalam to the north—and the Cheras on the west coast, were regularly at war. To prosecute these wars, they all recruited help from the chieftains of the plains. At the end of the thirteenth century this pattern of constant warfare resulted in a total collapse. Ambitious plains chieftains, rebellious frontier guards and vengeful Sinhalese forces ganged up to overthrow the Chola kingdom and usher in a period of political confusion.[30]

This military débâcle brought to an end the period of valley dominance. The society of Brahman and Vellala remained but it would also change, and if we are to understand the origins of these changes, and to trace the subsequent history of society, state, and commerce in Tamilnad, we must turn away from the valleys and look to the plains and to the curious military history of the south from the fourteenth century onwards.

INVADERS AND PLAINSMEN

The history of Tamilnad is often written as though it were simply the history of the valleys, but in fact the valleys contribute only one of the two major strains of the region's past. The plains contain over half the land area, and have sheltered a very different population, culture, and social structure. For much of the past, however, this society has left little in the way of literary or archaeological record and thus its history is somewhat obscure. But it is nevertheless important all the way through and, from the fourteenth century onwards, it becomes increasingly dominant and increasingly influential in the history of Tamilnad as a whole.

The Tamilnad plains are divided into eastern and western parts by a broken line of hills (the Varushanad, Andipatti, Palni, Kollamalai, Pachamalai, Shevaroy, Kalrayan, Javadi and Nagari ranges) and rough country (the saline, infertile soils of Pudukottai and southern Tiruchi). To the west of this line there is a series of small upland plateaux divided from one another by spurs of broken hill ranges straggling away from the Eastern and Western Ghats. The largest of these plains is that of Kongunad, which we have mentioned already. To the north of this, there are the tracts loosely known as the Baramahal, and to the south the Dindigul country. To the east of the line, are the slightly lower plains lying between the three main valley systems—the Arcot plain lying between Tondaimandalam and the Kaveri, and the dry south-east, lying between the Kaveri and Tambraparni. There is also a small tract between the Tambraparni and Cape Comorin. These areas to the east are flat, open expanses, broken by the occasional stark outcrop of rock.

With low rainfall, high temperatures and, for the most part, only thin and sandy red soils, the plains were hardly attractive to early agricultural settlers. Certainly millets have been grown in the plains as far back as archaeological memory but it is doubtful whether this was the region's major form of economic enterprise until very late in its history. Large parts of the plains were covered with scrub and dense forest and the sparse population depended for its livelihood on herding and hunting. Cattle seem to have been especially important within this economy. The early inhabitants of the plains were almost certainly immune to the Vedic interdictions against eating the cow. Certainly they regularly replenished their supplies by raiding one another's herds and pilfering other stock from the valleys; the fringes of the valleys were littered with 'hero-stones' which marked the spots where noble warriors had died in the attempt to stave off cattle-rustlers, and the ritualized way to start a war between plains peoples was by seizure of the opponents' cattle. The favourite sport of the plains, which also had some of the character of an age-ceremony, was a form of bull-fight.[31] This *jallikattu* is preserved to this day, as are many other remnants of the plains dwellers' involvement in a herding economy.

We know little else of this society. We know that the valley settlers were impressed by the plainsmen's primitive ferocity, that the two regions were intermittently at war, and that the more astute valley kings tried to draw the plains chieftains into diplomatic alliance. We know too that the plainsmen worshipped gods which were mostly animistic images of local agents of misfortune—snakes, smallpox, fire—and which had nothing to do with Aryan mythology.[32] In the medieval period, there are glimpses of powerful plains chiefs. As the medieval period entered on its military spiral, these chiefs were drawn into closer alliance with the valley kings. As the fighting became more desperate there were even attempts to solidify these alliances by techniques of ritual incorporation and marriage alliance which had been unthinkable in previous centuries.[33] But the plains do not make their definite appearance in the historical record until the pressure of Muslim invasions began to make significant differences to the demographic, military, and political development of Tamilnad.

The effects of the Muslim invasions on Tamilnad were nearly all indirect, and to understand this we need to look at the peculiar military geography of medieval south India. In the early fourteenth century, the Delhi Sultanate conceived plans to expand into south India. The Muslim invaders possessed new resources which enabled them to overcome that hitherto effective political boundary—the Deccan—though their difficulties showed how effective a frontier it had been; the leader of an early expedition to the south, which had penetrated nowhere near as far as the Tamil country, noted on his return that the journey was like crossing the 'razor-bridge of hell'.[34] The most important part of these new resources seems to have been camels, which were quicker and more durable than elephants for long-distance travel over harsh terrain, and also more useful in battle.

The early expeditions onto the Deccan contented themselves with carrying off gold, jewels, and elephants to enrich and empower the Sultanate. On the return from one journey, 'a thousand camels groaned under the weight of treasure extracted'.[35] By the time the Delhi leaders considered the possibility of establishing more settled control and more efficient tributary relations, their empire had been stretched too widely over the north Indian plain and was falling apart at the seams. A Delhi envoy for the first time reached through to the Tamil country and established a viceroyalty at Madurai in the 1310s, but very soon after the Delhi empire fell apart and the viceroy was left without a roy. A contingent of Muslim soldiers and nobles remained in nominal command of Madurai for half a century, but spent most of that time intriguing against, and murdering one another, and thus had very little effect on the general politics of the region. Meanwhile the Islamic spearhead across central India splintered into a series of Muslim states on the Deccan—Ahmednagar, Bijapur and Golconda—north of the Tungabhadra river. This division of strength, and the mutual jealousies of the three states, eased the pressure on south India.

Between the Muslims and the Tamils lay the Telugu and Kannada peoples on the southern Deccan. For almost 300 years, this remained an effective barrier. For the first 200, three lines of Kannada chiefs managed with considerable difficulty to organize a coalition of Kannada and Telugu nobles on the Deccan to keep the Muslims out. The first line of chiefs became known as the Hoysala kings; the latter two have been dignified by history as the emperors of Vijayanagar. These warrior-states protected the south of the peninsula but did not try to rule it. The Vijayanagar emperors looked on the Tamil districts as a source of troops and military supplies and while these demands had repercussions which we shall consider below, they in no way amounted to direct imperial rule. In the middle of the sixteenth century, the three Muslim states on the Deccan finally came together and then quickly disposed of the fragile rampart that the Vijayanagar empire offered as the defence of the south. The battle of Talikota in 1565 reduced the Vijayanagar emperor to a fugitive prince, and brought the Muslim frontier down to the southern edges of the Deccan. Yet once again the Tamil region was reprieved. The two remaining Deccan Muslim states, Bijapur and Golconda, now had the south at their mercy but a new threat from the north prevented them from moving in for the kill. The next generation of Muslim invaders, the Mughals, was following closely in their predatory footsteps.[36]

In the next few decades, the Bijapur and Golconda rulers looted the south for resources to use in warfare against the Mughals, but made no attempt to occupy the region. The irony was that by the time the Mughals got round to prosecuting their designs on the south at the end of the seventeenth and start of the eighteenth centuries, they too found themselves just as overstretched, just as much prey to centrifugal tendencies, and just as hampered by rival dynasts, as the Delhi sultans had been before them. The rise of Sivaji's Marathas and the growing power of Mysore, meant that the submission of the far south of the peninsula would not be a simple matter. No single one, or small combination, of the various forces drawn up in the southern reaches of the Deccan—Bijapur, Mughal, Golconda, Mysore, Maratha—was going to be allowed to seize the rich rice-lands of the far south without arousing the jealousy of the others; and soon the advanced fighting forces of British and French trading companies added an extra dimension to an already complicated picture. Although the major rivalry over the fate of the south took place 300 miles to the south of the rivalry of Vijayanagar times, it was still on the Deccan. It did not flow into the Tamilian area, and then only the northern fringes, until the middle of the eighteenth century, and by then of course the British had become an interested party. Even then it was the British successes in northern and western India and in the centre of the Deccan that finally decided the fate of the Tamil region. For 500 years, the political fate of Tamilnad was effectively decided by battles and rivalries taking place beyond its northern border. The Tamil region, as we shall see

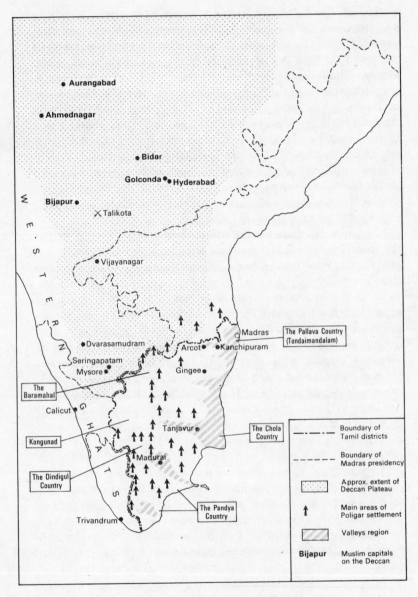

Map 3   Southern India: historical

below, was often a source of supply, of loot, of recruitment, but it was almost never directly involved in the rivalry. This fact is of immense importance in understanding the evolution of state-systems in Tamilnad, the shifts in the control of land and the relations of different communities.

The first important reaction to the pressure, however remote, of Muslim invasion came in the sphere of military organization. Changes had begun during the military disorders of the eleventh and twelfth centuries, but were rapidly accelerated once it was found that Muslim armies, so long as they were not inhibited by internal rivalries, made short work of the southern militias. The Muslims introduced camels, relegated elephants to the baggage train, made far greater use of cavalry, and trained platoons of expert bowmen. Moreover, the Muslim armies consisted of professional soldiers. The southern militias of the medieval period were part-timers equipped with sword and lance and accustomed to overwhelming any opponent by sheer weight of numbers rather than by tactics or military technology. The medieval Cholas started to transform these militias, principally by investing heavily in the expensive business of importing horses. This innovation proved so important that the Chola kings placed contracts in which they agreed to pay even for the horses which died on the journey from Arabia, and the importers of the west coast became very rich men indeed.[37] However it was the Hoysalas, the thirteenth-century Deccani Hindu kingdom which controlled parts of Tamilnad after the Chola collapse and which carried the defence of the Hindu south in the period before the rise of Vijayanagar, which made the first significant responses to Muslim military might. They made careful arrangements to import horses, hired cohorts of Muslim mercenaries, and trained platoons of elephant-borne bowmen. They also started a move towards standing armies, by providing state pensions for the families of slaughtered veterans, and began a trend towards enormous armies; one estimate of the Hoysala forces reckoned 120,000 men. Eventually the Hoysalas became a virtual military state, with the king constantly on horseback, and military governors for each of the kingdom's provinces.[38]

The Vijayanagar dynasts started out as officers in the Hoysala armies and naturally they adopted a similar pattern. For much of the fourteenth century Muslim pressure was mitigated by the mutual jealousies of the three Deccani Muslim states and there was little incentive for further military reform. But by the fifteenth century, pressure was renewed, and the introduction of gunpowder brought yet another new dimension to warfare. Thus the great Vijayanagar emperor, Krishnadevaraja, not only imported horses and trained bowmen but also built forts and cast cannons. Even with this new technology, the Vijayanagar forces still relied mostly on sheer size. The forces of Krishnadevaraja were simply enormous and estimates range between a hundred thousand and a million.[39]

To achieve this military build-up Vijayanagar required unprecedented supplies of men, food and other forms of tribute. Naturally enough, the Vijayanagar emperors looked to the southern lands, which they were protecting from Muslim intrusion, to help provide these supplies. In two important ways, these demands on Tamilnad tended to increase the importance of the plain tracts. Firstly, the peoples of these regions were suitable material for recruitment. Secondly, this relatively unoccupied tract provided a frontier for expanding agriculture to produce the supplies demanded in the north.

The mobilization of the plains was achieved partly by the immigration and settlement of Telugu warrior chiefs and clans, and partly through the medium of the existing plains chieftains. The latter were either lured into co-operation by the grant of titles and other favours by the Vijayanagar emperor, or battered into co-operation by a Vijayanagar army. The Telugu warriors and clans either filtered into the Tamil country in flight from the disorders on the Deccan, or arrived with the Vijayanagar envoys who came down to organize the resources of the south and who soon supplanted the remnants of the old valley dynasties. They set up as Nayaks or Viceroys in the major valley centres. These Nayaks set about mobilizing the plains through a set of slightly varying systems that were variously known as *amaram, candashara, kattubadi* or *palaiyam*. Under these systems, a warrior chief was settled on a portion of plains territory. These settlements were mostly ringed around the valley centres and were designed firstly to provide a much firmer defence of the valleys than had been possible hitherto, and secondly to send armed recruits to the Vijayanagar armies. These levies were sent initially to the Nayak who in turn was supposed to send his contingent to help the emperor when demanded. In order to support the system the grantee—*amaranayak* or *palaiyagar*—was required to remit little or no tribute in return for his grant of territory, but was encouraged to build forts, organize levies, and push forward cultivation by constructing irrigation works and forcing cultivation. The grantee in turn settled clans and families on the land on the stipulation that they would push forward cultivation and would provide recruits when necessary. The basic unit for measuring land in these settlements was the *al jivitam*, which meant the extent sufficient to support one (fighting) man.[40]

The *amaranayaks* and *palaiyagars* introduced two new techniques to enforce the expansion of production. The first was the village headman. In each locality, the grantee appointed a headman who, in return for privileges which guaranteed the prosperity of his family, organized the other inhabitants for production and military service.[41] The second also entailed a much greater degree of intervention by the state (via its dependants such as the *palaiyagars*) in the business of agriculture than had been seen before. The state took a considerable role in organizing within the village basic services necessary to sustain village production. It appointed various ancillary workers in the villages—irrigation overseers, guards, priests, washermen, blacksmiths, carpenters, potters and so on— and provided them with special grants of land or doles of paddy for their support. Under the pressure of this new and rigorous system, large parts of the harsh and unpromising plains were opened up for cultivation.[42]

In roughly half of the plains, the grantees were immigrant Telugu warriors. They settled with their followers in the outskirts of Madurai district, western parts of Tirunelveli, and on the outskirts of Tondaimandalam in North Arcot and the northern part of Salem. They tended to settle on the tracts of black soil. These were generally much harder to work than the thin red soils, because they quickly became heavy and waterlogged in the monsoon, and tended to dry out and tessellate in a drought. They had therefore attracted almost no settlement by the Tamil plainsmen, but the Telugus were accustomed to such soils in their homeland, knew that they rewarded the extra toil and expense needed with a gratifyingly favourable yield, and were experienced in the particular techniques of their cultivation. Elsewhere on the plains this military settlement incorporated the local chiefs—in much of South Arcot, north Tiruchi and contiguous areas of Salem, the southern outskirts of the Kaveri through south-west Tanjavur, Pudukkottai, and parts of Ramnad.

The Vijayanagar period saw a dramatic change in the balance of power between valleys and plains. The main centres of political control still lay in the valleys—the Nayak viceroys had their headquarters at Madurai in the Pandya country, Tanjavur in the Kaveri, and Gingee in Tondaimandalam—but the military power which now underwrote the political status of the region clearly lay on the plains. This was even more noticeable after the Vijayanagar rampart was swept away in the mid-sixteenth century and the warrior-chiefs of the plains became the only defence of the valley principalities against the depredations of Muslim, Maratha and Kannada forces from the north. The civilization of the valleys was thus obliged to show a greater respect for the peoples of the plains and consequently made efforts to incorporate them into valley culture, or at least to bring the culture of valleys and plains into some form of alliance.

This was most noticeable in changes in religion and temple worship. From the fourteenth century, the enthusiasm of *bhakti* worship was directed into cults centred around the more martial aspects of some of the Vedic gods, particularly Vishnu. These cults attracted the warrior chieftains. Next, the temples which in the medieval period had emerged as crucial institutions for advertising gradations of social status, could now be used to smooth the alliance between the proud valley-dwellers and the warriors they had hitherto despised. In return for the protection which the warriors afforded to the temples and to the valleys as a whole, the temple priests accorded to the warriors a high social status within the pecking order of the valleys.[43] While this strategy helped to incorporate the leaders of the plains society, there was other evidence that this process of accommodation extended to commoners as well. In the Vijayanagar period, the practice of the temple-building, hitherto a part of valley culture, spread widely on the plains. In this process there were dramatic attempts to bring the gods and goddesses of the plains people into some form of correspondence with the Vedic pantheon. Some of these plains deities were accorded kin or marital ties with Vedic gods. In the case of some of the plains' folk goddesses this was found impossible or undesirable, but still it was possible to incorporate a shrine to these goddesses (*amman*) in the major Vedic temples.[44] Major festivals were restructured in a similar way. The most famous example was the Chitrai festival in Madurai which was completely re-orchestrated by Tirumala Nayak in the mid-seventeenth century. Lord Alagar, the personal god of the Kallar people of the plains outside Madurai, was dubbed not only a incarnation of Vishnu but also a brother-in-law of Siva. He was thus invited to the annual Chitrai festival to celebrate the marriage of his sister Minakshi with Siva but, in a ceremony which spectacularly dramatized the wish of the valleys to incorporate the plains people but still keep them slightly apart, he regularly turned up late and never got further than the outskirts of the city before returning home.[45]

In the Vijayanagar period the temples were extraordinarily active. The immigration of new peoples (for masses of artisans, merchants and other service groups accompanied the Telugu warriors, and other migrants came as refugees from the disorders of the Deccan) and the rapid changes in the local balance of power, inflated the temples' role as a social arbiter. This period thus saw the final hardening of the *bhakti* movement into a hierarchically-minded temple-oriented ritual system, and made the Brahmans peculiarly important as the arbiters of social standing. They had to bow to the new political facts of life, but somehow keep the cultural dominance of the valleys intact. They thus had to admit the warrior chiefs to some form of ritual pre-eminence, and make an adjustment for the other plains people which drew them into close alliance but also kept them just beyond the pale. As a result the temple, both in the capital towns and in the localities, became the focus of a subtle and enormously varied system of social gradation.[46]

Thus the pressure of the Muslim presence on the Deccan caused changes in military organization and social adjustment further south. The main points of these changes, and the crucial role of the state in pushing them through, were summed up by the Vijayanagar Emperor, Krishnadevaraja in his work of political theorizing known as the Amuktamalyada: 'The expenditure of money which is utilised in buying elephants and horses, in feeding them, in maintaining soldiers, in the worship of Gods and Brahmans and in one's own enjoyment, can never be called a waste.'[47]

The period had an enormous effect on the society of the plains. The exact processes are obscure but they can at least be guessed. Through the period a rather fluid society of hunters, herdsmen and marauders 'precipitated out' into something which looked more like a society of lineages and castes. There is evidence of some tribal or tribal-like divisions of the plains people before this period, but it is not clear how strong it was.[48] The Vijayanagar period and after, however, saw three important pressures on the plains peoples.[49] First there was a large amount of migration around the Tamil country, presumably as a reaction to Telugu immigrations and warrior raids, and these are graphically recorded in the mythologies of some plains settlements. This probably entailed a considerable reorganization of whatever social bonds had existed beforehand. Secondly, there was large scale recruitment into the Nayak and Vijayanagar armies. One commentator estimated that the Tamil Nayaks had to supply 600,000 foot soldiers and 24,000 cavalry[50] and this must have constituted a significant portion of the able-bodied population of the plains. The process of recruitment probably gave some new shape to the population of the plains and there is some evidence that the three main divisions of the plains peoples (Padaiyichi, Kallar, Maravar) originated from the division into three Nayak armies (Gingee, Tanjavur, Madurai). Thirdly, the *palaiyagari-amaram* settlement shifted the emphasis of the plains economy away from animal husbandry towards arable agriculture and in the process forced more people to settle on and work the land. Those peoples who evaded this settlement seem to have been gradually confined to the diminishing area of forest and mountain where they continued as primitive hunters and herdsmen. Those who did settle elaborated new forms of social organization to suit their new calling as farmers-cum-soldiers. The crucial unit of this new social system seems to have been a lineage or a group of kin and affinal relations. The land was probably distributed on the basis of clans and then re-distributed within the clan on the basis of kinship. There is evidence that the word for a lineage, *karai*, was used to denote a share in a clan landholding.[51] Modern anthropologists have noticed that despite the obscuring effect of time it is still possible to trace the congruence between clans and land settlements in certain parts of the plains.[52] Within the clan, social and political organization probably depended on kinship. Again there is still evidence of plains peoples using marriage alliances among exogamous lineages within the clan to construct an intricate pattern of political relationships around a graded hierarchy of lineages. Each lineage or each family was obliged to supply a certain number of recruits for the military subvention but was left to do this in its own way; families probably divided up the duties so some served on the land while others went to the army.[53]

All of this, however, was subsumed under a political structure which, in its emphasis on state intervention and military duty, tended to be organized on the bases of merit and power rather than on kinship. There was indeed a hierarchy which stretched from the Vijayanagar court, through the Nayaks, to the poligars and so to the village headmen, and however imperfectly this structure of command may have been realized it was nevertheless important. Men were appointed to positions in this hierarchy because they achieved the upwards flow of resources which the system demanded. Thus political power in the plains came to depend not so much on ancestry or lineage as on the backing of superior authority. Most of the chiefly families of the plains trace their pre-eminence back to some form of grant from the Nayaks or from Vijayanagar. This was equally true for Telugu immigrants and local chieftains, even if the latter had obviously been significantly powerful previously, and it was also true to some extent for the village headman families in the villages.[54] Of course the two systems—the local one based on kin, and the over-arching one based on merit and power—inter-penetrated one another to some extent, particularly in the middle levels. *Palaiyagars* would sometimes select lineage heads as village headmen in order to draw on their authority to get things done in the village, and clans would sometimes promote their military talents to local headship or invent fictive kinship ties to underline a relationship between clan and *palaiyagar*.[55]

The demands of warfare and production had gathered scattered groups of herders and huntsmen together into armies and then separated them out again as agricultural settlers. The muddling effects of this process can be glimpsed in the confusion of names and titles among the plains peoples, and in the variety of their myths of origin. The caste names and titles which have persisted on the plains show up the different stages of their history: Valaiayan, Vedan, Urali and Vettuvan clearly denoted hunting; Idaiyan referred to herding; Kallar, Maravar, Vanniyan and Padaiyichi had associations with soldiery and plunder; Ambalagar, Muttiriyan, Mutrachi, Palli, Agamudaiyan, Udaiyan and Nattaiman betrayed claims to village dominance in an agricultural society. Many of these castes as they are now defined were probably cobbled together from a number of different groups. Among the Udaiyans, for example, there are some who have historical memories of descent from Vedar huntsmen, and others who claim descent from the army of a south

Arcot chieftain. Moreover among the sub-groups of the Udaiyans, there is a definite record of their historical development; some call themselves Malaiman (hill-dweller), others Sudarman (hero or warrior), and others Nattaiman (settler). As already noted, the three major plains castes of Padaiyichi, Kallar and Maravar were probably the result of the aggregation of separate groups into the three armies of the Tondai, Chola and Pandya kingdoms respectively. The extent to which pre-existing groups were muddled up and re-divided in this process of recruitment and settlement can be seen in the confusion of sub-caste names. A member of one of these castes, and of many others in the above list of plains castes, is liable to carry the name of a different caste as his sub-caste name.[56]

With the establishment of firm chieftaincies, forts, and considerable organization of local militia in the fighting of the seventeenth and eighteenth centuries, these new settlements agglutinated into something like local communities—'commonwealths of contiguous tribes' was the description of one nineteenth-century historian.[57] Most of those north of the Kaveri fell into a related group of Palli, Vanniyan and Padaiyichi; most of those to the south into the related group of Kallar, Ambalagar and Agamudaiyan; and most of those even farther south into the category of Maravar. It was hardly surprising that the early British anthropologists found it difficult to understand the organization of these groups and to trace from them trees of descent leading back to common ancestors. Nor was it surprising that they found significant traces of 'tribal' customs. Among many of them, for instance, it was still common for youths to compete for wives through shows of physical prowess, generally associated with the local form of bullfight, the *jallikattu*. Nor was it surprising that they found immense variety among the family customs, marriage ceremonies and alliances, personal appearance, deities and religious ceremonials of the various settlements of these 'castes'. Finally, the plains people had made some adjustment to the Brahmanism of their new allies in the valleys but this was uneven and imperfect. They still kept their local rites and ceremonies and most of their social customs. They often grafted onto these a readiness to acknowledge the Brahman's role and a respect for Vedic temples.[58]

While the most important developments of the Vijayanagar period came in the expansion on the plains, there were also significant repercussions in the valleys. The defenders of the Deccan and the chieftains of the Tamil plains demanded agricultural supplies in return for their protective services. They secured these either by trade, by raiding for tribute, or, increasingly as time went on, by devising more settled systems for extracting a surplus from valley agriculture. These demands quickly breached the proud autonomy of the valley villages and buckled the structure of corporate localities.

From the end of the medieval period, the inscriptions relating to village corporations tail off and the last of these from the early Vijayanagar period find these institutions in a state of financial crisis; temples had suffered from the looting of Muslims and mercenaries, and beleaguered corporations were selling villages into private hands.[59] Undoubtedly the decline of these corporations was a result of the attempts of the new outside political forces to break down the relative autonomy of the village political system in order to be able to extract its surplus resources. It is probable that this period saw a diversion of many of the corporations' village taxes into state coffers. The period also saw a subtle but significant change in the relationship between state, village, and temple. Whereas the medieval rulers had assumed the duties of 'protectors' of local temples and had gone on to offer the temples endowments and to arbitrate in temple disputes when so requested by the locality, the Nayak and Vijayanagar overlords transformed this role of protector into a much greater degree of central control over the vital material and ritual resources of the valley's local temples. As the villages came under financial pressure, so the considerable resources of the temple became even more important for local survival. In this situation the rulers' willingness to donate to the temples was a way both to sustain the local economy and to exert a much greater degree of control over it.[60]

The Nayaks also placed state officials in the valley countryside to oversee the business of production and to ensure a steady rate of surplus extraction. The duties of some of these officers whose role survived into the eighteenth century were to supervise the irrigation sources, encourage the villagers to extend cultivation, and keep the upper levels of the state administration informed about local affairs; in return they were awarded a share of the grain-heap. Sometimes these officials were military outsiders, and sometimes they were leading local families who were elevated by state authority to a position of primus inter pares. The Nayaks also began to build up the notion that all valley land was somehow under the control of the state.[61]

Yet all these trends were softened by the very strength of valley traditions and by the readiness of the overlords to adjust their innovations to local circumstances in order to achieve their overall goal. Although the corporations dwindled away there was little attempt to disrupt the power of the land-controlling elite of Brahmans and Vellalas. Their control of village resources was still recognized. The heirs of the corporate controllers were known as the *kaniyatchikarans*, land-controllers, or in the more usual Persian form, mirasidars. These terms defined those elite families who held a share (*pangu*) of the rights to control the village. These rights were jealously guarded, even though in this period they almost certainly became more individualized and also more easily transferable.

WAR AND SOCIAL CHANGE

The events which followed the collapse of Vijayanagar accentuated the pressure on the valleys. After the battle of Talikota in 1565 wiped Vijayanagar off the map, there was a steady decentralization and disintegration of political control. The Tamil country was finally wide open to the invading armies and by the mid-seventeenth century the north of the region was little more than a highway for foreign soldiery—Golconda forces in the 1640s and '50s, Maratha chiefs in the 1660s and '70s, and Mughal generals in the 1690s and 1700s.[62]

The residual power of the valley kingdoms which had survived in the guise of the Nayak viceroys because the Vijayanagar emperors persuaded the local chieftains to uphold them, now fell away and political power became extremely localized. The Nayakship of Madurai survived longer than most because the local chiefs of Kannivadi, and Ramnad endeavoured to uphold it. These chiefs could mobilize remarkable guerrilla armies in the plains countryside and harass the invading armies. But by the 1730s the local chiefs could no longer see any point in maintaining this residual centre of authority at Madurai and were more interested in their own independent power.[63]

Power drifted to the local chieftains of the plains and the late

seventeenth and early eighteenth century saw a continous, debilitating struggle of local potentates. There were definite atempts to
arrest this process and find a means of settlement. These attempts
showed in the remarkable, unprecedented rate of temple-construc-
tion, which had now become the time-honoured tactic in Tamilnad
for translating military authority into political legitimacy.[64] But the
dispersal of military power and the pressure of the invaders made
settlement impossible. The Maratha, Muslim and Kannada forces
to the north found the Tamil south so disorderly that they made only
limited and rather ineffectual attempts to establish control over the
region and contented themselves instead with lightning raids to
raise tribute to fuel the real conflict in the Deccan and the north.
These raids set off domino wars within the south as the aggrieved
parties attempted to recoup their losses.

In this period the interior of Tamilnad became an exceptionally
perilous place. Few of the European travellers who visited south
India at this time set foot in the interior, and those who did reported
mainly that it was disorderly and dangerous.[65] The problems of
invasion were compounded by the problems of dearth which
inevitably followed. Throughout the late eighteenth century there
were reports of major famines,[66] and clearly many of the invading
armies declined to stay and consolidate their gains because their
arrival so easily precipitated famines. But it is important not to
overdo the picture of 'anarchy', as the British conquerors tended to
do in their attempt to draw a contrast between pax Britannica and
the era that had preceded it. The warfare took place mostly on the
plains and seems, except for occasional tribute raids, to have
avoided the valleys. Even on the plains, wars and famines were
intermittent and sporadic, and for long periods powerful local
chieftains or invading generals were able by sheer military might to
carve out havens of peace. Nevertheless, the expansion of plains
settlement was decisively halted and may even have gone into
reverse, particularly in the north-west which acted as the gateway
for invading armies.[67]

The troubles flowed into the valleys because the valley peoples
now relied so utterly on the plains chiefs for protection. They were
obliged to call on the unruly plains chiefs to extend their guardianship, *kaval*, over the valley villages and in return to pay them a fee.
Increasingly this system of *kaval* came to resemble an extortion
racket as much as a policing system. And as the disorders of the

plains increased, remnants of the plains armies strayed into the fringes of the valley settlements. *Kaval* duties grew into effective political control and eventually resulted in settlement and often displacement of the old valley population.[68] In parts of the valleys in the eighteenth century this resulted in a considerable shift of population and of rural control. It accelerated in the second half of the century when the Mysore forces led by Hyder Ali and Tipu Sultan began to raid into the valleys with more deliberation. The Mysore rulers had geared up their forces to face the full might of the Mughal and Maratha armies and against such forces the consequences of Tamilnad's insulation from the rapid advances in military technology in the north were only too apparent. Moreover, Tipu was carving out his empire with single-minded intent. The raids into Tondaimandalam and the Kaveri valley caused considerable havoc.[69] The scale of bloodshed clearly surprised the local population, besides, in the case of the 1780 raids, forming the basis for Burke's oration in the House of Commons. Large numbers of people fled from the Mysore forces and in the wake of the raids certain areas were taken over by new populations in which the remnants of the poligar armies figured quite prominently. Padaiyichis from Salem and the Arcots moved across into the outer reaches of the Tondai country, and down into the north and east of the Kaveri delta. The Kallars in the woods of Pudukkottai moved north into the fringes of the Kaveri delta, and south into the edges of the Vaigai basin. The Maravars of the Ramnad forests moved into some of the richer lands in Tirunelveli. These movements were often complex. The oral history of a Kallar village studied by Louis Dumont recorded five changes of local mastery in what (with the usual chronological distortion and elongation of such memories) was clearly a short period. [70]

Thus these final years before the arrival of British rule had quite dramatic effects on the demographic pattern and the reproductive potential of the Tamil countryside. They also had repercussions for the political establishment of the region and for the relationship of the state with the countryside.

Over a long period the increasing demands of defence and the increasing specialization of military talents had tended to transform the state structure into a markedly military affair and to set it apart from the countryside, particularly the valley countryside. At the same time it had increased the demands which the state placed upon

the countryside for supplies. There was, in fact, a growing antagonism between the state and rural society.[71] Meanwhile the state
had had to seek out new sources on material support and increasingly it had come to rely on the profits of trade. In the medieval
period, as we have seen, the rulers had taken care to organize,
police and profit from overseas trade. From the sixteenth century
onwards, the irruption of the Europeans into Asian trade contrived
both to increase the volume of trade on the Tamilnad coast and also
to improve the balance of trade as well.[72] Tamilnad exported both
raw materials and manufactured goods (mostly cloth) to Arabia and
southeast Asia and the favourable balance of trade created an
inflow of specie and jewels which the political authorities soon saw
the advantage of taxing and controlling. The rulers preferred this
foreign trade to be in the hands of foreigners rather than local
inhabitants. Thus it was north Indians, Arabs and, increasingly,
European trading companies who were encouraged to settle in the
Tamilnad ports and conduct a trade from which the ruler could
extract a tribute.[73] In the end of course, the competition of foreign
trading companies reacted with the competition of local political
authorities and encouraged the foreigners to play a role in local
politics. Meanwhile, the prosperity of the enormous city of Vijayanagar helped to create a considerable flow of internal trade which
continued after the fall of Vijayanagar though it was constantly
being re-oriented along new routes.[74] In the seventeenth century
the intermittent European control or blockade of west-coast ports
created a sizeable flow of trade from the east-coast ports over the
Ghats and down into the kingdoms of Kerala.[75] In the eighteenth
century, the rising power and prosperity of Mysore created a
lucrative trade up from Tamilnad to the north-west.[76] Local rulers
were quick to levy tolls on this inland trade. In the seventeenth
century the Tanjore ruler was said to raise a toll on every conceiv-
able type of goods transported, 'even on the very cow dung'.[77]

The warfare and disorder of the late seventeenth and eighteenth
centuries seriously threatened this source of prosperity and revenue. The marauding activities of rival chieftains, plains armies or
just simple robbers made internal trade difficult, and caused the
political authorities who aspired to rise above petty military hegemony to concentrate their best attentions on policing the frontiers
and highways in order to keep up a decent flow of trade. There were
three such authorities—Tipu Sultan of Mysore, the Mughal emis-

sary who as the Mughals crumbled became the independent Nawab of Arcot, and the British East India Company. All three paid significant attention to trade and all three became fixated with the question of internal policing. The Nawab's police system in the north of Tamilnad was one of the few successes of his rule.[78] Tipu wanted to build up a navy to assist foreign trading, and set up a system which combined the functions of forwarding contractors, customs officers and espionage agents to ensure the flow of internal trade.[79] The British company's concern with trade hardly needs describing.

Thus the state systems which were emerging in the eighteenth century were very different from those which had developed up to the medieval period. They had become enormously distanced from agriculture and from the populations of the countryside. They were concerned with trade, policing, taxation, and military might. They looked on the agricultural society of the valleys chiefly as a source of revenue and supplies and as a result centralized taxation increased enormously in the seventeenth and eighteenth centuries. They looked on the chieftains of the plains as disorderly intruders. By the middle of the eighteenth century Tipu was committed to abolishing or at least controlling the *palaiyagars* in the north-west of Tamilnad[80], and the East India Company with the Nawab in tow were starting the long business of reducing the *palaiyagars* in the south.[81] From the *kaval* system of the *palaiyagars* themselves, to the red-coated sepoys of the company, the efforts of political authorities were bent on the construction of systems of political control. In the countryside this meant a strengthening of those devices by which political overlords attempted to enforce their control over the villages—the post of village officer in the plains villages and the post of local overseer in the valleys.[82]

Two periods of early south Indian history had seen the emergence of two different social systems in two geographically different areas. The first, in the valleys, was based on settled rice agriculture. Here the social structure reflected the dominant importance of the 'control of land', and was characterized by a marked dual stratification underwritten by Brahmanical ideas of deep ritual division. The second, in the plains, was moulded more by animal husbandry and warfare than by agriculture, and led to a society marked by a military-style hierarchy which was buttressed not so much by ritual exclusiveness (although this was of course not absent) but by

kinship rules and pyramidical systems of patronage and redistribution. These systems were far from static. Early on they spawned a
hybrid version in Kongunad and as the region became steadily more
integrated so the systems clashed and influenced one another on the
margins. Within each region there was an enormous amount of local
variation. This trend of mutual adjustment accelerated remarkably
in the disorder of the eighteenth century, yet however much the two
systems had been thrown together, they were still separate and
distinctive. The distribution of different communities in the late
nineteenth century (see map 4) still showed the separateness of the
two systems; the valleys were still largely populated by Brahmans
and Vellalas, while the plains were shared by immigrant Telugu
communities and Tamil herder-warriors. Meanwhile the map also
shows the evidence of change. The plains communities had nibbled
into the fringes of the valleys, as had other communities like
Chettys, Nadars, and Muslims whose vocation lay mostly in commerce.

This was certainly not an insulated, egalitarian, unchanging,
traditional peasant society. Change was rapid and accelerating.
Warfare, the state, and commerce penetrated far into the countryside. Strategies of ritual and social exclusiveness, military bravura
and political favouritism had created enormous inequalities of
wealth and status.

In the early modern period, from Vijayanagar onwards, warfare
and commerce had become peculiarly important as agents of social
and economic change. Warfare had encouraged social mobility,
redistributed population, and distanced the state system from the
countryside. Commerce had been the natural ally of warfare. Army
camps and political headquarters created pools of commercial
demand. States cultivated overseas trading as a way to earn revenue
as well as a way to secure vital military supplies. The increased
tempo of warfare from the late seventeenth century onwards
accentuated all these trends. States became more ambitious, taxes
multiplied, and with the multiplication of taxes went the development of systems of banking and trading necessary to convert
revenue in kind into expenditure in warfare. The natural corollary
of these developments were attempts by states to extend their
tentacles more directly into the villages, and to push forward the
frontiers of the agricultural economy in order to produce more
supplies and to provide support for more men. New systems of

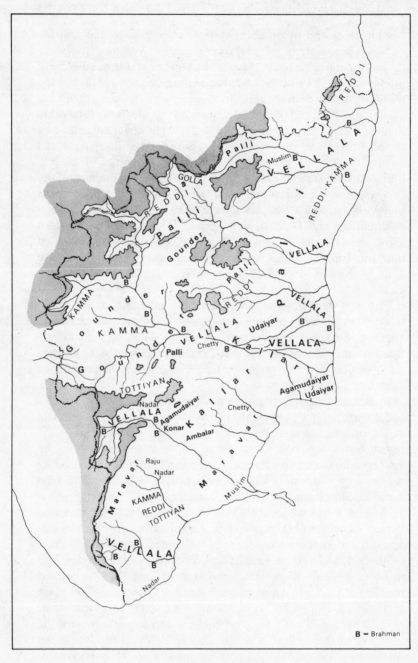

Map 4   Tamilnad: settlements of main agrarian castes

Table 1: Caste types as percentage of the population of each district

	Madras	Chingleput	South Arcot	Salem	Coimbatore	Tanjavur	Tiruchi	Madurai	Tirunelveli	Tamil Districts
Priest	4	4	3	2	2	6	6	2	4	3.09
Vellala	12	7	7	16	31	10	8	9	9	12.42
Militiaman and Immigrant	13	25	36	29	10	24	31	23	18	24.61
Field Labourer	12	26	24	13	9	22	21	13	16	17.59
Hunter and Herder	4	7	7	7	3	9	6	11	5	7.02
Artisan, Weaver and Service	9	14	10	18	26	10	9	16	28	16.32
Merchant	28	5	7	.7	8	10	4	12	8	9.64
Total in categories shown	82	88	94	92	89	91	85	86	88	90.69

Note: This table groups the castes shown in the 1891 Census into some rough occupational types, as denoted by their caste-name and their current status. Castes were aggregated as follows:

Priest = Brahman, Pandaram, Valluva

Vellala = Vellala

Militiaman and Immigrant = Agamudaiyan, Ambalākkaran, Kallan, Kshatriya, Maravar, Palayakkaran, Kamma, Reddi, Nattaiman, Tottiyan, Vokkaliga, Malaiman, Udaiyan, Kappiliyan, Lingayat, Palli, Vannian.

Field Labourer = Vettuvan, Urali, Paraiyan, Mala, Pallan, Holeya, Muppan.

Hunter and Herder = Idaiyan, Yadava, Golla, Kurumban, Malaiyalan, Vedan, Villiyan, Karalan, Valaiyan.

Artisan, Weaver and Service = Kammalan, Ambattan, Vannan, Vaniyan, Kusavan, Uppiliyan, Uppara, Shanan, Chakkiliyan, Odde, Izhuvan, Devanga, Sedan, Kaikolan, Patnul.

Merchant = Balija, Chetty, Kavarai, Sheik, Labbai, Pathan, Saiyid, Vadugan.

Source: *Census of India 1891*, Volume XIV, Pt. ii, 358-77.

state-appointed village officers, revenue farmers, revenue agents and ancillary workers were set up to help expand the agrarian base, by coercion where necessary, and to extract the state's portion of the surplus. More resources were dragged out of the villages, but with some reaction in terms of local resentment. At the turn of the nineteenth century Buchanan talked of a local incident on the borders of Kongunad when

Eight chiefs of villages went to the insurgent Dindia and procured from him an order to plunder the country. Having returned with this commission they collected about five hundred ruffians and plundered Sati-mangala...Had not very vigorous measures been taken to repress their barbarity, every farmer in the district was ready to have joined them, in order to share in the plunder of the towns.[83]

It was hardly a great break with recent tradition when at the very end of the century Tamilnad was finally taken over by a commercial company with an inflated army and an idea of setting up a centralized and supremely elevated state system on the returns from an expanding agricultural base.

THE COLONIAL SETTLEMENT

Yet the establishment of British rule promised to bring many changes. The long period of intermittent but debilitating warfare gave way to a long period of internal peace. The foreigners were committed to replacing Tamilnad's fragmented framework of political authority with a more centralized and efficient government. They reckoned, moreover, to use the centralized state structure to pursue the goals of utilitarian political economy. They believed that through legal, educational, and financial innovations they could create an environment in which the agrarian economy could grow at the behest of the market. These notions were laid out explicitly in the writings of the man who played the single largest part in the design of the early colonial settlement in Tamilnad, Thomas Munro.[84] Moreover from the start of the British period, and more especially in the later part of the nineteenth century when the steamship began to shrink the globe, Tamilnad's farmers began to find their new niche in the international division of labour. They started to buy more of their *veshties* from the stocks made in Lancashire, and to sell more of their crops to the agent of the export house.

The next chapter is devoted to the history of Tamilnad's international trade. The last two sections of this introductory chapter carry forward into the colonial period the history of the development of government and its relationship to the agrarian economy. This section deals with the British attempts to devise a system for taxing and governing rural Tamilnad, while the final section traces the consequences for the development of the region's agriculture.

The Madras Presidency, the East India Company's southern province, was largely put together between 1792 and 1801 as a collection of those bits of peninsula India which had not been left in the hands of the native rulers of Hyderabad, Mysore, Cochin, Travancore, and a handful of smaller states. It consisted of a small Malayalam-speaking portion on the west coast, a large Telugu portion on the southern Deccan with a spur stretching up the east coast towards Orissa, and the Tamil districts with which we are concerned. The core of the Tamil portion—and indeed the core of the province—was Fort St George which the Company had occupied (with intervals) since 1638, the city of Madras which now surrounded it, and the Jaghir of Chingleput which the Company had held, officially as a subordinate of the Nawab of Arcot, since 1765. In 1792, the first defeat of Tipu Sultan had given the Company Salem and Dindigul, and in 1799 the second defeat added Coimbatore. These districts covered the Kongunad region, and most of the plains to the west of the line of Tamilnad hills. Also in 1799, the Company took over the Kaveri deltaic district of Tanjavur from its Maratha prince, and in 1801, with the collapse of the Nawab of Arcot, added the rest of the eastern districts. The southern portion of these districts had not been under the effective control of the Nawab, but rather in the hands of the poligar (*palaiyagar*) chieftains. These had been reduced slowly and painfully since the 1760s, and were finally subdued after a war of attrition between 1799 and 1801.[85]

The British thus inherited the remains of several different ruling systems. The Nawab, a Mughal viceroy, had introduced some but not much of the Mughal style of bureaucracy, and some but not much of the Mughal system of land-tax. Along with the other rulers and pretenders of the period, his concern had been to keep an army in the field rather than to establish a system of administration. His treasury had never functioned well (which had resulted in the debts to the Company on which their claims to cession were mounted) and he had tended to raise taxes casually but cruelly when they were needed. He established few courts, and did little for irrigation or other public works, but managed in 1744 to bring the Hindu temples of the region under a greater degree of central control than they had ever experienced before.[86] Tipu had been somewhat more single-minded, if only slightly more efficient. He was intent upon raising the wealth of the country that he commanded in order to be able to cream as much of it off as he could. He encouraged trade (which led to a large trade over the Ghats between Tamilnad and the Mysore Deccan), and tried to extend the area of cultivation, particularly in cash-crops that might be useful for commerce. He also tried to establish a firm system of land revenue, based on land assessment, and to collect these revenues through a bureaucracy rather than tax-farmers. This was never as regular or successful as it might have been. There was a reasonably sophisticated and complete scheme of land-assessment and of other tax-assessments, notably *moturpha* (professional) and *sayer* (transit) dues, but the demand was pitched enormously high and only the irregularity of collection allowed the system to survive.[87] Meanwhile the poligars of the south, particularly once they were under pressure from the British, Tipu and others, abandoned any pretence of settled administration in favour of a sort of guerrilla state.[88]

This was not very hopeful material but it was not entirely unpromising. Indeed, in the opening years of the nineteenth century, Fort St George's governors adopted the better bits of each of their inheritances and seemed set fair to establish a state structure that was stronger than anything previously seen in the region. From Arcot, they adopted the Mughal system of courts and seemed ready to improve and strengthen it with elements from the more advanced Mughal system of the north. Also from the Nawab, they inherited the important care of religious institutions. As the East India Company, they already had a virtual monopoly of the region's external trade. By adopting Tipu's *sayer* and *moturpha* taxes they took a strong grip on internal commerce, while in the south of the peninsula they had taken over the grain trade as a safe method to supply the troops fighting the poligars. As for revenue, the Company's officers, Read and Munro, found the remnants of Tipu's sophisticated, strict and bureaucratic system in Salem, dubbed it 'ryotwari' and argued that it was the proper system for the whole region.[89]

But very soon, Fort St George drew back from the possibilities of oriental despotism. Largely this was a decision dictated by resources. It would almost certainly have been expensive to establish such a system, and the East India Company was suffering financially from two decades of intermittent warfare. Bombay and Bengal had already emerged as the most important centres of the commercial and political empire, and begun to overshadow Madras. Further, there was not the manpower. Tipu and the Nawab did not leave behind many officials or official institutions that could be drawn into the framework of Company Raj, and the poligars had left absolutely none. Finally there was a growing ideological objection: India, it was thought by many in Calcutta and London, should be ruled lightly and by and large conservatively. Within twenty years the Company's commercial monopoly was gone, the judicial system had been allowed to languish, most of the troops had been withdrawn to the north, every effort had been made to free the government from any involvement in the grain trade, the idea of perfecting Tipu's revenue system had been abandoned, and plans were afoot to extricate the Company from the administration and care of the temples. The Raj, in the south at least, was in retreat.

For the first half of the nineteenth century, then, Madras enjoyed a fairly minimal form of government. Imperial rule amounted to raising enough revenue to support the army and the Company's central administration, to send a slender bureaucratic and judicial presence into the districts and to provide a small surplus for public works.

The Government of Madras's first attempt to create a systematic revenue system reflected this desire to leave well alone. No sooner had they fought the poligars into submission than they set about resurrecting them as the agents of imperial control in the countryside, and even extending the poligari system to parts of the region which had never experienced it before. The idea was that poligars would act as a combination of estate owners and revenue farmers and would thus provide government with a flow of revenue without the need for government itself to interfere too deeply in the affairs of rural society. Thus when the Government of Madras sat down to make its treaty with the poligars at the end of the war in 1801, it borrowed from Bengal the Permanent Settlement regulation, which had guaranteed the Moghul-appointed zamindars possession of their territories in return for a fixed annual tribute, and applied it to all the remaining Madras poligars, except those whose part in the war had been especially flagrant. Then they began carving up parts of Chingleput, Salem and Dindigul into blocks known as mittas, and offered them at auction as estates under the same Permanent Settlement system.[90]

The policy had a mixed success. Most of the old poligari estates survived through into the twentieth century. It proved difficult for the warlords of the eighteenth century to transform themselves into the revenue-managers of the nineteenth but it did not prove impossible. Their authority over men, which was bestowed by lineage, tradition, and terror, and which had once been used to raise troops, could be harnessed to collect the revenue, and by and large government left them to do it in their own fashion. For the newly-created mittas, however, the matter was far less simple. The auction-purchasers of the new mittas included old officials, merchants, and local cultivators. They did not have sufficient authority to mobilize men and resources in the manner of the established poligars. Given the harsh conditions of the plains, it was necessary to have some special authority to push cultivation forward, create a surplus, and draw a revenue from it even in the best of times. And the early nineteenth century was not the best of times. Much of the plains had not recovered from the era of intermittent warfare; the population was sparse and irrigation works in bad repair. The government did not give the newly created mittadars much time or leeway to build up their estates, but insisted on an immediate flow of tribute. As a result, the people who took on the mittas looked on them as a short-term speculation rather than a long-term investment. The demand for mittas was so low that they could be secured at auction for ridiculously low sums; it was possible to recoup this and make a reasonable profit by taxing the peasantry; and there was little obligation to pass much of the proceeds on to government. When the mittadar reneged on his obligation to remit revenue, there was little the government could do but take back the estate and put the mittadar in jail; many of the speculators found a short spell in jail a reasonable price to pay for a quick profit; and thus the turnover of mittadars was astoundingly high. By 1818, there were only a few mittas which had acquired any sort of permanence, and they were mostly ones which had been taken over by local chiefs and lineage heads who were functionally equivalent to the poligars proper. Meanwhile the Madras jails were packed with the men whom the British were trying to mould into a new landed gentry.[91]

By and large the geographical distribution of estates (poligari and mittadari) followed a clear pattern (see map 9). They were all on the plains, scattered around the edges of the old valley territories. The old Pandya country, where the Madurai Nayaks had used a poligari settlement to the greatest extent and where the invaders had least successfully penetrated, was almost completely ringed by estates, while there were broken rings around the Kaveri and Tondai territories. There were none in the valleys, and very few in those areas of the plain that had been recently ruled by Tipu or the Nawab. In other words, the estate system worked in those areas which had long been under the control of local military chieftains. These estates covered roughly a quarter of the Tamil country.[92]

By the time the failure of the Permanent Settlement was apparent, the Madras Government was already experimenting with other revenue systems. Indeed the problem of devising a suitable form of revenue system for Madras had quickly become a matter for considerable dispute. While this dispute was conducted mainly in the realm of ideological argument (thereby creating the source material for countless studies of policy-making), the actual evolution of the revenue system on the ground depended on practical experimentation rather than on theoretical nicety. Between 1800 and 1820, the Madras government tried out a host of revenue systems. Moreover, each 'system' was not systematically applied, but was passed out to the Collectors of the various districts as a set of guidelines which the Collectors were required to interpret and implement according to local conditions.[93] The result was an enormous variety of local practice. Different systems worked in different areas largely, as in the case of the Permanent Settlement, according to the dispensation of local society to accept or reject; and every system was modified slightly to suit the contours of the local landscape. The process was rather like the craft of batik. Fort St George poured numerous variously coloured revenue systems over rural Madras and each adhered in a different area, according to the way the local material had been prepared by its own social history.

There was some experimentation with watered-down versions of the Permanent Settlement in which villages were leased out singly rather than in estate-size aggregations, and for fixed terms of three or ten years rather than 'permanently', but the experiment had all the disadvantages and none of the merits of the Permanent Settlement and was soon condemned to failure. At the ideological level, the victory in the dispute over the most suitable revenue system was won by the advocates of 'ryotwari' which was, in theory at least, a form of collection direct from the cultivating peasant without the intervention of any feudatory chief, tax-farmer, co-sharing brotherhood, or village lessee. It was, in other words, a system of direct settlement between government and the farmer.

The system originated from the settlement work done by two officers, Read and Munro, in the Baramahal and Ceded Districts in the 1790s, and was destined to become the characteristic revenue system for Madras after Munro became Governor of the Presidency in the 1820s. Read and Munro argued that they found in operation, in the Baramahal and Telugu Ceded Districts, a system in which each peasant paid revenue for his own holding, that this revenue was calculated according to the extent and productivity of his land and reckoned as a percentage of the yield, and that this holding and revenue demand might alter from year to year according to the decision of the cultivator. Most important was the idea that the system was based on accurate village records, which showed individual plots and their revenue liability, and that these records provided both the charter of the individual peasant's freedom and the means by which the state might collect the revenue regularly, fairly and without assistance of intermediaries.[94]

Munro and Read argued that ryotwari was the indigenous revenue system of rural Madras. But it is important to realize that their evidence for this claim stemmed from one particular sort of region with certain very special local characteristics. Firstly, both the Baramahal and the Ceded Districts were plains areas; land was relatively freely available and there were none of the co-operative *kaniyatchikaran* village elites or tied labourers of the valleys. From such an environment Munro and Read could derive a system centred on the model of an individual peasant farmer who could vary his landholding from year to year. Secondly both the Baramahal and the Ceded Districts had been ruled by Tipu Sultan who had dismantled the poligari superstructure which had stood over these villages and often humbled local lineage heads as well. It was thus possible to derive a system in which there were no political intermediaries in the revenue system. Finally Tipu had also tried to perfect the system of village office and improve local records, which meant that there were village registers which Read and Munro could present as the lynch-pin of the relationship between government and cultivator. It was noticeable that in their arguments about the 'traditional' character of the ryotwari system, Munro and Read brought forward hardly any evidence which predated Mysore rule.

In other words, the ryotwari system, as Read and Munro found it, was the product of the recent local history of a specific part of the plains. But Munro argued that it was traditional, and characteristic of the south as a whole. He also argued that, in its elimination of wasteful intermediaries and its reliance on records of actual culti- vation, it was a beautiful example of the principles of Ricardian economics. It was thus both conservative and utilitarian. This was an irresistible combination of arguments.[95]

From 1822 onwards, the ryotwari system was applied to all the areas of the province which were not happily marshalled under the Permanent Settlement. However, few of these areas resembled Read and Munro's description of the Baramahal and Ceded Districts. There were co-sharing villages, gentleman farmers, village chiefs, systems of revenue payment in kind, and a host of other characteristics which found no place in the theory of ryotwari tenure. Yet ryotwari was applied; not because it successfully submerged all theoretically embarrassing local practices, but rather because it was bent to local circumstance. This flexibility was achieved by two devices. Firstly government did not bother too much with the survey of land and the establishment of proper land records, and was quite happy to allow individual Collectors to implement the ryotwari principle according to their own interpreta- tions. Looking back from 1855, Fort St George confessed that the early ryotwari settlement had been a rather slipshod affair:

In some districts attempts were made in the years immediately succeeding the British assumption to establish something like a register of lands, and fixed rates of assessment, founded on actual measurement and valuation. But these measures were in every case carried out in haste, with imperfect agency, and in many respects in a very defective manner. The surveyors, so called, were wholly ignorant of any correct methods of measuring, and were under no effective control; there were no maps, either field, village or talook, and no permanent boundaries; and even the records of the surveys have been imperfectly preserved.... But these defective and imperfect surveys extended to only a few Districts; and there are many even at the present day wherein the land revenue demand is based merely on the unchecked statement of the Curnum, who thus has vast opportunity both of making exaction on the Ryots, and in collusion with them of defrauding the government.[96]

Secondly, despite the fact that the point of the ryotwari system was that government should deal only with the ryot or actual cultivator of the soil, the government made absolutely no attempt to define exactly who the cultivator was or to identify him among the complex ranks of rural Madras.

It was necessary to ignore this latter problem because it simply was so vexed. In both the plains and valley villages there were several different sorts of people who had some hand in the management of land. In the plains there were the local chieftain and the village officer whose role stemmed from the political settlement of the area, the lineage head and family head whose role stemmed from the kin-based organization of the clan territory, and finally the man who stood behind the plough.[97] In the valleys, there were the government agents often known as *nattars* or *pattackdars* who had been appointed by the post-Vijayanagar political authorities to organize production on behalf of the state. Then there were the *kaniyatchikarans*, better known to the British by the Persian title of mirasidars, who might have either individual, joint or rotating claims in the management of a certain piece of land, and who played absolutely no part in the labour of cultivation. Next there was the Pallan labourer, who might or might not have a hereditary right to work on the land and be supported by a share in the produce. Finally there might also be *kavalgar* who had established himself as the guardian of the land.[98] Who was the 'cultivator' in either of these cases? The answer of course was he who could claim the title without fear of contradiction within the locality, and could amass the revenue which the government demanded. In other words, it was the political elite of the village.

This meant that in neither plains nor valleys did the practical operation of the ryotwari settlement match the theoretical pattern very closely. In both cases the application of ryotwari evoked local protests and the settlement then had to be modified to suit local taste. In the plains this was reasonably straightforward. As we have noted above, the people of the plains did not place a high social value on the control of individual plots of land. The territory of the village fell under the management of the lineage head and state-appointed village officers, who maintained their authority through control over men rather than over land. This political elite was however worried that with the ryotwari settlement government would interfere with their management of land, undermine their own privileges, and contrive a much more fixed pattern of land distribution within the village than was usual. They were worried about the consequences of issuing pattas (land deeds) to each 'ryot'. They soon found however that they had little to fear. The government agreed to issue pattas each year, which meant that there was no trouble about changing the pattern of land occupation within the village from year to year because of lineage reorganization or shifting cultivation.[99] It also left the business of keeping the records, issuing pattas, and collecting the revenue up to the village officers. In practice the ryotwari system in the plains meant a settlement with the village headmen. They were left in much the same position of control which they had occupied in pre-British times, and they were also rewarded for their co-operation with government in much the same way as before. Previous states had rewarded village headmen and other village officers and artisans by granting them pieces of land and discounting their revenue liability. These lands were known as inams. In the first half of the nineteenth century the British by and large left these inam lands alone, even though they suspected that village officers had successfully inflated their holdings during the troubles of the eighteenth century and during the confusion of the early British rule, up to a point where in some villages over forty per cent of the land was held by village officials as inam.[100]

In the valleys, the administration of ryotwari was much more difficult. Here control over land was greatly valued; indeed it did in itself define the political elite of the village. The ryotwari settlement aimed to assign each plot of cultivated land to each individual 'cultivator', but the mirasidari (*kaniyatchikaran*) elite of the village claimed to control all the village land, not just that part which was cultivated; they sometimes managed the land jointly or by some form of rotation, and they took little part in the business of 'cultivation'. Nor was there any strong tradition of village office. The mirasidars had in the past managed to forestall government attempts to place in the village its own officials who would inevitably compromise their own claims to absolute control. Finally the ryotwari settlement prescribed revenue payments in cash whereas the mirasidars preferred to pay in kind as a share of the harvest and thus oblige government to bear some of the brunt of the fluctuations of the season.[101]

Throughout the valleys there were sporadic protests against the implementation of ryotwari. Attempts to collect revenue in cash were constantly frustrated by the mirasidars' refusal to comply. A Collector in South Arcot who tried to break up the mirasidars' control of the uncultivated land of some villages provoked such a riot that he had to be quickly transferred out of the district.[102] An attempt to conduct a field-by-field survey of land in the Tambraparni valley faced such local oppposition that it ground to a halt after only fifteen villages had been completed.[103] In Mannargudi taluk in the Kaveri delta government officials did, with great difficulty and much expense, compile a survey which showed in detail each field, each boundary and each 'owner'. Some years later when they wanted to refer to this survey, they found that the several copies, which had been lodged in government offices in the taluk and district headquarters, had all been systematically destroyed. A survey of South Arcot district suffered much the same fate.[104]

For the British, as much as for previous governments, the importance of drawing the revenue out of the rich valley areas dictated a careful settlement with the mirasidars. Rather vaguely in law, and rather more openly in administrative practice, they recognized the mirasidars' claim to manage the whole lands of the village. Government officials indulged in a constant and massively irrelevant debate about the exact nature of the mirasi right, particularly about the remnants of its corporate aspects, and the ways in which these might be accommodated with British-based land laws;[105] meanwhile in practice the government allowed joint systems to continue in the villages by not enforcing a distribution of pattas. Sometimes the mirasidars took the village on one 'joint patta', sometimes a head mirasidar merely took up the whole village on a single patta and then organized internal affairs without reference to the government's ryotwari rules, and sometimes the government simply allowed the village to be assessed as a whole as though the ryotwari principle did not exist. In Tanjavur, where the mirasidar protests were strongest, most of the villages remained under *mottamfaisal* or lump-sum assessments until the 1890s and those few conversions to a ryotwari approximation were achieved by negotiation with the mirasidars and 'made largely in accordance with their wishes'.[106] Government also gave way substantially on the question of cash assessments and until the 1830s was still assessing and collecting rents in kind in large tracts of the valleys.[107] In the Tambraparni, for instance, the government gave way to such an extent that for some time the mirasidars were allowed the best of both worlds: the annual demand was collected each year as a share of the harvest, which enabled the mirasidars to pass on the effects of seasonal misfortune to the government, and the grain thus collected was then handed back to the mirasidars who acted as contractors for converting the grain into cash. Eventually by the 1820s the villages where the annual yield was fairly steady and predictable agreed to accept a cash demand based on an average rather than an annually adjusted share of the harvest, but because prices were dropping government had to agree to index-link this cash demand to current grain prices. The less secure villages resisted such transformation until the 1830s and then only capitulated after the government promised to be very liberal with remissions in bad years.[108]

The executive arm of the government was not apparently very anxious to foist a new tenurial system on rural Tamilnad. Nor were the British courts going, in this period at least, to act as agents of social reformation. The British created very few law-courts in the rural areas, indeed far fewer than were wanted. Every time a new type of court was instituted, it quickly became jammed with business, and there was a constant stream of petitions demanding more facilities for legal dispute. Furthermore, Munro insisted on keeping the revenue and judicial parts of the administration together. While this suited his image of an all-powerful, paternal administration, it also ensured that the higher courts would be managed by people with no special knowledge of or training in law. It became a standing joke that decisions in the Madras courts, even the Supreme Presidency court, were more a matter of luck than judgment, and the overall effect was to confine most matters of dispute settlement to the locality.[109]

From about mid-century, however, the government began moves to tighten up the administration.[110] In the early part of the century, when the air had echoed to the sound of utilitarian argument and reformist fervour, the administration had in fact accommodated itself to local circumstance. Ideology had been a surrogate for implementation. After mid-century, when the utilitarian ardour was spent, and the officers of the new Imperial Raj were informed merely by an ideal of 'good administration' , governmental measures began to bite, though not always exactly as intended. The pressure for change came initially from individuals who were disgruntled or outraged about the conduct of imperial rule. Later the pressure became more clearly financial; revenue administration would have to be more efficient if the precarious finances of the Raj were to survive the cost of the Mutiny, Afghan wars and the like. Finally there was also a humanitarian motive for reform; the Indian Empire should be made as upright and warm-hearted as its Queen-Empress.

These early pressures for change came from many sources. The prospect of the revision of the East India Company's charter in the mid-1850s occasioned widespread reflection on the state of the Empire. A number of European lawyers practising in Madras wrote humorous and outraged pamphlets about the farcical state of British justice in India.[111] A number of departmental investigations revealed the extent to which the fragmentation of the revenue system allowed those at the lower levels—powerful payees, village officers, and subordinate officials—to divert a considerable slice of government dues into their own pockets.[112] Administrative experience showed that zamindars tended to be steely rack-renters or incompetent bankrupts, and that the lack of any proper tenurial law was probably the reason.[113] A rather half-hearted attempt to control the scandals of inam tenures created a bitter agitation.[114] Collectors' reported that the boundary stones laid to record the facts of early field surveys had often been systematically destroyed, rendering the rest of the survey material absolutely meaningless.[115] The summary conclusion was that the early settlement of the region had been achieved under pressures of time, poor resources and insistent revenue demands, and that its shortcomings were now too obvious. So, the Raj started again.

Between 1855 and 1870 there was a flurry of new administrative initiatives. The foundations were laid for a new pyramid of law courts.[116] A new central police force was established.[117] Judicial activity began to involve government again in the business of temple management.[118] The Inams Commission investigated every claim to a preferential tenure, abolished all those that were suspect or which had been invented illegally since the British arrival, and regularized those remaining.[119] The Revenue Recovery Act of 1865 laid down, for the first time, a strict legal picture of the rights of the zamindar in levying rent from his tenants, and the rights of the tenant to resist eviction.[120] Most significantly of all, 1865 saw a decision to submit the entire 'ryotwari' area to a precise survey, and on the basis of this survey to mount a new ryotwari settlement with standard rules and practices for the whole province.[121]

None of these moves was an unqualified success. There were more courts available, but it was still reckoned that Madras justice was little better than a roulette wheel and litigants aproached the courts with a studied callousness which was neatly captured by the observations of a cheerful Irish official, J.T.Gwynn, in 1908:

Just been having a most interesting interview with a sub-magistrate who was explaining to me why so many more witnesses are cited in cases in this town [Tiruchi] than elsewhere. It appears that there is in this town a recognised establishment known as the Witness Depot. You do not here bribe your witness yourself. You send a note through your lawyer to the Depot specifying the grade of witness you want and the facts to be proved. The lowest grade is a 5 rupee man. Grades run from that upwards. Rs 5 for a cooly (of course a trained man warranted to stand cross-examination), Rs 10 for a varam [crop-share] cultivator or petty shop-keeper or a Christian, Rs 20 for a ryot paying kist [land-tax] to government, a railway employee or Eurasian out of work and so on up to Rs 50 which is the price of an income tax payer. Trichy is a very advanced town.'[122]

The revised police force was too small to patrol the entire province. It was hoped that it would be able to supervise the village watchmen and use them to provide more effective police control in the countryside, but this proved a pious hope and the police remained an urban force which was useful in the rural areas only in an emergency and even then with mixed results. This was illustrated by an incident in Ramnad in the early twentieth century. The head of the district police found out that trouble was brewing in the countryside only when a remote missionary sent a message to tell him that his girl converts were unaccountably reluctant to come to school. He immediately swung the forces of law and order into action: that is he sent thirty-six constables down to the station to wait for the next train while he sought around the town for a car to replace his own (which was out of order) and spent some time haggling over a suitable rental fee. By the time the police arrived in the affected area on the following day, they found that the half-mile length of main street in the market town had been completely burnt out, that there had been riots and looting in nearby villages, and that an area of twenty or thirty villages had been in uproar for the last three or four days. The head of police was a little suprised by his ignorance of these goings-on, but admitted that it was a good thing he had not turned up earlier since the hundred troops sent from the neighbouring district to help turned out to belong to the same caste (Maravar) as those on the rampage and might well have added to the disorder rather than quelling it.[123] The might of the Empire was rather obscured in the countryside.

The Inams Commission was not able to uncover as many fraudulent titles as government supposed to exist. In advance of the Commission's investigation, Fort St George had reckoned that some hundred lakhs of rupees of revenue had been alienated under inam and that much of that could be recovered, but the commission only managed to increase the revenue by eight lakhs.[124] After looking at the variety in the customary relations between zamindar and tenant in different parts of the province, government shied away from a strict charter of rights and obligations and merely passed an Act stating that all contracts for rent 'express or implied' should be respected. It took only a handful of contradictory High Court decisions to put the state of the law back into exactly the same mess it had been in before the Act.[125]

Government might not be gaining a much greater grip on rural society, but was at least trying. The sum total of these measures brought government more firmly into the countryside than before. The new courts broadened the scope of governmental arbitration. The Inams Commission's enquiry went far beyond any previous governmental investigation in both width and depth. The Revenue Recovery Act at least meant that the courts and government would henceforth be almost constantly involved in the technicalities of zamindari law, and that a series of further enactments would follow around the turn of the century. The police did occasionally enter the villages and bring the heavy hand of government to bear in a local dispute; the angry reaction which such an action often evoked from the villagers showed how novel and significant such intervention was. Much the same mixture of failure-but-change marked the imposition of the new survey and settlement.

Between 1862 and 1890, Fort St George compiled an accurate survey of all the ryotwari land in each of the Tamil districts, and recorded the results in a variety of maps, registers, and accounts. Henceforward, each 'ryot' was to hold a patta deed for the lands he occupied (the old pattas had been little more than receipts for revenue paid at the end of the season); each strip of land was assessed for revenue at a rate of (usually) thirty per cent of the net yield of the land, calculated according to a complex formula which theoretically took account of the productivity of the soil, the expenses of cultivation, the level of prices, the facilities for marketing, and other similar factors. These assessments were to be revised every thirty years. The thirty per cent net rate was lower than previous rates, and it was decreed now that remissions would only be available when the climate was unusually harsh.[126] Fort St George now knew what the land was (the surveys revealed enormous extents concealed from view) and knew who the 'cultivators' were. Munro's dream of a peasant society could now be realized.

Or could it? The Madras administration remained sensitive to its own weaknesses, and anxious not to prejudice the collection of revenue by dogmatic innovation. What is most remarkable about all the discussions surrounding the introduction of the new surveys and the 'late-ryotwari' settlement, was that there was still absolutely no discussion of who the 'ryot' was. It was simply assumed that the earlier settlements had fixed this satisfactorily. Moreover, there were still strenuous attempts to satisfy those elements, chiefly the deltaic mirasidars, who disliked the notion of a ryotwari settlement. Thus government accepted the idea that villages could still be held jointly, even if to some extent this position had to be fictionalised in the records. The rules for *darkhast*—that is for the assignment of newly occupied land—were framed so that the right of assignment rested in theory with government, but in practice with leading men of the village.[127] And finally the settlement of the most truculent mirasidari area, Tanjavur district, was left as late as possible. It was not completed until the 1890s, and still provoked such an effective protest that some villages were left out of the ryotwari settlement.[128]

Thus throughout the century the British settlement of rural Tamilnad depended on an accomodation with the political elites of the countryside. In a way that was not very different from previous regimes, the British left the mirasidars in reasonably untrammelled control of the valley villages, while putting their weight firmly behind the chiefly families and village headmen of the plains. Indeed, as the century progressed and the British administration of rural Madras became marginally more deliberate, this pattern of connection between state and rural elite was strengthened rather than weakened. In the valleys, where previous states had under-written the dual stratification of society by confirming the ritual division between the mirasidari elite and the rest of the village, the British achieved much the same result by granting effective recognition of mirasi claims and by issuing pattas only to mirasidars and not to other members of the village. In the early settlements they accorded preferential rights to some local Brahman and Vellala notables who based their claims on caste privilege, and towards the end of the century they began to give greater acknowledgement to the entire structure of caste which emphasized the stratification of the village into high-caste land-controllers and outcasted subordinates.[129] In the plains, they confirmed the chiefs in the Permanent Settlement and gradually added to the powers of the village officer.[130] They thereby extended the tendency of previous rulers to build up the hierarchical structure of plains society by political grant.

There were two consequences of this pattern of governmental accommodation which require special emphasis. The first is the simple point that the nineteenth century did not see a wholesale reconstruction of Tamil rural society along 'colonial lines'. Indeed in this period Tamil rural society looked very much as it had done in previous centuries. There were of course adjustments and portents of the future, but these were for the moment relatively unimportant. In the valleys the mirasidars were firmly in control. In the plains government recognized (by implication) that it was only possible to extract revenue by the use of an authority which was derived from some combination of past military glory and present political force. The zamindars were allowed to run their own police and judicial systems and government did not interfere too closely even when zamindari officials wielded the baton a little too wildly. When certain estates got into trouble and the government was forced to take over the administration for a short time, the government officers often found that cultivation contracted and revenue fell.[131] In other words it still required a heavy hand to keep much of the rough plains territory under cultivation.[132] In those parts where the old chiefs had been removed, the government's own local officer, the tahsildar, often assumed the role of coercive chief. The Torture Commission Report of 1855 revealed that tahsildars and village officers in the plains were often just as brutal as any military chief in their attempts to raise revenue.[133]

The second point is that the uncertainties of the ryotwari settlement combined with the chaos of legal procedure to thwart any notion that the colonial state was introducing anything like a western, capitalist concept of property. When the government gave up its attempt to mould society to the ryotwari system and effectively allowed the ryotwari system to be moulded by the contours of local society, it thereby assured that local notions of rights in land would not be immediately superceded by notions of 'ownership' and 'title' which the ryotwari settlement envisaged. Government expected that the detailed survey and the issue of pattas to each 'ryot' in the post-1850s revenue resettlements would not only facilitate revenue collection but would also provide cultivators with a secure title in land. But in fact the pattas failed to acquire a legal status.[134] As we have already seen, the allocation of pattas in the first place only bore a tangential relationship to the locally-recognized distribution of control over land. There was no way in which this single deed could cope with the various layers of rights in land, and the various subdivisions of these rights according to the complex Hindu law of the family. Moreover, if in the first place these deeds made only a very rough attempt to describe and to guarantee local rights, with the passage of time the position became worse rather than better. The main trouble was that the procedure for transfer of patta deeds operated through the taluk office and, as a government committee noted in 1915: 'Disposals in the Taluk Offices mean the intervention of greedy, unintelligent or jaded Taluk subordinates'[135] and thus most ryots found it simpler not to bother about the patta at all: 'Very few pattas are granted nowadays and very few ryots come to the jamanbandi camp to receive patta. Why should they? How does it improve their position?'[136] The result was that the patta registry contained the names of many who had long since lost any interest in the land. It also became more and more difficult to match the piece of paper to the land to which it referred. It was reported that a large amount of the government's work in launching legal process for recovering arrears of unpaid revenue arose because individuals who acquired land deeds by inheritance or settlement of debt found that one of the few reliable ways to discover what land the deed referred to was simply to neglect paying the revenue and allow the government to undertake the work of identification.[137]

But control of land was important, particularly in the valleys and, as we shall see below, increasingly in Kongunad and the plains as well. Since the patta offered no evidence of title, it was necessary to resort to the courts. Here the position was only marginally better. There were few civil courts set up and, since the imported legal procedure allowed virtually limitless resort to adjournment and appeal, they were always crammed with business and decisions could not be achieved promptly. In the lower courts the judges were legal amateurs, there was little attention to laws of evidence, the mixture of English property law and Hindu family law created innumerable contradictions, and the lack of written evidence of title placed a premium on oral evidence which was notoriously open to corruption.[138] It was thus dificult to predict the court's decision. Finally, the procedure for enforcing court decrees was notoriously unreliable. Here the agency was the court amins, who were few in number, ill-paid, and famous for their venality. 'At their hands', wrote one exasperated litigant, 'the Decrees even of the High Court become waste paper.'[139]

There were a large number of cases over land ownership submitted to the Madras courts and of course many were successful. Indeed, they helped to make the patta registry even more inaccurate:

Another cause of divergence between the revenue registry and the facts is furnished by proceedings of Civil Courts, which necessarily take place behind the back of the Revenue Department. Private suits affecting boundaries or rights to ryotwari land and therefore affecting the entries in the revenue registry constitute a substantial part of the litigations of the Presidency. In disposing of such suits, the Judge is not bound to take cognizance of the revenue registers or to communicate his findings to the Revenue Department.[140]

But resort to the courts was an expensive, lengthy, and unreliable business. It was certainly not secure enough to constitute an effective guarantee of rights in land. 'As things stand at present', noted a Tamil banker and lawyer in 1930, 'it cannot definitely be said who is the owner of a particular bit of land.'[141] As a result of this confusion in the courts and in the administration of ryotwari, it was not so much the state which acted as the guarantor of property, but the local community. The government itself had to admit that this was so. 'The system is ryotwari,' noted one Collector, 'but no officer of Government knows who the ryot is, in about fifty per cent of the cases or more, except the village officers. I have never asked a village officer how he knew from whom to collect. I do not allow collection to be impeded.'[142] Village officers kept private notebooks, and of course never showed them to higher officials. When the Collector made his annual tour of the district to close the accounts, he frequently came up against disputes which could only be decided by recourse to the true record of affairs in the village officers' private records. At this point the representative of the Queen-Empress had to stand embarassedly to one side while the village officers got out their own records and settled the matter.[143] One official put the ratio of 'government-settled' villages to 'village-officer-settled' villages at about two to three.[144]

In some cases, the dominance of local law over state law created special difficulties for government. The inhabitants of plains village occasionally hit on a brilliantly simple way to reduce their revenue demand; they simply omitted to pay revenue, the government moved in and sold up the land for arrears, at auction the land was knocked down for a trivial sum which was much less than the original revenue demand (and which in some cases was raised by public subscription in the village).[145] The result was that land titles circulated around the village, but, to the government's dismay, this seemed to make little difference to the actual disposition or usage of land in the village.[146] There was also a constant trickle of reports of civil court decrees which had been unceremoniously overturned by a local panchayat. The government was constantly puzzled by the fact that the courts (and executive officers) were constantly being requested to adjudicate in seemingly petty disputes over, for instance, minute pieces of property. It was clear in such cases that the plaintiff could not make an economic gain from such a case and British officials simply concluded that such people were 'litigious' by nature.[147] But this conclusion simply misunderstood the way in which people were using the courts. They were often pursuing litigation in order to achieve a political advantage. Local political elites had in the past looked upwards to the state or overlord to underwrite claims to local political pre-eminence. The executive arm of the British state was notoriously unwilling to perform this sort of service in a systematic fashion, but victory in the courts seems to have come to act as a form of surrogate. A court victory, however pyrrhic, represented a governmental endorsement of local domination. It was ironic but entirely logical that this curious form of endorsement remained important precisely because government failed to replace local systems of law with effective systems of its own. There was a concept of property in nineteenth-century rural Madras but it was one which was operated by the political system of the locality and only occasionally modified by the larger political system of the colonial state.

In sum, the style of rural administration in colonial Tamilnad was decided more by the constraints of local circumstance than by the reforming ideologies of nineteenth-century Britain. The state system settled down gently over the varied contours of local Madras. In the second half of the century there were some attempts to tighten up the systems of governance which led on to a considerable process of reorganization, centralization and professionalization of the upper levels of government in the last quarter of the century. But this process of administrative reorganization for the moment stopped short of the village. Government continued to deal with rural Madras through the agency of the local political elites, and as the superstructure of government became more powerful, this merely tended to strengthen the position of these local elites and to give added emphasis to the local pattern of political control—the stratification of the valleys, the pyramidical hierarchy of the plains.

It was not however that nothing changed in nineteenth-century rural Tamilnad. The rapid pace of social change in previous centuries had not suddenly ground to a halt, though it is possible that with the virtual elimination of one of the major agencies of social change—warfare—there was some slowing of the pace. But these developments within the political framework of rural Madras did not take place in isolation. We must now look at the agricultural economy.

AGRICULTURAL GROWTH

Tamilnad's agriculture expanded through the nineteenth century. The expansion was far from steady for it was punctuated by a price slump in the 1830s and by bad bouts of famine in the 1860s, 1870s and 1890s. Nor can the expansion be quantified; there are simply no reliable figures. Yet there was a succession of favourable influences. British rule did bring to an end the tendency of foreign warriors to use the plains as a battleground and the valleys as an informal commissariat. The high level of land revenue demand probably impeded expansion for much of the first half of the century but from the 1840s onwards prices were slowly but steadily improving and British land revenue officers were becoming marginally more sensible. Then the 1840s saw a noticeable change in British government expenditure. From that decade onwards, small but nonetheless significant sums were spent on major irrigation works and on roads and other forms of communication. From the 1860s on, Tamilnad began to feel the pull of increased international demand for agricultural raw materials.

In the valleys this expansion meant a return to settled conditions and a gradual but definite expansion of the region's habitual regime of paddy cultivation. The crucial decade was the 1840s. By then the government's assault on the mirasidars had petered away, and it had begun to realize its responsibility for irrigation. District Collectors had all along been organizing the repair of existing irrigation works in a piecemeal fashion, but in the 1840s Arthur Cotton and his associates among the Madras engineers began to turn irrigation into a Victorian crusade:

So long as one drop of water is allowed to run waste into the sea, we must take blame to ourselves for not exerting our best efforts to obviate the evils of poverty or the dreadful effects of famine.[148]

Cotton and his colleagues concentrated on large-scale works on the major river-systems of the region. Some were constructions of considerable technical bravura, others merely repairs and extensions to old irrigation systems. The most important in Tamilnad fell on the Kaveri and Tambraparni rivers. At the same time, government attempted to oblige local landowners to honour their presumed responsibilities, known as *kudimaramat*, to maintain smaller irrigation works.

The response of the valley mirasidars was enthusiastic. They magnified the government's efforts by contributing their own funds to assist the major government projects and raising further sums for totally private projects. The mirasidars were also happy to act as labour contractors and to offer their tied labourers to work on government irrigation repair schemes at a price. Finally they were ready, at the deliberately low water rates fixed by government, to take up every cusec of water provided.[149] As a result the irrigated area expanded significantly in the second half of the century. Srinivasa Raghavaiyangar estimated that the acreage under government works in Madras Presidency grew from 2.3 million to 3.4 million between 1852 and 1890 while the acreage under private irrigation grew from 0.4 million to 1 million.[150] While these figures are government's own records as interpreted by its most enthusiastic local employee, and must therefore be treated with some care, there are others who corroborate the general pattern. In his study of Tirunelveli district in the nineteenth century, David Ludden has estimated that the irrigated acreage under the Tambraparni river system was growing at something like 1 – 1½ per cent per annum through the middle of the nineteenth century.

David Ludden's study points out two other important features of this expansion. Firstly, it was concentrated in the heartlands of the valley regions, where cultivation was already at its most secure. Government concentrated on such regions because the water supply was comparatively reliable and the technical problems were by and large minimized so that projects would achieve the greatest expansion of cultivation (and thus also the greatest return in water dues) for the least outlay. Government devised a quasi-commercial system for assessing irrigation projects and this pattern of location was the inevitable result. Secondly, the lion's share of the expansion of irrigated cultivation under these new works was achieved not by the incorporation of new lands but by double-cropping on existing irrigated fields. These valley heartlands were already densely settled and thus the chief avenue for expansion was inevitably intensification of cultivation practices rather than extension of area. The expansion of valley agriculture in the mid-nineteenth century, therefore, did little to disturb the existing pattern of society. Government irrigation works merely added to the prosperity of those who were already in control of the most secure and fertile tracts in the region. Indeed, for the valley mirasidars the nineteenth century was something of a golden age. The Government junked its own utilitarian principles to give them the revenue settlement they wanted, supplied them with better irrigation, employed them first as grain contractors then as irrigation contractors and later as servants in the expanding bureaucracy, built roads and railways which took their surplus paddy to markets in Madras City, Ceylon and south-east Asia, provided courts which were thankfully inaccessible to their dependents and which thus could – with skill – be used to confirm mirasidari privileges, and finally flatterred their social pretensions by honouring the notions of the Sastraic caste system which had long underwritten the stratification of valley society.

In the plains, the expansion of agriculture was greater both in its extent and in its social impact. Here government assisted the expansion not through irrigation but through communications. Indeed it did little or nothing to assist irrigation outside the valley centres except for some rather half-hearted attempts to repair tanks and to encourage landowners to fulfill their *kudimaramat* obligations.[152] Communications, however, were especially important for the plains. Their economy, as we have already seen, had always depended on a considerable volume of trade round the periodic marketing circles which passed through the *kottai-pettai* settlements and the temporary local markets or shandies (*sandais*). The plains were a poor place for producing food, but were a good place for growing certain other crops such as spices, oilseeds, cotton and pulses, for producing building materials such as bricks, tiles, stone, and timber, and for breeding cattle. The expansion of the plains economy depended crucially on the ability to import food to supplement local production of poor millets, and on the ability to export the range of local produce.

In the eighteenth century, local trade was hampered by warfare, by the attempts of local rulers to raise tolls, by the predations of disorderly militias and other highway robbers, and by the state of the roads; in 1800, 'there was not one complete road throughout the whole Presidency on which it would have been possible to employ wheeled carriages' and one of the main roads down to the south was said to be difficult going 'owing to the frequent intervention of paddy fields'.[153] The chief means of internal transport were the pack-bullock and the ass. These were slow, had a limited capacity, and were expensive. It was estimated early in the nineteenth century that the cost of carrying grain just eight miles added one third to the price. Under these conditions, most of the trade was in the hands of people who were very close to being robbers themselves—the gypsy-like Brinjaras and Lambadies—and the only articles carried over any distance in any considerable quantities were salt, which was a necessity, various luxury items which commmanded a good price, and cattle, which transported themselves. The only exceptions to this pattern were the extraordinary pockets of demand created by mobile armies, or by the resplendent courts of successful rulers, such as Tipu in Mysore and Martanda Varma in Travancore.[154]

From the beginning of its rule, Fort St George repaired certain roads for military use, but the major change came in the 1840s when the government set about turning the straggling mule tracks into passable roads. Some, like the 'cotton road' built down through Madurai and Tirunelveli to the port of Tuticorin, were designed to encourage exports, but others were built merely to assist the passage of government officials, soldiers, and traders through the interior of the country. At the start of the nineteenth century, government reckoned, carts were used for local transport but were 'never used for distant journeys'. By 1850 there were an estimated 90,000 carts in the province, and by 1877-8 the figure had risen to 284,000.[155]

Cart freight was still expensive, and it made no sense to carry grain, particularly the coarse cheap millets of the plains, more than a few miles. Carting did however encourage the production and trade of articles with a better value-to-weight ratio, such as vegetables, spices, fruit, betel; and produce for local and export trade like sugar, indigo, tobacco and cotton. And as carts became more common, so they became cheaper, and one estimate reckoned that the cost halved between the 1840s and the 1880s.[156] Some of this reduction may have been caused by competition with the railways, for in the 1880s rail transport cost on average a quarter of the rate for carts per ton mile. But the railways did not wipe out carts; indeed they encouraged them since the railway network was skeletal and carts had to be used to carry from the interior to the rail-head. In the decade after 1877-8, the estimated number of carts in the province rose from 284,000 to 436,000.[157]

Railways did make it economic to carry bulky goods like paddy and oilseed over considerable distances. The early network, built between 1860 and 1880, merely linked together the three valley centres, Kongunad and Madras City, connected them to routes to the north and west, and in so doing joined the cotton and rice-growing areas to the main ports. Between 1880 and 1900 there were just two lines built across the groundnut-producing area; and after 1900 there were several small lines added, mainly in the Kaveri and Tambraparni deltas. By 1920, the network covered the main cities and ports, and the rice and cotton areas in some detail, but there was only a handful of lines branching into the plain.

Peace and roads were the conditions necessary for expansion. It is not possible to give a statistical account of this expansion because the government's surveillance of the dry cultivation of the plains was nowhere near as good as the monitoring of irrigated areas in the valleys. However, a number of reports by travellers between the late seventeenth and early nineteenth centuries indicate that at this time considerable areas of the plains were still either scrub, forest, or wasteland. In the mid-seventeenth century, Tavernier found the western fringe of the Tondai country covered in impenetrable forest infested with monkeys. The south-eastern coastal region was still covered in jungle and inhabited by tigers, and the black-cotton soil in the north of Tirunelveli was still covered with forest in the mid-eighteenth century.[158] The British troops had enormous difficulties in penetrating stretches of forest in the Arcots plain and in Ramnad during the fighting of the second half of the eighteenth century.[159] Buchanan found traces of past cultivation but little current agriculture during his traverse of north and north-western Tamilnad around 1801.[160] Elija Hoole passed through jungle continuously except in the immediate vicinity of the rivers in his journey down the coast southwards from Madras in 1820, and found much of southern Salem covered by jungle and inhabited by the ever-threatening tiger.[161] There is piecemeal evidence that these areas were being cleared very rapidly in the early nineteenth century. Much of the expansion was no doubt the recouping of lands lost in recent fighting, but some represented new clearances. In the 1790s, Read abandoned the idea of a permanent settlement of the revenue and moved towards the idea of the more flexible ryotwari system when he discovered just how fast cultivation was expanding in Salem and realized that a permanent settlement would deny government the benefits of a similarly expanding revenue.[162] Arrowsmith's map of Tamilnad in 1822 suggests that forests in the Arcots and Ramnad, which the troops had had to hack their way through half a century earlier, had already been rapidly cleared.[163] The resettlement party in Salem in 1861 reckoned that cultivation had grown twelve per cent in ten years, and another estimate of 'dry' cultivation in Salem in the late 1860s reckoned that acreage had grown from 6½ to 10¾ lakh acres in under twenty years.[164] By the time of the surveys of the 'late ryotwari' settlement, all the areas mentioned as forest in the travellers' accounts cited above had been largely cleared and submitted to the plough.

For most of the century, the plains seem to have acted as an internal frontier. Land was relatively freely available and had almost no market price.[165] Cultivation was still to some extent operated on a shifting system. In 1855 in South Arcot government reckoned that the area under cultivation shifted by about ten to fifteen per cent a year.[166] Times of adversity would produce massive movements of population. According to one report some 150,000 persons, or half the population, quit Ramnad after a series of bad rainfalls, and both government and zamindars found that cultivators would protest with their feet if the revenue demand was too high.[167] In these conditions, the expansion of acreage seems to have run ahead of the population. The Collector of Tirunelveli reported that the barrier to increased cultivation of cotton was not the availability of land but the provision of labour.[168] The number of pattas or land deeds issued by the revenue administration increased steadily in the second half of the century.[169]

Commercial activity expanded in parallel. Settlement reports regularly spoke of the increasing number of shandies—the number in Tirunelveli rose from thirty-five in 1823 to seventy-six in 1880—[170] and although some of the expansion can be attributed to the greater watchfulness of the enumerators, much of it was undoubtedly real. Meanwhile the first of the all-India censuses taken in 1871 and 1881 showed that plains Tamilnad was scattered with burgeoning small-towns. The 1881 Census found eighty-two towns in Tamilnad with populations between five and fifteen thousand; many of these were old *kottai-pettai* settlements, perhaps now swollen by the location of a railway station, road junction or government sub-office. The commerce of these local markets and small towns consisted in local exchange, reciprocal trade with the valley regions, and, increasingly as the second half of the century wore on, supply of commodities for overseas trade. The communities who handled this trade were two sorts.[171] Firstly there were the 'immigrant' merchants, mostly Telugus and Kannadas, who had come south with the warrior expansion of post-medieval times and had established themselves in the business of periodic marketing as part and parcel of the process of settlement on the plains. The Devangas and Balijas dominated the markets in Salem and Kongunad; the Komatis and Beri Chetties who had long dominated the peddling markets on the Arcots plain now also moved into the channels of long-distance trading and some of them settled in Madras and the other ports of Tamilnad's east coast. Secondly, there were local communities who expanded the other way from the ports to the interior on the impetus of expanding overseas trade. The Labbai Muslims moved inwards along the routes of the hides and skins trade and took a considerable role in the markets of the Arcots and Madurai.[172] The Shanars, who were branded as toddy-tappers but who had long since diversified into landholding and local trade in the far south, expanded northwards into the growing cotton-marketing towns of Tirunelveli and Madurai.[173] A number of fishing communities from the littoral, notably the Paravas in

Tuticorin, also built on a long history of activity in the colonial ports and moved into commerce in the immediate hinterland.[174]

While there is (albeit circumstantial) evidence to suggest that the plains economy expanded quite freely and easily for much of the century, there is (equally circumstantial) evidence that the expansion had begun to reach some sort of ceiling by the last quarter. Clearly peace and economic expansion resulted in a considerable growth of population, although the exact statistical outlines of this growth cannot easily be made out. Government took censuses of Tamilnad's population regularly from 1823 onwards, and according to these estimates the population of 1823 had doubled by 1866-7 and almost tripled by 1901. It is certain that the earlier censuses under-enumerated and thus tended to accentuate the rate of increase. It is noticeable that the recorded increase in districts which the British knew well early in the century is much less than that in those which they hardly knew at all. In Salem, which had been Read and Munro's stamping ground and which remained of interest to British officials throughout the period of the early settlements, the census reckoned that the population had just doubled between 1823 and 1901, whereas in South Arcot, which remained a blank on most British administrative maps until mid-century, the recorded increase was five times. The Salem figure is probably nearer the truth. Anyway, this was still a considerable increase and the censuses suggest that much of it was concentrated on the plains.[175]

In Salem, where officials had commented on the rate of agricultural expansion since the 1790s, a revenue officer noted in 1870 that 'almost every inch of cultivable land is now taken up'.[176] Between then and the end of the century, many other officials reported on the declining availablity of new land in the plains.[177] Certainly the expansion was not punctuated quite so neatly or so conclusively, but it is still probable that whereas land had been expanding faster than population until the 1860s or 1870s, thereafter the roles were reversed. Dharma Kumar calculates that over Madras Presidency as a whole, land and population were moving roughly in parallel between 1884-5 and the end of the century.[178] Meanwhile on the plains the surest signs of the closing of the frontier were the gradual disappearance of shifting cultivation and the increasing saleability of land. In the early part of the nineteenth century there were numerous reports that dry land had no pecuniary value.[179] As the Tiruchi Collector reported in 1826, 'the ryots are poor, cultivate a small extent of land each, and are not considered to have any proprietary right in it'. By the 1890s figures of around ten to fifty rupees an acre were beginning to be mentioned.[180]

These were just the outward signs of a major shift in the foundations of plains society, away from the flexible, militaristic society of old to one which depended on agriculture. This was not of course just a sudden switch. Agricultural expansion had from the very beginning formed part of the military colonization of the plains. But the nineteenth century still saw a major change of emphasis. The profits of warfare had declined, while those of agriculture had increased, and by the end of the century the dependence on agriculture was such that the scarcity of land had become noticeable. In this period, there were many signs of the strains of transition. The military character of the plains had not been immediately submerged by pax Britannica at the start of the nineteenth century. Because the British made virtually no attempt to provide for the policing of the rural areas, there was still a call on militia services. The zamindars continued to use their military peons to keep peace, encourage cultivation and drag out the revenue in their estates, and other villages were still ready to hire *kavalgars* to protect their crops and cattle; indeed the partial demobilization of the poligar armies after 1801 initially increased the threat to law and order and raised the premium on *kaval* · services.[181] As the century wore on, however, the demand for military services declined. The zamindars relied more on the assistance of the British administration to coerce recalcitrant tenants, and allowed their private armies to decay. Except in the more remote regions, villagers came to rely more and more on the ability of the roads and railways to bring the government's police into the countryside when necessary. The 1870s, 80s and 90s were clearly years of transition, for in the period there were many of the signs of local militias being carelessly demobbed. These were the great years for 'dacoity' in the south, and the police force spent much of its energy capturing militiamen who had taken to marauding.[182] There were also reports of villages rejecting the services of their *kavalgars*,[183] and more and more reports of the institution known as *tuppukuli*, a mixture of rustling and protection racket which was clearly the last resort of unemployed *kavalgars*. The disorders of this period lingered on until, with the help of the obtuseness of the police department, large sections of the Kallars and the Padaiyichis were labelled as 'Criminal Tribes'.[184] Among all these ructions, the most eloquent evidence of the social transition of this period was offered by the violent clashes in the southern districts between Shanars and Maravars. The Shanars belonged to a community which was considered low in status because of its association with toddy-tapping, but which was rapidly growing richer on the expanding commerce of the plains towns. The Maravars looked back to a high status as warriors, but looked forward to a more equivocal future in an increasingly cramped agriculture, and they bitterly resented any attempts on the part of the Shanars to convert new wealth into new status. This see-saw movement in the prospects and self-images of the two communities provided the background for a series of communal incidents and communal riots in the last quarter of the century.[185]

CONCLUSION: THE THREE REGIONS

The history of Tamilnad passed through three distinct phases. The first was dominated by the agricultural civilization of the river valleys, and saw the elaboration of a material culture centred on rice and irrigation, and a political culture structured around temples and Brahmanical codes of social status. The second was dominated by the military talents of the plains and saw new forms of social organization formed in the process of military colonization, and a new political culture which emphasized the importance of military power. This new material and social culture was laid over and reacted with that of the valleys; the social organization of the plains was influenced by some of the notions of status so important in the valleys, and the valleys in turn had to find some form of accommodation with the military and political systems of the plains. The third period brought the two societies even closer together. The inroads of foreign invaders broke down the land and sea boundaries which had kept Tamilnad in relative isolation, and set off internal movements of military mobilization and demographic resettlement which blurred the boundaries between valleys and plains. Moreover while in the short-term this period saw a fragmentation of political authority and a drive towards local autonomy, in the long term it encouraged the growth of a centralized political authority.

Yet despite these rapprochements and overlays, at the time of the British conquest there were still marked differences between valleys and plains, while Kongunad had emerged as a third region with distinctive characteristics of its own. The local variety of the region's history has meant, as many have observed, that each Tamil village is somehow different from every other one, yet it is still possible to describe two very different cultures which the British found in the valleys and plains at the outset of the colonial period, and a third variant in Kongunad which is in many ways a hybrid of the other two. Given the local variety, and given the tendency of the regions to merge fairly gradually into one another at the frontiers, any description of these separate regions must deal only in archetypes and must admit that there is an infinite number of variations which combine different features of the two systems in a different distinctive mix. Yet deep in the valleys, way out on the plains, and far off in Kongunad there were societies which were modelled by their distinctive geographical setting and their particular historical experience.

Valleys

The rivers made possible a relatively secure agriculture based on rice and permanent irrigation works. Over the years the valleys had become prosperous and relatively densely populated. The ability to dominate the region and to benefit from its fertility had long depended on control over the one resource which was in finite supply, land, and the ability to use the one resource which required careful, co-operative organization, irrigation water.[186]

The settlements of population in the valleys were distributed along the water-course in a close stipple of small hamlets. These settlements were dominated by the Vellalas and Brahmans who had been the earliest settlers and who had first devised forms of co-operative management to control the land and organize the flow of irrigation water. The social organization of the valley villages still contained elements of these systems of management. The organizing notion was *kaniyatchi,* literally control of land. The leaders of the village still expressed their privileged rights in terms of a share (*pangu*) in this control (*kaniyatchi*), as heirs, literal or metaphorical, of the original settlers. Although the resources of the village may once have been managed completely communally by the association of *kaniyatchikarans,* the *pangus* had generally speaking been divided into individual units. However the remnants of corporateness often remained in the form of some village council of *kaniyatchikarans* and, more particularly, in the idea that *kaniyatchi* entailed not only a claim on a cultivated plot but also a share in the control of the entire territory of the village including waste-lands, roads, house-sites, and grazing grounds.[187]

This claim to total, exclusive control of the village on the part of the *kaniyatchi* elite had to be buttressed by ritual exclusiveness as well. The fecundity of irrigated rice agriculture attracted many people to the valleys and made it possible for the *kaniyatchikarans* to distance themselves from cultivation. The land was worked by non-*kaniyatchikarans* who accepted a serf-like status in return for a share (however meagre) in the valleys' reliable harvests. With the help of the state authorities, which underwrote *kaniyatchi,* and with the help of Sastraic sociology and its emphasis on hierarchy, the *kaniyatchikarans* could not only keep the labourers outside the village by forcing them to dwell in separate hamlets, but also keep them outside Hindu society, by labelling them as 'outcaste' or 'untouchable'.

The valley villages were thus divided into two exclusive sections—the privileged corporation of Brahman and Vellala *kaniyatchikarans,* and the outcaste labourers who were usually Pallan or Paraiyan. The maintenance of exclusive land control also dictated a series of different social and political strategies. The first line of defence was created by rules for marriage and inheritance which confined the right to privilege within narrow limits. Cross-cousin marriage was favoured by the valley elite, and marriage circles were relatively small.[188] But varna rules and tight marriage patterns could not cope with the strains imposed by the expansion of the valleys through the extension of irrigation or the swelling of the valley population with the irruption of military adventurers. In response, the concept of Vellala developed into a flexible status-category which could admit acceptable or irresistible newcomers without causing any damage to the notion of stratification which buttressed the valley's system of agricultural production.[189] Over the years the ranks of the Vellala swelled to include many who had no connection with the early settlers. The early inhabitants merely retained sub-caste names which reflected their claims to noble ancestry—Choliya, Tondaimandalam, Tuluva, Pandya, Karaikatha, Kondai-

kottai. Meanwhile most of the immigrants readily adapted themselves to the norms of valley culture. Even those who were
originally just land-grabbing plains soldiery or upstart recipients of
royal grants, often grew into Vellala-hood by changing their gods,
their food habits, their funeral rites and other distinctive customs.
Some of the later waves of settlers, particularly those who moved
into the valleys in the disorder of the eighteenth century, still had
their original names and titles, but had so changed their social habits
that they had nothing in common with their erstwhile kinsmen who
still lived on the plains. This was most noticeable among the various
settlements of the Kallar. Others who had moved into the valleys
somewhat earlier had even adopted a new title which stressed that
they were separate from their cousins remaining on the plains;
generally this title was one which had denoted a noble rank in their
old community (Agamudaiyan, Udaiyan) or one which meant
village lord or village head (Pillai, Mudaliar, Nattaiman, Nattar).[190]
Finally some had made the full transition to Vellala with the result
that the British census in its attempt to count 'sub-castes' found
over 900 units among the Vellala.[191] These niceties of nomenclature
meant that the route through which a rough plainsman could find
his way into valley society had become proverbial: 'A Kallar may
come to be a Maravar, turn into an Agamudaiyan, by slow degrees
attain the title of Vellala, and then set out to be a Mudaliar.'[192]

Thus by the end of the eighteenth century the exclusive land-
control of the Brahman-Vellala nobility had been considerably
dented. Newcomers had been able to buy, seize or be granted a
place in the hierarchy of valley society. Merchants had bought their
way in; rulers had settled warriors, revenue farmers or other
intermediaries; and plains militiamen had moved from providing
kaval guardianship to exerting firmer and more permanent political
control.

The prosperity of the valleys also made them fairly cosmopolitan
in outlook. There was considerable commitment to foreign trading.
The valleys exported rice to Ceylon and the east, and imported
metals, precious stones and all sorts of luxury goods. The ends of
the various river deltas were scattered with seaports. Besides these
port towns, there were also a number of inland towns which grew up
as administrative and religious centres. The country-dwellers maintained close links with these towns through their participation in the
external trading economy, through their commitment to temple-

based religion, and through their association with state authorities. The latter had developed in the early period because the complex society and economy of the valley countryside demanded the services of powerful outside arbitrators to settle potentially debilitating disputes over matters like irrigation and social status. It changed somewhat in the later period when the state wanted to extract a greater flow of surplus out of the delta economy. The growing military power of the state meant that it could impose closer control over the valley countryside, but the threat of withholding vital supplies of food remained as a declining yet residually effective bargaining counter which mitigated the move towards centralization. Except in difficult circumstances, the state generally got its way most effectively by cajoling the support of the *kaniyatchi* elite, and the proverb admitted that 'the Vellala's goad is the ruler's sceptre'. Thus just as much as the state came to impose greater central control over the valley countryside, so the elite of the valley villages penetrated into the ranks of state personnel. It was mostly members of the Brahman-Vellala elite who came to act as state agents in the valley villages and who filled the places in the growing central administrations in the capital towns. Moreover state systems (and trading systems) were inherently and, as times went by increasingly, unstable. The sites of the administrative capitals in the valleys shifted rapidly with the rise and fall of dynasties, and the location of ports was only a little more stable since there were lots of potential harbours though none with particularly outstanding advantages, and the patterns of overseas trade shifted rapidly, particularly from the sixteenth century onwards. In the valleys, the urban centres had none of the fixity and cultural ferocity of the countryside.

Plains

While the productive base of the valleys rested firmly on irrigated rice agriculture, the economy of the plains was very different and somewhat varied. The combination of the harsh climate and (generally) poor soils meant that arable agriculture was not the original, and never the sole support of the population. Rather there was hunting and herding and later more developed forms of animal husbandry. Then there was some inferior cropping of millets which, in the early days, was almost certainly conducted in a shifting, slash-and-burn system. The expansion of settlement from the Vijayanagar period on expanded and stabilized agricultural practices but there were still elements of long-fallow cultivation in the plains agriculture of the nineteenth century. Finally there was the provision of specialist goods and services which could be exchanged with the surplus food of the valleys. These goods and services fell into three categories. Firstly, there were livestock. Cattle were bred on the plains and on the edges of the hills and annually taken along drove-roads which led down through a series of markets in the valleys where they were sold for use in valley agriculture. Sheep and goats were also kept for penning on valley fields to provide manure, and mules and horses were raised for transportation. Secondly, there was protection. From the late medieval period the plainsmen acted as mercenaries for the valley lords in times of war and, under the *kaval* system, gradually came to work as their policemen and defendants in time of peace as well. Thirdly, there was a whole range of ancillary services. The principal of these concerned construction. The plainsmen quarried stone, felled timber and later manufactured bricks and tiles and smelted iron. They sold these and other manufactured products in the valleys.

The importance of agriculture in the valleys made control of land the crucial feature of social organization. By contrast the crucial feature in the plains was control of men. Land was poor and abundantly available to anyone who would clear the scrub, and thus had little or no social or pecuniary value. The importance of military service and, to a lesser extent, the production of goods and services, laid great stress on the control of men and their ability to work or fight. Even agriculture depended to some extent on the ability of controllers of men to force their subordinates to work the rather hopeless soil.

In contrast to the close stipple of agrarian settlements along the valleys, the plains were settled in compact, isolated and fortified villages. Francis Hamilton Buchanan who toured the Tamil districts (and beyond) immediately after the imposition of British authority, left a graphic description of this pattern of settlement:

The country is exceedingly bare and population scanty. All the houses are collected in villages; and the smallest village, of five or six houses, is fortified. The defence of such a village consists of a round stone wall, perhaps forty feet in diameter and six feet high. On the top of this is a parapet of mud, with a door in it, to which the only access is by ladder. In case a plundering party comes near the village, the people ascend into this tower with their families, and most valuable effects, and having drawn up the ladder, defend themselves with stones which even the women throw with great force and dexterity. Larger villages have square forts with round towers at the angles. In those still larger, or in towns, the defences are more numerous, and the fort serves as a citadel; while the village, or Pettah, is surrounded by a weaker defence of mud.[193]

These latter were the fort-mart (*kottai-pettai*) towns which usually marked the headquarters of a local chief or *palaiyagar*.[194]

The social structure of these villages revolved not so much around the management of land as the organization of people. This was achieved through two interlocking systems, one based on kinship and the other on military hierarchy. By the time anthropologists came to study them in the mid-twentieth century, certain of the plains communities had only a skeletal organization at the local level. But in parts of the region there were remnants of an organization based on lineage, lineage heads and clans. Often in such cases, the ambitious families and lineages did not limit themselves to the narrow pattern of marriage which was common in the valleys, but rather sought further afield for alliances which helped to raise or substantiate the status of the individual family and lineage, and which also helped to knit the clan together as a unit.[195] While this system based on kinship grew up from the base, the other system based on military merit and political achievement grew down from above. At the top were chiefs and *palaiyagars* whose families had originally gained their status by military might or royal appointment. In the middle levels of the society, the two systems met and accommodated one another. It was not uncommon, for instance, for the overlord to raise up individuals or whole lineages, because of their talents and services, and endow them with functions and privileges which they did not qualify for on grounds of kinship. Equally, the lower levels of society often invented fictional kinship ties to explain the dominance of political leaders.

The authority created in this hierarchical system was used, not to hold on to land, but to exercise forms of jurisdiction over people and to some extent to control the distribution of food and other scarce resources among the whole population. Leaders at all levels of this society acted as judges over matters concerning the personal conduct of their subordinates. They also operated systems of redistribution. The *palaiyagari* town invariably contained a market which was under strict political control. The village heads operated redistributive systems which closely resembled the jajmani systems of northern India.[196] The surplus of local agriculture, dues from trade and ancillary services, and profits from *kaval* fees were centralized under the control of the village heads and redistributed to labourers, artisans and other subordinates in customary amounts. The chief members of the village would also store any excess produce from a good year, in order to sustain the village through the bad years which, predictably in this region, would follow. The system of economic redistribution was likely to be buttressed by a series of ritual performances which emphasized the centralized character of the village.

The relationship of the countryside to the state and to commerce also differed between valleys and plains. While the valleys sported a small number of large religious and administrative capitals, the plains had numerous small towns, mostly the *kottai-pettai* settlements described above. While the valleys were firmly oriented towards external trade, the plains participated mainly in local trading. The highly dispersed and nucleated pattern of settlement encouraged the growth of a structure of periodic markets. Merchants and artisans trekked round circuits of *kottai-pettai* towns. Moreover, these merchants and artisans rarely belonged to the local rural community. Many of them had entered the country as migrants from the Telugu and Kannada regions, either as refugees from warfare or as camp-followers of the northern armies, while others had probably used the opportunities provided in times of political disorder to quit a lowly calling, enter commerce and thus clamber slightly up the social scale.

As we have already seen, the state-system in the plains from the Vijayanagar period on interfered considerably in the internal organization of the plains countryside in order to achieve its aim of expanding production and creating the basis of a military supply and recruitment system. This meant placing officials, artisans and other ancillary personnel in the villages. Thus besides the groups of Telugus, Padaiyichis, Kallars and Maravars who formed the 'dominant castes' of the plains villages, there was a varied population of outsiders. In many parts, the emphasis on the importance of *men* meant that village leaders provided incentives to attract immigrants to the locality; often, for instance, *parakudi* or outsider-tenants were allowed considerable discounts on local rents and dues against the sums paid by *ulkudis* or insider-tenants. Plains villages thus often include immigrant *parakudis*, 'foreign' merchants who lived and transacted with the locally dominant population but clearly did not belong to it, and state-appointed officials and artisans. The population of the plains countryside was thus often split ritually and socially into two distinct parts, which were often described as left-hand and right-hand. On one side was the dominant warrior community with assorted labouring, artisans, and service personnel who had been part of the original or early settlement, and who were part of the jajmani-style redistributive system centred on the dominant lineage. On the other side was a rather more casual organization of the disparate peoples who were late-comers to the society and who often owed their status and wealth to the state, commerce or some other system beyond the village.[197]

Kongunad

The history and the settlements of Kongunad contain features of both the valley and plains type, but the region is sufficiently distinctive to demand a short treatment on its own. Its physical geography resembled the other regions of the western plains, but with important differences. It was much larger and better defined than the Baramahal or Dindigul country, being a large upland plain almost entirely surrounded by small hills. Its rainfall was lower and even less reliable than the rest of the plain, but it was traversed by some of the important tributaries of the Kaveri, had considerable patches of good black soil and also of good red soil washed down from the Ghats. It also had good reserves of subsoil water and when these could be tapped, the one barrier to a considerable fertility disappeared.

Thus it was a much more promising area than other parts of the plain. It was also more susceptible to invasion. The main east-west route of the southern peninsula passed through the Kongu country in order to cross the Western Ghats through the Palghat gap. Routes from the western Deccan to the Pandya country and parts of the Kaveri crossed it from north to south. For much of its history it had been marched across by traders and armies. Moreover, standing right in between the Kaveri, the Pandya country, the Chera country of the west coast and the Mysore country on the southern Deccan, it had spent most of its history acting either as battleground or a buffer state.[198]

Its society and culture were thus a unique combination of elements of the plains and valley models. Although geographically Kongunad belonged to the plains, its historical role brought it into close contact with the valleys, particularly the Kaveri. The Chola kings made a deliberate attempt to settle and rule the region and the combination of Chola-induced immigration and incorporation of the local population created a majority community which laid claim to Vellala status. These Kongu Vellala, often known as the Gounder, adopted many of the Brahmanical customs and social pretensions of the valley Vellalas. But unlike the latter they also had a history as warriors. They thus had the plains-style social structure based on patrilineage and a hierarchy of supra-lineage political chiefs, known as pattagars, who traced their political status back to military service under the Nayak rulers and political grants which came by way of reward.[199]

As in the plains, the local economy had clearly once been involved chiefly with livestock. The subordinate castes in Kongunad carried names which revealed their early vocations; the most numerous were Valaiyans, which meant hunters, and Chakkiliyans, which meant leather workers. Moreover some of the most important and richest of the Kongu Vellala had become, not big arable farmers, but cattle-ranchers breeding specialist animals for sale both inside and outside the region. But unlike the rest of the plains, Kongunad had also developed a successful agricultural economy. Because rainfall was exceptionally low, and the area which could be watered by local rivers exceptionally limited, cultivation depended on the development of irrigation from wells. Well-building seems to have begun from the time of the early Chola settlements in the medieval period, and to have grown slowly but gradually despite the difficulties of sinking wells in the region and despite the disruptions of intermittent warfare. Wells were a capital investment which made agriculture profitable and thus gave the land they watered a degree of attractiveness and value that was unusual in the rest of the plains. Thus as in the valleys, land-control had become important.[200] Feuds over land were common and had led to the growth of a local customary law over land and land transfer. Thus a history of purchase and seizure had tended to obscure, though not completely destroy, the relationship between kinship and territory which marked most of the plains.

The patterns of trade and of settlement reflected this intermediate position between the valleys and the plains. Kongunad had, like the plains, a number of local chiefly towns connected by circuits of periodic marketing, but it was also crossed by long-distance routes conveying trade from north to south and east to west. As on the plains the settlements were isolated, compact, fortified. But rather in imitation of the valleys peoples who lived close to their fields rather than on a nucleated pattern, the Gounder often deserted his village in the busy agricultural season and went to live in a field-hut on his plot. Similarly as in the valleys the cultivation was rich and intense enough to merit the employment of hired labourers; but unlike the valley mirasidar the Gounder himself was not distanced from cultivation—he proudly stood behind the plough—and unlike the valley pannaiyal the Kongunad labourer was virtually adopted as another member of the Gounder's family rather than being condemned to a separate, low, outcaste, and serfish status.

There was an equally complex mix of ritual attachments. The Gounders venerated household gods, the local deity Murugan who was generally popular among Vellalas in the valleys, and the Vedic deities on top of that. The villages were often divided on the left-right pattern noticed on the plains, but with one curious difference; the Brahmans stood outside and above this division and appeared to function rather like the Brahman of the valley village who stood above the rest in order to be able to confirm the supremacy of the Vellala and give ritual endorsement to their *kaniyatchi* style of land control.[201] The pyramidical hierarchy of the plains was buttressed by the dual stratification of the valleys. The Gounder enjoyed control over both land and men. They were exceptionally powerful.

Until the last quarter of the eighteenth century, so far as the European traders were concerned southern India was merely a rather useful factory for muslins, chintzes, and calicoes. Once the East India Company had fought and bargained its way into governmental control of the region, there was a tendency for the Company's policy-makers to think of it as something of a *tabula rasa*, a convenient laboratory for experiments in colonial government. Yet those who had to implement the Company's policies found that they were dealing with a complex and ancient society whose history had an impetus of its own. As many historians of colonial India have

pointed out, the colonial transformation was tardy and inconclusive. The East India Company was able to centralize control over
its south Indian possessions only slowly and tentatively. It was able
to build on the efforts of the military state-builders of the last three
centuries, but it found it difficult to acclimatize imported ideas and
institutions. The notion of achieving a social and commercial
revolution through legal and political innovation 'from above'
faded gently into the footnotes of intellectual history. There was no
sense in which a new rule of law, concept of property, or framework
of capitalist relations was thrust down upon south India's rural
society.

The agrarian economy did indeed expand, but on a rhythm that
reached back at least into the region's medieval history. The
pressure of an aggressive state system with expansive military aims
continued to push out the frontiers of cultivation just as it had since
the time of the Hoysala and the Vijayanagar warriors. Like its
predecessors, the company based its power in the valleys and spent
money on irrigation to encourage more intensive exploitation of the
valleys' remarkable natural endowment. Similarly the Company
completed the efforts of its predecessors in finally incorporating the
plains and encouraging the extension of arable agriculture into the
remaining reserves of forest, waste and pasture.

The Tamilnad countryside responded well to these demands
partly because it was a flexible society which had grown accustomed
to rapid change, but partly because it forced the colonial rulers to
meet it half way. After a brief initial period of aggrandizement, the
colonial state was obliged to accommodate itself to the contours of
local society. Authority was allowed to fragment, and power was
allowed to devolve onto the leaders of local society. Through its
hit-and-miss efforts to find methods of taxation and policing *which
worked,* the colonial state became a remarkably conservative force.
It succeeded in pushing forward the agrarian economy by identifying the leaders of local society and then abetting their influence.
The valley mirasidars in the nineteenth century were generally
speaking well off, socially as powerful as ever and, by the latter part
of the century, politically ambitious as well. The chiefs and mili-
tarized clansmen of the plains faced pacification, domestication,
and settlement, and this made the transition less smooth and
peaceful; but once they realized that the British posed no threat to
established local notions of privilege and hierarchy, they generally

both co-operated and profited. The accommodation struck with local leaders, and the expansion of the agrarian economy along well-rutted tracks, meant that there was no dramatic reorganization of production. Society was not turned upside down. The century saw the further multiplication of the number of small farmers who used various combinations of family, tied, and paid labour and who grew variously for subsistence, for the state, and for the market.

The last third of the century witnessed a new complex of changes. Firstly, the colonial government set about a new round of centralization and integration. Secondly, the pace of agrarian expansion slowed. In the earlier part of the century, expansion had been particularly rapid as there was room to take up the slack caused by the disorders of recent decades. But the steady erosion of reserves of good land turned the path of expansion metaphorically uphill; the tortoise of demography started to overhaul the hare of cultivation. Thirdly, the ports of the coromandel coast began to welcome more of the new steamships on the rapid run through the Suez canal from Europe. Before going on to consider the history of rural Tamilnad in the twentieth century we must inspect the accounts of colonial trade.

Colonial Trade

In the middle of the nineteenth century Madras slid into a classically 'colonial' pattern of foreign trade. At the start of the century, the Madras ports were mostly exporting the handloomed textiles made on 'Company investment' to a variety of destinations in Asia and Europe, and importing a range of mainly luxury goods from both east and west. By the 1850s, however, Madras was exporting raw materials and importing manufactures, and her dominant trading partner was Imperial Britain. The export of handloom goods had dwindled from the Rs 85 lakhs annual average at the turn of the century to nearer Rs 50 lakhs by 1850 and had been replaced by a massive inflow of Lancashire cottons and a trickle of the metal-ware and other manufactured products of Britain's industrial revolution.[1] Meanwhile the ships leaving the Madras ports were now loaded with a variety of agricultural produce. Madras had long exported grain, mostly to Ceylon, but this rose from Rs 20 lakhs to Rs 50 lakhs per year in the first half of the century, while in the same period raw cotton, indigo and sugar rose from negligible amounts to annual averages of 40, 25 and 20 lakhs respectively. As Madras agriculture was thus introduced more emphatically than ever before to international trade, there was a massive jump in the prices ruling in the internal markets as they made a once-and-for-all adjustment to the prices ruling in the new, encompassing international market.[2] But beside that one major adjustment, prices were reasonably stable and fluctuations mostly reflected seasonal changes.

WEST AND EAST

Madras was only very tentatively drawn into international trade. Around 1900 exports from the Madras Presidency were worth around Rs 12 crores a year, which was roughly equivalent to Rs 3 per head of population. Moreover, between the mid-nineteenth century and the first world war, when Britain moved from the era of Hanoverian expansion to the era of Victorian high imperialism, Madras's fledgling colonial economy failed to mature along the apparently predictable lines. Of course the imports of Britain's textiles and metal-ware gradually increased and were soon supplemented by railway goods, while cotton exports surged in the US Civil war boom and Europeans came to plant coffee, tea, and rubber on the Western Ghats and Tamilnad hills. To that extent, Madras followed the classic pattern of the era. But in the extension of the field of British capitalism and in the ramification of Britain's imperial economy, Madras was hardly a startling success. The Madras farmers failed to grow a suitable long-staple cotton and thus their product interested the Lancashire mill owners only in times of crisis. Madras sugar production could not compete with Java or the Caribbean, indigo could not compete with north India, and tobacco could not compete with Java or North America. The conditions for planting coffee were much inferior to those in Latin America and the Caribbean, and for tea were much worse than Ceylon or the eastern Himalayan foothills. Most of the big companies soon sold up their plantation interests and the south Indian estates were largely the province of small European companies and indigenous entrepreneurs.[3]

Even if Madras was not being drawn more closely into a convenient relationship with British capital, yet she was not immune to the important trends of late nineteenth-century international commerce. The spread of steam shipping and opening of the Suez canal brought down freight charges; the 'second industrial revolution' and rising living standards in Europe increased the demand for the raw materials for consumer industries; and these two factors together exerted a gentle upwards pull on the terms of trade for primary produce, and encouraged European capital to migrate to exotic parts of the world. This period introduced two new trends in Madras's external economy. First, the new incentives to east-west trading resulted not in a closer relationship with the imperial mother-country but rather with other industrial regions of northern Europe and, to some extent, America. Madras's most successful exports in this period were hides and skins and oilseeds, particularly groundnut, and both found their major markets in France and Germany, while much of the region's expanded export of raw cotton went to Belgium and France. Similarly, the companies which invested in and controlled this rising export business were often European rather than British—the Greek Rallis, Swiss Volkarts, French Dreyfus.

Second, within the outer shell of the European-dominated international economy, Madras began to acquire much closer links with the rest of Asia. To some extent, this was a matter of closer links with Asia's only industrializing country, Japan, which was prepared to take supplies of the region's short-staple cotton. But more it consisted of closer ties with the regions which surrounded the Bay of Bengal—Ceylon, Burma, the Straits Settlement and other parts of southeast Asia. Madras had always had strong political and commercial links with these regions, but the late nineteenth century saw a massive change of scale. This was part and parcel of a complex but rapid process which saw different parts of south and southeast Asia develop, under the aegis of European capital, into complementary partners in a new trading system.[4]

European plantation capital moved into sparsely-populated parts of Ceylon, Malaya and Indochina. This created a demand for labour and for the provision of various services, and this in turn created a demand for food and other consumer goods for the labourers and the personnel of the service towns. The deltaic portions of southeast Asia's major rivers—the Irrawaddy, the Chao Phraya and the Mekong—were capable of producing the region's staple, rice, but as yet the deltas were barely utilized and in parts virtually un-populated. With some nudging from Britain and France, these regions were rapidly opened up in the late nineteenth century and soon produced the food necessary for the new agglomerations of plantation labourers and for the growing populations of the ports and service towns attached to the plantation economy. The rice acreage of Cochinchina expanded from 0.5 to 2.2 million between 1880 and 1937, that of Thailand from an estimated 2 million in 1855 (when the Bowring treaty dragged the country into the inter-national economy) to over 7 million in the 1920s, and that of Burma from 600,000 to 8 million over the same period.[5]

At first Madras contributed something to this new supply of food and her exports of rice to Ceylon and elsewhere grew steadily up to the first world war. In this role, however, Madras was rapidly overhauled by the frontier economics and virgin soils of the new rice deltas. Where Madras was much more successful was in providing a supply of labour and, to a lesser extent, a supply of services and consumer necessities. The site of the new European plantations in southeast Asia was dictated largely by the availability of land (and thus by the absence of a dense local population) and for that reason they quickly exhausted local supplies of labour. The expansion into the rice deltas also soon gathered momentum and ran beyond the existing reserves of mobile labour. Here was clearly a frontier of opportunity which looked remarkably deep and wide to those who viewed it from the cramped conditions of eastern India.

Madras already had some experience in exporting labour to southeast Asia and elsewhere. In the seventeenth century, the Dutch had found that spice production exhausted the local labour supply in Java and had imported some labour from south India, while for many centuries Tamils had been trading, working, and settling in Ceylon. In the early nineteenth century the British soon got used to the idea of despatching their Indian subjects to labour for British capital in far-flung parts of the world. Some Tamilians went to the West Indies in the 1840s, and some to Mauritius, British Guyana, and Natal in the 1850s and 60s.[6] The development of plantations and rice deltas in southeast Asia quickened the pace. There was a drift of Indians into Malaya continuously from the eighteenth century; from 1844 government and planters began to assist passages and the numbers rose to 4-6,000 per annum between the 1860s and 1890s. Most of these were Tamils, and most worked on sugar and (later) coffee estates. The development of rubber production saw the numbers shoot up and reach a peak of 160,000 in the mid-1920s.[7] Migration to the coffee estates in Ceylon picked up from the 1830s, and expanded rapidly when tea and rubber were planted from mid-century. The annual movement by the 1880s was in the region of 40,000 a year.[8] When the Burma delta was opened up, south Indians, mostly Telugus but also some Tamils, went as frontiersmen, labourers and urban workers. By 1921 there were 387,509 Tamils in Malaya, 275,000 south Indians in Burma and some 600,000 Tamils in Ceylon.[9]

Trade followed the migrant. The Kaveri and Tambraparni deltas had long supplied Ceylon with rice, and this export trade boomed as the migration increased. In occasional years, there was also export of grain to Malaya, but this was rare. Much more significant was the trade in textiles. The efforts of the European traders had already made a market for south Indian weaving in the spice regions and this market grew, partly to supply the new south Indian migrants in the region, but also to supply an expanding market among the indigenous population. While rice and textiles were the most important exports, there were many others, for south Indian tradesmen followed the labour migrants to supply them with their accustomed foods and accoutrements.[10] By 1901 Indians formed about half the population of Rangoon; another 35,000 lived in Penang; and both Kuala Lumpur and Singapore also had strong concentrations. Indeed, by the early twentieth century, Penang was on its way to becoming the second city of Tamil India.

After trade came investment. The most noted of the overseas Tamil investors were the Nattukottai Chettiars, bankers from Ramnad district. Most probably they were drawn into this business through their involvement in financing the Kaveri rice trade, which took them to Ceylon, where they started up in local finance, and then extended similar business to Malaya and, in particular, Burma. Their enormous involvement in Burma probably began in earnest around 1880.[11]

The scale of their operation is of course difficult to measure with accuracy. One estimate dating from the early twentieth century reckoned that there were 750 Chettiar firms registered in Ceylon, with an aggregate capital of 7½ million pounds. This investment covered almost every commercial activity from lending small sums to estate workers, to large trading concerns, and the odd industrial enterprise.[12] Besides the Chettiars there were a number of other south Indian trader-financiers on the island, and the 1933-5 Census found 76,947 Indians of trading caste, over a third of the total Indian population.[13] In Malaya, there were also a number of small-scale south Indian financiers in the later nineteenth century, most notably acting as middlemen in the fishing business. Then Chettiars came in to finance small-holding, to make loans to the Malayan princes, to supply working capital for some estates, and to lend to labourers. There are no early estimates of the scale of the enterprise but three estimates between 1946 and 1951 put total Indian investment in Malaya between Rs 170 million and Rs 1,000 million, with about three-quarters of this owned by Chettiars.[14] In Burma, the Chettiars were active in financing trade in Rangoon, and in providing capital for Burmese money-lenders to use in the country-side. In the 1880s they moved out into the frontier towns in the expanding rice acreage of the Irrawaddy delta and lent directly to those clearing and tilling the land. By 1910 there were 350 Chettiar firms, and by 1930 that had risen to 1,650. At that date, they commanded nearly sixty per cent of short-term agricultural lending and forty-five per cent of long-term finance in the Lower Delta and their capital was estimated at between 450 and 500 million rupees.[15] Finally there was investment in land. Some of this evolved out of the lending by Chettiars, who had acquired six per cent of the cultivated area of Lower Burma by the early twentieth century.[16] But there were also a number of Indian peasant settlers both in Burma and Malaya, as well as the large settled Tamil agricultural community in northern Ceylon. By the 1930s, Indians held 235,000 acres of small-holding in Malaya, which was eight per cent of the small-holding area, and also 242 rubber estates, mostly quite small ones.[17]

It is tempting to describe this connection of India, and parti-cularly Tamil India, to the expanding economy of southeast Asia in the language of economic imperialism. The flow of trade was clearly asymmetrical: India exported mainly manufactures—chiefly tex-tiles but also a variety of artisan produce—and imported mainly primary produce such as arecanut, spices, metals and later Burma rice. Although most of the Chettiar capital was generated in southeast Asia itself by the high rate of return, there was initially some export of capital. Furthermore most of the Chettiar firms kept their headquarters in south India, developed a sophisticated system of out-agencies, and remitted considerable funds home. There was also a growing movement of colonization. Although in the nine-teenth century most of the migration to all three territories was short-term and migrants returned within one to four years, from the turn of the century there was more and more settlement. Finally the remittances back to India, particularly those by the educated south Indians whom the British brought in to help administer the terri-tories in the late nineteenth century, could be construed as the 'home charges'. Again there is no accurate information on the level of remittance. The Malayan Year Book put the total for the years 1935-40 and 1946-7, admittedly years when there was a net outflow

Table 2: Distribution of foreign trade of Madras Presidency, 1886-7 to 1955-6

Trade (imports + exports + re-exports) with each country as a percentage of total trade

	Britain	France	Germany	Belgium	Italy	Netherlands	USA	Canada	Australasia	Japan	Ceylon	Burma	Straits Settlement	Malaya	Indonesia	China and Hong Kong	Iraq	Egypt
1886-7	62.5	9.5	0.1	0.5			2.2		0.6		9.0	3.6	3.3		0.1	0.2	0.1	2.9
1890-1	59.7	9.5	0.7	1.3			3.1		0.3		8.4	5.3	2.8		0.1	1.0	0.1	2.4
1895-6	52.5	8.0	2.1	2.4		0.2	5.7		0.3	2.3	8.4	7.4	3.0		0.1	1.6	0.1	1.6
1900-1	49.0	4.3	3.0	3.7		0.3	4.1		0.7	1.0	9.2	12.9	4.9		0.1	0.2	0.1	1.3
1905-6	42.3	7.5	5.2	4.9		0.4	5.2	0.6	0.7	3.2	9.7	11.1	3.4		0.6	1.1	0.1	0.4
1910-1	35.7	9.3	5.7	4.7		0.7	4.2	0.6	0.8	4.1	11.3	13.7	3.6		1.2	0.8		0.1
1915-6	42.2	7.9	0.1	0.1	0.1	0.3	5.5	0.1	0.9	2.6	17.6	10.7	4.9		1.0	1.0		0.1
1920-1	44.1	3.7	1.0	3.5	0.3	1.0	6.2	0.2	0.7	2.7	8.7	14.9	5.8		0.9	1.4		0.2
1925-6	29.9	8.3	5.6	3.7	2.5	3.7	5.3	0.2	0.4	5.9	8.9	15.9	4.3	0.3	1.1	1.3	0.3	0.1
1930-1	32.1	5.9	6.9	2.2	1.6	5.2	5.1	0.4	0.3	2.5	9.6	17.4	2.5	0.4	2.4	1.0	0.6	0.1
1935-6	33.7	5.0	5.6	1.6	1.0	3.0	4.2	0.3	0.4	4.1	6.1	25.4	1.4	0.3	1.1	0.3	0.4	0.4
1940-1	37.1	1.1		0.4	0.5	0.1	10.4	0.9	1.6	3.4	22.6	22.6	3.7	0.7	1.1	4.3	0.5	0.5
1945-6	34.2	0.5			0.1		24.1	2.4	2.4		16.6	1.5				0.2	11.6	0.3
1950-1	25.4	1.6	2.2	2.1	3.2	2.3	17.6	3.3	4.3	1.2	5.4	6.8	1.8	1.4	0.7	1.6	3.7	2.4
1955-6	31.6	2.2	6.7	2.8	2.6	3.4	10.7	1.2	1.6	6.6	8.9	2.6	1.4	2.1	0.7	1.2	0.8	0.9

Sources: *Annual Statement of the Sea-Borne Trade of India*; *Annual Statement of the Sea-Borne Trade of the Madras Presidency*.

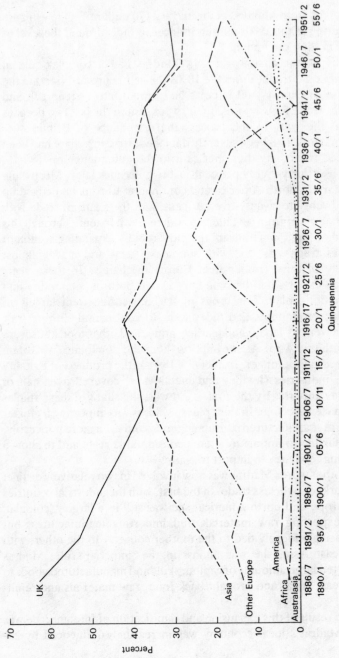

Graph 1   Shares of Madras Presidency trade by continent 1886-7 to 1955-6

Note: The graph shows the percentage of total trade (exports, imports and re-exports) with each continent and with the UK.

Source: *Annual Statement of the Sea-Borne Trade and Navigation of the Madras Presidency.*

of Indians from Malaya, at around Rs 170 million.[18] One estimate for Burma in the 1930s put remittances to India around the level of Rs 30 million per annum.[19]

Thus by the first world war, Madras had a complex role in international trade. From the 1890s the gentle upward trend in the volume of exports and imports had turned into a steep rise and Madras trade grew by roughly fifty per cent in the last two decades before the war. In the process the dominance of Britain over Madras trade had been severely damaged; Britain's share had been reduced from sixty-three per cent in the quinquennium 1886/7 – 1890/1 to thirty-eighty per cent just two decades later. Meanwhile the share of north America and continental Europe had edged up from twenty to twenty-five per cent, and the share of trade with Asia had risen from seventeen to thirty-five per cent. Through this period of 'high imperialism' the most rapidly expanding section of Madras trade was that with southeast Asia; and it was almost entirely in local (rather than European) hands. In these years Madras exports had become very varied both in commodity and destination—plantation crops of tea and coffee went largely to Britain; groundnuts and hides went to continental Europe; raw cotton went to Japan; and textiles, grain, and other foodstuffs went to southeast Asia. As for imports, here the dominance of Britain lingered rather longer. In 1886/7 – 1890/1, the products of Britain's staple industries (textiles and metal-ware) covered over half of Madras imports. By the first world war, the share of these staples was in clear decline. In their place, Madras was importing a greater range of manufactured consumer goods, and even more noticeably, was starting to import food on a considerable scale and to show a growing tendency to import treasure.

In other words Madras was now involved in two relatively distinct networks of overseas trade. In the first, with the industrial countries of Europe and north America, she was still in a largely 'colonial' role exporting raw materials and importing manufactures, but increasingly loosely tied to the mother country. In the other, with southeast Asia, she was almost in the 'imperial' role; Madras exported large amounts of capital, skills and manufactured goods to southeast Asia, and brought back food, raw materials and remittance.

The result of this expansion and ramification of foreign trade was that Madras's local economy was increasingly influenced by external factors. By the end of the century there was hardly a single product grown or made in Tamilnad which was not, in some quantity great or small, loaded onto a ship and sold abroad. As a share of the region's total production, exports were not especially significant. Estimates of this proportion, for India as a whole, range between ten and thirty per cent, and the difference between these estimates indicates the problems of calculation.[20] If, however, we were to remove from the calculation those items which were produced for susbsistence and which only entered the marketplace in the tiniest quantities—in particular, the coarse millets—then the share of exports would rise significantly. Moreover, there were other factors which exaggerated the importance of the external economy. Several of the crops and other items produced for export enjoyed little demand in the local economy. Groundnut oil was not appreciated locally, until the 1930s there was not the industrial capacity to absorb local cotton production, and there was only a limited market for hides and skins. Furthermore, the sale of these items was often the only means available for the Tamilnad culti-vator to realize the cash he needed to cover certain unavoidable expenses. Thus in the short term, the supply of these products was very inelastic, and the internal level of prices was very vulnerable to external fluctuations. Finally, the handling of export produce quickly became the most lively and probably the most profitable element of local commerce. The prosperity and the confidence of export trading thus sent ripples through the local trading sector as well. The two sectors were often dominated by the same whole-saling firms at the top, borrowed much of their funds in the same money-market, and worked through the same local traders at the bottom. If export trading was in a healthy state, then the local money-market would be easy, wholesalers expansive, local traders active and Tamilnad commerce as a whole would look bullish and buoyant. If export trading looked sickly, the banks and money-lenders would withdraw their funds from the bazaar and this would affect local trade as much as export trade. In the later nineteenth century, local prices in Madras were drawn into line with foreign price-levels and from then onwards the fluctuations of international markets, and the international purchasing price of the rupee gradually supplanted the weather and local supply conditions as the major ruling influence over local prices.

The international levels of Madras's major export products were decided in the major clearing markets in Europe.[21] Liverpool oversaw the market in cotton, London dominated hides and sugar, Hamburg and Marseilles dealt in oilseeds. In these markets, Madras was usually a very minor supplier and thus had little influence on the overall level of activity. The case of hides was something of an exception, but for cotton the market was dominated by the supplies from America, and for oilseeds there was chaos of competition between west African palm-nuts, Egyptian cotton-seeds, north Atlantic whales and many other oil-bearing products.[22] In the case of rice there was no dominating marketplace but as time went on the price in Madras was increasingly influenced by the mobile supplies from Burma and the other southeast Asian deltas.[23]

Thus by the turn of the century Madras was in a position where the level of her trade and the level of her prices were largely influenced by conditions in some of the primary produce markets in Europe. Moreover Madras was a minor participant in these markets and thus had little leverage in their workings. Then in the early twentieth century these international markets began to wobble and Madras started to experience the effects.

AN UNSTABLE WORLD

From the early years of the twentieth century, the prices of Madras export goods began to rise. This was a worldwide event which resulted chiefly from the circumstances of the primary produce markets. These were markets which received supplies from various, scattered parts of the world, and which distributed them to various industrial countries. Largely because climate and other factors ensured that the supplies from different sources were irregular from year to year, these were usually rather speculative markets where prices were continually re-negotiated by auction and where forward-contracting and other forms of market-control had little success in damping down speculative tendencies. In the early twentieth century, demand from the increasing ranks of industrial countries was strong and growing, and this tended to bid up the prices of primary produce. This was particularly noticeable in the markets for the kind of materials which Madras provided—cotton, hides, oilseeds—for they supplied low-technology, consumer industries which could be (and were in this period) built in many countries with a minimal industrial base. Moreover, the fact that supplies of these products responded slowly to increases in demand, tended to increase the bullish character of the market.[24]

Thus the years before the first world war served as a prologue to the conditions Madras would have to deal with throughout our period. Export prices climbed by around twenty-five per cent in the first decade of the century. From then on the prices ruling in Madras were on a roller-coaster. After this preamble of pre-war inflation, prices went through the roof in the first world war, came back through the floor in the slump of the thirties, and returned through the hole in the roof in the second world war. Moreover these price movements bore no relation to changes in supply in Madras as a result of, for instance, good or bad harvests. They were even only partially related to changes in demand. Mostly they were created by unstable conditions in the industrial economies, by chaos in the non-system of international settlements, and by the wartime financial strategies of the British imperial rulers. They were particularly dramatic for Madras for many reasons. The fluctuations were novel in their rapidity and intensity. Prices doubled in five of six years around the first world war, fell by a third in five or six years of the depression, and multiplied two and a half times in five or six years of the second world war. Next the government did little to defend the internal economy against the full force of these external fluctuations. And finally, the fledgling economy of Madras was too immature to deal with the rapid swings of price. Those internal prices, wages and other costs which were in monetary form adjusted slowly and often cantankerously to imported fluctuations. It made it necessary for the contractors to any monetized economic relationship to organize machinery to adjust their levels of payments according to a remote and often obscure yardstick. It made difficulties, and created wayward tendencies, in internal markets. It caused short-and long-term shifts in income and wealth.

One major theme of the rest of this book is the attempts to cope with these fluctuations and their results. This theme will be taken up in later chapters, but for the moment we must examine the major fluctuations of prices and external trade from 1914 to 1950. In order to do this properly we shall have to look at movements in Madras's foreign trade and, most importantly, decompose these into changes in volume, and in prices, and look at shifts in the terms of trade and in the pattern of trade goods.

Colonial Trade

Table 3: Madras Presidency foreign trade 1886-7 to 1955-6;
basic indices of value, volume and price

Quinquennium	Exports Value	Exports Volume	Exports Price	Imports Value	Imports Volume	Imports Price	Terms of Trade
1886/7-1890/1	85	91	93	86	87	99	94
1891/2-95/6	97	96	101	91	91	101	100
1896/7-1900/01	99	99	100	97	100	97	103
1901/2-05/6	120	114	105	126	122	104	101
1906/7-10/11	159	130	122	195	157	125	98
1911/12-15/16	197	148	133	229	137	167	80
1916/7-20/1	205	115	178	275	108	256	70
1921/2-25/6	313	151	207	396	163	244	85
1926/7-30/1	344	176	195	484	262	186	105
1931/2-35/6	215	152	141	367	273	135	104
1936/7-40/1	295	234	126	375	228	165	76
1941/2-45/6	290	122	238	271	85	321	74
1946/7-50/1	719	150	479	1174	230	512	94
1951/2-55/6	698	120	582	1253	195	646	90

Note: All figures are quinquennial averages. In the original data, figures for trade with Burma were classified as 'Coasting Trade' until the separation of Burma from British India in 1936-7; these figures have been added in so that Burma trade is included throughout. The indices of value and price have been constructed so that the first four entries in each column average 100. The volume indices were created by dividing value by price. The terms of trade index was created by dividing export price by import price. The price indices were constructed using material from the *Index Numbers of Indian Prices*, and from the Indian and UK trade statistics (through working out unit values by dividing value by volume or number). Weights were worked out specifically to suit Madras trade. For the export price index the weights were: grain (7), leather (24), groundnut (13), gingelly (4), sugar (2), tea (9), oils (5), raw hides and skins (2), coffee (8), raw cotton (11), twist and yarn (2), piece-goods (9), tobacco (4). For import prices, three overlapping indices were compiled to take account of the changing commodity composition.
1886/7-1920/1: iron and steel (10), other metals (5), liquor (4), provisions (3), kerosene (5), betel (6), twist and yarn (21), piece-goods (42).
1906/7-1935/6: iron and steel (10), other metals (6), liquor (2), provisions (3), sugar (6), kerosene (5), betel (4), twist and yarn (12), piece-goods (26), paper (4), dyes and chemicals (3), instruments (2), railway plant (6), machinery and millwork (11) [electric motors (3), sewing machines (2), lathes (1), textile spinning machinery (5)].
1921/2-1955/6: iron and steel (6), other metals (5), liquor (2), provisions (3), sugar (3), kerosene (7), betel (2), twist and yarn (5), piece-goods (8), paper (4), dyes and chemicals (6), instruments (3), railway plant (3), machinery and millwork (16) [electric motors (4), electric switch gear (2), sewing machines (1), lathes (1), textile spinning machinery (4), oil engines (2), sugar machinery (2)], petrol (2), vehicles (3), grain (21).

Source: *Annual Statement of the Sea-Borne Trade and Navigation of the Madras Presidency*

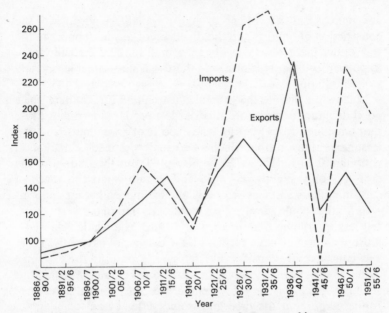

Graph 2 Madras Presidency: indices of exports and imports at
constant prices 1886-7 to 1955-6

Note: Trade with Burma is included throughout. The published data on the value of
merchandise trade was deflated with separate indices for export and import prices.
The construction of these indices is described in Table 2.2. The indices of exports and
imports presented here are aligned so that the first four entries of each index
averages 100. There is no attempt to show the relative level of exports vis-a-vis
imports.

Source: *Annual Statement of the Sea-Borne Trade and Navigation of the Madras
Presidency.*

The first world war

During the first world war, India's financial stability and trading
prospects were subordinated to the needs of Britain's war aims.
This meant that India's trade was constricted by the closure of
markets and lack of shipping, while India's currency was manipulated to provide the government with the funds to buy wartime
supplies in India.

Britain secured her war supplies by printing rupees against pieces
of government paper held in London and Delhi.[25] The gross note
circulation in India rose from Rs 66.12 crores in 1914 to Rs 153.46
crores in 1919. Since this increase in currency was not matched by

any increase in the volume of goods available—indeed with the constriction of imports and the diversion of certain supplies to the war effort there was probably an overall fall and certainly some important individual shortages—there was an inevitable, money-stoked inflation.

Meanwhile despite the general constriction of trade there was a good demand for many of India's export products, including those that emanated from Madras. The exports of groundnuts, and to a lesser extent raw cotton, which were usually destined for markets in continental Europe were badly disrupted, but the trade with the east was only slightly damaged and Britain wanted as much of certain military supplies—notably textiles and leather for uniforms —as Madras could supply. Thus in the early part of the war, exports fell less in volume than imports and India as a whole achieved a more than usually large surplus on the balance of payments. There was consequently considerable pressure to push up the exchange value of the rupee. However the British government resisted this strongly, since this very government was the major purchaser of Indian exports at the time and would suffer by any such appreciation. As a result the exchange value of the rupee was kept firmly down until 1917, and the terms of trade moved sharply against Madras products. Thus Madras, and India as a whole, was being forced to loan its current prosperity to the war effort. Poor terms of trade and constricted imports meant that living standards in India were being depressed against a future credit in government paper in London.

This situation was peculiarly disruptive because the government was achieving its wartime supplies by the haphazard method of stoking up inflation and distorting the terms of trade. The combination of an externally-induced decline in real income with an externally-invented inflation spawned social tensions. By 1917 there were some novel moves towards trade unionization in the towns as workers sought ways to make wages chase after prices.[26] And by 1917 there were also signs of food shortages and food riots in parts of the countryside as inflation distorted the marketing structure and encouraged speculation and hoarding. Government had to step in to control the distribution of essential commodities in short supply (kerosene and cloth), to damp down social tension, and to prepare for a new spate of nationalist pressure.[27]

The Government's wartime economic policy ended in a horrible heap between 1917 and 1922. After a short post-war boom, India's trade collapsed in price and to a greater extent in volume in a worldwide post-war slump. The Government had been forced to take the brakes off and allow the rupee to rise in 1917. It shot up and then shot down again in the trade slump as London and Delhi thrashed inconclusively around looking for a theory of currency management which would suit the imperi? i Government's needs. In this tangle, the Indian people lost most of the 'credit' that they had built up during the war; some of the Government of India's reserves were spent on railway goods, but much of the real value of these reserves seems to have been lost in the chaos of trade and the rupee exchange. Yet by 1923 matters had settled down somewhat. India still effectively had an unusually low exchange rate in the early 1920s, but the potentially harmful effects of such an exchange rate were submerged by the exceptionally good demand for Madras's export products, and by the low prices and reasonable supply of import goods.

In the 1920s the rapid re-tooling of European industry and the phenomenal rates of growth in America, Russia, Japan and Germany created an immediate demand for raw materials. As supplying countries adjusted slowly to the rapid change from the constricted conditions of wartime, the markets for primary produce again became bullish and speculative.[28] The terms of trade moved dramatically in Madras's favour. Exports climbed to new levels. The trade with Asia was more or less retained, while there was renewal of demand in Europe. Exports of textiles and leather more or less maintained their wartime-inflated level, while exports of oilseeds returned and climbed to an unprecedented level. In the late 1920s the volume of exports had reached twice the level of the 1890s and with the favourable movement in the terms of trade this meant an era of unparallelled prosperity for the region as a whole. The volume of imports soared—to three times the level of the 1890s— and there was a quite unprecedented import of treasure.

None of this had essentially changed Madras's role in inter-national trade. The pattern of demand for Madras products had changed little in the pre-war boom, the wartime inflation and the 1920s boom. As table 4 shows, the profile of Madras exports had remained remarkably constant, with only a slight tremor in the war years, while the scale had gradually and sporadically increased. Regularly some forty-five per cent of Madras exports came from

Table 4:   Madras Presidency; exports by type of goods 1886-7 to 1955-6

Quinquennium	Percentage of total exports in each quinquennium			
	Farm Produce	Plantation Produce	Other raw material	Artisan and Factory goods
1886/7-90/1	46.3	13.9	0.1	33.2
1891/2-95/6	36.5	17.4	0.2	38.5
1896/7-1900/01	35.8	14.2	2.1	40.4
1901/2-05/6	41.7	13.2	5.4	34.4
1906/7-10/11	45.3	10.9	6.3	32.2
1911/12-15/16	46.1	14.0	3.1	29.8
1916/17-20/1	30.0	16.2	5.0	44.0
1921/2-25/6	45.0	13.6	3.9	28.9
1926/7-30/1	45.7	15.6	2.8	28.3
1931/2-35/6	38.4	20.3	3.0	30.2
1936/7-40/1	38.9	16.6	2.9	30.2
1941/2-45/6	34.8	19.7	4.4	29.5
1946/7-50/1	24.7	10.2	3.7	46.6
1951/2-55/6	20.5	3.7	5.0	48.5

Note: Farm Produce = grain, fruit and vegetables, oilseeds, spices, raw cotton, raw tobacco, animals, dyes.
Plantation Produce = rubber, coffee, tea.
Other raw materials = fish, raw hides and skins, timber, manure.
Artisan and factory goods = sugar, twist and yarn, piece-goods, manufactured tobacco, oils, oilcake, coir, manufactured hides and skins.
Sources: *Annual Statement of the Sea-Borne Trade and Navigation of India; Annual Statement of the Sea-Borne Trade and Navigation of the Madras Presidency.*

farm agriculture, another fifteen per cent from plantation agriculture and along with another five per cent consisting of other raw materials most of this went to the markets of Europe; meanwhile some thirty to thirty-five per cent consisted of artisan produce which mostly travelled eastwards. Imports had changed rather more; the massive import of textiles had dwindled away and been partially replaced by an increase in the imports of food and fuel oils. While this change had important aspects which we shall consider later, it was for our purposes at the moment little more than the exchange of one consumer item for another. Overall, Madras trade was remarkably stable, even in view of the increasingly eccentric fluctuations in price. The next fluctuation, that of the 1930s slump, would bring about more marked divergences.

Table 5:   Madras Presidency: imports by type of goods 1886-7 to 1955-6

Quinquennium	Percentage of total imports in each quinquennium				
	Food	Raw materials and intermediate goods	Fuels	Capital goods	Consumer goods
1886/7-90/1	6.9	26.5	1.5	8.4	42.8
1891/2-95/6	12.1	26.4	2.3	8.3	43.9
1896/7-1900/01	17.0	26.3	1.6	7.0	40.1
1901/2-05/6	15.4	22.0	0.5	10.6	41.2
1906/7-1910/11	25.6	19.5	0.9	6.2	35.0
1911/12-15/16	18.9	20.4	1.1	10.0	36.8
1916/17-20/1	23.6	21.3	2.0	8.0	31.9
1921/2-25/6	23.0	20.2	4.5	14.4	27.2
1926/7-30/1	26.5	17.7	5.7	10.6	24.9
1931/2-35/6	28.2	14.4	9.6	7.6	26.7
1936/7-40/1	29.8	12.4	8.2	10.1	22.6
1941/2-45/6	15.9	9.1	33.3	9.3	15.7
1946/7-50/1	35.6	13.6	6.5	16.7	15.7
1951/2-55/6	25.3	16.2	7.1	19.6	18.3

Note:
Food=grain, betel, provisions, sugar.
Raw materials and intermediate goods=raw cotton, timber, iron and steel, other metals, twist and yarn, chemicals, dyes
Fuels=coal, fuel and other oils
Capital goods=building and engineering materials, machinery and millwork, railway plant, vehicles
Consumer goods=matches, kerosene, manure, instruments, drugs, hardware, liquor, tobacco, piecegoods, paper, glass.
Sources: *Annual Statement of the Sea-Borne Trade and Navigation of India; Annual Statement of the Sea-Borne Trade and Navigation of the Madras Presidency.*

The depression

Much has been written about the great depression in recent years, and there are some well-laid lines of academic battle. However, most of these studies are designed to explain why the investors of America (and to some extent the labourers of America and the investors and labourers of Europe) had such a bad time between 1929 and 1933, and they are somewhat irrelevant to our purpose. We do not need to enter into these controversies or to attempt to explain 'why the depression happened', particularly in so far as it affected the industrial economies. We do however need to understand the origins of shifts in prices and demand and this will unfortunately lead us into the edges of this academic minefield. We should however remain on those edges, and view the event from the paddyfields of Asia rather than from the pavements of Wall Street. The depression clearly consisted of both an immense cyclical crisis in the world's industrial economics, and an equally immense crisis of production and prices in the world's agriculture. These two events were inextricably connected, but for analytic purposes we will have to try to keep them a little apart. We are interested in explaining how the fluctuations in trade and prices affected the internal economy of Madras. For this we will have to delve a little into the origins of the agricultural depressions, and also consider a little of the changes in demand from the industrial nations.

The second half of the 1920s saw a dramatic change in the conditions in the world's markets for primary produce. The bullish atmosphere which had prevailed since the 1860s (despite several short-term slumps) was abruptly terminated. In brief, where once demand had seemed to be increasing rather faster than supply and where this had pushed up the prices in the characteristically speculative primary produce markets, there now seemed to be more supplies than demand. This position was reached earlier in the case of some commodities than others, but the slide of these particular prices managed to prick the bubble on which all the markets were floated. This stage had been reached by mid-1929. When the industrial economies then faltered and attempted to solve their problems by deflationary policies, prices were pushed down further. In the third and final stage, from 1933-4 onwards, the industrial economies recovered but the old links of trade and the old arrangements of marketing were not simply restored.[29] In each of these three stages the configurations of prices and demand facing the Madras rural economy were rather different and need to be considered separately.

The conditions facing primary producers in the European markets might have been expected to deteriorate rather sooner than they did. After all, the high prices which prevailed, particularly from the late 1890s onwards, might have been expected to increase supplies, and the era of high imperialism certainly brought more areas of the primary-producing world more firmly into the international markets than ever before. Further, it might have been expected that the markets would before long become more 'transparent' for purchasers, and that techniques of market-control would iron out the bullish fluctuations. Yet the deflation of the primary produce markets was delayed by two factors. Firstly, the first world war cut back agricultural production within Europe and inhibited the growth of production elsewhere because of the difficulties over trade. Secondly, when supplies threatened to outdistance demand in certain products in the mid-1920s, there was no immediate effect on price levels because countries built up stocks or erected price-support schemes and were able to finance both these devices with loans which, at this time, the industrial countries seemed only too willing to give.

Yet by the second half of the 1920s the bubble under the primary produce markets was beginning to bulge. After the post-war reconstruction, the rate of growth of population and of manufacturing in the industrial west both slackened.[30] Although primary production and trade were clearly dependent on this source of demand, they responded slowly to this change of pace. This was partly because production was so scattered through the world, partly because of the lags in agricultural investment, partly because, as we shall argue below in the case of Madras, the way in which the demand in the European markets was transmitted to the local markets was bound to induce delays in response. The weakening of demand was felt earliest and most forcibly in the market for those primary products which were produced in both the industrial countries and elsewhere; in such cases the disruption of European production during the war had inflated demand and encouraged production outside Europe and the return of European production post-war led to a keen competition in the markets. Thus it was the markets for wheat, wool, and meat which first began to look bloated, and it was the good wheat harvest in Europe and North America in 1928-9 which, coming at a time of unprecedented levels of wheat stocks, started the downward spiral of prices and also stampeded the U.S. towards protectionism.[31]

For tropical products there was not such an obvious rivalry between different economic regions, yet there were still signs of increasing competition in the markets. The market for oil-bearing materials was always particularly volatile because of the variety of substitutes, and although the available figures suggest that the world production of linseed and cotton, hemp and rape seeds was declining in the late 1920s, there were marked opposite movements in the supply of soya beans, copra, olives and, particularly, groundnuts and whale blubber.[32] In the southeast Asian rice market, there were also signs of increasing competition. India had long ago been replaced by Burma as the major trader and from the first world war on Thailand, Indochina, Taiwan, and Korea were placing increasing amounts of rice in maritime trade.[33]

While the competition was less fierce in these 'tropical' markets as compared to the 'temperate' markets, the weakening and then the collapse of prices for wheat and other temperate products had a chain reaction throughout primary-produce trade. By 1927-8 prices were generally tumbling. This was not a question of 'overproduction' as such. Rather the rate of growth of demand in the industrial countries slackened, while a number of different producers were still responding haphazardly to a tug of demand created by a bullish market and good terms of trade. The weakening of the market in certain products exercised some downward pressure which ramified through the characteristically unstable markets of all primary products.[34]

The weakness of primary produce prices undoubtedly contributed to instability within the industrial economies themselves. After all, a considerable proportion of their populations, particularly in the U.S., derived their income from agriculture, and a sizeable proportion of investment was in raw material futures and similar ventures. But the crash of 1929 and the monetary disorders of 1929-31 in the industrial nations had many other causes and we do not need to list them here. It is important to note only two things. First, the slump spread so universally and assumed such catastrophic proportions because of the basic instability of the international trading system in the post-war era. Since the war most currencies had been effectively 'managed' but there was no universal yardstick and no machinery for policing parities. While Britain had been *the* dominant world trading power, with over half the total volume of world trade, then the pattern of international settlements had been made to balance without too much trouble; Britain had balanced accounts within her own multilateral trading system, and all other systems had been essentially grafted onto that of Britain. But the decline of Britain from her position of dominance—the USA's share of world trade overtook that of Britain in the late 1920s—and the ever-increasing complexity of world trade patterns undermined the apparently automatic working of the system. Through the 1920s, international settlements were squared only through eccentric movements of specie and, more importantly, foreign lending. This state of affairs was inherently unstable—as the era of 'hot money' made only too clear. There was no real reason why movements of capital and gold should, without regulation, serve to counteract imbalances in trade patterns and indeed there were good reasons why they should react to completely different stimuli. This is of course what happened in 1928-9 in the succession of national banking scares and the domino flight of international capital. The result was that the crisis of confidence which came to a head in 1929 would quickly and dramatically damage the smooth working of world trade. Second, the industrial countries all reacted to the troubles of 1929—the stock market crash, the primary produce slump, the disordering of world trade, the chaos in currency markets—with deflationary policies. High interest rates, restrictions on money supply, protective tariffs and unemployment were seen as the recipes for internal stability.[35]

The result was a curious hiccup in the pattern of world trade. While world demand was squeezed by the competitive deflations and by the collapse of the trading system, it was the industrial countries themselves which absorbed most of the impact. Many countries reduced industrial production, at the cost of unemployment and social unrest, and erected tariffs to protect the rest of their industry. There was thus an overall fall in manufacturing production and, as many countries sought for a greater degree of self-sufficiency, an even greater fall in trade in manufactures. In one estimate, world production of manufactured goods fell twenty-two per cent between 1926-30 and 1931-3 and world trade in these goods fell twenty-eight per cent.[36] Primary produce behaved rather differently. In the case of plantations, where the organization of capital and labour followed many of the lines of industrial units, investment could be withdrawn and labour dispersed and the logic of capitalist accounting dictated that it should be so. Peasant production was not so elastic. In this sector production fell very little. In cotton, for instance, the League of Nations figures of world production suggest that the average level in the years 1930-8 was roughly six per cent *above* the level in 1925-9. In the case of groundnuts, the rise over the same period was of the order of twenty-three per cent, in the case of rice five per cent. Overall there was some slackening in the rate of growth of primary production but this was mostly accounted for by plantation crops.[37] Similarly, the overall decline in the volume of trade did affect primary produce, but the fall between 1925-9 and 1930-3 was around six per cent and was nowhere near as steep as the twenty-eight per cent fall in the trade of manufactures.[38]

There were several reasons why production and trade in primary products fell far less than production and trade in manufactured goods. To some extent there was a growth of local industries to absorb the primary produce not wanted by the slump-ridden industries of the west, and in some items there was an expansion of trade between the primary producing countries themselves. But the largest reason was that the inelasticities of supply had forced prices right down. The slump had taken up the slack in the primary produce markets in the west. In some instances the depression had seen the emergence of cartels or monopsonistic combines which could manipulate prices down. In 1929 and 1930, when everyone was talking about the high level of stocks, when flows of overseas capital had dried up, and when interest rates were high, the primary markets had seemed to be glutted and prices had dropped like a stone. Production, however, had been maintained for many different reasons—because it was not easy to reduce production in the short term, because farmers assumed that the depression was temporary and of minor importance, because one of the basic 'costs' of peasant production was food and that fell in price too, and so on.[39] The general level of primary produce prices halved between 1929-30 and 1931-3, while manufacture prices declined around thirty per cent. Prices dropped so dramatically that primary produce remained cheap and continued to find a reasonable market in the depressed economies of the industrial west.

From 1933, the industrial economies began to climb back towards recovery. The immediate problems over international trade and payments were, temporarily at least, brought under control, and government economic policies began to urge national economies onto an upswing. But as the world trading pattern was reconstituted in the mid-1930s, two differences were apparent. Firstly, while industrial production returned to its old rate of growth, *trade* in industrial products was more sluggish. Policies of tariff protection and import substitution in both the industrial and backward countries had meant a once-and-for-all shift towards self-sufficiency.[40]

Secondly, the trade in primary products, which between 1880 and 1925 had tended to follow the index of manufacturing production like a faithful dog, was this time not dragged along by the west's industrial growth.[41] The immediate crisis of the depression had disguised a more long-term shift in demand. There were many reasons for this new disjunction. The new wave of industrial growth in the west was based on armaments, on construction, and on the manufacture of consumer durables. These items did not require the same level of inputs of primary produce as had the food, cosmetic, textile and naturally-based chemical industries which had played such a part in the industrial growth of the late nineteenth and early twentieth centuries. Moreover, even in some of the old food, oil, and textile industries there was now competition from synthetic products. Further, many industries were making more efficient use of raw materials. And finally, the continued deceleration of population growth in the west was reflected in the slower rate of growth of demand for food and other basic raw materials. Thus demand for raw materials remained sluggish, the primary produce markets remained relatively slack (there were still considerable stocks of cotton and other primary materials) and prices of primary produce remained depressed long after the economies of the industrial west had picked up.[42]

In order to understand how the depression bore down upon Madras, we shall have to look in more detail at the ways in which the demand and price for Madras export products were transmitted from the external to the internal economy.

As noted above, the prices for cotton, groundnut and other Madras export crops were fixed in the auction-markets of the west. Madras was only a minor figure in these markets and thus the level of her supplies had little effect on the performance of the market. Producers in Madras thus had to accept whatever price the world market offered them. The prices in the European markets were closely watched in the primary markets in Madras and although (as we shall see below) individual markets had different characteristics and showed different styles of short-term fluctuation, in the long-term the prices in Madras followed those in the western markets very closely indeed.

The connections between the external and internal economies need to be examined to show how international prices were transmitted to the internal markets. The liquidity of the internal economy was influenced by the supply of money, by the availability of credit, and by the rate at which money and credit instruments circulated. Since export crops were for the most part cultivated on credit, it was credit that played the most important part in this relationship. While the cultivator himself got the credit from a number of different sources, mostly close at hand, the overall flow of credit was decided by the actions of three institutions: the export houses (and their asssociated banking agencies), the bazaar money-market, and the government.[43] The lion's share of credit was provided by the export houses who each year moved funds to India to perform their business, and supplemented with local borrowing from the 'formal' banking sector. Some of these funds were channelled into the local economy through forward contracts, while more was deposited in the 'formal' banking sector where it provided reserves against which the banks made loans to and discounted bills for the local money-market. The flow of this sort of credit was decided from year to year by the export-houses' expectations of the future state of the European markets.

Other credit was provided through the bazaar money-market itself. In this sector (as we shall see below), the turnover of funds and the circulation of credit instruments was exceptionally rapid. Most of the bazaar bankers specialized in short-term lending and discounting and dealing in hundis (a form of short-term trade bill), while a large number of merchants specialized in commission business, operated entirely on credit, and possesssed very little capital of their own. The liquidity in this sector depended crucially on the rate of circulation of credit instruments. This in turn depended on two further items: confidence in the future, and gold. In such a volatile market, gold was the one form of security which was considered fairly reliable. It could be used by bankers as a security to raise loans from the formal banking sector. It was accepted by bankers as hypothecation for loans from the bazaar to the countryside. Cultivators invested in stocks of gold because it represented a form of life insurance; it could be used as security to raise loans, in hard times it could be turned into cash at a moment's notice, and at death it passed by law to one's wife. The stocks of gold in the countryside depended on the profits of export production and trade in previous years. Thus the liquidity in this part of the market depended in part on the bazaar banker's estimation of the future state of the market, and in part on the longer-term trend of trading performance.

The government, meanwhile, could affect internal liquidity by influencing the rate of interest and the supply of currency. In two somewhat haphazard ways government acted as a uniquely sensitive mediator in the commercial marketplace. The first way operated through its budget. By the time of the first world war, the Government of India's revenue had come to depend heavily on customs receipts and other heads such as income tax; thus the level of revenue was uniquely sensitive to the conditions of internal and external trade. So long as trade was good it was relatively easy to balance the budget, the government deposited its surplus revenues in the short-term in the formal banking sector, and these deposits helped to keep liquidity good and interest rates low. If, on the other hand, the budget fell into deficit, then government had to raise loans from the banks and the internal money-market and that had the opposite effect on liquidity and interest rates. The second way operated through the balance of payments. Although there was no formal accounting of India's balance of payments, the Government of India was in fact sensitive to its fluctuations and passed those fluctuations on to the internal economy. If the balance of payments was healthy, then there would be a good demand from foreign export-firms to purchase rupees from the Government of India in London, and the proceeds created reserves against which government could issue rupees in India. If on the other hand the balance of payments was in deficit, then the Government of India would find it difficult to secure foreign exchange for transmission to London to cover the 'home charges'. In such a situation it would have to raise interest rates in order to attract capital from abroad, or run down the paper currency reserves and effect a corresponding contraction in the volume of rupees circulating in India. There was a third alternative—to allow the value of the rupee to fall in the hope that it would stimulate exports—but this was generally unacceptable since in the short-term it merely made it more expensive (in rupees) to cover the 'home charges'. The government's influence on the liquidity of the internal economy was thus sensitive to the immediate state of the commercial economy.

Until the 1920s, this rather haphazard system worked reasonably successfully. War, bad harvests, or instability in the international exchanges from time to time affected the immediate state of

commerce and impelled the government to contract the currency or
to push up the rate of interest. It is important to see that while these
devices helped to solve the Government of India's own immediate
problems over the budget and the exchange, they were on their own
quite likely to exacerbate the problems in the longer term since they
tended to choke off commercial activity. The system survived in
these years, however, because the long-term prospects of India's
export trade were good. That meant that the bazaar money-market
and foreign export firms could absorb the shocks of temporary
crises, even when those shocks were exacerbated by the actions of
government. Demand for Indian produce in the west was good and
the trend in the terms-of-trade was favourable. That meant that for
the most part the balance-of-payments was in surplus and there was
a steady inflow of gold which went to build up the stocks held by
cultivators and local bankers and so oil the wheels of the bazaar
money-market. As tables 3 and 6 show, there was a close correspondence throughout the period between the movement in the
terms of trade and the direction of gold flows. From the 1880s to the
1920s Madras was steadily accumulating gold, and in the mid-1920s

Table 6:   Madras Presidency: imports and exports of treasure 1886-7 to 1955-6

	Average annual movement of treasure in Rs lakhs		
	Export	Import	Balance
1886/7-1890/1	17.27	25.48	+ 8.21
1891/2-1895/6	11.28	16.53	+ 5.25
1896/7-1900/1	13.50	44.27	+ 30.77
1901/2-1905/6	17.03	101.72	+ 84.69
1906/7-1910/11	49.09	88.00	+ 38.91
1911/12-1915/16	55.76	20.76	− 35.00
1916/17-1920/1	26.42	10.82	− 15.60
1921/2-1925/6	16.26	38.95	+ 22.69
1926/7-1930/1	10.21	388.77	+378.56
1931/2-1935/6	207.04	63.98	−143.06
1936/7-1940/1	35.34	30.28	− 5.06
1941/2-1945/6	71.97	35.88	− 36.09
1946/7-1950/1	152.94	4.00	−148.94
1951/2-1956/7	77.75	.01	− 77.74

Source: *Annual statement of the sea-borne trade and navigation of India.*

the flow reached extraordinary levels. Although it is rather a crude and dangerous yardstick, it is probable that this figure is the best representation we have of the build-up of commercial capital in Madras agriculture and agrarian trade. Meanwhile, during a short-term crisis, the foreign firms generally overrode the government's potentially deflationary effect on currency and interest rates, by importing enough capital to maintain the liquidity in the internal trading economy.

In the second half of the 1920s, however, the system came apart. In short, the long-term faith in the strength of Indian exports faded away as the demand for primary produce slackened in the mid-20s. Thus when prices dropped and government faced difficulties over both the budget and the balance of payments in 1929, foreign firms did not have the confidence to countervail the usual deflationary actions of the government. Indeed they added to the deflationary trend by themselves withdrawing credit.

Confidence in the future of Madras's exports dwindled away from the middle of the 1920s. The prices of the three main export crops of Madras agriculture all weakened from 1925 onwards. World supplies of groundnut were rapidly expanding in the 1920s, and were competing against other rapidly expanding sources of natural oils including soya beans, copra, olives, and whale blubber. Cotton stocks were building up as cultivation expanded in new areas such as Uganda as well as more established areas such as Egypt and USA.[44] As for rice, Madras had already lost many of her export markets to the Burmese producers and now the competition between Burma and other expanding export areas in Indochina and Thailand, was bringing down prices to the level at which southeast Asian rice could displace local supplies in the Madras home market.[45]

At first, India was shielded from the effect of weakening prices. Foreign firms were still importing the capital to carry out their business and in 1927, when government apparently realized the consequences which would follow if the flow of foreign funds was cut off under these conditions, the Government of India raised short-term interest rates to attract foreign capital. In 1929, however, the balance of payments turned sharply towards a deficit. The fall in export prices reduced trade receipts while, on the impetus of the recent boom, imports were at the highest level ever. In the circumstances this led to two deflationary developments. First, India could not escape the effects of the worldwide contraction of foreign lending sparked off by the repatriation of American funds. India's poor trading position meant that there was little confidence in the rupee, and the prospect of imminent constitutional reforms added to the trepidation of foreign lenders. Second, the Government of India reacted in its usual fashion by realizing the sterling necessary to remit to London by running down the reserves and contracting the money supply in India. In 1929-30 and again in 1930-1, the supply of currency fell by about six per cent. This in itself was not too severe, especially considering the decline in prices. But government's difficulties were not over. Its revenues depended heavily on customs revenues and other indirect taxes and these were badly hit by the onset of depression. Government expenditures did not respond so readily to the slump of prices, the budget lurched towards a deficit, and the Government of India was forced to borrow short-term funds in India to meet the gap. These borrowings not only pushed up interest rates, but reduced the stock of funds which the banks could make available for the commercial sector.[46]

The government's actions were not swingeing in themselves. The contraction of currency was far less than the fall in prices, and the upwards pressure on interest rates lasted only until 1931. These actions, along with the tentativeness of foreign firms, did however contribute to the general undermining of confidence in India's export prospects. That in turn slowed down the activity in the bazaar money-market which led to a much greater reduction in the liquidity of the internal economy.

The crisis thus deepened and lengthened. The reduction of liquidity helped to push prices down even further. The lack of confidence, the continuing spiral of prices, and the worsening terms of trade meant that the balance-of-payments problem remained. By early 1931 the Government of India had virtually exhausted its usual strategies for finding remittance in difficult times and now had to face the fact that this was not a short-term exchange crisis which would be surmounted by a revival of trade and foreign lending, but a major disjunction in foreign trade which would need a more substantial, longer-term solution. By May 1931, the rupee exchange rate was looking extremely insecure and the Government of India had to contemplate the possibility of seeking such a longer-term solution by devaluation. In September 1931, the rupee was linked to sterling as the latter was taken off the gold standard, and as a result the rupee was devalued against gold.

The devaluation had the desired effect of easing the Government of India's problem over the balance of payments by increasing exports and reducing imports. But this was achieved principally by cutting the import bill—the devaluation accentuated the already deteriorating trend in the terms of trade—and encouraging exports of gold itself. Massive exports of gold began in the final months of 1931 and continued for much of the decade. At first, this outward flow brought in a windfall profit, for in rupee terms the stocks of gold purchased in the late 1920s were sold at a considerable profit after the devaluation in 1931.[47] But on a longer-term view the sales of gold represented a considerable dissaving by the agricultural sector and a considerable reduction in the capacity of the bazaar money-market. Although the process is obscure, it seems probable that much of the gold which appeared on the export market in the early 1930s found its way there through a pyramidic process of foreclosure on the security for loans which could not be repaid when crop prices went through the floor. The proceeds of these sales seem to have been dispersed in two different ways. First, some went to pay for imports and other necessities which had become enormously more expensive as a result of the rapid decline in the terms of trade. Second, some seem to have accrued to the banks, bazaar money-lenders, and other intermediaries in the credit pyramid. Because the prospects for investing the proceeds in local trade were currently so poor, much of these profits seem to have been transferred into other forms of investment, mainly in the urban sector.[48] Both forms of dispersion moved gold out of the ambit of the bazaar money-market and thus represented a reduction in the liquidity available for rural commerce.

Thus from the late 1920s onwards a succession of factors reduced the volume of funds available to finance the production and handling of cash crops. The immediate effect was a contraction both in the price and in the volume of exports. However, production barely adjusted to this fall. The reduction in credit and capital for cultivation meant that landlords, traders, cultivators and government took a smaller income from business but that the flow of produce into the market was maintained. The reduction in liquidity in the market meant a drastic fall in price. By 1933-4 the price had fallen so low that in terms of volume exports were climbing back to the levels of the 1920s.

The second world war

For the remainder of the 1930s, the prices offered for Madras export crops remained low, and the terms of trade continued to drift against Madras. In terms of volume however, exports returned to the trend of gentle increase which had marked the period leading up to the depression, with the result that the volume of exports reached unprecedented levels towards the end of the decade. The advent of war in 1939, and more particularly the spread of war to the east in 1941, subjected Madras's external economy to a new series of shocks. Whereas the past decade had seen a modest expansion of the volume of demand for Madras exports at a greatly reduced level of prices, the early 1940s saw a constriction of demand coupled with a dramatic inflation of price levels.

Both factors resulted from the special demands of wartime. The war closed off markets in Europe and to some extent in the east and, as we have seen, these had consistently been the most expansive of Madras's trading partners in the relatively 'normal' years of the twentieth century. While Britain was anxious to buy supplies for the war effort, this was not enough to counteract the decline in the European and Asian markets. Madras export trade was rapidly cut back to almost half the level it had assumed on the eve of the first world war.

Thus the markets for Madras produce were weak. In the case of certain items—notably cotton and rice—there was some compensation in the form of increased internal demand, but generally speaking the market was so slack that government stepped in to attempt to limit the production of certain items (groundnut, short-staple cotton) which could not be expected to find a market.

But the overall slackness of demand was to a large extent obscured by an enormous inflation of prices. The background to this inflation was similar to the pattern in the first world war, only exaggerated many times. Britain required considerable help from India during the war both as a supplier of war materials and as a base for the eastern theatre. Almost Rs 3,500 million was spent on defence between 1939 and 1946 and while half of this was debited to the British government, it virtually all had for the moment to be paid for with rupees in India (while sterling credits built up in London).[49] No government could have contemplated raising the sums necessary by taxation and thus the Government of India again resorted to the device of printing money (against the sterling balances in London). The scale of the operation made the currency manipulations of 1914-18 look like minor tinkerings. The supply of money climbed from Rs 317 crores in 1939 to Rs 2,190 crores in 1945.[50]

The war effort was in fact being financed in a covert way by a combination of forced loans and forced taxation. On the one hand, there were simply less goods around in the economy. A combination of a continued deterioration in the terms of trade and strict government control of shipping choked off imports in an even more dramatic way than exports. The volume of imports into Madras in the quinquennium following 1941-2 was lower than at any time since the 1880s. Meanwhile government bought up £3,000 million of war materials in the course of the war and in many cases (for instance textiles) this represented a diversion of production away from the home market. There was some expansion of production in India during the war, but it nowhere near matched the expansion of (overseas) demand. In certain basic commodities such as textiles, food, and kerosene there were real shortages and government was obliged to police the market in such items. On the other hand, there was much more money around in the economy. The result was a massive inflation of prices which only flattened out after the war at three to four times the level of the late 1930s. Most of the population were simply seeing a reduction in their volume of consumption (because there were less goods to go round) while having to pay out just as much of their income (because the market pushed up prices to levels where they absorbed virtually all the volume of demand).[51] Of course some people were able to gain in the process from speculation in the market in particular, and some of the gains were transferred into savings (bank deposits rose) and capital investments (particularly in war supply industries). But in macro terms there was a decline in living standards. Some of the decline represented a simple transfer of income to the government for the prosecution of the war, and some was covered by the sterling balances building up in London. Effectively the people of India had lent money to the government for the war effort, and held an IOU in the form of the sterling balances. Under these conditions 'real' incomes in rural Madras remained low, and the gold continued to flow out of the countryside.

Thus while the period from the mid-1920s onwards saw two very different movements of prices—a steep drop and then an even steeper rise—there were many ways in which this period of two decades may be taken as a whole, and there was through the period a gradual trend of change in the region's external economy.

First, throughout the period export prices in real terms were low, or, in other words, the terms of trade were moving against Madras and particularly against its rural sector. As a result the volume of imports plummeted downwards, and gold continually drained away from the economy. The fall of imports affected manufactured consumer goods most sharply; their share of Madras imports halved between the late nineteenth century and the years of the depression and second world war. Most of this fall was contributed by the drop in the import of piece-goods.

Secondly, the 'traditional' pattern of Madras exports was substantially disrupted. The market for primary produce became insecure in times of war and financial instability. The market for manufactures in Asia was also badly hit. The depression saw a massive contracting of the plantation economies in southeast Asia with a corresponding halt in the flow of migrants from India to the east, and a general loosening of the ties of commerce which, over the past decades, had gradually been binding the countries around the Bay of Bengal closer together.[52] The Japanese irruption into the southeast region completed the decay of this arm of Madras export trade.

Thirdly, as in many poor countries of the world, the 'effective protection' provided by the disruption of trade in the depression and war, the change in the terms of trade between industrial and agricultural goods, the difficulties and expense of securing imported consumer goods, and the poor prospects for investment and growth in local agriculture, dictated an internal shift of resources away from the countryside to the town. It is important to see, however, that the 'effective protection' was not very strong, and that it came at a time when the local economy was far from healthy. Thus while there was some momentum to shift the emphasis of the economy away from its heavy dependence on agriculture and towards import-substituting manufactures, this movement was constrained by the low level of demand and the relative dearness of capital imports. This state of affairs tended to encourage growth only in those industries which required little or no imports of capital, and which produced 'necessities' which would still find a market even in a depressed economy. This favoured low-technology, often handicraft industries producing foodstuffs, apparel, and low-level luxuries like tobacco.

Fourthly, these factors encouraged a marginal but nevertheless significant withdrawal of Madras from its involvement in international trade. Exports did not recover quickly after the war, and although a rapid and impressively favourable movement in the terms of trade (associated with the post-war boom and the release of some of the sterling balances built up during the war) saw a steep rise in imports in the late 1940s, by the early 1950s the terms of trade had reversed yet again, imports again declined, and the volume of imports per capita was no higher than it had been at the end of the first world war.

Fifthly, along with this marginal withdrawal there was also a change in the character and direction of Madras trade. The emphasis shifted right away from the earlier staples of the Madras export houses—groundnuts, raw cotton, and rice. Between the wars these three items had supplied between a third and two-fifths of Madras exports; after world war two they contributed only one or two per cent. Their place was to some extent filled by other crops—notably spices, fruit and vegetables, and tobacco; over the same period their share rose from three or four per cent to around a fifth of the total exports. As a whole, raw agricultural produce now formed a much smaller proportion of total exports. It had fluctuated around forty per cent of the total from the 1880s to the 1920s and then fallen steeply to a level of roughly twenty per cent. Given the contraction of export volume, and the rise in population, this meant a massive fall in per capita exports of rural produce.

Meanwhile exports of artisan and factory-made produce had risen, particularly in the aftermath of the second world war. These consisted mostly of textiles, oils, and leather. Along with this shift in the pattern of export products, went a marginal shift in trading partners. The market for raw materials in Europe declined, the market for manufactures in eastern Asia ceased to expand, while new markets for manufactures and for a range of primary produce opened up in North America and to a lesser extent in Africa and Australia. The character of imports had changed accordingly. The decline of imports of consumer goods had been matched by a small rise in imports of capital goods, raw materials and fuels—all of which went largely to the new industrial sector—and a much more impressive rise in imports of food.

If we are to characterize the change in Madras external economy between the 1880s and the 1950s, then it can be seen as two distinct phases. The first began with Madras in the classical position of a colonial economy, tied closely to the imperial mother-country, exporting agricultural produce and importing consumer goods. The region's external economy was very much the province of the rural sector—the main exports were cash crops, and a high proportion of imports (particularly textiles) were 'wage-goods' for rural labour. Throughout this first phase this essentially colonial and agrarian external economy expanded and ramified. More countries of the industrial west were inducted as trading partners, while Madras also built up an interesting 'sub-colonial' trading system of its own under the wing of European capitalist expansion further east. In the second phase, there was a bumpy retraction from overseas trading and a shift of emphasis from the countryside to the town. The 'sub-colonial' portion matured and ramified while the Madras countryside steadily became insulated from world trade. By the end of the period, in total contrast to the start, the external economy was much more a matter for the region's urban as opposed to its rural sector. Artisan and factory goods contributed a rising portion of exports, while imports were now dominated by the capital goods and raw materials required for urban industry, the petroleum required for urban transport, and the food required for urban survival.

CONCLUSION

The British settlement of southern India had done little to prepare the ground for colonial exploitation. The government built ports, roads, and later railways but it eventually abandoned its more ambitious plans to bounce the region into the nineteenth-century era of 'progress'. Against this local background, European commerce turned out to be a pickpocket rather than a smash-and-grab artist or an elegant embezzler. The agency houses originally sunk some capital in the production of crops in demand in Europe—notably cotton and sugar—but by the later part of the century they had been convinced that Tamilnad's ancient agriculture would resist wholehearted recruitment. Most of the agency houses gave up the venture as unprofitable and concentrated instead on establishing a small enclave of plantation agriculture on scattered parts of the Western Ghats and Tamilnad hills. From the 1860s onwards the exports of rice, cotton, groundnut, and a few other crops grown by Tamiland farmers increased steadily and promisingly. The trade in rice, however, remained wholly in indigenous hands, while cotton and groundnut were taken up by a scattering of small European firms which for the most part operated 'offshore' and invested no more than a small amount of turnover capital in the region. By the last few years of the century the most expansive part of Tamilnad's trade was not that which stretched west to the docks of London, Hamburg, and Marseille but rather that which stretched east to Colombo, Rangoon, Penang, and Singapore. In this trade Tamilnad was sending out capital, labour, professional skills, and manufactured goods and receiving back food, assorted luxuries, and remittance.

However limited, tentative and unusual were Tamilnad's overseas relations, they nevertheless dragged the region into unavoidable contact with trends of economic change of international rather than local significance. Up to the mid-1920s, demand for agrarian produce expanded on a worldwide scale, trade increased, and prices rose. The effects were felt both in Tamilnad's westward trade, which supplied consumer industries in Europe, and in her eastward trade, which ultimately depended on the west's demand for southeast Asia's plantation produce. From the mid-1920s onwards, the pendulum swung back, demand decelerated, international trade became less reliable, prices dipped. Both arms of Tamilnad's trade contracted. These long-term swings were broken up by more ephemeral oscillations caused by international wars or the quirks of imperial currency management. The effects of these eccentric movements were magnified by the way in which rural Tamilnad was attached to the international economy. The international markets in which prices and openings for Madras goods were decided were remote, complex, speculative, and unstable. Tamilnad's produce was often pushed out onto the speculative fringes of these markets because her old and tired agrarian system found it difficult to compete against younger and fresher production regimes in other parts of the world. Moreover the way in which the colonial government reacted to changes and crises in India's trading performance tended to accentuate the eccentric movements of price and demand rather than smoothing them down.

The following chapters examine how Tamilnad's agriculture reacted to the swings and roundabouts of international commercial fortune. The first task is to look at the agricultural sector itself and in particular the organization of labour, the provision of other productive resources, the management of finance and marketing. This forms the subject matter of the next two chapters. The second task is to look at the relationship of the countryside with the town and with government, particularly in the period after the depression when the pull of international demand had weakened, local urban demand had become more important for Tamilnad's agriculture, and the consequences of the instability in the markets were beginning to demand the attentions of government. These matters form the subject matter of the final two chapters. We must now turn away from this survey of the over-arching trends of history, and look at how things were produced.

3

Agriculture: labour, resources, production

Between the 1880s and the 1950s Tamilnad's agriculture had to adjust to two unavoidable influences—increased pressure on natural resources on the one hand, and increased opportunities and difficulties in the market on the other. Yet these two influences must be fixed in the proper perspective. There was no question of a new and sudden intensification of population pressure, or of a new and sudden reorientation away from subsistence and towards commercial agriculture. Southern India counted among the world's older areas of settlement, and in global terms already had a dense population and intensive agrarian system before the start of the British period. Similarly, agrarian society had for a long time been producing commodities for the market. We are not concerned here with an 'agricultural revolution', but with subtle changes of degree.

The rural population of Tamilnad increased steadily through the period. The decennial rates of growth from 1881 onwards (to 1961) were 16.9, 1.4, 7.2, 2.5, 5.3, 9.4, 7.8, 7.6.[1] If we smooth out the oscillations caused by the famines of the 1890s and the influenza epidemic of 1917-18, we are left with a remarkably steady rate of expansion at a bit over seven per cent a decade. These figures relate to the *rural* population; the *total* population of the region was accelerating, particularly after the influenza epidemic, but the excess was absorbed into the towns and cities.[2] It is not easy to explain the demographic growth in the countryside by reference to increasing land, food, or medical care. Rather it must be seen as part of a long-term trend of expansion which extends back into medieval history. Peace and agricultural expansion had probably occasioned some quickening of the pace in the nineteenth century.[3] Better transport, better organization of famine relief and some limited success with epidemic diseases, (plague, smallpox, cholera) seem to have contributed to the rate of growth in the twentieth.[4] While demographic growth provided more agricultural workers, the increasing urban population and the overseas markets demanded more food and raw materials from agriculture. There was thus great pressure to exploit the region's productive resources. As a result, productive resources were rapidly being made scarce. By the end of the nineteenth century it was becoming difficult to find spare lands which were capable of cultivation. The average size of a farm was already pretty small. If we set data on occupation (male, actual workers only) from the 1911 Census[5] against data on cultivated area from the contemporary *Season and Crop Report*[6] we find that each landowner (cultivating and non-cultivating) had on average 5.38 acres, while each cultivator (landowning or tenant) had just 4.53. To pursue this averaging a bit further, only about a third of each holding would be irrigated, and without irrigation yields in Tamilnad agriculture were bound to be low.[7] Meanwhile, land was not the only productive resource which was obviously in short supply. Agriculture required water, manure, and cattle. The increased demand for food and cash-crops and the absence of reserves of land dictated more intensive use of existing land. More intensive use of land meant increased inputs of ancillary resources like water, manure, and cattle-power, and more intensive and effective use of labour. This chapter looks at changes in the usage of natural resources and at changes in the organization of labour.

The three regions—plains, valleys and Kongunad—reacted very differently to the combination of the increased level of demand with the natural constraint on the supply of land and other productive resources. This was a result, firstly, of their very different natural endowments and social histories. The valleys had been densely populated and intensively cropped for centuries, while in the plains and Kongunad there had still been considerable room for expansion in the nineteenth century. The valleys lacked land while the plains and Kongunad still to some extent lacked labour. Secondly, each region was suited to a different cropping regime with different markets. The plains grew cotton and groundnut for the westwards trade; the valleys grew rice for the towns and for the eastwards trade; Kongunad grew cotton, sugar, and other crops mainly for the local urban market. The combination of different natural endowments, different styles of agrarian organization, and different markets dictated rather different strategies of productive investment, different extents of agrarian change, and different types and intensities of social conflict.

LABOUR AND RESOURCES

Plains

The nineteenth century saw the gradual dismantling of the military systems which had formed the backbone of life in the plains tract. The decline of the income from warfare and plunder, coupled with the increasing opportunities in cash-cropping for export, dictated a shift of emphasis into agriculture. There had always been agriculture on the plains in association with the herding peoples and the military colonies, and there had probably been tracts of permanent cultivation around the *kottai-pettai* settlements for many centuries.[8] But until the nineteenth century agriculture at any distance from these settlements was probably sparse and shifting. This was not surprising in view of the harshness of natural conditions. The rainfall of the region was around 30 inches per annum and unreliable, the temperatures tropical or sub-tropical and the dominant type of soil was red, light, and fairly thin. Under such conditions it was not possible to grow much other than one crop of coarse grain per year. However parts of the tract were slightly more favourably endowed by nature, and throughout the plains tract it was possible to effect some improvement by simple investments. There were some large areas of black soil and smaller patches of it throughout the tract. Such soil was markedly more fertile and retained moisture much better than the light, red varieties. Meanwhile even on the worst soils, the addition of bulky humus-making materials improved both fertility and the vital property of moisture retention at the same time. There were also occasional seasonal streams and rivulets which could be tapped by simple irrigation works, and the gentle slope which characterized most of the plains encouraged the construction of 'tanks'—small reservoirs restrained on the lower edge by a simple, crescent-shaped bank—which retained the water from rainfall or streams. Better soils, regular manuring, and simple irrigation devices could make cultivation rather more secure, and extend its range to include better millets like cholam, perhaps small areas of paddy in the immediate vicinity of tanks, and a number of pulses, spices, oilseeds and other crops.[9]

In such a habitat, two basic agricultural strategies were available. On the one hand, it was possible for the individual cultivating family with little or no capital and no assistance from non-family labourers to eke out a living which would barely rise above subsistence. The military colonization of the plains with the parcelling of the land into *al jivitams*,[10] or units to support one soldier, had probably been based upon this style of cultivation. On the other hand it was possible to farm the land much more intensively, but that required a substantial amount of capital and a considerable command of labour.

The former, or 'minimal', strategy concentrated on the cultivation of poor millet crops. Varagu, samai, korra, and even the slightly better millets like cumbu and ragi, had a very high tolerance of drought conditions. Scattered into a poor soil with little more assistance than a prayer for a good monsoon, they would generally produce some return although the yield would always be hopelessly low. This sort of cultivation needed almost no capital. The seed could be retained from the previous crop; the soil was light enough to be roughly ploughed with the poor specimens of cattle bred in the locality and fed on the local scrub; and the ground needed little or no manuring so long as it was allowed to lie fallow quite often. Naturally enough, this sort of agricultural practice tended towards a form of impermanent or long-fallow cultivation. Buchanan noticed quite a lot of this in 1801 in the Baramahal,[11] and the resettlement officer in Salem in 1916 noted that there was still a tendency to shift the area under cultivation quite dramatically from year to year, particularly in the specially arid taluk of Attur.[12] Around the same period, the Collector of North Arcot noted that about 30,000 acres, or five per cent of the cultivated area in the dry part of the district, was taken up annually on *sivoijama*; this term meant that the farmers were not prepared to take up the land on a permanent land-deed, but were happy to pay a higher rate of revenue just so that they could give up the land in the following year (and not incur a continuing obligation to pay revenue on it).[13]

This form of 'minimal' cultivation also tended to orient towards subsistence. Millets did not demand a great input of labour and there was no need for a farmer to look beyond the labour resources of his own family. There were of course some cash needs—cloth, salt, perhaps an iron tip for the plough, and certainly the government's revenue—but these could generally be provided for by two different methods. Firstly, because cultivation was confined to one crop per year and concentrated in the period of the monsoon, there was a long 'off-season' when the family could seek out various forms of wage-labour. Secondly there were certain crops which were barely more demanding to cultivate than poor millet and which could be sold for a meagre cash return. Castor-seed and horse-gram were the most popular and they were grown in minute plots all over the plains. Unless they were well watered and manured, the yield from castor-seed and horse-gram was very low, but so long as ground-space was not difficult to find it was cheap and easy to grow enough to yield an adequate return. There was also no difficulty over realizing the cash, for the produce could be sold in the local shandy. So long as land was fairly easily available (and throughout most of the plains that seems to have been the case until the end of the nineteenth century) the land devoted to this sort of cultivation acquired little or no value. The revenue department, which prided itself on the high ratio of collection to demand, was constantly annoyed when small farmers on the plains refused to pay the revenue demand, simply abandoned a plot, and allowed the government (vainly) to put it up to auction to realize the arrear which was a mar on their accounts.[14] As an experienced local official noted at the turn of the century:

It is certain from local inquiries and experience during several years that much dry land has no sale value though frequently under cultivation; a ryot will let it be sold for trifling arrears and at the sale there will be little or no competition.[15]

The other cultivation strategy required much larger inputs of capital and labour, and thus aimed to secure some form of commensurate profit. Even the poorest red soils repaid investment in the provision of manure and water, so long as the two things were done both together and on a sufficient scale. The black soils were more expensive to work in the first place; they were heavy and thus needed better bullocks and stronger ploughs, and they were liable to waterlog if too wet or tessellate if too dry and so needed better provision for irrigation and drainage. But they also had more natural humus and retained moisture better than other soils; thus they were rarely taken up by the exponents of 'minimal' cultivation but were favoured by intensive farmers. The necessary inputs on both black and red soils, however, required some investment of cash and considerable command of labour. Manure came either from animal-dropping or from leaves and grass gathered from the wastes and forests. Graziers had to be paid to pen their animals on the land, or labour had to be mobilized to move cartloads of manure from the forests or cattle-stalls to the field. Intensive dry-land cultivation required something like two thousand sheep-days of penning, or forty cartloads of farmyard manure, for each acre.[16] The provision of water differed according to location. In some areas there were seasonal tanks or streams, and here the farmer would have to dig channels, perhaps build an annual temporary dam on the stream or a 'spring channel' to catch the water that ran along below the surface of the river-bed, build the bund (bank) of the tank, and clear the silt from all the reservoirs and channels in each season. In much of the area, however, water was not so easily available and could only be reached by digging down to the sub-soil deposits.[17] Sinking wells was expensive, particularly on the uplands towards the interior of the peninsula where the water-table was low and the gneiss old and hard.[18] Moreover, raising the water required either a considerable expenditure of human labour or, more commonly, the services of some strong bullocks. These animals were expensive to buy, because they had to be bred carefully in selected parts of the region (notably in Mysore, the interior of Kongunad, or the uplands of the Deccan rim), and needed more careful feeding in order to repay the considerable initial investment.[19]

The returns came in several ways. The yield per acre of millet crops could be more than doubled by careful cultivation, and the investment in well-irrigation provided an insurance against all but the very worst seasons. Water and manure also made it possible to grow more valuable cash-crops—high-quality oil-seeds such as gingelly, chillis, spices such as turmeric and coriander, cotton, tobacco and sugar-cane. All of these found a local market although it would probably require a further investment with a carter, commission-agent or local dealer to convey the crop to the local market-town.

Compared to the 'minimal' strategy of cultivation, the more intensive strategy required a continual investment in the improvement of the land, a regular supply of working capital, and a significant command over labour. It is difficult to compare estimates of cultivation costs for different crops because of the vast differences in local conditions, but roughly speaking between the wars it required 1½ to 2 times the outlay necessary for careful cultivation of millet to grow gingelly, 2 to 2½ times to grow cotton, 6 to 9 times to grow tobacco, and 10 to 15 times to grow sugar-cane.[20] It is important however to understand that 'investment' in 'fixed capital' and 'working capital' in this economy was not mainly a matter of deploying sums of money. Both forms of 'investment' did of course require some cash outlays—the purchase of brick or stone to line a well, the purchase of special seeds, the payment of day labourers—but it also required two other specific things: a command over considerable supplies of labour and a privileged access to certain locally scarce resources, notably those provided by the forests and wastelands.

Many of the investments in 'fixed capital' required not so much the purchase of artefacts as the deployment of labour—to dig a well, build up and maintain a tank bund, clear scrub, level ground, or plant protective hedging. Similarly many of the advances in 'working capital' were simply a matter of deploying more labour—to bale water, carry loads of green manure many miles from the forest, hoe and weed more often, and harvest more carefully. Besides this deployment of labour, the other major element of 'investment' in intensive plains agriculture concerned cattle and forests.

Cattle, and other forms of livestock, were an indispensable part of the plains economy. There were many families who lived entirely or mainly by breeding cattle, sheep, goats, and even ponies, and others who worked as drovers and graziers. Livestock in some cases formed an economy in its own right—as a source of milk, meat, leather, and draught power[21]—but chiefly it was important as an adjunct of the arable economy. A traditional unit of land measurement in the plains was the *kota*, which represented the area which could be cultivated with a single team of bullocks. This unit varied from place to place according to the demands of the land—roughly speaking it was around five to six acres where there was a well or water-course, and ten to twelve acres where there was none—and the fact that it was considered in some senses as an optimal size of holding indicated the expense and the importance of cattle and the need to adjust other factors of production to suit this one particular input.[22] Cattle were required not only for ploughing and other jobs in preparing the land, but also for lifting water and transporting produce. Besides, animal manure was the single most important fertilizer in the plains and was provided by cattle and by sheep and goats which were penned on the fields in the off-season. Many plains villages had enormous numbers of livestock. In one Ramnad village in 1916, there were about 400 head of cattle and 1,200 sheep and goats between 780 inhabitants.[23] The government's livestock census in 1921 counted in the district of Salem 1,188,433 cattle, 131,732 buffalo and 1,281,934 sheep and goats among a rural population of just under two million.[24] 'The ryot's wealth' noted one official in 1913, 'seems to be reckoned by the size of his herd and in consequence he is very loath to part with his animals.'[25]

The importance of cattle points also to the importance of the land which was not actually cultivated—that is, the common or waste ground in and around the village, and also the more remote areas of forest mostly on the hillsides. These were indispensable as grazing grounds both for the local cattle, and for those driven up from the valleys during much of the cultivation season. The forests also provided grass and green leaves which were widely used for manure, particularly on paddy land. Cart-loads and head-loads were taken down and sold in the valleys. Finally they provided timber which was the raw material for buildings and for agricultural implements; again it was both used locally and provided an inflow of cash through sale outside the zone.[26]

The more intensive the strategy of cultivation, the more desperate the need for good cattle and good access to the forests. Any plains cultivation which used water, whether from tanks or wells, needed good cattle to lift or impel the water from irrigation source to field. The black soils favoured by the more intensive farmers were heavy to work and thus demanded sturdy draught animals. Intensive cultivation tended to include direct involvement in marketing and that meant cattle for transport. The need to keep cattle led to the need for good access to grazing grounds while the crops were on the field.

In sum, the more intensive strategy of cultivation on the plains required three things. It required cash to buy seed, purchase cattle, pay wage-labour. It also required a command over labour; this did not only mean the wealth to pay wages, but also the ability to secure labour when it was needed. This was always going to be somewhat difficult in a region where it was reasonably easy (at least in theory) for any man to set up as an independent cultivator, and it was particularly difficult at certain peak times in the agricultural calendar. Since the cultivation season for most farmers was strictly dictated by the timing of the monsoon, and since the crop range of most farmers was limited to a few particular crops, many cultivators would find themselves planting at roughly the same time and harvesting at roughly the same time. Finally it required good access to the resources of waste land. It was no good if you could buy good cattle but could not find a place to graze them.

While the 'minimal' and 'intensive' strategies of cultivation were enormously different in goal and scale, they in fact existed side-by-side in the same tract, within the same village, and on adjacent plots. Neither was self-sufficient. Each could exist only if there was an exchange of goods, labour, and services between them. The result was a complex pattern of redistribution within village society. It is easy, when describing such patterns of redistribution, to give the impression that they were ordained by some benign communal ethic. That impression would in this case be highly misleading. The practitioners of the 'intensive' strategy concentrated control over the local surplus in order to be able to 'buy' the labour of their lesser neighbours. The relationship was not benign and 'moral', but tense and fractious.

In the nineteenth century the hierarchical society of military chiefs and settler-militiamen was translated into a society of dominant and dependent cultivators. Although economic roles were substantially transformed in this shift of emphasis away from warfare and towards farming, the hierarchical structure which had underlain the military settlement provided a mould for the organization of agricultural production. The majority of plainsmen fell into a pattern of simple cultivation that required minimal inputs, no more than family labour, and only a marginal contact with the monetized economy. They also engaged in a number of subsidiary occupations (mainly concerning livestock farming and the production of construction materials) which both provided important supplements to the local way of life and also created articles for exchange in the valleys. This form of economy, however, could not provide a secure income in such a harsh tract. One or two years in five the rains would fail. Cultivation in the other years would not provide the individual farmer with a surplus which could keep him alive and pay his cash dues in the bad years. For this he had to rely on the exchange of ancillary produce in the valleys, and on the bounty of the village leaders' more intensive and secure cultivation.

The poligars and other military overlords of the plains tract took little interest in the shift to agriculture, but the lineage heads, village headmen and others who had provided the middle ranks of the politico-military hierarchy of the tract were well placed to adopt the role of intensive cultivators. In the earlier pattern the village chiefs had commanded the labour of the villagers for military service, and in return had protected the village against marauding and adversity. In the new pattern the village heads commanded the labour of the village for intensive cultivation, and in return protected the village against seasonal fluctuation and other hardships. They provided a market for the artisan work and ancillary services which the subordinate villagers undertook to supplement their income from minimal cropping, and they drew on the labour services of the subordinate villagers to effect the capital and current improvements necessary for 'intensive' cultivation. In return the village chiefs were responsible for the maintenance of the village economy. Each year they redistributed the surplus product of intensive cultivation to the artisans and servants, such as the carpenters and washermen, whose services were necessary for all the villagers, and to those cultivators and labourers who did not on their own plots produce enough for subsistence.[27] Furthermore they dug grain-pits, often beneath their own houses, in which they stored grain against the possibility of bad seasons.[28] In the more backward parts of the south Indian plains, the basic outlines of this jajmani-style system of redistribution were still visible recently. In the 1950s Scarlett Epstein investigated a plains village in the Kannada tract to the north of Tamilnad and deliberately chose one that had been relatively untouched by commercialization. She found that the traditional payments made by the village leaders to artisans, labourers, and dependents of all kind were clearly calculated to equalize the distribution of resources in a bad season so that all might have the chance to survive, but at the same time to enable the village leaders to skim off the surplus in the good years.[29]

Thus the society of the plains tended to divide into 'big men' and 'little men'. It was not necessarily the old chiefly families which became the new intensive farmers, though there is some considerable evidence of family continuity of this sort. Families could rise from the ranks by luck, clever investment, and marriage alliance, and equally families could fall because of financial misfortune or demographic disaster. The point is that the hierarchical mould of old-style plains society, with its emphasis on the importance of control over manpower, could be adapted to operate the new agricultural economy. The institution of village office, which, as we have seen, remained important in the political ordering of the plains tract in the nineteenth century, helped to strengthen this hierarchical mould and, in certain cases, to maintain the continuity of old chiefly families.[30]

It was not, however, a completely smooth transition. In particular, towards the end of the nineteenth century and the start of the twentieth, two new factors began to affect the plains economy. Firstly, the tract became much more closely involved in foreign trade. The crops demanded by the export houses were those which, for the most part, could be grown in the plains rather than the valleys. Secondly, the reservoir of spare land was gradually exhausted and there was pressure not only on arable land itself but also on the resources of the remaining forests and wastelands.

In the far south there had long been a considerable tract of cotton and it was already expanding significantly in the second quarter of the nineteenth century. In parts of the far south and the Arcots plain, there were significant increases of sugar cultivation in the 1830s and 1840s, and there were some advances in tobacco, spice, and indigo in mid-century. The major expansions came, however, with the growth of world demand after 1860 and the most important crops were cotton and groundnut. In the 1850s, groundnut was already recognized as a paying crop in South Arcot.[31] It was relatively cheap to cultivate, liked the light soils that prevailed on the plains, and tolerated any variation in rainfall from 55 inches to the low figure of 20 inches. It was also a legume and therefore kind to the soil and useful in a rotation. It even provided a reasonable amount of fodder and a very useful manure in the form of oilcake left after pressing out the oil. The demand in Europe grew with the development of food and cosmetic industries, mostly in France and Germany. Successive pressings of groundnut yielded raw material for cooking oil, margarine, and soaps.[32] By 1870 there were 20,000 acres in South Arcot and a large export from the ports of Cuddalore, Pondicherry, and Madras, and by 1882 the acreage had more

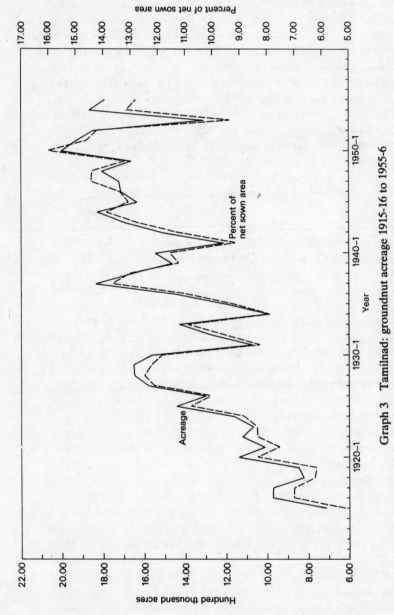

Graph 3   Tamilnad: groundnut acreage 1915-16 to 1955-6

Note: Groundnut acreage was not reported separately before 1915-16.

Source: *Season and Crop Report.*

than doubled to 48,000. In the 1890s, the yield began to decline because of poor cultivation practices. However, one of the main export firms, Parrys, introduced a new strain from Mauritius, the world market kept the prices rising, and although there was little improvement in cultivation practices the new strain was rather more hardy.[33] By the first world war, there were over 300,000 acres under groundnut in South Arcot. From the 1900s there were also significant increases in North Arcot, which had 200,000 acres by the end of the first world war, and to a lesser extent on the plains areas of Salem, Tiruchi, and Madurai. By the first world war, there were roughly 850,000 acres under groundnuts in the Tamil districts, and between then and 1955 the acreage continued to increase, with large fluctuations, at a trend rate of an additional 23,000 acres a year. The proportion of net sown area devoted to groundnuts rose from seven per cent in the first world war to twice that figure in the second. In parts of the Arcots plain and the central plain it was, between the wars, the largest single crop, occupying rather more than a quarter of net sown area.

Cotton acreage increased in the price boom of the American civil war, but then declined down to 1900. World prices for cotton were improving after the post-civil war slump, but Tamilnad mostly grew short-staple cotton and this was not greatly in demand on the world market. The agricultural department had however been attempting for some time to develop strains of long-staple cotton that would thrive on the poor soils and low rainfall of the plains. In 1900 they finally had success with an imported plant which had an American style of foliage and staple, but in place of the shallow roots of the American plant, had a long tap root which could reach down to the rather sparse moisture in the soils of the plains. It did well on red soils with a limited amount of irrigation, and provided a quality of cotton that was much better than anything else produced in the region. The Buckingham and Carnatic mills in Madras immediately offered to pay a premium for cotton from this plant, known as Cambodia, and helped popularize its use.[34] While it became most important in the Kongunad tract, where it was grown under well-irrigation, it also did well on the western part of the far-south plain, where there were red soils and water percolated from the Ghats. Meanwhile in the same period, the department also developed a new strain from the local varieties in the far south. This karunganni plant had a better staple and fibre quality than the local

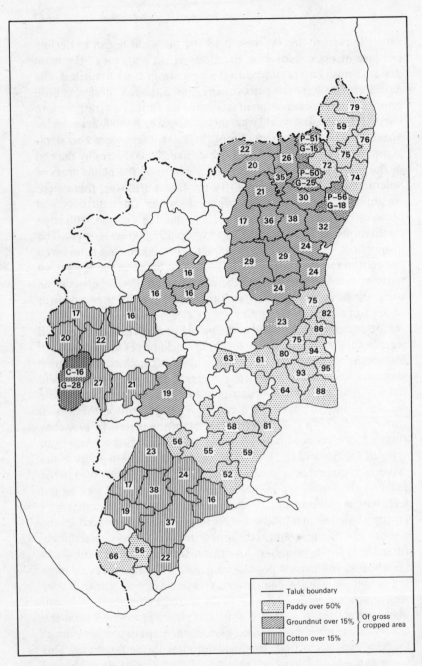

Map 5   Tamilnad: main areas of paddy, cotton and groundnut

varieties, and could be grown on the heavy, moisture-retentive black soils without additional irrigation. The spinning magnates of the far south, Harvey and Co., promoted this strain from 1907, and it quickly spread through the black soils in the centre of the far south.[35] With these new strains, good international prices, and demand from Bombay and the slowly developing local textile industry, the acreage under cotton expanded rapidly from four per cent of the total net sown area of the Tamil districts around 1900, to eight per cent in the first world war and nine to ten per cent in the interwar years. In the far south, cotton occupied roughly a quarter of the acreage between the wars, and in the centre of the black-soil tract the proportion rose to fifty per cent.

While these two were by far the most important cash-crops in terms of acreage on the plains, there were also smaller areas under tobacco, spices, vegetables, and sugar, and these showed sporadic but definite increases after the first world war. These late nineteenth-century demands for export crops promoted a last spurt of expansion of the acreage under cultivation in the plains. The new crops did not necessarily take acreage away from grain and in many instances they actually created net additions to the total acreage. Groundnut was so hardy that it could be grown on land which could scarcely support any other crop and which was barely worth clearing simply to grow millet. The returns on cotton cultivation made it worthwile clearing more of the difficult black-soil tract. Thus the government's settlement reports in the plains districts in the late nineteenth century recorded significant expansions of acreage: sixteen per cent in North Salem in 1872,[36] seven in South Arcot in 1887,[37] eleven in North Arcot in the 1870s.[38] In Salem as a whole, where officials in the 1860s ventured that all cultivable land had already been taken up,[39] the acreage expanded by about 400,000 acres, or an increment of one third, between the 1880s and the first world war. In the same period the proportion of the reported acreage that was under cultivation in the two southernmost districts rose from forty-five to fifty-five per cent.

By the end of the first world war, this expansion had reached some form of natural limit. Officials who were asked to find unused land to allocate to demobbed soldiers could only come up with small patches of dubious utility.[40] As export demand had increased the monetary value of plains farming, and as the expansion of acreage approached this limit, so ordinary plains land took on a cash value.

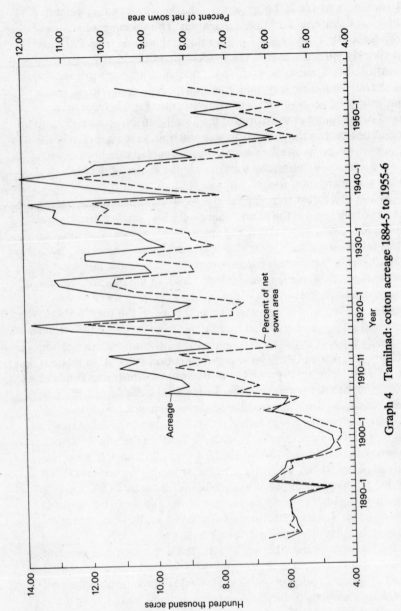

Graph 4 Tamilnad: cotton acreage 1884-5 to 1955-6

Source: *Season and Crop Report.*

Land which had been somehow 'improved', by the construction of a tank or well, or by constant manuring, had for a long time commanded a value and entered into the market. The ordinary, poor land which predominated in the plains, however, did not really enter into the market until the last quarter of the nineteenth century.[41] In the years leading up to the first world war, the nominal price was advancing rapidly, but it was still low in absolute terms—around Rs 50 an acre—and the volume of transactions was very small.[42] The commercial expansion on the plains did not lead to a crisis over land, so much as over labour and waste.

The agricultural economy of the plains, as it developed in the nineteenth century, revolved around the interdependence of 'minimal' and 'intensive' styles of cultivation. The 'intensive' cultivation depended on the ability of the village leaders to command the labour of the smaller cultivators. However, the commercial expansion at the end of the century was accessible to all cultivators without restriction as to size. Groundnut in particular could be grown virtually by anyone and anywhere. As one observer noted about groundnut cultivation in the southern portion of the Arcots plain:

The cost of production is exceptionally low. It is possible for one man with a pair of oxen and a single plough to do all the work necessary—cultivation, manuring, sowing, weeding, reaping etc., for from five to eight acres of groundnuts and other grains, with the exception of some assistance at weeding and harvest. This is not uncommon in this locality.[43]

Groundnut cultivation was so simple and, in the first quarter of the twentieth century, so profitable that even many small farmers would borrow the capital necessary to get started. 'It is now grown', noted the government, 'on all kinds of soil from the poorest to the best black-cotton and repeated sometimes on the same fields year after year, regardless of rotation, due to the short-sightedness of ryots.'[44] Cotton was a little more expensive but still possible for a small farmer. In the far south in 1919 it was noted that : 'Petty ryots, especially those who lease land, and ryots who are in financial difficulty, will grow cotton every year as this is the money crop of the tract.'[45] Most cultivating families, however poor, could raise the money capital necessary to enter into export cropping of groundnut, either by saving the proceeds of wage labour, or by raising a loan. At the climax of the period of booming prices and good foreign demand, even some of the most lowly of the plains population were clearly profiting. In Ramnad in the 1910s a student noted:

Most of the villagers own some land at least. In fact buying land has become almost a craze in the village .... Some have even gone to the length of buying land with money borrowed at from twelve to eighteen per cent though the yield can never be expected to be beyond four or at the most six per cent. Even the Pallans and Chakkiliyans invest their surplus money in land.[46]

Just as the export demand stimulated the production of cash-crops on small holders' plots, so it also encouraged the more intensive farmers to expand their operations. While groundnuts and cotton could be grown in a small-scale, cheap fashion in the 'minimal' pattern, they responded well and delivered much higher yields if they were supplied with fertilizer, irrigation, and attention. As we have already seen, the expansion of the more intensive style of cultivation entailed the application of more and more labour—to carry water and manure, to weed and hoe more attentively, and to harvest more carefully. The expansion of cash-cropping greatly increased the demand for labour in the tract and led to competition between the 'intensive' and 'minimal' cultivators for control over the latter's labour.

By the late 1920s there were sporadic local reports about the difficulty of securing labour for intensive cultivation. Large ground-nut growers in Salem complained that it was difficult to get labourers whenever there was an unusual demand for labour on public works and government projects.[47] In statements which eloquently displayed the relative importance of labour and land in the plains agrarian economy, several observers pointed out that the price of land in any tract often depended to a large extent on the local availability of labour. In Tirunelveli, one official ventured that the value of land in different villages depended firstly on irrigation sources but then on the 'existence of capitalists and traders in the village', that is, the penetration of the market, and finally on 'the abundance of labourers and cultivators'.[48] The value of land in Salem, according to one leading resident, 'depends upon the amount of labour that is available in each place and also on the richness of the soil'.[49] In some areas there were reports of rises in cash wages. In one plains village in Madurai, surveyed in the early 1930s, the large landholders complained that wages were very high and the surveying student concluded that :'As a matter of fact, sometimes the labourer is better off than the cultivator.'[50]

It is not possible to discover how large or how widespread such wage rises were. There does seem to have been some increase in the ranks of wage-labourers but it was not overwhelming and most plains residents still seemed to have access to some land.[51] There were however signs of a reorientation of the relations between 'big' and 'small' men. One of these was the development of a form of labour contracting, disguised as a form of tenancy. Up to the 1890s there was little tenancy in plains villages except for some waram (crop-sharing) arrangements on patches of paddy land. In the years that followed, however, there was a small but significant expansion of tenancies. In one Ramnad village, for instance, there was no land under tenancy in 1916 but by 1936 thirteen per cent of the village land had been leased.[52] Although there were numerous local differences in the form of leasing, there was an overall pattern. The lessor was only rarely an absentee and generally took a close interest in the tenanted holding. Very often he provided not only the land, but also the bullocks (or perhaps a loan for the tenant to buy the bullocks). Often too, it was written into the contract that the lessor would also provide the manure, and sometimes even the seed and other inputs. As for the rental, this was usually a fixed cash payment, known in this tract as *kuthagai*. Most of the tenants were small landholders and cultivators in their own right. In sum there had been a shift from the old system in which 'intensive' farmers commanded the labour services of the sub-subsistence cultivators and rewarded them with grain, to a new system in which the 'intensive' cultivator parcelled out surplus land, often in units which could be worked with one pair of bullocks. By continuing to provide inputs of seed and manure, he kept a close control over the usage of the land, solved the problem of securing labour, and sacrificed very little of the profits of cultivation; by all accounts the remuneration of the *kuthagai* tenant was only a fraction above the level of payments to a tied labourer.[53]

While such tenancy was one form of adjustment to the demands of expansive cash-cropping, it was never particularly widespread. Most village surveys reported between ten and twenty per cent of their area under contracts of this form.[54] Money-lending, however, was much more extensive. The whole subject of money-lending in rural India has been hopelessly obscured by a succession of different commentators, and must therefore be treated carefully.

The British administrators of the late nineteenth century seized on money-lending as a simple explanation for the torpidity of agriculture. It was easy to blame usurers for the poverty of the average rustic, and it also helped to justify the levels of land revenue if it could be shown that revenue payments hurt the ryot far less than interest payments.[55] Administrators and economists elaborated a picture of predatory money-lenders, seizing the profits and often also the land of the downtrodden cultivator. The picture also proved amenable to nationalist ideologues, who could find the origin of the money-lender in the supposed creation of a land-market under British rule. From there, the argument was passed to the Marxists and 'rural romantics', who saw in the money-lender the extension of capitalism into the rural, peasant-based economy. Most of these analysts have condemned money-lending as 'usury' with little attention to its context or purpose. It would, however, seem more sensible to examine the role of money-lending against the background of the local society and economy.

It is necessary, at the outset, to distinguish between money-lending which forms part of trade and commerce, and money-lending which forms part of the internal system of redistribution of the village. The former sort will be considered in the next chapter. The latter sort was by far the most important in plains south India. Given the questionable character of land as a form of surety, it was dangerous for an outsider to lend money directly in plains villages. The only people who were really capable of assessing a villager's creditworthiness and compelling repayment were other villagers who could rely on personal pledges for security and who could use the village's internal government to sort out any dispute.

Such lending from cultivator to cultivator had existed at least since the advent of British rule and both Munro and Buchanan noted it.[56] Credit transactions between cultivators are best considered as part of the hierarchically-ordered system of redistribution within the village, and it was hardly surprising in a tract which used cash extensively before British rule, that parts of this redistributive system should be monetized. The village chiefs concentrated wealth —from plunder, local taxes, trade, cultivation—and redistributed it in the form of grain doles, wage payments and loans. Frederick Nicholson, who made the first systematic study of rural credit in Madras in 1895, noted that 'as between ryot and ryot, credit is often a mere friendly office without documents or accounts, based upon village good feeling, local knowledge of character and status, and even custom; it is not so long even in this Presidency, since the revenue default of one ryot was regularly made good by his co-villagers.'[57] Indeed 'big men' were *expected* to provide credit to 'small men' and in certain cases seem to have been virtually obliged to do so. Often these transactions involved no real computation of interest payments and no real expectation of repayment; just as the village leader was expected to distribute grain to keep the village alive, so he was expected to distribute capital resources to keep the village lands under cultivation.[58]

The late nineteenth century saw a definite increase in this form of credit. As cash-cropping increased, and as the market for grain improved, so the village leaders transformed more of their 'savings' from grain to cash, and changed the 'currency' of the redistributive system from grain and other kind payments to money credit. The transfer was slow, sporadic and incomplete, however it was clearly quite advanced by the late nineteenth century. It was probably miscalculations in the process of transition that caused unusually high levels of death from famine in these years. Village leaders were growing more cash-crops and less grain-crops and holding more of their savings in cash rather than kind. They still held 'insurance' stocks of grain but these would last no longer than one bad season and in each of the last three decades of the nineteenth century there were large numbers of deaths from famine when the rains failed in more than one year in succession.[59]

The growth of money-lending went hand in hand with other advances of monetization—waram to *kuthagai* rents, kind to cash wages. The pace of change differed from locality to locality, yet by the early twentieth century a large part of the internal redistributive system of plains villages was in cash. In 1930 it was reported that a large number of plains villagers went regularly to the village leaders to borrow sums of money which they needed to bridge the gap between their ordinary income and their outgoings.[60] Such lending, as one witness told the Banking Enquiry, was not simply an entrepreneurial activity but represented 'the survival of ideas of communal life by which the villagers were bound together as a definite entity.'[61]

The village leaders who handed out these loans often extracted their return not so much in interest as in labour services. As Nicholson noted, 'there are numerous unexpressed services and dues which custom requires of the debtor; e.g., presents of fodder, vegetables, delicacies, services in repair of tanks, etc., services in faction disputes and in the giving of evidence'.[62] Often it gave the creditor a lien on the labour of the debtor and his family:

The tenant and the farm servant will take advances of grain between twenty-five and fifty per cent interest and cash advance at twelve per cent interest during the slack season to be adjusted to their produce. A certain amount of grain and money debt as due to the landholder will always attach to these classes. In general they are willing to pay certain perquisites and do extra free service for the landowners. Free supplies of vegetables for festive occasions, the bullock carts for Divali, marriage and other ceremonial occasions, free fuel, free labour for house repairs, fencing or erection of mud walls, fodder for cattle, watching of the farm and crops, staying on the field with cattle, service at a lower wage for cleansing canals and tanks of silt and payment of a higher *salami* are some of the forms which these perquisites and free labour have taken in different areas.[63]

Often it would enable the creditor to direct the debtor's labour on the latter's own land; the patron would supply the credit for cultivation, would then be in a position to order the nature of cultivation, and would take repayment in kind. In many cases these loans were carried over from year to year, waxing and waning according to the character of the season, and with little attention to the niceties of book-keeping. British officials were constantly puzzled by the fact that such loans were never given to finance improvements in the debtor's land, such as the sinking of a well or the levelling of a field,[64] but this puzzlement resulted merely from their inability to understand the logic of the system. Creditors gave out 'loans' in order to be able to secure dependants and it would have been foolish to make 'loans' which, by improving the productivity of the debtor's land, helped him to become more independent. In extreme cases the debtor would become little more than a tied, client labourer. 'Certain ryots', as one official noted, 'attach themselves permanently to a particular leading ryot who finances them throughout the year and takes in return all the produce grown by them.'[65] There was however a countervailing tendency which prevented any generalization of this form of tight clientage. Anyone who made a cash profit from agriculture immediately set about lending some of this to his neighbours. Thus as cash-cropping spread, so lending became more competitive and debtors could under certain circumstances switch their patrons.[66]

While the increasing commercialization of plains agriculture led to a competition for labour which in turn fostered 'tenancy' and 'money-lending', it also led to competition over access to pasture, forest, and waste land. As we have seen, these tracts were a vital adjunct to the arable economy and had particular importance for the business of cattle-keeping. Until the last quarter of the nineteenth century, there was little problem about access to pasture and forest. However the increase in arable cultivation not only increased the demands for pastures (and other uses of forest and waste lands) but of course caused a straightforward reduction in the amount of such land available. Meanwhile the area of forest available to the plains economy was diminished not only by the simple business of clearing and planting, but also by the activity of a government anxious to protect the areas that remained. The Madras government set up a forest department in the 1850s, passed an Act to enable it to conserve forests in the 1870s, and began setting up the machinery to put the Act into operation in the 1880s. The department aimed to develop the remaining areas of *major* forest as economic resources in their own right, and thus tried to separate them off from the plains agrarian economy. The Government declared these areas as 'reserved forest', restricted access to them completely, prohibited the casual use of many of their resources, and allowed a strictly limited use of other areas on the payment of fees and issue of licences.[67] This was the theoretical story; the reality was one of the great running sores of the Madras administration.

Although it is difficult to judge the extent to which the area available to ryots diminished, the figures given as 'waste' give us some indication. In this classification came land that was not cultivated but not demarcated as forest (nor entered as 'not available' because it consisted of house-sites etc.). Although it is a category of government statistical record that is peculiarly vulnerable to error, the graph does show a remarkable decline in the plains districts from the 1880s to the first world war. The resources of the forests were too important to the economy of the plains to be foregone, yet just at the time when the forests were being ploughed up or reserved, so the advent of cash-crops was increasing their importance as sources of leaf-manure, grazing for work-animals, and timber for implements. Thirty years after the government had reserved the forests, villages still retained a memory of their traditional use-rights, and of the boundaries between their patch of the forest and those commanded by neighbouring villages. When

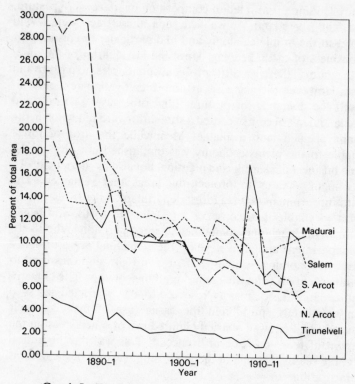

Graph 5   Waste land in selected districts 1884-5 to 1915-16

Source: *Season and Crop Report.*

the government investigated the administration of the forests in 1913, it was bombarded with requests for freer access:

> In the districts...where the demand for free grazing was met with, it was almost invariably accompanied by a demand for free fuel, free leaf manure and free agricultural timber—in fact a demand for the abolition of all control.[68]

The ryots based their claim on 'immemorial custom', while the government saw it as a claim 'for the right to use or to destroy the forest property of the State without any restriction whatever'.[69] Meanwhile some government officials from the district rather than from the central offices recognized that the forest administration ensured that people were 'driven by poverty to be dishonest'.[70]

Naturally the ryots fought bitterly to retain their continued rights to use forest produce. The number of offences against the forest rules and restrictions ran at the level of 30,000 a year, and instances of violence were legion. Forest department subordinates and graziers fought pitched battles and often murdered one another with alarming frequency.[71]

In 1924, the government was obliged to change its policy and release areas of forest which were so close to villages that proper policing was impossible. Some were now placed under the supervision of the revenue department while others were allotted to panchayat councils of local villagers.[72] But while the government gave with one hand, it took away with the other. The forest and agriculture departments took a dislike to the careless breeding of local cattle. The results of such breeding were admittedly poor specimens and the departments felt that they used up valuable grazing resources and carried diseases which were easily transmitted to better stock. Thus from 1917 government permitted village waste lands, which hitherto had been conserved as grazing grounds, to be assigned away for cultivation.[73] On the same principle, in 1933 they contemplated raising the fees for grazing in reserved forests.[74]

Although the ryots' determination did keep open some access to forest resources, partly through bribery and partly through sheer force,[75] yet still the available resources were dwindling and thus the costs of using them rising. At the resettlement of North Arcot in 1913, the government officials calculated that cultivation expenses had increased much faster than the general inflation of prices, largely owing to the restrictions on access to the forests; manure had got more expensive and so had the maintenance of plough-bullocks.[76] At the government enquiry into forest administration in 1913, the costs of manure and grazing were a repeated source of complaint.[77] In the 1930s, when the slump of prices pushed farmers back onto slim margins of profit, the plains farmers petitioned, not for a reduction of land revenue, but for reduction of grazing fees and for easier access to the forests; the costs of cattle and manure were clearly seen as a more imposing part of their personal economies than the govenment *kist*.[78] One petition complained of the exorbitant fees paid to contractors who had secured concessions to supply grazing, firewood, timber, and manure and argued that: 'The maintenance of the cattle which is the backbone of the agriculturist has become very difficult for want of facilities as in the old days.[79] Some zamindars who had maintained private forests began to find a reasonable income from carefully selling off the rights to graze and take manure.[80] But for most ryots, the upkeep of cattle in particular became difficult and expensive. The lack of grazing land forced many into the expensive expedient of growing crops specifically for fodder.[81] The total area under fodder crops in the Tamil districts was roughly 30,000 to 40,000 acres at the turn of the century; it rose steadily to 150,000 in the late 1930s and then jumped to 200,000 during the second world war.[82] The latter jump was probably the offshoot of a bad spate of cattle disease in the early 1940s, which enormously raised the purchase price of cattle and therefore made the cattle economy as a whole necessarily more expensive and intensive.[83] Half of the acreage and most of the increase came in the single district of Tirunelveli, while there were also substantial and increasing areas under fodder in other parts of the plains—Madurai, Ramnad, and Salem.

As the services provided by the forest became more scarce and more valuable, so not everyone could gain access to them. The ability to keep cattle, collect manure and so forth came to depend more and more on a combination of financial and political power. The main result of the forest regulations had been to make the forest department 'peculiarly corrupt'.[84] Ryots could get access to the reserved parts of the forest, but it required an outlay. 'In one or two cases', noted the 1913 forest report, 'villagers admitted quite frankly that they had paid the guard and the watcher, and having so paid, did what they liked in the forest.'[85] Others admitted it by implication. 'I have arranged that they do not impound [the illegally grazing cattle]', said one substantial ryot.[86] The purchase price of cattle rose much more rapidly than crop prices in the early twentieth century. In the 1890s Nicholson estimated the cost of a pair of good bullocks at Rs 40; a Court of Wards officer in 1913 reckoned Rs 150-200; and witnesses at the Banking Enquiry in 1929-30 estimated Rs 600.[87] Moreover, the advance of well-irrigation for intensive agriculture placed a very heavy strain on the cattle which worked the *kavalai* lift; a probably rather exaggerated estimate reckoned that the life-span of a good pair of working cattle was once eighteen years, but had now been reduced to two or three.[88] The combination of high purchase and maintenance costs meant that it was not possible for every ryot to buy and keep his own cattle. The settlement officers in northern Salem in 1934 reckoned that the number of cattle and ploughs in the tract had declined 7½ per cent in the past thirty years, despite a considerable expansion in both population and acreage.[89] In villages surveyed in the 1920s and 1930s, roughly half the number of operational holdings had plough-cattle, and in surveys in the 1950s the proportion was closer to one third.[90] Many cultivators then had to hire their plough-cattle, sometimes from a professional cattle-keeper in the village or locality, but more often from the more prosperous neighbours. There were also more cases of a form of tenancy in which the tenant borrowed money from the landlord specifically to purchase the cattle necessary to work the plot. Such a form of agreement not only carried a high rate of interest but often bound the tenant to a higher rental or an extra provision of services for the patron.[91]

The Government took a periodic census of livestock and other forms of agrarian capital.[92] These statistics suggest that in Tamilnad as a whole the number of livestock was increasing steadily in the early twentieth century, but such statistics must be treated with care. Firstly there were considerable difficulties in estimating the number of livestock in each village; secondly the coverage of these livestock censuses gradually expanded to include more and more of the villages within zamindari estates. We cannot eliminate the first source of error but we can try and control for the second. Table 7 shows the census estimates of livestock and ploughs in all those taluks which had less than five per cent of their area held under zamindari (and inam) tenure. While the table does not present anything like a clear picture (and many of the taluks fall in the valleys or Kongunad rather than the plains) the overall suggestion is that holdings of livestock were not increasing anywhere near as rapidly as was population.

Only the richer cultivators, the 'big men' could afford to bribe the forest officials and purchase the expensive cattle. Meanwhile they secured privileged rights to forest by certain other means. From the mid-1920s the government was forced to recognise that it had enclosed too much of the forest and waste lands, and thus started to release small areas for use by the plains villagers.[93] From the '20s, the graph of 'waste' land started to turn upwards again. However, some of this was classified as 'village forest' and placed in the hands of 'forest panchayats', which inevitably were controlled by the leading villagers. Meanwhile in some parts of the plains, village

Table 7: Livestock in selected taluks, 1891-1951

Taluk (District)	Year	Cattle %	Buffalo %	Sheep & Goats %	Ploughs %
Dharapuram (Coimbatore)	1891	155	19	276	28
	1911	159	20	345	33
	1931	126	21	332	32
	1951	135	23	258	41
Nannilam (Tanjavur)	1891	84	28	57	26
	1911	81	29	75	21
	1931	91	23	52	25
	1951	98	29	64	26
Perambalur (Tiruchi)	1891	87	18	261	17
	1911	94	23	269	25
	1931	92	19	297	32
	1951	114	28	253	43
Melur (Madurai)	1891	91	12	137	28
	1911	106	12	106	31
	1931	93	8	119	28
	1951	146	18	133	49
Villupuram (S. Arcot)	1891	124	21	64	20
	1911	127	22	83	33
	1931	124	13	87	30
	1951	86	16	96	30
Wandiwash (N. Arcot)	1891	96	40	95	25
	1911	78	17	79	21
	1931	87	15	85	25
	1951	90	14	96	33
Gudiyattam (N. Arcot)	1891	92	22	79	23
	1911	84	16	98	22
	1931	90	15	95	22
	1951	113	24	87	32
Kollegal (Coimbatore)	1891	96	5	48	9
	1911	99	10	46	13
	1931	89	8	41	15
	1951	106	21	75	24
Tirunelveli (Tirunelveli)	1891	43	11	121	9
	1911	40	11	123	10

	1931	41	17	105	10
	1951	46	18	98	13
Nanguneri	1891	67	13	182	13
(Tirunelveli)	1911	62	13	186	14
	1931	88	21	213	19
	1951	111	25	236	27

Source: *A Statistical Atlas of the Madras Presidency*, 1895, 1913, 1936 and 1963 editions. The data originate from the government's quinquennial livestock censuses.

leaders began to 'enclose' the waste lands which were adjacent to the village site and which had generally been considered as a communal resource. They took out land-deeds, and thus contracted to pay revenue on the land, which was an indication of the readiness of the 'big men' to pay a premium to secure rights which had hitherto been available gratis.[94] In some zamindari areas it was reported by the 1930s that all the communal lands had been assigned away in this fashion because the zamindars were anxious to get the extra revenue and because the leading villagers were prepared to pay to secure grazing grounds.[95]

The 'little men' were well aware of their loss. The 'minimal' form of cultivation became more and more difficult to maintain. The fence which defined the government's forests came to symbolize the closing of the land frontier and the increasing scarcity of ancillary inputs. There were many petitions from poorer villages asking for government to release reserved forest in order to allow extensions of cultivation. One such petition claimed that the particular forest had once been cultivated and contained wells and temples as a clear proof of that. They begged:

The population has now increased more than thousandfold and they [the petitioners] are unable to find cultivable lands and are anxious to get these lands which their ancestors had once abandoned... The villagers are very poor cultivators, who have no lands of their own. They are depending on the doubtful charity of rich landlords, who own an unnecessarily large extent of lands for their living and keep it as close preserves.[96]

Moreover, the closing of the frontier encouraged the price of land on the plains to increase. At the resettlement of Salem district in 1934, the government reckoned that the price of dry land had increased up to six times in the previous thirty years, while rental values had increased up to ten times and the overall price-level had no more than doubled.[97] Comparing surveys of tenancy rentals made in 1918 and 1947 the largest increases were in the dry and well-irrigated lands of the plains tract; the increase in the dry lands on the Arcots plain was 5.5 times.[98] It was getting both more difficult and (in real terms) more expensive to gain access to land and to the other resources necessary for even the 'minimal' style of agriculture.

It was left to the depression and the following period of unstable prices and uncertain foreign demand to work through the consequences of this increasing pressure on resources. The immediate effect of the depression was to inhibit the flows of credit within the village with the result that there was a definite drop in the acreage under cultivation in the plains in the three years after 1928-9. The commercial crops suffered most. The acreages under groundnut and cotton fell sharply during the depression, and while there was a recovery of commercial cropping from the middle of the decade there was also a significant shift of character. The crops which were cheap to cultivate were displaced by those which were more expensive.

The trend of increase in groundnut, which was the poor man's crop par excellence, peaked in the late 1920s and then petered away. Foreign demand thereafter was erratic and acreage oscillated wildly without any upward trend. Besides, yields began to fall off from the mid-1930s;[99] this resulted probably from the exhaustion of land which had yielded well while it was newly cleared but which had deteriorated rapidly under intensive use. The cotton acreage also peaked in the late 1920s, and but for a secondary peak in the late 1930s declined badly until the 1950s. Meanwhile government and the cotton-buyers were discouraging cheap production of poor varieties of cotton and encouraging the comparatively expensive business of growing good long-staple cotton. Government tried to ban coarse cottons, and introduced new varieties of Cambodia cotton seed (Co2 and Co4), while the Japanese market for short-staple cotton was disrupted and the expanding home market wanted only long-staple.[100] At the same time the nascent sugar industry in the region created a demand for sugar-cane, and the rapid growth of the urban population provided a market for spices, fruit, and vegetables. Thus the overall acreage under commercial crops did not decline after 1930, but the changing pattern of demand dictated a transfer of acreage from crops that were relatively cheap to produce, such as groundnut and local cotton, to crops that required more expensive inputs such as good quality cotton, sugar, spices, fruit and vegetables.

Local credit was not so freely available after the depression. Cultivators who had prospered in the 1920s, and had immediately lent out their profits to their neighbours, fared very badly between 1929 and 1933 when the steady contraction of prices made it impossible to gain any reasonable return from this form of money-lending.[101] In the aftermath, there was much less competitive money-lending, and consequently a much greater chance of dependence on a few sources of credit. One Ramnad village surveyed in 1916 had showed no evidence of monopolistic control over local credit, but a resurvey in 1936 found that one Konar landholder was the village's principal money-lender and also the sole channel for marketing the cotton grown in the village; many smallholders were constantly in debt to the Konar and their only form of repayment was to surrender the crop to him immediately after the harvest. [102]

Thus after the depression many factors made it especially difficult to maintain a 'minimal' style of cultivation and aspire to any sort of economic and social independence. The market wanted the more expensive cash-crops but these required an intensive style of cultivation; it was difficult for the 'little man' to command credit except under stringent conditions; it was difficult to secure adequate grazing and other important wasteland facilities unless one had capital or influence. Thus in this period, the ties of dependence became stronger. Outwardly, plains society retained its usual form. There was some small increase of landless labourers, but most families still had access to some land. However a high proportion of the landowning families were obliged to supplement their income either by working outside agriculture, or by working as labourers for the leading families of the village. In one plains village surveyed by the Madras University's Agricultural Economics Research Centre (AERC) in the 1950s, for instance, there were 140 families which cultivated, 64 which worked solely as labourers, and 129 which supplemented cultivation with wage-labour.[103] In this and other plains villages surveyed by AERC, a considerable number of cultivating families had had to resort to labouring full or part-time within the past generation. Similarly, it was estimated that a sizeable proportion of the villagers' combined income from all sources was earned outside the village. In the AERC-surveyed villages the figure was usually beween a fifth and a quarter. Some villagers commuted to work in the towns, some supplied carts, cattle, building materials and so on to the towns and to the deltaic tracts, and others went to neighbouring villages to work as day labourers for prosperous cultivators. Indeed it seems that the success or failure in adapting to the new demand for expensive crops had brought about a considerable geographical shift of labour demand. Vadamalaipuram was a village which had adapted well throughout the early twentieth century and had shifted its acreage first to groundnuts, then to cotton, then to chillis and finally to plantains and onions. The village had thus imported thirty-five men to work as permanent farm servants and also attracted casual labour at peak times.[104] Meanwhile the village of Sengipatti had not adapted at all well and by the 1950s had a swollen force of 621 casual labourers who nearly all did some work outside the village.[105]

Meanwhile the management of the land was coming more and more under the control of the oligarchy of village leaders. Some of the less prosperous families who had enthusiastically bought land in the optimistic years in the first quarter of the century were forced to sell up and there is some evidence of land being transferred from smaller to bigger farmers. This, however, does not seem to have been very widespread.[106] Yet the growth of small tenancies, which allowed a labourer to gain a marginal advantage of independence and control over the crop, was abrogated. It was thus very difficult for 'small men' to build up a holding by purchase or lease. Instead, the lease market now served to convey land which was still owned by smallholders into the managerial control of large cultivators. In many of the plains villages surveyed by the AERC in the 1950s there were many cases in which the holders of small plots leased their land to more substantial cultivators while they themselves worked as labourers.[107] In the 1951 census a remarkable number of people returned their occupation as 'rentier' (or equivalent) and offered a secondary occupation in some menial job—labouring, construction, small artisan work.[108] It seems that many families which had aspired to smallholder cultivation in the early part of the century were now obliged to abandon their land to their more substantial neighbours who could command the facilities necessary to maintain cultivation.

The supply of labour for the more intensive farming of the leading cultivators thus improved enormously from the depression on-

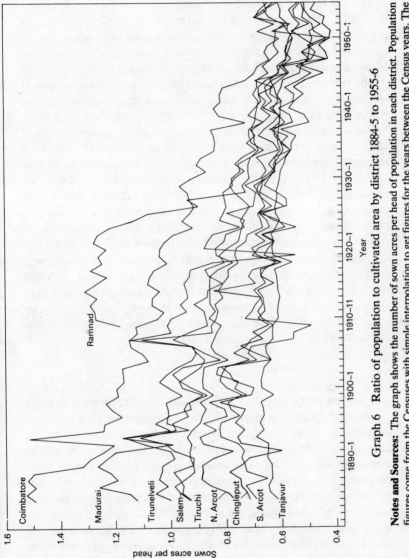

Graph 6 Ratio of population to cultivated area by district 1884-5 to 1955-6

Notes and Sources: The graph shows the number of sown acres per head of population in each district. Population figures come from the Censuses with simple interpolation to get figures for the years between the Census years. The data include both urban and rural population. Acreage figures are 'gross sown area' from the *Season and Crop Report*.

wards. Firstly, there was a significant increase in population. In the 1880s the density of population per cultivated acre was much higher in the fertile, well-watered valleys compared to the dry plains. By the 1950s, however, this differential had virtually disappeared (see graph 6). It was as if demographic increase made population 'find its own level' of density in the various tracts. Secondly, the possibilities of independent smallholder cultivation dwindled away. By the end of the period the leading cultivators of the plains could command labour from their smallholder neighbours and supplement this where necessary from a floating and mobile pool of casual labour. While the demand for cash-crops remained good, and the supply of labour was so amenable, there was little incentive to revolutionize the pattern of agricultural organization. By concentrating on a new commercial variant of the old style of political domination in the locality, the leading men of the plains had retained their strong position and strengthened the hierarchical backbone of local society. Where once the chiefs had operated a jajmani system of local redistribution, now the commercial cultivators managed the flow of credit. Where the lineage heads had established a claim to reign over a certain territory, now the commercial cultivators kept a firm hand on waste lands and access to forests. Through this control of credit and waste lands, the leading cultivators retained their control over the lesser men of the village and thus could manage the agricultural economy of the tract.

The valleys

The history of the plains in the transition from the nineteenth to the twentieth century was marked by two major changes: the increased importance of cash-cropping, and the slow buckling under the weight of growing population pressure. In the valleys the picture was very different. The valleys had been relatively crowded for many centuries and although the population did increase in this tract in the twentieth century, there was no sense in which population pressure was a novel factor. Similarly the change in cropping patterns was much less significant. Seventy-eight per cent of Tanjavur's acreage was under paddy in the mid-1880s, and seventy-six per cent in the mid-1920s. In Tamilnad as a whole the acreage under paddy increased from about 4 to about 4½ million acres between the 1880s and the 1950s and over four-fifths of this acreage fell in the valleys tract.

Within the valley villages there were some dry lands which grew millets, cotton and other crops characteristic of the plains, and there were considerable stretches of garden lands which grew spices, vegetables, sugar and many other crops in intensive fashion. Even so the dominant cultivation of the entire valley tract was paddy. A large part of the tract was incapable of supporting any other crop. The irrigation systems were mostly designed to collect the monsoon rainfall and flush it down through the irrigated tract using the fields themselves as the chief means to conduct the water. The water supply was highly seasonal, and at the height of the season the fields were swamped. The system was designed to irrigate the greatest possible area of swamp paddy with a fairly meagre flow of river-water and in this it was remarkably efficient. The engineers on the Kaveri river system were proud that the water passed through literally thousands of fields and that hardly a drop reached the sea. But any crop which did not like inundation or which required a supply of water for longer than two or three months in the year could not be grown—at least not without further works of engineering to improve drainage and storage. Most other potential 'wet' crops such as sugar-cane, betel, plantain and some spices, needed good drainage and long periods of water-supply. They were also much more profitable than paddy. They could be grown in some of the upper reaches of the riverine systems where the water supply was rather more secure and long-lasting, and where there was rather more slope to the land, and thus better natural drainage than further down in the delta. There was some sugar-cane on the upper reaches of the Palar-Cheyyar and Ponnaiyar-Gadilam systems, and at the head of the Kaveri delta around Tiruchi town. There was some plantain and betel on the river banks (*padugais*) in the same section of the Kaveri, and on the upper reaches of the Tambraparni-Chittar. Elsewhere, such cultivation required some further capital input.[109] In the Tondai area, where the irrigation system generally worked through tanks which collected water from the rivers and directly from rainfall, the position was a little different. The tracts near larger tanks were well-suited to crops other than paddy, but on the whole the system was less secure than the riverine version, and as one moved further away from the tanks the possibility of poor water-supply in years of low rainfall increased, and thus the economics of investing in expensive cultivation became more doubtful.

There was, as we shall see, some increase in other forms of

cultivation, but mostly it waited until the later part of our period. Paddy was far and away the principal crop, and the number of sowings a year depended mainly on the supply of water in the particular tract. On the very best plots on the upper reaches of the Tambraparni-Chittar there could be three crops a year, or at least five crops in two years, but this was very rare. The western part of the Kaveri delta, most of the Tambraparni-Chittar and Periyar systems, and parts of the smaller river systems supported two crops, one in each monsoon. The eastern Kaveri delta and most of the remaining valley tracts grew one crop on the north-east monsoon, but in the Tondai region there were large areas which, in years of low rainfall, would have to be transferred from paddy to millets and other dry crops.[110]

Two factors shaped the characteristic production system in the tract—the density of population and the small–scale nature of paddy cultivation. Firstly, as we have already seen, the signal benefits of a relatively secure food supply had for a long time attracted a large population into the valleys and this had enabled those who, either by ancient right or military might, exercised a control over the use of land to distance themselves from the work of cultivation and to rely instead on the labour of subordinate groups. The society of the valleys was thus severely stratified into two levels—those, known as *kaniyatchikarans* or mirasidars, who controlled the land, and those who offered their labour in return for a share of the land's product. Secondly, there were good reasons why, in growing paddy under flush irrigation, the basic unit should be characteristically small. In order to control the flow of water it was important to have small, level fields surrounded by bunds (banks). The area which could be worked by one plough-team, consisting of one or two men and a pair of buffaloes or cattle, was usually in the range of one to four acres, depending on the particular conditions of the locality. Paddy fields had to be ploughed several times over, and then the water supply had to be carefully regulated, and finally the harvest had to take place promptly. Larger cultivation units did not offer any gains to scale; every additional plot (of one to four acres depending on locality) simply required the addition of another plough-team and labouring family.[111]

The mirasidar was rarely competely distanced from the cultivation. Even under a waram (share-cropping) system, he often took some responsibility for organizing the inputs of water, manure and seed;[112] in one Tambraparni village it was noted that:

The landlord must see that the tenant cultivates the land properly, sows enough seed, manures the field sufficiently and spends liberally on all necessary items. If the manure is wanting, it is in the owner's interest to give the tenant manure and debit it to his account; or if the tenant has no money, he sometimes pays him for necessary expenses and gets it back at the harvest time.'[113]

Similarly in the Kaveri delta, it was often the mirasidar's responsibility to advance seed, manure and *thaasu kuli* or cultivation expenses.[114] Commonly the mirasidar also made several stipulations in the lease deed with the aim of ensuring good and profitable cultivation and minimizing any potential harm to the land; there were often clauses restricting the cultivation of crops like plantain, sugar, casuarina or gingelly which could exhaust the soil, and other clauses enjoining the tenant to prepare the seed-bed, weed, manure, hoe and level up the land in the proper manner.[115] Finally many landlords who let out on waram, each year took back a different portion of the land according to a rotation so that they might repair any deterioration caused by the waramdars and thus keep up the yield and value of the land.[116]

The production system thus contained two and sometimes three layers. At the bottom was a layer of labourers. Above that was a layer of 'agricultural managers'. These were the people who generally organized cultivation but who themselves rarely touched the plough. They might control only one 'labouring unit' of land, or they might control up to thirty or forty. In most cases they held the patta for the land and considered themselves the mirasidars. In a significant number of cases however, they were themselves tenants (*porakudis*). Such substantial tenants, however, supplied much of the working capital for the land, usually had a pretty autonomous control over the land and its usage, had effective fixity of tenure and were in much the same position as the patta-holding mirasidar.[117] Such substantial tenants rented the land from 'estates' which might cover several hundred acres. A few of these were zamindaris and other forms of political grant, and many were the endowed lands of temples and other religious and charitable institutions. They were scattered throughout the tract, but were particularly numerous in the east of the Kaveri delta.[118] The institutions or individuals who held these estates rarely took any part in the management of cultivation. They might play some role in marketing and storing the grain, but often they acted merely as rentiers and revenue intermediaries.

The crucial relationship was that between the mirasidars (or their tenant equivalents) and the labourers. This differed enormously from place to place, depending on the contribution which each party made to the business of cultivation. Formally there were two systems: waram and pannai. Waram was a form of share-cropping tenancy in which the waramdar and mirasidar divided up the grain-heap at harvest according to set proportions. Pannai was a system of tied labour in which the pannaiyal (or *padiyal*, or *adumayal*) was paid daily or annually in measures of grain. In effect the two systems were not at all sharply distinguished. The remuneration of the labourer, whether he was a pannaiyal or waramdar, was much the same. The plentiful supply of labour meant that the mirasidars could force the remuneration down close to the level of subsistence. As a report on tenancy in 1947 noted:

In this province, the prevailing notion of rent among the land-owning classes is that the tenant is merely a wage-earner and is not entitled to any appreciable margin of profit over and above what an ordinary agricultural labourer will get for cultivating the land... The main difference between the tenant and the actual labourer is that the former is independent and has a better status than the latter. In waram (crop-sharing) system particularly only a small margin of net profit is allowed to the tenant.[119]

The crop-share of the waramdar and the grain-doles of the pannaiyal rested at virtual subsistence level, with suitable additions made to cover any part of the capital or working expenses which the labourer or tenant himself supplied.

There was a range of labour relationships which began with pannai at one end and merged into various stages of waram at the other. Pannai was essentially a form of indenture. In return for a low but secure wage, the pannaiyal undertook to work as a tied labourer on the plot. The indenture was such that the mirasidar could virtually insulate the pannaiyal from the wider economy. The wage payments generally came in grain, supplemented with bonuses in the form of other necessities like cloth and salt paid in kind on festive occasions. In certain areas, the mirasidar also paid the pannaiyal 'toddy money' not as cash but in the form of an account at the local liquor shop. The mirasidar would also meet any extraordinary expenses of the pannaiyal and the 'debt' thus incurred would substantiate the pannaiyal's dependence. The largest of such extra-ordinary payment was often the expenses of marriage and many pannaiyals began their indenture when they wanted to get married. These were not really debts, because the pannaiyal generally had little chance of finding the money to pay them off, yet these payments gave the contract the appearance of debt-slavery and certainly that is how many official observers interpreted it.[120] The conditions of service differed somewhat from tract to tract. Gilbert Slater described the form in South Arcot:

As a padial he would receive a definite allowance of grain every month and a present of clothing once a year, and in return be bound to render the creditor any service he might require. His wife also could be called upon to serve, but if so her labour has to be paid for. By law such debts cannot be passed on to the next generation, but the employers preach the doctrine that a padial's son ought to regard them as debts of honour.[121]

In the Kaveri delta, the conditions were often more harsh:

The general stipulation connected with such debt bondage is that the man, his wife and his children yet to be born are all to serve as agricultural labourers of the landlord, who allots a site to the labourer for residential purposes and a piece of land for use as a backyard for cultivation purposes. The remuneration for the service rendered is generally half of the wages of an ordinary independent labourer and, as a result, an indebted labourer of this type is said to be unable to repay the debt.[122]

While the contracts outlined above were permanent, even heredi-tary, there were other pannaiyal contracts which were much more short-term and which differed very little from the most subordinate forms of waram tenancy.

The waramdar's percentage share of the crop fluctuated accor-ding to the fertility of the land and according to the amount of fixed and working capital he provided. At one end of the spectrum, where the land was exceptionally good and where the mirasidar provided all of the capital so that the waram tenure was 'little more than a form of inclusive contract for a certain proportion of the labour of cultivation',[123] then the waramdar's share might be as low as twenty per cent. At the other end of the scale, the land might be so poor that fifty per cent of the yield would be necessary to maintain the labourer's family at subsistence level, and the waram-dar's share would rise higher if the mirasidar contributed little to the organization of cultivation; negligent absentees, Brahmans who stood completely aloof from agriculture, and widows often received very small shares indeed.[124]

There were generally other labourers in the valley tracts who were not directly attached to the land either by waram or pannai contract. This untied labour force included the wives and other dependents of pannaiyals and waramdars and also many men who could not get, or did not want to be tied down by, a waram or pannai contract. They were paid wages by the day, and the rates were rather higher than those for the pannaiyals. The mirasidars liked to keep a slightly excessive supply of labour in the village and thus they not only welcomed any expansion in the number of day labourers, but also tended to employ more pannaiyals than was absolutely necessary. Although this looked profligate, it was preferable because of the difficulty and importance of securing labour at the peak seasons, particularly the harvest. Many mirasidars would take on pannai almost as many labourers as they needed just for the harvesting period, even though they could not find profitable employment for most of them for much of the rest of the year. In most of the valley tracts the labouring people (including waramdars) accounted for over half the total population.[125] The continuity of this highly stratified system depended on the success of the mirasidars in retaining sole control over the land and its product, and thus being able to dictate terms to the lower levels of valley society.

Within this basic framework, however, there was considerable change over time. In the early nineteenth century, the subordinate groups were in an exceptionally depressed state. Pannai contracts were often written up in a formal fashion, and in certain cases the pannaiyals could be bought and sold with the land. The moralizing British interpreted these facts as evidence of a system of slavery. But the tight subordination of these years was probably a fairly temporary consequence of the eighteenth-century disorders and the willingness of subordinate groups to purchase subsistence in the relatively secure and unwarlike valley tracts even at a high price. As the century wore on, the indentures relaxed somewhat, partly as a result of governmental antipathy, but more because of the expansion in the demand for labour both in the expanding agriculture of the valleys and beyond.[126] There were signs towards the end of the century that wage rates in the valleys were being edged slightly upwards in real terms.[127] There was also some evidence that members of subordinate groups were taking land on patta; the government complained about the massive expansion of small holdings and worried that the new 'pauper ryots' would not be able to pay their revenue regularly.[128] But this was probably not evidence of a significant relaxation of mirasidari control. It was common for mirasidars to grant allotments (*maniams*) to their labourers for them to grow their own vegetables and other necessities. It was one way to simplify the costs of keeping a labourer, and to tie him down more firmly to the village. As long as the allotment was insufficient for subsistence, then there was no real change in the relations of dependence.

In the transition to the twentieth century, the expansive trend in valley agriculture dwindled away. It had been based on good prices and a growing demand for rice in the towns, among the prospering elite of the plains, and in export markets mainly in Ceylon. But by the turn of the century, both price and demand for valley rice were suffering from competition with the produce grown in the new deltas of southeast Asia. By the 1880s, Burma was placing large amounts of rice in international trade, and by the early twentieth century Thailand and Indochina had followed suit.[129] As we shall see in more detail in the next chapter, these supplies quickly undermined Tamilnad's rice markets in Ceylon and other parts of southeast Asia, and were soon competing for the market in Tamilnad's own towns. This competition dragged down prices and except in those years when war or other factors disrupted the import trade, the price of rice fell relative to other crop prices throughout the early twentieth century. Southeast Asian rice was cheap because it was grown on virgin land, with good water supplies, under 'frontier' conditions. The costs of producing rice in the Tamilnad valleys were so much greater that, even with the cost of freight, southeast Asian rice arrived cheaply in the local markets and thus acted as a drag on local prices and on the profits of paddy cultivation.[130] The reasons for relatively high costs in Tamilnad were legion. The mirasidars blamed the revenue demand but this was only one, small contributory factor. The valleys, just as much as the plains, faced rising costs for manure and other ancillary materials that came from the forests and grazing grounds. These costs were in some cases even magnified for the valley cultivator. When the forest department marked off the forests and began charging fees for access, it levied specially high fees for 'non-local' cattle, which usually meant beasts brought up by graziers from the valleys to the forest areas on the plains.[131] Following this ruling, many valley mirasidars switched their attention to the forests within the zamindari tracts, but by the 1920s this strategy was bankrupt since the zamindari forests were quickly devastated by over-intensive use. The difficulties of owning cattle meant that many valley cultivators chose not to own them permanently. Rather they purchased from an itinerant trader at the start of the cultivation season and sold them back once the fields were prepared and the cattle were no longer necessary; this worked out as a very expensive hiring system.[132]

Moreover, while the southeast Asia delta tracts were new land, the Tamilnad valleys were old and exhausted. Paddy lands under flush irrigation had a very considerable capacity for recuperation. The nutrients were easily replaced in the soil by the river-borne silt, by the assistance of water-borne algae for making and fixing fertilizing chemicals, and by the rapid decomposition of simple manurial materials such as paddy-stubble.[133] Under these circum-stances, local cultivators paid only minimal attention to manure and fertilizer. If only one crop of paddy was being grown in the year, it was considered adequate simply to puddle in the paddy-straw and perhaps add further manure once every five years or so. It was only a second crop which was reckoned to need more attentive ma-nuring.[134] Thus two-crop land was prepared in the dry season by penning animals, carting leaf-mould or cattle manure, digging silt out of tanks and channels, and occasiohally growing crops of 'green manure'. But while this regime was reckoned to maintain an equilibrium level of soil fertility, there seems to have been a deterioration of cultivation practice as the land was farmed more intensively from the nineteenth century onwards. Much of the expansion of cropped acreage in the nineteenth century was achieved through double-cropping, and the trend continued into the twentieth.[135] There was also around the turn of the century a rapid if uneven spread of the practice of transplanting paddy. Both innovations raised the yield per acre, but both increased the demands made on the land. There is some evidence that cultivators increased the attention they paid to manure but it seems unlikely that, given the contemporary increase in the difficulties of securing manure, that it matched the increasing intensity of use.[136] Certainly there is evidence that yields per acre in the valleys began to decline in the early twentieth century. According to Blyn's figures, the yield per acre of paddy in Madras rose rapidly until the first world war and this was probably the effect of the conversion to transplantation. But from then on, the decline was steady and by the time of the second world war yields had fallen by something like ten per cent.[137] It is usual to doubt the yield data upon which estimates such as those of Blyn are based. Yet in 1946 a suitably sceptical new Director of Agriculture in Madras initiated some sampling experiments to check the yield estimates of the revenue department; 954 experiments indicated an average error factor of only 2.3 per cent. Moreover, this same Director was inclined to believe the recorded evidence of declining yields because of corroborating evidence from a half-century of experience in growing paddy under research conditions. Even on the research stations, paddy yields had declined and tests were beginning to explain why yields might be declining generally throughout the paddy tract. The strains of paddy grown in the valleys were very susceptible to a decrease in the supply of water and to a delay in the timing of transplantation. If an increase in cropping meant that the water was spread more thinly and that cultivation in some fields was delayed, then yields could well fall. His own calculations from the Madras statistics showed that yields of paddy declined sharply from the mid-30s.[138] Thus it seems that the increasing intensity of valley agriculture had led to carelessness about manure supplies and water usage and thus had set the valleys on a trend of agricultural decline.

The overriding reaction to this state of affairs was not any enthusiasm for agricultural improvement, but rather a resigned negligence. As we saw above, the mirasidari society of the valleys had for a long time maintained an outward orientation, towards the state and towards urban society in general. Against this background of agricultural difficulties, it was not surprising that the mirasidars reacted in two particular ways. Firstly, they estimated that they had a better chance of improving their margin of profit, not by intensifying cultivation, but by demanding assistance from the state. Whereas the real incidence of the land revenue demand was undoubtedly declining in the face of inflation and most non-valley dwellers recognized this and entered no complaint about land taxation, the mirasidars of the valleys kept up a constant agitation. It was by no means an illogical strategy. Throughout the nineteenth century the Kaveri and Tambraparni mirasidars had managed to delay the proper implementation of the ryotwari system.[139] In the

1890s the Tanjavur mirasidars had embarrassed the government into tempering the proposed increase in revenue rates.[140] Thus again in the 1920s the Tanjavur mirasidars made an enormous fuss over the resettlement of the revenue,[141] and in the 1930s over the new water-rates under the Kaveri-Mettur project.[142] Secondly, the mirasidars invested much more heavily in securing non-agricultural occupations rather than in promoting agriculture itself. Mostly this meant an investment in education. Most of the new colleges founded in the late nineteenth and early twentieth centuries were located in the old valley-centres. By 1935-6, eighteen of the Tamilnad colleges (first and second grade, men and women) were in the valleys and only two were outside. These colleges were filled with members of the major mirasidar castes—Brahmans, high Vellalas and a scattering of Reddis, Kammas and others.[143] While many of these students came from families which had been settled in towns for several generations, there was a constant influx from the mirasidari valleys. British officials and local observers were forever remarking that valley families who seemed loath to cultivate their land with care, would ruin themselves borrowing money to put their son through college. As one Kaveri lawyer commented:

[Education] is one of the chief reasons for the indebtedness of the agriculturists. They even sell their lands to educate their children. Nowadays, education has become very costly, especially higher education. Many small landholders have been ruined by this.[144]

Recruitment to the services, the legal profession and other professional jobs was dominated by men from these origins. While professional occupations of this sort were the favourite resort of the mirasidari family, there was also some attraction in commerce. Many found their way from control of the local grain-heap into grain trading and perhaps from that into different sorts of mercantile activity.[145] Others moved from local money-lending into more formal banking.

Before the first world war, few mirasidari families moved completely away from the village. Some members of the family would be left to supervise the lands. But urban earnings were a useful supplement to the income from cultivation and they enabled the creaking agricultural system of the valleys to survive. 'Most of the richer agriculturists', noted the Collector of Chingleput in 1930, 'have got other avocations in Madras from which they are able to meet the land revenue and other expenses.'[146] 'Here', noted a student in his study of the Tambraparni tract, 'tenancy is resorted to not out of unwillingness on the part of the landlord [to cultivate himself], but out of the necessity of being absent from the place, because most of the landlords are bankers or traders in Travancore and outside the tract.'[147]

To provide a counterweight to local agrarian decline, the mirasidars looked not only to the state and the urban economy but also to frontiers of opportunity outside Tamilnad and outside India. Moreover, it was not only the mirasidars but also, and to a much greater extent, the labourers and bankers of the valleys who sought this avenue of escape from local stagnation. Just as the plains economy became closely associated with the increase of Tamilnad's westward trade, so the valleys were involved in the expansion of Tamilnad's overseas interests to the east. The movement of mirasidari scions into education, public service, and trade took many of them overseas, particularly to Ceylon and to some extent to Burma, where they were either employed in British service, or pleaded, taught, and traded on their own accounts. However, it was the labourers of the valleys who joined most enthusiastically in the move to the east.

The expansion of tea, coffee and rubber estates on the Western Ghats and in Ceylon and Malaya, and of rice farming in Burma, opened up a demand for labour, and from the 1880s the surplus labour force of the valleys provided one of the largest elements in the migration. The statistics do not enable us to identify the geographical and social origins of the migrant force with any great accuracy. However, it was the ports at the ends of the valleys which carried most of the migrants—Negapatam on the Kaveri to Burma and Malaya; Tuticorin by the Tambraparni and Dhanushkodi on the Vaigai to Ceylon; Madras and Cuddalore in Tondai to Burma— and most of the migrants came from the immediate hinterland of the ports. A good many of the migrants had urban and artisanal skills—cooks, carpenters, pedlars—but the hard core consisted of agricultural labourers. From the early years of the century, observers of the delta tracts noted the regular outflow of labour.[148] In 1910, a sub-Collector in the Tambraparni tract noted:

We are near famine conditions after a five year drought. It would have been famine long before this but for the lucky proximity of the Ceylon and Travancore planters estates. They can absorb an unlimited quantity of labour [and] pay a good wage. The people have long ago acquired the habit of emigrating to get a little capital and returning to live on it.[149]

In Palakkurichi, a Kaveri village, the population changed little between the times of surveys in 1916 and 1936 despite the region's trend of demographic growth, and mostly this was due to emigration to the estates which had, by 1936, caused a shortage 'of labour in the locality.[150] In one Tondai village, by 1916 several of the poorer agriculturists had sold their land and emigrated to Ceylon.[151] In a village in the Periyar tract surveyed in the 1930s, it was said that a large proportion of the labour force had migrated to Ceylon and this had pushed up the local cost of labour.[152] In another Tambraparni village, it was reported that the Maravar and Parava labour force regularly migrated to Ceylon and that some of the oilmongers went to Penang.[153] At the resettlement of Tanjavur in 1922 it was reported that the only villages where wage-rates had risen were those where there had been heavy emigration.[154] Indeed, every single survey of a valley locality in the early twentieth century mentioned emigration of labour.

Very little of this migration was permanent. While there was a steady build-up of the Tamil population in Ceylon, Burma, and Malaya, there was a much larger flow of short-duration migrants. In some cases, particularly the migration to rubber estates in Malaya and to the paddy harvest in Burma, the seasonal migration could be timed to fit in with the off-season in the Tamilnad valleys, but in most cases the labourers in fact were absent from Tamilnad for a season or two. Thus the migration was important in two ways. Firstly it drew off much of the growing excess population in the valleys. The scale of this operation is difficult to quantify because of the nature of the statistics but it is possible to hazard an informed guess. By the 1920s, there was in any one year something like a million and a half Tamils overseas, mostly working as labourers; 600,000 were in Ceylon, 500,000 in Malaya, 300,000 in Burma, and roughly 100,000 in Fiji, Thailand, Indonesia, and elsewhere.[155] Probably at least two-thirds of them, or one million, came from the valley tract. The total population of the valley tract, meanwhile, was in the region of ten million at this period. It is clear that a very high proportion of the valleys' labour force was involved in the movement of migrant labour.

As we have seen, there were sporadic complaints that this migration caused a shortage of labour in the delta villages, and that this raised the level of wages. While it is doubtful if such wage rises were general throughout the valleys, yet it seems probable that migration prevented the level of wages falling as population out-stripped production. The migration must also have supplemented the incomes of a very high proportion of valley families. Just as for the mirasidars urban employment filled the deficit caused by declining per capita production, so overseas earnings enabled the lower levels of the population to survive.[156] As we shall see in the next chapter, there was also a considerable migration of capital from the deltas. As the local economy of the valleys deteriorated, the rise of opportunities in the towns and overseas provided a safety valve which filtered away all the pressures for effecting any serious change.

Thus while none of the parties involved took an interest in revolutionizing the pattern of production and social relations in the valleys, there were important internal adjustments which followed from the growing involvement of valley peoples in affairs beyond the tract. A certain political tension was endemic in a society which was so starkly stratified and there seems to have been a fairly continuous murmur of protest which emerged occasionally in local jacquerie or in more general movements for caste and religious reform. In the early twentieth century, there were good reasons why this sort of tension should have increased. Firstly, the attention of the mirasidars was being deflected away from their local concerns. Secondly, migrant labouring enabled the subordinate groups to circumvent the mirasidars' attempts to insulate them from the cash economy and to prevent any accumulation of wealth.

The slackening of the mirasidars' local attentiveness was revealed in the extent to which fixed grain-rents, known in the valleys as *kuthagai*, began to replace *waram* crop-sharing. The move from *waram* to *kuthagai* was commonly associated with the mirasidars' drift towards absenteeism. There was almost no move to cash rents, and this must have been because the urban-based mirasidar looked to his landholding to supply him with grain; the grain-market in the towns could still falter badly in years of poor harvest, and anyway if the mirasidar secured the grain at putative farm-prices rather than purchasing at a much higher rate in the bazaar it amounted to a premium on the rental. Lease-deeds commonly stipulated such conditions as: 'the grain to be delivered at the lessor's house in Egmore [a Madras suburb]'.[157] Nor was the transference from *waram* to *kuthagai* anywhere near complete. It was most common in the most secure tracts of the valleys, where mirasidar and tenant could arrive at a fairly accurate assessment of the average annual yield under waram and, probably with some discount, use this as the level of the *kuthagai*. In areas where the annual yield was erratic, it was much more difficult to persuade the tenants to accept a fixed annual payment.[158] But even with these qualifications, there was clear evidence of change. In one Tondai village, it was reported in 1916: 'There are about eight non-cultivating landowners, and they are employed variously. One is an Assistant Inspector of Salt and Abkari Department, another is a District Munsif, some are employed as petty officials in Madras. These eight landowners hold about 100 acres of wet land, and lease it on the "kuthagai" system.'[159] This represented about a seventh of the village's land. By 1936 the number of absentee landholders had risen to 107 and the proportion of land now on *kuthagai* was roughly a half.[160] In another Tondai village surveyed on the same two occasions, the number of non-cultivating landlords rose from nought to nineteen, and the proportion of land under *kuthagai* from a negligible amount to a quarter of the total.[161] In a Tanjavur village, there were only three non-cultivators in 1916 and they were all resident, while by 1936 there were ninety absentees.[162] In a Tambraparni village, it was already the case in 1916 that there was a clear division between the resident holders, who let on waram, and the absentees who let on *kuthagai*. In the next twenty years, the pattern of landholding changed quite dramatically and the number of tenants, mostly on *kuthagai*, rose to include over half the agricultural population.[163] In two villages of the Periyar tract surveyed by the Banking Enquiry in 1930, there were many absentees with occupations in the nearby towns of Madurai, and the proportions of land under *kuthagai* were thirty and fifty per cent respectively.[164]

The migrant labourer who returned with cash in his pocket naturally often aspired to buy land, for this was not only an investment in economic security but also a claim to social standing. In certain parts of the valleys they appear to have had limited but significant successes. The Kaveri valley mirasidars seem to have fought hard to retain their exclusive control over land but in the Tondai and Tambraparni regions subordinate groups did acquire lands. In the Tondai region, mirasidari society was never as fully formed as it was further south, and by the 1920s a number of Paraiyan and other labouring groups had acquired land.[165] In the

Tambraparni, the ease in shuttling back and forth to Ceylon meant that subordinate groups were quite active in the land market. In the 1920s, a student observed:

Going through the pattas in the [Tambraparni] villages we find that the labouring classes like the Shanars, the Chettis, the Barbers, the Thotians, Nayakans, the Goundans and the Vellalas, who were originally field-labourers, have become peasant-proprietors. The Sub-Registrars say that in the majority of sales documents registered, the claimants happened to be agricultural labourers having no pattas previously.[166]

While there is limited evidence of labourers' success in buying land, there is much more evidence of the efforts on the part of the mirasidars to prevent excessive social mobility. This entailed several attempts by the mirasidars to deploy new methods to control land and to dominate the subordinate levels of valley society. Firstly, there were attempts to replace the patronal control of pannai labour with more formal versions of debt bondage. In parts of Tanjavur, the relationship of labourer to landlord became substantially monetized and the old rituals of imprecation and donation were translated into a system of book-keeping. As the Tanjavur Collector noted, service agreements had largely been replaced by debt-bonds, often reinforced through a pro-note:

In some cases of hereditary service families regular bonds and pronotes are not insisted on. A sort of ledger account is maintained; periodically these accounts are struck and the signatures of the debtors are taken thereon. The accounts are never cleared or closed... The debt bondage system enables the mirasidars to keep in hand a number of labour families for ready supply of cheap labour. The mirasidar does not object if these people seek work elsewhere and earn something when they have no work under him; but when he has work on hand, they are bound to work for whatever wages he will allow (generally half of what an independent labourer would be paid) and if they do not do that, persecution and harassment and even corporal punishment are often meted out with a view to cow down and bring round the rebellious element.[167]

Secondly, there were attempts to restrict the mobility of labour. As part of their claim to control the entire territory of the village, not just their individual cultivated holdings, the mirasidars argued that they controlled the sites on which labourers' houses were built. One tactic which the mirasidars used to curb the possibilities of short-term migration and to tie down their own supply of labour was to threaten labourers with eviction. As one Revenue Inspector reported from the north of the Kaveri tract:

These sites belong to the ryots [i.e.mirasidars] of the village and since the cheri people [i.e.labourers] are working in their lands, they have been allowed to occupy and live in lands belonging to the landholders. The cheri people bound down to a long continued system of short wages paid and distributed by their ryots have found themselves of late unable to meet the growing needs of their family and have resorted to work elsewhere also. This has met with oppression and some trouble to the cheri people from the ryots....[168]

By the 1910s, the issue of house-sites had become one of the major political wrangles of the Kaveri delta. In 1917, the government undertook to acquire house-sites for the labouring population to prevent this form of mirasidar oppression. The policy proved difficult. 'At the commencement', noted the Collector, 'the caste ryots were so opposed to the ameliorative operations that even criminal proceedings had to be resorted to keep them away from interfering with the work. In some cases, civil suits were launched by the ryots questioning the validity of the action of government.'[169] The government's plan was to buy up the house-sites and then let the labourers buy the sites from them on a form of long mortgage. But they soon found that the mirasidars obstructed their attempts to acquire the sites through court proceedings, and that even when government secured possession the High Court kept insisting on a steadily higher price to be paid to the mirasidars. Unsurprisingly, there was then difficulty getting the labourers to pay off the mortgage amounts.[170] When the government then tried to find alternative sites, this proved equally difficult. The Commissioner of Labour, who oversaw the scheme, concluded: 'The fact appears to be that in the deltas the caste ryots and the landholders have in the past obtained or annexed free of cost house-sites and porambokes which might be capable of being converted into house sites—with the result that no house sites are now available in the deltas.'[171] Before the second world war, the scheme had not enjoyed much success.

Thirdly, the mirasidars manipulated their role as government's intermediaries in the village to limit the labourers' ability to acquire land. The mirasidars controlled the land records of the village and thus could make it difficult for an upstart to secure a land-deed. Labourers who sunk their capital in clearing, irrigating and culti-vating new land often found that when they subsequently applied for a patta (title deed), they discovered that one had already been issued to an established mirasidar even as they were engaged on the work of reclamation.[172] If they tried to purchase land at a sale for arrears of revenue, the village officers who administered the sale would simply not permit it. If they purchased privately, they might have difficulty taking actual possession. While these obstructive practices are often associated largely with Brahman mirasidars, they were in fact by no means exclusively associated with the high caste. In the tract newly watered under the Periyar scheme, the warlike Kallar adapted themselves to these mirasidari methods within a single generation. 'Five years back', noted K.G. Siva-swamy in the 1940s, 'the Kallars prevented the Valayans from ploughing without their permission in a place in Melur taluk on the ground that they were the leaders of the village who had the authority to control the Valayans... Where they are in a majority the Kallans will prevent the grant of land by absentee landholders to lower classes (untouchables) or to any community excepting them-selves.'[173] The government attempted to give some assistance by altering the rules for assigning new land so that after 1918 the established landholders of the village had no priority, and by initiating special schemes to assign lands to members of the 'depressed classes'. Again, these schemes had only a marginal impact, because 'depressed classes' schemes had very little funds, and because the procedure for assignment was still controlled by the village officers.[174]

Against this background of agricultural stagnation and social tension the depression of the 1930s had a peculiarly unsettling effect on the valleys. The price of paddy fell no more steeply than any other crop-price but whereas in the case of cotton and to a lesser extent groundnut, there was still a reasonable demand for the crop at the lower price fixed by international conditions, the volume of demand for Tamilnad paddy was severely reduced by the compe-tition with cheap imports. By 1930, the Director of Agriculture reckoned that the slump and the imports had pulled the price below a level at which the mirasidars of Tanjavur could make any kind of profit,[175] and for the next three years the price continued to fall. At the end of the crop year in both 1930 and 1931, mirasidars who were holding up stocks in the vain hope that the price would rise could find no market for their produce and eventually had to dump their stocks at the time of the next harvest. In real terms, the income from paddy cultivation was badly cut.[176]

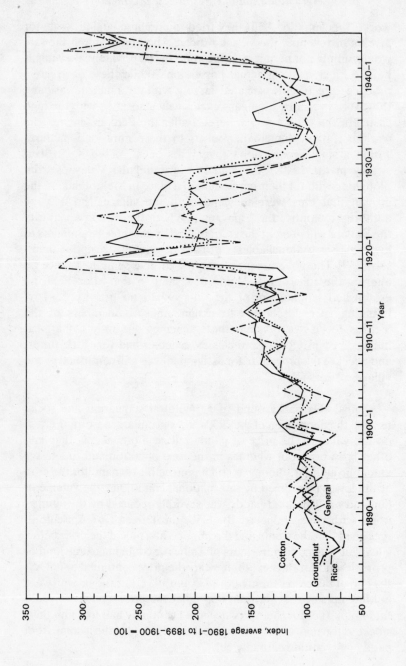

Graph 7 Price indices 1884-5 to 1944-5

Notes: The price indices shown in the graph are supposed to be an approximation to prices ruling in Tamilnad's urban markets. The basic data is bitty and fallible and the graphs are only illustrative approximations. The main technique used in constructing the indices was to compare as many available indices as possible (by graph-plotting and regression) in order to reach the most likely approximation. The cotton index up to 1940 is the index of Bombay Broach prices from the index numbers; this did not differ substantially from the movement of harvest prices in the main cotton-producing districts as published in the *Season and Crop Report*, or from unit prices of raw cotton export calculated from the *Annual Statement*. The cotton-index was extended beyond 1940 (rather shakily) with the help of these two sources and with figures from the Reserve Bank, P. V. John and *Measures of Food Control*. The Groundnut index comes mostly from unit values of Madras exports (value divided by volume), checked and modified in years when the low level of exports produced a statistically suspicious result by comparison with data from John, Reserve Bank, *Season and Crop Report*. The Rice index comes from the Chingleput chapter of the *Statistical Atlas*. It is slightly more erratic than the index for Tanjavur from the same source, largely because of the greater variability of rice production in Chingleput and because of the proximity of the Madras market. The general index is the general weighted index from the *Index Numbers of Indian Prices*, extended past 1940 by the Reserve Bank general price index.

Source: *Annual Statement of the Sea-Borne Trade and Navigation of the Madras Presidency; Index Numbers of Indian Prices, 1861-1931* and annual addenda; Reserve Bank of India, *Report on Currency and Finance* (annual); *Measures of Food Control*; P. V. John, *Some Aspects of the Structure of the Indian Agricultural Economy 1947/8 to 1964/5* (Delhi, 1968); P. J. Thomas and N. Sundarama Sastry, *Commodity Prices in South India* (Madras, 1940); N.V. Sovani (ed.), *Reports of the Commodity Prices Board* (Bombay, 1948); *Statistical Atlas of Madras Presidency; Season and Crop Report*.

The mirasidars reacted in a predictable way: they looked to the government for assistance. They demanded land revenue cuts, reductions in water charges, embargoes or tariffs on imported rice, devaluations of the rupee, reductions in railway rates which would bring down the price of valley rice in the retail market, and many other measures. While the government brushed these demands aside as merely examples of the usual vociferousness of the valley dweller, it seems probable that the discontent was reasonably well justified.[177] When in 1933, the Board of Revenue asked the various Collectors to comment on the impact of the depression, it was only the report from Tanjavur that stood out in a series of rather bland and dismissive replies:

The tenant cultivator and the small cultivator generally have no reserves worth the name on which to fall back. The cultivator on a larger scale, i.e. the mirasidar, has exhausted the majority of his reserves. In the Tanjore division the extent of exhaustion is estimated at 80% in the case of owners of less than 10 acres and 50% in the case of owners of more than 10 acres.... In the case of piece-goods, the sales at last Dipavali fell, according to one account, by 70%....[178]

Others took a rather more moral tone: the high price since the first world war had raised the mirasidar's income without any substantial effort on his part; he had consequently raised his style of life and was now finding it difficult to retract.[179]

The strains of depression led to several subsequent effects. Firstly, the mirasidars cut down their outlay on cultivation. As one Tambraparni man noted in the first year of the depression:

It must be said in this connexion that the sudden fall in price of paddy in this year without any corresponding reduction in the price of all other cereals and pulses, has benumbed the enthusiasm of the agriculturists to spend more money on cultivation.[180]

At the end of the decade, another man of Tambraparni mirasidari family noted that the rice-growers 'have held up improvements of their lands and expansion of cultivation and postponed even very necessary annual repairs of bunds and balks, thus reducing the volume of work available to the agricultural workers'.[181] The Kaveri-Mettur project from 1934 provided water for another 330,000 acres in the south of the old delta, but by the coming of the second world war less than half of the new supply of water had been utilized; this was largely because the cultivators in the 'new delta' neither possessed nor could raise the necesssary capital to build channels and level fields for wet cultivation.[182]

At the same time there was an abrupt change in the pattern of migration. The depression hit the plantations of Travancore, Malaya and Ceylon and the rice industry of Burma with special severity. European capital was withdrawn, output choked off, and labourers dismissed. The great flow of migrant labour was thrown into reverse. Each year in the 1920s something like 800,000 Madrassis had got on the boats to either Burma, Malaya, or Ceylon. Between 1930 and 1933 that figure was reduced by more than half. Besides that, in each of these years there were more people returning than making the outward journey. There was a net return of Indian migrants in 1930-3 to the tune of about 250,000 from Malaya and 125,000 from Ceylon. In 1933 the Malayan and Ceylonese planters found that they had overreacted and began to take back some of the labourers they had recently repatriated, but the flow never resumed its old proportions and with the added complication of the war and Japanese occupation in the 1940s the flow of migration was seriously disrupted for two decades. The number of south Indians in Burma dropped from 240,000 in 1930 to 150,000 in 1950, while the numbers in Ceylon and Malaya remained more or less static over the same period.[183]

The valley labourers not only lost an important source of income—remittance from Ceylon dropped from around Rs 14 million in 1929 to around Rs 7 million per year between 1931 and 1933[184]—but also faced a glut of labour at home. An official in the Kaveri tract produced figures which showed a net annual migration of 4420 persons a year from the Tanjavur district alone in the years 1923-30, and a net repatriation of 4141 a year in 1931 and 1932, and commented:

With emigration to Malaya stopped and that to Ceylon greatly reduced and a large number of labourers repatriated from Malaya during the years 1930-2, we have now a larger number of agricultural labourers in this district than there was for the last twenty-five years or more.[185]

There is some evidence that this glut of labour exerted downward pressure on wage-rates. In parts of the central Kaveri delta, the Collector thought that the daily payment was reduced from 2½ to 3 Madras measures of rice to 2 to 2½.[186] In the Tambraparni, one observer reckoned that the competition for tenancies pushed the waram rental down from 8/21 to 7/21.[187] These appear to have been local effects and most wages seem to have stuck at customary levels, but in many places there were fears expressed about a glut of labour.

When the coming of the second world war finally brought the period of depression to an end and brought the price curve out of its hollow and sent it up on a steep ascent, the consequences of the depression in the given context of production and rural relations soon became apparent.

The depression put enormous pressure on the mirasidars—not only on their capital assets, but also on the remnants of their corporate organization. In the Tanjavur village of Palakkurichi, there was still in 1916 'a non-official panchayat board, which practically settles all disputes arising among the villagers, manages communal affairs, administers communal income, supervises large undertakings, such as temples, roads, tanks, dams, etc.'[188] In the 1930s, this panchayat had collapsed and the resurvey of the village concluded: 'The village has been drifting towards economic deterioration. An important cause of the setback is the existence of party cliques and lack of union among the members of Nayudu caste who form the predominant landowning class.'[189] In Chingleput, the Collector reported at the end of the decade: 'The tendency is for the educated ryot to drift to the towns or busy himself with politics. The result is that the villages in many cases, have no important resident ryot to act as leader and organize the rest of the ryots to do work necessary for their common good, such as Kudimaramath work in tanks and channels and there is no cooperation in the villages themselves.'[190]

The combination of economic strain and social discomfort encouraged many of the mirasidars, who already had both urban and rural interests, to free themselves of their rural commitments. This disengagement began in the early years of the depression but was stifled by the tightness of credit and the consequent slowness of the land market. It picked up in the war when prices rose rapidly, credit eased slightly, and wealth made either out of urban business or out of blackmarketing crops was rapidly sunk in land. The land market was very slow throughout the 1930s, but in the early 1940s it was more lively than it had ever been before. While there was some investment by urban people and in particular by Nattukottai Chetties recently turned out of Burma, such speculative investments were generally short-run and the land soon found itself in the hands of agriculturists again.[191] It is difficult to estimate the extent of land transfer in the delta tracts in the fifteen years after 1930, but a rough guess would be in the region of one-third of the total cultivated area. Most of the big 'estates' of several hundred acres remained as they were; such institutions were relatively remote from the practice of agriculture and were little affected by the short-run vicissitudes of price and season. Rather, a section of the mirasidars who had cultivated urban interests now moved more completely into an urban life, and allowed others to take control of the land.

In Eruvellipet, in deltaic South Arcot, the number of land-owners fell from 165 in 1916 to 148 in 1936 and to 50 in 1961. In Gangaikondan in the Tambraparni tract, virtually all the land at the turn of the century was owned by a clutch of 120 Brahman mirasidari families. By 1936, the number of Brahman families left in the village had been reduced to 75 and their land-holdings had been reduced to a fifth of the previous extent. Most of the land had passed into the ownership of tenant families from the Maravar and Vellala castes. In Dusi in North Arcot, in 1916 all the land had been owned by Brahmans and worked by non-Brahman tenants. By 1936, a large proportion of the land was owned by the non-Brahmans and much of the rest worked by them on *kuthagai*. The village had lost nearly a quarter of its population in the early 1930s, and one significant part of this loss came from the migration of Brahman ex-mirasidari families to Madras and other nearby towns. Here, unlike in Eruvellipet, the effect was to increase the number of landholders from 65 in 1916 to 326 in 1936. After 1936, a number of the absentees cut their links with the village; between 1936 and 1961 the number of absentee landlords fell from 107 to 20 (yet these 20 still owned half of the total land) while the number of resident landlords rose from 219 to 381.[192] In the village of central Tanjavur described by Kathleen Gough in the 1950s, a large number of Brahman mirasidari families had departed for urban occupations within the previous generation. They had been succeeded in the ownership of land by those members of the old tenant stratum who had oriented themselves most clearly towards the market economy.[193] In the nearby village studied by André Béteille, most of the old mirasidari families were still resident in the early 1960s but they had lost most of their land and had now come to rely heavily on urban incomes.[194] In the Kaveri village of Kaliyanapuram, 79 households left the village in the early 1950s and a very high proportion of these seem to have been mirasidars.[195] While some of these latterday shifts may have been due to the 1952 land legislation (which placed a very permeable ceiling of thirty acres on a single holding) and may, for that very reason, be more apparent than real, it remains true that a sizeable proportion of the old mirasidari stratum was moving from the village.

By itself, this shift of personnel was no more than the final stage in a very limited social revolution which had begun some time before. With the drift towards absenteeism and the consequent growth of *kuthagai* tenure and gradual purchase of land by subordinate groups, the share of mirasidar and tenant groups respectively in the management of cultivation had been gradually shifting for many years. On its own, this limited social revolution did not guarantee any change in the style of production. But in the 1930s and 1940s there was also a move to effect a more significant transformation of valley agriculture. This too had a history. From the beginning of the century small enclaves of entrepreneurial farming had grown up within the valleys' general pattern of stagnant agriculture. There were some cultivators who could see that the market for paddy looked bleak while the growth of overseas trade and urban consumption was creating a good demand for certain products which could be grown on irrigated land—sugar, betel, plantain, spices. Such crops required heavy investment and careful attention and thus they had limited appeal for the average mirasidar. But credit was available and, increasingly, so was leased land. In some cases, it was established mirasidars themselves who entered upon a pattern of more intensive cultivation, but generally, in the early days at least, it was individuals from the stratum of tenants, or men from outside the village, who took the lead. These were men who took on land which absentee mirasidars no longer wanted to cultivate directly, raised capital largely from urban sources, hired labour more in the style of the plains with permanent farm servants and casual labour rather than tied pannaiyals, and grew mainly cash-crops.

In the Tambraparni, this practice began around the turn of the century, with mirasidars buying up plots in remote villages, growing cash-crops and making a large profit.[196] In the Kaveri, there was a similar development in the upper reaches of the delta. The favourite crop here was plantain, which could be easily marketed to the growing urban population. The costs were, however, extremely high. One estimate reckoned that the cultivator would have to spend Rs 250 on labour, Rs 30 on plants, Rs 100 on manure and Rs 100 on fencing and miscellaneous items for each acre, and then wait for two years before he got a return. Then when the harvest arrived, it needed more than the local labour-supply could stand and thus required some considerable organization:

There are a dozen planters or more in every important village growing plantains who each take up on lease fifteen or twenty acres for cultivation, and there are a few who take up even fifty or sixty acres each. As wages have to be paid each week, and there are several items of purchase, one succeeding the other like suckers, manures and bamboos, the need for ready money is quite great. Few, indeed are owner-cultivators. The more common practice is for the lands to be leased to some enterprising men with capital, partly owned and partly borrowed, and of great capacity for superintendence of work on the garden and for bargaining with buyers who are agents of firms in Madras and other big consuming centres.[197]

Betel cultivation was similarly expensive and in the Tambraparni owners of lands suitable for betel gardens charged Rs 325 per acre as rental.[198] Such cultivation required considerable resources of credit, but those with access to urban credit-institutions could manage this. In some parts urban merchants and bankers took a very direct part in financing such cultivation, as in parts of the Tambraparni valley where, according to V.S.Krishnan: 'Some daring wholesalers of Virudhunagar have gone to the extent of actually financing the cultivation of chillies themselves.'[199] More often, however, it was groups of tenants who built up a reputation for reliability and entrepreneurship who could command the necessary funds. In many cases, these were plains dwellers with experience in the business of garden cultivation, who migrated into the valleys. 'The Kammas of Tirumangalam (Madurai district)', noted K.G.Sivaswamy, 'have purchased wet lands in the Periyar area. They are efficient garden cultivators, investing large sums in deepening wells, using oil engines and electric pumps and raising paying crops all round the year.'[200] While this pattern became most common in the cultivation of expensive crops, it was also applied to paddy. Sivaswamy also noted: 'The Pillais have established a reputation for supervising share-tenants and untouchable farm-labour. They take large areas of land in Tanjore on lease. They pay cash deposits and take on lease temple lands in the Tanjore district on a low rental for a period of seven years. They have purchased land in the Periyar tract.'[201] In the Tambraparni it was often Nadars filtering in from the harsh dry tracts to the south, and finding credit with their mercantile caste fellows in the towns to the north, who became the leaders of this managerial style of cultivation.[202]

Again the development was limited. By 1930, only about 1¾ per cent of the total area of Tanjavur and two per cent of Tiruchi were growing spice, fruit and vegetable crops. But in the 1930s and 1940s there were good incentives to expand this more concerted style of valley cultivation. The splintering of mirasidar society made land more readily available. The continued upwards drift of prices of necessary inputs—cattle costs in particular rocketed after an epidemic of disease in the early 1940s—made it ever more necessary to drag a better yield out of the land. The market for many cash-crops expanded with the rapid expansion of the town population in this decade, and then the market for rice improved after the Japanese disrupted southeast Asian imports from 1940 onwards. After this, as we shall see below, the government began chivvying agriculture into action and helped by easing the supply of certain important inputs. Finally, there was a plentiful supply of labour during these years.

The acreage under sugar, spice and vegetable crops more than doubled in the 1930s and 1940s, yet it still remained a small fraction of the total area. There were enormous difficulties in converting flush-paddy tracts to other forms of cultivation and thus the process was inevitably slow. Moreover, the government was desperately trying to discourage cash-cropping in favour of food production in the 1940s.[203] But, to its horror, the acreage under paddy actually dropped during that decade. This was largely due to some particularly unkind seasons in middle and late 1940s and possibly also to the internal turmoil of valley society in these years. For while the overt signs of a shift in agricultural practice were severely limited, there were several signs of social conflict brought on by a clash between old and new styles of entrepreneurship and production. These came in two forms. Firstly there were clashes between the old mirasidari order and those who wished to seize hold of production and push it more towards the market. Secondly, there were protests by labouring groups who feared that they would lose most in the course of this transformation of production.

The first type of conflict erupted most obviously in the Periyar tract at the end of the war. Here the mirasidars had mostly drifted to the towns, particularly the nearby city of Madurai, and allowed the control of cultivation to fall gradually into the hands of the waram tenants. Thus it was the tenantry that was confronted with the imperatives for changing agricultural practice. In 1946, under encouragement of the government's food production drive, the tenants invested in an extra crop, and argued that they deserved a greater share of the return since they, rather than the mirasidars, had taken the decision to make the extra investment and had also found the inputs. The customary level of the tenant's share was one-third of the produce, but they wished to push this up to a half. When the mirasidars objected, the tenants simply seized the entire produce. At the next normal harvest, the tenants extended their claims. War conditions, they argued, had inflated the cost of inputs and these costs were borne by the tenant; thus the contract of tenancy ought to be substantially changed. Ten thousand acres of the Periyar tract around Sholavandam were soon involved. The tenants again threatened to seize the crop, and the mirasidars quickly brought in the Collector and local political figures to arrange an arbitration.[204]

The result was an agreement which in principle recognized the extent to which the mirasidars had lost control of agriculture. Customarily the landholder made certain deductions from the total yield of grain before the waram division began; these deductions represented payments for his services as leader and protector of the village. These were now abolished. Customarily too, the mirasidar took a large part of the straw, since he needed this for the cattle which he supplied for draught and manure. Since he no longer kept the cattle, the straw was now allotted to the tenant. The arbitration however left the waram shares the same as before, with the result that the agitation started up again in the following year. According to the mirasidars, the tenants became well organized, on independence day they 'not only cried down every landowner in indecent language, but also pelted stones on their person and on [their] houses'.[205] Twelve tenants' leaders were arrested, and in some villages the mirasidars were intimidated into accepting a fifty-fifty division of the produce. The mirasidars again called out for official assistance. 'They said they were quite willing to have an arbitration,' noted the Collector, 'but it must be an arbitration which will have a legal basis and which can be enforced.'[206] At the 1947 harvest, the government appointed a retired judge as arbitrator and he raised the tenant's share of the grain upto forty-five per cent. Although it was only a slight increase, along with the concessions won in the previous year, the tenants had won recognition of the fact that they effectively controlled the agricultural economy, and they had also gained control over a bit more of the grain heap. It was also significant that this adjustment had been achieved through the mediation of the governmental machinery.[207]

The Periyar tract was a very 'new' valley area where mirasidari power was only a couple of generations deep. Even so this dispute was not necessarily untypical. There were similar troubles in the bastion of mirasidari society, the Kaveri delta, and even in the Mannargudi taluk, where the mirasidars had most forcefully resisted the imposition of ryotwari revenue principles in the nineteenth century. Here cantankerous tenants argued that the landlord's crop-share should be reduced on the grounds that the prices of agricultural inputs (which the tenants bore) had risen during the war. The dispute was aimed mainly against the Uthirathi math, which had large holdings in the district. The disputes spread over two years, 'leading to assaults and breaking of heads', and in the end the landholder was obliged to reduce the rental from a two-thirds to a three-fifths crop-share, and forego execution of decrees for Rs 9000 of rental arrears.[208]

The second set of disputes arose out of pannaiyal labourers' fears about security of employment. The move to make valley agriculture marginally more intensive and more commercial entailed a desire to rationalize the use of labour. The extraordinary glut of labour, from the depression years onwards, gave the employing mirasidars considerable opportunity to alter the pannaiyal system. It became ever easier to rely on the supply of casual labour to cover the workload during the peaks of the cultivation system, and this made it possible to dispense with a large number of pannaiyals who were maintained under-employed for most of the year simply in order to ensure a labour supply at the critical times. By the mid-1930s there were well-organized gangs of casual labour who moved upto a hundred miles between different tracts in order to find work. They were arrayed under foremen who bargained for a good wage-rate; they shuttled back-and-forth between plains and valleys taking in cotton and groundnut harvests and the paddy transplantation and harvesting seasons.[209] The pannaiyals first sensed the competition from this new form of labour when they discovered that they had lost their own bargaining power in the harvest season. Traditionally pannaiyal tied labourers achieved their most substantial remuneration at this time when their labour was most in demand. Generally they could demand something like one-seventh or one-eighth of the produce as a harvest bonus. By the 1930s the mirasidar could refuse to pay this bonus and bring in a gang of casual workers by lorry.[210]

By the late 1930s the relations between mirasidars and pannaiyals in parts of the Kaveri tract had reached a particularly low ebb.[211] In 1943 the nascent Communist Party organization in the province began to take an interest in the social conflicts of the Kaveri. At a conference of the Provincial Agricultural Labour Federation in 1943, there was a series of resolutions protesting against the maltreatment of pannaiyals and demanding higher wages. By 1944, the Madras government was concerned about the increasing politicization of the pannaiyals' position. Then the disputes between tenants and the Uthirathi math sparked off a wave of protest by the pannaiyals in the same clutch of villages, and the communist organisers quickly moved in and lent assistance. The pannaiyals were anxious to raise the level of wages, but they were also badly worried about their security. In the past few years under the cover of the government's food production drive, the mirasidars had made a much more extensive use of imported labour for the harvest, and as a result many of the mirasidars were now anxious to cut down their complement of permanent tied labourers. In 1944, the district authorities intervened and arbitrated an agreement. Daily wages were increased from two to three local measures of paddy, but the most important parts of the agreement were those that guaranteed to the labourers their share of the harvest, banned the import of labour from outside, and bound the mirasidar not to dispense with his tied labourers and evict them from their house-sites.[212]

By the harvest of 1945, the agitation had spread to cover most of two taluks in the east of Tanjavur district. The mirasidars refused to honour the 1944 agreement, imported labour for reaping, refused to pay the pannaiyals at the harvest, and used the subsequent protests as an excuse to evict the surplus pannaiyals. Against a background of mounting violence, the government externed the two principal communist organizers and instituted special conciliation machinery. As the Collector explained:

The labour meetings were allowed for some time but on this pretext the leaders got together a large number of Pannaiyal labourers who attended the meetings armed with deadly weapons. Clashes between kisan [i.e. politically organized] and non-kisan [i.e. imported] labourers were reported. Several weapons including bugles used for war cries, have been seized from the kisan labourers. They were also prosecuted and convicted. As meetings became a regular menace to the peaceful countryside faraway from the Police stations, they were banned. But the mischievous activities of the leaders did not cease. They were found to be visiting labourers stealthily and giving them evil advice, the worst of it being that they would get a share in the landed property of their masters, if they kept up agitation and also began to make objectionable speeches.[213]

As the agitation spread towards the north, certain mirasidars attempted to forestall trouble by getting the mirasidars to agree to raise wage rates. They formed an association 'to prevent the agricultural labourers from being enlisted as members of the Communist Party and thus creating disruption between the mirasidars and the labourers'.[214] Before the harvest in 1946, government sent in a district magistrate to attempt to consolidate the ad hoc arrangements of the previous two years into a more steadfast agreement. The magistrate set up a permanent wage board, guaranteed the tenure of house-sites, and enjoined the mirasidars to consult the conciliation machinery should they wish to import labour or dispense with the services of a waramdar or pannaiyal.[215] The mirasidars, particularly those from beyond the area where the agitation had been serious, were horrified and flooded the Secretariat with protests. They were particularly disturbed by the provision that the government could fine them if they furtively imported outside labour and could restrict their control over house-sites. The communist leaders, meanwhile, spread their agitation further north into the taluks of Kumbakonam and Mayavaram. At the harvest, the mirasidars continued their usual practices. After a fracas at Konerirajapuram, one of the newly elected ministers went to investigate: 'The difficulty', he reported, 'arose however in the fact that the landlords had already imported labour from outside the villages and had employed them for cultivating the lands, which were about to be left fallow, on a co-operative basis.' His attempt to make a local agreement failed utterly because the mirasidars refused to accord the pannaiyals and small waramdars any kind of occupancy right. Despairing of success, the minister started to lead his Congress government towards a position of supporting the mirasidars' case. He argued that the government should protect the right of the mirasidars to import labour since that 'will at least bring the Kisans to their senses and help also in disuniting the present leadership of the Kisans, which I feel is absolutely necessary in the interests of harmony'.[216]

There is no real ending to this tale. In the 1950s things settled down slightly. Emigration to Ceylon and southeast Asia started up again and began to draw off some of the surplus labour. In one Tanjavur village surveyed in 1959, emigration to Malaya and Indochina had made the most significant contribution to a decline of the village's population by seven hundred persons in eight years.[217] The government passed a Pannaiyals Protection Act and then started on land-ceiling legislation and the two Acts together encouraged valley mirasidars to revert to the old style of cultivation—with resident mirasidars, tied pannaiyals, and little use of casual labour. The cultivated acreage which had declined badly in the 1940s now started to rise again. As Gough and Béteille noted in their studies of Kaveri villages in the 1950s and 1960s,[218] the new generation of valley mirasidars, many of whom had only recently risen from the ranks of the tenantry, soon began to cultivate a life-style and concern for political and social status, which was little different from their predecessors. The relationship between mirasidar and pannaiyal remained sullen and fractious and there were sporadic outbreaks of serious trouble throughout the next two decades. In the end the valleys resisted the lure of economic rationalization and opted instead for the remnants of the past.

Compared to the plains, the history of the Tamilnad valleys in the late nineteenth and early twentieth centuries emphasized continuity rather than change. There was no dramatic shift in settlement patterns or in cropping and only a marginal adjustment to the market. The valleys' economy was based on a guaranteed market for the major crop, paddy, a fairly inflexible production system based on riverine flush irrigation, and a stratified socio-economic organization buttressed by a large supply of hopelessly poor labour. The system adjusted quite quickly and quite often over time in response to changes in markets, labour supply and other factors, but the basic outline seemed to have a self-righting quality of its own. In the late nineteenth century and early twentieth century the external economy in southeast Asia provided a safety-valve which dispersed any pressures building up inside valley society which might have provoked change. The depression of the 1930s provoked a crisis since labour supplies improved and markets declined at the same time. Consequently there were attempts to rationalize the production system, and there were also political troubles which mostly surfaced in the following decade. But not much really changed. By the end of the period the valleys had lost their role as the most important agricultural region in the area. The conflicts inherent in valley social organization were creeping ever closer to the surface and minor breaches of the surface were becoming steadily more common; but now the state was at hand to deal with this.

Kongunad

Kongunad was in many ways geographically and historically similar to the plains region. It was simply the largest of the upland basins lying between the Tamilnad hills and the Ghats, and it had low rainfall and little riverine irrigation. It had also been only sparsely settled until very late in its history and had an 'internal frontier' for expansion in the nineteenth century. But it also shared some features of the valleys. Historically it had been closely associated with the premier valley region, the Kaveri. It had acted as a buffer state for the Kaveri kings and as a frontier of settlement for Kaveri colonists, and thus the leading Kongunad community, the Vellala Gounder, had many of the social pretensions of the valley mirasi-dars. In reflection of this unique mixture of local archetypes, Kongunad had an unusual history in the passage from the nine-teenth to the twentieth century. There was neither the sluggishness of the mirasidar economy of the valleys nor the tensions of the new commercial economy of the plains. Rather there was a remarkably successful growth of entrepreneurial farming. It is important to stress that this was a recent transformation, for it has been easy for other commentators to find a great continuity in Kongunad's agrarian history: nineteenth-century British writers commonly noted the intensity of cultivation in Kongunad and praised the expertise and application of the 'sturdy' Gounder peasant;[219] twentieth-century observers have noted their enterprise and wealth, and it is easy to paint this as a simple and unchanging picture in which hard work (and a little bit of help from a good resource-endowment) was rewarded with success in both periods. Yet until the late nineteenth century, Kongunad still concentrated on the production of food crops, and only in the mid-twentieth century did it emerge fully as the most commercial zone in the region.

When Buchanan passed through Kongunad in 1801, he noted that the population was sparse and vast tracts of land, although showing signs of cultivation in the past, now lay unused.[220] The area had supplied food, spices, and textiles to the eighteenth-century Mysore court, but this had been difficult because of the lack of good roads and with the collapse of the market in Mysore, trade had fallen off badly. He noticed several large landowners, employing labour on an annual contract or occasionally letting land on a share-cropping system, but most of the land was worked by individual families with a single plough and something like eight acres. He attributed the prevalence of family farms to the sparseness of the population and the easy availability of land. Agriculture was very varied, especially in the *thottam* gardens under the 20,000 or so wells in the district; tobacco, cotton, chillis, and spices were grown as well as many varieties of grain, but the commonest pattern of agricultural production consisted in a large amount of coarse grain (notably cumbu) accompanied by small amounts of cotton, castor, and horse-gram in rotation.[221]

There was little sign of the 'minimal' style of cultivation which characterized so much of the plains tract. The fact was that the land of Kongunad would not support such a regime. The rainfall was lower than anywhere else in Tamilnad and was inadequate for most types of cultivation. The black-soils which dominated the centre of Kongunad were heavy, liable to waterlog when wet and tessellate when dry, and thus impossible to work with just some scrawny local cattle and some 'minimal' input of labour. The red soils were light, thin and thus usually unproductive unless assisted by irrigation. As a result of these deterringly harsh characteristics, the cultivable soils of Kongunad had not already been overworked and so retained a lot of natural fertility. To come to terms with this tract, the farmers had to commit themselves to an expensive, and thus necessarily intensive, style of cultivation. In the black soils they had to use strong, expensive plough cattle, and they had to weed and tend carefully to sustain the natural fertility and to provide as far as possible against the drastic effects of flood or drought. In the red soils, they had to supply water. Irrigation by tanks, which were the characteristic device of the plains tract, was simply not possible. The soils were absorbent, rainfall low, and mean temperature high, so that tank-water quickly evaporated or percolated away. The only other possible source of water lay under the soil. Thus from medieval times, Kongunad's agriculture was built around wells. This had a profound effect on the pattern of settlement and the style of cultivation. Well irrigation was expensive to install and expensive to work. The local gneissic rock was hard and the water-table deep, so the initial construction of wells, and the periodic maintenance necessary to prevent deterioration, required skilled stone-masons. The usual way to lift the water was through bullock-power and this made it even more necessary to keep good cattle. These high initial costs dictated an intensive style of agriculture. A good well could provide water virtually all the year round and thus could yield a return commensurate with the investment so long as it was worked carefully and constantly. This encouraged a pattern of smallish farms, focused on the *thottam* or well-irrigated garden, and worked by family or tied labour.[222]

Under the protection of the pax britannica and later the stimulus of demand in world markets, agriculture in Kongunad expanded faster than in any other part of the region in the second half of the nineteenth century. In his classic manual of Coimbatore district (which covered the greater part of the Kongunad region) written in 1887, Frederick Nicholson noted that the southern tracts 'forty years ago were virgin forests' and that the western part of the district as a whole had been more famous for teak than for grain. This had changed rapidlly from around mid-century:

In the time of Colonel Fullarton (1770) and Buchanan (1800) a vast teak forest extended between Pollachi and Palghat and troops traversing it had literally to cut their way through; so recently as 1840 herds of elephants might be seen in the virgin forests, which then extended up to the Anaimalai village bungalow; this tract is now an open plain, destitute of all except ordinary trees, cultivated and traversed by good roads.[223]

This expansion had gone hand-in-hand with an increase in the number of wells. Observers reckoned there were around 18,000 to 22,000 wells in Coimbatore district at the start of the nineteenth century and a census in 1814 put the figure at 27,097. By 1854 the number had risen to 35,411. In the following year, the British abolished special rates of assessment on garden cultivation, and by 1872 the number had risen to 57,437 and by 1880 to 64,985.[224] Thus the number had roughly tripled to the point where there was roughly one per cultivator. While still rapid, the expansion of cultivated area was rather steadier than it was on the plains. There were still tracts of good black soil being newly submitted to the plough in the 1920s.[225] There was no rush into the 'minimal' cultivation of the plains. Rather, the agriculturists concentrated on the better lands, while the poorer land was devoted to cattle-raising and thus complemented the intensive arable cultivation of the good land by providing the vital livestock.

There were three main centres of cattle-raising. The first, in the middle of Kongunad, bred the large and strong Kangayam breed on tracts of pastures often sown especially with *kolukkattai*, a special fodder grass. Here two important men in the locality—the pattagar of Palaiyakottai (a Gounder clan head) and the village headman of Kadiyur—emerged as massive breeders with herds of 500 to 1,000 head of cattle, while many other inhabitants reared smaller herds of ten or twenty head. Secondly, in the southeast, on the dry and stony tracts of Dharapuram taluk, there were several large holdings for grazing. The enforcement of the ryotwari system after 1855 made the breeders take up these open pastures on a formal title with the result that the acreage of revenue-paying dry land in this taluk increased by fifty per cent in the next twenty years.[226] Thirdly, there were the outcrops of hills, mostly round the edges of the Kongunad basin. Here the cattle were often of the Alambadi breed, which were not so well-favoured within the Kongunad region because they were marginally less sturdy than the Kangayam, and could not survive, as could the Kangayam, on the poor fodder available in local pastures. However, the cattle-breeders of Kongunad also exported their stock both through sale at local fairs and through peddling at a series of local fairs and markets which stretched along the roads leading away from Kongunad towards the rich valley regions.[227]

Thus Kongunad largely (but of course not completely) avoided the rapid spread of virtual subsistence cultivation on poor land, and the growth, as on the plains, of a system in which minimal and intensive styles of cultivation existed side-by-side and complemented one another by exchanging surplus labour for surplus food. Rather, a system of a careful agriculture on good land was complemented by a system of careful animal husbandry on the poorer tracts. In both cases the rate of capital formation was pretty high. Moreover, Kongunad also avoided to a great extent the crisis which came about when the forests were diminished on the plains.

This was partly because the nearby Western Ghats and some local hills were covered with forests that were not threatened by the encroachment of arable cultivation, but mostly because cattle-raising was an intensive, profitable business with an export outlet and it was worth retaining certain lands for the purpose. Indeed such grazing lands had by the 1880s acquired a value (Rs 25-30 an acre) which was well above the value of cultivated dry lands throughout much of the plains.[228] The cattle produced were expensive and the price in the twentieth century was rising rapidly, but they were also good cattle and would repay the investment if they were inserted into a suitably intensive scheme of production.

The expansion of the nineteenth century saw mainly the multiplication of small farms based on a well or a tract of good black soil, rather than the spread of large holdings. Of course there were many areas where new arable farms were formed on lands that were originally part of large grazing holdings and where the cultivator assumed the status of a tenant. Yet most observers in the late nineteenth century commented on the prevalence of small owner-cultivator holdings in Kongunad, just as Buchanan had at the start of the century.[229] Moreover, these holdings produced mainly grain. In the 1880s, Coimbatore had a larger proportion of its ground area covered by crops of dry grain and pulse than any other district of Tamilnad. Cumbu was the most common millet, followed by cholam, which was less susceptible to drought but also less productive, and then by ragi which flourished under well-irrigation. Castor and horse-gram were the most common crops grown for cash-sale, followed closely by cotton and gingelly. The well-irrigated gardens were then clustered with a variety of other crops—tobacco, sugar, chillis, vegetables—all grown in small amounts and generally sold in the plethora of shandies spread through the region.[230]

In other words, the expansion of owner-cultivator farming had meant an expansion of semi-subsistence farming in which grain overwhelmingly predominated. Many other crops were grown to pay the revenue and the high capital-costs of farming in this tract, but they were generally grown in small amounts partly to maintain a correct rotation, partly to provide insurance against perverse fluctuations of price and demand on any single product. It was a strategy of survival which was reflected in the parsimonious, unostentatious habits of the Gounder peasants, so often praised by the British officers who reacted badly both to extremes of poverty and to conspicuous displays of wealth. As part of the same regime, local social relations remained largely in a traditional mould. Labourers were generally tied and paid mostly in kind and perquisites. Rentals were nearly always in kind, often on a crop-sharing agreement. There was still a considerable cohort of village functionaries—particularly guards for crops and livestock and repairmen for the irrigation works—paid out of the grain-heap. Moreover, especially among the Gounders, the lineaments of caste and clan organization were well-preserved. Clan organization reflected (or was made to reflect) the distribution of land within the locality; lineage and clan leaders had their ritual powers substantiated with material influence and retained a considerable social and judicial role; and this organization extended beyond village and clan to knit the region together more closely than any other part of Tamilnad.[231] Agrarian society in Kongunad thus had many unusual characteristics which were born from its 'frontier'-like development and its peculiar ecological demands. By the late nineteenth century there had evolved a society of small owner-cultivators largely oriented to farming for survival yet necessarily doing this at a higher level of capitalization than was usual in southern India and with a limited but important orientation to the market.

The provision of better transport and thus the penetration of local and world demand had a peculiarly stimulating effect on this production regime. Kongunad farmers were accustomed to working at relatively high levels of capitalization and intensity and thus it was comparatively easy—and very profitable—to move towards a far larger proportion of cash-crops. As we have seen, they already knew the techniques for the production of cash-crops on *thottam* gardens and on the black-soil tracts; what was required was a change of scale. This came about very rapidly once improved transportation and trade facilities made it easy for them to export their crops and to import food. Thus the advent of the railways in the last quarter of the nineteenth century had a very rapid and substantial impact. The rail-heads quickly emerged as major entrepot markets—Erode for chillis and tobacco, Tiruppur and Coimbatore for cotton, Avanashi and Pollachi for groundnut—often in the process effacing other market-towns which had not been blessed with a railway-line.

The most important cash-crop was cotton, which had been grown in the region for a long time and had spawned a considerable industry of local hand-spinning and handloom-weaving. But, as in the far south, the type of cotton grown in Kongunad was of peripheral importance to European markets, and the attempts by the British in the mid-nineteenth century to introduce new varieties and new techniques for processing came to nothing.[232] The American civil war created an overseas demand for Kongunad cotton, and the Kongunad farmers responded remarkably quickly. But once the war was over, the cotton acreage lapsed. From the 1870s, however, the railways and the gradually increasing trend of world prices saw a rapid increase in the acreage under cotton and other cash-crops. Coimbatore had sported some 150,000 acres of cotton in the early part of the century, but this had risen to over 200,000 by the 1880s.[233] The discovery of the Cambodia strain in the early years of the twentieth century had a particularly marked effect on Kongunad for the strain grew especially well on the submontane irrigation systems in the west and on the *thottam* gardens throughout the red soils of the area. It also provided a better yield and had a ready market in both Madras (Binnys specifically promoted the spread of Cambodia in Kongunad) and Bombay.[234] The hike in prices and demand in the first world war brought the Coimbatore cotton acreage up to 300,000 and the spread of the local cotton-mill industry in the 1930s moved it nearer to 400,000. The collapse of the international market, difficulties of the local industry and cropping policies of the government (which favoured grain) during the war caused a dramatic decline in the 1940s, but this was rapidly made good in the following decade.

Meanwhile, there were increases in other crops. Tobacco was particularly well-suited to the Kongunad *thottams*; it was very expensive to grow and needed careful watering, but it gave a remarkably high monetary return per acre. The acreage doubled in the 1880s (from fifteen to thirty thousand acres) and then fluctuated around the same level for the rest of the period. Sugar-cane had similar characteristics and its acreage advanced slowly but steadily from 4,000 in the 1880s to 8-10,000 between the wars and then doubled to 20,000 in the post-war period. Meanwhile Kongunad had largely ignored the rapid spread of groundnut which affected the plains around the turn of the century; it was a cheap, easy crop not well-suited to local conditions. But around the first world war it was discovered that in the western part of Kongunad, around Pollachi, it was possible to grow a form of groundnuts quite different from that grown in the 'minimal' style on the plains. This was a different strain, and it was grown under irrigation.[235] The result was a superior yield and a superior quality, and the acreage in Coimbatore leapt to 175,000 in the boom of good prices in the late 1920s, fell back in the depression, but then increased rapidly in the 1940s when much land was transferred from cotton to groundnut because of price and marketing advantages.

The enthusiasm for these new crops meant that some of the crops previously grown to yield a monetary income declined very rapidly. The area under horse gram halved between the wars and the area under castor seed was reduced to a third of its previous level. But in terms of acreage this decline did not compensate for the increase in other cash-crops. In the late nineteenth-century, the acreage devoted to cash-crops in Coimbatore (roughly eight per cent of the total) was very close to the average for Tamilnad as a whole. The proportion in Coimbatore increased steadily thereafter, but because of the rapid spread of groundnut elsewhere, Coimbatore fell behind the regional average. But this conclusion is misleading since the cash-crops which were grown in Coimbatore—irrigated Cambodia cotton, irrigated groundnut, chillis, sugar and tobacco—gave much more valuable yield per acre than the extensive groundnut cropping on the plains. In terms of value of output, the proportion contributed by cash-crops was increasing much faster in Kongunad than elsewhere. Then from the mid-1920s, Coimbatore overtook the regional average in terms of even the simple proportion of total acreage devoted to cash-crops and by the 1950s it had the largest proportion (around twenty per cent) of any single district.

The difference from other zones was much more than a simple question of scale. Because Kongunad started out with a more intensive style of farming, it was simpler for the farmers in this region to respond to new stimuli by increasing the intensity. As elsewhere, land and other inputs rapidly became more expensive in the early twentieth century, but whereas elsewhere the farmers often responded by reducing their usage of expensive items and attempting to cut costs by depressing the price of labour, in Kongunad they tended instead to move towards a system of production that was dictated more and more by economic rationality and less and less by the demands of subsistence and tradition.

Thus Kongunad in the transition to the twentieth century faced much the same problems as those experienced in the other regions —the fluctuating demand for specific crops, the difficulties over forests, the problems of labour management—but overcame them in its own way. Just like the other regions, Kongunad experienced unusually rapid fluctuations in demand for different crops. However the characteristic unit of Kongunad agriculture, the *thottam*, was extremely flexible. Because of the secure and virtually continuous irrigation from wells, it was possible to grow almost any of the crops known in the region. Cultivators normally spread their risks by growing many different varieties simultaneously in order to ensure against vagaries of climate and market and it was comparatively easy to change the emphasis. Thus the pattern of cropping in Kongunad responded quickly to the fall in demand for cotton and the rise in demand for sugar, vegetables and spices. The shift to these new crops often required extra investment, but this did not inhibit change.

As elsewhere, the cost of buying and maintaining cattle rose rapidly in the early twentieth century, and since the cost in Kongunad was already unusually high this was particularly significant. The cost per pair of plough-bullocks rose from something like Rs 100 at the turn of the century to Rs 600 by 1930. Moreover, the increased use of wells and the associated *kavalai* bullock-powered water-lifts, and the expansion of black-soil cultivation (particularly of karunganni cotton) put a greater strain on the animals. One report (which seems rather exaggerated) reckoned that the working life of a plough-team had once been reckoned as eighteen years, but in the previous generation had been reduced to two or three years. Straw for cattle-feed became scarce and expensive, particularly in the Pollachi areas where, by the 1930s, cropping had become particularly intense.[236]

There were several responses to these difficulties. In some areas there appeared professional plough-teams. Individual farmers (presumably those with no wells needing bullocks to lift water) ceased to own cattle, but hired from specialists who made their living from keeping cattle and hiring them out. Elsewhere there were attempts to command a supply of fodder. From the late 1930s there was a significant increase in the cultivation of fodder crops but this was in fact a rise from almost nothing to only three to ten thousand acres and was nowhere near as important as in the far south. It was however noticeable that cumbu, which was originally considered

the most suitable and best-quality millet in the tract, declined
significantly compared to cholam; the latter provided much better
straw and this may have been the reason. Finally, there were
instances of farmers taking plots of paddy-land on expensive leases,
largely so that they could secure the paddy-straw for their
bullocks.[237]

In the late nineteenth century, the pace of expansion caused
difficulties over procuring labour, just as in the plains tract.
Garden-cultivation was especially labour-intensive. In the 1880s,
Nicholson noted that labour seemed to be scarce and attributed this
to the fact that labourers generally had the chance to set up their
own holdings.[238] In both the valleys and the plains, the subsequent
period saw village elites attempting to use the tools of local political
power and local economic clout to coerce labour, with predictable
consequence in the form of heightened social tension. Kongunad
responded, however, not by manipulating old forms of social
dominance or new forms of debt clientage, but by moving slowly but
significantly towards a more commercially rational use of labour. In
the early twentieth century, landless labourers in Kongunad were
generally paid better, and accorded a better local status, than their
counterparts elsewhere in Tamilnad.[239] From the mid-nineteenth
century there was an expansion of the ranks of 'permanent farm
servants'. These were attached labourers, sometimes indebted to
the landlord, but in other ways quite unlike the pannaiyals of the
valley zone. They were more like an extension of family labour. The
thottams needed a constant, year-round attention and thus it was
appropriate to have a constant labour force. The permanent farm
servants were often lodged in the cultivator's house and fed with the
cultivator and his family. Their pay, moreover, was not unlike a
family share of the proceeds of cultivation. They were generally
paid a regular dole of grain, but for labour specifically on the
cash-crops they were likely to be paid in cash, or in a portion of the
produce which they could dispose of at will. Sometimes they also
received a cash-present at the end of the year, and since this might
fluctuate with the annual fortunes of the farm it was thus to some
extent in the nature of a dividend.[240]

The number of these permanent farm servants appears to have
increased quite rapidly. In one village surveyed in the 1930s there
were a hundred cultivators and 160 permanent farm servants, and
no nineteenth-century report on Kongunad leads us to expect such a

high ratio of labourers to landholders.[241] Many observers reckoned that the Kongunad labourers were better off than their counterparts in other parts of the region,[242] and it was noticed that while wages were pulled down by prices during the 1930s depression in most part of the region, in Kongunad wages rose in the same period.[243] Towards the end of the period, there also appeared well-organized gangs of day-labourers. These toured the villages at the times of peak labour-demand, mostly at the harvest. They were led by foremen who generally demanded a good price in return for the contract to work on a particular farm.[244] The AERC surveys of the 1950s showed that the wage rate for casual labour in Kongunad was significantly higher than in the rest of Tamilnad—Rs 0.87 was the average figure, and Rs 1.50 was the figure in one Kongunad village.[245] Kongunad was thus able to attract labour to overcome any potential shortage. In terms of density per acre of cultivated land, the population of Coimbatore (in which district most of Kongunad lay) was growing faster than that of any other district in the early twentieth century (see graph 6). The Census has obscured the businesss of internal migration, but it seems clear that part of this increase was due to an immigration from the other regions, particularly towards the end of the period; in the 1930s and 1940s the population in the taluks of Kongunad, and of north-western Tamilnad in general, showed rates of increase significantly higher than the average.

Thus towards the end of the period, Kongunad had a large, reasonably well-paid and apparently reasonably well-satisfied labour force. Certainly there were less disputes over the problem of access to land, and in keeping with the general commercial character of Kongunad's development, there was a highly commercial market in land. Between the wars, the price of land in Kongunad was comparatively high and increasing comparatively rapidly . A tenancy survey in 1946 found that the average rental value (which was closely associated with sale value) of garden land in Coimbatore was Rs 80.9 per acre which was virtually the highest figure in Tamilnad and had, since a (not strictly comparable) tenancy survey in 1918, increased more rapidly than any other category of land in Tamilnad. Moreover there is an interesting comparison of the ratio between these average rentals and the average land revenue demand, which reflected government's assessment of the land, its value, and its productivity. In Coimbatore in 1946, the average rental of garden land was around forty times the average revenue demand, while in no other district was the same ratio above sixteen times.[246] The difference reflects both the eagerness for land in Kongunad and also the perceived value of the capital invested in construction and improvement of wells and other capital inputs on Coimbatore gardens, for these investments were not taken into account on government's evaluation.

In other zones, even though land prices were high the market in land was generally slack. In Kongunad the market was much more active. Already in the 1880s Frederick Nicholson reckoned 'the traffic in land is very large' and estimated that two per cent of land was sold in any one year.[247] By 1925, according to the registration figures, there were sales of immoveable property worth Rs 5.4 crores in Coimbatore and this figure was substantially above those for other districts, even those with large tracts of valuable wet land.[248] In other districts, it was commonly reported that the auction of land for non-payment of revenue was a farce; either it was stage-managed by the village-headman or no one came forward to bid, and the amounts realized by such sales were risible. Yet in many parts of Kongunad, it was reported that these auctions excited considerable interest and there was a lot of competitive bidding.[249] Similarly in other districts it was commonly reported that the govenment's fear that money-lending was often the prelude to land transfer was ill-founded. Yet in Coimbatore, this fear appears to have been justified. Creditors would foreclose in order to get control of land. As one prominent Coimbatore banker and politician reported: 'Practically the whole of the land in the village changes hand once in forty to fifty years. You first lend the money, then the interest accumulates, and then you become the owner of the land. In turn you begin to borrow or the [next] generation begins to borrow and the story is repeated.'[250] As a result, Kongunad farmers were wary of mortgages and considered them 'shameful'. Borrowers were reluctant to raise money on mortgage for fear of losing their land, and creditors were reluctant to lend on mortgage for fear of being portrayed within local society as a land-grabber.[251] Such reluctance helped to make institutions such as indigenous banks and co-operative societies more popular in Coimbatore than elsewhere both as creditors and as places to invest spare funds. Yet even with these cautions, there was a high rate of transfer for good land. 'Not even one inch of land in the fertile Nallar valley', noted a prominent Kongunad historian in 1937, 'belongs to the original or indigenous owners today.'[252]

Like other dry regions, Kongunad was notorious for its crime rate. As the economy became more markedly commercial, this was reflected in the type of crime. Murder was a local pastime and Coimbatore had for a long time led the province in this respect; by the 1930s many of the murders revolved around land. The same local historian noted that the Gounder farmers were 'easily affected by land disputes. Even an inch of ground or a small water-course or the right to a palmyra tree or a tamarind tree standing on the edge [of a plot] would result in the chopping off of a head...Kanurkkana, a village at the north-east extremity of Avanashi taluk which gave rise to a number of murders recently, has tobacco garden lands worth Rs 6000 to Rs 10,000 per acre.'[253]

There was also a flourishing commercial market in tenancies. The settlement officers in the 1880s estimated that fifteen per cent of all land was leased and the customary rental had risen in the past half-century from half of the *net* produce to half or even two-thirds of the *gross*.[254] The officer who conducted a survey of tenancies in 1918 found more lease-deeds to examine in Coimbatore than in any other district except Tanjavur and reckoned, as we have already seen, that rentals were exceptionally high.[255] Some of these tenancies were covered by agreements which maintained the owner's effective control over the land. The owner dictated how many acres would be laid down to different crops, made his own arrangements to manure the land, and even stipulated that the tenant could keep any grain grown on the plot but should allow the lessor to take the marketable produce such as the cotton kapas.[256] But others were straight commercial agreements, which were generally organized so that the land was divided up into the sort of plots which could be worked by one family with its usual complement of cattle and permanent farm servants.[257]

There were other ways in which Kongunad farmers proved responsive to economic incentive. It was not uncommon for farmers to exchange plots of land so that they might consolidate their holdings and thus facilitate irrigation from a single well.[258] When the Madras Agricultural Depatment put out improved varieties of seed, these were readily adopted. By the mid-1930s the department was running a scheme to multiply and distribute improved Cambodia cotton seeds (Co2) on farms in central Coimbatore. The farmers who planted these improved varieties took the kapas to special gins which extracted the seeds and returned them to the farmer for the next year. The co-operative societies which ran these schemes out of four cotton-marts in Coimbatore had nearly 5,000 farmer-members by the end of the decade.[259] Chemical fertilizers and powered water-pumps were eagerly adopted in Kongunad towards the end of our period because they provided an economic alternative to the increasingly expensive business of keeping cattle for lifting water and providing manure.[260]

Kongunad did not escape the dislocating effects of the 1930s and 1940s, or the strains of increasing pressure on natural resources. From the 1880s the bigger landlords had been enclosing grazing grounds and taking them on patta in order to establish exclusive rights.[261] Many of the smaller farmers, who were as committed to the market as their larger neighbours, were badly hit by the fluctuations of price from the first world war onwards. One local banker and honorary magistrate commented on their distress in the depression in suitably moralistic terms:

For the past two decades and particularly since the advent of the Great War of 1914, owing to the fabulously high prices at which the ryots sell their cotton and other produce, there was an abnormal rise in the income which gave an impetus to a high standard of living.... More than one-half of the ryot population strictly adhere to the time-honoured tradition and they are in a prosperous condition. It is the middle-class people with small holdings, owing to high standard of living, improvidence, inordinate expenses in marriage ceremonies and dowries, that are deeply involved in debt and are sadly wanting the wherewithal for cultivation. They go about borrowing from money-lenders, bankers, banks and nidhis at random.[262]

There were other reports that small men were being squeezed out by the price depression and were having to sell their lands. But these shifts seem to have been marginal rather than basic. The independent, commercially-oriented landholding remained the most characteristic production unit. It was not an egalitarian society, and indeed there were many villages which were held wholly or substantially by a single landed magnate. But most holdings clustered around the optimum size for a single family, well, and team of cattle. In a village surveyed in the 1950s, only 29 of the 370 holdings were over 15 acres, and there was a considerable amount of leasing which ensured that by far the majority of holdings were close to the optimal level of five to ten acres. The number of cultivators' sons who had fallen into agricultural labour and the number of emigrant labourers were well below the average found in this series of surveys.[263]

In sum, Kongunad survived the commercial fluctuations of the twentieth century rather better than the other regions precisely because it was more committed to the market. It was thus able to profit from the other regions' fumblings. Because it went farther towards an untrammelled commercial method for attracting labour, it was able to use the surplus labourers from the other tracts. Because it was dependent on the market, it adjusted more quickly than the other regions to the markets' vagaries and was better able to exploit new opportunities. Because it was prepared to invest in agriculture it was able, as we shall see in the next chapter, to attract capital even from outside the region. Kongunad became a land of commercially-minded owner-cultivators.

LAND USE AND FOOD SUPPLY

The relationship between cash-cropping and food supply has become part of the debate about the impact of British imperialism in India. The debate has focussed on the quesion of whether or not the expansion of export-trading and the construction of railways to open up the interior subordinated Indian agriculture to the needs of western markets rather than the needs of local consumers. Studies of this question have examined whether export crops drew acreage away from grain. The debate, like so many in Indian economic history, was begun by R.C. Dutt who thought there was a direct link between the spread of railways and the incidence of famine in the last three decades of the nineteenth century.[264] Recently Michelle McAlpin has argued that Dutt's case is far from proven; while cotton cultivation expanded in the late nineteenth century, there was no fall in grain acreage in absolute terms and only a marginal fall of the proportion of cropped area devoted to grain. McAlpin ends by suggesting that we must look at distribution rather than production as an explanation of the famines, and thus we must look at social relations in the countryside.[265] I do not wish to get involved in the debate over the great nineteenth-century famines. In fact I wish to begin, both chronologically and methodologically, where McAlpin's work comes to an end. My emphasis here is on the twentieth century, whereas McAlpin's study ended in 1900. Moreover whereas McAlpin's statistical investigation ended with an invocation to look at social changes in order to understand the background to distribution problems, I wish to start out from the assumption that the statistics of production are only comprehensible when they are predicated on a knowledge of the organization of agriculture. Thus I wish to examine the main statistical trends in Tamilnad's agriculture from the 1880s to the 1950s in the light of the foregoing discussion of agricultural organization and practice. To construct a completely circular argument, the statistical data on agricultural trends provides confirmation of some of the social changes outlined above, and also indicates the results of those changes.

Some convenient simplifications have had to be used to reduce the statistical data to some sort of order. In particular, I refer throughout to a category of 'commercial crops' which is far from analytically precise. All crops were potentially commercial; some portion of every crop grown was sold in some market somewhere; there were several different levels of marketing which could be adopted by way of definition – the local shandy, the urban retail and wholesale traders, the export houses. I shall simply use as a rough classification all those crops which were sold mainly for use outside the countryside itself—either for consumption or industrial raw material in the towns, or for export. This division is reasonably clear in the case of Tamilnad since the major commercial crops under this classification were not ones which might be absorbed in local markets (such as, for instance, wheat in the case of the Punjab). Rather they were cotton, groundnut, sugar, spices, fruit and vegetables. The latter three were of course items which might be consumed in the countryside but most of the supplies used locally were grown on backyard plots which did not figure in the agricultural statistics and thus we can assume that most of the acreage recorded under those heads was 'market gardening'. The only major problem arises with paddy, which was grown for local use, urban consumption and export, but it is impossible to slide a statistical knife between these categories and we shall instead use a simple division into 'commercial crops' and 'grain' and put paddy into the latter category. Furthermore, there are other problems about statistical coverage. Government's statistical net broadened over time and , in particular, in the early twentieth century many of the zamindari areas were being newly inducted into the business of

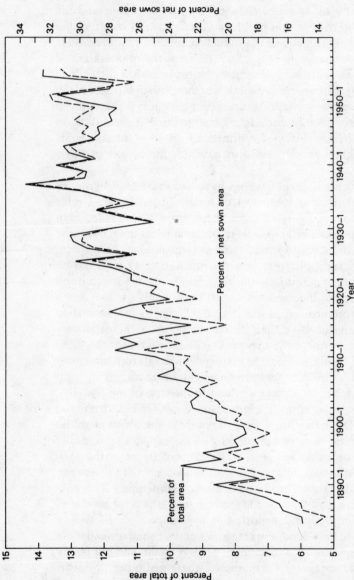

Graph 8   Tamilnad: commercial crops 1884-5 to 1955-6

Note: Commercial crops are defined in the widest possible way to include: cotton and other fibres; sugar-cane and other sugars; chilli and other condiments and spices; plantain, mango and other fruit and vegetables; groundnut, gingelly, castor, coconut and other oilseeds; dye crops; tobacco. The definition excludes all grains and pulses, and also fodder crops and plantation crops such as tea, coffee and rubber.

Source: *Season and Crop Report.*

statistical surveillance. Besides, the boundaries of districts shifted from time to time. In order to counter these fluctuations, we shall often express acreage *as a proportion of the total area*, that is as a proportion of the entire territory, including forests, waste ground and so on. This form of expression presents its own problems, but it is less open to error than the presentation of absolute figures.

The dominant trend in the agriculture of the period under review was the increase in commercial crops. The proportion of Tamilnad's total area under commercial crops rose from around four per cent in the 1880s to around twelve per cent in the mid-1920s and around fourteen per cent by the end of the period. As a proportion of the gross sown acreage, commercial crops rose from rather less than a tenth at the start of the period to rather more than a quarter at the end. The major contributors to this increase were groundnut and cotton. Groundnut acreage rose steadily until the first world war, slumped badly in the depression, and recovered from the second world war onwards when the local oilseed crushing and hydrogenation industries got off the ground. Between 1915-16 and 1954-5 groundnut occupied on average 10.8 per cent of the net sown area of Tamilnad, and on trend the groundnut acreage increased at a rate of 1.7 per cent a year. On the Arcots plain, which was the heart of the groundnut-growing tract, groundnut covered nearly thirty per cent of the new sown area on average. The acreage under cotton, meanwhile, was less affected by the depression, owing to the simultaneous growth of the local cotton industry and the spread of new long-staple varieties. The long-run increase of acreage was finally disrupted in the latter part of the second world war when the export market for the short-staple cotton was lost and government was urging cultivators to devote land to food crops. On average through the period from 1885-6 to 1955-6, cotton occupied seven per cent of the new sown area and on trend the cotton acreage increased at a rate of 0.6 per cent a year. The proportion of acreage was greater, and the rates of increase faster, in Kongunad and the far south.

While these two crops provided the bulk of the commercial crop acreage, there were in the latter part of the period significant increases under other crops. From the late 1930s, the expansion of a sugar industry in the province induced an increase in the acreage under sugar-cane, mostly in the valley areas and to some extent also in Kongunad. Up to 1930, sugar-cane had occupied no more than

0.2 per cent of the region's acreage; by the end of the decade, the acreage under sugar-cane had doubled and with another spurt after the war it more than doubled again by the mid-1950s to reach a share of almost one per cent of sown acreage. In the same period, the rapid acceleration of the urban population induced an increase in the acreage devoted to certain crops destined for urban consumption—notably chillis and other spices, betel-gardens, mango and plantain groves, and plots of other sorts of fruit and vegetables. By the end of the period, such crops occupied almost four per cent of the sown area. Since most of these crops required considerable amounts of water, the plots were mostly in the valley areas, especially in the Tambraparni region and the hinterland of Madras City both of which had considerable and expanding urban populations.

These figures on the adoption of commercial crops only confirm the finding of several other studies that southern India seemed more readily responsive than other regions to the demand for marketable agricultural produce.[266] We can now see some of the reasons for this. Population and cropped area were both increasing fairly rapidly in the nineteenth century and this meant that local production regimes were somewhat flexible. The plains and Kongunad, where the expansion of commercial cropping was most striking, were areas which were accustomed to commerce, although this had generally been associated more with armies than foreign shipping. They had for a long period produced saleable goods—specialist crops, construction materials, artisanal artefacts—and traded them for the surplus food of the valley regions; and thus found it easy to adapt to market agriculture when they found that the crops in demand could be grown on local soils.

Commercial crops were thus adopted fairly smoothly within the context of local production regimes. There was no move towards large-scale commercial farming; rather commercial crops were grown on a fraction of holdings of every possible size. Up until the first world war, the increase in commercial cropping seemed to work in favour of the more subordinate members of rural society. There was an increase in the need for labour and in certain areas this nudged up wage rates and improved conditions. There was also a growing possibility of finding tenancies in certain areas, and more chance for small cultivators to carve out an independent cash income through petty cultivation of cheap crops like groundnut and short-staple cotton. These influences were by no means universal and they were often countered by the deployment of financial and political power on the part of the village elites. Then in the later part of the period, the process of commercial growth clearly began to favour the more substantial cultivators. This was the result of the interlocking of three important trends. Firstly, the growing pressure on resources, both of land and most importantly of the ancillary inputs from forests and waste lands, allowed a premium to those who could establish a privileged right of access—either by dint of ancestral rights or by virtue of political clout or financial power. Secondly, the market for commercial crops was shifting slowly but steadily towards items which were more expensive to produce; common groundnut and short-staple cotton were gradually giving way to long-staple cotton and new varieties of groundnut which both needed specially selected seeds and more careful cultivation; meanwhile sugar, tobacco, spices, fruit and vegetables were also increasingly in demand. Thirdly, the growing instability of prices and demand favoured those farms which could diversify pro-duction, and absorb the shocks of short- and long-term fluctuations. It also, as we shall see in the next chapter, favoured those with secure access to capital and marketing arrangements.

Conditions favoured those cultivators who could command the resources to farm moderately intensively, who could secure inputs and use them efficiently, and who could mobilize sufficient labour. The substantial cultivator, whether he was owner or tenant, pros-pered, but those at either end of the rural social spectrum tended to suffer. Those large landholders who were excessively distanced from cultivation were unable to profit; 'estate mirasidars' in the valleys and zamindars in the plains actively resented the growth of commercial cropping because it loosened their remaining grip on their prospering subordinates and on the products of agriculture. Both of these groups suffered a rapid decline in political and economic fortunes in this period. At the other end of the scale, labourers and small cultivators were drawn into closer ties of dependence which differed enormously from tract to tract de-pending on the social and political inheritance from the past. Ironically it was those tracts which were most wholeheartedly committed to the market which were most prosperous and most free from social and political tensions, while it was in those tracts where the elites attempted to use the resources of the past—autarky,

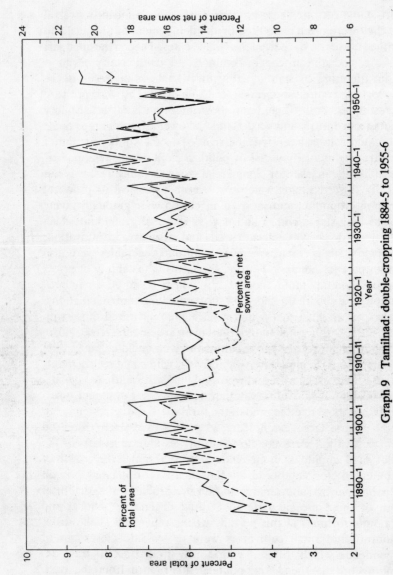

Graph 9 Tamilnad: double-cropping 1884-5 to 1955-6

Source: *Season and Crop Report.*

political hierarchy—to combat the difficulties of the present—market fluctuations, labour's demand for a fair share—which prospered least from commerce and had the worst repercussions.

The trends in the use of land differed significantly in the early and later parts of the period. In the early period, the increase of commercial cropping provoked an expansion of total area under cultivation. It is difficult to quantify this increase because the geographical units employed for statistical collection changed quite a lot up until about 1910, and there is probably some (though not by this time very much) exaggeration of the increase due to improvements in statistical surveillance. Roughly speaking, an extra four per cent of the region's total area was taken into cultivation, raising the sown area from about forty-three per cent to about forty-seven per cent of the total between the mid-1880s and the first world war.

Much of the expansion may be attributed to groundnut, for this crop could be grown on poor dry soils which could not grow anything else besides very poor millet and which were hardly worth clearing for that purpose. In the groundnut-producing districts, the expansion of cultivated acreage was much more startling than the overall trend of the region. In South Arcot it rose from about thirty-eight to fifty per cent of the total over the same period and in Salem from about twenty-six to thirty-five per cent. While the extension of acreage provided the avenue of expansion for commercial cropping on the plains, this was rarely possible in the valleys. Here there was a marked spread of double-cropping, which roughly doubled from three or four per cent of Tamilnad's total area in the 1880s to six or seven per cent between the 1890s and 1930s. On trend an extra 0.3 per cent of the total area was double-cropped in each year, and in Tanjavur the rate of increase was four times as fast.

There was a further process which was clearly associated with the expansion of acreage and increase of commercial crops. Each year more land was being left fallow. The logic of this was reasonably clear. When left alone for a period, tropical soils quickly recuperate the nutrients lost in the process of crop growth. Throughout the tropical and sub-tropical belt there is a tendency to use fallowing as the cheapest and easiest means to conserve the fertility of the soil.[267] In the Tamilnad plains, as we saw above, there was still a tendency towards long-fallow cultivation in the nineteenth century. This however had been restricted by the obligations imposed by the later ryotwari settlement and by the increasing pressure of population on

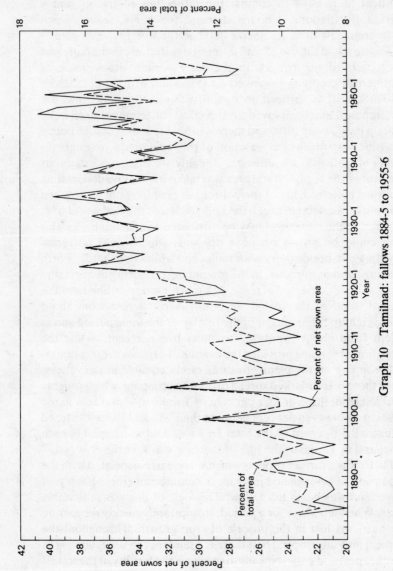

Graph 10 Tamilnad: fallows 1884-5 to 1955-6

Source: *Season and Crop Report.*

the margin of land. Even so, cultivators still knew the value of fallowing and local agricultural practice favoured rotations with regular periods of fallow. Naturally enough the increasing intensity of land-use under commercial crops dictated an increasing care about fallowing. Although there were reports that cultivators grew cotton and groundnuts recklessly without thought for the future, the statistics show that the increase in fallowing was concentrated in the parts of the plain which grew cotton and groundnuts, and that there was a strong statistical correlation between the expansion of these crops and the increase in fallowing. Between the 1880s and the first world war, the proportion of the land in use (that is, sown area plus fallow) which was left fallow each year rose from about a sixth to about a fifth.[268]

After the first world war, there were significant changes in the trends of land-use. The steady expansion of the cultivated area came to an end. There was still territory available and indeed after the end of our period there would be further expansions in cultivated area. But these depended on secure markets and government assistance. Most of the land that remained to be taken up was poor, expensive to clear, and difficult to irrigate.[269] So long as the market was so unstable, and so long as there was no assistance from government for irrigating unpromising tracts, then cultivators were unwilling to extend the acreage. Double-cropping continued to increase, but the trend was now less regular and reflected the fluctuating state of markets, prices and climatic conditions.

Meanwhile the practice of fallowing continued to grow. The trends differed greatly between districts and it seems that in the plains the increase was sustained, with a dip during the second world war, until the early 1950s. There remained a close correlation between the increase in fallowing and the increase in both commercial cropping and in the practice of double-cropping. The suggestion is clear. The uncertain conditions of the later period dictated a rationalization of land usage. Firstly, some of the poor land which was taken up, mostly by small cultivators, and farmed repeatedly with groundnuts or short-staple cotton was now getting exhausted, could no longer be used as profitably so long as the market was uncertain, and thus was allowed to recuperate longer or simply to drop out of cultivation altogether. Secondly, the increasing domination of the village elites was reflected in a reorganization of land usage to suit their needs. In parts of the plains and Kongunad there

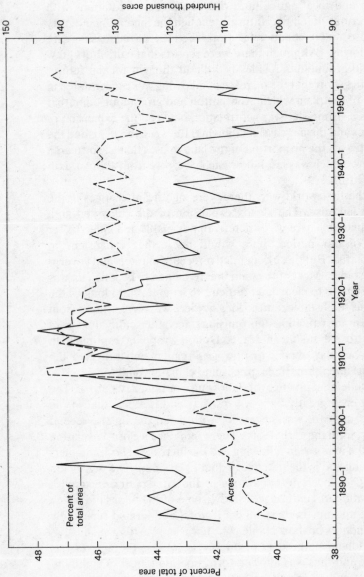

Graph 11 Tamilnad: net sown area 1884-5 to 1955-6

Note: The sharp rise up to 1915-16 in the graph of acres of net sown area is greatly assisted by the extension of statistical coverage. The other graph, which allows for this extension by displaying net sown area as a proportion of the total area under statistical coverage, gives a more realistic picture.

Source: *Season and Crop Report.*

were reports that lands which had once been used for dry grains or poor commercial crops were now left for grazing since for the substantial cultivator the upkeep of his cattle was more important than the produce of a few scrappy acres of groundnut or grain.[270] The proportion of the land in use which was left fallow each year rose from something like a fifth in the 1910s to something over a quarter in the period from 1920 to 1950.

The area under crops declined. The net sown area dropped steadily from a peak of roughly forty-five per cent of the total area of Tamilnad at the end of the first world war to a trough of forty per cent at the end of the second. Something like a ninth of total acreage was lost, and from 1930 onwards there were fewer acres submitted to the plough than in the latter years of the nineteenth century. Double-cropping continued to expand, but it was not significant enough to counter the overall decline. Besides, the extension of double-cropping occurred most forcibly in the valley tracts which were currently benefiting from new irrigation works. In the plains, the decline of gross sown area was particularly marked.

In other words, after the first world war, the area submitted to cultivation was declining in just those areas which were expanding their production of commercial crops. The decline of acreage meant a decline of acreage under grain. Up to 1920, the expansion of commercial crops had not intruded on the acreage under grain. Every year, some forty per cent of Tamilnad's area was growing grain—twelve to fifteen per cent under paddy and twenty-five to twenty-eight per cent under coarse grains and pulses—and there was no significant drop in the absolute level. After that, however, the acreage under grain dropped steeply and steadily through to the late 1940s. It was not the good qualities of grain which suffered a decline. The continued expansion of irrigation works and of double-cropping edged up the paddy acreage slowly but steadily. Similarly there was no decline in the acreage under cholam, the best variety of millet. The decline came in the pulses and in the poorer millets—cumbu, ragi, korra, varagu, samai. Up to the first world war these crops had covered roughly twenty-two per cent of the total ground area of the region. By the 1930s they had been pushed back to around sixteen per cent and in the slump of the late 1940s they dropped to twelve or thirteen per cent. These crops provided the staple diet of the poorer members of rural society. They were rarely marketed in any substantial quantity but were consumed

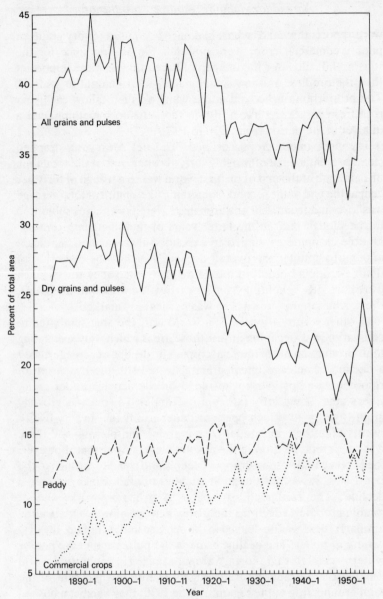

Graph 12   Tamilnad: food and commercial crops 1884-5 to 1955-6

Note: 'Dry grains and pulses' includes all pulse crops and all grain crops other than paddy. 'Commercial crops' are defined as in Graph 8.

Source: *Season and Crop Report.*

locally. Thus while the population of Tamilnad grew by about eighty per cent, the acreage devoted to the crops which supported the bulk of the region's poor fell back by rather more than a third. The per capita acreage under dry grains and pulses had more or less halved within thirty years.

The implication is clear. In the tough conditions after 1920, the desire to cultivate more and more commercial crops dictated that resources of labour, manure, and managerial attention should be concentrated on these crops. It was not just that there was a simple transfer of acreage from grain to commercial crops; rather there was a tendency to concentrate resources on the production of 'good' crops on 'good' land to the extent that the production of 'poor' crops was neglected and thus overall acreage declined. For it was not only the acreage under grain which declined but probably also the yields. The official yield figures are of uncertain value; certainly before 1916-17 they were collected very sloppily, but after a reform in the Board of Revenue's procedures they became rather more reliable from that year onwards. Blyn's analyses of these figures suggest that yields of grain crops climbed slowly upwards until the 1920s but then fell away. Blyn used the government's own provincial aggregates, which apparently averaged district figures without bothering about weightage. I analysed the figures on a district basis and looked only at each crop in the districts where it was particularly concentrated. The general impression was not dissimilar to that which emerges from Blyn's analysis; yields tended to be steady or rising until some point between the wars when they started to fall away quite rapidly; after reaching a trough during the years of bad rainfall in the late 1940s, they mostly recovered slightly in the early 1950s. The trend in paddy yields in Tanjavur and Tirunelveli held up quite well until the second world war, but in Chingleput there was a definite break in the mid-1920s and a fierce decline which had almost halved yields by the late 1940s. As for the dry grains, cholam appeared to be in decline from the early 1920s onwards, particularly in Coimbatore where yields again halved by the late 1940s, but rather less steeply in Tiruchi. Data on cumbu yields revealed no trend, but for varagu, ragi, and horse-gram the (rather dubious) early data showed a rise until the early 1930s followed by a steep drop thereafter (see graph 16). Out of eleven district-war analyses of grain yields from 1918-19 to 1953-4, eight showed a definite and statistically significant decline (see table 30).[271]

The official figures were corroborated by local surveys. In one village near Erode, the 1930 Banking Enquiry investigators found that the yield of coarse grains grown on dry lands was abysmally low 'due to the fact that dry lands are neglected by the ryots who devote their attention almost entirely to garden lands from which they expect a greater yield'.[272] In Vadamalaipuram in Ramnad, which was surveyed four times between 1916 and 1958, there was a noticeable decline in grain yields alongside a steady increase in the intensity of commercial cropping. In this village, there was no significant shift of acreage from grain to commercial crops, but there was a steady progression over time towards the cultivation of more expensive commercial crops; groundnuts gave way to cotton, then to chillis and finally to onion and plantain. By the 1950s, the commercial acres were being farmed intensively with manure and chemical fertilizer, but there was not enough manure left over to treat the grain acreage. Between the 1930s and 1950s, the yield of paddy in the village had declined by twenty-five per cent and the yield of cholam by thirty-three per cent.[273]

These trends can also be seen on the larger scale. The biggest declines in grain acreage and in total acreage under cultivation came in the districts which also had the most intensive regime of commercial cropping—notably the district of Coimbatore. Statistically it is clear that the increase in fallowing was the major cause of the decline in grain acreage and total cultivated acreage. Furthermore, there is a strong positive correlation between the trends of commercial crop acreage and the trends of fallowing. Fallowing tended to increase in parallel with the expansion of groundnut acreage in the Arcots, cotton acreage in Kongunad and in the far south, and sugar acreage in Tiruchi.[274]

There are a number of reasons why the decline in the availability of dry grains may not have been quite so steep and stark as the acreage figures suggest. Tastes may have shifted; imports may have grown; more of the dry grain acreage may have been irrigated and thus more productive. On the first point, there clearly was some shift in tastes. The people of the towns and the elites of the villages generally ate rice rather than millets. For the former it was largely a matter of costs—the addition of freight charges incurred in moving grain from country to town eroded the margin of price between rice and millets; for the latter it was largely a matter of pretension—it was a mark of status to eat rice rather than coarse grain. Certainly the slow but steady increase in the urban population and the expansion in the ranks of successful commercial-cropping farmers shifted several people from the ranks of the millet-eaters to the ranks of the rice-eaters. By the late nineteenth century the growing prosperity of Kongunad was reflected in the volume of grain being brought in by rail.[275] Yet it is impossible to quantify this shift. Besides it is not clear where this expanding market for rice could secure its supplies. Local rice production was increasing but nowhere near so fast as the population. There was however a significant growth in the imports of rice. Madras Presidency changed from being a net exporter to being a net importer in the first two decades of the twentieth century, and the volume of imports increased rapidly after the first world war (see table 8). Between the

Table 8: **Madras Presidency, overseas trade in grain**
1886-7 to 1955-6

Quinquennium	Exports in Rs lakhs	Imports in Rs lakhs	Balance, Rs lakhs	Balance in estimated tons of rice
1886/7-90/1	65.42	9.60	− 55.80	− 60 000
1891/2-95/6	65.36	44.34	− 21.02	− 20 000
1896/7-1900/1	96.04	76.02	− 20.02	− 20 000
1901/2-05/6	138.37	83.50	− 54.87	− 60 000
1906/7-10/11	208.91	268.54	+ 59.63	+ 50 000
1911/12-15/6	260.11	170.65	− 89.46	− 60 000
1916/7-20/1	170.81	281.64	+ 110.83	+ 70 000
1921/2-25/6	122.05	470.00	+ 347.95	+200 000
1926/7-30/1	303.85	613.14	+ 309.29	+200 000
1931/2-35/6	88.51	568.81	+ 480.30	+500 000
1936/7-40/1	121.70	671.25	+ 549.55	+500 000
1941/2-45/6	121.00	240.13	+ 119.13	+ 60 000
1946/7-50/1	0.74	2612.60	+2611.86	+650 000
1951/2-56/7	41.65	1801.41	+1759.76	+300 000

Notes: The table covers all shipments of grain between Madras and foreign countries, including Burma. There has been no attempt to adjust for the difference between f.o.b. and c.i.f. prices. This means that the final column understates the (negative) balance of exports and overstates the (positive) balance of imports. The estimate of tonnage is in any case a rough calculation based on trade unit prices. Minus sign=net export.

Source: *Annual statement of Sea-borne trade and navigation of British India.*

1920s and the 1950s around 350,000 tons of rice was imported on average each year and this represented an addition of about eight per cent to the local supply. On the third point, there were scattered examples of farmers growing cholam under irrigation and getting an increased yield but again quantification is difficult and it seems probable that, given the competition for irrigation water, the practice was unlikely to be extensive.

In sum, shifts in taste, increases in irrigation, and growth of imports probably did little to counter the steep fall in supplies of grain. The weakening in the position of the lower ranks of rural society was revealed in the sharp decline in the production of their staple foods. The poor must have had much less to eat.

CONCLUSION

The expansion of overseas trading from the late nineteenth century onwards caused an increase in Tamilnad's commercial agriculture. The plains and Kongunad were closely connected to westward trading, the valleys were involved in eastward trading. The plains and Kongunad readily responded to the western demand for certain industrial raw materials. The valleys sent rice, labour and other services to the expansive areas of southeast Asia. Commercial crops never occupied more than a minor portion of total acreage, but in terms of the diversion of resources other than land—labour, fertilizer, water, managerial skills—they bulked much larger in the rural economy. The enthusiasm with which the foreign markets gobbled up the produce which Tamilnad could send in the late nineteenth and early twentieth centuries meant that there was little need to overhaul the systems of production completely. For a long time Tamilnad's farmers had produced goods in some quantity for the market, and it initially made little difference to them that the market was now more remote, more demanding, and more rewarding. The three regions made marginal internal adjustments to their production regimes, and contrived to accommodate a closer attachment to the market without any substantial reorganization of local society.

The dominant groups in local society prospered most to begin with. The leading villagers in the plains and the mirasidars in the valleys had the best initial opportunities to profit from the market.

But as demand rose and prices increased in the early twentieth century, the delights of market farming percolated gradually down through the ranks. The 'minimal' cultivators of the plains could start out with a small borrowed capital, a small plot of groundnut or short-staple cotton, and large hopes for future prosperity won by a combination of divine benevolence and steady accumulation. In the valleys, migrant labourers could come back with the profits of exile and buy their way into the fringes of landed society, while enterprising tenants could tap urban capital and launch bravely into high-cost, high-return farming. In both areas, the advance of the market and the steady upward movement of population growth brought increasing competition over scarce resources of land, labour and other productive resources. The increase of demand *made* the supply of these inputs scarce.

Competition and conflict were obscured by the feeling of general well-being as long as profits were good and the frontiers of opportunity seemed wide open. But between the wars the character of the market changed. The tug of demand slackened, profit margins were pared down, competition among Tamilnad's producers became more fierce and desperate. The scales were now tilted against those who could not deploy some privileged advantages against their neighbours and rivals. Some of the leading villagers were ruined by this new climate of rivalry, and some just withdrew and transferred their interests to other parts of the economy. But those who suffered most were those clinging most precariously at the bottom of the ladder of commercial success. Small farmers now found it more difficult to get an independent foothold on the ladder. Meanwhile their more powerful neighbours now used all their powers to secure their own control over the scarce resources necessary for production. They sought to engross the ancillary resources such as manure, grazing land, and cattle power, to exercise a command over available labour, and to dictate cultivation on as much land as possible, whether they owned it or not. In this period the leading men in both the plains and the valleys used old-fashioned types of political and social power to engross resources and coerce labour. The dominant figures of the plains used the remains of their hierarchical privileges and their financial importance within the local economy. The valley mirasidars deployed ancient rights and the backing of the state. In Kongunad, however, the enterprising farmers did not react to the instability of the market by junking capitalist principles in favour of an exercise of patrimonial privilege, but rather set out to be more efficient and 'rational' at the business of commercial agriculture. The strategies of the plains boss and the valley mirasidar spawned social tensions which, in the valleys in particular, led to the first of a spate of class battles in the countryside. The strategies of the Kongunad farmer produced profits and relative peace.

These trends of adjustment within agrarian society were reflected in the usage of land. Up to the first world war commercial crops had expanded, food production had been pretty well maintained, agriculture had been both extended and intensified. The period from the end of the war to the depression proved to be a period of transition. From then on, commercial cropping continued to expand, agriculture continued to become more intensive, but now at the cost of the production of food. This change reflected the increasing weakness of the lower strata of rural society and the growing success of the dominant groups in engrossing resources and subordinating labour in order to sustain the growth of the commercial economy.

So far we have been necessarily vague about the market and the ability to take profits from it. So far we have viewed the process of commercialization from the angle of vision of one standing in the cultivator's field. Now, however, it is time to abandon the plough and climb up on the trader's cart.

4

The Markets

At the end of chapter two we discussed movements in foreign demand, and in chapter three we looked at the countryside's response. In this chapter, we look at the bit in-between—the mechanics of the marketplace. There is virtually no attempt to unravel the arcane business of local trade; the emphasis is firmly on the institutions and economic roles involved in the removal of rural produce to the markets of the towns and ports. The first section traces the selling of commercial crops, the second examines the accumulation of capital and provision of credit, and the third briefly examines the market for the most important agricultural resource, land.

SELLING THE CROPS

There is really no reliable way to estimate the proportion of all agricultural produce that was sold on the market in the early twentieth century.[1] Exports of rural produce per head of population in the Madras Presidency were very low—around Rs. 1.2 per head in 1891, Rs 2.9 in 1921 and Rs 3.2 in 1951[2]—but that calculation of course excludes produce sold to the local urban market and the market elsewhere in India. We have also seen that a rather arbitrary definition of commercial crops as virtually everything other than grain would include between a fifth and a sixth of total acreage in the first half of the twentieth century[3]. As indications of the importance of the market in the countryside, these figures are probably misleadingly low. Certainly the bulk of agricultural produce consisted of dry grains, and to some extent paddy, which were grown and consumed within the village. Since over four-fifths of the population lived in the countryside, this is hardly surprising. Even so, virtually all cultivators grew some produce which was sold, and, as we have seen, many cultivators were increasingly concentrating their productive resources on just these items. The importance of the market was in no way new. In his study of Tirunelveli district in the early nineteenth century, David Ludden has listed the products which were bought and sold in the countryside; they include articles exchanged between different agrarian tracts, articles exchanged between countryside and town, and articles exchanged with overseas regions, and the list is remarkably long.[4] The easing of difficulties over transportation in the nineteenth century, both internal and overseas, widened the range and extended the frontiers of trading. By the end of the century, there was probably no single agricultural crop which did not find some small market somewhere beyond the locality—even the poor millets in probably minuscule amounts[5]—and the imported goods available in the countryside now included a fair range of the products of Europe's industrial revolutions.

There were three main sorts of marketplace for the countryside— the shandy, the fair and the market-town. The shandies were periodic markets which gathered at small villages or even at lonely crossroads. The transactions were small-scale. The shandy was visited by the agriculturist with small amounts of produce to dispose of, and by the petty trader who progressed round a series of shandies 'like a tramp vessel'.[6] The prices offered for the small lots of agrarian produce were usually very low. The fairs were usually annual meetings associated with the cattle trade, with religious festivals, or with both.[7] There was a series of fairs held in the agricultural off-season along the roads which led down from the cattle-breeding grounds in Kongunad and in the Mysore Deccan to the valley areas of the Kaveri and far south. The bigger cattle-fairs along this route were associated with major religious events, particularly the Chitrai festival at Madurai. While cattle were the major article of commerce at these fairs, there was also considerable dealing in cloth and other consumer goods. The market-towns acted as wholesale points for the shandy traders and as bulking points for crops that were to be exported from the tract. The shandies dominated the plains tract; periodic marketing had been a natural adjunct of the sparse military colonization of the region and the need for an arena in which to exchange the goods and services of the plains tract with the foodstuffs of the valleys. In the denser settlement of the valleys, with their numerous political and cultural headquarters, the market-town was more common. Both the number of shandies and the number and size of market-towns grew rapidly in parallel with the increase in commercial activity.

Here we are not concerned with the pattern and the hierarchy of the markets themselves. No hexagons will appear. Rather we are concerned with the relationships involved in marketing. The participation and the relative power of different groups involved in commercial transactions has a bearing on several important questions: the distribution of wealth, the accumulation of capital and capacity for investment, the consolidation of political and economic power. Indian historiography has often been peculiarly antagonistic to the rural market; on the basis of rural-romantic or primitive-communistic views of rural self-sufficiency, it has viewed the market as a specifically alien institution. In particular it has often portrayed the denizens of the market as low types who were able to steal the major part of the peasant's produce. To a large extent, of course, this view is justified. The market certainly did grow under the impetus of the expanding external economy, and those who controlled the market were able to make fortunes beyond the avaricious dreams of the two-acre farmer. But a blunt view which opposes 'the market' and 'the peasant' does scant justice to the complexities of rural commerce. The produce broker, just like the money-lender, often turns out to be a peasant in disguise. It would be nice to calculate the margins of profit secured by the various participants in market transactions, but the evidence available cannot really support such an analysis. We are bound to use a more impressionistic approach.

While all sorts of rural produce were brought into the shandies, fairs and market-towns, three particular commodities dominated rural commerce in the late nineteenth and early twentieth centuries. They came from different regions and were destined for different final markets and thus they present a varied view of marketing relationships. The three were paddy, groundnut and cotton. Paddy came from the valleys and found its market both within the region and in the 'eastern arc' of Tamilnad's trade. Groundnut came from the plains and was, until late in the period, sold exclusively in westward trade. Cotton came from the plains and Kongunad and was destined both for westward trade and increasingly for a local industrial market. In each case—and with two variations in the case of cotton—the market was elaborated rather differently in the largely benign period before the first world war; but all suffered major crises of reorganization in the years of instability and depression. The period as a whole witnessed a complex and important change in the commercial and social relationships between countryside and town.

Paddy in the valleys

Paddy was the only foodgrain which was marketed in any quantity, and in terms of weight it was the single most important item of Tamilnad's internal trade. In the 1930s, the railways carried roughly 400,000 tons of paddy around the Tamil districts and, since the cart was cheaper than the railway for journeys up to forty or fifty miles, the addition of shorthaul trade would increase this figure substantially.[8] But despite its importance, the paddy trade was curiously disorganized. There were no really big bulking centres, no 'rice barons', no dominating trade routes. The characteristic contract in the Tamilnad rice trade in the late nineteenth century was a deal between a rice-miller and a retailer for the supply of ten bags. Most of the trade remained like this into the twentieth century and a local official described the chaotic state of the paddy trade in this fashion:

But one peculiar feature of the paddy trade in the southern districts of the Presidency is that, while all these districts enjoy quick transport facilities by rail and sea, the trade itself has no organization behind it. Immediately after harvest, hundreds of paddy merchants go round villages and even to other districts with hundreds and thousands of rupees on hand, purchase paddy for ready money payments from the ryots and then arrange to carry it to their destination, partly by road and partly by rail. The ryots in the rural parts are also eagerly waiting for the arrival of these itinerant merchants or their agents and then dispose of the paddy for whatever prices the merchants may dictate. If the merchants do not visit any villages or tracts, the stock on hand in those localities remains idle. When the prices are high, the merchants are slow to purchase and when the prices are low, the ryots are not eager to sell, with the result that the stocks in the rural parts very often suffer loss by warehousing, depreciation, damages and theft, not to say loss of interest during the period of immobilisation. The merchants themselves sometimes do not know where to buy cheap and where to sell dear and are, not infrequently, put to much loss. Somehow the trade is still going on, sometimes too briskly and sometimes too slowly according to the immemorial custom of the Nawab days. Though the southern districts are often called the Granaries of the Presidency, there is nowhere any granary worth the name.[9]

This apparent disorganization was a result of the scattered nature of the market and the geographically unstable nature of the supply.[10] The people who bought rice on the market were the local elites in the non-rice growing areas of the plains and Kongunad, and the inhabitants of towns and cities. The former were scattered thinly over a wide area. They purchased their supplies irregularly in the shandies and market-towns. The towns of Tamilnad, as we shall see below, were small and numerous rather than big and few. The demand for rice was thus not aggregated but dispersed. Moreover the demand was also very complicated. There were many different varieties of rice, and as in most societies where the staple is rice, they were considered very different products. The strain of rice planted, the mode of cultivation, and the primary processing all affected the finished product. On the first point, there were an enormous number of strains, each better suited to a particular soil, rainfall pattern and time of year. On the second point, the length of cultivation (which generally depended on the time of year) and the practice of harvesting early or late, could make an enormous difference to the coarseness or fineness of the grain. Finally, there were numerous ways of treating the rice before it reached the consumer. It might be 'cured' for some weeks left standing in the shock in the field, or for a year or more stored in a granary, or it might be consumed immediately. Then it could be sold simply as unhusked paddy, or it might be husked at source. Also it could be parboiled, or milled, or both, and there were many different techniques of parboiling and milling. The variety of possibilities created a variety of demands. There was a basic division between fine and coarse qualities. The cheaper coarse product came either from a poor sort of paddy plant, or consisted of grains broken in the process of threshing or milling, and it was usually parboiled. The finer varieties were immensely varied and the wealthy of Tamilnad society were often extremely pernickety about their staple food.

Meanwhile the sources of supply were very variable from year to year depending on the vagaries of climate. Paddy was grown throughout the region, though mainly in the river valleys and on the north-east coastal strip. Only a very small fraction of the total production, that grown under wells, delivered a steady and assured yield from year to year, and such supplies were almost exclusively grown for local consumption by the cultivator or his neighbours. The rest was in some way dependent on the year's rainfall, not only for directly watering the fields but also for filling tanks and swelling rivers. Some of the paddy-growing regions were more reliable than others. The best was the upper Tambraparni, where the river regularly deposited fertile alluvium and where two crops a year were virtually assured, and three were possible. This area was closely followed by the middle-reaches of the Kaveri—in the taluks of Lalgudi, Tiruchi, Tanjavur, Papanasam, and Kumbakonam— where again the river helped to fertilize the land and where the supply of water was moderately secure. Yet in bad years, perhaps one in ten, the river could supply too little or too much water, and the usual two (or very rarely three) crop regime might be reduced to one. Further east in the Kaveri delta, the normal year saw only one crop, and the danger from drought or flood was considerably increased. The tracts irrigated from the other smaller rivers—Palar-Cheyyar, Ponnaiyar-Gadilam, Vaigai, Vellar—were in much the same situation as the lower Kaveri. Finally there were large areas, particularly in Ramnad and in the Tondai area (North Arcot, South Arcot, Chingleput) where cultivation relied heavily or exclusively on the supply of rain to tanks, and these areas were particularly unstable. In good years they might produce two crops of paddy, in bad years none at all.[11]

Not only was the supply variable according to weather, but weather patterns could be extremely localized. A year of abundance in the southern districts might be a year of drought in the Kaveri. In the rain-fed areas, the monsoon storms could often prove exceptionally capricious, watering one village and completely starving its neighbour. Some areas on the fringes of the valleys, particularly in the Tondai region, would export in good years and import in bad years. Until some way through the agricultural year, the traders had no way of telling which particular region had surplus stocks and, within that region, which particular villages and cultivators had not already sold off the stocks. Thus the pattern of paddy marketing consisted of a large number of fine strands, knitted together each year in a complicated and slightly different pattern. As a government report noted:

In the producing areas there are a number of milling centres and in the districts of deficit production there are a number of importing centres. It is found that every importing centre has dealings with a number of milling centres from which it draws its requirements in small quantities and in a similar way every milling centre supplies produce in small quantities to a number of importing centres in a particular area... The merchants or commission-agents both at the producing as well as the consuming centres keep in touch with each other regarding the fluctuations in the market. The merchant at the consuming centre compares the prevailing prices at all the producing centres and [places] orders for the rice or paddy from a particular centre where the prices are most favourable to him. The merchant at the exporting centre usually sends samples of the produce when he quotes prices. The business is mostly transacted by individuals and not by any organized body of people.[12]

The trade was so fragmented that during the great famines of the late nineteenth century, markets quite close to the famine zone were relatively unaffected; merchants in Madras City explained that they got their supplies from areas other than those which supplied the famine-prone Deccan and thus barely noticed the effects of high prices and shortages little more than a hundred miles away.[13]

Because of this fragmented character, there was a distinct pattern to the annual marketing cycle. There were four stages.[14] The first stage came immediately after the main harvest in the months from January to April. This was the time when cultivators had to pay their government revenue and service their debts. Many cultivators, particularly the smaller ones, were obliged to unload their produce immediately. Perhaps half of the entire crop was sold at this point and naturally enough the prices were low. The purchasers included merchants, rice-millers and substantial mirasidars. Merchants and millers often went round the villages in this season, or sent commission-agents, and bought up stocks for cash. Sometimes the merchant would park his cart at the threshing floor itself. At this stage the merchant or miller would buy enough to cover the immediate, assured market. He would send samples of his stocks to retail dealers and take orders to supply a few bags to each of a number of centres. Substantial mirasidars, meanwhile, would procure stocks of rice in order to store against an expected price rise. They accumulated stocks through the crop-shares they received from their waram tenants; the mirasidars who were really interested in the market would have provided the seed and the cattle for the waram tenant in order that they might take away a very substantial crop-share. Meanwhile, both mirasidars and some merchants lent small amounts in kind and cash to the lesser cultivators to cover their expenses in the few months leading up to the harvest; these loans were then repaid from grain on the threshing floor.

In the second stage, mirasidars who were not pressed to sell immediately at the harvest, released their stocks bit by bit to cover their occasional family expenses. In some cases they took the paddy, or sent it through a commission-agent, to one of the *nellu mandis* (rice marts) which existed in all the towns of the valley tract. Here the stocks were bought by merchants or millers' agents. In some places, the sale would be achieved by auction:

In some big centres... the produce from the surrounding villages is brought by the cultivators to a common spot called *mathsulu* or *chavadi* every morning. Buyers and brokers collect there and the grain is actually auctioned. Either each consignment is auctioned separately or the amounts realised in auction for the first consignment of a particular variety is taken as the price for that variety for the day.[15]

By this point in the year, the merchants would have some idea of what had happened in the post-harvest sales and where there was still a demand. Often they merely acted as brokers for retail shops and bought paddy at the *nellu mandis* on commission against retailers' orders.

Up to this point, the pace of the market had been dictated by the rate at which supplies were released. In the final part of the year, however, it was the residual demand which began to dominate affairs. Prices began to rise, and merchants and mirasidars with speculative aims came forward into the market. Several mirasidars acquired crops from their own and neighbouring villages, either through money-lending activities, or perhaps through spot sales at the harvest. Generally speaking, these activities were not financed on personal capital, even if the mirasidar-dealer was wealthy enough to do so. While loans given early in the season might come out of the mirasidar's own hoard, once the harvest approached (and yield and prices could be gauged) he would raise money from a banker. Some of these bankers were the estate-owning mirasidars, some were rice mill-owners, while others were professional bankers. Nattukottai Chetties were active in this way in the Kaveri delta and in the riverine tracts of Madurai district. In the Tambraparni there were a number of Brahman banking communities, notably the Kallidaikurichi Iyers.[16] In Tondaimandalam, there was a wide variety of bankers, including Muslims and Marwaris as well as men of agricultural caste, working out of Madras City and its hinterland towns.

In certain cases, the mirasidars simply waited in the village and 'the consumers also directly go to the very doors of owners and buy in cash'.[17] Merchants too would circle round the villages looking for stocks. Then in the final stage of the marketing year, the big estate-owning mirasidars and the big millowners would release stocks on the eve of the next harvest when prices reached their peak. Very little rice was stored from one year to another. There were hardly any proper granaries in the Tamilnad valleys, only some pits and *puris*, circular straw huts, where paddy could be stored for one season but which would not withstand the assault of the monsoon.[18] The big growers and dealers, who could command sufficient finance, would hold stocks as long as possible. Banks and urban money-lenders would lend up to eighty per cent of the value of rice stored. Thus as the year progressed, the remaining stocks of rice were concentrated in fewer and fewer hands. The latter stages of the marketing year depended utterly on credit supplied by joint-stock and indigenous bankers and only those who could command credit and find storage could benefit from the annual upturn of the price curve. Generally this was the larger mirasidars and some big mercantile firms.[19]

Between the late nineteenth century and the 1920s there was a significant expansion in the volume of paddy marketing. The expansion was based on growing demand in the towns, among the prospering cultivator elites in the plains and among the Tamil labourers who migrated to plantations in Ceylon and southeast Asia, and who also helped to extend the market for Tamilnad paddy among their new neighbours. It was assisted by the elaboration of the railway network which made the business of moving paddy to the towns and ports much easier and cheaper. The harvest price of paddy rose three-and-a-half times between 1880 and 1925, which was a much steeper rise than that experienced by other grain crops (around two-and-a-half times) or by imported goods (around two times).[20] The height of the boom came in the first world war when inflation pushed up prices and when there was a rapid increase in the demand in Ceylon. Ceylon took 67,114 tons of rice a year in the quinquennium before the war and 131,570 tons in the war years.

It was not only an expansion of trade but also a significant change in its character.[21] In the earlier period, most of the movements of paddy were over quite short-distances and most of the paddy involved was of 'fine' quality. The movements were from the valley tracts into the local towns and westwards into the adjacent parts of the plains. The principal consumers had been urban-dwellers and plains notables. But in the late nineteenth and early twentieth century, expansion was based largely on demand for coarse rice in three specific centres: Madras City; the Ceylonese plantations; and the towns of Kongunad, particularly Coimbatore, where the demand came from a growing industrial population as well as from prospering cultivators. There were also increases in demand for fine varieties on the old, sporadic pattern, but it was the growth of these more concentrated, down-market pools of demand which was the most substantial change. The Tondai region was best placed to serve the market in Madras City and here there was a growth of production in this period based on the spread of wells and major irrigation works. The Kaveri region benefited most from the demand from Kongunad and Ceylon,[22] because the Kaveri was the largest tract and, ironically enough, because it produced some of the lowest grades of rice. The harsh exploitation of pannai and waram labour, which was the hallmark of the production system in this quintessentially mirasidari tract, led to some careless and wasteful cultivation practices. The Kaveri mirasidar 'cannot be sure of realising his legitimate portion of the produce unless he is actually present during harvesting and threshing operations'.[23] Big mirasidars, in particular, had to harvest the fields when it was possible for them to be present, rather than when the timing was exactly right for the crop; they also had to thresh the grain immediately, rather than leaving it to cure, since poor pannaiyals and hungry cattle would prey on any stacks left in the fields. The result was a coarse grain, which broke easily, was difficult to mill, and which usually had to be parboiled. The Kaveri did produce some fine varieties—*muthu samba* and *white sirumanai*—but also much of the coarser *sembalai*.[24] As a general rule, the bigger the mirasidar and thus the greater the problems of supervision, then also the greater the proportion of coarse paddy in the total produce.

Thus it was the Kaveri that acted as the major supplier of paddy to the new markets. As the table of paddy movements by rail and canal in 1933-4 shows, the Kaveri was despatching 51,938 tons to Coimbatore and 44,719 tons to Ceylon and these two amounts together made up two-fifths of the entire total of paddy which was grown in Tamilnad and put on the market via rail and canal.

There was no significant expansion of the Kaveri's rice acreage in this period to meet the expansion of demand. The market-oriented mirasidars and merchants invested not in any expansion of production but rather in techniques to increase their command over the crop. The buoyancy of the market attracted indigenous bankers, particularly Nattukottai Chetties from neighbouring Ramnad and Marwaris from northern India. They provided credit to the mirasidars to enable them to increase their lending to their waramdars and lesser neighbours. They also provided credit which enabled both mirasidars and merchants to make more forward loans to secure the crops on the eve of the harvest and then hold it in store.[25] Finally they also invested heavily in the building of rice mills. Owning a rice mill enabled the mirasidar or merchant to enlarge his share of the profit by cutting out other levels of the marketing process and dealing directly with the retailers. It helped him to judge the fluctuations of the scattered paddy market better since he could hold stock of unmilled rice and then mill small amounts to order. It also represented a capital holding against which the mill-owner could raise extra amounts of working capital from banks and from the bazaar money-market. All in all, it increased the leverage which an individual could exert in his attempt to gain greater control over the essentially static suppply of Kaveri valley rice. In 1910 there were only four rice mills driven by oil engines in the Kaveri tract. By 1917-18 there were 215.[26]

The boom in the paddy market brought some prosperity to the valleys. Looking back from 1930, one Tambraparni mirasidar noted:

Except some cots, benches, boxes and shelves, there was no furniture worth the name in 1900. The number of cots has now very much increased. Almirahs, books, safes, chairs, tables, clocks, watches and every other furniture required for making life comfortable can also be found in the house of well-to-do persons now.... In 1900 mud vessels were used freely in every home and they were also used to some extent on special occasions.... But now, even poor persons handle some metallic vessels in their daily life. Middle classes use mud vessels only to a very small extent and the rich have given them up entirely. Instead of one set, four or five sets can be had for special occasions.[27]

Such prosperity of course depended on success in the market. For some of the subordinate members of valley society the boom meant less economic security. The fact that the mirasidars managed to

Table 9: Movement of paddy and rice by rail and canal, 1933–4

Destination	Madras City	Chingleput	North Arcot	South Arcot	Salem	Coimbatore	Tanjavur	Tiruchi	Madurai	Ramnad	Tirunelveli	West Coast	North India	TOTAL
	Source													
Madras City	2607	2031	506	628			4477		15				7 5562	8 3219
Chingleput	1445		9	796			5353						204	7807
North Arcot	4353	289	625	267	24		3622						2548	1 1103
South Arcot	1976		89	1754			3113	60		77	63		45	5423
Salem	1222	16	15	4938	2818		5752	26			11	1768	2675	1 6423
Coimbatore	28	30	884	394	999		5 1938	7811	72	27	629	4 0545	7838	11 1195
Tanjavur	115		19	1091			8998	43	7		51		155	1481
Tiruchi	403		21	386	22		1 1106	931	11	156	116		388	1 2609
Madurai	154	65		179	23	14	6397	5768	143	184	7094	108	1666	2 1652
Ramnad	15	2	9	167		22	4310	418	1105	1787	1 2046		1086	1 9180
Tirunelveli	17		11	127			2305	43	668	78	5307		377	3626
West Coast		111	230		11	457	1170	60	827	100	1196			4162
Pondicherry & Pudukottai	827	3	51	625			2704	75	32		22			4339
Ceylon				9450			4 4719							5 4169
North India	2 7061	1484	4334	31			3410							3 6320
TOTALS	3 7616	4031	6178	1 9079	1079	493	15 0376	1 4304	2737	622	2 1228	4 2421	9 2544	39 2708

Note: The original data distinguish between paddy and rice. Here paddy has been added to rice, after deducting a third to account for the loss of weight in husking and milling. The unit is thus tons of cleaned rice. The figures in square brackets indicate movements *within* districts; these have not been added to the totals. The total of these movements within districts is 25,992 tons, which is equivalent to 6.6 per cent of the total movements outside districts (as shown in the table). 'West Coast' includes South Kanara, Malabar, Cochin, Travancore and The Nilgiris. 'North India' includes everything north of the Tamil districts; most of the imports from the north come from Nellore or the Kistna-Godaveri deltas in the Andhra districts; most of the exports to the north are destined for Mysore or the Andhra Ceded Districts. The rice which is indicated as originating from Madras City (and probably much originating from the West Coast) was imported from Burma etc. If we eliminate this presumably imported rice we reach the following abstract figures:

Rice grown in Tamilnad and marketed outside the district of origin	220 127
Rice grown in Tamilnad and transported to market within the district of origin	25 992
Total rice grown in Tamilnad and taken to market by rail and canal	246 119
Portion of above total which is exported from the Tamil districts	98 990
Amount imported from outside	172 581
Total available on the market	319 710

Source: Computed from tables in GOM: *Report on the Rice Trade of the Madras Presidency* by C.R. Srinivasan (Madras, 1934).

market increasing amounts of paddy, while production remained
more or less stagnant, meant that locally supplies of food were
reduced. This became clear in 1918 when, at the height of the
wartime inflation and the exporting boom to Ceylon, there was a
poor harvest in parts of Tamilnad. To the government's surprise,
the signs of distress appeared not in the dry tracts which were prone
to famine, nor even in the towns which depended wholly on the
market, but in the valley areas themselves. Local labourers protested that the merchants and mirasidars were busy exporting stocks
with the result that local supplies were low and prices unbearably
high. They rioted and attacked stores of grain awaiting despatch at
the railway stations.[28]

While labourers were becoming insecure, the opportunities for
cultivators, even small cultivators, were considerable. The readiness of banks, bazaar bankers and merchants to invest money in the
paddy trade meant that by the early 1920s even quite small
cultivators could command enough credit to hold up stocks and play
the market to some extent. The merchants found it more difficult to
secure stocks at a premium by lending to small cultivators on the eve
of the harvest against a contract to supply their produce, because
small cultivators found it possible to take several of these loans from
different sources and then oblige the rival creditors to bid against
one another to secure the crop. It is not at all clear how extensive
such participation in the market by small cultivators was, but it
certainly increased with the general expansion in the paddy market
around the first world war.[29]

But in fact the valleys' prosperity in these years was very fragile.
The valleys made no real attempt to adjust to the new demands of
the market, either by raising production to match the new level of
demand, or by streamlining marketing arrangements to suit the new
shape of the market. The fragmented nature of the valleys' marketing
arrangements was inefficient, expensive and quite inappropriate
to the new aggregated markets which had grown up in Ceylon,
Madras and Kongunad. There was some growth of wholesale
trading; agents in the importing region started to collect orders in
advance from many of the retail centres and shandy traders, and
then procure stocks on bulk order from big mirasidars and merchants in the valleys.[30] But this process had not gone very far. As a
result, other paddy-producing areas outside Tamilnad were able to

invade the market. They were able to produce rather more cheaply than the valleys' own careless system, and market more efficiently by exploiting the possibilities of bulk trading to the areas of concentrated demand.

The first of these external regions was the Andhra deltas to the north. Although a valley tract which was at least as productive as the Tamil valleys, the Andhra deltas were not saddled with the same society and production system. Until the British built irrigation works on the Kistna and Godaveri rivers in the 1860s, and Nellore district was equipped with wells and minor riverine systems in the later nineteenth century, the Andhra deltas were mostly too dry or too prone to flooding to support a dense and stratified society. The coming of secure irrigation brought prosperity and social change, but it did not create a mirasidari society. The land remained with enterprising cultivators driven along by the gains from the market and the demands of the most truculent labour force in the region.[31] By the turn of the century, the Andhra regions were sending rice by rail to Madras City and to Kongunad in increasing amounts. The rice differed little in price from that produced in Tamilnad but it was much better in quality—there was none of the careless and inefficient production associated with mirasidari supervision.[32]

Andhra rice was quickly followed by southeast Asian rice. In the Irrawaddy delta, which Tamil labour and Tamil Chetty capital helped to open up after 1852, the paddy acreage expanded from 600,000 to 8 million by the 1930s. The Mekong and Chao Phraya were only just behind. Thailand's rice acreage went from about 2 million to 7 million acres over the same period, while in Cochinchina the acreage grew from ½ to 2¼ million acres between 1880 and 1937. Burma was placing 2 million tons of rice in international trade by the end of the nineteenth century and Thailand and Indochina were not far behind.[33] These expansions brought virtually virgin lands into paddy cultivation. The costs of production were much below those in the exhausted soils of the Tamilnad valleys, and the keenness of marketing had all the marks of a frontier economy. In the 1930s it was calculated that paddy cultivation cost Rs 13 an acre in Burma and Rs 24 in Tanjavur, while the mark-up on every 160 lbs brought into the market was fifteen annas in the scattered marketing system of Tanjavur and eleven annas in the wholesale methods employed by the Burmese exporters. The rice produced in Burma was poor quality, often broken, and it competed directly with that grown in much of the Tamilnad valleys.[34]

By the 1870s, Burmese rice had started to erode Tamilnad's hold on the Ceylonese rice market, and by the early twentieth century had limited Tamilnad to about an eighth of the market—mainly the good quality strains and some coarse rice for the Tamilian labourers.[35] Increasing amounts of Burmese rice began to arrive in south India, principally on the west coast (which was usually supplied from the Kaveri and Tambraparni) and in Madras City. By the first world war, rice prices in Tamilnad were largely controlled by Burmese prices.[36] 'The price of rice in India', reported a gloomy mirasidar later, 'drops immediately a Rangoon steamer is sighted from the Indian coast.'[37] The import of rice in bulk also affected the style of marketing in Tamilnad. Entrepreneurs in the final retail markets started to build rice mills so that they could 'finish' the imported supplies to suit local tastes; the demand for rice that had already been milled fell away and by the mid-1920s many of the rice-mills which had been built in the Kaveri tract during the first world war were standing idle for much of the year.[38]

Thus even before the depression, the failure of the valleys to adjust to changing conditions of demand meant that they now faced the fact that prices and marketing methods were being dictated to them by imported supplies. There was downward pressure on rice prices in Asian markets from 1925 onwards but for a time local conditions obscured this trend; in 1925-6 there was a poor harvest in the Kaveri, and in 1926-8 there was a boom in migration to the Ceylonese plantations and thus an increased demand for rice exports.[39] But further east, large surpluses of rice in international trade were leading to intense competition, price-cutting and dumping. Japan, which was a large market for southeast Asian rice in the 1910s and early 1920s, had almost succeeded in procuring all its supplies from its own empire. Thailand and Indochina were successfully displacing Burmese rice in the Malayan market. The slump in sugar prices encouraged Javanese cultivators to grow rice instead, and thus closed the market there. These tremors precipitated an avalanche of market competition.[40]

Burma responded by shipping large amounts of cheap rice to Ceylon and India, particularly Madras City and the west coast. Rice from the Kaveri and Tambraparni valleys was quickly pushed out of the markets in Ceylon and on the west coast. In Madras City,

Burmese rice competed with supplies from the valley areas of Chingleput and the Arcots, and also displaced much of the supply from the Andhra deltas. The Andhra rice promptly sought a wider market in Salem and Coimbatore, where the Kaveri had hitherto commanded much of the demand. Then in 1927-8 Thailand and Indochina also began dumping cheap rice onto the south Indian market. In response Burmese rice moved further into the markets in the interior. In 1928-9 382,077 tons arrived from Burma and 6,416 from Indochina and Thailand, and the amounts swelled in subsequent years. Imports from Indochina and Thailand reached a peak of 80,327 tons in 1933-4, dipped for two years, and then shot up to 249,764 tons in 1939-40. Imports from Burma meanwhile rose steadily to a rough average of 700,000 tons a year in the second half of the 1930s.[41] It is difficult to judge what proportion of the market was supplied by southeast Asian rice; however when in 1943-5 the government attempted to monopolize the movement of rice above the level of the village, the quantity handled was in the region of one to one-and-a-half million tons in Madras Presidency.[42] The southeast Asian imports of the mid-1930s represented rather more than half this figure.

The price of rice in Tamilnad was weak in 1928, and in November 1929 it began a slide which continued, without serious interruption, for four years. At the bottom of the trough in mid-1933 the price was just half the level it had been before the harvest in 1929, and thirty-seven per cent of its level before the harvest of 1927. It did not show any significant rise until war was approaching in 1939.

Southeast Asian rice invaded the Tamil market as easily as it did for a number of reasons. It was, as we saw above, much cheaper to produce than Tamilnad rice. It was even much cheaper to transport. Freight charges were ridiculously low, initially because Japanese steamers calling to buy scrap-iron in Madras, and Tamilnad shippers taking cloth and other goods to southeast Asia, would offer very favourable rates to secure return-cargo, and later because the general recession of trade led to a rate-war among the major shipping companies. Since the Tamilnad rail network was still sparse, cart-charges fairly high, and rail-rates only low on the routes to and from the ports, it was cheaper to transport paddy from Rangoon to many of the interior parts of the province than it was to get it across country within Tamilnad.[43] Southeast Asian rice was cheap also because it arrived in large quantities and aimed mainly at

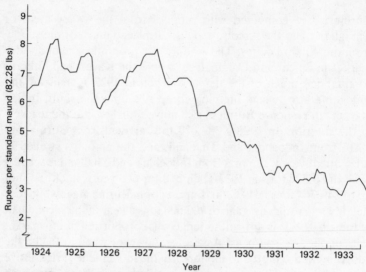

Graph 13   Monthly movements of rice prices 1924 to 1933

Note: Graph shows the movement of rice 'second sort' in Chingleput district.
Source: *A Statistical Atlas of the Madras Presidency.*

the concentrated markets in Madras City, Coimbatore and the west coast. Because of the wholesale, high-turnover nature of the trade, dealers would take smaller commissions and smaller profits per bag than was usual on the small consignments from the many *nellu mandis* of the valleys.[44] But the penetration was so easily achieved mainly because of the failure of the Tamilnad valleys to supply their old, and now expanding, markets—to increase production and to adapt the supply to the markets to match the new conditions of demand. Once southeast Asian rice was established in the Tamilnad market, it proved impossible to dislodge it, despite weighty political reasons and strong agitational pressure to do so. Throughout the early 1930s the mirasidars raised strong agitations for revision of the railway-rates, and a ban (or duties) on the import of rice.[45] Eventually the government made two revisions of railway-rates but they had little effect. A government-sponsored scheme to rationalize the system of marketing valley rice collapsed. A scheme for better dissemination of information on prices to growers and dealers was equally ineffective.[46] A duty imposed on imports of broken rice in 1935 had to be removed within a year when a poor season on the Kaveri threatened to create a serious shortage of supply,[47] while the disruption of the Burma supplies in the second world war (though other factors were also at work) caused a major crisis. [48] The 'boom' of the years 1880-1925 had clearly been created by the unwillingness of the valleys to supply an implicitly protected market.

Finally the penetration of foreign supplies was helped by the way in which the marketing of valley rice was disordered by the onset of the depression. As prices weakened and markets were stolen by imported supplies, the merchants and financiers, on whom the valleys' marketing network depended, withdrew their services. The bazaar bankers who provided most of the finance for holding stocks of rice became increasingly nervous in the later 1920s. By 1930 one Kaveri mirasidar could report that 'the old Nattukottai Chettiar', who had been the mainstay of paddy financing, 'is practically a vanishing factor in this business.'[49] By 1933 he had disappeared altogether; another mirasidar reported in 1933: 'Formerly there were Nattukottai Chetties who used to be given credits from the Imperial Bank and in their turn used to advance money to the millowners, thus facilitating the latter to do their business. All these failed. There was no credit at all.'[50] For a time the Marwari money-lenders remained. They made their best profits from charging penal rates of interest on loans which became overdue and normally the merchants and mirasidars only resorted to them in special circumstances. In 1929 and 1930 they did a lot of business. Yet soon their debtors found that they were ruined by their inability to meet the deadline for repayment, and the Marwaris themselves found their capital congealing in overdue loans which were profitable on paper but not in practice. By 1931-2 they had also withdrawn.[51]

Small mirasidars immediately found it more difficult to enter the paddy market when supplies of credit were so tight. Merchants and millowners were also obstructed and in 1931 it was reported that three-quarters of the rice-mills in the Kaveri were not working at all.[52] In both 1929-30 and 1930-1 several of the big mirasidars and merchants held up their stocks in the expectation that prices would rise towards the end of the agricultural year when supplies were usually short. But in each year the imports of Burmese rice prevented the upturn; prices slid steadily downwards (see graph 13). The big mirasidars and merchants were forced to unload stocks

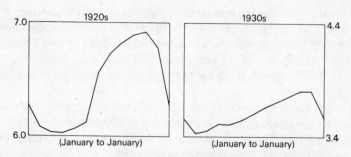

Graph 14   Average monthly movements of rice prices
in the 1920s and 1930s

Note: Units are rupees per standard maund (82.27 lbs); data are from
Chingleput; '1920s' is average of 1920-1 to 1929-30; '1930s' is average of
1930-1 to 1939-40.

Source: *Statistical Atlas of the Madras Presidency.*

at a loss at the tail of the agricultural year.[53] When government
made a cursory investigation of stocks of paddy held in the Kaveri
region in March 1933 it uncovered twenty-five millowners each with
stocks between 50 and 2,000 tons and an average of 543 tons, and
twenty big mirasidars with stocks between 30 and 1421 tons each
and an average of 573.[54] Only in 1934-5, a year of poor rains, did
prices achieve their normal seasonal fluctuation, and the difference
of the two decades of the 1920s and 1930s is obvious from the
profiles of the averaged monthly movement of rice prices (see graph
14). 'A large number of these people', noted a government report
on the big mirasidars and rice traders, 'came to grief during the early
part of the depression period as there was no rise in prices
subsequent to the stocking of the produce. This business has now
gone down considerably and the landlords do not take any risks by
handling any more stock than they themselves produce.'[55]

The valleys' rice trade stumbled through the 1930s. There was
nothing like a complete collapse but there was a general shrinkage.
Small mirasidars now found it difficult to get credit at reasonable
rates to enable them to play the market. Big mirasidars were badly
hit financially but survived because their reserves were good; yet
they retracted their activities and were reluctant to buy in supplies
and speculate. The urban merchants who had not lost their capital
and credit in the initial swoop of the depression did reasonably well;
they could not secure credit easily but, if they had their own funds,

'on account of the low price of rice they are able to turn out twice as much business as they used to for the same amount of capital'.[56] Thus more and more it was the independent urban merchants who came to dominate the market with the big mirasidars pushed back into a subsidiary role and the smaller mirasidars more or less excluded. The complex marketing system which had connected each valley region to each retail centre shrivelled up. There was still a complex market for the finer grades of rice, but the valleys' coarse rice was not able to dislodge southeast Asian supplies from the urban markets. Increasingly the valleys were feeding just them- selves and their neighbouring areas. The consequences would become clear in the 1940s. When the southeast Asian supplies were disrupted, government found that there was no marketing system to get the locally-produced supplies into the major urban markets in Tamilnad and there were threats of an urban famine unless government itself entered into the rice market.[57]

Cotton and groundnut in the plains

The two major commercial crops of the plains were cotton and groundnut. Both were grown in some quantity throughout the region but each had a specific, compact area where it was parti- cularly important. Groundnut dominated the Arcots plains where, by the 1920s, it occupied about a third of the acreage. Cotton was grown in the far south, particularly on the black-soil tract between Madurai town and the Tambraparni basin. Here too it was over a third of the acreage by the 1920s. In both cases, production on this scale was a relatively new development, dating from the 1880s, and was absolutely dependent on foreign encouragement. Acreage had expanded in parallel with the penetration of foreign commercial influence and foreign firms dominated the marketing of the crop. In the case of groundnut the most important companies were Rallis, a Greek company, Volkarts, a Swiss company begun in 1881 and established in Madras in 1888 and, for a short time, Madras City's premier British agency-house, Parry's. Both Parry's and Volkarts entered upon groundnut commerce in order to expand their export business to match the scale of their import business, so that they should not, in the precarious world of late nineteenth-century trade and finance, get caught by a vicious swerve of the terms of trade with all their capital tied up in moving goods in one direction only.

Their main interests were elsewhere—Parry's were an established agency-house, Volkarts imported steel and exported cotton—although for Rallis and Volkarts groundnut became their most important concern in south India.[58]

The cotton business dated back to the building of the 'cotton road' down through the southern districts to the port of Tuticorin.[59] The business expanded in the American war boom, and matured in its aftermath. In the fall of demand that followed the American war boom, several of the export firms built powered ginning factories in the hope of improving the quality of their product and thus gaining a better international market. In Tuticorin, Volkarts built a gin in 1876, A.& F. Harvey followed a couple of years later and then Dymes & Co; while elsewhere Rallis built gins in Sattur, Virudhu-nagar, and Tirumangalam. Harveys then built the first spinning-mill of the region at Papanasam in 1883, five years later another at Tuticorin, and the next year one at Madurai. Other mills started up in the early twentieth century, but by this time Harveys' operation was one of the biggest in the entire Indian cotton industry, and Harveys dominated the cotton market in the tract. The ginning factories of Harveys, Dymes, Volkarts, and Rallis supplied the Harveys' mills and also a steady export trade in raw cotton.[60]

The rapid growth of the export trade and the domination of foreign interests helped to ensure that the method of marketing cotton and groundnut by-passed the existing pattern of local markets.[61] The foreign firms did not operate through the shandies but helped to set up marketing channels of their own. In the case of both cotton and groundnut the foreign firms were prepared to push considerable amounts of finance into the local market in advance of the harvest to ensure that the crop could be purchased and moved to the port (or mill) with comparative ease. As we have already seen, the firms either shipped their own funds to India, or borrowed locally from the European-owned banks in India. In the early years—in the American war boom for cotton and in the initial phase of groundnut expansion in the 1880s—the foreign firms were prepared to lend forward finance right down to the level of the village. But they soon discovered that this was a very insecure practice and settled instead for lending to town merchants.[62] This practice led to the growth of market-towns as bulking centres and commercial entrepôts. In the case of groundnut, the export firms advanced money to established local merchants who bought in the crop, often shelled the nuts, and stored them in godowns until they could be moved to the port. These merchants were known as shedmen. Sometimes they were effectively only commission agents and operated entirely on the firms' capital, but more usually they merely used the forward finance provided by the exporters to supplement their own capital. The international groundnut market was very irregular because of the many different areas of supply. The export firms would generally wait until they could gauge the state of demand and price in that year, and then place forward contracts, with finance attached, for the supply of a certain quantity on a certain date at a certain price. The merchants would buy in and store to meet these contracts and also to cover any urgent demands which might arise in the course of the marketing season.[63] These bulking markets were all spread along the railway lines. There were ten of these towns in the Arcots tract and they were all growing rapidly through the turn of the century.

In the case of cotton, the four ginning centres—Tuticorin, Virudhunagar, Sattur, and Tirumangalam—became virtually the sole centres of the cotton trade until the first world war. Harveys and the export firms bought cotton in these four markets almost exclusively on forward contracts. Here the crucial men were the kapas-dealers. The European firms usually bought kapas (unginned cotton) direct from the kapas-dealers[64] and then ginned it either in their own gins or, under lease, in their colleagues' gins; alternatively the firms put out a contract to a ginning factory to suppply them with lint on a specific day and the factory then dealt with the kapas-dealers. The ranks of kapas-dealers were dominated by the Nadar community. There were also several Kammas, whose community dominated the business of growing cotton in the far south, but the overwhelming number of them were Nadars. They had started in the nineteenth century as upcountry agents and carters for the European firms. Towards the end of the century four Nadar families had come to monopolize the business of supplying kapas in Tuticorin, while in Virudhunagar ten Nadar families, which were already established in local trade and finance, moved wholesale into the cotton trade. These premier Nadar families, and others in the markets of Sattur and Tirumangalam, were linked by marriage ties and caste institutions.[65] In his famous work on the Nadars (Shanars) in 1849, Bishop Caldwell reckoned that there were roughly twenty of these trading families and that they were substantially richer than

their caste-fellows.[66] As Hardgrave has shown, they built fortified
pettais from which to carry on their trade, established staging posts
down the main carting routes, and levied a communal tax to support
this commercial infrastructure.[67] In Virudhunagar they consciously
modelled their financial activity on that of the handful of resident
Nattukottai Chettiars, and it was the marriage of this financial base
to the trading agencies stretching out from Tuticorin which gave the
Nadars their dominance of the cotton business. It was no coincidence
that the European exporting firms built their gins in the towns
already occupied by the Nadar traders, and both sides profited. The
opening of the railway in 1876 made Virudhunagar the most
important of the cotton towns and the chief centre of Nadar
business.[68] Between 1871 and 1911, its population quadrupled,
while Sattur and Tirumangalam also grew faster than other towns in
the region (tripling and nearly doubling respectively). By the first
world war, the annual turnover of the Tuticorin market was 60,000
bales (of 400 lbs), that of Virudhunagar and Sattur 35,000 bales and
that of Tirumangalam 10,000 bales.[69]

Although the groundnut shedmen and the cotton kapas-dealers
were tied down by forward contracts and liberally provided with
forward finance from export houses and local bankers, they made
little attempt to lend money into the villages to ensure cultivation
and to secure a hold on the crop. This was largely because for the
town merchants, almost as much as for the foreign firms, the plains
countryside was an alien and commercially dangerous place. It was
not really possible to secure loans on landed or other forms of
property, partly because the property held so little real value and
partly because the legal system provided no easy method to
substantiate any such contract. There was thus a hiatus in the
marketing structure. It was not that the lower level of the market
did not need finance. In the case of both groundnut and cotton the
harvest required a considerable cash outlay; day-labourers had to
be hired and paid in cash; carters had to be hired and paid in cash;
the petty produce of many different cultivators had to be brought up
and amalgamated. The finance for cultivation, harvest and primary
bulking was found in the locality and only very rarely came from the
marketing network. Such finance was usually marshalled by a
village dealer, who was usually the local shopkeeper, perhaps a
professional rural money-lender, and most often simply a substantial cultivator. These dealers often lent out sums midway

through the cultivation system with stipulations about delivery of the crop, and perhaps also with devices to ensure that they could buy the crop at a premium. Village-dealing was a pivotal role, with enormous opportunities for profit, but it depended on a unique blend of skills. Since it required some ability to judge the risks of cultivation and to gauge the creditworthiness of the debtor cultivators, it was generally only a local cultivator with good standing who could take on the job. But the village dealer's role also required some knowledge of the market and some skill in getting a good deal from the shedman or kapas-dealer. The most successful took a considerable interest in the state of the market, and perhaps themselves took the crop to the market town. In the process they might build up contacts in the town and thus find that they could, on the necessary personal security, borrow· funds from indigenous bankers and so expand their operations at the village level. Some even passed into the ranks of urban trade, and got involved in building groundnut decorticators and cotton gins. It was difficult if not impossible for a town merchant to move down the marketing chain into this role, but it was not impossible for the village dealer to go the other way.[70]

Even so, for the most part the village dealers seemed content with a more limited role. Most of the crop in the far south and Arcots' groundnut tracts was sold in the village. At the harvest, and sometimes just before, the town merchants—shedmen and kapas-dealers—sent out agents to buy up the crop from the village dealers. Several reasons were given why the village dealers were, for the most part, happy to sell in the village rather than going themselves to the market-town where, it might be thought, they would have a chance of securing the best possible price. The first reason was that the countryman's distrust of the town was often just as strong as the town-dweller's uncertainty about doing business in the rural areas. Many a farmer believed that if he went to market 'the buyers combine so cleverly that for all the trouble he takes he gets a meagre price'.[71] The second was that the market, being so dominated by foreign demand, was known to be rather inflexible. Although there was considerable competition between rival merchants to control the flow of produce from field to port, so far as the cultivator was concerned the price and the volume demanded were fixed by remote processes in foreign markets and there was nothing he could do to alter the fact. He could trust to the competition between

merchants to ensure that he himself got a reasonably good deal, but
could expect no speculative advantage from trying to play the
market. In the case of the far-south cotton tract, the market had
become very steady by the early twentieth century. The demand,
dominated by Harveys, was very regular. The supply too was
comparatively regular since there was no serious alternative to
growing cotton as a commercial crop in the black-soil tract. In the
case of both cotton and groundnuts there was little advantage to be
gained from holding the crop in the village and seeking to time the
sale to the best advantage.[72] Groundnut required moisture at the
end rather than at the beginning of its cultivation period and was
harvested in the monsoon. It was difficult to store the nuts and to
protect them against the rains and they soon deteriorated if they got
damp.[73] The groundnut was thus cleared out of the village very
quickly at harvest. As for cotton, the picking season was long and
again storage was difficult because of bulk and vulnerability to
damp and to pests. Both groundnut and cotton tended to be sold in
the village, immediately after the harvest, to agents and town
merchants.

Thus village dealers tended to try to expand their business, not by
penetrating the upper levels of the marketing system, but rather by
elaborating their network for securing the crop in the village. It was
generally the substantial cultivators, who were accustomed to
lending in cash or kind to their lesser neighbours, who emerged as
the village dealers. In the early twentieth century many people
commented on the rate at which money-lending within the villages
was growing in the plains tract. Estimates of the proportion of
cultivators who were in debt ranged between seventy and ninety-
five per cent.[74] Resettlement parties working in the groundnut tract
in the 1910s and 1920s all reported that the debt per head and debt
per acre were growing one-and-a-half to two times faster than
prices.[75] Credit expanded as more and more village dealers became
known in the urban market and were able to borrow extra funds
from the indigenous bankers. The growth of debt in this case was
not evidence of a peasant economy sinking under the predatory
weight of the rapacious money-lender, but of rapid growth of a
commercial economy.

In the period from the first world war to the mid-1920s the plains
markets were exceptionally prosperous and this prosperity caused

significant changes in their operation. In the case of groundnut, it created a sellers' market. The value of groundnuts exported from the province had risen from Rs 17 lakhs in the 1850s to Rs 1.19 crores by 1890 and touched Rs 14 crores in the best years of the 1920s. In the 1920s the price was fifty per cent above the pre-war level and estimates of the clear profit on an acre of groundnut cultivation ranged up to Rs 60.[76] Trade in groundnuts was so profitable that everyone wanted to be in on the business. In the growing tracts, almost anyone who made a profit from these boom years attempted to lend his surplus cash to increase production on neighbours' lands. In the bulking marts there was hardly a single businessman who had not put some capital into speculation on groundnuts.[77] While the majority of the trade was still dominated by the big agents and shedmen, there was a mass of part-time operators. In the towns of South Arcot there were two established systems—*kashtakootu* and *vasakkattu*—by which a businessman lent his excess funds to family and friends to deal in commodities, and in the 1920s such small dealers were in the groundnut market.[78] The big firms, the agents and the part-time speculators became so anxious to secure a decent share of the trade that they dropped many of their inhibitions about doing business in the countryside. The export firms such as Louis Dreyfus and Volkarts began, through agents, to offer advances to groundnut cultivators.[79] These funds were offered in the hope of extending cultivation and winning good will, and they were not at all closely tied to a contract to supply groundnut at the harvest. Town merchants also became more daring about lending in the countryside and before long the groundnut grower discovered that he could easily borrow money right at the start of the cultivation season; previously creditors would not lend out until two months before the harvest when the prospects for the crop were reasonably clear. A Tiruchi man listed the various sources of local credit: 'There are the agricultural moneylenders, the dealers of requisites [such] as leather and hardwares in rural markets, the brokers in the towns who advance money on the commercial produce, the retail village dealer who exports the produce, and a few Chetti shops here and there, a few nidhis and private or company banks, and lastly the co-operative societies which issue rural credit.'[80] There were so many agencies anxious to lend to the cultivator in the vague hope of securing the crop that the cultivator was able to raise credit with fewer strings attached than ever before. When he came to market the crop, again he was well placed. When the Banking Enquiry Committee asked a groundnut merchant if he believed the cultivators got a good price for their produce, the merchant replied gloomily: 'There is competition and as a result of it sometimes there is even a loss [for the trader].'[81] The cultivator still had no reason to leave his *pial* to sell his groundnuts, and if he did venture to the market-town he ran the risk of being manhandled by anxious traders. A government report later talked of 'the disorder that prevailed in the markets...such as using physical force in dragging groundnut carts and groundnut sellers by traders and their employees, every one to his premises, and thus creating all sorts of hubbub to the utter confusion of the stranger sellers from distant villages'.[82] Another observer in South Arcot noted that: 'The brokers meet the carts even on the road and try to take the carts to their respective mandi merchants, promising very often a good tiffin in a hotel, or offering some such temptation.'[83] In the bulking markets a new institution grew in importance. This was the *tharagu mandi* or brokerage market, where the village dealers, or commission agents working on behalf of the groundnut cultivators, brought their stock and put it up to auction before the competing ranks of shedmen and agents of export companies.[84] During the groundnut boom of the 1910s and 1920s even the smaller growers had the chance to secure relatively cheap and untrammelled credit and to get a pretty good selling price.

In the case of cotton, it was the *kapas*-dealers rather than the cultivators who rode the boom most successfully. Many of them made windfall profits during the first world war and its aftermath and attempted to use these to strengthen their position in the market. To do this, they built cotton gins in the outlying villages of the cotton tract. They aimed to intercept the cotton before it went to the European-owned gins, and thus to be able not only to take the profits from ginning but also to play the market for ginned cotton. In 1911 there had been just twenty-four ginning factories in the far-south cotton tract and most of these were owned by European export firms and concentrated in the four main market-towns. By 1921 the number of gins had risen to thirty-eight and by 1933 it reached 105. The additions were virtually all Indian-owned and were scattered through forty-six different towns and villages.[85] Many were built by Nadars and a few by the Kammas.[86] The Nadars also built new marketing yards, particularly in the black-soil tract, and the addition of new gins and yards altered the whole geographical pattern of marketing.

Whereas the average annual turnover of the four old marketing centres in the war-years had been 140,000 bales, and this represented ninety per cent of the local cotton business, by the early 1930s the turnover had fallen to 90,000 bales and represented roughly fifty per cent of the business. Tuticorin was no longer such a dominant market, Sattur's business had more than halved, and Tirumangalam had become a minor market. Only Virudhunagar survived, and this was largely because the wealth of the town was based on more things than the cotton trade and this gave it a foundation from which it could be transformed into a centre of the spinning industry in the critical years. Meanwhile seven new marketing centres of some importance, and seven other smaller ones, emerged and took over roughly half the cotton trade.[87]

The diffusion of markets was accompanied by a change in structure. The rising cotton-dealers who had established the new markets and built the gins were able to force better terms from the buyers. In 1924 they successfully forced the buyers to accept a code of business conduct.[88] But the dealers still needed to stay on the buyers' 'approved lists' and so had to maintain quality and meet forward contracts promptly.[89] They thus needed to build up an elaborate system of forward-financing designed to ensure that, in what was now a highly competitive market to secure kapas, they could find the supplies to meet forward contracts. In the 1920s, the dealers in the many markets lent, through sub-agents, large sums of money in the villages to try and secure the crops. Such loans helped to secure the crop, but they gave no guarantee of the price that the dealer would have to pay, nor did they get him any discount. There was such competition between rival ginners and rival markets that the growers—or at least those who assembled the crops in the villages—could be sure to get the appropriate price.[90] Ninety per cent of the cotton was still sold in the village, but under highly competitive conditions. In one survey it was found that each village had on average three large and six small dealers working as agents or contractors for the ginning markets.[91] The standard method used for deciding the price at which a cultivator (or his agent) sold the crop was an arcane system of secret negotiation conducted by hand-signals under a cloth; it was essentially a one-shot auction which put considerable pressure on the dealer anxious to meet a for-

ward contract and it was generally believed to favour the grower.[92]
In cotton just as in groundnut the 1910s and 1920s were good years
which saw profits percolate down through the layers of the market
to reach even many of the less substantial farmers of the plains.

The character of the 1920s boom in the plains' markets made
them specially vulnerable to the collapse of the 1930s. In both the
cotton and the groundnut markets, there were by the late 1920s
large numbers of speculative dealers and agents, working on small
amounts of capital and small percentages of profit, borrowing funds
from bazaar bankers and prosperous merchants, and attempting to
gain a larger stake of the market by lending daringly.[93] Prices of
both crops slipped downwards from the mid-1920s and then crashed
decisively from 1929. Yet from 1931 onwards the experience of the
two markets was rather different. The price of groundnut fell more
heavily than the general price index. By 1934 the price stood at forty
per cent of the level of the mid-1920s. There was some recovery in
the middle of the decade and then a secondary crash on the eve of
the second world war. The acreage under cultivation responded
very quickly to these price movements. Over one third of the
groundnut acreage disappeared between 1928-9 and 1934-5. On the
Arcots plain, the groundnut acreage was almost halved in this
period. From 1935 onwards, acreage recovered again and continued to grow after a slump on the eve of the war. In the early years
of the depression, groundnut was competed out of European
oilseed markets by supplies from Africa and the middle east,[94] and
only recovered its stake once as an agricultural student noted in
1935, 'the price of groundnut is so low that its cultivation is hardly
worth the trouble'.[95] In the case of cotton, the price fall was neither
so steep or so long-lasting, and the fall in the volume of demand was
very temporary. The simultaneous expansion of a local cotton
industry sustained demand for Tamilnad's cotton and throughout
the 1930s the cotton markets were active, even if the price was
depressed. The acreage under cotton also slumped at the onset of
the depression but this movement was no more dramatic than the
usual year-to-year oscillations of cotton acreage and the average
acreage in the 1930s was as high as in the previous decade. The
slump of acreage came later, during the second world war. The
differing profiles of price and demand had rather different effects
on the local markets.

For the Arcots' groundnut market, between 1929 and 1934 the turnover was roughly halved in volume and halved again in value. This sharp contraction quickly crumpled up the elaborate chains of forward financing. Export firms withdrew funds, joint-stock and bazaar bankers held back. All except those with substantial personal resources were cut out of the market. The commission agents, small-time traders, and speculative dealers who specialized in forward finance and relied on bazaar credit, were quickly removed from the marketing yards. The small cultivator who had sat independently in the village waiting for men to come with finance and offers to buy the crop was now immensely disappointed.[96] The towns which had acted as the principal bulking markets and which had grown spectacularly in size in the 1910s and 1920s stagnated in the 1930s.[97]

Out of the wreckage emerged a much simplified system of marketing. The number of export firms involved was greatly reduced. For instance, before the first world war there had been seven companies dealing in groundnut at the port of Negapatam— Rallis, Bests, Volkarts, Parrys, Gallois Montbaur, Kuppuswami Aiyar and Pernon Bayal; by 1933 there were only three—Rallis, Louis Dreyfus and the East Asiatic Company.[98] Parrys said they had withdrawn because the groundnut market was 'speculative in the extreme' and because they could not cope with the competition in international markets and the sharp fluctuations of prices for this product.[99] The few firms which remained took a much tighter grip on the market. To a large extent they now by-passed the bulking-centres altogether. They sent agents into the villages, bought the crop directly and arranged for transport straight to the port. They lent no forward-finance in the villages, except on the very eve of the harvest.[100]

The shedmen from the market-towns and their agents were also again reluctant to lend in the villages. Their share in the market was much reduced by the direct buying of the export firms and many of them went out of business. There was still a large number of people in all the market towns with some stake in the market but, as a government report noted in 1943, 'barring a few established traders in every market the rest cannot be considered to be permanently trading in groundnut'.[101] A survey in 1939 found 153 full-time groundnut dealers in the groundnut tract.[102] These dealers who survived the crash were now much less troubled by competition and they set to work to invest in ways which would recoup some of the decline in trading profits. In Salem there was an enormous increase in the construction of groundnut decorticating plants. In the southern part of Salem, for instance, there had generally been two new mills (designed not only to shell groundnuts but also to husk paddy and to gin cotton) built every year in the 1910s, and three a year in the 1920s. In 1929 twelve were built, in 1930 nineteen, in 1931 nine, in 1932 eleven, and in 1933 nine.[103] In five years of the depression, the number of decorticating plants in the region had more than doubled. In north Salem, meanwhile, there were only twenty mills in 1929, and another thirty were built in the next nine years.[104] In South Arcot, the dealers made an even more dramatic attempt to rescue their fortunes by technological innovations. Here they built groundnut oil-presses, hoping perhaps to divert some of the excess production of groundnuts to local consumption as domestic oil, and also to secure the profits of pressing the oil in India rather than allow this profit to fall to the European pressing factories. For a short time the strategy was moderately successful, and South Arcot was quickly flooded with small rotary oil-presses. But at the end of the decade, demand shrank and Hyderabad State, which had also invested in an oil-pressing industry, subsidized its export production and pushed Tamilnad groundnut oil out of the export market. In the last two years of the 1930s, over 100 oil-presses, each worth about 1,000 rupees, were sold off for scrap in South Arcot alone.[105]

In the case of cotton, the depression had a similar scything effect on the elaborate pattern of marketing. Here too the ultimate buyers, which in this case meant some export companies, one or two new cotton-mills and still, overwhelmingly, the Harveys spinning empire, took a stronger grip on the market. They cut many of the middlemen out of the marketing process and dealt directly with the growing tract. Many of the old ginning centres, both the original four and the later markets built in the 1920s, went into decline, while almost every village in the cotton tract emerged as a market where the agents of the buying companies dealt directly with cultivators and village dealers.[106] 'Primary markets,' noted a report on cotton in the late 1930s, 'are too numerous to mention for in almost every cotton-growing village are to be found active local buyers of cotton.'[107] Each market, both these new village centres and the remains of the old ginning markets, was dominated by a small number of merchants who managed most of the finance, and undertook all the functions of the market between grower and mill. They lent money to the villagers, bought and sold on their own account, and acted as commission agents for large growers who wished to sell direct to the ultimate buyers. In Sattur, which was still a fairly large example of these markets, there were just twelve of these businessmen, and one of them had far and away the biggest turnover. A study of six of these showed that they had an average capital of around Rs 35,000, sixty per cent of which was their own, and that they lent almost half of this in the villages. The most important dealer lent out a total of Rs 95,000.[108] In other areas, the domination of the market by a handful of firms was even more marked. The Virudhunagar market was dominated by ten firms, and these firms had developed a system of 'chain shops', which were really agencies reaching out into the smaller markets.[109] Similarly, three or four Nadar firms from Tuticorin had dominated the building of new markets in the villages of the Koilpatti tract to the north of the port.[110]

The strings of independent middlemen between grower and market, market and buyer had been squeezed out as prices fell and profit margins were cut. Indigenous bankers who provided most of the finance for such operations had, like indigenous bankers everywhere, got into difficulties at the onset of the depression, stopped lending, and withdrawn from the cotton trade. The extra finance needed by the dominant merchant firms was now provided by specialist institutions, and they lent only to the established firms which already had a high capital of their own. In Tuticorin, the Nadar Bank served this purpose. In Virudhunagar there were twelve specialist bankers concentrating entirely on the cotton trade.[111]

In the period from the first world war onwards, the commercial crop markets on the plains had proved very wayward and this character had been emphasized by the simple geographic instability of the place of sale. Towns had quickly boomed and then stagnated as the market had come and gone. The trading communities of this region reacted by seeking out forms of investment which would act as an insurance against the market's volatility. Although they might build gins and oil-presses to strengthen their hold on the commercial crop market, these investments often proved short-sighted. Thus they placed most emphasis on diversification. The cotton dealers and groundnut shedmen moved their own capital into sugar and alcohol businesses (a reflection of the Nadars' toddy-tapping connections), into general wholesaling and the growing business of retail agencies, into transport companies, and into small-scale factories making matches or some other mass consumer product.[112] These were mainly investments in local consumer industries and services; such businesses were more reliable and had a more visible market than the commercial crops which seemed at the whim of European mercantile fortunes. The plains tract thus sported many small towns, rather than a few large ones, and each town contained a wide range of small-scale enterprises.

The instability of the market emphasized the gap between town and countryside. While there were some local dealers and substantial cultivators who moved from the countryside into marketing and into urban occupations in the earlier period, by the 1930s this route had become much more difficult. The commercial crop markets were under the control of the export firms and major Indian merchant houses in the local towns, and it was much more difficult for substantial country-dwellers to raise the capital and forge the connections to enter into the marketplace. The difficulties of the 1930s were reflected in political tensions between countryside and town in the plains. Cultivators complained about the unreliability of merchants, the avarice of urban money-lenders, the upstart arrogance of successful urban communities; the townsmen talked of the backwardness and unresponsiveness of the countryside. From time to time these tensions erupted in political troubles. The 1930s saw a resurgence of the petty criminal activities which caused the British to label the Maravars of the far south and some of the Padaiyichis of the Arcots plain as 'Criminal Tribes'.[113] It also saw sporadic outbreaks of communal tensions which reflected the urban-rural division. In the far south there were incidents involving the urban Nadars and Rajus on one side with the rural Maravars and Vellalas on the other. On the Arcots plain there were Hindu-Muslim disputes; these often began among urban groups but sometimes spread to involve the largely Hindu countryside against the Muslims who were concentrated almost exclusively in the towns.[114]

Kongunad cotton

The history of cotton marketing in Kongunad was in bare outlines little different from the history of the commercial crop markets on the plains; there was a period of rapid expansion leading up to the depression and then a dramatic rationalization of the marketing pattern in the 1930s. But in detail the style of marketing, and in particular the relationship between cultivators and the market, was substantially different. The Kongunad market was much more speculative than the cotton market in the far south and the cultivators took a much more active interest in the business of marketing. The depression did not deepen a rift between urban merchants and rural producers, but rather precipitated the cultivators into an even closer involvement in the urban end of the cotton business.

The involvement of Kongunad cultivators in marketing was in large part a development of well-established local practices. The independent-minded Gounder cultivating households had usually marketed their own produce at the shandy; it was traditionally the role of rural women to manage the marketing. But the involvement in cotton marketing was encouraged by the particular character of the market. Most of the profit on producing cotton in Kongunad was to be gained by selling at the right moment and thus cultivators rarely left this business to merchants.

Until the 1890s there was no organized cotton market in the Kongunad tract. Local produce was either ginned and pressed in four local factories and then railed to Madras, or it was taken down by cart to the nearest markets (usually Dindigul) in the far-south tract.[115] In the early twentieth century, the discovery and spread of the Cambodia cotton variety completely transformed the position. The Cambodia plant produced a long-staple cotton which was in rising demand in Bombay and the markets of Britain and Europe. It was grown not only on the black-soil tract, where there were no serious alternatives as a cash-crop, but on the red soils under streams, channels, wells or even on a gamble on the south-west monsoon.[116] As such, it competed for space in the fields and well-gardens with a number of other commercial crops—sugar, tobacco, plantains, oilseeds, and various spices and vegetables. In such a tract, the supply of cotton was liable to vary from year to year according to the weather and also to the price relative to those other crops.[117] In the 1910s and 1920s the proportion of the net sown area under cotton in Kongunad fluctuated between about ten and twenty per cent.

Those who wanted to secure the Cambodia cotton crop had to send agents into the tract to encourage cultivation and convince the cultivators that there was a good profit to be made. The first to promote Cambodia was the firm of Binnys which owned two spinning mills in Madras City.[118] By the time of the first world war, export companies had also moved into the tract. Then during the war, the Bombay mills enjoyed a sudden surge in demand to supply both the gaps in the home market for cloth vacated by the belligerent states of Europe, and also indents for military supplies for the British government. In 1916 thirty Bombay merchants descended on the Kongunad tract looking for new sources of raw material. They were so anxious to expand production that they went round the villages with bags of rupees handing out loans to any one who would promise to grow and deliver some Cambodia cotton.[119] By the end of the war, cotton occupied a third of the sown area and had roughly doubled its coverage in a quarter of a century.

The Bombay merchants settled their headquarters at Tiruppur, one of the small ginning towns in the heart of the cotton tract, and succeeded in making it the chief, and indeed virtually the sole, market for cotton in Kongunad until the late 1930s. Tiruppur grew from a small town with a river-crossing, rail-junction, railway station and 6,000 inhabitants at the turn of the century, to a marketing centre of 18,000 people in 1931 and 52,000 by 1951. It was easily the fastest growing town in Tamilnad in the first half of the twentieth century. Several gins were built in Tiruppur during the first world war, and several others were built in villages in the cotton tract. But only Tiruppur emerged as a market.[120]

This was because Tiruppur became the centre of speculative interest in Kongunad cotton. The supply of cotton, as we have seen, was very variable because of the susceptibility to changes in the weather and because of the possibility of substitution by other crops. The demand too was extremely erratic. Even after the arrival of the Bombay merchants, Tiruppur still supplied some cotton to Madras and to the export trade. Nevertheless it was the demand from Bombay which set the style for the market. The Bombay merchants were not regular purchasers and they did not buy on contract nor, after the initial profligate enthusiasm, push out much forward finance. Rather they bought on the spot. During the war years and after, the Bombay merchants were using the Kongunad market to top up the supplies of raw cotton from Bombay's usual catchment areas in Maharashtra and Gujarat. The merchants purchased, on telegraphic order from brokers or millowners in Bombay, usually at no more than fifteen days notice. The Bombay market itself was erratic and speculative; there were a large number of supplying markets and a large number of competing mills; stocks could be built up and dissipated very quickly and both the price and volume of demand for raw cotton could alter quite suddenly. At Tiruppur, which was right at the fringe of Bombay's supplying system, these characteristics were exaggerated. After 1922, when the Bombay textile industry went into a long-term decline, Tiruppur's supplies were channelled more towards Madras and the expanding local mill industry. But the early years had set the pattern of marketing. Besides, the new mills which appeared in the south were small and their mutual competitiveness helped to sustain Tiruppur's character as a speculative market. There was some growth of forward contracting in the late 1920s, but the majority of contracts were still made on the spot. Prices could thus still move quickly and spectacularly; if there were dealers anxious to make rapid purchases because they were committed to forward contracts the price could be pushed upwards, if there were none it would fall.[121]

Before long Kongunad cotton-growers developed a keen sense of the market. In their occasional bursts of enthusiasm to assist agriculture, the Madras government would hatch schemes for spreading market intelligence in the interior, but were regularly forced to scrap such schemes when they discovered that even in the most remote villages of Kongunad the cultivators had weekly, if not daily, information about the Bombay market.[122] The Kongunad growers by and large kept themselves free of those debts which amounted to a mortgage on their cotton crop and which committed them to sell at someone else's leisure. Indeed they found the cultivation of Cambodia so profitable that they called the crop 'Marvadi Paruthi', or the 'money-lending cotton', and sang its praises most fulsomely:

Raising an acre of Cambodia cotton is as good as insuring oneself for an income of Rs 100 per annum and such a steady annual income is bound to revolutionise his [sic] economic position. If you want to clear your debts, raise cotton; if you desire to free yourself from the clutches of your village sowcar, grow cotton. If you like to celebrate the marriage of your son and daughters, without borrowing, grow cotton. If you want two square meals a day, and enjoy the fruits of your hard labour and lead a contented life, grow cotton. If there is a Kamadhenu [a mythological cow which supplies every want] on earth it is cotton and cotton alone.[123]

Thus a significant number of cultivators loaded their cotton onto country carts and brought it into the Tiruppur market yard themselves. In 1919 a sample survey showed that a third of the cotton sold in Tiruppur was brought in by cultivators; most of them had brought not only their own crop but also that of their neighbours.[124] Yet in the market they still required the services of a commission agent who understood the workings of the market, was sensitive to the fluctuations of demand, and could help the grower secure the best deal. The Tiruppur market yard was soon swarming with such agents. Often it was also necessary to hold the cotton at the market-place in order to wait for the opportune time to sell. Thus a number of the agents built godowns where, for a fee, the cultivator could store the cotton until the agent felt it was the right time to sell.[125] These commission agents built up close relations with different villages in the growing tract. Indeed many of the agents originally came from the cultivating villages and cultivating communities. Once the growers felt they could trust these agents to look after their interests, then they no longer felt it necessary to come to the market yard themselves. They could send the cotton kapas to the agent, perhaps with a stipulation about the minimum selling price, and either leave the rest of the transaction to the agent's discretion, or remain in constant telegraphic contact with the agent about the state of the market. By the late 1920s, according to J.S. Ponniah, ninety-five per cent of the cotton kapas were sold in the market by commission agents and only five per cent directly by the cultivators. Yet this did not mean that the cultivator had abandoned his control over marketing. The agent was usually working on his strict instructions.[126]

Soon many of the villages in the cotton tract acquired their own small cotton ginning factories. There were five gins in Coimbatore district in 1911, forty-seven in 1921, ninety in 1933 and 149 in 1941.[127] These gins were generally built by substantial growers and occasionally by local merchants. They enabled the cultivators to sell their cotton as lint rather than kapas and thus gain the extra value-added from the ginning process. Some cultivators would merely take their kapas to the local gin, pay a fee to have it processed, and then sell in the usual manner. In other instances, the gin owner became another link in the marketing chain. He would take over the crop, put it through the gin, and then send it to his commission agent at Tiruppur. Occasionally he might buy the crop from the cultivator before ginning, but usually he merely worked on a commission basis.[128]

For the cotton growers and local gin-owners to play the market in this fashion, there was a need for considerable sources of local finance. Soon after the Cambodia market got under way, Nattuk-kottai Chettiar bankers settled in Tiruppur and Coimbatore in large numbers and were joined by Marwari and Multani bankers from north India. They specialized in lending against stocks of cotton held in the Tiruppur market. The business seemed so secure that before long the joint-stock banks also became involved;[129] this was unusual since in most of south India the joint-stock banks were reluctant to lend directly on agricultural produce. All these agencies still did not meet the demand for finance, and the gap was filled by a form of co-operative bank known as the nidhi. These institutions, which will be described in more detail in the next section, were a development from local savings funds. They acted as a store of savings for traders and professional men in the locality, and they were often used by traders and growers who wanted to raise short-term loans against stocks of cotton deposited in the market. By 1930 there were about 125 of these nidhis in Coimbatore district with an estimated total capital of two crores of rupees. Not all were connected to the cotton trade, but many of them were and their mushroom growth in this district alone in south India was clearly connected to the expansion and to the special character of the Tiruppur cotton market.[130]

In the late 1920s, just as in the case of other commercial crops, the bullishness of the market saw an expansion of forward financing and a swelling of the ranks of speculative dealers. A number of commission agents transformed themselves into brokers by raising their own capital and trading on their own account. Again as in other crop markets, the depression rationalized the marketing system. Many of the sources of liberal credit simply disappeared. Of the fifteen bazaar banking firms operating in Tiruppur in the late 1920s, not one was still in business a decade later. Most of the nidhis either collapsed or withdrew. Next, the Bombay merchants, who had helped to establish the Tiruppur market and had dominated its early years, now closed up shop and went home. They had been declining in importance through the 1920s and the combined effects of the price-fall and labour troubles in the Bombay mills finally precipitated their departure. Their role as the main buyers in the Tiruppur market had been gradually taken over by the forty cotton-brokers who had emerged from the ranks of commission agents, and by the twenty owners of ginning factories in Tiruppur town. However, a number of these new buyers did not survive the depression. By 1934 the brokers had lost their important role as purchasers and by the end of the decade only two of them were left. Similarly the number of gin-owners had been reduced to sixteen, and only twelve of them were of any importance. Along the same lines as the other crop markets, the depression left Tiruppur under the domination of a small number of powerful mercantile institutions. The twelve major gin-owners were now the most important purchasers, and they acted as the channel for a good deal of the market's finance, which now in the absence of the nidhis and bazaar bankers came almost exclusively from the joint-stock banks.[131]

But this rationalization of the market did not distance the cotton cultivators. Indeed many of them reacted to the disruptions of the depression by moving more firmly into the market and into the textile business. In the 1930s, a number of substantial Kongunad families, who already had interests in growing cotton and who had developed interests in the cotton market, now started to build cotton mills. This was a rational and far-sighted decision. Textile mills were a relatively cheap investment, and the collapse of the local cotton trade meant that there were considerable amounts of idle capital in the region. The expansion of Cambodia cultivation had provided a source of raw material, while the market had been temporarily opened up by the disruption of Bombay's textile output and the implicit protection of the depressed state of foreign trade. There were five mills in Kongunad in the 1920s and thirty-six by 1940. Most of them were built by some combination of Kamma and Gounder rural families with Chettiar bankers, urban professionals, and the remaining two Bombay merchants.

Other substantial cultivating families moved more definitely into the role of cotton ginners and traders. With the collapse of the brokers and the indigenous bankers, certain rural entrepreneurs began to take a more active role in providing the finance and organization to get the cotton crop into the market and to wring a good deal out of the purchasing agents. Often these were the owners of local cotton gins.[132] Surveys of Kongunad villages in the depression found that there were still good supplies of local credit for cultivation and much of this came from the local cotton gins. In other cases, the finance for production and marketing was found from co-operative societies. The government had, by 1930, been promoting co-operatives for a quarter of a century and only in Kongunad had they had any substantial degree of success. The societies were not 'co-operatives', properly speaking, but they did provide a device through which members could borrow funds quite cheaply from the government. There were several sorts of society which flourished in Kongunad. One was the seed society, which grew up with the spread of the Cambodia cotton plant. Cultivators delivered their crop to a co-operative society which ginned the cotton and returned the seeds to the cultivators so that they could plant a pure strain in the coming year without resorting to the seed-dealer. There were four of these societies in the Tiruppur tract in the 1930s and their annual turnover of business had risen to Rs 20 lakhs by the end of the decade. These seed societies often organized the sale of the lint, though this was usually the province of the other sort of co-operative organization, the loan-and-sale society. These institutions lent to cultivators during the growing season, then took over the crop at harvest and managed the business of sale. The society not only had the advantage of dealing in bulk, but it also provided a means for raising the credit to hold the crop in the market until the price was right. These societies had started up in the 1920s and by the early 1930s there were twenty of them in the rural areas around Tiruppur.[133]

The cultivators, local gin-owners, and co-operative societies still sold directly in the market. Indeed after 1934 they almost always sold directly to the Tiruppur gins or to the agents of the new cotton mills. A survey in the late 1930s reckoned there were 537 dealers in the Tiruppur cotton market, most of whom can have been no more than substantial cultivators and local commission agents,[134] and a survey in the 1950s reckoned that the proportion of cotton sold directly in the market by the cultivators themselves had risen to a half.[135]

The expansion of the local mill industry sustained the increase in the demand for Cambodia. In the late 1920s about a third of the cotton grown in the Madras Presidency went to supply mills within the province (mostly Harveys and Binnys) and by the end of the 1930s the proportion had risen to two-thirds. If Cambodia alone is considered, the rise was from about fifty to ninety per cent.[136] Estimates of the yield and consumption of Cambodia, even though the figures are very rough, show that the demand rose faster than the supply in the second half of the 1930s.[137] New primary markets grew up in the Kongunad countryside but these did not undermine Tiruppur's position; Coimbatore emerged as a market for the cotton imported to cover the local shortfall in the supply to the Kongunad mills, and new markets at Pollachi, Udumalpet, Gobi-chettipalaiyam, Dharapuram, and Erode grew up to supply specific small mill-centres on the fringes of the Kongunad tract. Tiruppur remained firmly at the centre of the cotton trade, and it was clearly dominated by the families of rural Kammas and Gounders in the roles of producer, trader, and now industrialist.[138]

The major crop markets showed a similar trend, though great differences of detail, in the early twentieth century. From the 1880s through to the first world war and the 1920s they enjoyed a boom based at least in part on foreign demand. The systems and institutions of marketing which emerged to meet this demand were fundamentally new. For the most part they were elaborate and disorganized. It was open for any entrepreneur to find some niche in the marketing process whether as a broker, carter, or commission agent, and the chains of marketing lengthened as the prosperity of the market increased. The business of marketing attracted finance from many sources—foreign firms, joint-stock banks, bazaar money-lenders, urban and rural traders, cultivators themselves—and to-wards the end of the boom it was relatively easy for any cultivator or trader to secure finance, perhaps at a good price, but without uncomfortably extenuating conditions. The markets were thus characterized by a large number of small operators—growers, agents, dealers—operating on small sums of personal capital, large amounts of borrowed capital, small margins of profit, and high rates of turnover. Such a system was peculiarly vulnerable to the slump in prices and the slump in the volume of trade in the late 1920s. The systems of marketing were rationalized and restructured. Although none of them collapsed completely, and although the mass of small dealers would return as soon as there was credit and opportunity, the depression did see a concentration of control over the market by a small number of commercial and financial institutions. At the same time, the major destination of most of the goods marketed ceased to be the international markets in east or west, but was increasingly the home market. Supplies of paddy were completely absorbed by local demand, groundnut was diverted to local oil-pressing, oilcake and hydrogenation industries, cotton went more and more to the nascent mill industry in the region. The towns of the tract were being gradually transformed from entrepôts in the overseas-oriented marketing chain, to centres of industrial and domestic consumption for rural produce.

This altered the relationship between countryside and town, and altered the relationship of rural marketing with the government. The detailed pattern in each market was very different. The valleys' paddy had become a secondary source of supply for the province's towns and when the primary supply (from southeast Asia) was cut off in the war, then government had to step in to procure valley production and move it into the towns. The plains market came more and more under urban control, with a consequent growth in urban-rural tension, and with a new readiness on the part of the government to take a regulatory role. The Government of Madras passed a Commercial Crops Marketing Act in 1933 and started to put it into operation with the building of marketing yards and formation of marketing committees in the groundnut and cotton tracts in the later 1930s. The aim of this Act, and several subsidiary pieces of legislation, was to provide a state-controlled institutional base for marketing commercial crops in order to regulate abuses in marketing, monitor the volume of turnover, and lay down rules about the quality of the product.[139] In the Kongunad cotton market, however, there was less incentive for government to take a hand. The market was less disrupted in the depression, largely because the producers themselves moved in and took a more substantial role in the whole of the cotton business.

Meanwhile there had been a massive crisis in the business of bazaar banking. From the 1880s to the 1920s, bazaar banking had provided the majority of the credit on which the whole marketing system operated. In the 1930s, it all but disappeared. In the early period, the profits of bazaar banking represented the most substantial accumulation of capital in the course of the produce boom.

What then became of this accumulation? We shall now have to look at the history of the creditor.

THE MONEY-MARKET

In the period leading up to the first world war there was an enormous growth in the volume and value of internal trade. Foreign demand was the prime mover of this expansion but many other factors contributed—the rise in population, slow but steady concentration in towns, the extension of the railway network and steady reduction of railway rates (from 54 pies a mile around 1880 to 8½ pies a mile in 1920),[140] the spread of prosperity among the rural elites. The expansion of export business, and the improvements in transport, stimulated local commerce as well. The number of shandies in southern Salem, for instance, increased from eighty at the turn of the twentieth century to 136 thirty years later.[141] Trade needed finance and this rapid extension of trade required an equally rapid growth of financial institutions. Of course external and internal trade were not at all new, but there was no sense in which they had over the years built up a firm institutional base. The European companies which had been involved in the ports of the Tamilian coast for over three centuries had done little to elaborate financial and commercial networks reaching into the interior. In the seventeenth century they had used the devices of the 'chief merchants' and dubashes to conduct business in the interior, and in the eighteenth and early nineteenth centuries these institutions had crumbled away.[142] When produce exports expanded in the second half of the nineteenth century, the export companies found that they had to import their own funds to finance the movement of goods from interior to port. Meanwhile the major internal trade routes, stretching from the Tamilnad interior over the Ghats to Mysore and the west coast, seemed to have even less institutional provision. Goods were carried on the bullocks of the gypsy-like Banjaras and Lambadis, and Buchanan, who has left the most extensive account of this trade, found no evidence of any substantial financial organization.[143] Thus the extension of the market in the late nineteenth and early twentieth centuries prompted a rapid expansion of financial institutions and financial networks.

The exchange banks which serviced European enterprises, and

the state banks (the Presidency banks, amalgamated in 1920 into the Imperial Bank, transformed in 1935 into the Reserve Bank) did not act as a primary source of finance for internal trade. They provided loans which reached the internal money market but then only by indirect routes and only through the mediation of men whose personal financial standing was well assured.[144] The initial sources of finance had to be found without the external economy's assistance. In this period there were only three groups which were accumulating savings on any significant scale—urban professionals, the elites of the countryside, and the bankers and merchants involved in trade.

The urban professionals were the least important of these groups, both in numbers and in volume of savings. Yet it is clear that the rise in the number of government servants, and the expansion of the legal profession, did create some significant stores of wealth. Much of this went into urban property but some at least was used more flexibly. Generally speaking it was stored carefully, in bank accounts and later in post office savings, and the early joint-stock banks found a large share of their investment among these groups.[145] Yet the apparent safety of such investment was badly undermined by the collapse of Arbuthnots, a major finance house in Madras, in 1907. While this crash suggested that the established banks were not as secure as advertised, the rising trend of inflation simultaneously encouraged urban professionals to find a more lucrative form of investment. The rapid inflation of the first world war, coupled with the evidence of speculative mercantile profits, pushed urban savings into new channels. Several Madras witnesses before the Indian Industrial Commission of 1916-18 noted that urban professional groups were really the only people willing to invest in joint-stock enterprises, and several of the most noted professional families in Madras (notably the Vembakkam Iyengars) were personally involved in the founding of Indian joint-stock banks and Indian joint-stock trading and manufacturing companies in the period between the Arbuthnot crash and the collapse of the post-war boom.[146]

Among the rural elite, wealth was clearly growing throughout the period. A good deal went directly into consumption—better houses, expensive ceremonial, donations to temples, pilgrimage tours—but even this was in some ways economically instrumental: such spending could (as long as the gentle boom continued) earn status, and status was a prerequisite for credit. Much more, however, went into buying insurance or into expanding enterprise. While some kept their hoard in a trunk under the bed, most found better ways to cushion themselves and their families against disaster. Buying land was, in some senses, an expansion of enterprise, but it was also a useful form of insurance. It was an asset which seemed to appreciate regularly, and it could be used as a security for raising funds up to fifty or even seventy per cent of its value in some places. Investment in gold or jewellery, meanwhile, was slightly less troublesome, was equally good as a security for raising loans, and provided even more of the characteristics of a life insurance policy:

There is always an inclination to make large presents of silver and gold vessels and ornaments on marriage and other occasions. This is due to the fact that these articles in specie will be ear-marked as those of the person to whom they are presented while presents in cash will get merged in the general assets of the family...and if the family is indebted the cash presented will be applied to bring about relief to the family from its general indebtedness...Further, owing to the right of survivorship obtaining under the law in Hindu joint families, the only resources available to the widow of a sonless deceased co-parcener are her jewels and vessels and naturally the sonless husband and wife are anxious to increase the investment in that form to save something for the widow in case of the husband's death without diversion. Also, in cases where the husband is a trader whose fortunes are uncertain, wife's jewels are a good savings bank on which the family can fall back when the creditor has taken away everything else of the trader's property.[147]

In this situation it is not surprising that as major agriculturists became steadily more involved in marketing, so investments in jewellery increased. In the 1890s, Nicholson wrote about Coimbatore:

The following statement of a Goundan's mode of allotting his net profit is interesting, not as an exact statement, but as indicating the objects of expenditure, viz., one-eighth for charity, three-eighths for gold and silver ornaments (a mode of hoarding), one-fourth for buying land, and one-fourth hoarded. The records of trials and complaints show that a good deal of silver is secreted in the walls of houses etc.[148]

Many rich agriculturists placed their savings in productive enterprises but the results often did not encourage any expansion in this form of investment. Cultivators involved in growing and trading commercial crops naturally thought of investing in processing factories but in many cases they found that their knowledge of the market was imperfect and their calculation of its stability was sadly misjudged. In only eight years around the first world war some 7 lakhs of rupees were sunk in the construction of powered rice mills in the Kaveri delta, but before long the rural entrepreneurs discovered that their enthusiasm had been misplaced; there were now too many rice-mills, and anyway the demand for milled rice was falling away and being replaced by a demand for unmilled paddy, and thus few of the rice mills could be run at a profit. Those cultivators in the far-south who invested in cotton gins in the 1920s, and those on the Arcots plain who invested in groundnut decorticators in the 1930s had similar experiences. Moreover, these were investments in processes situated close at hand and allied to the agriculturist's own activity. The rural elites also put money into urban-based businesses, and here the disillusion was even greater. A Tirunelveli landowner and lawyer, looking back from 1930, noted:

Like South Sea Bubble many short-lived and never-to-be-started-with companies are started and people's money to a large extent has been wasted if not actually swindled. The Arbuthnot, Alliance [another company that crashed], the sale of the Koilpatti and Mysore Tanneries, and scandals about the Tinnevelly sugar and failure of a Chettiyar and the insolvency of the so many indigenous banking agencies, rightly, I think, make the people think twice before they put their money in the hands of unknown institutions with their headquarters in distant places. Further the callousness of those who swindle and live a life of waste deters any simple-minded agriculturist from having anything to do with so-called banks and insurances, industrial companies and indigenous banks.[149]

In these circumstances most of the rural elites stuck to local money-lending and dealing in commercial crops. 'As regards the money-lending individuals', one Kaveri dweller told the Banking Enquiry, 'they do not form a separate professional class. Roughly speaking all those who have spare money—ryots, merchants, retired officials, shop-keepers and vakils—lend it.'[150] In the prosperous years, many of the richer cultivators who dabbled in such money-lending in the normal course of events emerged as rather more elaborate local bankers; the same commentator continued: 'It is not unusual for a wealthy landlord to receive deposits of cash from widows, orphans or poor relatives, who have money to deposit and who require some trustworthy person to take charge of their money and also allow interest. The wealthy man receives these deposits not because he has need of them for his banking, or more strictly lending business, but because he inspires trust in this class of depositors and because it is more or less accepted in usage as a social obligation.'[151] It was generally reckoned that if the rich cultivators 'are not too avaricious and pay only an ordinary amount of care in choosing their customers, they can make higher profits in this rural banking than in any other business'.[152] Certain landowners found it so congenial that they allowed money-lending rather than cultivation to become their major activity. 'Fifty per cent of big landholders', reckoned one observer of North Arcot, 'have lent their savings to the other cultivators of the village and in the surroundings and eventually become the indigenous bankers of the village.'[153] They lent short-term to cover cultivation expenses, for rather longer-term for the expenses of a marriage or other family crisis, and they invested money in buying and holding produce destined for the market.

By far the most important stock of capital used in internal trade was generated within the commercial community itself. The demand for finance for internal trade was so strong that those who were prepared to take the risks of lending liberally and flexibly could earn a substantial profit. As a response to this demand, a number of banking groups severely modified their mode of operation. In the mid-nineteenth century the characteristic loan by an urban money-lender was a term-loan, secured on property, and earning between nine and twelve per cent interest.[154] By the first world war, mortgages had been replaced by pro-notes; borrowers did not wish to put their property at risk while speculating on the produce market, and creditors were not anxious to see their liquid capital solidify into land and thus preferred personal security. Term-loans had become more or less open-ended, since traders preferred to be free to play the market. In return for these facilities, the creditor could charge a higher rate of interest. The rate on pro-notes was generally over fifteen per cent and sometimes as high as thirty-six.[155] The rise had come about because the creditor was now taking more risks, because there was increasing demand for loans, and because, as a result of these two things, the creditor was more likely to be involved in legal proceedings to recover his loans and the legal process had not expanded in parallel. As one landlord and trader observed: 'The dilatoriness of the Civil Courts shows no signs of improving and it was said shortly after the War that the openly agreed rate of interest in Salem district had risen by no less than three per cent as an offset to the creditor to compensate him for this delay and added expense in seeking a decree and in the difficulty in executing a decree when obtained.'[156] There were high profits to be made by bankers who were prepared to take the risks involved in this system. A number of banking communities had devised procedures for coping with the demands of this style of banking and had accumulated large profits.

These groups had had to develop several specific devices. Firstly, they had to evolve methods for transferring funds between different markets. 'Owing to the paucity of banking organisations in many of the muffassal towns', noted one banker as late as 1930, 'the question of transfer of funds from one town to another is still a matter of great difficulty.'[157] Except between the few places which had an office of the state bank, postal money orders and insured post were the only official systems available for remitting funds and these were very clumsy to operate.[158] Secondly, they needed a procedure for fixing interest rates, and adjusting them in tempo with the fluctuations of the market. And thirdly they needed machinery to shuffle funds between different individual bankers so that they could share the risks involved in lending on such a fluctuating business as the crop markets and dissipate the risks of individual failures. Those banking communities which evolved these procedures soon did so well that they could attract deposits and later even borrow money from the formal banking sector to expand their business. An early bridge-head quickly opened up into a major territory.

There were a fair number of independent banking families among such communities as the Labbai Muslims, Nadars, Devangas, and Vaniga Chetties, but by far the majority of the indigenous bankers of Tamilnad came from two specialist banking communities—the Nattukottai Chettiars and the Kallidaikurichi Brahmans. There were many similarities in their growth.

Both, for instance, seem to have been involved in the cloth trade in the mid-nineteenth century and to have made a strategic transfer into produce-broking as the internal cloth market declined. The Nattukotai Chettiars claim a commercial history that takes them back to medieval times, when they were expelled from the Chola country and settled in a remote corner of Ramnad.[159] From then until the eighteenth century their history is mysterious. In the early nineteenth century they appeared as cloth-traders who extended their business in the wake of British expansion in Ceylon and southeast Asia, and moved into financing many of the growth-points of the new colonial economy around the Bay of Bengal: they financed the rice-trade to Ceylon, the expansion of the agricultural frontier in Malaya, Burma and Indochina, lent on trade in export-produce within Madras, and found their way to the commercial heart of British India in Calcutta. Their strategy was simple and remarkably effective. They lent mainly on the security of tangible assets (jewels, property), they provided only working capital and never contributed towards plant, and they chose businesses that were clearly expanding. They generally lent in small amounts and for short periods and because this meant a rapid turnover of business they could afford to be accommodating to their debtors over the exact date and manner of repayment; for this attractive service, they could charge a high rate of interest. They provided easy, but expensive, money. As they expanded, they evolved a suitable set of communal institutions. They had a council to fix interest rates, and a tribunal to sort out disputes without recourse to law. They evolved a system of agency which allowed an apprentice (generally a kinsman) to work for three years on the capital of the parent firm, in which time he either proved his unworthiness or made the necessary profits to become a banker (or partner) in his own right. They also developed a system for circulating money among Chettiar firms, both within southern India and across the Bay of Bengal, through agents known as *adathis* who worked as clearing houses for Chettiar bills in each of their major centres of business.[160]

By the 1890s it was reckoned that the Nattukottai Chettiar community, which consisted of some twenty to thirty thousand people, commanded a capital of some 10 crores of rupees, somewhat more than the annual revenue of the Government of Madras.[161] In the early twentieth century, they expanded their business much more rapidly outside India than within it.[162] This was largely because of the better opportunities provided by the expanding plantation-economies and rice-deltas in southeast Asia, but it was also due to the superior legal protection for lending that they found in countries outside south India. As one Nattukottai Chettiar told the Banking Enquiry:

Formerly we were doing much business here but owing to difficulty in recovery of loans and persons declaring insolvency, we have discontinued more or less our business here and extended our business there. There is also great complexity with regard to encumbrances, inheritances, etc. here...[In Burma] if you file a suit you can be sure of getting the decree within six months or at the most within eight months you can realise the money. I know in Southern India cases have taken ten years and sometimes even centuries to be finally decided. Even in the Munsifs' Courts cases are generally decided not earlier than five years.[163]

The faster rate of economic expansion and the better legal protection offered in southeast Asia as compared to Tamilnad meant a better rate of return. Nattukottai Chettiars reckoned that they could earn only eight to nine per cent return on their capital in south India, while in Ceylon the return was ten to twelve per cent, in Burma twelve to fifteen per cent, and in Malaya fifteen to eighteen per cent.[164] Naturally, by the end of the 1920s, most of Chettiar capital had gone in search of the higher rates; yet wherever it was used, it was clearly delivering a high return. Even at the south Indian rate, the capital could be doubled within eight years, and at the Malayan rate in less than five years. No one, then, was surprised at the estimates of the Chettiars' gross capital by this time.

The Nattukottai community in the 1920s numbered around 40,000, and according to tax returns there were 2,882 of them active in banking in south India (with branches abroad) and 1,600 based solely in Burma.[165] Estimates of their capital varied. The Assistant Commissioner of Income Tax reckoned that they had 50 crores of rupees invested in loans, $14\frac{1}{2}$ crores in houses and jewels ('in Devakottai alone there are said to be 300 houses costing not less than a lakh each...') and 15 crores in lands and plantations. Besides their own working capital, they had another 25 crores of loans and deposits. Of the resulting 75 crores, roughly 66 were in liquid investment, distributed geographically as follows: 23 crores in Burma, 20 in Malaya, 5 in Indochina, 10 in Ceylon and 3 in Madras.[166] Other, roughly contemporary, estimates differed very slightly, and in particular gave slightly higher estimates of Chettiar capital deployed in south India. V. Krishnan estimated the Chettiars had 75 crores of their own capital, supplemented by 9 crores from the Imperial Bank and 8 crores of other deposits and a total of 11 crores was used in Madras.[167] M.S. Natarajan inflated their total resources to 140 crores, with 75 in Burma, 25 in Malaya, 14 in Ceylon, 10 in Indochina and 16 in Madras.[168]

They had been helped to this extraordinary wealth by some particular windfalls. A large number of Indo-Burma Petroleum shares fell into their hands (as security for loans) just before the price of these shares rocketed in the years leading up to the first world war. A number of rubber plantations, acquired similarly as security on bad debts, multiplied in value up to ten times during the short time that the Chettiars held them. And they did very well out of financing the black market in rice during wartime controls in Ceylon.[169]

Although most of their business was outside India, in Tamilnad they continued, up to the early 1920s, to have a substantial stake in urban finance and also to lend a bit in the rural areas, though that was mostly confined to their home-region of Chettinad. In the towns, their activities ranged from the *kandu* hand-loans offered to shopkeepers and repaid on a daily basis at what amounted to huge rates of interest,[170] to large-scale financing of the trade in imported cloth.[171] They also lent considerably to produce-merchants, and often dealt in the hundis or notes of hand which traders used both as a pro-note for a simple loan and as a crude bill of exchange to cover a commercial transaction.[172]

One or two of the Kallidaikurichi Brahman bankers also took their business abroad, yet most remained in the province. They originated from an inam village in the Tambraparni valley, and up to the early nineteenth century had been involved in the trade over the Ghats to the west coast, particularly in cloth. Like the Chettiars, when foreign demand for cloth deteriorated, they moved across to financing the burgeoning trade in agricultural produce, and soon found this much more profitable. By the early twentieth century, the number of Kallidaikurichi Brahman banking firms was variously estimated at between 100 and 175, and their personal capital at between 5½ and 7 crores of rupees. They continued to do some lending in the villages of Tirunelveli and Ramnad, but most of their business was in the larger towns of southern Tamilnad—Madurai, Tuticorin, Tirunelveli, Tiruchi. Here they lent mostly in the short-term to produce-merchants, to allow the latter to acquire, hold and resell goods with very little personal funds. Their business relied on very fast turnover, and, rather more than the Chettiars, they borrowed heavily from depositors and from modern-style banks to inflate their own funds.[173] In 1930, S.N. Subba Iyer, one of the biggest Kallidaikurichi firms in Madurai, had a personal capital of just 3 or 4 lakhs of rupees, supplemented by 6 lakhs of deposits and 2 lakhs of Imperial Bank loan. Working with 1½ lakhs in cash and the rest out on loan, he reckoned to have a daily turnover of 2 to 3 lakhs of rupees, and to handle in a single year hundis valued up to a crore.[174]

Most of the business of town-based bankers like Subba Iyer consisted in lending money on the security of crops held in the market (sometimes locked in godowns and the key handed to the banker); lending out money to commission agents who went out into the villages to collect crops; and transmitting funds from town to town by holding running accounts with bankers in other places. Most important of all, they discounted hundis or bills of exchange; this facility, in which they lent short-term funds to merchants against evidence that the merchant was expecting payment on a prior transaction, enabled a large number of small merchants, commission agents and the like to operate on an extremely meagre personal capital, or possibly none at all.[175] The fragmentation, novelty, and rapid growth of the market encouraged this position. Trade, both internal and external, increased rapidly and gave opportunities for more and more people to take a part in it as forwarding agents, commission agents, produce brokers, wholesalers, and retailers. Yet most of these had to discover finance and thus had to go to the indigenous bankers. There was thus enormous competition for the bankers' facilities, and because of this and the unsteadiness of the market in most agrarian produce, the bankers could charge high rates. Loans on crops locked in a godown might start at nine per cent, but the *kandu* hand-loans ranged up beyond fifty per cent, and most lending from indigenous bankers to ordinary merchants and agents came in the range of twelve to twenty-five per cent depending on the security of the deal and the time of year (rates rose significantly at harvest times). In other words, by providing the facilities and the flexibility which would allow almost anyone to take a part in produce-broking, the indigenous bankers ensured that competition among the many agents and brokers cut their margins of profit to a minimum, and enabled the bankers themselves to take the lion's share and grow steadily rich. Once their wealth and respectability seemed assured, they attracted deposits. Urban professionals and those wealthy landowners with extra funds to invest often deposited with indigenous bankers.[176] Moreover, as the Imperial Bank and new joint-stock banks ventured warily into the business of short-term lending, they tended to lend only to these indigenous bankers, and so increase the

Table 10: Indigenous bankers 1928-9

	Number of Bankers	Estimated Capital	Estimated Net Interest
	URBAN		
Madras	89	34 532 000	1 010 400
Chingleput	79	5 000 000	198 741
North Arcot	137	8 044 937	411 577
South Arcot	117	3 596 996	400 609
Salem	103	3 476 279	302 401
Coimbatore	412	22 821 817	1 940 821
Tanjavur	125	8 632 129	664 874
Tiruchi	70	10 833 686	442 292
Madurai	45	5 814 095	431 297
Ramnad	139	21 541 212	683 727
Tirunelveli	22	7 380 000	140 000
	RURAL		
Chingleput	51	1 500 000	144 732
North Arcot	253	15 168 544	826 734
South Arcot	347	9 720 448	1 077 903
Salem	505	16 730 329	1 657 573
Coimbatore	339	19 215 926	1 739 516
Tanjavur	252	11 489 037	988 511
Tiruchi	304	13 502 517	1 264 178
Madurai	18	7 255 626	400 749
Ramnad	572	98 420 487	2 495 004
Tirunelveli	160	15 861 000	1 002 351
TOTAL	4129	340 567 065	18 223 990

Notes: The original data for North Arcot and Ramnad lacked full details on estimated capital, but included estimates of interest. I have used these estimates of interest, and the average capital:interest ratio of the other districts to calculate an estimate of capital for these districts.

Source: Figures supplied by F.H. Sennick, Commissioner of Income Tax, *MPBC*, III, 1090-4.

latters' hold. The modern-style banks had neither the expertise nor the daring to deal directly with all and sundry in the bazaar. Instead they kept lists of approved borrowers, and generally required signatures from two approved persons before they would offer a loan. Even many Nattukottai Chettiar bankers were not found to be suitable customers for the Imperial Bank, and this allowed one approved Chettiar firm to make a colossal fortune by simply borrowing from the Imperial Bank, adding half a per cent to the interest, and then distributing the loan amongst other bankers in Chettinad.[177] As one witness told the Banking Enquiry:

Indigenous bankers can be said to be practically helping agriculture, trade and industry of the district [Tanjavur], say to the extent of 60%...The indigenous bankers generally start with a very small capital. The Imperial Bank of India and joint-stock companies [he means banks] help them to a certain extent. They easily influence the public and get deposits which, in some cases, rise to several times the capital. There are instances where private bankers started business with a nominal capital of Rs 10 or 20 thousands and transacted more than Rs 15 lakhs within a period of fifteen years. Finally when the accounts were closed they had a surplus of Rs 1, 2 or even 3 lakhs in some cases.[178]

In 1929, an income tax officer made an attempt to calculate the capital involved in indigenous banking, and the results are shown in table 10. The division between urban and rural seems to refer to residence rather than to any qualitative difference in the style of operation. Since this is evidence calculated from tax records we can assume that the estimates of capital and interest are rather low; the figures show a net interest rate of around five per cent, which is, by all accounts, much too low. The number of bankers, meanwhile, is certainly overestimated, for it clearly includes many 'intermediary' operators, who were mainly borrowing and re-lending the assets of the principal bankers (this is clear from other figures on 'expenses' which include the interest *paid out* by the bankers themselves—this will of course act as some corrective to any underestimation of total capital).

Besides the indigenous bankers, there was also a number of independent merchants (or merchant firms) who traded on their own capital and were also drawn into financing other smaller traders, taking deposits, dealing in hundis, and undertaking other banking functions. A number of Nattukottai Chettiars who still found their main occupation in dealing in cloth operated like this, as did a number of wholesalers in the larger cities and some Indian export-import merchants in the major ports.[179] What marked out these merchant princes, like the indigenous bankers, was the size of their personal capital and the manner in which they financed the operation of other dealers and agents. Where they differed from the indigenous bankers was in the fact that they also dealt in produce and, because of their extraordinary commercial dominance, carried on a wide range of mercantile activities. A number of them acted as wholesalers in such goods as cloth, chillis, gram and other agricultural produce. Operating from the mid-point of a commercial chain stretching from producer (or port) to consumer, they proffered finance both backwards to the brokers, sub-merchants, and commission agents who supplied the goods, and forwards to the retail shops that sold them.

The Chettiar cloth wholesalers in Madurai bought imported cloth by advancing loans to import-firms in Madras City, and then offered the goods to retail shops on credit. Retailers could theoretically buy in much more cheaply if they dealt directly with the import-house, but generally speaking that would have forced them to operate on a much lower scale. The Chettiars allowed them thirty days of cheap credit, and let them keep running accounts. Thus one cloth retail firm which had only Rs 100 of its own liquid capital had an annual turnover of Rs 20,000 and an annual profit that was equal to its own capital.[180] S. Venkatachelam Chetty, one of the biggest dealers in chillis and other produce in Madras City, operated a similar system: 'We generally advance about seventy-five to eighty per cent of the market price of goods to the commission agents who send us the goods...We sell mostly on credit...We send our own men to each of these bazaars for collection daily and sometimes weekly.'[181] Venkatachelam Chetty admitted that such a style of operation tied up an enormous amount of capital, but pleaded that this was the only way to keep things moving. A.R.A.S. Doraisami Nadar, a big timber-import firm in Tuticorin, went into banking on the profits of the war-time boom and began to finance the dealings of lesser local merchants:

Most of the merchants here have only a limited amount of capital in cash, but a large amount of property, jewels etc., and the [modern-style] banks here do not advance them money though they have property. We know the value of their property and their standing and we advance them... We watch over their business every day and we do not often lose.[182]

Doraisami Nadar could borrow from the Imperial Bank and the

joint-stock National Bank at eight to nine per cent, and he re-lent large portions of this credit to other merchants at nine to twelve per cent. In the same town, M.C. Muthukumaraswami Pillai held a similar position, except that he had diversified his commercial business as well as entering into banking:

We have been merchants for a long time past. We have both export and import business besides commission business. We have branches at Colombo and Tuticorin and deal in onions, oil-cakes, chillies, besides exporting into Colombo potatoes from Naples, Marseilles, Malta and Bangalore; chillies from Calcutta; coriander, sugar and other such commodities from various parts. We also deal in rice on a large scale. For our abovesaid trade we have invested a capital of Rs 75,000 in addition to a borrowed capital of about the same sum...There are plenty of merchants who trade with a capital not worthy of being called so; and there are many more whose actual investments and borrowed capital stand in the ratio of one to ten. So, trade here to a large extent is dependent on the money lent to them and on the banking facilities afforded to them.[183]

And, he added, much of this credit had to come from Nattukottai Chettiars, or other major merchants like himself:

Inland traders, however rich and honest they may be, are looked upon with suspicion. The [modern-style] bank limits allowed to them are very low...these branches of the Imperial and other foreign banks are not able to understand the local needs. They cannot know well the status of the different merchants and also the nature of the several trades.[184]

Thus the large and growing trade in the interior of Tamilnad was floated on the finance of remarkably few entrepreneurs. The speed of the growth in trade from the mid-nineteenth century, the accumulation of savings in the hands of agriculturists and professionals, the provision of extra funds by modern-style banks, the profitability of produce-dealing and thus the multiplication of small traders, all tended towards the concentration of finance in very few hands. For example in Madurai, the largest town outside Madras City, it was estimated in 1928-9 that the total capital in trade amounted to 140 lakhs of rupees. Of this 46 lakhs were provided by modern-style banks; of the remaining 94 lakhs, just 64 were provided by six banking firms.[185] By this time, the modern-style banks had not penetrated far beyond Madras, Madurai, and two or three other large towns, and thus in the rest of the province the dominance of a handful of firms was even more remarkable. The very profitability of produce-dealing, both for the export market and for the local bazaars, tended to attract funds away from any

other business. Indeed from the 1880s to the 1920s the *real* value of
registered mortgages on agricultural land in Madras did not rise at
all, and entrepreneurs wishing to start industrial enterprises found it
immensely difficult to raise capital.[186] P. Thyagaraja Chetty, the
premier handloom-weaving magnate and city politician of Madras,
tried in 1910 to start a company to build a cotton mill but could only
raise a third of the 12 lakhs of capital needed; next year he floated
the idea of a cement company but only managed half of the requisite
3 lakhs; and in 1913 he proposed a match factory, requiring only 2
lakhs, but again failed.[187] The problem was not some culture-bound
'shyness' of Indian capital; indeed the manner in which the savings
of agriculturists and urban professionals found their way into
deposit accounts with indigenous bankers was proof of the readiness of savers to invest in the most profitable manner available. As
Thyagaraja Chetty himself concluded:

There is no flow of capital for industrial enterprises, and if there is any, it is
only for petty industrial concerns from the small savings of middle-class
population. The wealthy classes comprising the zamindars, Guzaraties
[mainly jewel dealers], Marwaris, Nattukottai Chetties and the lawyers
generally, look for what they consider safe investments on mortgages of
land, houses and jewellery. With the rates of interest that are easily
obtainable, money-lending is a favourite occupation.[188]

Indeed the period from roughly the 1880s to the early 1920s was
an extraordinary time for the money-market. The multiplication of
Chettiar capital (admittedly largely outside India), the expansion of
the Kallidaikurichi firms, the emergence of merchant princes like S.
Venkatachelam Chetty and A.R.A.S Doraiswami Nadar were all
evidence of the scale of expansion. More and more institutions were
drawn into produce-broking. After the first world war, the Imperial
Bank and the joint-stock banks were prepared to risk more of their
funds in this business. The Tanjore Permanent Fund, a mutual
savings-and-loan association begun in the 1880s and hitherto lending mostly to its largely professional membership, started laying out
loans on produce in the early 1920s.[189] Perhaps the most sensitive
indicator of the attractions of bazaar banking in this period is the
migration of bankers from other parts of India. In the Census of
1901, there were 571 Marwari-speakers listed in the Tamil districts,
and few of these lived outside Madras City and its environs. By
1931, the figure had risen to 1252 and they were spread rather more
widely through the province. The number of Multani bankers also

increased; these are rather more difficult to trace through the Census, yet in 1901 there were only eleven Punjabi-speakers listed in the Tamil districts and in 1931 there were 181 in Madras City, 743 in Chingleput district and 647 in Trichinopoly. There were also significant rises in the numbers speaking Gujarati, Hindi and Sindhi; although not all of these need have been bankers, it is probably safe to assume that many were.

These north Indian bankers were agents of firms with head-quarters in Bombay and other north Indian cities, and they brought their capital from there, and rarely tried to attract local deposits. Indeed, because of the size and security of their parent firms, they often found it easier (and cheaper) to secure funds from the Imperial Bank. In most ways, their operations resembled those of the Chettiar and Brahman indigenous bankers, but with some important differences. They tended to move into those areas that were newly attractive and thus did not have an established local bazaar banking sector. Fifteen or so Marwari firms moved into Coimbatore and four others into Erode around the turn of the century when the cotton trade was beginning to pick up, and ten to twelve Marwari firms began operating in the groundnut trade in the Arcots plain from around the time of the first world war. The Shikarpur Multanis came rather later, were barely settled by the 1920s, and tended to use local sub-bankers because their lack of local knowledge placed them in some danger. By the early 1930s, there were forty-five Multani firms in the province, with about 110 branches. There were also six major Marwari firms and four major Gujarati firms, as well as a number of lesser Marwari and Gujarati entrepreneurs who generally lent small amounts to shopkeepers and other members of the urban lower middle class.[190] One estimate put the total capital of these 'foreign' bazaar-bankers at 10 crores.[191] A lot of their business was at the expanding and speculative edge of the market. In the larger towns they commanded a lot of the business in discounting hundis for small traders. Since many of their clients were fairly small and speculative operators, these north Indian bankers took considerable risks and charged high rates of interest. The presence of such foreigners, charging twenty-five per cent and more, was further evidence of the desperate search for capital and the remarkable buoyancy of produce-trading.

The period also saw the elaboration of a pyramid of credit which stretched all the way from the Imperial Bank to the lowly strata of the countryside. The Imperial Bank and other modern-style banks lent to substantial traders, prominent Nattukottai Chettiars, and other indigenous bankers. The substantial bankers lent to their lesser colleagues in the bazaar, who in turn lent to prominent rural-dwellers. The latter lent to their neighbouring cultivators, tenants and even labourers. At each stage of the pyramid, the creditor supplemented the loans coming from above with at least as much capital of his own, and made a small addition to the rate of interest. The building of this pyramid ensured that the finance of the urban sector and European business, of internal trade, and of cultivation were to a considerable extent interconnected.

The machinery of bazaar-banking had been built quickly and rather shoddily; by the end of the period, and particularly after the spurt of the first world war, it was beginning to overheat. A fairly small number of large cogs was driving an ever-increasing number of small cogs at an ever-increasing rate and with ever-diminishing lubrication. Such a machine was bound to overheat. The rapid development of the nidhis and chit funds provided the clearest evidence of the peculiar pressures placed on the money-market, and the consequent growing insecurity that marked financial dealings.

Both nidhis and chits began as forms of co-operative saving. The chits were funds subscribed by members at the rate of one or two rupees a month and then distributed to each of the members in turn by a variety of systems, some depending on a simple rota, others on a lottery (in which those successful were omitted from later draws), and some by auction (in which subscribers offered competitive discounts on the pay-out share). They had their origin in village saving funds, but in the early twentieth century became a common feature of the urban bazaars. Here they were less co-operative in character, and resembled more a device for small-time entrepreneurs to raise capital (usually around Rs 1,000) for some business deal. The possibilities for swindling were immense. People would be prepared to invest in these funds to find a place for spare savings (and sometimes, if properly managed, these funds could yield a high return—particularly the auction chits) and also to oblige the fund's promoter.[192] But it became a commom device for traders and bankers to use chits to try and bale themselves out of financial trouble, and thus failures were frequent. A Tirunelveli man, who insisted that failures were not common in his area, did nevertheless put the ratio of chits that failed as one in ten.[193]

Nidhis began in 1858 in a similar if slightly grander way, as mutual loan societies based on monthly subscriptions stretching over a four to seven year period. Their assets were originally lent only to members and, at the end of the period, the fund was wound up and profits re-distributed. With the foundation of the Mylapore Hindu Permanent Fund in 1872, the character changed. This fund did not terminate; individual subscribers could wind up their connection with the fund, but they were then replaced and the number of subscribers, and the capital stock, remained roughly the same. From the 1880s, such 'permanent funds' spread throughout the Presidency, but at first remained as associations of merchants or professional men helping one another out by this form of co-operative finance.[194] In the early twentieth century, there was a further development, originating in Kongunad and connected closely to the expansion of the cotton business there. In these nidhis, the subscriptions were partly or wholly replaced by a share issue. The shares were not returnable, but were negotiable and on top of the shares the nidhis accepted short-term deposits.[195] Generally still they only lent to members, on the security of land or jewels, but in the over-heated atmosphere of the early 1920s they began to lend to non-members, and also to lend on the profitable and fashionable business of crop-dealing.[196] By the end of the 1920s there were two or three hundred nidhis in Tamilnad, with a high proportion in Coimbatore, and their subscribed capital amounted to around 100 to 150 lakhs of rupees.[197] Several of them particularly in Coimbatore, were dominated by a handful of big bankers, who clearly found this a clever device for expanding their personal capital. Three of the big nidhis of Coimbatore town, for instance, were dominated by one man who owned forty-eight per cent of their total capital, and one observer suggested that 'in Madras Presidency there may be said to be a new caste named "Fund-Office Caste" or "Directors Caste", for the very simple reason that the very same gentlemen, or their relatives, and later on their descendants, would be found on the boards of several directorates.'[198] In some cases these directors creamed off as much as seventy-five per cent of the profits of the nidhi and only paid out the remaining twenty-five per cent in dividends to the other shareholders. One knowledgeable local banker reckoned that only four or five of the 125 Coimbatore nidhis were secure organizations while in many cases 'the nidhi really helps one or two people to become office-bearers and is started for that purpose. It is just to

oblige a particular man that his friends and other people join as
shareholders.'[199] Another Coimbatore nidhi manager confessed
that the chief reason for starting such a fund was 'to provide
employment for relations and friends'.[200] Yet the nidhis obviously
provided a service. They attracted considerable deposits, largely
from urban professionals and from merchants anxious to find a
short-term investment for funds in slack periods. A study of twenty
nidhis (in Coimbatore, Madras and elsewhere) found that of the
4,022 depositors, 1,837 were either officials or professional men,
another 520 were merchants and shopkeepers and the remaining
701 were agriculturists. They lent at nine per cent, which was
reasonably cheap, and had, between the twenty nidhis, 45,864
clients, mostly merchants (11,560) and agriculturists (17,415).[201]
Finally, the financial entrepreneurs liked them. Those few men of
the 'Fund Office Caste' who gathered control of several nidhis were
able to use them to great effect. Besides the advantage of controlling
the savings of others, the direction of a nidhi had other benefits. A
shareholder could borrow back from the nidhi, sometimes up to the
extent of ninety per cent of the value of his share, and if he was careful the difference between the interest on his lending and borrowing
was minute; nidhis made most of their profit by charging penal rates
of interest on overdues and thus were able to keep their normal
deposit and loan rates roughly equal. Besides that, the director could
then use his share certificate, and his status as a director, as security
to raise extra funds elsewhere, from indigenous bankers and even
from some of the modern-style banks.[202] In other words, the nidhis
provided a productive investment for the savings of agriculturists,
merchants and urban professionals; an additional source of loans
for many small produce-brokers as well as some growers and others;
and a useful field of enterprise for the merchant-financier.

The rapid rise of the nidhis thus exemplified the most significant
trends in the money-market; the availability of savings, the attractions of speculative lending on produce, the tendency for the
management of investment funds to concentrate in few hands. They
also showed another important characteristic, clearly in evidence by
the mid-1920s: the extreme insecurity of financial institutions.

The nidhis had very meagre reserve funds. This was of course a
result of their historical evolution: they had begun as joint-savings
enterprises lending only to their own members, and had only later
come to resemble joint-stock banking concerns. Yet while they had

made the transition to a banking format in so far as they had achieved some form of permanency, transformed the subscription funds into share capital, accepted deposits and begun lending to non-members, they had not also acquired substantial reserves. The Tanjore Permanent Fund was one of the oldest and most solid of the nidhis, yet even that institution kept virtually all its funds in current circulation. Its subscription capital (it had not fully made the transition to share capital) amounted in 1930 to 23 lakhs, and its deposits to 3 lakhs; meanwhile its total lending amounted to 25 lakhs, its investments (largely in government paper) to 3½ lakhs, and its reserve funds to a meagre Rs 186,000.[203] Many of the less prestigious nidhis were reluctant to let any of their funds drop out of circulation; they listed a reserve fund in their accounts but then merrily lent out the contents just·like all their other money. One estimate reckoned that the nidhis as a whole had capital of 4 crores, deposits of another 1.2 crores, and reserve funds of just 35 lakhs.[204] In certain cases, the readiness of nidhis to accept large amounts of short-term deposits and then re-lend the entire sum, made them peculiarly vulnerable to a run; one Coimbatore banker offered an instance of a nidhi which had share capital of Rs 8000 and deposits of 1 lakh.[205] Considering that the nidhis got their funds from subscriptions or shares which could fluctuate, and deposits which could be quickly withdrawn, and considering that they lent out as much as possible with little thought for reserves, they were clearly sailing very close to the wind.

While the nidhis were most obviously precarious in this respect, the rise of joint-stock banking in the early twentieth century had taken place under exactly the same conditions as those affecting the rise of the nidhis and, though more carefully regulated by the law, the joint-stock banks still had certain wayward characteristics. By 1919-20, there were 223 joint-stock companies involved in banking and loan business, with an aggregate paid-up capital of 247 lakhs. By 1929-30, the number had risen to 343 and the paid-up capital to 430 lakhs.[206] Most of these companies were either nidhis or partnerships of indigenous bankers, and only sixty-six might be considered as 'modern-style' banks, and only one, the Indian Bank, was of any size. The Indian Bank had been founded in 1907 (following the Arbuthnot crash) on an alliance of the premier professional family of Madras City and the premier Nattukottai Chetty family. It found most of its capital from the communities

headed by these two families, served as a deposit for the funds of the
professional people of Madras City, and acted mainly as the reserve
bank of the Nattukottai Chetty, Multani, and other indigenous
banking firms. It grew steadily and evenly up to the end of the war,
but then started to go a little awry. Its paid-up capital reached 12.79
lakhs in 1923 and stuck; deposits however grew rapidly throughout
the 1920s. The law required the bank to increase its reserves at a
suitable rate, but they rose only from 6 lakhs in 1923 to 15 lakhs in
1931, while deposits climbed from 41 lakhs in 1917 to 68 lakhs in
1923 and 193 lakhs by 1930. At the same time, the cash balances of
the bank had grown, and also the need to find some productive
outlet for funds. Inevitably, the Indian Bank was drawn into lending
on produce. It opened branches in the mofussil (notably at Coimbatore) and began to lend on rice, groundnut, and cotton stored in
the market, as well as continuing the indirect finance through
indigenous bankers. By the late 1920s, a large part of the bank
officials' time was spent visiting godowns to make sure that the
goods were not deteriorating.[207]

Other local joint-stock banks enjoyed rapid increases in deposits.
While in the 1920s deposits at the branch of the Imperial Bank in
Madras barely increased, and those with the foreign exchange
banks grew only slightly from 364 to 425 lakhs between 1920 and
1929, those with the joint-stock banks rose from 137 to 585 lakhs.[208]
Moreover most of these institutions had evolved out of indigenous
banking concerns, and still operated in a similar fashion. They lent
in the produce market, they discounted hundis, and they stretched
their assets to the limit. When the Banking Enquiry asked the director of the Nadar Bank about the contents of that bank's reserve fund,
he thought for a bit and then suggested the fixtures and fittings.[209]

Between 1926 and 1930, the produce market lost its extraordinary buoyancy. Indeed, it sank. It took down with it most of the
final security on which credit had been supplied. Advances against
produce often extended up to eighty per cent of the value, but as
already noted, in years like 1929, 1930 and 1931 the drop in prices
exceeded the twenty per cent margin of allowance. Mortgages on
landed property ranged up to seventy per cent of the estimated
value, but in the same three years the price of land halved. Jewels
had always been considered the most rock-like of securities, yet by
1930 they also suffered from the same trouble:

There is always difficulty in getting them valued. There are various qualities of jewellery and there is always fluctuation in the market with regard to their price. From the last few years the price of gold has been going down and we regard that business as dangerous... Certain jewels which have been valued at Rs 1,000 some six years back are now valued only at Rs 400 or Rs 500.[210]

Once it was clear that the depression was not merely a short-term cycle, there began a series of desperate and hopeless attempts by all those in the credit pyramid to retract the funds lent to those below them and to get out of the produce market. By 1929, the Imperial Bank had virtually stopped providing any credit to the Nattukottai Chetties[211] (who were one of the most speculative elements in the market and were also more encumbered than other bankers because of their southeast Asian connections), and by 1931 when the combined attempts of Delhi and London to deal with the international aspects of the financial crisis resulted in a rapid contraction of Indian currency, the Imperial Bank had become very sticky about lending to any of the bazaar bankers. The other modern banks quickly followed suit and one of Madras's leading merchants, S. Venkatachelam Chetty, complained that they were acting just 'like a panicky private money-lender'.[212] He went on to describe the repercussions in the bazaar:

The local money-lenders who generally discount the hundies and bills of their borrowers with the Banks, had to withdraw their credit facilities from the market, as those Banks would not freely discount their bills as previously. The pressure for repayment of loans aggravated the trouble with each stage in the fall of prices of commodities. Properties and jewels which had to be disposed of to meet dues have come in a rush into the market, which was already short on money, could not secure the purchasers even at a depreciated value of nearly 50 per cent. In the result the extent of security which these investments offered for loans against them became considerably contracted.[213]

At first the indigenous bankers were hesitant about calling in their own loans. They were used to riding out temporary financial crises and anyway with their heavy deposits, slight reserves and over-extended credits they could not afford to precipitate a run on deposits. But when the crisis lasted longer than initially expected the strain became too great. By mid-1930 there were sporadic reports of failures among indigenous banking firms.[214] Local investors did start to withdraw their deposits and bazaar banking firms were obliged to resort to the law in an attempt to maintain their own liquidity. In parts of Tamilnad the number of cases of lands distrained to realize mortgages doubled in the early 1930s and in the civil courts there was a rapid rise in the number of debt suits and insolvency petitions. But this recourse to law was not very large and not very effective. The number of mortgages called in was still very small compared to the total number; and the rush to the courts merely clogged the machinery. While the number of suits filed rose rapidly, the number satisfactorily concluded was completely stationary, and by 1932 it was reckoned that 400 days was the minimum time necessary to bring a debt suit to any conclusion at all.[215]

Given these difficulties and the importance of confidence, most indigenous bankers did not try the courts. Some simply tried to achieve some sort of turnover which would allow them to continue in business. One Ramnad Nadar who had 2 lakhs out on loan was prepared to ignore interest and just take repayments towards the capital, in order to achieve some sort of flow of funds; if this failed he negotiated private purchase of lands mortgaged to him and then set about leasing these lands as another way to achieve some liquid returns.[216]

But not all indigenous bankers were so accommodating and further down the credit pyramid there were merchants and sub-lenders who depended to a greater extent on borrowed funds and on the confidence of their customers, and here collapses were more common. As one merchant said of the indigenous bankers in 1930: 'Their overvigilance to guard their interests proves a thorn in the sides of merchants. Even a slight rumour of loss is sufficient to disturb their mental equilibrium and they will insist upon immediate payment and thus precipitate matters to a crisis. Merchants failing thus is a common feature.'[217] Those who borrowed from the modern-style rather than the indigenous bankers were often in much greater trouble, for the modern-style banks were less flexible and rather more sure of their own status. L.K. Tulsiram described the fate of the Chinnia Komba merchant family:

They were a noble family and had a very good business for years together. The man who was conducting the family business was not able to meet the demand one day and all the officials [of the bank] went to him and demanded payment. Naturally he could not meet all their demands and they locked his shop and one of the biggest families, the owners of the Chintadripet market in Madras, was ruined.[218]

The Nattukottai Chettiar firms in general felt the pressure of the downturn in the market right from the middle of the 1920s. The

Chettiars had suffered an earlier crisis around 1910, when a number of firms suffered from a bad speculation in Burma oil, and when firms working in Calcutta were enticed into the management of zamindari estates, got caught with too much of their capital locked in land, and were ruined.[219] Because of the close relations and mutual accommodations between Chettiar firms, such crashes were liable to have widespread effects, but in the conditions of 1910 the matter was soon forgotten. From 1926, however, the Chettiars faced a more serious crisis. It began with the failure of the Chettiar company that managed the Choolai cotton mill in Madras, one of the few Chettiar industrial concerns. The trouble was that, as the produce market turned down, this firm, like the unlucky Calcutta firms, found too many of its assets tied up in a solid form, and had to put itself in the hands of a receiver.[220] Two years later, another Chettiar firm which had speculated in landed property, faced the difficulty of meeting its normal day-to-day obligations when a large number of the merchants who had borrowed from the firm could not repay on time. Once again, it learnt to regret its fixed investments. In fact the Imperial Bank was persuaded to bail out the firm, but the damage to Chettiar prestige was substantial.[221] In the next couple of years, a number of smaller Chettiar firms failed because of the lack of confidence, and the level of deposits in Chettiar concerns dropped sharply. The reaction of the Chettiars was simply to withdraw even further from dealings in south India. In the mid-1920s they had sensed the coming crisis in the Kaveri rice-trade and had stopped supplying working capital to the rice mills.[222] By 1928 they were moving completely out of rural finance, even in their home area of Chettinad; twenty-eight firms in Chettinad were winding up their business and preparing to transfer funds to southeast Asia.[223] They had also eased out of the Ramnad and Madurai cotton trade and thus had most of their south Indian business in urban finance. Here too they got into difficulty when the onset of the depression made their business debtors 'very slow to pay' and caused a string of Nattukottai Chettiar failures. There was a 'consequent heavy loss incurred by a variety of capitalists here' who had invested with the Chettiars and this had 'resulted in the withdrawal of the money invested with them by the capitalist public and its deposit with the joint-stock banks'.[224] The withdrawal of the Chettiars from south India to concentrate on the foreign concerns proved of course to be extremely short-sighted. When the crash

Table 11: Marwaris in Tamilnad 1901-51

	1901	1931	1951
Madras City	455	919	–
Chingleput	86	191	48
North Arcot	13	35	–
South Arcot	–	25	3
Salem	8	3	–
Coimbatore	9	33	32
Tanjavur	–	–	6
Tiruchi	–	24	8
Madurai	–	19	–
Ramnad	–	3	–
Tirunelveli	–	–	–
TOTALS	571	1252	97

Sources: *Census of India.* 1901. Volume XV-A, Pt ii, 115. *Census of India 1931.* Volume XIV, Pt ii, 282. *Census of India 1951.* Volume III, Pt ii-B, 104.

came in Burma, Malaya and Ceylon they found themselves in severe political as well as economic difficulties.[225]

Other indigenous bankers fared no better. There were reports of crashes among the Kallidaikurichi Brahman first operating in the Tambraparni valley, and among the Kallidaikurichi Brahman firms who had moved into the Kaveri rice business when the Chettiars had withdrawn.[226] The Marwaris, meanwhile, simply quit the region. Whereas there had been only 571 Marwaris in the Tamil districts in 1901, the number had risen to 1,252 in 1931, and fell to ninety-seven by 1951 (see table 11).[227]

The nidhis were particularly badly hit. Because of the fly-by-night character of these institutions the rate of failure had always been high. Yet until the late 1920s, the number of new nidhis formed continued to exceed the number collapsing. Yet in the first year that the produce market slipped (1926) there were twenty-three failures, and from 1928 the steady increase in nidhi profits turned down into a loss.[228] By 1930, the nidhis (including those that had virtually become joint-stock concerns) were in exactly the same position as the indigenous bankers. One Coimbatore banker noted:

Table 12: Development of joint-stock banking in Tamilnad 1900-51

Banks listed as in operation in 1952, classified by year of incorporation

Year	Number	Year	Number	Year	Number
1900-9	7	1933	10	1943	2
1910-19	13	1934	1	1944	2
1920-5	11	1935	9	1945	4
1926	5	1936	10	1946	4
1927	1	1937	1	1947	–
1928	1	1938	1	1948	1
1929	1	1939	–	1949	–
1930	1	1940	–	1950	–
1931	6	1941	–	1951	–
1932	3	1942	1		

Source: Reserve Bank of India, *Banking and Monetary Statistics of India.* (Bombay, 1954), Table 22, pp. 279-81.

There is always a feeling of insecurity in the minds of depositors, I can refer to two or three cases in the district that ended in failure because they were not able to command public confidence. The Erode Bank Ltd. is doing only collection work. The Ratna Deepika Nidhi Ltd. is in a similar condition. Joint-stock enterprises which started with high trumpets have not been able to successfully appeal to the imagination of the people.[229]

When, in the middle of these difficulties, the High Court adjudged that the liability of nidhis was unlimited and extended even as far as past subscribers who might have ceased their connection with the nidhi for many years, there was visible alarm among banking and investing circles in Coimbatore.[230]

A large number of nidhis failed between 1929 and 1933, and those which remained were substantially changed. A few became trading companies and rather more transformed themselves into joint-stock banks. This gave them rather more status and rather more protection under the law than they had had as nidhis, but it also required them to conform to the Companies Act and in particular to build up decent reserve funds. In several cases a number of nidhis merged together, amassed a reserve fund, adjusted their rules to conform to the Act, restricted their speculative lending, raised their lending rates above their deposit rates, and became joint-stock banks. Several indigenous banking firms pursued the same course and as a result the ranks of the joint-stock banks swelled in the middle of the 1930s.[231]

The carnage in the money market had different repercussions for the urban and rural ends of the business. After 1929 the rich cultivator-traders found it much more difficult to secure urban finance to complement their own resources. A number of them were bankrupted when local depositors lost confidence in them and tried to withdraw their funds, while at the same time their urban creditors were pressing for repayments and their own debtors could not find any cash.[232] In late 1931, following the British government's retreat from the gold standard, there were enormous sales of gold from India. Between 1932-3 and 1934-5, Madras made a net export of treasure to the extent of 8 crores. Much of it undoubtedly came out of the hoards of bankers, traders and cultivators involved in the pyramid of rural credit. The retreat from the gold standard meant that the sellers made a considerable profit on the sum which they had paid for the gold in recent years, but this immediate profit-taking disguised a long-term loss of security. Gold had always formed one of the most important forms of security offered in the rural money-market and thus the sale of gold meant a loss of capacity to borrow. By 1933, there were frequent reports about the torpor of the rural money-market and government was forced to take notice. It made a gesture of assistance by giving 10 lakhs for the co-operative societies to channel into rural credit, but this was rather like throwing a bucket of water onto a drought-ridden field.[233] A series of books, pamphlets, speeches and intercessions in the legislative council told government that it was part of their responsibility to help unglue the money market.[234] Gradually government lumbered into action; but it took so long to formulate and enact legislation, and was so unskilled in such delicate matters, that its debt acts were almost certainly counterproductive. Legislation did not become effective until 1938, by which time prices had begun to rise, internal and external trade were growing, and the money-market showed all the signs of recovering some of its old buoyancy. Under such conditions, government intervention made creditors wary, and thus inhibited the revival.

The first legislative move came in August 1932, when government published the Madras Money-lenders Bill. This measure merely obliged all bankers and money-lenders to keep accounts, and imposed a ceiling of eighteen per cent on the rate of interest. A

Select Committee tampered with the provision about the interest-ceiling, and then the bill was put on the shelf on the grounds that the Government of India was thinking about an all-India bill on interest rates. When this latter measure failed to materialize, the bill was taken down off the shelf, given to a Select Committee weighted heavily with financiers who tore up the provision on the interest ceiling, and emerged in 1935 as the Madras Debtors Protection Act. This Act obliged all money-lenders to keep accounts, but suggested no sensible way of enforcing this stricture, and gently passed into the dusty, inert pages of Madras legislative history.[235] In 1933, a prominent Coimbatore banker wrote a bill to set up conciliation boards to scale down the arrears of debt which were blocking up the credit system. Government officials did not like the bill, partly because it was a private bill rather than a government one, partly because (they suggested) there was no evidence of demand for the measure and largely because they were worried about embroiling the machinery of administration so deeply in the entrails of the local economy: 'The Board [of Revenue] is inclined to believe that the debtors and creditors might resent this sort of interference. The landholders and the ryots may be expected to settle their differences between themselves without the intervention of Government.'[236] They were particularly worried about the provision that an arrear of debt, after it had been scaled down by a conciliation board, should be collected by government on behalf of the creditor.

Two years later, however, the government felt obliged to adopt the bill; it was passed in April 1936, yet only came into action, district by district, in the later months of 1937. The Act established, in each district, a Debt Conciliation Board consisting of a deputy collector, and two non-officials appointed by government;[237] one of the latter was usually a retired judge or government officer, and the other a major landowner. These boards were to interview those debtors and creditors who brought their cases up for arbitration, and suggest a reasonable settlement. Since the agricultural and financial future looked much rosier in 1937-8 than it had in 1931-2 when both debtors and creditors had been clamouring for such an Act, it was hardly surprising that the response was very cool. Government had been careful to remove from the Act the provision in the original bill that made government responsible for collecting the conciliated debts and therefore few creditors could see any point in coming for arbitration. The Act had been drafted in such a way that creditors who had mounted the loan on some sort of security (land or jewels) were quite at liberty to reject the settlement of the board and go to law. Of course, some such creditors did agree to come before the conciliation boards, in the hope that this would help them collect from their debtors, and when they found the settlement not to their liking, they went to law. Other cases brought to the boards were mainly attempts by debtors to complicate legal proceedings that were already in motion. All but one of the eighteen cases filed in Coimbatore in the first six months had been brought up by debtors

solely with a view to defeat proceedings in the Civil Court and to delay execution petitions, sales for attachment of decrees, confirmation of sales already held etc. Even an adjudged insolvent came up with a petition after all his property had vested in the official Receiver and he was no longer qualified to enter into contracts. The Act at present is abused by cantankerous debtors to gain time and if possible keep their creditors out of their dues.[238]

The activities of the Debt Conciliation Boards however changed substantially in 1938 when government passed some new legislation, the Agriculturists' Relief Act.

This measure, by far the most important piece of all the debt legislation, was contrived to scale down the arrears of interest that had been accruing during the depression. It ruled that all arrears of interest dating from 1932 and before should be wiped out, that all interest from 1932 until October 1937 should be calculated at five per cent and all interest thereafter at six and a quarter per cent, and that any debt on which the interest paid already amounted to twice the original loan should be deemed discharged. This was a serious measure. In the first fourteen months of the Act's operation over 100,000 cases were filed, relating to more than Rs 200 lakhs of debts. Government arranged that the Debt Conciliation Boards could act as tribunals to hear cases under the Act and this gave the Boards a new lease of life.[239]

In the business of simple conciliation, the Boards were an enormous failure. Between 1939 and their abolition in 1944, 24,464 conciliation cases were submitted to the Boards (in all Madras Presidency) and only 3,113 reached any conclusion.[240] But as a tribunal for the Agriculturists' Relief Act, the Boards were rather more active and successful. In the ninety-one months of its operation up to the end of the second world war, there were 203,874 cases involving 955 lakhs of debt, and the resulting court decisions reduced the total dues by 52.1 per cent—wiping away almost 5 crores of accumulated interest.[241] This represented a considerable legislative success, but it of course created its own problems. Money-lenders were not anxious to do business when their profits were liable to be reduced by this (or future) legislation, and when the official limit on the rate of interest was 6¼ per cent. As prices began to rise in 1939, and then rocket in 1941, this ceiling on the rate of interest became somewhat stupid. Very soon after the Agriculturists' Relief Act came into operation, the professor of economics at Annamalai University made a survey of the local credit market in the University's hinterland. Lenders were generally apprehensive about lending; after the succession of four pieces of legislation on debts they were worried where the next act would lead, and despite rising prices and rising internal trade the credit market was as slack as at any time since 1930.[242] It was a measure of the shortage of rural credit that the number of application for government's *taccavi* loans (which were meagre, hedged about with regulations, and thus usually unattractive) had risen to twice the normal level.[243] Government had been aware of this difficulty since its first consideration of debt legislation in 1932, and in 1935 had passed yet another debt act, the Agriculturists' Loans (Madras Amendment) Act, which made provision for more substantial supplies of credit from government agencies. In 1938, they put the final touches to the measure and put it into operation; the results speak eloquently for themselves. In four years of operation from 1938-9 to 1941-2 there were a total of 5089 applications for loans out of which only 640 were approved, and while the budget provisions for the scheme totalled Rs 142.5 lakhs only Rs 2.98 lakhs was actually spent.[244] The trouble was the rules under which these loans were granted. They were offered only to agriculturists, who had been through the machinery of the Debt Conciliation Boards, and who still wanted loans to discharge debts to money-lenders which they had contracted before 1937 and for which they had offered security valued at two-and-a-half times the value of the loan.

It was, in fact, Catch 22. To get one of these loans, one had to be both a virtual bankrupt, and possessed of property worth two-and-a-half times the value of the loan. As the Board of Revenue concluded:

The system is completely machine-like, demanding official and public enquiries into the ryot's private affairs. Often he is at the mercy of the local officers who take no personal interest in his welfare. Months lapse before loans are sanctioned and even when received he remains constantly subject to official supervision. The slightest default results in summary recovery where no personal consideration is allowed or shown...If a loan is granted with what proves to be later inadequate security the official is held responsible. Government have never admitted the principle that in lending money there must be some bad debts.[245]

Thus debt legislation had contrived to reproduce, in the potentially buoyant conditions of wartime inflation, the problems of 1931, for again lenders were reported to be 'recovering dues and keeping them safe'. As in 1931, lending had of course not completely stopped; the rural economy of Tamilnad simply could not work without some redistribution of funds, but it required considerable ingenuity and registered a considerable change in the character of the money-market. One young economist reported in 1939:

But it is not as though private moneylending vanished from the villages....In order, however, to escape the effects of the regulation of rates, creditors get deeds of sale on land for moneys lent but promise to reconvey the land to the borrowers at the old price on payment of interest stipulated. Meanwhile they are supposed to be tenants, paying rent to the fictitious landlords.... Money is also lent on mortgage with possession, and interest is secured in kind, as usufructuary mortgages are not brought within the scope of the Act. Money is lent on gold with or without documents; if former, the higher rate of interest demanded is deducted from the principal in advance....It is on unsecured loans that the greatest ingenuity has been exercised: the borrower is an accomplice. Short-term loans are given on pro-notes for one or two years; the interest agreed to orally is taken in advance for the stipulated period...the legal rate of 6¼ per cent is of course found on the pro-note.[246]

The need for such ingenuity had important consequences. It represented a return towards the conditions in which the only reliable security for a loan was the creditors's personal knowledge of the debtor, in other words, a position where credit not only operated as an important element of social power, but also would not be offered outside a context of social power. Lending substantiated dependency, but was also not possible without dependency. Since the late nineteenth century, with the extension of trade in agricultural produce and the keenness of entrepreneurs to offer loans in the countryside to secure produce, this characteristic of the rural money-market had been being gradually eroded; now the uncertainty created by the depression and legislative interference pushed matters backwards. Lending continued, but it was more of the character between neighbours, than between entrepreneurs and producers.

This meant that although the conditions of the second world war were, in many aspects of trade and finance, similar to those of the years of the first world war only in a more extreme measure, the reactions of the rural money-market were very different. Between the mid-1930s and the early 1950s, the prices of food grains roughly quintupled. Yet while debts had grown during the inflationary period which preceded the depression, in the 1940s they shrank in real terms.

All statistical estimates of the debt of rural Madras must be treated with some caution. Each of the estimates below was calculated in a different way, and in the middle of all these calculations there were 'correction factors' of quite frightening proportions. Yet as indicators of general trends, they may be accorded some respect. The first was the work of Frederick Nicholson in 1895, and relied on an abstraction from official records on mortgages, and some rather cursory sample surveys. It yielded a figure of Rs 45 crores as the total debt.[247] The Banking Enquiry in 1930 relied on a roughly similar method of estimating, though using rather larger and well-investigated samples. It reached a figure of Rs 150 crores,[248] though a later student thought this too low. Zacharias pointed out that sample surveys in settlement reports in the early 1920s had shown a debt per head of Rs 51, and the sample surveys of the Banking Enquiry itself showed a figure of Rs 61—and these two calculations would have yielded figures for the total debt of Rs 214 crores and Rs 256 crores respectively.[249] Two studies in 1934-5—one by the economist P. J. Thomas and one by a government commissioner, W. R. S. Sathyanathan—both working basically from the material in the Banking Enquiry, reached a figure around Rs 200 crores. They argued that there had been little repayment of debt during the depression, and that the rise had been largely due to the accumulation of interest.[250] Another economist, B.V. Narayanaswami Naidu, reckoned that for similar reasons the total debt by the end of the 1930s had risen to 271 crores. He then went on to conduct a very rigorous survey of a sample of one thousandth of the Presidency's population in 1945 and came to the conclusion that the total had fallen to 217 crores. His surveys showed, with some considerable conviction, that larger landowners in particular had prospered on wartime inflation and had devoted much of their profits to purchasing land and reducing their burden of debt.[251] Zacharias objected to some of Narayanaswami Naidu's arithmetic, and reduced the totals for 1939 and 1945 to 210 and 175 crores respectively, but he launched no objection against the general argument.[252] Even allowing for these differences of calculation and also large margins of error, the figures pointed to a large reduction in the real value of rural debts. Comparing 1935 and 1945, prices had more than tripled, and the value of debts had possibly shrunk slightly. Even comparing 1930 and 1945, the statistics suggest that the real value of debt had at least halved.[253]

B.V. Narayanaswami Naidu's 1945 survey went into considerable detail. It suggested that there had been no reduction in the *proportion* of the rural population that was in debt, and it argued that the debts of the lower strata of rural society (small tenants and landless labourers) had increased in absolute terms. The major change had come among landholders, and particularly those with more than five acres. Few of them had annulled their debts, and it was still generally the case that the richer one was, the bigger was the debt and the bigger also was the ratio of debt to income. Yet Naidu's survey suggested that a large number of landowners had partially reduced their debts, with the result that for large landowners (over twenty-five acres) the per capita incidence had fallen by forty per cent, and for slightly smaller landowners (five to twenty-five acres) it had fallen by twenty-five per cent.[254] The next investigation of rural debt was the All India Rural Credit Survey in the mid-1950s. This survey, conducted in 1952-3, produced a figure of Rs 483 for the average debt of each rural family in the Madras Presidency which compared to Narayanaswamy Naidu's figures of Rs 255 in 1945 and Rs 319 in 1939, and to the Banking Enquiry's figure of Rs 194 in 1930. The estimate of debt had thus risen eighty-nine per cent between 1945 and 1952-3 while the Reserve Bank's price index had moved up sixty-seven per cent, and this comparison suggested that debt was once again increasing. Yet the level of debt was still below the estimates made in the 1930s in real terms.[255]

Given the rise in prices and demand for food crops during the war, and given the expansion of commercial cropping in the post-war period and the Korean war boom, this sluggishness on the part of rural credit suggested a clear difference from the pattern at the turn of the century. The figures suggest that while during the war trade and prices recovered, the provision of credit did not rise on the same scale. The rupture of the money-market was to some extent permanent; and in particular it meant less lending from town to countryside. Capital still circulated fairly freely within the close confines of rural society, but less was being advanced from the commission agents, brokers, indigenous bankers and professional sowcars. The boom of the 1914-18 war had found recent immigrants from Bombay wandering around the villages of Kongunad recklessly handing out rupees. There was nothing comparable in 1939-45.

The loss on the part of the rural money-market was to a large extent a gain for urban finance. The collapse of the institutions which had channelled finance from the towns into the countryside meant a build-up of capital in the towns. Even by 1930, observers were noting a shift in the location of savings. Two witnesses before the Banking Enquiry—one a rural and one an urban banker—saw matters in roughly the same light:

On the one hand we find a large number of moneyed men and institutions in cities who are at a loss to know where to invest their moneys and how to get a fair return by way of interest on such investments. Nattukkottai Chetti firms which used to take in large deposits at what is called "the nadappu rate of interest" which generally worked out to 9 per cent per annum have latterly been unwilling to accept deposits, at any rate it is difficult to get firms of established reputation and credit to take deposits in the usual course. The banks in Madras have been steadily lowering the rate of interest at which they are prepared to accept deposits from the public. Loans on first mortgages of immoveable properties in Madras have proved to be a disappointing source of investment, as in most cases the lender had to take the immoveable properties himself as no purchasers are available to take them in auction. Further, owing to the fall in the value of these properties after the war, persons who lent on this kind of security and even institutions like the Mylapore Hindu Permanent Fund [an unusually good and prestigious nidhi] which is well known for its cautious valuation of houses have found to their cost that the security has failed to satisfy the loan in full. Insurance companies which always have large funds on their hands and rich temples and mutts are also finding the same difficulties with respect to the investment of their large surpluses.[256]

Till recent times the indigenous banking firms of Chettis or of hundi merchants of Tinnevelly have been commanding immense credit in the market. Investors preferred to leave their moneys on deposit with these bankers because of their high reputaion and secondly of the liberal terms offered by them. The moneys were generally taken by the indigenous bankers payable 'on demand'. Such moneys were earning as much as nine per cent. However, during the past five years there have been two crises amongst Nattukkottai Chetty firms. These have led to failures of some well-known banking firms. Consequently, the public have lost confidence in the stability of these firms. This has led to withdrawal of large deposits from other indigenous bankers as well. These moneys have found their way into two channels. Large depositors have preferred to put their savings on fixed deposits with reputable banks. The middle-class and small investor in his anxiety to make his savings earn as much as they were doing while on deposit with indigenous bankers has turned his attention to stock exchange securities. During the past few years this tendency has become pronounced.[257]

Bank deposits were increasing rapidly during the late 1920s. There was a slight fall-off in 1930 and 1931 because of the general international uncertainty, the failure of banks and bankers to recoup their recent outlays, and the overall financial stringency caused by the attempts of Delhi and London to preserve the stability of both pound and rupee through the international crisis.[258] But by early 1932 the urban end of the money-market began to ease. The Imperial Bank of India bank rate reached it highest point, at eight per cent, in December 1931 and then fell away rapidly to four per cent by the following July and 3½ per cent from February 1933 onwards.[259] By December 1932 the exchange banks in Madras had cut their interest rates because of the embarrassing flood of deposits which they found difficult to use.[260] The flow of gold from the rural areas to the export market also helped to transfer creditworthiness from countryside to town. The gold passed upwards through indigenous bankers and pawnbrokers to the jewellers and specie-brokers in Madras and Bombay. As the 1934-5 Income Tax Report noted, the funds which these urban dealers realized from the sale of gold often went into gilt-edged securities—assets which urban operators could use as security for loans from the modern banks.[261] 'The loss of confidence in the indigenous bankers', noted a Kaveri valley man in 1930, 'has resulted in the withdrawal of the money invested with them by the capitalist public and its deposit with the joint-stock banks who as a consequence suffer from the glut.'[262]

The main sources of urban savings had prospered from the conditions of the depression. Big merchants who survived the rationalization of the produce markets were if anything in a stronger position than before as a result of the carnage among their lesser colleagues. Government officials and professional men, many of whom were on fixed (or nearly fixed) incomes, became richer in real terms as prices fell. At the same time, rural savings began to gravitate more towards urban institutions. One economist noted that cultivators' and money-lenders' nervousness about produce prices and about government debt legislation had by 1938

to some extent diverted savings into the purchase of land and houses. But here again fear of tenancy legislation on radical lines checks the tendency to invest in lands. Some of the prosperous joint-stock banks and the well-established co-operative banks, Provincial, Central and Urban, have attracted deposits even from the villages at low rates of interest. There is indeed a glut of money and the problem is to find safe outlets.[263]

Largely because the depression also saw a spurt in urbanization, one investment that still seemed secure was urban land. The scheme to expand Madras City, and particularly to build a new middle-class suburb in the west in Mambalam, attracted investments not only from city landholders and financiers, but also from upcountry bankers and landowners.[264] Much more capital than before was, however, diverted towards joint-stock enterprises. The total number of joint-stock companies registered in Madras rose from 679 in 1925-6 to 1577 in 1939-40, and their paid-up capital from Rs 1233 lakhs to Rs 2,209 lakhs.[265] This was, of course, not really a revolutionary transformation, and even these figures tend to over-estimate the extent of change. A large proportion of the capital (about a quarter) was in banking institutions, and much of the rest was in small trading companies—mostly old family businesses which had been fitted into the legal framework of joint-stock enterprise. Yet there was a significant increase in speculative, institutional investment in urban rather than rural enterprise. From the early 1930s the major newspapers catering for an Indian readership began to carry advertisements for share-issues in new public companies. These were most commonly for cement agencies and electrical supply companies[266] (both an offshoot of urban growth), cotton mills (on which more below), and banking companies,[267] but there were also flotations to start sugar mills, steel plants, paper mills, and cinema companies.[268] Some indication of the different interests that combined to float these enterprises can be had from the lists of their directors. Madras Sugar Ltd, which planned to build a large sugar mill in the Arcots plain, included a major zamindar from the region, two principal merchants from Madras, and four retired government officials.[269] The Srimati Sugar

Mills Ltd which planned to build a similar mill in Tiruchi district, had three of the biggest landholders of the district, a Nattukottai Chettiar banker, and two Muslim merchants.[270] The directorate of the East Ramnad Electrical Supply Corporation included two local landlords, six professional men, two local merchants from the produce-market, and one banker from each of the Chettiar, Marwari, and Kallidaikurichi Brahman communities; each had subscribed Rs 3,000.[271] Madras Pictures Ltd, set up to make and distribute cinema films, was led by one of the biggest Vellala landowing and professional families of the Tambraparni valley, and had two other local landlords, a lawyer, an engineer, and a produce merchant on its directorate, and had already attracted investments among the landholding community of the far south.[272] National Movietone Company Ltd represented an alliance between some of the biggest landholders of the Kaveri and Kongunad areas, a Chettiar banker, a Marwari banker, and two small-town merchants.[273]

'The year 1933-4', recorded the report of the Madras Department of Industries, 'witnessed the highest number of new registrations [of companies in Madras] since the Indian Companies Act came into force, namely 167, as against 152 in the previous year.'[274] The number of registrations continued to be high in subsequent years: 196, 185, 236. The increase of investment in joint-stock companies soon led to the formation of a stock exchange. Earlier an exchange had been formed in Madras during the speculative boom following the first world war, but it had quickly stumbled to a halt and been closed down in 1924.[275] One Indian and two European broking firms continued to operate in Madras after the exchange closed, but business was slow.[276] However, as the pace of investment increased in the mid-1930s, four new broking firms were founded and several other small firms began to deal in shares. Without regulation and with a lot of money chasing investment outlets, the way was paved for a rather unruly market. As a government official noted on the subject of the smaller broking companies, 'their means are meagre and they cannot be relied upon for regualr deliveries and fulfilment of obligations'.[277] In September 1937 the major firms established a stock exchange association as a tactical ploy to force the less substantial and wayward firms out of business. The Association dealt little in exchange and transfer of funds, and functioned more as a channel for initial investment:

The business on the Madras Market is 90% investment as the type of investor in South India is more conservative than elsewhere and desires to invest money only hoping to obtain regular returns against uncertain returns he used to get on his private loan and mortgage investments. His anxiety has also been to invest money in a manner he can easily liquidate into ready cash should need arise.[278]

The bullish character of the market enabled the small firms to continue in business, outside the new association, and to continue to operate rather waywardly. As the Madras Mail reported: 'Then there is the flotation racket. It has been stated that there have been a large number of companies promoted during the boom, and the public have invested in these companies and lost money by heavy depreciation.'[279] There were a number of accusations that small broking firms acted as the paid agents of companies anxious to raise capital, and that the naive investor was consistently in danger.[280]

Much of the footloose capital in the mid-1930s gravitated not towards industrial or trading enterprises but towards new sorts of financial institutions. One set of institutions which profited from this trend, and did help to channel finance back to the countryside, was the co-operative movement. From 1905 to the depression the Madras government put a lot of money into forming co-operative credit societies, which it hoped would replace the perfidious money-lender in the business of rural finance. There was, of course, no such benevolent transformation; the co-operatives were by and large taken over by money-lenders and dominant landlord-cum-lenders in the villages, and their mode of operation began to approximate to those of local money-lenders despite the panoply of regulations designed to force them to operate otherwise. Several reports noted that the co-operative societies had not become communal societies of independent growers, but rather rings of money-lenders, who found the lendings from central banks to local co-operative societies a useful way to swell their own capital.[281] In one of Gilbert Slater's surveyed villages, for instance, the head of the co-operative was also the biggest local landlord-cum-money-lender and the village headman.[282] Co-operative loans fitted well into the pattern of local finance. While they were supposed to be fixed term for productive purposes, more and more they became, in effect, long-term loans to keep small landholders and tenants afloat. By the mid-1920s, forty-eight per cent of all borrowings were to cover old loans, in other words, to sustain an existing indebted position.[283] The result was that when the depression struck, they suffered in the same way as other credit institutions. Government discovered that the expansion of co-operative credit (such as it was, and it was not yet a significant figure in overall terms; the Banking Enquiry reckoned seventeen per cent but this was certainly an overestimate)[284] reflected not a steady increase of enthusiasm among landlords for the co-operative principle, but a growing dependence of certain debtors on the co-operatives; interest rates were low so debtors rarely repaid, but re-negotiated their loan at a higher level. When the depression forced the co-operatives to restrict the gross expansion of loans, there was immense trouble. The proportion of overdue repayments to total loans outlaid rose from twenty-six per cent in 1919-20 to forty-seven per cent in 1929-30 and seventy-one per cent in 1933-4. Between 1929 and 1937, a fifth of the credit societies had to be wound up, reducing the number from 12,478 to 10,041, and even among those that remained it was reckoned that only one quarter were really at work, while the others were hide-bound by a total of 5 crores laid out in loans that had become frozen.[285]

But while the idea of Raffeisen-style co-operative credit societies had apparently proved a great failure, in the 1930s the co-operative movement devised institutions which proved useful because they filled gaps created in the credit-market by the peculiar strains of the depression. One was the co-operative marketing societies, which we have already noted. Advocates of the principle of co-operation disliked these institutions, because they were 'impure'. They provided, in effect, a way for grower-traders to market their crops, and find the finance for marketing, when the indigenous bankers had withdrawn from the market and the urban merchants were reluctant to make advances against crops. They worked on funds that were raised partly from local deposits, but mainly from the modern-style banking sector. These societies began in the mid-1930s and by 1942-3 they had 61,118 members, made loans of Rs 196.76 lakhs against stocks of goods and handled 5 crores worth of produce.[286] They were still only a small part of the marketing structure, but in some places (particularly the cotton area of Coimbatore, and sugar-growing areas in Coimbatore and the far south) they were of considerable local importance.[287] The other new co-operative institution was the Land Mortgage Banks. These were set up to provide larger, longer-term loans than those offered by the ordinary credit societies. For the investor, they provided a means to lend money, essentially on the security of land, but with the added attractions of greater institutional security than was usual and, in the first year of their operation, a government guarantee of the rate of interest. Land Mortgage Banks were started in the districts from 1925, but made little progress because of their failure to attract deposit and share capital. In 1929, however, a Central Land Mortgage Bank was established. This central agency, raising money on debentures, proved much more successful, particularly in the conditions of easy money in the towns in the 1930s. It started out offering a rate of interest of 6 or 6½ per cent, but after 1934 this dropped rapidly and by 1936-7 was at the very low-level of 3½ per cent. By 1940 the Central Land Mortgage Bank debentures had attracted 168 lakhs. Roughly half of this came from short-term deposits of local government boards and another 38 lakhs came from within the co-operative movement. However 12 lakhs were from individual depositors and 22 lakhs were channelled through joint-stock banks and insurance companies. It was still a small institution in the context of the overall money-market of the province, but it had grown quickly and successfully against the background of the depression.[288]

Meanwhile, by far the biggest expansion among financial institutions came in the business of joint-stock banking. The new joint-stock banks grew directly out of the wreckage of the bazaar money-market. Local joint-stock banks were not entirely new. The Indian Bank dated from 1907, and by 1925 there were eleven other small joint-stock banks with paid-up capitals ranging up to Rs 3 lakhs apiece in the upcountry towns of Tamilnad.[289] These banks expanded in the 1930s and several new ones were founded. The first and biggest of these new flotations was the work of the leading member of the Nattukkottai Chettiar community. The Chettinad Bank began in 1929 with one crore of paid-up capital and immediately became the second biggest of the joint-stock banks based in the Tamil districts. In 1929 it attracted deposits of 109 lakhs.[290] It was quickly followed by the Bank of Hindustan, formed by the leading north Indian indigenous banker of Madras City, in association with some professional colleagues, to take over the work of the Madras branch of the Central Bank of India. Its paid-up capital of 10 lakhs, while much less than that of the Chettinad bank, immediately made it the third biggest of the joint-stock concerns.

By 1939 it had attracted deposits of nearly half a crore.[291]

Each year of the mid-1930s saw the flotation of a large number of joint-stock banking enterprises. In 1933-4 there were sixty-four (this refers to banking, loan and insurance), in 1934-5 there were forty-four, in 1935-6 thirty-five and in 1936-7 forty-seven.[292] While some of these were associations of nidhis or indigenous banks transformed, others offered shares on the open market. These included the Indian Relief Bank, whose directorate consisted of landowners, lawyers and jewellers; the Indo-Commercial Bank which was essentially founded on the capital of the Kallidaikurichi Brahman community; and the Indo-Carnatic Bank which included lawyers, landlords from the Kaveri delta and the northern portions of Andhra, and merchants from Madras and Bangalore.[293] Some of the companies floated were very small and others simply did not succeed, but forty-one new joint-stock banks were founded in the Tamil districts between 1931 and 1938. Most of them were small affairs, with paid-up capital and reserves of between ½ and 5 lakhs. Only eight of them were in Madras City itself while twenty were in Kongunad and the remainder were scattered through the other mofussil towns. The number of bank *offices*, including the various branches of each bank, in Madras City had grown from seven in 1916 to twenty-two in 1931 and then spurted to eighty-six in 1946. Meanwhile the number in other parts of Tamilnad grew from seventeen in 1916 to forty-five in 1931 and then raced ahead to 276 by 1946.[294] Moreover, while the investment in banks' joint-stock capital thus increased, the volume of deposits rose even faster. Merchants, money-lenders and rich agriculturists were clearly now placing their short-term savings with the banks rather than with the local money-lender or bazaar banker. On an all-India scale, the total volume of deposits in the Imperial, exchange, joint-stock, co-operative, and post-office savings banks rose from Rs 292.66 lakhs in 1930 to Rs 427.03 in 1939.[295]

This flood of capital into intermediate financial institutions—insurance companies also enjoyed a boom and several of them were floated on the open market by similar alliances of directors[296]—suffered a set-back in 1937-8. As with the rush to the produce-market in the pre-depression days, the rush to the security of banks, shares and insurance policies proved too erratic and uncontrolled. The crisis was sparked off by the failure of the Travancore National Bank with its headquarters in Trivandrum, the capital of the

Table 13: **Bank failures in Madras Presidency 1921-45**

	Madras Presidency		Rest of India	
	Number of banks	Paid-up capital (Rs 000)	Number	Capital
1921	1	11	6	114
1922	2	17	13	313
1923	3	203	17	46 143
1924	6	26	12	1 108
1925	–	–	17	1 876
1926	5	323	9	75
1927	–	–	16	311
1928	2	52	11	2 260
1929	2	6	9	813
1930	1	3	11	4 057
1931	4	83	14	1 423
1932	9	300	14	492
1933	6	108	20	192
1934	9	245	21	378
1935	10	153	41	6 443
1936	11	99	77	401
1937	21	839	43	313
1938	19	698	54	2 302
1939	45	1506	72	985
1940	19	555	88	1 835
1941	17	369	77	870
1942	11	239	39	1 168
1943	10	232	49	517
1944	3	175	25	452
1945	7	277	20	197

Source: Reserve Bank of India: *Banking and Monetary Statistics*, table 22, pp. 279-81.

princely state of Travancore on the west coast. The failure of this bank was to a large degree the result of a feud between the Dewan of the State and a group of Syrian Christians which included the owners of the bank.[297] Yet whatever the proximate cause, the failure was to some extent the result of the eccentric expansion of investment in Travancore National as in other banks. A handful of new, small banks in Tamilnad, including A.K.Shah and Komala Vilas,[298] and one of the major broking companies in the Madras Stock Exchange Association (Hudson, Tod and Co.),[299] went down in the same crisis of confidence. And there was a general run on bank deposits that threatened to undermine even the prestigious Bank of Hindustan. Eleven lakhs of deposits were withdrawn from this bank in three months in the middle of 1938. Four directors resigned when it was discovered how reckless the bank's officers had been in lending out, and how many bad debts the bank had acquired.[300]

This crisis completed the process of attrition which had begun in the depression. Many of the nidhis and indigenous banks which had only shakily made the transition to the joint-stock format at the onset of the depression now staggered into failure. The number of banks which had closed their doors each year had been growing since 1931 and it reached a climax in 1939 when banks with paid-up capital totalling Rs 1½ million joined the ranks of the failures.[301]

The collapse of the bazaar money-market had paved the way for the growth of a modern banking sector in Tamilnad. As we shall see in the next chapter, this not only assisted the growth of urban industry but also helped to mould the shape of the industrial sector. Meanwhile it also had a bearing on rural credit and the business of produce trading. The co-operative societies channelled funds back into the countryside and a few of the joint-stock banks specialized in lending in the commercial crop markets; the Nadar bank in the far-south tract and a number of restructured nidhis in Kongunad were active in financing the cotton trade. But most of the joint-stock banks, even most of those which had recently evolved out of the bazaar trade, were much more careful than before about lending on agricultural goods. They preferred to lend working capital to industrial concerns and provide turnover facilities for the urban retail trade. They would generally only lend on produce when it had advanced fairly far through the marketing process, and then only through trusted intermediaries. Rural money-lenders and cultivators who wished to play the produce market now found it much more difficult, though of course not impossible, to command credit from urban sources. The rural money-market had been thrown back more on its own devices.

THE MARKET IN LAND

The expansion of the rural economy through the nineteenth and early twentieth centuries put considerable pressure on natural resources. The increasing commercialization of agriculture ensured that rights of access to land, water, and grazing would become increasingly expensive and saleable items. The government, and the government's subordinates, could charge for access to water and forests.[302]Manure and cattle rose rapidly in price from the turn of the century. Land prices also began to climb upwards from the same period. In Tanjavur, the price of two-crop wet land was reported as Rs 441 to Rs 771 per acre in 1899-1903; in 1929-30 it had reached Rs 1,000 to Rs 5,000.[303] Dry land in backward parts of the plains such as the north of Salem could hardly be credited with a price in the 1880s but by the 1930s it commanded up to Rs 250 an acre.[304]

However it is very difficult to make any reliable statements about the nature of the market in land. This is largely due to the continued failure of the government to provide an effective machinery for substantiating titles in land. The only land deed distributed by the government was the patta issued by the revenue department, but this document conveyed absolutely no guarantee of land title. The register of pattas was so inaccurate that the courts would not accept them as evidence and many landholders simply did not bother to acquire their patta.[305] 'We have a considerable body of evidence', a government report on land records concluded in 1912, 'to show that the existing state of things causes general uncertainty as to title, gives scope for oppression and favouritism on the part of village officers, leads to excessive litigation, frequently based on improperly drawn up documents or on oral evidence, true or false, and helps to explain the somewhat contemptuous attitude sometimes adopted by Civil Courts towards revenue registers, maps and proceedings.'[306] There were countless suits submitted to the courts over the question of landholding, but recourse to law over land in British Madras remained an expensive, lengthy, and hazardous business. The All-India Civil Justice Committee of 1924-5 painted a chaotic picture of the administration of civil justice throughout the sub-continent; the village courts were staffed by local recruits with virtually no legal training and promotion was by seniority rather than merit, while the higher courts were manned by British revenue officers with little specialist knowledge of the law; the number of courts was so inadequate that delays were inevitable; evidence was often heard piecemeal over many months and in many respects court procedure was clearly 'illegal'. But the Committee reserved its most trenchant criticisms for the state of affairs in the Madras courts. Here there was little chance of getting a judgment in the lower courts within less than a year. If one went to the High Court then it would take a minimum of eighteen months before the case appeared before the court and seven to ten years was reckoned to be a good run. Then again, the procedure for enforcing High Court decrees was so feeble that only one in six was ever implemented.[307]

This chaos in the courts and in the machinery for land registration had several effects. Firstly, it ensured that the Madras government's records on the distribution of land and the rate of land transfer are extremely dubious. Government compiled and published data on the distribution of the patta land-deeds but we have no real way of knowing how many families owned several pattas, how many transfers of land were simply not recorded in the patta register, and how much or how little the distribution of pattas reflected the real distribution of land within the village.[308] Dharma Kumar has shown that the distribution of pattas among different size-classes changed remarkably little between the 1850s and the 1940s,[309] but we cannot in fact tell from the patta records whether this impression was secured through an equilibrating force in rural society or a simple inertia in the statistical machinery. We can however use other evidence to examine the suggestions of the patta tables. Here the first conclusion must be that differences which the patta tables (and Census material on the occupational distribution of the rural population) indicate in the different regions of rural Tamilnad seem to accord fairly well with other evidence on the historical and economic development of the various tracts.[310] In the valleys, there was a sharp division between the comfortable few and the subordinated many. About half of the population was landless and another third had plots of little more than an acre which was not really enough for survival. The remaining sixth consisted of a gentry of mirasidars which included most of the wealthiest landlords of the region. In the plains meanwhile there were fewer landless—perhaps a fifth of the total families—and a rather flatter distribution of land. Almost two-thirds of the population consisted of smallholders who were at or just below the subsistence level. The ranks of the gentry were much thinner than in the valleys—they were perhaps only a twentieth of the total—but their scarcity served to emphasize their dominance. Kongunad fell between these two extremes. It had rather more landless than the plains, rather fewer gentry than the valleys. The different distributions of land in the various taluks of the region accorded very closely with differences in natural prosperity. The most unequal pattern of distribution occurred in the Kaveri, Periyar and Tambraparni river valleys, followed by the rather less secure river valleys of the Tondai region and by the tracts at the foot of the Western Ghats where irrigation came from hill-streams. The most egalitarian patterns were in the most arid parts of the plains in Salem and the western part of the Arcots plain.

The second conclusion drawn from examining other materials on land ownership must be that the rather static picture indicated by Dharma Kumar's study of the patta tables over ninety years is by and large justified. Descriptions of the pattern of landholding in the 1810s and in the 1930s differ remarkably little. The Abbé Dubois, writing in 1818 and probably referring to the Madurai region, divided the rural population into several classes. First came the 'paupers' who included labourers, artisans and itinerants and who accounted for forty-five per cent of the total; then another thirty per cent of cultivators whose holdings would not yield subsistence and who had to live on loans and handouts from their richer neighbours; a further ten per cent were more or less subsistence cultivators, and seven-and-a-half per cent had a comfortable income from a combination of cultivation, local trading, money-lending, and village office; three-and-a-third per cent constituted the rural elite of large cultivators, traders and money-lenders; two per cent were Brahmans and bureaucrats; and a final one-and-a-half per cent were urban traders and various others.[311] The descriptions are loose, and the figures do not add up, but the profile is very clear. K.S. Seshachela Ayyar of South Arcot district gave a similar description to the Banking Enquiry in 1930. He omitted the labouring classes and concentrated on those with a stake in land. One per cent of these were big landholders who hired labour, and another five per cent were small-time rentiers with about ten acres of wet land apiece. Forty-four per cent were smallholders with less than an acre and thus little chance of subsistence, and finally fifty per cent were tenants in more or less the same state.[312]

It might seem naive and unconvincing to quote two such impressionistic local accounts as evidence for the rather static nature of the pattern of land distribution. But the point is that while many sorts of evidence—spot surveys, village investigations, patta tables, officials' casual observations—all attest to some local, short-term changes in the pattern of land-ownership, no evidence, observer or authority cares to assert that these local and ephemeral movements added up to any over-arching trends in land transfer. The comparison of the remarks of Dubois and Seshachela Ayyar over a period of more than a century is meant to emphasize that there is no obvious sign of any revolution or even evolution in the pattern of control of land.

It does indeed seem fair to assume that government's failure to provide reliable machinery for guaranteeing land titles should have dampened the market in land. There were many reports of the difficulties which holders of land titles experienced when they wished to find out simple things, such as where the land exactly was:

...even a learned man is not able to know sufficiently of his properties. If he wants to know anything he has to go and fall at the feet of the karnam and that officer rarely obliges him...Whether you consider it [patta] as a title deed or evidence of title, much of the present litigation arises on account of the ignorance of the people who do not know what they own.[313]

And prospective purchasers or creditors faced similar uncertainties:

Want of separate registration of holdings, absence of record of rights, the pernicious but time-honoured system of benami sales, the uncertain laws as to the liability of the members of joint families for payment of debts, the law relating to the disability of females, the future rights of reversioners—these make any dealings in land uncertain and speculative. Again the difficulty in obtaining decrees on mortgages, defences put forward, want of sanction for false defences, difficulties in execution [of decrees], the cumbrous law relating to exemption—these scare any investor.[314]

Leading Nattukottai Chetty bankers explained that their preference for lending money in southeast Asia rather than in Tamilnad rested in good part on the difficulties of the Anglo-Indian legal system. It was far too treacherous to lend money against land in Tamilnad.[315] The Chettiars pressed government to improve the machinery for registering land titles but government adamantly refused; they believed that such registration would make it possible for outsiders to buy up village land and thus they opposed the idea.[316] As a result, the guarantee of rights in land was still largely provided by the local community rather than by the state. Throughout the revenue department's horrified view of its own methods of revenue collection and throughout the court cases concerning land titles, the karnam's private notebooks, the evidence of the village headman, the decisions of the local panchayat, and the evidence of village neighbours play a substantial role.[317]

This had particular significance for three processes which, it might be thought, could have substantially altered the pattern of local landholding—the sale of land in cases of bankruptcy or default, foreclosure by creditors, and colonization of hitherto unoccupied land. Forced sales of land were notoriously covert affairs; as one observer reported: 'No due publicity is given of the sale. Some hangers-on of the village officer are collected together and a farce of the sale is gone through.'[318] The result, as another noted, was inevitable: 'Land in government auctions is chiefly bought by the big landholder of the village...and in the case of the absentee landlords even the sale is not known.'[319] Several other reports confirmed that it would be difficult for anyone outside the village elite to gain knowledge about such a sale, and if someone did by some means manage to buy land at such an auction he might find it very difficult to occupy the land because of local resistance.[320] Foreclosure on mortgages was difficult because of the tardiness and hazardousness of the courts, and again because of the chances of local resistance. In most cases of hopeless default by a mortgage-debtor, urban money-lenders would not try to take over the land themselves but rather would try to transfer the holding and debt together to another party; sometimes they would even increase the amount of credit made available in order to secure this solution.[321] As for colonization of new lands, this gave rise to difficulties because of the processes devised for *darkhast*, or the assignment of patta for new lands. Firstly, the procedure was carried out by the village officers and secondly, the *darkhast* rules stated that the cultivators of adjacent plots should have a preferential claim to take up any piece of hitherto uncultivated land. The result was that the established landholders of the village, and especially those with power to influence the administration of village office, held a virtual monopoly over new lands. Village labourers or outsiders could theoretically establish a claim to unused lands by using their own resources to bring them under cultivation, but in practice this was a difficult business. Firstly, local landlords would combine to prevent such an intrusion. Secondly, once they brought the land under cultivation they risked the possibility that the village officers would grant the patta for that land to someone else.[322] A government officer described the technique:

A was allowed by the village officers to clear the prickly pear off a field and cultivate it. *A* paid them half waram and they paid the sivoijama charge [revenue for temporary cultivation] out of this. When the land had been brought to a "clear" state, the village officers came to terms with the adjoining pattadar who darkhasted for and got the land. *A* remained on it as cultivating labourer...The demand for what cultivable land is available is very great and the chief obstacle to its being all greedily taken up are the various provisions of the darkhast rules, all intended to promote the interests of the ryots, but all worked in practice chiefly to subserve the interests of the village officers or individual influential ryots.[323]

In 1918, government modified the *darkhast* rules so that the village officers' control of the process was less absolute and so that established landholders had a less obvious claim to precedence.[324] But in fact the system changed very little and fifteen years later a senior official noted:

It is true that in the matter of obtaining vacant land whether for cultivation or for dwelling, the existing landholders or pattadars of a village have been able to monopolise whatever land might have been available. This had been due partly to the existence for many years of the preference given by the darkhast rules...to the possessors of 'lakti' rights [i.e. adjacent land-holders], partly to the fact that the village officers on whose reports decisions as to darkhasts and encroachments largely depend, have been as a rule in sympathy with, if not actual sharers in the interest of, the pattadars. But the monopolising tendency has not in the past operated to exclude [only] the depressed classes as such: it tends to exclude any 'outsider' whatever his caste who is not wealthy enough to acquire land in a village in the ordinary way.[325]

All these factors lessened the extent to which land would be accumulated by greedy bankers, parasitic landlords or other pre-dators lurking in the baggage train of the advancing market economy. The state simply did not provide the armaments for Mammon to blast open the village. There was of course a market for land but it was not a universal, open market. Indeed there seem to have been three separate and rather different types of land transfer. The first was simply the ordinary circulation of land within the cultivating community of the village. This was such a normal part of rural life that when people were questioned about the rate of land transfer they generally omitted to mention such transactions and spoke only of transfers outside this system. Very little of this process was mediated through governmental machinery and thus almost none of its effects are visible. We really have no idea whether land was being concentrated or not. There are suggestions that the control of the village elites, largely through village office, over the procedures of revenue-collection, *darkhast*, and land records would tend to concentrate land, but it is not possible to assess the strength of this trend.

The second market was in mirasidari titles and in other forms of 'landlord right' in areas where occupancy and cultivation on the one hand and the political control over land on the other had become separated. The transfer of such 'landlord rights' as the mirasidari tenure did not necessarily affect cultivation or the cultivator. Mirasidari titles had probably been commonly transferred for a long time whether through sale (there is evidence going back to the late Chola period) or, more often, by military action or political dictate. Indeed, the *Fifth Report* in 1818 suggested that the mirasidari elite in the Tondai region was almost completely swept away and replaced during the Nawab's administration on the eve of the British acquisition, and Tipu's invasion in 1784 probably had a similar effect in the Kaveri.[326] Moreover, mirasidari titles could serve as a savings bank. From the late nineteenth century, hoards of wealth were increasingly stored as holdings of valley wet land under mirasidari title. This form of investment was particularly attractive since the land could serve as security for raising a loan. From this period onwards, the attraction of this form of investment served to push up the price of mirasidari titles to good wet lands with the result that the price far exceeded the value of the land as an agricultural investment. As one landholder noted:

No actual cultivator will pay the fantastic prices which are necessary to buy the land in these areas. Here the purchasers are Vakils, merchants, and retired officials who wish to acquire land and in doing so are not, at the time, guided by the economic aspect of the purchase. In these tracts the agriculturist is content to take up a lease of whatever land he wishes to cultivate without any intention nor desire of purchase.[327]

People would not purchase mirasidari title in the hope of a gain from agricultural profits. It was generally reckoned that at best valley agriculture yielded a four per cent return to the share-cropping landholder and this was much lower than the return from money-lending and other forms of investment. People bought valley land for reasons of status and insurance. The official observers of the process tended to concentrate on the transactions to 'money-lenders' and other *bêtes noires* of the official mind but many of the purchases were effected by prosperous landholders from neighbouring, or even from very far distant, villages.[328]

Absentee landlords were not always resented so much as the British administrators expected them to be. To begin with, they found it very difficult to collect rents. Of course there were many absentees who were simply old residents, who left kinsmen and retainers behind in the village and were able to control their lands and rents almost as well as a resident.[329] But outside purchasers had much more difficulty, and it was commonly reported that the rents paid to such men were quite derisory. Moreover, there were indications that the loss of land to an outsider, even to a predatory money-lender, often occasioned little change in the relationship between the parties:

Where small ryots sell away their lands, they often continue to hold on to the land as tenants. In such cases, in some places, the rent is not generally the prevailing rate but it represents the interest on the old debt. Even after the sale is effected and the sale deed is executed, the ryot continues to pay the interest which is generally much higher than prevailing rent…Virtually he continues to be a debtor.[330]

In other words, the financial relationship tended to override the legalistic one.

Thus once land prices had soared beyond the ceiling of the village economy's logic, the fact that an outsider owned the land made little difference if the tenant was secure, the rent was low, and the credit-relationship was moderately unchanged. Obviously, things could not have been quite so hygienic and simple, and obviously attachment to land might have emotional consequences way beyond its economic logic. Yet, there is no obvious evidence of local resentment against outside purchasers in the period under study.

So to some extent, land in the valleys had become important as a good investment, rather than as a productive asset. As an investment it appreciated faster than prices, provided a form of life insurance, and conveyed some prestige. Bankers in some of the Periyar villages in the 1910s managed on the security of the 237 acres which they had purchased, to borrow 3½ lakhs of rupees which they could use as capital in trade and banking.[331] This worked out at almost Rs 1,500 per acre, which must have been close to the purchase price. It was an exceptionally good investment and it obviously made little odds to the absentee holder if he could not manage to collect much in the way of rent. This market in mirasidari title slumped during the depression but then boomed in the early years of the war. The rise in agricultural prices stimulated the market. It also enabled several agriculturists to pay off old debts which had stagnated during the depression, and the creditors sunk some of these funds in land. They were joined by Nattukottai Chettiais returning from southeast Asia anxious for an outlet for their capital.[332] The wartime boom of the mirasidari land market was, however, relatively short-lived. Nattukottai Chettiars and other creditors soon sold up their holdings and withdrew their funds once good opportunities for urban investment became available in the post-war years.[333] Thus in these years the price of mirasidari titles levelled out.

The third market was operated by enterprising agriculturists who were seeking good lands for commercial agriculture. This market was active in the most secure and adaptable parts of the valleys, and in the tracts under wells, particularly in Kongunad. Entrepreneurial farmers would take up good land on purchase or lease. The effects were visible in the government's survey of tenancy carried out in 1947. Between the valley districts (such as Tanjavur) and the plains districts (such as Salem) there was not a great deal of difference in the average holding of an owner-cultivator, despite the enormous difference in the fertility of the lands which they worked. In Coimbatore, the district which included most of Kongunad, the average holding was considerably larger. Next, across the plains and valley districts there was a rough correlation between the number of absentee landlords and the number of landless tenants; the valleys had significantly more of both categories, and the implication was that absenteeism and tenancy were closely linked. In Coimbatore, however, there were very few absentee owners, but at the same time there was the highest proportion of tenants among all the districts. Konguand also had a more active market in land titles than the other districts. The value of lands in Kongunad accelerated more than in any other tract; in the mid-nineteenth century good Konguand land had little more value than land in the plains whereas by the end of our period it was amongst the most valuable in Tamilnad. The rise in the price of Kongunad land was due to capital improvement rather than to any scarcity value.[334] When purchasing a well-irrigated *thottam* in Kongunad, a man was paying for the construction and maintenance of the well and its subsidiary channels, the history òf careful manuring of the land, the care in fencing to provide protection against stray animals, the work

Table 14: Landholding and tenancy 1947

Tenure category	Tenure categories as percentage of total owners and tenants in each district									
	Chingleput	North Arcot	South Arcot	Salem	Coimbatore	Tanjavur	Tiruchi	Madurai	Ramnad	Tirunelveli
Absentee landowners	12.5	6.4	6.7	5.1	6.7	13.2	5.0	7.7	8.8	7.7
Owner-cultivators who do not lease land	43.8	56.2	55.0	64.2	54.0	55.4	67.5	53.7	53.9	51.8
Owner-cultivators who lease out some land	8.5	6.3	7.7	2.8	7.2	5.2	4.4	5.7	8.6	8.5
Owner-cultivators who lease in some land	16.4	16.7	17.0	22.2	8.6	10.5	12.5	19.1	16.5	13.8
Tenants who own no land	18.8	14.4	13.6	5.7	23.5	15.7	10.6	13.8	12.2	18.2
Average holding of an owner-cultivator who does not lease (acres)	2.4	2.4	2.6	3.3	6.3	2.0	2.9	2.4	3.2	1.9
Average holding of an owner-cultivator who does lease (acres)	3.5	3.3	3.0	1.8	7.4	4.9	3.0	3.6	2.7	3.3
Percentage of owned land in an owned-cum-leased holding	45	50	45	64	53	34	47	53	52	53

Notes: Data were drawn from a survey of about a hundred villages in each district.

Source: Computed from data in GOM: *Report of the Special Officer on Land Tenures* (1951), Vol.III.

in levelling the land, and infrastructural benefits such as good local transport and marketing facilities. In Kongunad, much more than elsewhere, the price of land varied enormously from field to field, and here it reflected differences in capital value rather than anything else.[335] The price of betel gardens, sugar-cane fields and plantain plots in the valleys was similarly affected.

This latter style of land market does not seem to have affected the crude distribution of land. The entrepreneurial farms were generally quite small in terms of acreage, and most entrepreneurs restricted themselves to a size which could be comfortably managed as a unit; the intensity of garden cultivation required very close management and thus the units were rarely more than fifteen acres. But while the distribution altered little, the economic reality which it portrayed changed very substantially. In 1917, when government was attempting to estimate the number of substantial cultivators which in each district might qualify for an electorate, they placed the Kongunad district of Coimbatore mid-way between the valleys and the plains in terms of numbers. Yet just thirty years later a preliminary survey for an (aborted) scheme to introduce an Agricultural Income Tax found more potential assessees in Coimbatore than in any other district. Coimbatore had 1,574, the great mirasidari estates of Tanjavur yielded 1,511 and no other district had more than 700. The two investigations had rather different methods of assessment nevertheless the change in Coimbatore's rank is very striking. People in Kongunad were growing wealthy, not through the accumulation of land, but through the accumulation of capital improvements.

CONCLUSION

Tamilnad's agriculture became significantly more commercial during the period of high colonialism from the late nineteenth to the early twentieth century. Yet Tamilnad's accommodation to the expansive world economy was not simple, but complex and varied, and the variations matched closely with regional differences. The plains produced for the markets of Europe in the classic fashion, but Kongunad produced increasingly for the home market, while the valleys evolved a little 'sub-colonial' relationship of their own in the eastward trade. The system of production in each of the three regions was closely intertwined with the mechanics of marketing. Indeed the organization of production and the organization of marketing are best viewed as two parts of the same process. The character of both depended crucially on the leading groups in local society in each region and how they reacted to the opportunities and difficulties created by increasing demand. The mirasidars of the valleys faced the least promising market for agricultural produce owing to the competition of southeast Asian producers in agricultural tracts with considerable natural advantages. The mirasidars tended to ignore the lures of the market and to neglect the possibilities of transforming the local production system. The leading men of the plains made a much more substantial adjustment. Demand for groundnut and cotton was growing rapidly and they eagerly used their command over labour and the local surplus to fulfil this demand. But in their case the market was the most obviously 'colonial' in character; the products were destined for foreign consumers, the local buying agencies were chiefly foreign either in ownership or capital provision, and in the case of the far-south cotton tract one foreign company dominated and dictated to the local marketing machinery. In such a situation, the cultivators saw little point in penetrating the marketing structure. Cultivators were insulated from the buyers and exporters by a layer of intermediaries, who cushioned agrarian society against the transformative potential of commerce. In Kongunad, however, the cultivators were increasingly growing for a local urban market which they could play to their own advantage. Their more wholehearted involvement in the business of commerce was reflected into their strategies of labour organization, into the local flourishing of credit institutions, and into the local growth of a proper market in land.

Rural commerce proved to be very unstable, and the state did little to check this instability or to create and sustain institutions which would help farmers and traders to withstand the shocks. Commercial law and commercial institutions were badly underdeveloped and this underdevelopment encouraged instability. Between 1880 and 1950 there were major reorganizations of the marketing structure in each of the regions. Each reorganization saw startling shifts of geographic location and large changes in the personnel involved. The early phase, when foreign demand was growing for the first time in a substantial way in the late nineteenth century, saw the emergence of a loose and scattered marketing structure in which foreign companies played a large direct part and to which virtually only the privileged elites of the countryside had any independent access. The second phase, during the extraordinary growth of price and demand in the early twentieth century, saw the multiplication of marketing centres, the multiplication of financial institutions and financiers, and the appearance of strings of commission agents and other intermediaries. While of course this swelling of the ranks of businessmen was evidence of the success of the market machinery in engrossing much of the value of agricultural produce, the end result of this proliferation was to make the market more transparent and eventually to allow a wider section of the rural population to make a profit from commercial agriculture. In the third phase of contraction and rationalization after the depression, many of the smaller marketing towns were by-passed, many of the intermediaries were cut out of the marketing chain, many speculative financial institutions and operators were swept away by the cold wind of competition. This latter phase pushed the cultivators and local dealers of the valleys and plains back into a more remote, circumspect, and subordinate relationship with the marketing machinery; but at the same time it dragged the Kongunad farmers stumbling forward into a greater involvement.

Money-lending and banking were intimately connected with the growth of rural commerce. Just as it is difficult to separate the business of selling the crop from the business of producing it, so also it is difficult to separate the business of financing the crop as well. In many cases, of course, the three roles of grower, trader and financier were concentrated in a single man or family. This did not necessarily mean that a few prominent individuals had a stranglehold over land, trade, and credit. There certainly were many big "bosses' of this sort, particularly in the dry parts of the plains, but they were not unqualified despots and they were not without a good number of lesser rivals. Virtually everyone who realized a surplus from agriculture tried his hand at trade and money-lending, and thus there were many apprentice despots who created a competitive commercial environment, particularly during the expansive phase which preceded the depression.

In a countryside such as this it makes no sense to view agriculture through the theoretical retina of the individual, independent peasant, toiling away in the fields and wrestling hopelessly with the *external* forces of trade and money-lending. It does not really make sense to seize on the individual landholding, or individual cultivating family, as the crucial unit of production. Few farms enjoyed any chance of economic and political independence. It would perhaps be best to view individual holdings as work-units in a complex production system. The principal unit of organization was an 'agrarian manager'—a landlord, trader, or creditor who provided the facilities (credit, ancillary resources, perhaps land, decisions) necessary for production and who encouraged or forced other farmers to provide the labour. But then that view is too simple, for these units of agrarian management themselves were not discrete. Farmers might take tenancies, loans, assistance from several different patrons, and might produce for several different marketing chains. Intricate patterns of money-lending and clientage traced out these interwoven networks of agrarian management. Money-lending was an intrinsic part of the system of production. Of course it served to concentrate control over wealth, over the surplus, but in doing so it was reflecting the fundamental inequalities of local society, not creating them. To understand the full import of money we need to know not only how wealth was concentrated, but also how it was dispersed again. To understand the role of credit, we need to look at the circuits of agrarian capital, not just at the predations of the money-lender. This can, however, only be done in a very impressionistic way.

The expansion of demand for rural produce required an expansion of liquid capital—both to finance a larger annual turnover in the market, and to expand productive facilities. In the early years, much of this extra capital was provided in annual advances from foreign banks and companies. As time went on, more was accumulated among local traders, financiers and growers from the profits of previous years' transactions. Certainly the control over this local capital was exceptionally concentrated in the hands of the landed and commercial elites. Even so, very little of the accumulated capital was allowed to leak out (I am, of course, discounting here the profits made by foreign banks and export houses). Some was undoubtedly diverted into hoarding, as the rising stocks of imported gold clearly show; yet as has already been pointed out the value of gold stocks was not necessarily removed from the circuit of active capital since it was substantially replaced by credit instruments. Some was undoubtedly spent on consumption goods and luxuries, but again there seems to be little evidence of profligate spending on conspicuous items. Most of the profits of production, trade and finance seem to have been ploughed back into the local economy. Much of this remained in the form of merchant capital, but some also went into sustaining and expanding the productive base of the agrarian economy. Acreage was extended, wells sunk, more expensive seeds used, more acres double-cropped, and these and other forms of extension and intensification required increased spending on fixed and working capital.

The tremors of the depression broke open the circuit, and occasioned a considerable shift of capital resources. A large amount of accumulated capital was simply wasted—lost in the slide of prices, stranded by the shifts in market-location, by-passed by the changes in market-demand, consigned to the scrap-heap after the speculative booms in rice-milling, oil-pressing, and other investments in processing. The swing in the terms of trade between rural and urban goods, the attrition of money-lending and bazaar-banking, and the uncertainty about the future of demand for agricultural produce, destroyed much of the machinery which had redirected such a large proportion of the local profits of agriculture back into the cycle of production. In the aftermath of the depression there was almost certainly a decline in investment and reinvestment in agriculture which caused acreage to slump and acreage under commercial crops to slump even further. The decline of investment may very well have encouraged the move towards increased fallowing as a technique to maintain productivity without heavy financial outlay. Meanwhile, from now on capital was drained away from countryside to town much more emphatically than before. In much of the region rural marketing came more under the ultimate control of urban financial institutions which channelled much of the returns into the urban sector. A rentier economy, staffed by speculators in good-quality land and investors in joint-stock banks, started to take a much firmer hold. At the same time the rural economy was becoming steadily more dependent on the demand issuing from the local urban economy rather than directly from the overseas market. The future of the countryside now rested on the success with which the region's urban economy tranformed the value extracted from agriculture into a generator of prosperity. We must now escape through the back gate of the marketing-yard into the shops and factories of urban Tamilnad.

5

Towns

There have been towns in southern India for almost two millennia. The Sangam poets talked of cities, emporiums and resplendent capitals, and described their busy streets and tall buildings. Yet even in the late nineteenth century Tamilnad was not a very urbanized society. Only about a tenth of the population lived in towns, and most of the towns were little more than large villages. The 1871 Census counted only seventeen places with over 15,000 people. Moreover there was little sign that town and countryside represented complementary economies, each creating its own particular products and exchanging them for those of the other. The towns were rarely manufacturing centres. To a large extent this must be attributed to the slackness of rural demand for urban goods. The countryside did consume various manufactured items, but most of these were produced by local artisans and there was comparatively little aggregation of manufacturing in urban areas. Cloth, the most important single manufactured item, was produced by handloom in literally thousands of different villages throughout south India. There was even relatively little demand among the rural elite for luxury goods. Rural wealth was typically expended on services rather than goods. The rich landlord or cultivator would buy the labour of barbers, washermen, carters, household servants, priests, and other ritual and domestic functionaries rather than equip himself with consumer goods. In part this preference was culturally determined; possessions were vulgar, flashy, unnecessary, while a train of servants added to one's status and self-esteem. But it also had an economic logic, however much a circular one. So long as labour was plentiful then services were cheap, and so long as there was no competing source of employment, such as urban industry, then the supply of labour would remain plentiful.

In such circumstances the towns which grew up in Tamilnad tended to be administrative and religious centres, extensions of an external economy, and occasionally transmission points for the trade between one rural region and another. For the most part, Tamilnad's towns were not tied into a close relationship with a fixed rural hinterland. Rather they depended for their existence on 'external' factors—the state or foreign trading—and this tended to make the 'urban material' of the region geographically unstable; there were many potential sites for ports, forts, capitals, religious centres, and marts, and over the decades shifts of political power, deflections of the routes taken by the bullock traders as they wandered across the plain, changes in the direction of overseas trading, could alter the site of the major towns. Forts have grown up from time to time on unremarkable strips of beach and at river mouths, and have been readily abandoned for other sites, no better or worse endowed. The coast is dotted with the relics of past mercantile glory, now reduced to fishing hamlets or archaeological curiosities—Mahabalipuram and Pumpuhar from classical times; Korkai, Tondai, Caturangapattinam, and Devanampattinam from the time of the early travellers; Porto Novo, Tranquebar, Pulicat, and Karikal from the time of European trade; Kayalpatnam and Kulasekharapatnam from the early colonial period; and many more. Conversely, of the two major ports of modern Tamilnad, Madras was no more than a deserted and malarial strip of beach in the early seventeenth century, and Tuticorin was little more than a quiet fishing village in the early nineteenth. Nor had politics encouraged large-scale urban growth. The plains had never supported major political regimes, and this tract was dotted with many small forts rather than few large capitals. The major river valleys had all formed the sites of kingdoms, but these kingdoms had rarely extended their sway beyond a single valley and its environs. Moreover they had fought one another and fallen prey to northern invaders, and this combination of outside aggression and local strife had caused political capitals to shift and crumble. Just as, the coastline was littered with the remains of old ports, the valleys were strewn with the shells of old political headquarters and temple centres—Kanchipuram and Arcot on the Palar-Cheyyar, Tiruchi, Srirangam, and a host of satellite towns on the Kaveri, Madurai and

Ramnad on the Vaigai, Tenkasi and Palamcottah on the Tambraparni.

After some initial uncertainty, the British established a new pattern of urban growth. They built up Madras City as the administrative and commercial capital of the region, and selected a number of lesser towns as sub-ports and sub-headquarters. But the British in the nineteenth century did little to alter the character of Tamilnad's towns. They did not with any success turn Tamilnad's towns into centres of production whether for the home market or for export. The desultory character of local demand, the absence of good sources of motive power, the difficulties of establishing industries in a region where there was no urban infrastructure, discouraged British attempts to reproduce Victorian prosperity in this part of the east. This conclusion was not reached without trial and error. Both of Madras's major agency houses, Parrys and Binnys, spent much of the nineteenth century searching for profitable types of urban enterprise.[1] Both firms began as general traders but before mid-century had tried to imitate their Calcutta colleagues by processing sugar, jute, and indigo for export. The ventures were so unsuccessful that they were virtually all abandoned after mid-century, when the two companies attempted to copy the north-Indian boom in plantation production. However, Parrys made a mess of coffee-planting on the Ghats and gave it up by the early twentieth century. They also had another unsuccessful experiment with sugar manufacture, and had finally to turn the factory into a pottery. During the American Civil War, they built several gins and presses to prepare raw cotton for export but were obliged to sell these off after the boom had collapsed. They were finally rewarded for their tenacity over sugar, and also found a profitable niche in the export of groundnuts. Binnys meanwhile made disastrous attempts to import coal and manufacture ice for the growing European population, and equally disastrous attempts to mine mica and export sugar. Similarly during the American Civil War, they invested in cotton processing but decided in the aftermath to expand rather than contract; they built a cotton mill to use the cotton which was no longer demanded on the world market and went on to become the largest cotton manufacturers of the region.

Both companies survived this succession of failures because of their good foundations in the more secure business of export-import agencies and services. Binnys ran the Madras port and had a considerable stake in shipping, insurance, and minor service engineering. Parrys had slightly smaller shipping and insurance interests but were also involved in organizing emigration to Natal, introducing Charles Ewing's Patent Single Rail Tramway to India, and importing European manufactures. By the end of the century Parrys and Binnys had been joined by a number of other European firms which exported raw produce, imported consumer goods mostly for the European community, and undertook various agencies and services.[2] But the difficulties which Parrys and Binnys had in expanding their interests into more substantial activities were testament to the difficulties which any entrepreneurs would face if they attempted to transform urban Tamilnad from a service sector into a productive machine.

The desultory character of the European commercial penetration left considerable room for Indian enterprise, but this tended to suffer from the same constraints and to follow the same lines of business as the European firms. In the 1850s, a prominent European lawyer found a substantial degree of Indian enterprise in the streets behind the Madras port:

Petty Native Shopkeepers have everywhere sprung up, in the closest imitation of the European Retail, Auction, and Commission dealers; establishments are now conducted by Hindus, wherein the customer meets with as much intelligence, and civility, and articles of just as good a quality, as in those kept by Europeans: nay, Houses of Agency, carrying on large export and import traffic, have opened as competitors with the old established English Firms.[3]

A number of Indian firms participated in the rising export of raw produce. Three or four large Muslim firms rivalled Gordon Woodroffe in the export of hides and skins. Kuppuswamy Aiyer and Co. were involved in groundnut export. Stanes started his cotton mill in partnership with V. Tiruvenkadaswara Mudaliar. Many of the European companies (for instance Innes and Co.) had Indian partners.[4]

While the European companies had some comparative advantages in trading to the west, they had almost none in the smaller but nonetheless flourishing trade to the east. Here local entrepreneurs dominated. They were not so prominent as the European firms, largely because the individual firms were smaller and were very often located outside Madras in the smaller ports of the Coromandel coast. The Muslim firms of Negapatam and Nagore exported cloth to southeast Asia and imported metals, spices, betel, and later rice.

The Parava firms of Tuticorin ran rice, dried fish, cattle, cloth, and spices across the straits between India and Ceylon. And in Madras itself there were Muslims, Beri Chetties, and north Indians who imported timber from Burma, sent lungis and kailis to Malaya and West Africa, and helped redistribute spices and condiments around the countries bordering the Bay of Bengal.[5] In the case of these articles of trade, Europeans played no part as suppliers or final markets, and consequently European enterprise had little advantage and little interest. Local bankers had set up the machinery for remitting funds, and local traders played the major role.

There was however one manufactured item which commanded a secure market in Tamilnad and which thus offered potential for industrial expansion. That was cloth. In the early nineteenth century, the cheapness of Lancashire textiles created a market for mill-made cloth in India and, by a variety of devices which are by now well known, the market was protected and expanded throughout the century. Tamilnad's handloom production was far from annihilated but it was certainly severely reduced. For much of the century, half of the foreign imports into Madras Presidency consisted of Lancashire textiles.[6] Once Tamilnad started growing increasing amounts of raw cotton for export, it became clear to European entrepreneurs, just as much as to critics of imperialism, that good industrial opportunities were being lost. As we have already seen, it was one of the major agency houses and cotton exporters, Binnys, who reacted to the collapse of the American Civil War boom in cotton exporting by building a cotton mill to supply textiles to the local market.

In the first half of the twentieth century, textiles would become the principal form of factory industry in urban south India. The prosperity of three major and several minor towns would come to depend in large measure on the cotton mill industry. Thus to understand the expansion of urban south India it is necessary to follow the growth of the cotton mill industry and other enterprises which were set up later on much the same pattern of import substitution. This chapter looks first at the cotton mill industry, and then at the statistical pattern of urban growth in the first half of the twentieth century. But factory industry played a relatively small part in the life of the Tamilnad towns. In the first half of the twentieth century the most rapid industrial growth was not happening in the modern factories but in thousands of little workshops. The latter part of the chapter looks at the expansion of the petty, handicraft industries and at the general profile of urban growth.

FACTORY INDUSTRY: THE COTTON MILLS

Binnys' was not in fact the first textile mill built in Tamilnad. The first two were little more than outriders of the expanding textile industry in Bombay. The boom in cotton prices caused by the American Civil War swelled the profits of many Bombay cotton dealers, and once the market settled down again after the inevitable post-war slump, some of the capital accumulated in the boom was sunk in the construction of mills in Bombay. The southern cotton-growing areas were already supplying the Bombay mills with a certain amount of raw material, and thus it was not surprising that some Bombay merchants thought of locating new mills nearer to this growing tract. The first mill was built in Madras City in 1874 by a Bombay Parsee company, and the second was built a year later by a Bhatia entrepreneur who had already built mills in Bombay and Gujarat since the American War boom.[7]

Neither of these two mills was very successful. They had to take on the expensive services of European managers and engineers, and they had to compete in the same markets (that is, largely the export of yarn to China) with the Bombay mills without the help of the ancillary services and shipping facilities which grew up around the much larger textile complex in Bombay. The Parsees soon withdrew, leaving their mill to the Bhatia company, and by the turn of the century this first mill had closed down. The Bhatias' original enterprise, the Choolai mill, kept going until 1939 but it was in difficulties from the early years of the century, failed to take the opportunities to expand, and remained a small spinning mill with antiquated machinery and absentee management. In the example of these two enterprises, there was little incentive for south Indians themselves to invest in the cotton industry.

Binnys started their Buckingham mill in Madras in 1878 and followed with the nearby Carnatic mill six years later.[8] Harveys, who had been involved in the business of exporting cotton from the far-south tract, followed suit with a mill at Papanasam in 1885, a second at Tuticorin in 1889, a third at Madurai in 1892, and a large extension to the Tuticorin mill in 1898.[9] The third of these

European enterprises was the Stanes Company of Coimbatore. Again they were a general trading company which like Binnys had sunk capital in the expanding coffee business, found that local investment was just as profitable as trade, and looked around for new avenues. Stanes had not only a coffee estate, but also a coffee-curing works in Coimbatore town, and in 1890 they built the Coimbatore Spinning and Weaving Mill nearby. They expanded in 1910 when they took over another mill which had been founded in Coimbatore two years earlier.[10]

Binnys, Harveys, and Stanes all prospered and expanded their businesses within a few years of foundation, yet again this provided little stimulus to Indian entry into the textile business. There were Indian imitators, but their fate seemed to suggest that this was a business best left to the big European companies. A mill begun by some Muslims in Koilpatti in 1892 had little success and went bankrupt in 1908. The Mall mill in Coimbatore only survived two years before being sold to the Stanes company. The Lakshmi mill, was floated in Coimbatore in 1910 but did not immediately get off the ground.[11] The only reasonably successful Indian mill in the Tamil districts was the Kaleeswarar mill in Coimbatore. The founder was a Nattukottai Chettiar banker and both he and his principal backer had been drawn into the textile business when they had taken over another mill on the other side of the Ghats in Malabar in 1902. This Malabar mill was another enterprise inspired from Bombay. The Chettiars had invested in the enterprise and moved into management when the Bombay Parsees withdrew. The venture was reasonably successful and they added the Kaleeswarar mill in Coimbatore in 1906.[12]

There were several reasons why the European enterprises turned out more successful than the Indian. The textile industry faced several difficulties in the south. Firstly, there were no easy sources of power. Harveys used the motive force of the Tambraparni river tumbling off the Ghats for its Papanasam mill, but there was no other river which could provide such a service without expensive engineering works. Stanes used firewood from the Palghat hills (and so did the Kaleeswarar) but this was already a diminishing resource that was rapidly becoming expensive and its use was soon to be restricted by the conservationist Forest Department. Binnys (and the Choolai mill) imported coal by rail from north India. There were no coal-fields locally and freights were expensive. Secondly, there were difficulties of marketing. Nearly all the raw cotton available locally was very short in staple and often very poor in quality. It was thus difficult to spin anything but low counts and at the turn of the century almost ninety per cent of the yarn produced in Madras mills was below 20 counts (the lower the count the thicker and coarser the yarn). This made it difficult to produce cloth that could compete in quality with that from Lancashire or Bombay, and it was barely profitable to produce coarse cloth at a price that made it competitive with the better-quality imports. Thus although all the early mills started out with both spinning and weaving departments, it was only Binnys that managed to sustain and expand the business of weaving, while all the other mills concentrated on spinning yarn that could be supplied to handloom weavers or exported to the far east. Roughly a fifth of the yarn was exported, mostly to China.[13] Here the European companies had an obvious advantage because of their experience in the import-export business and their links with the European commercial complex in the east. But the chief advantage of the European companies lay in the command of capital. In the spinning industry there were opportunities for very significant economies of scale in the matter of fuel costs and management costs. The European companies were able to set up units that were sufficiently large to reap these economies of scale. By 1890, Binnys were operating over 70,000 spindles in their two mills; Harveys had the same number by 1898; and Stanes had 50,000 by 1910. Such enterprises required large sums of capital, and these were mostly raised from European sources. Binnys relied on their experience as bankers and managing agents to raise their capital, mainly in Madras itself and mainly, though not entirely, from the local European community. Harveys raised much of their capital in England, while Stanes sold shares to the growing European planting community in Coimbatore and took into partnership the major European bankers of Madras, Arbuthnot and Co. Indian entrepreneurs bitterly resented the racial division of the capital market. A prominent businessman complained to the Indian Industrial Commission in 1916:

Enterprises—industrial and commercial—under Anglo-Indian control and management do not find any difficulty in securing financial help from the Presidency Bank and Exchange Banks. The customer and banker being intimately known to each other, perfect mutual confidence is established both in India and in England. One depends on and is supported by the other, their interests are identical. Further, the retired and working partners in England are able to exercise considerable influence in several ways, such as, securing financial help from abroad and arranging liberal facilities by the Exchange Banks through the London offices. The Exchange Banks get deposits from the Secretary of State for India out of Indian balances. (It seems to me that there is no reason why they or other banks in London should have deposits of Indian money at cheap rates of interest while the same if diverted to India would be of immense benefit to her. Indeed I do not see the justice or the necessity for the Government to finance trade through the banks anywhere in England)....They further enjoy liberal discount facilities from the big London banks.[14]

The Indian mill companies could not command these sort of resources and were consequently smaller, less profitable and, as is evident from the fate of the Koilpatti and Mall mills, more prone to failure. There was no institutional mechanism for prospective Indian entrepreneurs to raise capital. It was necessary to persuade kinsmen and friends to invest money, and this was difficult when the future of the enterprise was uncertain and there were much more secure and profitable outlets for investment in general trading and money-lending. It is noticeable that the most successful enterprise came from within the Nattukottai Chettiar banking community, which was at this time generating large profits from financing export-trading and from exporting capital to southeast Asia. Some of this capital was diverted into the Kaleeswarar mills, partly by the sheer enterprise of the manager P. Somasundaram Chettiar, and partly by the flair of his backers, the A.L.A.R. family who had already shown that they were less cautious about fixed investments than most Nattukottai Chettiars by buying a zamindari.[15]

Indeed, this enterprise on the part of the Nattukottais fore-shadowed the next wave of mill expansion after the first world war. The war itself had a curious effect on the Madras textile industry. Imports of cloth declined, prices rose, and the army required considerable supplies of cloth for uniforms. But while there was thus high demand for cloth production, not all the mills profited. Binnys was the only concern that had developed a large weaving department and it gained most of the profits of military supply.[16] But other mills suffered from difficulties in securing raw materials. There was a significant expansion of local supplies of raw cotton, but wartime controls gave priority to those mills such as Binnys producing for the army. Imports of dyes and supplies of specialist yarn and high-quality Egyptian cotton (needed for the production of specialist goods) were cut off. Many of the mills were forced to work intermittently and some closed down for a period. For many of the textile entrepreneurs, it was a time of acute frustration.[17]

After the war, it soon became obvious that there had been significant changes in the conditions facing the Madras textile industry. Firstly there had been a notable expansion in the local cultivation of cotton—the acreage in Madras had grown by some eighty per cent since the turn of the century—and an even more notable expansion in the cultivation of cotton of superior quality, particularly the long-stapled Cambodia cotton plant. By the early 1920s the Cambodia plant provided a third of the Madras-grown raw cotton consumed by the province's mills and by the early 1930s it supplied over half.[18] The Madras mills still needed raw cotton imported from other parts of India, but certainly the changes in local agriculture were making the mills' raw material costs steadily cheaper, and enabling the mills to produce better quality yarn; between the turn of the century and the early 1920s the proportion which yarn under 20 counts occupied in the total yarn production of the Madras mills had been reduced from almost ninety per cent to just under fifty per cent.[19] Secondly, there had been a shift in the market. The expansion of the cotton industry in Japan had begun to take away the market for Indian yarn in China and other parts of the far east. Meanwhile, the expansion of the handloom industry within the province, based both on home demand and exports, provided a growing market for mill-made yarn. Whereas the Madras mills had found it difficult to compete with the larger and more advanced industry of Bombay in the matter of yarn exports, in the matter of supplying the local handloomers proximity gave them enormous advantages over their Bombay rivals. Similarly, the European entrepreneurs' experience in foreign trading no longer provided any special advantages and the way was being opened up for more Indian enterprise. Thirdly, the war had exposed all the weaknesses of the Bombay textile industry. Throughout the 1920s it suffered from over-capitalization, labour disputes, high overhead costs and shrinking markets.[20] This not only meant that Bombay was less of a rival to the Madras industry, but also that the government was bound to take some measures to assist the ailing Bombay industry and in so far as such measures, like fiscal protection, had a national effect, they were bound to assist the comparatively healthy industry in Madras even more than they could assist the sick mills of Bombay.

Table 15: Dividend rates in selected spinning mills, 1919-48

	Buckingham and Carnatic	Madura (Harvey) (Binny)	Tinnevelly (Harvey)	Coral (Harvey)	Coimbatore Spinning and Weaving (Stanes)	Choolai	Pankaja	Radhakrishna	Rajalakshmi	Vasanta	Kaleeswarar	Lakshmi
1919		60	60	35	10	20						
1920		80	100	80	50	50						
1921	10	100	100	80	50	50						
1922	20	75	87½	*	75	40						
1923	20	20	30		50	12						
1924	20	20	40		20	12						
1925	20	22½	40		8	12						
1926	10	19	40		10	12						
1927	10	15	40		12	12						
1928	10	20	*		12	6						
1929	10	25			8	8						
1930	10	24			8							
1931	10	10										
1932	10	10			2½							
1933	10	10										
1934	10	5				6	13	12	9	20		
1935	10	10				6	12	8	7½	20		
1936	7½	10			5	7	9	8	6	15		
1937	10	10				7	8	9	7	15		
1938	8	10				7½	11	10	7	25		
1939	9	10			6	7½			7			5
1940	12	10			6	7			7		6	
1941	12½	15			12	16			12		6	10
1942	12½	20			50	25			25		56	45
1943	15	30			50	30			30		40	70
1944	16	30			15	15			15		24	7½
1945	15	30			19	15			15		24	7½
1946	15	30			20	15			15		24	10
1947	12½	20			6	3			5		24	5
1948	16	17½			4	6			5		12	4

*The accounts of Harveys' Coral and Tinnevelly mills were amalgamated with those of their principal Madura Mill in 1922 and 1928 respectively.

Source: Bhogendranath, 34, 46, 61, 74, 83.

In sum, the Madras mills now had more convenient raw material supplies, more convenient markets and less rivalry than ever before. These advantages now accruing to textile entrepreneurship in Madras were made quite plain in the figures of dividends paid by the existing mills during the post-war boom. From 1919 to 1922, Harveys' Madurai mill paid an average dividend of 78¾ per cent, Harveys' Tirunelveli mill 86 7/8 per cent, Stanes 46¼ per cent, and the Choolai mill 40 per cent. Although the boom cracked in 1922-3, the mills continued to pay reasonable dividends throughout the decade.[21]

There were two noticeably different trends in the building of mills in the 1920s. The first was a continuation of pre-war patterns; the second foreshadowed the boom of the mid-30s. Moreover, as in the pre-1914 period, the progress of the industry was halting and the expectations of the early 1920s were nowhere near fulfilled. The onset of the depression in 1929, again brought the expansion of the industry to an abrupt halt.

Table 16: Imports of textile machinery into Madras Presidency

	Imports, value in Rs lakhs	Price index	Index of imports at constant prices 1912-13=100
1912-13	16.3	47	100
1913-14	8.6	48	51
1914-15	117.1	54	625
1915-16	3.5	64	16
1916-17	5.9	80	21
1917-18	5.4	100	15
1918-19	5.6	120	13
1919-20	14.3	137	30
1920-1	33.8	156	62
1921-2	72.8	154	136
1922-3	105.8	129	236
1923-4	67.7	112	174
1924-5	38.6	104	107
1925-6	26.0	100	75
1926-7	19.9	101	57
1927-8	25.8	99	75
1928-9	22.6	93	70
1929-30	30.1	90	96
1930-1	24.8	94	76
1931-2	15.3	92	48
1932-3	16.4	89	53

1933-4	33.0	85	112
1934-5	28.5	89	92
1935-6	38.7	105	106
1936-7	43.4	111	113
1937-8	48.7	114	123
1938-9	44.4	126	102
1939-40	19.6	150	38
1940-1	19.0	179	31
1941-2	22.2	222	29
1942-3	20.5	311	19
1943-4	12.3	371	10
1944-5	18.4	356	15
1945-6	24.4	314	22
1946-7	45.6	285	46
1947-8	93.6	254	106
1948-9	157.1	280	162
1949-50	236.9	308	222
1950-1	126.7	306	119
1951-2	89.6	333	78
1952-3	144.2	388	107
1953-4	125.2	426	85
1954-5	71.9	442	47
1955-6	137.9	454	88

Note: The price index was worked out from unit prices of UK exports of the sort of machinery Madras imported (principally spinning machinery).
Source: *Annual Statement of the Sea-Borne Trade and Navigation of the Madras Presidency.*

The first of the trends was the continuation of Nattukottai Chettiar enterprise. The community had prospered in the war and its aftermath from the illegal trade in rice to Ceylon and from the boom in rubber prices in Malaya and Burma. In 1921, Karimuthu Thyagaraja Chettiar of Madurai started the Sri Minakshi mill, in 1925 some other Madurai Chettiars founded the Mahalakshmi mill, and a Ramnad Chettiar family took over the ailing Choolai mill.[22] Bankers also played a large part in the foundation of the Vasanta mills in Coimbatore in 1929. The moving force of this enterprise was R.K. Shanmugham Chettiar who was not a Nattukottai, but in so far as he received help and encouragement from contacts he had made in the western Indian mill industry in the course of his political career, and in so far as he was a banker himself and raised capital largely from Nattukottais and others of the banking (and professional) communities in Coimbatore, his enterprise summed up many of the trends of Indian mill-building up to this point: the only enterprises that succeeded in raising the necessary capital and getting off the ground were either those which were essentially extensions of the established industry of western India, or those which drew on the excess capital of the flourishing banking communities of the region.

The second of the trends set off by the post-war boom marked a large and significant departure from this pattern. The 1920s also saw three enterprises founded by families from the Kammavar Naidu community of Coimbatore district. The Naidus, originally though often very remotely immigrants from Andhra, were the second biggest agricultural community of the district and were the foremost cultivators of cotton on the black-soil tract. As noted in the study of cotton-marketing, the leading growers in the Kongunad cotton tract had been drawn into the business of marketing and processing the crop to a much greater extent than the cotton-growers of the far south. Many Naidu and Gounder families in Kongunad had acquired substantial interests in marketing the crop and had even constructed cotton gins and presses in many of the important towns and villages of the tract. In the 1920s, three of the leading Naidu cotton-trading families moved into spinning.

The first was the PSG family. Their founder was Peelameedu Samanaidu Govindaswamy Naidu who had a successful career as a cultivator and dealer in cotton before setting up the Sri Ranga Vilas Mill in the home village just outside Coimbatore town in 1921-2. The second was the family of V.Rangaswamy Naidu, again a cotton trader, who built the Radhakrishna mill (which gave the title 'RK' to this family's industrial group) in the same village of Peelameedu in 1923. The third was G. Kuppuswamy Naidu, whose family came from the neighbouring village of Pappanaickenpalaiyam. He had started out as a cotton dealer, developed an interest in hand-ginning, set up a partnership to start a power gin, and had a stake in five ginning factories around Coimbatore by 1908. He floated his Lakshmi mill company as early as 1910 but had to give up the enterprise before the war started and failed to raise enough capital until the mid-1920s. He finally started the Coimbatore Cotton Mills in the nearby village of Singanallur in 1929.[23]

Both the bankers' mills and the Naidus' mills founded in the 1920s raised the capital in the same way. They sold shares privately, firstly to their close relatives, and then to a wide circle of kin, friends and business contacts. Generally the family accounted for a significant

portion of the capital and the entire share issue was spread over
fewer than fifty persons. R.K. Shanmugham Chettiar and his three
brothers contributed a quarter of a lakh each to the Vasanta mill
and sold the remaining 9 lakhs of shares to their contacts in
Coimbatore town and its environs.[24] In most of the mills investigated by N.C. Bhogendranath in the 1950s, twenty shareholders
owned over half the shares and in the case of the Lakshmi group in
particular the founding family owned a large (but indefinite)
proportion.[25] This was not an easy way to raise capital and the
success of the flotation depended entirely on the wealth, status, and
contacts of the entrepreneur in the first place. The earliest companies were clearly more successful than those that came later—
among the bankers' companies the Sri Minakshi raised 14 lakhs in
1921, but the Mahalakshmi could manage only 6 in 1925, and
amongst the Naidus the PSG raised 11 lakhs in 1921-2, while the RK
mill found only 8 lakhs in 1923, and the Lakshmi mill only 6 lakhs in
1929. At least two companies floated in Madurai, one in Coimbatore, one in Salem, and one in Tirunelveli in the middle of the
decade failed to attract the capital to get started.[26] Those entrepreneurs who did manage to raise funds, however, were quite
confident about the size of the market and its ability to accommodate
newcomers. There was no need for these entrepreneurs to feel that
they were rivals with one another. Indeed R.K. Shanmugham
Chettiar was encouraged to start his mill by the Ahmedabad
millowner Kasturbhai Lalbhai, and Shanmugham Chettiar himself
lent a hand to the Lakshmi group by arranging their purchase of
machinery when he went to England to equip the Vasanta mill.[27]

Despite this confidence, the progress of the industry through the
1920s was not easy, and there were good reasons why there was not
a great rush of investment. Several mill flotations had not succeeded
in attracting sufficient capital. The ill-fated Koilpatti mill had
passed to a second Nattukottai Chettiar company, which found it
difficult to raise the capital to keep it going and eventually sold it
into European hands in 1929. The Pandyan mill started in Madurai
in the middle of the decade also had difficulty in raising funds and
was taken over by the Harveys empire in 1928. Furthermore, two of
the older mills were running into trouble. The Mall mill, which had
already passed from independent management to the control of the
Stanes company, was taken over by the Nattukottai Chettiar
Kaleeswarar group and then went into liquidation in 1930. Mean-

while the Choolai mill paid out its last dividend in 1929. The onset of the depression brought the process of mill expansion to an abrupt halt. Dividend rates fell off sharply and in 1931 the principal mills made a net loss. No mills were floated between 1929 and 1932.[28]

The lull, however, proved to be only temporary. Beginning in late 1932, there was a boom in the flotation of mill companies that reached a peak in 1935 and did not tail off until 1938. Whereas twenty units under thirteen separate companies had come into existence in the past half-century, thirty new units under twenty-five separate companies came into existence in the seven years following 1932. What caused this sudden boom?

The most obvious answer would seem to lie in tariff protection. The excise levied on Indian mill-made cloth to countervail the effect of import duties had disappeared in.1925; and a duty was placed on the import of piece-goods in 1930 and it rose from an original level of fifteen per cent of British manufactures and twenty per cent on non-British manufactures to a peak of twenty-five and seventy-five respectively in mid-1933.[29] Although this was an impressive tariff barrier, its effect on the investment in the textile industry in Tamilnad is rather uncertain. Certainly as the figures for dividends show, there was no sense in which the advantages of protection were reflected in increases of profits in existing enterprises which could be witnessed by potential new entrepreneurs and investors. Dividends were clearly in decline. Moreover, the tariff protection was specifically designed to assist the ailing industry in Bombay and therefore it related mainly to the production of mill-woven cloth. The abolition of the countervailing excise and the imposition of a duty on imported yarn in fact hindered the handloom industry, which was the major market for the yarn spun in Tamilnad's mills but which also needed some specialist imported yarns. If the new mill companies were a response to the advantages of tariff protection, we might expect that investment to result in the construction of more mills to weave cloth (for this market was protected by the tariff) rather than just to spin yarn (for the handloomers were not). But in fact nearly all the investment of the mid-1930s went into construction of spinning units.

Besides, the tariffs seem to have had little success in limiting the quantity of either yarn or piece-goods imported into the Madras Presidency. Between 1921-2 and 1928-9 Madras imported on average 677.4 lakh yards of piece-goods per annum, and the

Table 17: The textile mill boom 1932-9

	Coimbatore and environs			Other Tamilnad			
	Mill Name	Capital (Rs lakhs)	Ownership	Mill name	Location	Capital (Rs lakhs)	Ownership
1932	Dhanalakshmi	8	Chettiar				
	Pankaja	6	Banker				
	Sri Rajalakshmi	7	Naidu				
1933	Palani Andavar	6	?				
	Ramalinga Choodambika	5	Chettiar				
	Sri Venkatesa	6	Naidu				
	Pioneer	5	PSG Naidu				
1934	Balasubramania	4	PSG Naidu				
	Janardhana	4	Naidu				
	Sri Saradha	1	Gounder				
1935	Jayalakshmi	4	N. Indian	Sri Rajendra	Salem	5	Chettiar
	Kamala	3	Naidu	Trichinopoly	Tiruchi	5	N. Indian
	Murugan	5	Banker				
	Gnanambika	4	Gounder				
	Saroja	3	Chettiar				
	Tirumurthi	4	?				
1936	Lotus	3	?	Mettur Industries	Mettur	?	European
				Rajapalaiyam	Rajapalaiyam	5	Raju
1937	Asher Textiles	4	Muslim trader	Jawahar	Salem	4	?
	Kothari	6	N. Indian	Thirumgal	Gudiyattam	6	?
	Palamalai Ranganathar	2	Naidu	Lakshmi	Koilpatti	?	Lakshmi Naidu
1938	Kasthuri	3	Naidu	Soundararaja	Dindigul	3	?
1939	Kumaran	4	PSG Naidu				

Source: Ponniah, 'Production and marketing', I, vi and vii; Dalal and Co.

corresponding figure for 1929-30 to 1935-6 was 780.1 lakh yards. For yarn the equivalent figures were 80.5 and 73.8 lakh pounds per annum. Neither government fiscal policy nor the implied protection of a world depression in trade appear to have been giving much incentive to the investment of funds in the Madras textile mills.

Much more important seem to have been the advent of hydro-electric power and the availability of capital. The Pykara hydro project was conceived in the 1920s, built on the slopes of the Nilgiri hills, and began providing electricity in 1933. The first lines ran down to the region of Coimbatore town and before long the current was being used to power spinning machinery.[30] While this overcame one of the bottlenecks to the expansion of the industry, the access of Indian capital overcame another. Among the thirty mills started in Tamilnad between 1932 and 1939, there were two European flotations, one north Indian enterprise[31] and a sprinkling of local bankers among the directors and managers. But the dominant force in the expansion of this period was the agriculturists and traders from the cotton tracts, particularly of Kongunad. Two of the three Naidu groups founded in the earlier period made substantial extensions by building new mills, while other Naidu and Gounder families from

Table 18: Cotton textile companies in Tamilnad 1941

Company	No. of units	No. of spindles	No. of looms
1. The early European companies			
Harveys	4	465 424	
Stanes	1	46 434	280
Binnys	2	119 108	2 776
2. The early Naidu companies			
Lakshmi	4	105 672	
PSG	4	66 092	
RK	1	33 960	
3. The early 'bankers' companies			
Choolai	1	40 164	774
Karimuthu	3	63 540	
Mahalakshmi	1	10 240	
Kaleeswarar	2	63 200	644
Vasanta	1	28 104	270
4. New European companies			
Cambodia	1	29 284	
Mettur	1	24 252	603

5. New Coimbatore companies

Asher	1	12 000	
Kamala	1	9 304	
Murugan	1	11 480	
Dhanalakshmi	1	25 300	126
Gnanambika	1	11 200	
Janardhana	1	17 880	
Kasturi	1	7 940	
Kothari	1	13 824	
Lotus	1	12 512	
Palani Andavar	1	20 400	
Venkatesa	1	11 200	
P. Ranganathar	1	5 600	
R. Choodambika	1	13 124	
Saradha	1	11 424	168
Tirumurthi	1	11 200	
Vyasa	1	9 560	
Kuverraj	1	12 000	
Jayalakshmi	1	18 720	
Pankaja	1	21 200	

6. New non-Coimbatore companies

Loyal	1	24 242	224
Rajapalaiyam	1	12 300	
Sri Kothandarama	1	40 000	82
Soundararaja	1	6 400	
Trichinopoly	1	16 000	
Thirimasal	1	12 040	

SUMMARY

Class of company	Total no. of spindles in class	Average spindles per company in class
Early European	630 966	210 322
Early Naidu	205 724	68 575
Early "banker"	205 248	41 050
New European	53 536	26 768
New Coimbatore	255 868	13 467
New non-Coimbatore	110 982	18 497

Source: Most of the information comes from Ponniah, 'Production and marketing', I, ch. VI appendices i and ii; ch. VII, appendix I. Additional information from other sources cited in footnote 32.

Kongunad, and later some of the leading grower and trader families from the Raju community in the southern cotton tract, also made the move into the cotton industry. The mills which they built were mostly very small indeed. The average number of spindles worked by each of the mill companies already in existence by 1929 was 94,722; the average size of the new mills in Coimbatore in the 1930s was 13,647 spindles, and most were in the region of 12,000. The entire total of thirty-one new units not owned by Europeans had only just as many spindles as the Harvey company.[32]

The crucial factor in the foundation of most of the new mills in the 1930s was the availability of capital, indeed the readiness of investors to put their funds into this particular sort of enterprise. The cotton mills were probably not as obviously profitable a form of investment as they had been in previous years. But it was not the *absolute* level of profitability that was important. The drastic decline during the depression in the profits to be made from lending on and trading in raw agriculture produce left many local merchants and money-lenders with idle funds. Although cotton mills did not yield the sort of returns that trading and lending had done, particularly in the good years of the mid-1920s, the examples set by the Naidus' and bankers' companies showed that it was a fairly safe and paying sort of investment. Many of those who in previous years had taken a satisfactory profit from trading in cotton and then been happy to allow some other entrepreneur to take a further profit on the same raw material by spinning it into yarn, realized that the best way to counteract the fall in profits from raw-cotton trading would be to capture the profits from spinning.

The Naidu pioneers had demonstrated that it was not particularly difficult to establish a spinning mill. There was plenty of rough, inexpensive land on the outskirts of Coimbatore. Buildings and machinery were moderately inexpensive—the average cost of plant was in the region of Rs 100 per spindle—and a small mill could be set up on a fixed capital of 5 or 6 lakhs, and perhaps even less if the machinery was bought second-hand from a mill in Bombay which was either retooling or going bankrupt.[33] The few skilled men necessary for a spinning unit could generally be lured away from established mills in Madras City or Bombay, and the remaining labourers needed only a minimum of training and could be recruited easily in the neighbouring villages. Weaving required more skilled labourers but few of the new mills established in the 1930s bothered to install weaving sheds. There was a good market for yarn among handloom weavers and exporters.[34]

Thus many new entrepreneurs came forward from the ranks of the rural cultivators and traders. The mill industry could easily be seen as an extension of their existing activities rather than a qualitatively different ('industrial' rather than 'commercial') undertaking: the fixed capital was small, the working capital large and the turnover rapid. The problems of raising capital and organizing management became significantly different if the unit was large, but the Kongunad enterprises were all small, with a lot of the capital and most of the managerial talent supplied by the founding family. The cotton-growers of the Kongunad tract were much more intimately involved in the process of marketing and dealing in cotton than their counterparts in the far south. The major families of the Kongunad cotton-tracts already had considerable urban interests and considerable personal investments in the cotton business, and through their contacts of kin, caste and fellowship in village society they could command the investment funds of other growers and traders. In the far-south tract, by contrast, there was a layer of professional merchants and dealers who stood between the growers and the market. This tended to inhibit the agriculturist groups from reacting to the depression in the same way as the Naidus and Gounders of Kongunad. Both the Lakshmi and PSG from Kongunad set up mills in the southern tract before there was any significant flourishing of local enterprise. Only the Rajus who grew cotton in western Ramnad and dominated the cotton market in Rajapalaiyam town followed their example.[35] The Nadars who dominated the business of dealing in cotton in the southern tract reacted to the strains of the depression in a completely different way (as we shall see below) and did not promote a cotton mill until 1947.

The boom of investment in the cotton mills followed a pattern which had already been seen in the Kaveri rice-mill industry in the early twentieth century and in the oil-pressing industry on the plains in the 1930s, and which would soon be repeated in the leather business and in sugar manufacture. Once a particular enterprise had been revealed as safe, moderately profitable and easy to enter, capital was likely to flood in rapidly. Moreover, because there was as yet little development of financial institutions, and because investors preferred businesses with which they had some personal contact and some personal guarantees of security, this capital tended to be mobilized in lots of small industrial units rather than fewer big ones. In such a situation it was difficult for the various entrepreneurs to monitor the state of the market, and to gauge when that particular industry had become saturated. The flow of investment would therefore be very eccentric; it would snowball rapidly, continue beyond the point of saturation, and then cut off abruptly once the signs of over-investment were clear. Such eccentric patterns of investment left in their wake industries crowded

Table 19: Estimated production and consumption of mill-spun yard, 1914-15 to 1937-8

In 000 lbs

	Yarn spun in Madras mills 1	Yarn imports 2	Consumed in Madras mills 3	Consumed by Madras handlooms 4	Yarn exports 5	Balance (1+2)− (3+4+5)
1914-15	43 032	10 300	8 000	64 200	3 881	−22 849
1915-16	44 303	12 130	10 700	62 500	5 963	−22 730
1916-17	44 187	9 702	12 500	62 700	1 810	−23 121
1917-18	43 093	6 464	13 100	62 800	637	−26 980
1918-19	42 787	5 320	14 300	56 600	478	−23 271
1919-20	44 346	3 400	12 800	49 400	7 046	−21 500
1920-1	41 241	6 713	11 600	62 800	1 767	−28 213
1921-2	44 388	8 418	10 200	66 000	1 545	−24 939
1922-3	53 425	7 408	14 000	74 000	560	−27 727
1923-4	50 939	6 430	14 800	56 000	323	−13 754
1924-5	54 221	8 782	15 600	70 000	252	−22 849
1925-6	57 837	7 690	15 200	65 000	204	−14 877
1926-7	64 495	8 642	16 400	74 000	262	−17 525
1927-8	68 748	7 646	17 800	73 000	529	−14 935
1928-9	69 036	9 387	17 700	59 000	368	+ 1 355
1929-30	74 480	10 655	18 500	78 000	266	−11 631
1930-1	76 926	6 995	17 600	83 000	705	−17 384
1931-2	87 729	6 623	19 400	94 000	740	−19 788
1932-3	104 910	9 416	20 100	72 000	741	+21 485
1933-4	98 274	5 489	18 000	72 600	624	+12 539
1934-5	101 395	6 063	21 000	78 000	764	+ 7 694
1935-6	113 615	6 938	20 600	83 400	475	+34 078
1936-7	129 886	7 023	21 000	86 800	816	+28 293
1937-8	136 403	6 629	23 000	75 700	9 354	+34 978

Source: *Annual Statement of the Sea-Borne Trade and Navigation of the Madras Presidency*; Bhogendranath; Ponniah, 'Production and marketing'; *Annual Review of the Indian Central Cotton Committee*.

Table 20: Consumption of cotton grown in Madras Presidency 1928-9 to 1941-2

In thousand bales (of 400 lbs.)

	Consumption by Madras mills					Foreign exports					Consumption elsewhere in India					Totals				
	K	T	C	O	total	K	T	C	O	total	K	T	C	O	total	K	T	C	O	total
1928-9	30	52	66	26	174	17	54	21	74	166	11	1	41	125	178	58	107	128	225	518
1929-30	24	47	56	29	156	18	31	19	77	145	16	4	56	167	243	58	82	131	273	544
1930-1	30	41	60	32	163	3	24	10	44	81	14	6	38	131	189	47	71	108	207	433
1931-2	42	43	78	40	203	0	8	1	23	32	9	8	30	141	188	51	59	109	204	423
1932-3	43	52	93	27	215	10	35	2	81	128	11	4	48	136	199	64	91	143	244	542
1933-4	37	49	111	19	216	15	72	7	58	152	8	9	73	126	216	60	130	191	203	577
1934-5	30	36	117	41	224	16	49	20	13	98	10	19	91	180	300	56	104	228	234	622
1935-6	47	64	164	37	312	9	55	44	86	194	3	8	41	143	195	59	127	249	266	701
1936-7	58	53	151	32	294	11	27	51	111	200	2	0	38	131	171	71	80	240	274	665
1937-8	49	64	193	27	333	1	5	2	26	34	3	9	18	194	224	53	78	213	247	591
1938-9	55	58	141	34	288	9	8	1	125	143	4	7	20	186	217	68	73	162	345	648
1939-40	67	55	174	37	333	7	8	4	23	42	4	1	18	103	126	78	64	196	163	501
1940-1	73	68	226	64	431	10	8	10	31	59	13	1	36	116	166	96	77	272	211	656
1941-2	70	81	228	29	408	0	0	1	3	4	9	0	72	4	85	79	81	301	36	497

Note: K = Karunganni; T = Tinnevellies; C = Cambodia; O = Other.
Karunganni, Tinnevellies and Cambodia were virtually all grown in the Tamil districts, whereas the 'other' varieties (Salems, Westerns, Northerns) were mostly grown in the Telugu districts.
Sources: *Annual Report of the Indian Central Cotton Committee*; Ponniah, 'Production and marketing'; Bhogendranath.

Table 21: Supply and demand for cotton, 1928-9 to 1941-2

(In 000 bales of 400 pounds)

| | Supplies of raw cotton to Madras mills | | | % of total cotton grown consumed in Madras mills | % of Cambodia cotton grown in Madras consumed in Madras mills | Production and consumption of raw cotton grown in Madras | | | | | |
| | | | | | | CAMBODIA | | KARUNGANNI & TINNEVELLIES | | OTHERS | |
	from Madras	from rest of India	from abroad			Estimated out-turn	Out-turn minus Consumption	Estimated out-turn	Out-turn minus Consumption	Estimated out-turn	Out-turn minus Consumption
1928-9	174	207	1	34	52	147	19	162	3	391	166
1929-30	156	185	3	29	43	144	13	162	-22	210	-63
1930-1	163	200	5	38	51	90	-18	129	-11	218	11
1931-2	203	266	39	48	72	128	19	131	-21	254	50
1932-3	215	286	2	40	72	139	-4	139	-16	224	-20
1933-4	216	283	4	37	65	153	-38	130	-20	243	40
1934-5	224	285	9	36	58	208	-20	141	-19	173	-61
1935-6	312	406	13	45	51	209	-40	137	-49	318	52
1936-7	294	383	24	44	63	198	-42	138	-13	200	-74
1937-8	333	427	18	56	91	225	12	134	3	227	-20
1938-9	288	431	20	44	87	99	-63	123	-18	198	-147
1939-40	333	502	45	67	89	143	-53	158	16	177	-14
1940-1	431	595	na	66	83	208	-64	159	-14	169	-42
1941-2	408	na	na	82	76	256	-45	170	10	178	-142

Note: 'Out-turn' estimates come from Madras agricultural statistics. The minus signs in the 'out-turn minus consumption' columns suggest these may be under-estimates. Even if this is the case, there is still a clear trend.
Source: *Annual Report of the Indian Central Cotton Committee*; Ponniah, 'Production and marketing'; Bhogendranath.

with many small units all of which found it difficult to make a profit, and a residue of units which had not quite been completed when the boom cracked. The subsequent history was one of attrition and decline, and a reluctance among investors and entrepreneurs to look to this particular sector again.

The figures for the availability and consumption of yarn (see tables 19, 20, 21) should not be considered very accurate because they ignore details of coasting trade (which anyway was small), and lack data on rail trade (which the government decided not to collect in the crucial years) and because the major figure for handloom usage is a clever but fallible estimate. Nevertheless these figures tell a story which is clearly close to the truth. They suggest that the immediate consequence of the disorganized mill-building of the mid-1930s was that a deficit in the supply of yarn was rapidly turned into a surplus, and certainly this is what other evidence implies. From 1936 onwards, stocks of unsaleable yarn built up in the mill compounds. In fifteen mills surveyed by the government there were 5,476 bales of yard in stock in July 1936 and 13,116 bales in stock on the same date in 1939.[36] Mill-owners and politicians attributed this stock-piling to the dumping of cheap Japanese yarn, and to the consequences of the Indo-Japanese trade agreement of 1934, which obliged India to import 283 million yards of yarn from Japan.[37] But Japan was a convenient excuse rather than a convincing explanation. Imports of yarn had not increased significantly in the late 1930s, and certainly not on a scale to account for the large stocks in the compounds. In 1938-9, the year of the greatest outcry, imports accounted for only two per cent of the yarn available and the proportion had in fact been falling over the past four years.[38] Rather, demand had simply not expanded as fast as supply, and both the millowners and yarn-merchants were reluctant to reduce the yarn price in an attempt to disperse stocks. Instead they tried to get help from the government by summoning up the bogey of unfair Japanese competition, which had proved politically useful to other textile interest groups within the last decade.

There were good reasons why the mill-owners looked to the government rather than to price-reduction as a cure for their difficulties in the late 1930s, and to understand this we must examine their reaction to the ending of the mill-building boom. By the time it became obvious that the local market for yarn was approaching saturation, there were many mills in the course of construction, and many other mill companies still at the stage of flotation. Some of these companies folded, but many more just forged ahead. Since it was considerably easier to attract investment once the mill was actually in existence, rather than when it was just a paper proposition, many entrepreneurs set about building mills at the limit of their personal capital and with some assistance from short-term bank loans, in the hope of replacing much of their personal and bank-borrowed investment with share capital once the mill was completed. By the mid-1930s, many such enterprises launched into production with a paid-up capital that did not even cover the costs of the plant, and with a heavy reliance on expensive short-term bank finance to cover this deficit and to provide enough working capital to start operations. As a government official noted in 1939: 'The financing of the textile industry of Coimbatore is far from satisfactory. The paid-up capital of the [15] mills noted in the enclosure is about Rs 110 lakhs while their total block [i.e. fixed] capital is Rs 180 lakhs. The balance has been found partly from short-term borrowing and partly from revenues at the expense of reserves. In times of depression, the creditors generally withdraw their deposits.'[39] A cotton trader who had himself recently set up a mill added: 'Managing Agents of the Mills have unwisely extended their Mills beyond their capacities, and borrowed capital is being locked up in block [fixed] capital on machinery and buildings. Almost all the Mills in my District [Coimbatore] are placed in a great predicament, because they are not in a position today to arrange finance to meet the demands of borrowed capital.'[40] Banks might reasonably have been expected to be cautious about such loans, but then many of the promoters of the cotton mills, particularly in Coimbatore, had enough interest and influence in local banking circles to get over this wariness. Thus at least eleven mills started work after the existing units had begun to complain of rising stocks.

From 1936 onwards, the Madras textile industry advanced steadily into a state of crisis. Stocks built up; Harveys (which was big enough both to control the yarn price and to safeguard itself against disaster) initiated a cut in the price of yarn in July 1938 which made things increasingly difficult for the small mills; the advent of so many new mills increased the competition for raw cotton and pushed the ruling price in Coimbatore above the level of the Bombay market-price; then a bad cotton harvest in 1939 started to push the raw material price even higher, banks started to call in their short-term loans (particularly the Central Bank of India which had advanced over 70 lakhs to the Coimbatore mills), and the 1938 banking scare which followed on from the failure of the Travancore and Quilon Banks almost precipitated a wholesale crisis among mill-owners and bankers of Coimbatore.[41]

As the mills were forced back onto lower margins of profit, those companies with less advantages in the market obviously suffered first. The large European concerns and the well-established Naidu groups remained relatively secure. Among the other Indian mills, there were two categories which were badly in trouble. The first consisted of the very new mills built since 1932. They were especially anxious to display good profits and dividends in order to attract more share capital, but this was of course particularly difficult while they were paying out high interest charges for the bank loans which the share capital was supposed to replace. Besides this, many of the newer mills had had to hire managing agents, who put up some capital of their own and also lent an air of respectability which helped to attract further investment funds. But these managing agents demanded very high fees, often unrelated to the company's turnover, and this again put a strain on the company's working resources.[42] Many of the smaller mills tried to get over these problems by clever accountancy, and the balance sheets of the small Coimbatore mills acquired a certain fame as works of fiction. A 'leading auditor' of Coimbatore told a student investigating the mills that it would be 'a waste of time' to use the mills' balance-sheets as a source of statistical data since 'they often try to conceal information rather than reveal it'.[43] The second group of troubled mills included the older ones which had not taken the opportunities of the early 1920s or the early 1930s to expand their capacity or to renovate their plant. Both these categories suffered because of the small size of the units. They found that they paid much higher charges per unit of electricity than did the larger mills, and they seemed to require almost as many managerial staff as a mill several times the size. As the crisis deepened new mills such as the Saroja and Sri Saradha had to cut down production and lay off workers, one old and small mill the Coimbatore Spinning and Weaving paid almost no dividend throughout the decade, and the very early Choolai Mill finally went bankrupt.[44] But while the Choolai mill was the only major casualty, all the mills had to adjust to a situation of fiercer competition and lower margins of profit. Both the old mills worried about competing with antiquated machinery and the new mills, anxious to raise dividends and profits enough to overcome the shortage of capital, were obliged to run more 'efficiently'. That meant using the plant more intensively or driving down the cost of labour.

Thus in the later 1930s many of the mills tried to intensify their operations. In particular they favoured spinning yarn of higher counts since this was more valuable, and the proportion of yarn over 30 counts rose from 9.2 per cent of the province's output in 1928-9 to 29.8 per cent ten years later. This meant using better raw materials and thus the amount of Cambodia cotton consumed by the Madras mills rose from 66,000 bales in 1928-9 to an average of 162,000 in the years 1935-6 to 1938-9.[45] Similarly, the mills tried to increase the amount of work required of skilled personnel, particularly by doubling up the number of spinning frames which a single man supervised. And finally they introduced shift systems which enabled the mills to stay in operation for all or most of the day.[46]

They also drove down wages. In 1929, Arno Pearse reported that wages in the south of India were well below those in the cotton mill centres further north and that those in Coimbatore were the lowest in south India.[47] In 1930 and again in 1933, Harveys led the way in cutting mill-workers' wages on the grounds that food prices had fallen in the depression, despite the fact that Harveys (and many other mills) still had good profits and reasonable dividends. There was some resistance from the workforce but it was easily broken.[48] Then as food prices started to rise after 1934-5, there was no attempt to increase mill wages. Indeed, several mills tried to cut wages further, on the grounds that Japanese dumping was undercutting the price of yarn, and there were many complaints that the mills refused to give adequate compensation for the increases in the length and intensity of working brought about by the 'efficiency' schemes. Mills often sacked workers who protested about wage rates and about the increase in duties, and still found it easy to replace such men with new recruits from the surrounding villages.[49]

The result was a series of strikes. The Binny mills had suffered badly from labour trouble in 1919-21 when the cracking of the post-war boom coincided with the advent of constitutional reform, but apart from that and some trouble in the Stanes and Harveys mills in the late 1920s[50] mill labour in Tamilnad had been remarkably docile. But a wave of strikes which began in 1937 and climaxed in 1938 affected a large number of the south Indian mills, particularly those in Coimbatore. Some of these strikes resulted in very hasty lock-outs and there were good reasons to suppose that they were either promoted or at least quickly exploited by managements who saw the opportunity to restrict production and cut losses while the market was low. The mills hoped at the same time to get the sympathy of government, perhaps even for a further cut in wages. But most of the strikes were simply the result of friction and frustration. Indeed when the mill managements, encouraged by government's past record in labour matters and by its recent zeal in suppressing left-wing organizations in the province, appealed to the government for assistance in the war against labour, they were considerably surprised that it chose to attribute the strikes to inexperience and inefficiency of management and to the low level of wages.

The trouble began in September 1937 in the Lakshmi mill over the pay and duties of spinners, and quickly spread to ten mills, largely those of the Lakshmi and Kaleeswarar groups.[51] Fifteen thousand workers were involved for periods ranging up to six weeks. The government commissioned an enquiry into mill wages, but before the enquiry had reported, there had been a strike over wages and leave provisions in the Choolai mill and strikes in the Saroja, Sri Sarada, and Sri Ranga Vilas mills as a result of management attempts to cut down production.[52] The report appeared in April 1938 and recommended that wages be standardized up to the highest rates prevailing.[53] Many managers were horrified. A lot of the new Coimbatore mills had been deliberately located in the villages to take advantage of cheap labour at the cost of higher charges for transport and electricity, and they obviously could not compete on terms of equal wage-bill with mills located in the towns. Moreover, mill-owners argued that it would be folly to increase wages at a time when the market for yarn was falling. Hurriedly the government appointed another commission. By the time this reported in July there had been another spate of strikes, mostly arising from petty disputes between workers and supervisors or from individual cases of maltreatment and dismissal. Both mill-managers and the Collector of Coimbatore argued that the recent history of poor mill management and successful mill strikes had made local labour exceptionally volatile. The second wage report recommended moderate increases but was worried that even these might bankrupt some of the shakier mills.[54]

In most mills wages were increased along the lines of the government's recommendations, but the financial position of the mills remained weak and the desultory history of poor labour management continued. In 1939 the Murugan mill-workers struck work over wages and the management's attempt to abolish the night-shift; the Kaleeswarar workers struck over the payment of bonuses and provision of leave; the Choolai workers struck over the government's wage award and made the management decide finally to close the mill down. Later in the year there were small strikes at the Sri Ranga Vilas and Kumaran mills over the wage awards.[55] The officers of the Madras Government produced a whole catalogue of reasons for the unrest of mill labour. They recognized the effect of certain political 'agitators' on building up trade unions but were less than willing to blame the whole phenomenon on extraneous political influences. Rather they pointed to the rapid expansion of the industry, the instability of mill finance, the poor wages and conditions of labour, and the tendency of many of the new managers to treat the mill-workers like their field-labourers or domestic servants. Many of the strikes, they noted, began with minor shop-floor disputes and were fanned by the crass handling of both the supervisory staff and the management. They recognized that it would be difficult for the government to rectify the inexperience of management, but they started to erect a system for intercepting labour complaints in the hope that it would prevent many of the small examples of managerial incompetence resulting in major disputes. They also considered that a slightly richer labour force might well be generally more contented. Yet when the management argued that the state of the market precluded any possibility of a wage-rise, the government asked to look at some of the mills' books to verify this argument and reluctantly agreed that it was true. The government did however point out that the mills' difficulties were largely due to the uncontrolled expansion of the industry, the lack of a good capital base, and the high fees demanded by managing agents.[56]

This period was specially important in shaping the government's attitude to industry and industrial labour. The government was anxious for the mill industry to prosper, and to that extent it wanted to put profits in the pockets of the millowners. But it was also interested in public order and, particularly against the background of the later stages of the nationalist movement and the growth of left-wing politics, was concerned that discontented mill-workers might prove a peculiarly uncontrollable political force. Thus the government qualified its support of the mill-owners with three specific sets of conditions.

The first was that labour and management should submit their disputes to a kind of court set up by the government. During the disputes of 1938-9, the government threw together a skeletal procedure for conciliation while a more elaborate machinery was being devised. The second was that the mills should raise the general level of wages and standardize the rates paid for the same post in different mills. Many of the large, well-established mills were prepared to pay higher wages in order to stabilize their labour force and outflank their rivals; but the government eventually accepted the argument of the smaller, shakier mills that a high rate would drive them to bankruptcy. Thirdly the government recognized that there was considerable inefficiency and profiteering on the part of management, and thus demanded that managing agents' fees be reduced and linked more closely to the profit and turnover of the mill. This demand remained little more than a demand, since the government had no machinery to enforce such a stipulation. But all three sets of conditions set the tone for the government's involvement in industry, as personnel manager, accountant, and holder of the scales of industrial justice.[57]

In the end, Madras's bloated and fragmented textile industry was saved more by circumstances than by government policy. In 1938 Japan's distraction in war in northern China re-opened a market for yarn in the far east which had been lost to Japan thirty years before; and then the advent of the second world war sent prices and the demand for cloth spiralling. The price of yarn began to climb soon after war was declared, and by early 1941 it was soaring. The British again looked to the Indian textile industry to supply a large amount of cloth for military uniforms, while imports of cloth fell away and the decline in supplies from Britain, the United States, and Japan opened up large markets in Africa, southeast Asia, and Australia. The Tamilnad mills could sell all the yarn they could make. The only restrictions they faced lay in the supply of raw cotton and the inability to import new machinery to increase their capacity. The existing resources were therefore used with great intensity. By 1943, most of the mills were employing shift systems that enabled them to work most of the day and night. The average number of persons employed each day rose from 62,120 on the outbreak of the war to something over 90,000 at the end. The machinery was used so relentlessly, and in many mills without adequate maintenance, that by the end of the war it was in very poor condition.[58]

Profits were enormous, particularly in the year 1943, before the government erected a full array of wartime controls. In that year there was hardly a single mill that did not make a profit at least as large as its paid-up capital, and several mills made seven or eight times that amount. In 1943 among a sample of forty-one mills, twenty-two of them paid their managing agents a fee (related to profit and turnover) that was larger than their entire annual bill for wages, bonuses and salaries. And twenty-three of a sample of thirty-eight mills paid dividends ranging from thirty to seventy per cent. In 1944 and 1945, the imposition of taxes and controls dulled the rate of profit. Prices were supposedly fixed to prevent such high levels of profit although it was well-known that a large amount of cloth was sold on the black market. Many mills hid part of their profits, placed it in the reserve funds, or even paid higher wages, to reduce their liability for the new Excess Profits Tax. Even so dividends still ranged between ten and thirty per cent, profits per annum exceeded paid-up capital in about half of the units, and managing agents were not badly recompensed. One estimate reckoned that forty-five of the province's eighty cotton mills made a profit of Rs 20 crores between 1943 and 1945, and another estimate reckoned that the mills of Coimbatore alone made 13 crores in 1944-6 (that is, excluding the boom year of 1943). The firms that paid the biggest dividends in these years (averaging over thirty-five per cent per annum in the years 1943-5) were the big established companies of Harveys, the Kaleeswarar group, and the three Naidu groups of Lakshmi, RK, and PSG. The newer and smaller Coimbatore mills came next (between fifteen and twenty-five per cent per annum average) while most of the smaller mills outside Coimbatore were rather more conservative with their dividends and devoted rather more to reserves.[59]

Hardly any new mills were started in the early 1940s because of the difficulties over the import of machinery, but two earlier flotations did come into operation in 1942-3 and quickly made immense profits. Towards the end of the war, the PSG Naidu group

floated two new enterprises, but most of the other mill companies
were happy to use the windfalls of the war to stock up their reserve
funds, pay dividends that attracted investment to make up for their
early deficit in paid-up capital, and put money in the pockets of
owners, directors and managing agents. Mill shares did not increase
in value at anything like the same rate as profits, dividends or even
prices. On a base of 1935=100, an index of south Indian textile mill
shares stood at 85 at the outbreak of war, rose to the level of 191 for
one brief month in the middle of the 1943 boom, but fell away
rapidly thereafter. The fall was partly due to the effect of government controls, but more to public distrust of a share market which
proved particularly volatile; it was a small market and seemed easy
to manipulate, and after some people had fared very badly in the
fluctuations of 1942-4, interest in share dealing fell away. At the end
of the war, many of the mills dealt with the rather embarrassing
question of their enormous reserves and accumulated profits by
presenting bonus issues to their shareholders; this device enabled
them to increase the paid-up value of the company, soothe the
shareholders annoyed at the declining share values, and keep all the
accumulated profits within the company's safe.[60]

In 1945 the industry looked set fair for another bout of expansion.
But in fact, the coming of peace meant the re-emergence of all the
structural deficiencies of the industry that had been disguised by
wartime demand. The mills had worn out their machinery in the war
and had not been able to devote their profits to replacement. Now
the war was over they would face renewed competition from mills in
Europe, the United States and Japan. Moreover, India would be
obliged to import any new machinery from the very countries it
would now face as competitors, and it was reasonable to expect that
these competitors would re-tool their own industries before they
sold machinery to overseas rivals and that consequently India would
soon be left behind. India of course had the capital and the chance
to develop its own machine tool industry, but that would necessarily
take time.

There were also other old difficulties. The large number of small
units still made the industry very volatile. When government undid
price controls in March 1948, there was an immediate run on the
market creating a shortage, high prices, and rapid working in the
mills. By the time the government reacted and reimposed controls,
the market was glutted and government had to use the control

machinery to prevent more yarn entering into an already saturated market.[61] Stocks built up and by October 1948 it was reported that 'there is no more storage space in the mills.'[62] There was also an immediate return to the labour troubles of the late 1930s. Wages had been roughly standardized by the two government enquiries of 1938, but by 1945 there was again a chaos of different rates. During the war, wages had risen nowhere near so much as prices and profits, and various different formulae for 'dearness allowance' linked to the government's new cost-of-living index had brought about vast differences between mills. The 1938 reports had fixed basic wages between Rs 11 and Rs 16, depending on the particular task and on the location of the mill. When S.R. Deshpande made an all-India survey in 1946, he reported that wages in the south were still remarkably low in comparison to other mill centres, and wages in Coimbatore in particular were abysmal. Four-fifths of a sample of mill-workers in Coimbatore were still being paid between Rs 11 and Rs 16. The government immediately ordered that wage rates be moved up to a minimum of Rs 23, while they inaugurated a thorough investigation of the matter.[63] But before this was completed, there was another wave of strikes. The grievances were much as before—low wages and a variety of petty disputes over leave, dismissals, and shopfloor discipline—aggravated by the fact that the workforce was aware of the post-war shortage of cloth and the strength of their bargaining position in the short-term. The Harveys Mills raised their own wage rates above the government's required level and provoked a wave of envious strikes in the other mills in Madurai.[64]

From 1946, the dividends paid by the Tamilnad textile mills slid down from the dizzy heights of the war, and stock prices came tumbling down with them. Thus faced by declining levels of profit, labour trouble, shrinking markets, difficulties over retooling, and volatility in the market, few mill entrepreneurs were anxious to invest and expand. Besides, there was still a residue of wartime controls that surrounded any decision to invest with a tangle of red-tape. In 1946 the PSG groups set about building a new mill specifically to spin very high counts; it took them thirteen months to get the necessary government approval for their articles of association, application to import machinery, and licence to use electricity.[65] There were fifteen mills built in Tamilnad between 1945 and 1950, but only four of them were in Coimbatore and apart from the

PSG group (which built one mill in Coimbatore and one in Tirunelveli) few of the established textile entrepreneurs were interested in expansion. Most of these new establishments represented the tail-end of the expansion of the 1930s. Some were located in Madras City with an eye on the southeast Asian export market, but most were scattered around the weaving towns in or near the cotton tract so that they might gain the advantages of proximity to the supply of raw cotton, to a source of cheap labour, and to a market of handloom weavers.[66]

Few of the established mills were anxious to expand under these conditions. Most of the small mills in Coimbatore were not even anxious to retool. Such firms considered that a larger size meant a larger element of risk. They were reluctant to take on larger problems of labour control, and were uncertain how to make the transition from a small family business to a larger and more structured company. This transition presented very real problems in finding good and loyal managerial staff. If they had no wish to expand, then there was little logic in retooling; in the short-term it was always better to run the existing machinery, even at a gradually declining level of efficiency. Many of the small mills founded in the 1920s and 1930s were run down gradually to bankruptcy in the late 1960s (and nationalization in 1971-2).

The basic fragility of the textile industry's expansion meant that from the beginning most successful entrepreneurs had chosen not to reinvest profits in their own businesses but to spread their accumulating capital into a diverse range of interests in order to insure against localized disaster. Indeed, it seems likely from the figures of shareholding produced by Bhogendranath for 1951, that many of the original entrepreneurs, once their companies had prospered, actually reduced their own shareholding and their degree of control in their own companies.[67] Meanwhile, they spread their capital into service and retail businesses which could generally be assured of a reasonable turnover. The appearance of the motor bus and motor lorry in the 1930s meant that many successful textile entrepreneurs put their accumulated profits into small bus companies and trucking fleets. Later cinema halls and printing presses became popular, while agricultural land, urban property and general trading companies were always a favourite location for such diversifying investment. The boom in mill building in the 1930s ran out into a mass of small service enterprises in the 1940s and 1950s.

The three Coimbatore Naidu companies which had got under way in the 1920s were much more successful. They had of course some advantages from the fact that they established early and had reached a reasonable size by the time the industry became saturated. But they also accepted the logic of capitalist development to expand. They diversified like everyone else but they diversified in some ways that were beneficially linked to their original textile interests, and they overcame problems of management by manipulating ties of kin and caste. Both the Lakshmi and PSG groups expanded throughout the 1920s and 1930s and, as noted above, the PSG groups were quickly off the mark again after the war. The RK group took rather longer to get going, but then all three expanded in the mid-1950s, with financial help from the planning commission and technical assistance from foreign collaborators, while most of the other mill companies were resigning themselves to profitable decline. They expanded by founding new companies to occupy their sons, and the expansions of the '30s and '50s (and again in the '70s)· mark the passing of generations. By marrying within a close circle, employing sons within the family business, and expanding the family's interest at the same rate as the ramification of the family tree, the Naidus overcame many of the problems of management that confronted other mill companies. The Lakshmi group provides the clearest example. The founder, G. Kuppuswami Naidu, got started in the late 1920s by contracting a marriage alliance with a neighbouring Naidu family. He added mills steadily until the group commanded three by the end of the 1930s. His sons (four in all, but one died in 1952) took those over on his death in 1949. They added three more mills in the 1950s, and the next generation (two sons and a son-in-law) added three more factories connected to the textile industry in the '60s and '70s.[68] The PSG group was the biggest. The founder, P.S. Govindasamy Naidu died in 1926, four years after the foundation of the first mill. In the 1930s, four sons added two more mills, and acquired a further one by marriage. The next generation added another six mills to the group between the end of the war and the late 1950s.

From the beginning the families of these three leading Naidu groups, and their industrial interests, were closely intertwined. They invested in one another's enterprises, and exchanged company directorships. One of the biggest expansions of the late 1940s was a joint venture by the RK and Lakshmi groups, and in the 1950s the coming generation of the Lakshmi and PSG families cemented close marriage ties.[69] In the early years the Naidu families used their profits in the usual ways. The PSG family put a lot of money into land in the 1920s and 1930s and the two leading members of the second generation each had holdings of over a thousand acres. All three families took some interest in banking, bus companies, petrol bunks, and automobile repair works. The PSG groups also acquired some interest in fruit processing and fertilizers, and the Lakshmi set up a flour mill. But their diversifications were connected much more with the cotton industry in some fashion. Much of the PSG land was devoted to growing cotton and experimenting with new strains, and the RK family also had an experimental cotton farm. The PSG group started out with an 'Industrial Institute' in 1926 which made metal parts for factory construction, and expanded it to manufacture prime movers, lathes, and small machine-tools. Later they also added a bleaching and printing works in the weaving centre of Erode. The RK and Lakshmi groups reacted to the problems faced by the industry after 1945 by going in for the manufacture of textile machinery (to overcome difficulties over import) and viscose (to overcome problems of the supply of raw cotton).

Besides these major undertakings, many of the skilled employees of the Naidu companies hived off to set up small foundries, machine-shops and repair-works. The leading families did not try to prevent this leakage of skilled labour, but often encouraged it and lent capital to some of these workshop enterprises. This development not only provided many ancillary services for the local mills, but also helped to lay the foundations for light industries (notably the manufacture of irrigation pumps) which helped to make Coimbatore into the biggest and most varied industrial town of the south.[70]

But the success of the Naidu groups only served to point up the poor state of most of the other mill companies founded in the 1920s and 1930s. Except for a short boom in the mid-1950s, most of these mills were 'sick' from the end of the war to their takeover by the government in 1971-2. But while this final act made the government one of the biggest entrepreneurs in the textile industry, its involvement in the industry had advanced in line with the industry's growing problems from the time that those problems were generated in the expansion of the 1930s.

In the late 1930s, as we have seen, the government took over some responsibility for handling the relations between mill managers and their labour force. During the war, the government moved into control of the market for textile goods. In August 1942, it started moves to control the price of yarn and by August 1944 it had taken responsibility for the entire distribution of yarn. Mills had to reveal details of their production; all yarn produced by the mills went into a pool; and the government organized the distribution. The government also ordained the production of certain types of standard cloth and fixed quotas for production and distribution right down to the retail level. Decontrol in 1948 was a failure and the government had to retain control over the distribution of yarn into the 1950s, even though the provisions were quickly eased. The government also retained some control over the pricing of mill output. In 1948 it appointed a Tariff Board to enquire into the price structure of yarn and cloth. The Board evolved a formula for calculating the prices of yarn and cloth and set up machinery to monitor the working of this formula at regular intervals.[71]

The wave of strikes that marked the advent of peace meant that the government had to widen its role in industrial conciliation. In 1946 it raised the minimum wage to Rs 23 and then in 1947 increased that to Rs 26, with provisions for fluctuations according to the cost-of-living index. This settlement, however, led to a chain of new problems. Mill-owners complained that the fixing of wages without a parallel definition of the labourers' duties and obligations was nonsense, so in 1948 another government commission had to fix standards for each job in textile mills. This report occasioned another wave of strikes, and led to yet another series of commissions in the following year on the wages due to certain categories of skilled workers.[72]

Besides these questions of price control and labour conciliation there were many other ways in which the government was becoming involved in the textile industry. It was largely government capital which had founded the electricity-generating industry in the region, and with the increased use of electrical power both by industries and by agriculturists with irrigation pumpsets, the government found it had to take policy decisions about the distribution of scarce electrical output. The retooling of the textile industry required imported machinery and under the incipient planning machinery this presented the government with a decision over the use of foreign exchange.[73] Many mill-owners wanted to extend their interests into weaving as well as spinning, and this presented the government with the question of whether to favour the mills or the handlooms.[74]

While mill-owners complained bitterly about price controls and the advance of red tape, there were many that were aware that the clumsy structure of the industry would make it increasingly dependent on the assistance of the state. To the small mills which needed the government to handle their labour problems and to fix prices so that bigger neighbours could not drive them out of the market, this was obvious. But it was also clear to some of the bigger concerns. In 1945, the managing director of Binnys argued persuasively that the future of the industry would depend crucially on the assistance of the government, and he cited four main areas where government assistance was vital. The first lay in the development of more long-staple cotton. The finer types of yarn and cloth constituted the most promising part of the market and any extension of the supply of suitable raw cotton would require government investment in development of new strains, and government persuasion to spread their popularity among farmers. The second was the manufacture of textile machinery, which would probably require government initiative and investment. The third was labour relations, where the Binnys director argued, 'since the Government should guide, and, if necessary compel progress along the right lines, it follows that there should be a highly qualified staff in the Industries and Labour departments of the Provincial Government.' Finally, there was the need for 'extensive government measures of an anti-cyclical character designed to prevent those fluctuations in economic activity which have hitherto been accepted almost as if they belonged to the order of nature.'[75]

European entrepreneurs in India had generally been known for their extreme attachment to laissez-faire, yet here was the European manager of one of the oldest and largest companies in the south, on the eve of the transfer of power to Indian hands, arguing for greater state intervention in his own industry.

The cotton mill industry was not the only factory industry to grow under the strange conditions of the 1930s. Just as there was a rash of new textile companies borne up on the new availability of capital in the early 1930s, so there also appeared a number of flotations to build oil-mills, match factories, cement works, and sugar-processing plants. In all these cases, the new investment was to some extent attracted by tariff policies; sugar, matches, and cement all gained significant measures of protection in the 1930s. But as in the case of cotton, the growth of the 1930s had significant precursors in earlier years, and cannot be simply attributed to fiscal encouragement. Many of the cash-crop cultivators, traders and financiers from areas other than the cotton tract responded to the depression in the same manner as the cotton men—that is, by investing in manufacture. Moreover, they soon faced much the same problems. We have already seen that the groundnut trade invested heavily in oil-pressing factories in the 1930s. The number of oil-presses in the province increased from thirty-four to 238 between 1931 and 1938, and as in the case of cotton these were virtually all small units, each requiring about half a lakh of fixed capital. Again the investment overshot the demand. By 1938 it was reported that only half the capacity was being utilized and in 1940 it was reported that 100 small presses on the Arcots plain had been sold off for scrap.[76] The industry revived in the war, when government encouraged oil-pressing on the grounds that it not only supplied oils to the home market but also provided oilcake which the government required for manure as part of the Grow More Food campaign.[77]

The cotton tract in the far south reacted rather differently. Here, as we have noted, the cultivators were less involved in commerce than in Kongunad and did not for the most part make the transition into the mill industry. The Nadar merchants who handled most of the cotton trade in the towns of the far-south already had a wide range of commercial interests and were famous for the breadth of their enterprise. Under the encouragement of the 1930s tariff protection they sunk their idle capital, not in the textile trade, but in the manufacture of matches. Again, it was a case of many small units rather than a few big ones. By the 1960s, the town of Sivakasi had 800 small match factories. However there were also some unusual linkage effects in the match business. The manufacture of splints and boxes developed into a wide range of timber and furniture concerns. The production of chemicals for match-heads led towards firework, explosives, and other chemical industries. And the printing of matchbox labels developed into a litho-printing concern. Still the units were small. Sivakasi had fifty small litho-printing works.[78]

The major industry which developed beside cotton was white sugar. The history of the growth of the sugar industry in Madras is just as long and hesitant as that of cotton textiles. Both the European agency houses, Parrys and Binnys, had been attempting to develop a sugar industry in the region since the early nineteenth century when London abolished duties favouring West Indian sugar and for a short time encouraged import of sugar from India. Neither company was very successful. The total acreage under sugar-cane in the Tamil districts was quite significant—towards the end of the century it fluctuated around 30,000 acres—but there were great difficulties about using the cane for a white sugar industry. The sugar factories competed for supplies with the makers of the crude country sugar known as jaggery. The factory process was more efficient at extracting sucrose from cane and could afford to pay a premium to secure supplies. But in order to work efficiently and economically, a factory needed a convenient catchment area with enough cane to keep the factory in operation for a large part of the year. Sugar-cane deteriorated quickly after harvest and it was expensive and pointless to transport it over any great distance. If there were just isolated plots of cane then the jaggery-maker, who circulated from plot to plot and who processed the cane in the field itself, was in fact in a much stronger economic position. Yet in Tamilnad, the cultivation of sugar tended to be scattered in this way. Sugar-cane cultivation required large amounts of manure and long periods (up to a year) of steady water supply; without these conditions the sucrose-content of the cane dropped dramatically, and the advantages of converting the cane into white sugar rather than jaggery were correspondingly reduced. There were few places in Tamilnad which enjoyed both good supplies of water and good supplies of manure. Besides, sugar was an expensive crop to cultivate (because of the cost of seed and manure, the large use of water, and the long time needed in the field) and was very susceptible to drought. Few farmers would risk putting more than a small portion of their acreage to sugar-cane. And in the ideal tracts—the reliable parts of the valleys, the Kongunad *thottams*— sugar-cane had to compete for space with many other expensive and profitable crops (plantains, betels, vegetables). It was difficult for a prospective sugar factory to find tracts of cane that were extensive enough, compact enough, and of good enough quality, to render it sensible and profitable to pay the premium necessary to divert the cane away from the jaggery-maker.[79]

Binnys quickly gave up and sold their interests to Parrys. Parrys were more successful because they concentrated on distilling the sugar (and palm sugar) into alcohol as well as producing white-sugar, and the former had a more steady market. Thus their first plant at Cuddalore was later turned over completely to distilling; their second at Nellikuppam tried to produce both sugar and alcohol and had to be helped along by a considerable expenditure to improve the irrigation works for the local cane-growers. A third plant at Kallakurichi was closed down. A fourth at Ranipet (actually started by Arbuthnots and soon handed over to Parrys) had later to be converted to the production of manure, chemicals, and pottery. A fifth at Kulasekharapatnam also failed within thirteen years despite the company's construction of a light railway to transport the cane from the cultivating area.[80]

Parrys were not the only sugar company to be visited with failure and projected sugar mills in Coimbatore, Tanjavur, and South Arcot had all been abandoned. When the first world war cut off imports of sugar and the Government of India raised the duty on sugar to ten per cent in 1916 and then to fifteen per cent in 1921 in order to get more revenue, there was some impulse to investment. Two sugar factories were built in the Tirunelveli district, and there was a clear parallel to the development of the cotton mill industry. As in the case of many of the cotton mills built in the period, both the entrepreneurs came from the Nattukottai Chettiar banking community, and one was in fact the Nattukottai firm which had just taken over the Choolai cotton mill.[81]

Again the progress of the industry soon petered away. Although southern India still imported a lot of sugar, on a world scale there was imminent danger of a glut, and the Javanese were leading a race to improve the efficiency of production and cut prices. Although the government raised the duty to twenty-five per cent in 1922 and to fifty per cent in 1925 (again with the sole aim of increasing revenue), world prices of sugar were falling so rapidly that imports continued to increase. Both the Chettiar companies failed. By the end of the decade, Parrys again monopolized the field. By now they had spent considerable sums on irrigation and transport in the growing area for their Nellikuppam factory. They extended credit and arranged supplies of seed and fertilizer for their farmers. And they even acquired land and tried to grow high-quality cane themselves but

Table 22: Imports of sugar and sugar machinery into Madras Presidency 1920-1 to 1955-6

	Import of sugar (tons)	Import of sugar machinery, Rs lakhs	Index of machinery imports at constant prices, 1922-3=100
1920-1	19 212	2.6	199
1921-2	15 038	1.4	116
1922-3	9 864	0.9	100
1923-4	12 204	0.2	28
1924-5	30 584	0.4	57
1925-6	29 129	0.2	30
1926-7	54 253	0.2	31
1927-8	66 425	1.3	194
1928-9	71 765	0.2	29
1929-30	98 054	0.1	15
1930-1	88 291	0.1	15
1931-2	79 120	1.0	171
1932-3	55 613	4.2	825
1933-4	53 884	9.0	1 715
1934-5	49 793	16.2	2 936
1935-6	39 314	1.9	344
1936-7	773	4.4	726
1937-8	121	3.3	480
1938-9	6 708	2.9	412
1939-40	39 475	1.8	246
1940-1	59	9.7	1 203
1941-2	1 490	7.8	873
1942-3	4	1.0	103
1943-4		0.6	60
1944-5		8.2	773
1945-6		2.4	197
1946-7		9.2	683
1947-8		23.4	1 523
1948-9	10 034	55.0	3 227
1949-50		42.8	2 368
1950-1	6	12.5	630
1951-2	8 872	1.1	52
1952-3		18.6	769
1953-4	17 327	14.7	551
1954-5	8 139	4.8	183
1955-6	8 226	75.1	2 754

Note: The last column was calculated using an index of prices of sugar machinery based on the unit prices of sugar machinery exported from the UK.

Source: *Annual Statement of the Sea-Borne Trade and Navigation of the Madras Presidency.*

found it uneconomic compared to the less sophisticated but also less expensive methods of the ordinary farmer. At the end of the decade, they refitted their Nellikuppam factory and extended its capacity.[82]

After a series of tariff board enquiries, the government raised the level of duty on sugar to roughly 185 per cent in 1931-2. Although this was a substantial incentive to investment in sugar processing, and it had a clear effect on an all-India scale (the number of sugar factories in India increased from thirty-two to 152 between 1931-2 and 1935-6),[83] it did not have an immediately stunning effect on imports into Madras. These had stood in the region of 20,000 to 30,000 tons per annum between 1910 and 1925 and had been boosted rapidly to a peak of nearly 100,000 tons in 1928-9. They had started to decline even before the imposition of the tariff and continued to decline only slowly, so that even in 1935-6 imports still stood (at almost 40,000 tons) higher than in any year before the late 1920s boom.

Even so, investment had already begun to flood into the sugar industry. A large number of new joint-stock ventures to construct sugar mills were floated from 1931 onwards; the imports of sugar mill machinery soared; and thirteen new factories were built in the province (five of them in the Tamil districts) by 1937-8.[84]

The effect of the tariffs had been reflected in prices. While the price of jaggery fell in line with other food prices during the depression, the imposition of the huge tariff in 1931 halted the slide of white sugar prices. For the first time in many years, sugar factories could pay a sufficient premium to attract cane away from the jaggery-makers. The result was that the price of sugar, relative to other crops, rose slightly during the depression and there was a small but significant shift upwards in the acreage under sugar-cane in the early 1930s. From 1931-2 to 1936-7 the acreage under sugar-cane in the Tamil districts was consistently over 40,000, a level that had been reached before only in the latter years of the first world war. With the assistance of new varieties of cane developed on government's research farms the yield per acre advanced rapidly.[85]

The main problems facing the development of the sugar industry in Madras had always been the supply of raw material and the provision of capital. The dramatic change in the relative prices of white sugar and jaggery during the depression began to solve the problems of supply. The new-found readiness of trading groups to put their funds into manufacturing industry overcame the barrier of capital. As in the case of the cotton mills, it was bankers, traders, and growers who led the way, and in fact it was the Naidus of the Lakshmi cotton group of Coimbatore who established one of the new factories. Both the Nattukottai Chettiar sugar enterprises of the 1920s were re-opened under the control of different Nattukottai firms. A third Chettiar firm floated a company with local land-owners, traders, and prominent officials on the directorate, mentioned in its prospectus the new tariff and the high dividends now being paid by sugar companies in north India, and started a factory in North Arcot in 1935-6. A coalition of local bankers, traders and land-owners started another mill near the head of the Kaveri delta in Tiruchi district.[86]

Again the companies were small. The new flotations were in the region of 6 or 7 lakhs, and the combined crushing potential of the five new companies amounted in 1938-9 to 272 tons, which was insignificant beside the capacity of 1,000 tons possessed by Parrys' single factory at Nellikuppam, and clearly rather foolhardy since the estimated minimum size for an economic unit was in the region of 300 to 400 tons.[87] By the end of the decade, these small units were in difficulty. Production had risen quickly from the 15,000 tons produced by Parrys alone on the eve of their expansion in 1929-30, to 67,000 tons (in the whole province) in 1940-1. Madras was not yet producing enough to supply the province's total demand (which was around 100,000 tons) but the industry had expanded much more rapidly in north India and by 1936-7 there was a glut of sugar in India. Besides, the expansion of production in India in the 1930s had helped to undermine the attempts to stem world over-production of sugar by means of international agreements, beginning with the Chadbourne agreement in 1931. The result was a world sugar conference in 1937 that introduced measures to check any further expansion of production and effectively prevented any attempt to export excess sugar from India. The glut meant that sugar prices remained low when other prices started to rise. In 1938-9, the acreage under sugar in the Tamil districts fell by twenty-five per cent. Many of the factories made losses from 1937 onwards, and even Parrys cut their dividend down from the usual ten per cent to five per cent. Several newly floated sugar companies sank without trace. In 1938 the Tariff Board decided that even in view of the rapid growth of recent years, the industry still needed protection.[88]

Again the war acted as a saviour of an already badly balanced industry. Imports were now firmly ruled out, difficulties over rail transport cut down the supply of sugar from north India, and in 1941-2 and 1942-3 Madras made a large net export of sugar (16,291 and 11,822 tons respectively). Prices increased, even relative to other crops, and the acreage expanded dramatically despite the Madras government's attempt to encourage the production of foodgrains. At the end of the war, the acreage was double the high level of the 1930s and still growing. Parrys took most of the profits from the wartime boom. Unlike the small companies, Parrys were strong enough to plan an expansion during the doldrums of the late 1930s, installed new machinery in the early years of the war, tripled their production between 1938 and 1948, and bought out the largest of the new Indian sugar companies of the 1930s in the last years of the war. As with cotton mills, there was another boom in the construction of sugar mills on the impetus of high post-war prices, but by 1950 this too was punctured and the tariff board needed to take another look at the difficulties of the sugar factories.[89]

In Tamilnad the 1930s saw a boom of investment in local industry, producing mainly for the home market. To some extent, this was encouraged by the government's policy of tariff protection but, as Bagchi and others have noted, this policy was carried out rather half-heartedly and, as this study has pointed out, it was not clear that the tariffs in fact protected the home market. Much more important was a shift in the relative attractiveness of different sorts of investment. From the late nineteenth century onwards, considerable capital had been generated in commerce, particularly in the handling, processing, and exporting of cash-crops. This commerce offered several different opportunities for investment—ranging from lending money in the villages, to starting an account in a bank which lent on produce stored in the market—and these investments were more attractive than any others available. The depression of agricultural prices and the contortions of international trade from the mid-1920s onwards drastically reduced the profits in these forms of investment, and destroyed much of the institutional machinery which had channelled funds into this form of commerce. Considerable amounts of capital were probably lost in the slump, but much was simply conserved, stocked up in bank accounts or hoards, and

not pushed back into the cash-crop trade. A number of entrepreneurs from the old cash-crop business experimented in diverting
this capital into producing manufactured goods for the home
market. Generally these were cultivators and traders who decided
to undertake the industrial processing of the very crop which they
already grew and handled. They mobilized the idle capital of their
family and friends, and were able to tap other reserves of idle capital
which had built up in the joint-stock banks.

The enterprises which resulted had all the marks of merchant
enterprise. They favoured industries in which the ratio of fixed to
working capital was low, the turnover fast, the labour force
unskilled. They kept the units small, to minimize the problems of
raising capital and finding managerial talent from beyond the
original family. They were reluctant to reinvest profits in expansion, but rather sought forms of 'insurance' by diversifying
investment into retail and service trades which were reckoned more
secure than industry proper. The result was a rather unambitious
industrial sector. The nearest Tamilnad got to heavy industry in this
period were some cement works, which appealed since they had the
same characteristics of low capital and high turnover, and some
small engineering works which spun off from the textile industry.
The result too was eccentric swings of investment which created
rather fragile collections of small industrial units. This was wasteful
in the sense that the number of failures was high, and the amount of
fixed capital which was scrapped was considerable. It was also
politically significant in that it had, before the end of the 1930s,
brought the government to intervene in industrial management in a
way which would have been improbable a decade or so earlier.
Finally it was socially significant in the way in which it influenced the
pattern of urban growth.

THE GROWTH OF TOWNS

The 1871 Census listed forty towns with populations of more than
10,000 in Tamilnad. Although a century of colonial rule had
influenced the urban population, the pre-colonial pattern still
showed through in the distribution of these towns. Twenty-four of
them were situated within (or closely associated with) the valley
areas; six of these were ports with a history of overseas trading,

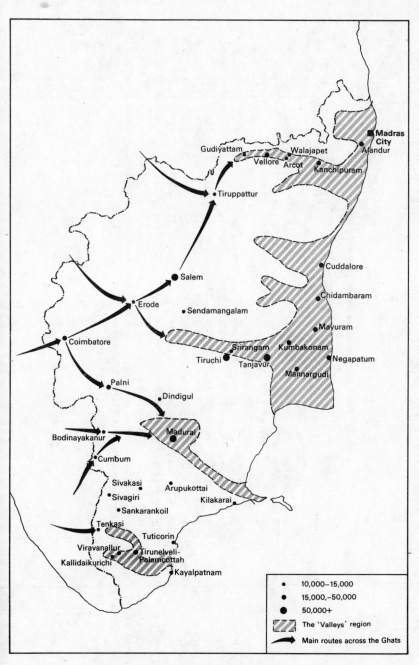

Map 6   Towns over 10,000 population in 1871

Table 23: Tamilnad: population and urbanization 1901-61

	Excluding Madras City					Madras City		Including Madras City				
	total population	% growth	urban population	% growth	urban as % of total		% growth	total population	% growth	urban population	% growth	urban as % of total
1901	18 227 601		2 130 648		11.69	552 899		18 780 500		2 683 547		14.29
1911	19 786 361	8.55	2 528 800	18.69	12.78	575 377	4.07	20 361 738	8.41	3 104 177	15.67	15.25
1921	20 416 338	3.18	2 733 353	8.09	13.39	591 536	2.81	21 007 874	3.17	3 324 889	7.11	15.83
1931	21 987 366	7.69	3 362 424	23.01	15.29	733 552	24.01	22 720 918	8.15	4 095 975	23.19	18.03
1941	24 499 338	11.42	4 127 466	22.75	16.85	881 485	20.17	25 380 823	11.71	5 008 951	22.29	19.74
1951	27 564 882	12.51	5 612 443	35.98	20.36	1 416 056	60.64	28 980 938	14.18	7 028 499	40.32	24.25
1961	30 551 589	10.84	6 931 891	23.51	22.69	1 729 141	22.11	32 280 730	11.39	8 661 032	23.23	26.83

Notes: The 1961 Census reworked the earlier population figures to match the districts as they stood in 1961. The 'urban' figure, however, is the sum of all those places which each particular Census decided to call a town.

Source: *Census of India 1961*, Vol. IX Madras, Pt II-A, pp. 143, 148-9.

while the others were inland towns which had all at some time been administrative or religious centres. The remaining sixteen were on the plains and in Kongunad. Generally the plains towns were smaller than the valley centres, and the location of many of them was clearly influenced by internal commerce. Ten of them lay on routes across the Ghats and were entrepots on the routes which connected the valley centres of Tamilnad to the political capitals of the Deccan and the West Coast. Many of these plains entrepot towns (Salem, Dindigul, Erode, Tiruppattur, Walajapet) had large Muslim trading communities which was probably evidence of participation in the flourishing internal trade of the seventeenth and eighteenth centuries. The other plains towns were remnants of the poligari system, with a fortified settlement (*kottai*) and a mart (*pettai*) for the peddling trade.

Throughout the period from the first Census in 1871, the Tamil districts presented a picture of steady urban growth. In 1891 (when the Census definition of urbanism had settled down a bit), 11.9 per cent of the Tamilnad population lived in towns and this proportion was high by contemporary Indian standards. Moreover, this urban population was not concentrated in a single dominant city, but was very well dispersed. Little more than two per cent of the population lived in the capital city of Madras and in 1871 the Census counted no fewer than 128 towns with populations of between 5,000 and 10,000. There were few parts of Tamilnad that were more than a day's bullock-ride from something that the Census of India could call a town.

By 1901, the urban proportion of the population had risen to fourteen per cent; some of this increase was undoubtedly real, but much was due to rearrangement in the definitions and categories of the Census Office. From 1901 onwards however, the figures became more reliable. The overall population, both urban and rural, advanced steadily up to the late years of the first world war, was then cut back badly by the influenza epidemic of 1917-18, began to increase rapidly in the mid-1920s, and accelerated steadily from then until the end of our period. Between 1901 and 1961, the total population increased by seventy-two per cent. The urban population accelerated more rapidly than the rural population from the mid-1920s, and increased its share of the overall population from 14.3 per cent in 1901, to 15.8 per cent in 1921, 19.7 per cent in 1941 and 26.8 per cent in 1961. But while these figures suggest a pattern of steady, accelerating urban growth, that impression is rather misleading. Firstly, the growth of urban population was not concentrated in a small number of truly urban centres but rather was scattered in a large number of small towns. The 1951 Census listed 266 towns and only one of these, the capital, had a population of over 1,000,000, and another six had populations of over 100,000. Over four-fifths of the urban population (and over a fifth of the region's total population) were still living in small towns. Secondly, the growth of these various small towns was uneven and discontinuous. The 1951 Census listed 253 towns with populations of over 5,000; 106 of these had grown twice as quickly as the overall rate of demographic increase since 1871 (or since the date when they were first listed separately as towns). Meanwhile as many as eighty-seven towns had over the same period grown less quickly than the overall rate of demographic increase and a further seventy-eight places had declined sufficiently to drop out of the Census classification of urban places altogether. In other words, some towns were growing meteorically, while others were stagnating. This is not at all surprising. But it is also worth noticing that the patterns of growth and decline were sporadic. For the purposes of an illustrative statistical exercise I divided the period 1871-1951 into four twenty-year sections, and defined a 'rapidly-growing' town as one where the population grew at twice the rate of the population of Tamilnad as a whole in the same period, and a 'stagnant' town as one where the population declined or grew less quickly than the rate of the total population of Tamilnad. Of the 173 towns listed in 1871 only five had consistent records of stagnation and four consistent records of rapid growth in the four subsequent periods. By 1911, 321 towns had been mentioned in the Census. Only fifty-five of these appeared in two or more of our periods and had a consistent record of growth (22) or stagnation (33), while just fifteen appeared in three or more of our periods and had a consistent record of growth (7) or stagnation (8). These categories and periods are admittedly arbitrary, and the calculations can easily be distorted by changes in the definition of the urban area of any settlement, yet the purpose of the exercise is only illustrative. Tamilnad was crowded with a large number of small towns which were growing sporadically and irregularly throughout our period. For most of the towns, periods of rapid growth alternated with periods of comparative (and sometimes absolute) stagnation.

Moreover if we examine the geographical distribution of town growth we can see that there were very different factors encouraging the accumulation of the urban population in each of the twenty-year periods. Between 1871 and 1891 the biggest single influence was the government. In these years, government started to expand the machinery of administration and to extend the network of railways. Most of the towns which grew rapidly in this period were either district or taluk headquarters, or railway junctions and halts, or both. In the period 1891-1911, the biggest factor was clearly the extension of cash-cropping and the emergence of marketing towns. The majority of the rapidly-growing towns were situated in the expansive cotton and groundnut tracts, or in the Tambraparni valley which in this period was enjoying a boom in the export of rice to Ceylon and the west coast. In the next period, 1911-31, commercial cropping was clearly still the main influence, particularly in Kongunad, to a lesser extent still on the plains, but no longer in the Tambraparni. At the same time there was also a boom in the towns of the Chettinad area which was the home area of the Nattukottai Chettiar bankers. Moreover this period saw the beginning of another trend which was much more obvious in the final period, 1931-51. Now urban growth was concentrated particularly in and around the major urban centres which were emerging as industrial towns—Madras City, Madurai, Tiruchi, Tuticorin, Salem and, especially, Coimbatore and the other cluster of Kongunad towns.

There was a similar, though less transparent, pattern in the distribution of urban stagnation. The stagnant towns of the period 1871-91 were mostly old political capitals—zamindari towns on the plains and old religious and administrative centres in the valleys—which were declining in the face of the new administrative and political assertiveness of the British. Many of the towns declining in 1911-31 were commercial centres which had boomed in the earlier period and which were now being by-passed by the rapid shifts of market-location. Finally in both 1911-31 and 1931-51, there was a clear concentration of decline within the valleys region. This was a clear reflection of the torpidity of the valley's agrarian economy, and of the readiness to export people and capital to southeast Asia or to other parts of India. By the last period, 1931-51, the distribution of urban growth and urban stagnation was sharply demarcated by the line of the Tamilnad hills. To the north-west of this line, in

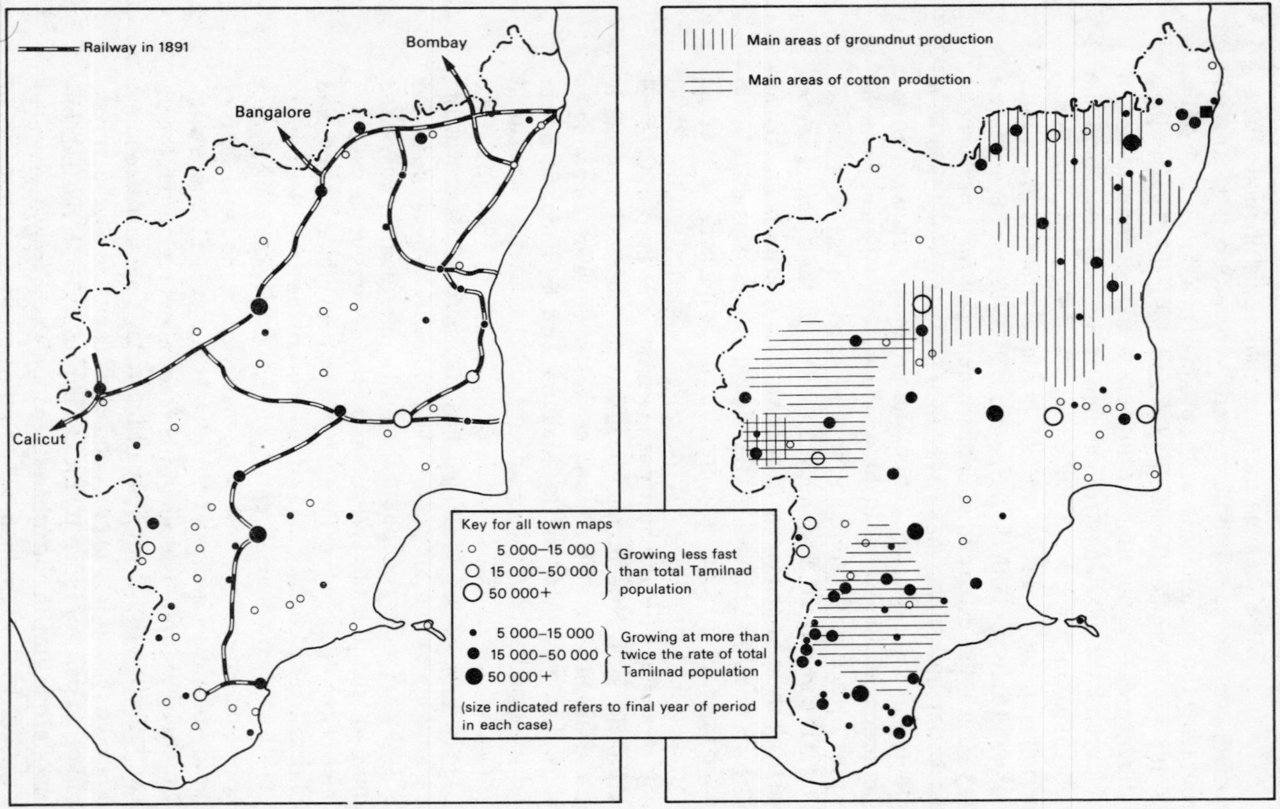

Map 7 b Towns 1891-1911

Main areas of groundnut production

Main areas of cotton production

Key for all town maps

○ 5 000–15 000
○ 15 000–50 000   Growing less fast
○ 50 000+   than total Taminad
                    population

• 5 000–15 000
• 15 000–50 000   Growing at more than
● 50 000+   twice the rate of total
                    Taminad population

(size indicated refers to final year of period
in each case)

Railway in 1891

Bombay

Bangalore

Calicut

Map 7 a Towns 1871-91

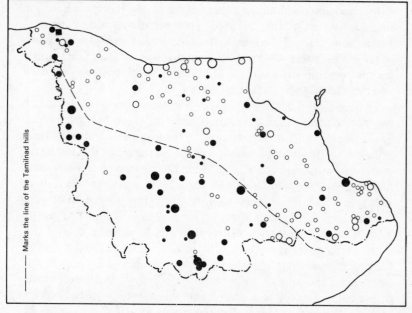

——— Marks the line of the Tamilnad hills

Map 7 d Towns 1931-51

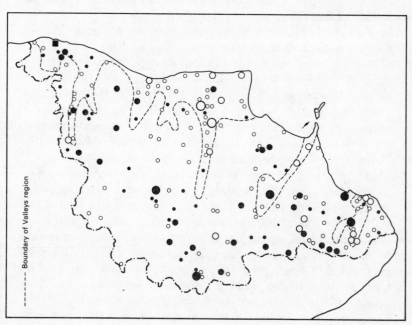

– – – – Boundary of Valleys region

Map 7 c Towns 1911-31

Kongunad and neighbouring areas of the plains, there was hardly a single town that was not counted in the 'rapidly-growing' category. To the south east of the line, in the valleys and some adjacent parts of the plains, there was hardly a town that was not 'stagnant' except for the two industrial centres of Madurai town and Tuticorin port and the hinterland of Madras City.[90]

The expansion of the population, particularly in the early part of the period, was chiefly due to outside influence—the spread of government and the penetration of the export economy. These influences were unstable and sporadic and the result was a shifting pattern of urban growth. Of course in this process of eccentric and unstable growth, some towns hit more ladders than snakes, but as we have seen, these were comparatively few. Those that grew consistently throughout the period were mostly old trading or administrative centres, which perhaps took on some role in the British administrative network, found themselves at the junction of the new railway lines, emerged as a cash-crop marketing centre, and later were the site of some form of industry. But most towns displayed bursts of sudden growth intermixed with periods of relative stagnation. In a closer examination of the patterns of growth of the different towns it is possible to see the effect of the erratic swings of investment in different sorts of enterprise. Each of the two wars produced a boom in building rice mills in the deltas followed by a long period of attrition when the demand receded in the post-war period. The location of cotton markets in the far south shifted three times in thirty years and similarly the location of groundnut markets in the Arcots shifted twice over the same period. The booms in textile mills, oil-presses, and sugar factories in the 1930s resulted in excess capacity and shrinkage in the aftermath. Towns rose and fell on these tidal waves of investment.

This pattern of urban growth also affected the nature of the town, its population and its functions. Three characteristics are particularly worth mentioning. The first is the important role of the state. Government employees constituted the single biggest category in the urban population. In the 1951 Census, those employed in health, education, public administration and rail transport constituted 11.4 per cent of the urban workforce. The expansion of government had also made a substantial contribution to urban growth. Although the following calculations are not quite honest, since not all administrators lived in towns, they are at least illustrative. In 1891, the number of government employees and their dependents represented roughly a fifth of the urban population. Between 1891 and 1951, the number of government employees and dependents in Tamilnad increased by some 875,000 and if we can estimate that each government employee gave on average employment to one other family (of traders, professionals such as teachers or lawyers, service personnel such as barbers, priests and astrologers, manufacturers and domestic menials) then we have an argument for one third of the addition to the urban population in that period.[91]

The second characteristic was the importance of retail and service occupations. Many of those involved in these spurts of urban growth seemed to be aware of their vulnerability. Those entrepreneurs involved in the leading sectors of urban growth took pains to insure themselves against imminent collapse. Many entrepreneurs preferred not to plough their profits back into their own original enterprise, but to deploy them into a range of other uses. Commonly they bought land and we have seen, for instance, how the PSG Naidu family of Coimbatore acquired thousands of acres on the profits of the textile booms of the early 1920s and 1930s. Other textile entrepreneurs became involved in minor engineering, fruit-canning and sugar-processing. But a far more common form of diversification was investment in general trading or in service industries.

In Coimbatore, the rise of the textile industry in the 1930s was directly associated with the appearance of a large number of small bus services and trucking companies, and in the second extension after the war most of the successful concerns invested in motor repair workshops and petrol bunks. Also after the war, there was a considerable expansion of investment in retail agencies for newly popular consumer goods such as soaps, detergents, and packaged tea; in wholesale agencies for industrial commodities such as cement; and in services such as printing presses.[92] Another prominent avenue was the cinema industry, both in the form of cinema houses and the growing business of film-making. Some of the first cinema companies in the region were begun in the 1930s by Nattukottai Chettiar bankers returned from Burma, and by members of the Coimbatore mill-owning community, while landlords and merchants from the successful cash-crop areas were prominent on the boards of film companies floated in the late 1930s.[93]

Table 24: Occupational distribution of the urban workforce 1951

Occupations as percentage of total urban workforce in each district

	Madras City	Chingleput	North Arcot	South Arcot	Salem	Coimbatore	Tiruchi	Tanjavur	Madurai	Ramnad	Tirunelveli	TOTAL
Owner-cultivator	0.3	6.4	4.7	9.5	6.0	4.8	7.2	6.1	6.5	9.1	9.3	5.5
Tenant	0.1	3.2	2.4	3.1	2.2	2.6	3.9	2.8	2.9	2.0	5.9	2.5
Rentier	1.0	2.3	2.2	3.4	1.6	1.1	2.6	6.1	1.4	1.1	3.2	2.1
Agricultural Labourer	0.2	7.0	3.4	10.0	2.7	5.7	6.0	4.9	3.7	5.4	5.5	4.1
Tobacco Manufacture	2.4	1.3	6.2	0.2	1.0	0.9	2.4	0.7	0.5	0.5	0.6	1.6
Leather Manufacture	0.5	1.2	3.3	0.4	0.9	0.5	0.7	0.3	0.9	0.3	0.3	0.7
Cotton textiles (1)	1.0	9.2	3.8	2.1	10.4	2.8	2.4	1.9	3.4	7.8	7.0	4.0
Cotton textiles (2)	3.0	3.7	5.3	2.8	12.5	9.9	2.3	1.1	12.7	4.8	6.2	5.8
Grain milling etc.	0.5	0.5	0.6	0.8	1.0	0.2	0.7	1.1	0.9	1.1	0.6	0.6
Oil-pressing and dairy etc.	0.3	0.1	0.3	0.4	0.2	0.9	0.2	0.3	1.5	0.8	0.3	0.5
Sugar manufacture	ns	ns	ns	0.6	ns	0.1	0.3	ns	0.1	0.1	1.1	0.2
Clothes making	2.0	1.0	1.6	1.2	1.3	2.0	1.1	1.1	1.5	0.9	0.8	1.4
Other processing of raw materials	0.7	1.6	0.7	2.6	1.4	1.5	0.8	2.0	0.9	1.2	1.1	1.2
Food trade	5.5	4.8	5.3	9.4	3.9	7.9	7.5	9.1	6.6	9.2	6.7	6.8
Textile and leather trade	2.4	2.3	3.0	1.3	2.6	1.6	1.5	1.7	1.3	1.6	1.0	1.8
Banking etc.	1.9	1.5	0.9	1.0	0.5	1.2	1.4	0.9	1.2	2.7	1.5	1.5
Other commerce	12.9	6.7	10.7	5.8	7.2	8.2	7.8	6.6	8.3	9.1	7.3	9.0
Road transport	4.3	2.5	3.4	2.5	3.4	3.7	3.1	3.1	3.1	3.0	2.5	3.3
Rail transport	2.3	2.4	1.3	2.8	0.2	1.8	3.7	1.6	0.9	0.5	0.6	1.7
Other transport	4.4	0.9	0.5	1.5	0.1	0.3	0.6	1.0	0.6	0.4	1.4	1.5

Manufacture of transport equipment	3.1	0.9	0.5	0.4	0.2	1.1	2.8	0.5	0.6	0.3	0.4	1.3
Stone-quarrying	ns	1.2	0.1	ns	ns	0.3	0.3	ns	0.1	0.6	0.9	1.0
Clay products	0.2	0.1	0.1	0.1	ns	0.1	0.2	0.1	0.8	0.2	0.1	0.2
Woodwork	1.7	0.9	2.0	2.0	1.8	1.7	1.6	1.9	1.8	2.1	1.8	1.7
Building construction	3.2	0.6	1.7	3.1	8.0	1.8	1.8	2.5	2.0	1.5	1.8	2.5
Other construction	2.8	2.2	1.6	1.4	1.2	1.5	1.5	1.6	1.5	1.9	2.6	2.0
Printing etc.	2.5	0.2	0.3	0.2	0.7	0.6	0.6	0.4	0.4	0.5	0.3	0.8
Domestic service	3.9	1.7	1.2	1.5	5.5	2.2	9.3	6.3	2.9	3.4	1.8	3.7
Hotels and restaurants	2.7	1.9	2.4	3.0	2.2	3.4	3.3	4.2	3.6	2.4	2.3	2.9
Laundry	1.6	0.9	1.1	0.9	1.1	1.2	0.7	0.6	1.2	1.6	1.4	1.2
Barber	1.0	0.7	2.5	1.5	0.7	0.7	0.6	0.7	0.7	0.9	0.9	0.7
Religion, charity and welfare	0.4	0.6	0.4	1.1	0.5	0.3	0.8	1.8	0.7	0.7	0.9	0.7
Health, education & public admin.	15.9	12.7	9.3	10.8	6.1	7.3	9.2	10.0	7.5	6.1	5.9	9.7
Law, accountancy etc.	1.6	0.7	0.6	0.7	0.7	1.0	0.7	1.0	0.9	0.6	1.9	1.0
TOTALS in categories shown	87.0	83.2	83.9	88.1	84.0	80.1	90.4	84.3	84.4	84.5	84.2	85.3

Note: The table includes 'self-supporting persons', both male and female, and exludes all 'dependants' whether 'earning' or 'non-earning'. 'Cotton textiles(1)' includes those described as 'independent workers' and is an approximation of the handloom industry. 'Cotton textiles(2)' includes those described as 'employers' and as 'employees' and is an approximation of the mill industry.
ns = not significant

Source: *Census of India 1951*. Volume III, Pt. II-A, Table B-III, pp. 200-333.

According to the 1951 Census over a quarter of the urban workforce was employed in various domestic services, in retailing food, in construction and in (non-rail) transport. The inclusion of other forms of retail trade would push the proportion nearer to two-fifths.

The third characteristic was that factory industry formed a very small part of urban functions and was indeed subordinate to other forms of industrial organization. Even in 1955, just 321,865 persons worked in factories that fell under the Factory Act. This was just 0.9 per cent of the total population, or about five or six per cent of the labour force. Moreover, not all of these were in manufacturing enterprises. By far the largest number, 118,076, were in textiles, and another 68,731 in agricultural processing plants which included sugar factories, oil mills, coffee curing works, and many others. Next came engineering works with 48,725; most of these were in the government railway works, or in scrap steel rolling mills established on the site of the abandoned railway workshops at Negapatam in 1936, and the rest were in the mass of small workshops around Madras and Coimbatore and the automobile repair shops in all the major towns. Meanwhile, many of those described as factory employees were in fact further additions to the ranks of the service industries. 9,441 of those employees listed under the Act worked in hotels and restaurants and another 13,465 in printing establishments.[94]

In terms of numbers employed, factory industry was overshadowed by the small-scale manufacture carried out in thousands of little workshops, back-rooms, courtyards, and stretches of pavement. The most prominent of these industries was handloom weaving, but there was also tanning, metal and wood work, rolling the cheap cheroots known as beedis, and a number of types of simple food processing. It is difficult to identify those employed in these activities in the Census categories, but a rough addition of those listed in the 1951 Census as employed in the manufacture of leather and tobacco, in the processing of foods, in the manufacture of cotton textiles as 'independent workers' (which roughly distinguishes handloom weavers from the 'employers and employees' in textile factories), and in other similar occupations, produces a total of about thirteen or fourteen per cent of the urban workforce. Handloom weaving alone, which employed something like four to five per cent of the urban workforce, was the single largest urban occupation and dominated a number of the region's towns.

What is more, these petty industries were not being driven out by the advance of modern industrial techniques and the advent of factory organization. Indeed many of them were expanding in the early twentieth century and were outpacing the growth of factory industry. On the eve of the second world war, the handloom industry still commanded sixty per cent of the market for cloth in the province.[95] Finally, these petty industries were not only expanding but also changing in character and these changes helped to shape the character of the region's towns and to draw the government into a deeper involvement in the urban economy. To understand the evolution of Tamilnad's towns we must now look at these petty industries and in particular at the most important one, the handloom weaving of cotton cloth.

PETTY MANUFACTURE: THE HANDLOOM INDUSTRY

The petty industries were an integral part of Tamilnad's uneven urban growth. They flourished on the unstable character of urban expansion, and in turn contributed to it. They flourished because they required little in the way of skill on the part of the labour and hence were flooded with recruits in times of local or general slump in the economy. They contributed to it because they evolved a form of production organization which was peculiarly fragile.

Tamilnad's handloom industry survived the onslaught of Lancashire in the nineteenth century fairly well. This is not to say that there was no distress among weavers in the nineteenth century. That part of the industry which in the sixteenth to eighteenth centuries had been organized by the European traders for export to the far east and elsewhere was badly hit, and imported mill goods of medium quality took away much of the market for cloth in the towns. But the market for coarse cloth in the countryside was reasonably well protected by the expenses of transportation and by the durability of the handloom product. The market for fine goods was preserved for reasons both of taste and technology. 'The handloom has held its own till now' a weaving magnate told the Industrial Commission of 1916-18, 'owing to the conservatism of our ladies'[96] while the manufacture of intricately designed border cloths defeated the power loom until quite late in the twentieth century.[97] Then from the late nineteenth century, the industry

Table 25:   **Export of piece-goods from Madras Presidency 1886-7 to 1955-6**

Quinquennium	Annual average in each quinquennium	
	Value in Rs lakhs	Quantity in lakh yards*
1886/7-90/1	43.09	129
1891/2-95/6	51.84	146
1896/7-1900/1	62.74	222
1901/2-5/6	91.09	304
1906/7-10/11	95.95	267
1911/12-15/16	106.06	289
1916/17-20/1	192.76	351
1921/2-25/6	274.68	449
1926/7-30/1	247.52	477
1931/2-35/6	148.41	339
1936/7-40/1	211.51	553
1941/2-45/6	398.43	437
1946/7-50/1	1116.57	786
1951/2-55/6	1044.58	660

* There is a small element of estimation in the calculation of yardage in the first ten quinquennia. In the original data, figures on yardage of exports to Burma were very disaggregated. Rather than waste time attempting to aggregate these figures, it was assumed that cloth exported to Burma averaged the same value per yard as cloth exported elsewhere (for foreign exports, rather than the 'coasting' trade to Burma, yardage was aggregated). The error will not be great. Burma accounted for about five per cent of exports at the start of the period and about twenty per cent of the mid-30s.

Source: *Annual Statement of the Sea-borne trade and navigation of India*

began to grow on the impetus of demand both home and abroad. The home market grew with the increase in population and with the increasing prosperity of the elite of town and countryside. As for exports, the highly coloured and highly specialized Madras lungis and 'Madras handkerchiefs' had long sold well in southeast Asia and the Persian Gulf, and now the market was improved by the fall in freight costs and by the advertizing of Tamilnad cloth by the migrant Tamils in Ceylon, Burma, the Straits and elsewhere. Trade figures do not enable us to separate handloom cloth from mill-made cloth with any accuracy, but it is unlikely that the Madras Presidency exported mill-made goods in anything but infinitesimal quantities until after the depression. Table 25 meanwhile shows that the volume of cotton piece-goods exported from the province almost quadrupled between the late 1880s and the late 1920s, and that the trend of growth continued thereafter with some slight disruption during the depression and the second world war.

In this favourable situation, the industry was very responsive to technological innovation. The Sourashtra community, whose members wove, dyed and dealt in cloth in Madurai and other Tamilnad towns, sent representatives to Europe in the 1890s to learn about new synthetic dyestuffs. The advantages in ease and cost of using these new chemical dyes meant that Madurai quickly became the dyeing centre for much of the province, the old natural dyestuffs rapidly disappeared from common use, and the Sourashtras prospered.[98] In 1901-2, the fly-shuttle was introduced to the region. This piece of string and elastic so important to Britain's earlier economic growth, was reckoned to increase the productivity of labour by something between fifty and two hundred per cent. By 1912, 20,000 looms in the province were equipped with the new device, by 1917, 100,000, and by the mid-1930s, seventy per cent of the province's total of around 300,000 looms.[99] Meanwhile the government took some interest in popularizing this and other technological improvements. From 1911, parties of government demonstrators toured the weaving centres to illustrate the advantages of the fly-shuttle and other small improvements. In 1917, the Government of Madras appointed a textile expert who helped to co-ordinate and disseminate information about technological opportunities and market fluctuations for the use of both the mill and the handloom sectors.[100]

The number of looms increased rapidly. There were several attempts to enumerate them, all of doubtful accuracy, but the overall trend is clear (see table 26), particularly if the Board of Revenue's suspiciously inflated estimates are ignored. While most of the expansion took place in the old weaving centres, there were some new settlements. Starting in the 1900s, Salem town grew a new weaving suburb which contained 2,000 weaving families by 1930s.[101] The amount of yarn consumed by the province's handlooms increased fairly steadily from an average of 62 million pounds in the four years leading up to the first world war to 80 million pounds in the mid-1930s.[102]

The looms were distributed throughout the region in a large number of centres ranging from the capital city down to small villages. As a government report noted in 1942: 'So many different types of handwoven cloth are produced in this presidency under so different conditions, to cater for varying tastes and needs and for markets wide apart and under widely different local conditions that each type and locality creates a separate problem of its own.'[103]

Table 26: Estimates of the number of looms in Madras Presidency

Year	Number	Enumerator
1856	197 000	Census
1871	280 000	Board of Revenue
1889	300 009	Board of Revenue
1901	167 806	Statistical Atlas
1921	169 403	Census
1921	242 000	Statistical Atlas
1929	260 000	D. Narayana Rao's Survey
1932	225 000	Tariff Board
1940	340 451	Fact-Finding Committee
1945	500 000	Yarn distribution scheme's census
1948	541 879	B.V. Narayanaswamy Naidu
1954	521 598 *	All India Handloom Board

Note: Figures include looms weaving wool, carpets and silk but these constituted only a small portion of the total.

* Figures for new Madras State, that is Tamilnad and West Coast only.

Source: Baliga, *Compendium*.

While there undoubtedly was enormous variety in the conditions of production and marketing, it is possible to reduce this to some sort of rough order.

Two factors helped to shape the organization of the handloom industry. The first was that entry into the industry was easy. In the early years of the twentieth century, the cost of a loom was estimated to be in the region of Rs 10-15.[104] By the late 1920s, inflation and technological improvement had driven this figure up to Rs 30 but this amount was still small enough to be found or borrowed without difficulty. Working capital was not necessary since most weavers operated on credit or on some form of putting-out system. Coarse weaving required little special skill, though complex fine weaving did require considerable expertise. While the weaving of luxury goods remained the province of specific weaving communities in which advanced skills were passed on from generation to generation, the manufacture of coarse cloths for the mass market was an occupation that many of the population looked on as a form of social security. Many families, particularly from the labouring, service, and lower-middle-class sections of the towns, looked on handloom weaving as a resort in time of hardship; if their employment ceased, or their small business collapsed, they could take to the handloom; as soon as the outlook improved, they might return to a preferred occupation.[105]

The second factor was that the most difficult part of the handloom business was marketing and that consequently those who had the knowledge, skills and resources to organize marketing tended to dominate the industry. So far as luxury cloths went, the demand was for small quantities in widely scattered final markets; slight shifts in taste, the advent of competition from new sources of supply, and innovations of transport meant that market demand might shift quite rapidly. So far as coarse cloths went, the market was again very complex. Most cloths were sold at festival periods. While some such festivals were celebrated simultaneously all over the region, others were much more localised. The traders had to attempt to get their cloths into the particular market to suit the rhythm of the local sacred calendar. Next, many communities which had become geographically scattered retained a preference for a certain sort of cloth. The result of these and other factors was that the trade even in coarse cloths was immensely complex. One estimate reckoned that three-quarters of the cloth goods sold in any retail market came from beyond the local producing areas.[106]

Besides this fragmentation of the market, there were other factors which put a premium on marketing skills. Firstly, handloom goods were produced rapidly and the handloom process added very little value to the raw materials. According to one estimate the cost of yarn represented over sixty per cent of the cost of the finished handloom product,[107] and the addition of other raw materials, such as size, would push the proportion even higher. Anyone who invested in the production of handloom goods had to take care not to build up stocks at a time when the price of yarn was falling for in such a situation it would not take long for a competitor to produce cloth at a lower cost. Secondly, the supply of labour in the handloom industry was perversely related to the home demand for the goods. As we have noted, labour would tend to flock into the industry just when the local economy was slack and thus demand was depressed. It thus required considerable capital and expertise to adjust supply to demand.

The raggedness of the market, perverse nature of the supply of labour, and low rate of value-added helped to make the classic organizational form in the handloom and other petty industries a putting-out system. A capitalist decided what goods should be made, supplied the materials and working capital to the craftsman, took back the finished product and conveyed it to the market. If the market slumped, the capitalist could cut off production simply by withholding advances; he had no obligation to support a permanent labour force and no 'plant' of his own. When the market revived it was easy to mobilize production because many weavers were in debt to the capitalist. A report in 1929 reckoned that the average debt of a weaver who owned his own loom was around Rs 50, and the average debt of a weaver who worked for wages was in the region of one to two months wages.[108] Generally the yarn-merchants or capitalists who financed production and marketing were able to claim a substantial profit, and to drive down wages whenever their profits were threatened. Various estimates reckoned that the yarn-merchant or capitalist made a profit of eighteen to twenty-five per cent on the articles that he commissioned and sold. Weaving wages hardly ever rose above subsistence.[109] As one weaving capitalist disarmingly told the Indian Industrial Commission, during the boom of the first world war: 'Weavers are not in such a flourishing condition, but the traders are in a somewhat flourishing condition.'[110]

There were many varieties of the putting-out system. Very often the capitalist supplied the weaver with working capital, mainly in the form of materials, and in such cases he was generally referred to as a 'yarn-dealer'; and sometimes he supplied in cash and was known as a 'sowcar'. Sometimes he supplied direct to the individual weavers, sometimes to a master-weaver who owned several looms worked by others, and sometimes to a further middleman who in turn contacted the weaver or master-weaver. Looked at from the bottom up, there were three situations in which the weaver might find himself. Firstly, he might be 'independent', owning his own loom, and receiving an advance of yarn or cash along with the commission for a particular job. Secondly, he might work for a master-weaver and receive piecework wages for each job; in this case either he or the master-weaver might own the loom. Thirdly, he might be a 'cooly weaver', working in a handloom factory under the direct control of a capitalist.[111]

Although local variation was enormous, it is possible to discern a difference between the organization of production in the case of fine and coarse goods respectively. The fine goods, which were mostly destined for export, were manufactured mostly in the ports and their immediate hinterlands. Madras City and the weaving villages of Chingleput district produced a high proportion of the lungis and handkerchiefs destined for Penang, Singapore, other parts of southeast Asia, and Africa, while the hinterland of the port of Tuticorin produced many lungis and saris for Burma and Ceylon. The requirements of skill, and the limited volume of output, meant that in these places the weavers mostly came from traditional weaving communities, notably the Devangas in Madras, Sengundars in Chingleput, Sengundar and Muslim weavers near Tuticorin. In these centres there were likely to be more 'independent' weavers (Chingleput had the highest proportion of 'independent' weavers in the region)[112] and more 'small-scale' master-weavers commanding up to twenty or thirty looms. In such places with the relative independence of craftsmen, the premium on skill, and the small-scale nature of organization, the master-weaver and yarn-merchant generally came from the same community as the weaver, and the local caste organization had at least some of the aspects of a craft guild. In particular, the capitalists and the caste organization were liable to provide outdoor relief in bad times, while in some particular cases such local caste organizations sponsored the technical education of weavers' sons.

Conversely, the interior districts produced mainly coarse goods for the local market. Here the weaving communities were liable to be much more mixed, containing a variety of different weaving castes and also a sizeable influx of people from other service communities, merchant groups, agricultural and labouring jatis. Here too the craftsmen were liable to be less independent and were more likely to be ranged in large groups (from two or three hundred up to a thousand) under master-weavers or big yarn-merchant capitalists.[113]

This division between coarse and fine production is not at all precise or clear-cut, either in style of organization or location. For instance, the biggest centre of production for export to northern India was at Madurai, right in the interior, while much of the export production in Madras City was organized in groups of several thousand weavers under major capitalists rather than in smaller 'guild' communities. There was, in fact, considerable 'overlap' between the two systems, yet even so the division is analytically useful and provides a necessary background to a discussion of the industry's history in the twentieth century.

This history centres on the reactions of the handloom capitalists to instabilities imported from an unstable world economy. Of course, the handloom industry in the region had had a large export component for at least three centuries and so was in some senses accustomed to the difficulties of dealing in a market that was remote, disorderly and thus difficult to predict. But conditions in the early twentieth century were essentially different from those of earlier periods. Firstly, under the regime of the European companies, it had generally been European capital which took the risks involved in selling in foreign markets, while in the twentieth century, particularly as a consequence of the post 1880s boom, it was increasingly local Indian capital. Secondly, the speed and scale of fluctuations of foreign prices and foreign demand were simply much greater than ever before. The price of cloth, particularly the price of cloth sold mainly to rural peoples both in India and southeast Asia, was closely tied to the (very unstable) level of agricultural prices. Meanwhile the costs of production were also vulnerable to international fluctuations. The Madras weavers had to import certain sorts of special yarn from Europe and Japan, while the local market for yarn was significantly affected by demand from Bombay and further afield. The weaving capitalists reacted to these imported fluctuations with great care. Whenever they faced a situation in which input prices were falling, or the market for cloth was slack, they would delay production for fear of being caught with heavy and increasingly expensive stocks. Whenever input prices rose so high that it was feared that they would be unable to compete with Bombay, Lancashire or local handloom weavers in the southeast Asian market areas, they again ceased production. Ceasing production meant throwing weavers out of work. The first world war, the early depression, the mid-30s financial crisis, the onset of the second world war, the post Korean war slump—each of these critical periods resulted in disorder in the weaving towns. 1930, 1934, 1936, 1940, 1941, 1942, 1948 and 1952-3 were bad years for the weavers. In each instance, there was distress in a large number of the weaving centres of the province, but it was in the major towns with large populations of weavers, such as Salem and Madurai, that the distress was most visible and most disquieting to the government and to other classes of society. In Salem town, for instance, roughly a third of the population was supported by the handloom and when the looms fell idle the entire economy of the town was dislocated and public peace threatened. Inevitably these instances of distress became linked to the political agitations of the period, most noticeably in Civil Disobedience.

By mid-1930, the effects of the world depression in prices had fed through to the handloom industry, and in many centres of the industry the capitalists withheld their advances. By July, there had been a large riot among the unemployed weavers of the small town of Komarapalaiyam in Salem and a crowd of 500 weavers had attacked the police in the North Arcot weaving town of Gudiyattam.[114] In Madurai, trade had fallen off so badly that 'a number of rich traders have filed insolvency petitions', and 2,000 Sourashtra weavers were idle.[115] Government soon woke up to the fact that Madurai formed one of the centres of Civil Disobedience and that the idle handloom weavers 'formed the bulk of the crowds in the town'.[116] It was much the same in another centre of agitation, Coimbatore, where the decline of the north Indian market for handloom saris was causing considerable distress. There was also some unemployment in the weaving suburb of Alwarpet in Madras City, and in many parts of the province government noted that handloom weavers took an especially zealous part in the Gandhian picket of foreign cloth shops.[117] During the next crisis, in 1934, a thousand Salem weavers rioted, looted the bazaar, and threatened to spread disorder into other towns of the district. The weaving industry of the town was still operating at a very slow pace when a local failure of the monsoon tempted the grain merchants of the town to raise their prices. The weavers responded by attacking and looting the grain shops.[118] Two years later, Salem and Coimbatore were again affected by a downturn in the north Indian market. Several of the merchants found themselves holding large unsaleable stocks, and again they reacted by closing down production and creating unemployment.[119] At the outbreak of the second world war, merchants in Madras City feared an abrogation of export trade and by November 1939 a quarter of the looms in the city were idle. The weaving capitalists of Madurai soon followed suit and over half of the 8,000 looms in the mofussil parts of the Madurai district had to stop work. Distress soon spread into other districts, most noticeably Ramnad where in the major weaving centre of Aruppukkottai a third of the population of 35,000 depended on weaving, and half of them were out of work by early 1940.[120]

In mid-1941, the industry was hit by a rapid rise in the price of yarn consequent on wartime shortages. The disruption of trade had cut off supplies of imported yarn and the Indian mills used this opportunity to recoup the profits they had foregone by price-cutting in the depression. By July, the price of yarn had multiplied two-and-a-half times in six months and was still rising. In that month, the peace of Salem town was badly disrupted by riots and looting expeditions by unemployed weavers. Matters quietened down as the weavers learnt to accept that capitalists were not going to risk their funds while yarn prices were so high, but later in the year large groups of weavers begging became a common sight in the town. Meanwhile in the nearby town of Rasipuram, the weavers set out to rectify the slackness of demand for their labour by systematically looting the cloth-shops of the town and burning the contents.[121] In December, this tactic spread to Madurai where the rioters stoned the police and firemen when they tried to approach the shops which the rioters had just set alight with the owners inside.[122] In early 1942, a very high proportion of the looms in the province were idle and the government was anxious about the possibilities of widespread disorder.[123]

The intermittent outbreaks of public disorder were just one form of reaction to the instability of the handloom industry. At the same time, the handloom capitalists were adjusting their style of operation to suit the new conditions. The efforts of the handloom capitalists gradually changed important parts of the structure of the handloom industry.

Firstly, over the period the number of looms weaving coarse goods rose much faster than the number weaving fine goods. To some extent this was because communities of skilled weavers were obliged by the instability of the market to transfer their resources to coarser production. The Devangas of Aruppukottai moved from the manufacture of fancy saris using mercerized Japanese yarn to the production of ordinary cotton saris. The Devangas of Tiruchi were still producing mainly silk saris in the 1920s but they moved from these to *angavastrams* (upper cloths) and then to cheap cotton saris by the time of the second world war. In the late 1930s, the weavers in Tiruchengodu gave up the production of medium-quality saris and took to the production of lower quality shirting. Madurai had produced mainly fancy dhoties and *angavastrams* around 1920 but by the second world war it had been reduced to plain saris.[124]

To some extent also the proportionate increase in coarse weaving was a result of the duties which the government imposed on imports of yarn as a measure of protection for the local spinning industry. A duty of five per cent was levied in 1922 and was modified in 1927 to become five per cent ad valorem or one-and-a-half annas per pound, whichever was the higher, and raised to 6¼ per cent or between 1½ and 1 7/8 annas per pound in late 1931. Most of the yarn imported for the use of handloom weavers consisted of specialist yarns used in the production of fine-quality goods, and these duties raised the price and hindered the availability of such yarns. The ranks of coarse weavers were also swollen by the influx of new recruits from the countryside and from the declining sectors of urban Tamilnad. As noted above, a series of (rather doubtful) counts of looms reckoned that the number in the province doubled between 1920 and 1940 and then doubled again by the mid-1950s. Local observations substantiate this picture of growth though of course they can give no guidance to the accuracy of its magnitude. The number of looms in Madurai, for instance, was said to grow from 3,000 to 5,000 between 1934 and 1941,[126] and between the 1921 and the 1931 Censuses the number of people in the province supported by the handloom industry rose by sixty per cent.[127] The consumption of yarn was not growing so fast as the number of looms; between 1921 and 1940 it rose slightly less than fifty per cent.[128] At the top end of the scale the number of weavers producing fine goods largely for an export market was slowly falling; while at the same time the ranks of weavers producing coarse goods was growing rapidly and their individual shares of production and their incomes were falling.

Secondly, there was steady concentration of control over the working capital engaged in the handloom industry. Of course, there always had been big handloom magnates. Pitty Thyagaraja Chetty commanded 20,000 looms in and around Madras City in the 1910s.[129] But around this time there were many smaller men, commanding only a handful of looms and working on a very low capital. While some of them survived, it is not surprising to find that these smaller operators found the price and demand instability of the depression and wars more difficult to manage than did their more substantial neighbours. Once the price instability had begun, it was difficult for those involved in the handloom industry to command outside credit. The banks would simply not lend to such

an unstable business, or if they did they imposed such tight
conditions and demanded such stringent securities that the handloom capitalists were wary of such loans because they themselves
knew that it was not possible to operate in such a strait-jacket. The
handloom capitalists, L.K. Tulsiram of the Madurai Sourashtras
told the Banking Commission, 'consider the bank as a serpent
which will bite them if they go near. They think if you go and borrow
they will come and sell your shop and put you to disgrace.'[130] The
yarn-importing firms allowed the weaver-capitalists a certain
amount of credit up to the first trouble in the first world war and
then withdrew that facility.[131] Some indigenous banking firms,
particularly Marwaris and Kallidaikurichi Brahmans who had caste
and kin connections in the handloom business, would extend some
credit but only when the market was extremely secure. Increasingly
it was men with substantial personal capital which would enable
them to mobilize production quickly when the market was favourable, and to hold considerable stocks when the market collapsed,
who dominated handloom production. By the 1940s, some forty
Devangas commanded the roughly 1,600 looms producing Rs 20
lakhs of goods a year in Coimbatore. Fifty yarn-dealers ran the
business in Madurai and an elite of four families managed most of it;
while in the largest single centre, Salem, there were a hundred men
handling an output worth half a lakh per diem.[132]

Thirdly, along with the trend towards 'coarse' production and
capital concentration went an inevitable shift in the organization of
the industry, away from the smaller 'guild-like' units that were
common among the skilled workers, and towards larger and more
loosely organized production systems. In no sense was this a
transition towards factory organization. A few more large workshops appeared,[133] but generally, in view of the instability of the
market, it had become even more important for the capitalists not
to commit themselves to regular working and expenditure on plant.
Large putting-out networks prevailed. In the periods of relatively
high demand, particularly during the second world war, many more
individual weavers managed to purchase their own looms and
become nominally 'independent'. Indeed one survey reckoned that
the proportion of 'independent' weavers had risen from twenty-
eight to forty-seven per cent between 1941 and 1948. But the (rather
contradictory) statistics produced by the same report pointed out
that these 'independent' weavers were in debt, generally to a yarn

merchant, on average to the extent of Rs 180; this figure represented the cost of the loom plus the income of about four months full-time working and so the independence was clearly very circumscribed. Besides, the income of these 'independent' weavers differed not one bit from the income of those working for a master-weaver or for cooly wages.[134] Several surveys of individual weaving centres in the late 1930s and early 1940s found that many weavers had lost what little independence they had, particularly as they moved from the production of 'fine' to the production of 'coarse' goods.[135] When yarn prices rose quickly in 1940-2, it was the truly independent weaver, working on his own capital, who first found it impossible to cope.[136]

Fourthly, the industry was becoming gradually (though by no means completely) concentrated in towns rather than villages, and big towns rather than small ones. There were several reports of weavers migrating in from villages to settle in towns, particularly in the main weaving centres such as Madurai, Salem, Coimbatore and Kanchipuram.[137] Many pressures were at work. Clearly when demand fell off, it was the outlying weaving settlements which suffered first. Weaving capitalists sent out middlemen to commission production in these centres and obviously the capitalists stopped production here first to save the costs of agency commission and transport. Furthermore, during the second world war the government did begin to provide welfare services in the towns and these were an incentive for immigration by distressed handloom weavers among various others. Finally, when producing in the towns, the capitalists were able to rationalize some of the ancillary processes. In the towns, warping and sizing were done by specialists and this saved both time and money.

The urbanization of the industry, concentration in bigger units, movement from complex to more standardized articles of manufacture and the attrition of individual, independent craftsmen, all these factors looked as if they might constitute a trend away from a 'traditional' towards a more 'modern' form of industry. But this would be to misinterpret the process of adjustment. There was no sign of a move into the factory and the production line. Indeed, putting-out remained the basic form of organization and in some respects the industry was becoming more part-time than permanent. Many weaving capitalists reacted to the instabilities of price and demand by diverting much of their capital into other forms of enterprise. In Chingleput in 1941 it was reported that 'the master-weavers and merchants are buying land and some are gradually becoming agriculturists and landlords'.[138] The yarn-merchants and capitalists who got caught with large stocks in the slump of 1936 in Coimbatore were, it was said: 'inclined to abandon the trade in hand-woven goods. They are not giving work to the weavers and are in fact only waiting to recover their dues from the weavers the moment the looms begin to ply. Many of the sowcars have turned their attention to other trades and some have invested money in the film industry and mill cloth trade.'[139] At the same time, many of the weavers were forced to look for secondary occupations in lean periods. The onset of the depression found many weavers trying to find jobs as conductors in the recently instituted bus-services in Madras City.[140] The troubles of 1941-2 in Salem and North Arcot coincided luckily with the groundnut harvest of the region and many weavers went to work in the fields and decorticating mills.[141]

The government's interest in the handloom industry increased throughout the period, and towards the end resulted in a heavy involvement. The Government of Madras took some interest in weaving technology from the early years of the century, notably through the efforts of the remarkable Alfred Chatterton as Director of Industries. From 1911, 'peripatetic weaving parties' toured the province popularizing the fly-shuttle and other innovations, but this service was swept away by government retrenchment in 1932. Meanwhile in 1917 the Government of Madras appointed a Weaving Expert and started a Textile Institute.[142] The evident involvement of handloom weavers in the agitations and riots of the early and middle 1930s ensured that the government transferred its attention from the technological to the economic aspect of the industry. Between 1930 and 1950, the rate at which the government instituted reports into the state of the handloom industry was almost biennial.[143]

At first, the government's interest did not result in any effective action. At a Textile Conference assembled in 1929, it rejected any possibility of assisting the handloom industry through changes in tariff or railway rates, and contented itself with some moralizing about the weavers' addiction to alcohol and with some pious hopes about the efficacy of co-operative marketing schemes.[144] In the same year D. Narayana Rao's *Report on Cottage Industries* also identified marketing as the main problem of the industry and recommended the extension of co-operative marketing schemes as the best method to expand demand for handloom goods and free the ordinary weaver from the control of the weaving capitalist.[145] But up to this time co-operative schemes had made little impact on the handloom industry and there was no attempt to translate the advice of the conference and of Narayana Rao into action. In 1930, the Director of Industries reported on the effect of the Indian yarn duties on the handloom industry,[146] and in 1932 government submitted a report to the Tariff Board arguing that the yarn duties assisted Indian mills in their competition with Indian handlooms far more than they assisted Indian mills in their competition with Japanese imports, and pressing for reduction or withdrawal of the duties.[147] But basically the Government of Madras accepted the need to balance the needs of the Indian mills against the Indian handloomers and entered little or no protest when Delhi refused to countenance any reduction in the cotton tariff, and in fact raised it in 1934. At this juncture, the Government of India agreed to divert some of the proceeds of the increased duty to handloom promotion schemes, and this enabled the Government of Madras to launch its vaunted co-operative marketing scheme. The Madras Handloom Weavers Provincial Co-operative Society was established in 1935 as a central marketing organization for affiliated societies of weavers, but, despite government finance, it made little progress before the second world war.[148]

In 1936, the attitude of the Madras government started to shift. In that year, the loss of markets in north India and overseas caused major distress and political disorder in the three main centres of Salem, Coimbatore and Madurai. The Director of Industries, the Registrar of Co-operative Societies and the Government Textile expert all made investigations into the state of the industry in the major centres and recounted the extent of unemployment and distress.[149] There was no attempt at welfare work but D.H. Amalsad, who had been the Madras government's Textile Expert with responsibility for both the mill and handloom sectors of the industry since 1919, came out with a tirade against the policy of protecting the mill industry at the expense of the handlooms, and this tirade set the tone of the Madras government's attitude in the years to come. Amalsad argued that the mills were not only capital-intensive and therefore inappropriate for a country where capital was scarce and labour plentiful, but also that they purchased

most of their capital equipment outside India and thus had no
linkage effects and a negative result on the balance of trade. The
mills were being protected, he went on, because they had political
muscle and the handloomers were being sacrificed because they
were politically weak. In 1938, he repeated the argument in a 'Note
on protection of hand-spinning and handloom weaving industries':

It is from the point of view of national economy that the Indian mill industry
had been protected against foreign competition. On the same ground the
handloom weavers now urge that their industry should also be protected
against Indian weaving mills. The public have now begun to evince greater
interest in the handloom weaver and the handloom weaving industry than
ever before. They realise that a large body of articulate interest is
benefitting at the expense of a larger but inarticulate community.[150]

In Madras, the handloom industry still produced four times as much
cloth as the mills and still employed far more people; and thus
government's priorities, Amalsad argued, should be clear.

Amalsad's tirade wandered around the corridors of the Secretariat collecting initials for a couple of years. But while the executive as yet took little interest, there were clear signs of a change of
attitude. One of the last acts of the Justice Party ministry before it
was swept out of power in 1937 was an attempt to introduce a
scheme of market-sharing through negotiations between representatives of the mill and handloom industries. These talks came to
nothing, but when the Tirunelveli District Association petitioned
the government to take steps to prohibit the mills from producing
certain sorts of goods which competed with handlooms, government
took the matter seriously and allowed the co-operative department
to commission a Special Officer to survey the province's handloom
industry and see if a scheme of market-sharing could be worked out
and enforced. Government was clearly moving towards a policy of
cultivating both a mill and handloom industry side by side.[151] The
Special Officer argued that the yarn duties had helped to make mill
cloth twenty to thirty per cent cheaper than the handloom goods,
and estimated that weavers' wages had been badly depressed in the
middle and late 1930s, by as much as fifty per cent in major centres
like Salem and Coimbatore. This report was quickly followed by a
Fact-Finding Committee under the Madras University's professor
of economics, P.J. Thomas, who again singled out the difficulties in
marketing handloom goods.[152] Finally R.D. Paul of the Department of Industry pointed out that government had so far done no

more than promote co-operative organization and the evidence showed that this affected a minute proportion of the weaving population.[153] This mountain of official reports, however, resulted in action only when the second world war began to play havoc with the Indian economy.

It was the Collector of Salem who unwittingly got government more deeply involved in the handloom industry. The rapid rise in yarn prices in 1941 turned almost a sixth of the population of his district town into unemployed beggars and he felt bound to act. To begin with he merely set up a rice dole, which from December 1941 supported up to 9,000 people, but soon he had more progressive ideas. Since the problem of unemployment arose because the yarn merchants were unwilling to make advances, he proposed that government should take over the yarn merchants' business and set the weavers to work. The scheme was proposed in haste and accepted in haste by a Secretariat and Board of Revenue who were horrified by the amounts being spent on outdoor relief. The Collector used government money to purchase yarn from the spinning mills, and to give yarn and wages to the weavers. By February 1942 there were 3,000 looms operating on government advances in Salem,[154] a similar scheme was getting under way in Madurai where distress was almost as bad,[155] and the Collectors of Chingleput, Ramnad, Tirunelveli and Coimbatore, who all by this time had considerable numbers of weavers living on government rice dole, were also thinking of similar projects.[156]

But the Salem scheme rapidly ran into trouble. The weavers soon realized that the government would accept anything they produced and continue to pay wages, and that the government officials supervising the scheme had absolutely no experience or expertise in the textile business. The weavers thus turned out poor quality cloth as rapidly as they could. Then in March, yarn prices started to fall. The yarn merchants now moved back into business, and soon were able to flood the market with handloom goods which were both cheaper and much better than those now piling up in the government godowns. Looking on its growing stock of expensive and shoddy cloth and its unused and expensive stocks of yarn, government began to realize the logic of the way in which yarn merchants worked. They invited local merchants to tender for the stocks but got a derisory response. They set up their own retail depot in Salem but the returns could not even pay the rent. They tried to unload the cloth onto various associations of government servants but had little luck. They tried to persuade the Government of India to take it away and use it for the army, but the army could find no use for such cloth. Finally they persuaded Delhi to take most of it away and give it free to refugees from Burma.[157] When other Collectors petitioned government for the funds to start similar schemes in their own districts, the Board of Revenue made its position clear:

It will be quite impossible for Government to finance all the handloom weavers of all the districts on the Salem model and acquire enormous stocks of cloth which may have to be sold at considerable loss, even if they can be sold at all in reasonable time. The essential weakness of the hasty Salem scheme is that in a very short time Government will find themselves in the position of merchants trying to sell crores worth of cloth and their ways and means position crippled till they secure disposal. The sooner we cut away from it the better.[158]

Thus ended Madras's first small venture into state capitalism.

But the handloom industry now had a charge on the government's attention. By the end of 1942, the government was aware that it would have to take a fairly prominent part in the organization of the cotton industry as a whole for as long as war conditions prevailed. The high price of yarn had induced many people to speculate in the yarn market, and this had caused a shortage of yarn supplies to weavers and a consequent shortage of cloth. This was not only pushing up the price of cloth on the home market, but making it difficult for the government to secure supplies for the army. Between 1942 and 1945 the government became more and more involved in the textile industry. It tried to regulate the supply of yarn to mills and handloom weavers, to control the prices of yarn and of retailed cloth, and to requisition stocks of cloth for the army.

In late 1942, the Madras government reorganized the Handloom Weavers Provincial Co-operative Society, and provided it with more capital, more paid officers, more borrowing capability, and a trained designer. It negotiated an arrangement with Harveys to provide yarn on forward contract at discount rates, and agreed to underwrite some of the losses that might be incurred in the attempt to make co-operative marketing work. But government also realized that any stimulus to the central co-operative organization was unlikely to prevent the cloth shortage that was imminent. So the government also established Collective Weaving Centres, where weavers manufactured goods for government requirements and also partly for the market, and, in an attempt to prevent speculation and hoarding, appointed a Yarn Commissioner to issue licences to all dealers and to oversee the movement of yarn in the province. These tentative steps proved ineffective and led to more stringent measures. In mid-1943 the government admitted that the licensing scheme did little to restrict profiteering, and now stipulated that all spinning mills should give regular accounts of their output so that the government might monitor stocks of yarn closely, placed a limit on the quantity of yarn that any dealer could hold in stock, and gave the Yarn Commissioner power to requisition yarn from the mills for use in the government's Collective Weaving Centres. Later in the year, the government provided extra capital through the Weaving Centres in an attempt to stimulate the handloom industry to produce cloth quickly to prevent a shortage. However, just as in the case of the Salem scheme, the private capitalists were quicker at responding to a clear marketing opportunity than were government officials. By the time the government scheme had resulted in stocks of cloth, the mills had already geared up production and flooded the market with cheaper material. To prevent any repetition of this competition between the mills and the handloom, the government now took steps to enforce a scheme of market-sharing. From early 1944 government ordered that mills could only manufacture certain prescribed sorts of standard cloths, and that the handlooms could henceforth have a monopoly in all other sorts of goods. While this at last gave the handlooms a guaranteed market, and ensured that they would enjoy reasonable prosperity until the late 1940s, there were still problems over the supply of raw materials. Under a new scheme begun in 1944, the government now attempted even closer control over the movement of yarn. All consumers of yarn, whether weaving mills, co-operative societies, or handloom capitalists were issued ration cards specifying the amount of yarn they were due and the source from which they could get it.

Thus in the last years of the war, government established close control over the textile business. Then came the problem of relaxing these measures. The end of the war and the restoration of export opportunities made the price of handloom cloth soar. In August 1945, the government stepped in and tried to lay down fixed rates of profit (fifteen per cent for the producer, four per cent for the middleman, and fourteen per cent for the retailer) to control prices. In 1946 the government issued an order fixing the wages of weavers, and setting up local handloom boards to frank and price all goods and to manage the rationing of yarn. These measures had to be tightened up further in 1947 when the government re-issued licences to all producers and dealers, ordered that the final retail price of handloom cloth should be equal to production costs plus a margin of 18¾ per cent, and appointed inspecting officers who had almost unlimited powers of entry and search. This was followed by another order enabling government to direct handloom weavers to manufacture certain items and not others with the aim of ensuring supplies to the home market before the manufacture of export articles.[159] Between December 1947 and February 1948 government dismantled many of these controls, but it left the scheme of yarn rationing in operation, and after prices had climbed by 200 per cent in the next six months, re-imposed licences and profit ceilings on all handloom producers and dealers.[160]

By 1948, the mills had returned to normal production and the market for handloom goods rapidly crumbled. By this time the government's interest in the handloom industry was considerable and it could not stand by and allow the industry to decline in the face of mill competition. From the time of the re-organization of the Handloom Weavers Provincial Co-operative Society in 1942, the government had used its panoply of controls over the yarn trade to encourage the growth of handloom co-operative societies. Co-operatives were given a better chance of getting supplies of yarn than private entrepreneurs, and also received considerable inputs of government capital. In 1936, there had only been thirty co-operative societies at work in the handloom industry. By 1946 there were 336 with 65,286 members and an annual turnover of Rs 373.09 lakhs. By 1953 the figures had risen yet again and there were 1,191 societies with 222,619 members, a working capital of Rs 394 lakhs and a turnover of Rs 538.53 lakhs.[161] Roughly a third of the province's looms were now connected to some form of co-operative organization and much of their operation was supported by government capital. Government had a direct interest in maintaining the industry, and now had the machinery to ensure that it would not decline. In the face of mill competition, government set up measures to encourage the export of handloom goods, and resolved to buy at least a third of government's textile requirements from the handloom industry.[162] In 1950 the government again took a leading role in ensuring that the handloom weavers were supplied with yarn, and, to protect the handloom market, persuaded Delhi to issue an order prohibiting the mills from manufacturing ten sorts of cloth.[163] The survival of the industry henceforth depended on government.

Although none of the other petty industries was quite so large and important as handloom weaving, many of them underwent similar processes of change in the early twentieth century. The tanning, carpet-making, beedi-rolling and metalwork industries were all organized on roughly the same lines as the handloom.[164] Each was scattered in numerous small workshops. On one estimate there were 400 small tanneries in the Tamil districts,[165] while beedi-rolling was carried out on the doorsteps and in the back rooms of thousands of poor households. The wages were generally pitifully low and the profits of the putting-out capitalists substantial. At the end of the 1920s a Tirunelveli man observed on the beedi industry that 'many have become suddenly rich by means of this trade',[166] while the wages paid to beedi-rollers were nowhere near enough to keep the worker alive. Many of the industries expanded in the twentieth century with some help from export demand. The hides produced by the Madras tanneries and known as 'East India kips' were always in demand in Europe and there were special spurts of demand in the twentieth century. In the first world war Madras (with a little help from Bombay) supplied three-fifths of the British army's boot uppers and even in the years following the armistice the war office bought Rs 6½ crores of tanned hides and skins in Madras.[167] The trade in beedis followed the Tamil migrants and expanded particularly well in Ceylon. At the same time that these industries became partially reliant on foreign markets, they also became more dependent on imported supplies. The metalwork industry was utterly dependent on imports of brass, copper, and iron. The beedi industry used local tobacco for the filling but imported wrapping leaves from Europe and Java.[168] The hides and skins industry imported cutch and other tanning materials. The involvement in overseas trading made Tamilnad's petty industries vulnerable to international instability and many of them experienced sharp swings of boom and slump. The tanneries slumped in the aftermath of the boom of wartime demand.[169] The beedi industry was in trouble when migration was disrupted in the thirties. At the same time the trend of long-term growth punctuated by short-term bouts of instability was associated with the concentration of the industries in major towns, the influx of more casual workers, and the growing dominance of a small number of putting-out capitalists. By the 1920s, the towns of Tirunelveli district were emerging as centres of footwear manufacture exporting to other parts of the region.[170] In Kumbakonam, traditionally famed as a metalwork centre, the number of workers expanded rapidly in the 1920s. By the end of that decade, nearly all the town's independent craftsmen had disappeared and the entire workforce of some 3,000 men was controlled by a handful of metalwork wholesalers.[171] Elsewhere, the influx of casual labourers disrupted the life of the independent artisans. Even the carpet-weaving industry of Salem, which required more skill than most of the artisan processes, developed in this way:

In former days, carpet-weaving was confined to the Pandaram caste. This industry has now been taken on by other caste people including agriculturists. This is mainly due to the agricultural distress prevailing everywhere. Coupled with this is the growth of a large number of carpet shops at Bhavani and the keen competition prevailing among the merchants. These merchants are underselling the carpets with the result that the wages are proportionately reduced.[172]

The towns of Tamilnad were rapidly becoming workhouses for the rural poor.

CONCLUSION: GROWTH AND STAGNATION

Up to the early twentieth century, urban Tamilnad consisted of a large number of small towns bobbing up and down on the tides of political and commercial fortune. Government, agrarian trade, retail and service industries, and petty manufactures provided the major functions of the towns. With a few notable exceptions, the urban centres had remarkable little fixity and the urban populations were remarkably mobile. Professional, clerical and service groups moved easily from the old political centres into the British capital at Madras when government began to centralize the administration from the late nineteenth century onwards. Traders shifted from town to town. As N.G. Ranga told the Royal Commission of Labour in 1930, it was only the most socially disadvantaged who cut their links with their native place in the countryside:

Most of the workers employed in the Coimbatore and Madura cotton mills and those working in the godowns of Coconada and Vizagapatam ports come from the nearby villages and are therefore living in their own villages. The toddy carriers of Madras go to the City for a stay of three to six months in the year and therefore expect to return to their villages, so soon as the specially busy season is over. But the scavengers of the Presidency capital have more or less permanently settled down in the city, and therefore visit their native village once or twice in every two or three years and that only for a few days. The cart-pullers, rickshaw-pullers and many of the casual workers of the city of Madras are also drafted from the village but they always keep on their relation with their villages. On the other hand, most of the Adi-Dravidas and Adi-Andhras who have gone to the city for work, are usually very reluctant to go back to their villages since they have come to take freedom in social matters which they are denied in the villages... The cotton mills of Madura and Coimbatore are mostly dependent upon the workers coming from the neighbouring villages and are therefore unable to work full time and at full speed during times of brisk work in the fields.[173]

A town could grow rapidly on a boom of trade, transport or professional functions. Then it would draw urban specialists from other towns and casual labour from the surrounding countryside. Once the town's burst of growth was over, the bloated nature of the population had become apparent, and stagnation had begun, it was possible for the more successful entrepreneurs and traders to move elsewhere, and for the casual labour-force to melt back into the countryside. Others were not so mobile. Less fortunate entrepreneurs would be forced back onto the investments they had made as insurance against just this eventuality. Thus it came about that towns became studded with absentee landlords and large numbers of competing businesses in such lines as general trading, transport companies, retail agencies and small service industries. The permanent labour force would be forced into those putting-out industries, particularly handloom weaving and beedi rolling, that acted as poor relief.

From the 1930s onwards, however, there was a significant change in this pattern of urban growth. The urban population began to grow more quickly, and increasingly the growth was concentrated in the major cities. The acceleration of urban growth was only partly related to the growth of modern industries. As we have seen, the new industries exerted a very limited demand for labour and were far from securely based by the end of the period. One reason for the acceleration was the advancing crisis in agriculture which cut off the line of retreat back into the countryside and induced even some of the most torpid towns to retain or even increase their populations after the town's economic base had been largely swept away. One

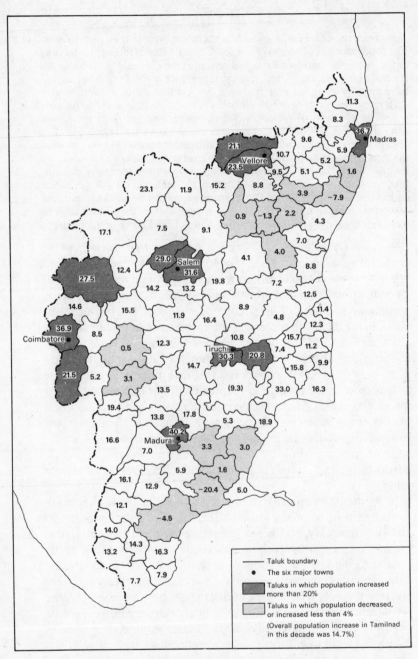

Map 8   Population increase by taluk 1941-51

reason for the concentration in large towns was the increasing importance of their petty industries as a form of outdoor relief for the region's poor, and the increasing importance of welfare services which government was providing only in the major towns. It was the economic strains of the second world war which helped to establish these welfare services. In 1943, government reacted to the threat of wartime shortages of food and other necessities by erecting systems of grain rationing and public distribution in the major towns. It also intervened in the management of the major urban industries with the aim of safeguarding employment and securing reasonable minimum wages. It was not long before government realized that such welfare activities attracted the impoverished of the countryside. Map 8 shows clearly that the areas where population was increasing rapidly in the 1940s were those in and around the major towns—Madras, the upper Palar, Salem, Coimbatore and the Kongunad towns, Tiruchi, Madurai. (The only exception to this pattern was the southern part of the Kaveri delta which had recently been provided with secure irrigation under the Kaveri-Mettur project.) Meanwhile, some of the areas of the poorest and most desperate agriculture in fact lost population during this decade, and some other poor, dry rural areas experienced virtually no growth. The parts of the coastal plain that fell between the Palar and Ponnaiyar basins, and between the Kaveri and Tambraparni basins, and also the poorer, upland part of southern Kongunad were clearly losing migrants to the burgeoning cities.

Thus the larger towns swelled in the 1940s, and most particularly those which enjoyed government food supplies, and those which were already known as centres of putting-out industry. The population of the capital increased by eighty-two per cent and passed the million mark. The influx of the poorer classes into Madras city had begun in the depression and the local proverb 'After ruin, go to the city' was frequently quoted in that decade.[174] In 1871 it had been estimated that one eighth of the city's population lived in the *cheri* hut quarters of the poor, but a further estimate in the 1930s raised that estimate to one third.[175] By the end of the war, the city had sprawled several new *cheris* and poor suburbs to the north and the east. While some of the influx into the capital was drawn into wartime manufacture, many migrants found their way into service industries or putting-out work, particularly the beedi-rolling industry. Other centres of coarse artisan industry also grew rapidly.

Salem, which was famous for weaving of coarse cloths and which had experienced hardly any population growth between 1871 and 1921, was now growing rapidly and increased its population by fifty-six per cent in the 1940s. Tanjavur, which had weaving, dyeing, and metalwork industries and which had been in decline since the dethroning of its Maratha Prince, grew by forty-six per cent and at last regained the size it had estimatedly been in 1780.

Finally, there was some new impetus to urban expansion from the increasing size of the administrative machine, both in the war and after independence. The sum effect of all these factors was that for the first time since 1871 the large towns grew rapidly as opposed to the small market towns. Besides Salem, Madras and Tanjavur, mentioned above, most of the other large towns that were district headquarters, artisan centres and magnets to the poor also grew rapidly in the 1940s. Tiruchi and its satellite towns added forty-five per cent, Tirunelveli-Palamcottah added twenty-four per cent, Coimbatore grew by fifty-two per cent and Vellore by forty-eight per cent. The seventeen largest towns (all over 50,000 by 1951) in sum added over a million people to their populations in the 1940s. This was an increase of fifty-five per cent and accounted for half the overall increase in the urban population of the region.

Only Coimbatore, with its satellite towns, was emerging as a centre of manufacturing industry. Twenty or thirty towns existed as collection points for produce destined for export. Other towns, even the large ones were mainly centres of administration, local exchange, and artisan manufacture. Even Madurai, the second largest town of the province, was more like an inflated village than a metropolis. It had four cotton mills, but the bulk of its population was in tertiary occupations; its most successful entrepreneur was merely running a mammoth version of the usual combination of bus companies, trucking fleets and automobile workshops;[176] and its size was due more to the sheer magnitude of the countryside it serviced (it commanded much of the southern tip of the peninsula), rather than to any autonomous urban function.

From the late nineteenth century there had clearly been some growth in the home market, both among the prospering commercial farmers of the countryside and among the ranks of traders, bankers, and professionals in the sporadically growing towns. Imports of consumer goods roughly doubled in value (at constant prices) between the 1880s and the late 1920s and it is doubtful whether the local European community accounted for more than a small portion of this increase. Moreover from the first world war, and more markedly from the depression, the conditions were favourable for local manufactures to replace imported goods. In the decade following the second world war, the volume of consumer goods imported had fallen back to the level of the 1880s. Meanwhile, imports of capital goods had started to increase.[177] The 1930s and 1940s offered many good opportunities for local manufacturers to capture the whole market. There was some incentive from the artificial protection of tariff barriers and from the implied protection brought about by the disruption of world trade. More importantly, the urban sector found itself in a newly favourable position to suck capital out of the countryside; in the 1930s and '40s the towns welcomed a flow of eager capital and cheap labour.

But there were enormous limitations on the potential for expanding the urban sector by import substitution against a background of agrarian decline. It was ironic that the three things which made urban investment look so attractive—the decline of alternative investments in agrarian commerce, the flow of cheap labour, the protection implied by the disordering of international commerce—were also signs that the future prospects for growth in the home market were very poor indeed. Agrarian decline closed off one important avenue for urban expansion. The decline in imports of consumer goods was only partially countered by increases in imports of capital goods; the major increase in imports consisted of the food which the Tamilnad countryside was increasingly failing to produce for itself. The other avenue for urban expansion lay in exports and here Tamilnad's industries had some marked successes, but only in a specific range of products. Tamilnad's export market in urban goods was pretty much limited to those items which the more established industrial nations would not or could not produce. That meant goods which were either handcrafted or at least had a high proportion of their value added by cheap labour.

Tamilnad's entrepreneurs invested eagerly in industry in the 1930s and 1940s but painful experience quickly taught them that their markets were restricted by the condition of the local rural economy and the competitive nature of international markets. The industries which emerged from these circumstances were of a particular type. On the one hand there were factory industries, mostly involved in processing natural products with a relatively simple technology. The units were generally small, the management based on family organization, the ratio of fixed to working capital very low indeed. On the other hand there were modified versions of 'traditional' industries which were characterized by intermittent operation, a reserve of cheap labour, and a putting-out system.

The result was a particularly torpid urban sector which by the end of the period consisted of a plethora of small towns, many of which had been tossed about and then stranded by the tides of commercial and industrial fortune, and a few emergent cities whose populations were mostly involved in trade, service occupations, and putting-out industry. Moreover the fragility and torpidity of this urban sector had begun to demand government's attention. The expansion of the 1930s had left behind a tentative urban capitalism and a poor and volatile urban working class. In the interests of its own revenues, and in the interests of political order, government was drawn into an active role in cossetting the region's urban economy. We must now leave the rather desolate streets of urban Tamilnad and enter the gloomy offices of the government.

6

The state and the countryside

In all the classic accounts of India in the second half of the nineteenth century, the state machinery which the British built is seen as a key instrument in the practice of a specific sort of colonial system. India was not a colony which was directly looted by mercantilist traders, greedy mine-owners, rings of fruit-canners or meat-packers. It was emphatically not a simple lucky-dip for imperial gamblers. India did not have the resources of vacant land or under-used raw materials to attract this form of colonial exploitation, and its social structure was reckoned to be too elaborate and arcane to bear much social and economic engineering. India therefore played a rather more subtle role in a rather more complex empire. It was the chief support of an extensive trading system in the eastern seas. It served as an important market for British goods and as an important testing ground for products and for marketing methods which Britain could deploy in other parts of the globe. It provided several key articles of trade which British ships could carry to customers in east and west. But most of all it was simply an invaluable overseas headquarters. It had port facilities, and it provided much of the military muscle for protecting Britain's eastward economic interests. The aim of the colonial state in late nineteenth-century India was thus to protect and promote this vital 'infrastructural' role. It had to maintain a military establishment, to build up the facilities for commerce and occasionally move to ensure that they were most helpful to *British* commerce, and, of course, to keep itself in existence.[1] Thus the state had two main activities. Firstly, it had to collect enough revenue to maintain the army and the administration itself and it had to be constantly on guard against economic or political changes which might undermine the revenue system. Secondly, it had to do the minimum necessary, in terms of state expenditure, to oil the wheels of overseas trade.

The government of late nineteenth-century Madras fits well into this pattern. With the completion of the 'late ryotwari' system it had become somewhat distinguished among Indian provincial governments in the matter of revenue collection and by the early twentieth century Madras could be described as the 'milch-cow'[2] of the Indian exchequer. As for commerce, the Madras government had for some time tried to encourage the production of the region's most promising product, raw cotton, had assisted in the movement of Madras labourers to regions where they could be especially useful to British commerce, and had built ports and railways systems to encourage trade.

However it is easy to suppose that between the elaboration of the late nineteenth-century pattern on the one hand, and the coming of independence and the orientation to economic development on the other, there was little or no change in the role of the colonial state. Indeed the history of the later stages of British colonial rule is often read as attempts to protect the nineteenth-century system under the thin and shabby cloak of laissez-faire. It may be heartening to assume that 'independence and development' represented a clean break with the bad old colonial past, but it may not be helpful. The colonial system did change remarkably in its latter stages, and the rulers and planners of independent, developing India did inherit not only much of the machinery of colonial India but also much of its 'work in progress'.

The classic, late nineteenth-century role of India's colonial state was formed against a specific background and it is hardly surprising that the activity of the government changed as the props of the nineteenth-century empire decayed. So far as Madras was concerned there were three important changes in the foundations of the region's economy. Firstly, the region's involvement in overseas trading reached a peak in the early twentieth century and then began to decline. Secondly, there was a sharp decline in the provision of food. This was not like the nineteenth-century famines — sporadic visitations of an unreliable climate which simply defeated the resources of a primitive system of transportation and a poorly organized market. Rather this was a steady decline in the average level of supply. Thirdly, industries had begun to grow and towns now played a much larger part in the region's society and economy. These changes not only played havoc with the classic colonial system, but they demanded some form of response from the colonial state. The Government of Madras could not ignore the fact that the foundations of the region's economy were shifting and that the survival of the state would depend on its success in understanding and exploiting those shifts. The Government of Madras could not neglect the consequences of a decline in the supplies of food, and it was of course especially sensitive to the social and political problems attendant on the spread of industry and the growth of towns.

The government became, reluctantly but ineluctably, more concerned about the health and prospect of the region's internal economy. This was not a simple or indeed a rapid transformation. The colonial rulers did indeed cling for a long time to the ideological comforts and the practical simplicities of a policy of laissez-faire. Yet gradually the dominating logic of the administrative apparatus ceased to be the collection of revenue and became the attainment of economic welfare or, at least, financial survival. The government's duty to assist the business of overseas trading declined in favour of a duty to assist the business of growing food. Moreover while it undertook its new duties as a response to unavoidable pressures, nevertheless the way in which it carried them out reflected a bunch of ideological assumptions about the future potential of the region's economy and about the kind of groups and classes in society which the government must look to for support. These assumptions of course helped to shape the future.

The first part of this chapter looks at the decline of the colonial settlement in the Tamilnad countryside by following the history of the two principal institutions which the British used to control the area—zamindaris, and village office. The later sections of the chapter look at the expansion of the government's involvement in the economy. Under this heading a number of items have already been noticed in previous chapters—debt legislation, industrial conciliation, some market regulation. This chapter looks at the two main areas which have not yet been dealt with—irrigation and food policy—and then attempts to sum up the nature of state interest and involvement by the time of Independence.

THE DECLINE OF COLONIAL CONTROL

For the British rulers of nineteenth-century Tamilnad, as of other parts of India, the chief function of the countryside was the generation of revenue. Land taxes were by far the most important supplier of government income. The collection of these taxes was the most important function of the rural arm of the bureaucracy, and the remaining apparatus of government was organized around the central pole of the revenue service. But if the flow of land tax was of so much interest to the organization of government, it was of course equally important to the organization of rural society. The extraction of revenue was the single most important transfer of resources in the village economy and thus those who in some way mediated the transfer were inevitably important members of local society. Indeed government's strategy of rural control was based on just this premise. Government gained leverage in rural society by allying with men of local power and influence, and sealed this alliance by an agreement to share the proceeds of revenue collection. The men who had authority and who controlled wealth tended to be those who were associated with government's revenue system.

By the twentieth century, however, the process of extracting revenue ceased to have such an important role. In part this was because the real value of the land revenue declined. In the second half of the nineteenth century the 'real' incidence of the land revenue had been erratic in the short-term (mostly because of fluctuations associated with famines) but fairly steady in the long-term. From the turn of the century, however, the incidence of land revenue declined. Mostly this was due to price inflation and the unwillingness of the government to risk the political consequences of raising the revenue demand in parallel with rising prices. The price-fall of the depression boosted the incidence of revenue demand back to the level it had been in the late nineteenth century, but this lasted for only a decade and merely constituted an exception to the trend which reduced the incidence of land revenue to one-third of its turn-of-the-century level by the 1950s.

Meanwhile the declining importance of the land revenue process was also in part due to the advance of commerce. By the early twentieth century in most parts of Tamilnad the economy of the

**Table 27: Incidence of revenue demand in ryotwari Tamilnad
1866-7 to 1950-1**

Quinquennium	Ryotwari Demand Rs per acre	Price Indices			Ryotwari demand deflated By each price index (1901/2-1905/6=100)		
		General	Rice (India)	Rice (Tanjavur)			
1866/7-70/1	1.9843	109	114		108	132	
1871/2-75/6	1.9904	100	104		118	145	
1876/7-80/1	1.9244	120	133	230	95	110	75
1881/2-85/6	1.9953	103	121	132	115	125	135
1886/7-90/1	1.9530	114	140	147	102	106	119
1891/2-95/6	2.0406	127	160	192	95	97	95
1896/7-1900/01	2.1861	136	172	216	95	96	90
1901/2-05/6	2.2405	133	170	200	100	100	100
1906/7-10/11	2.2767	162	220	304	83	79	67
1911/2-15/16	2.3013	182	244	281	75	72	73
1916/7-20/1	2.3690	255	306	444	55	59	48
1921/2-25/6	2.5453	261	336	536	58	57	42
1926/7-30/1	2.5732	229	305	436	67	64	53
1931/2-35/6	2.6114	145	166	264	107	119	88
1936/7-40/1	2.6367	159	188	234	108	106	101
1941/2-45/6	2.7460	247	344	617	66	61	40
1946/7-50/1	2.4562	420	644	723	35	29	30

Quinquennial averages

Notes and Sources: Ryotwari demand is calculated from 'settled demand ryotwari' and 'total acreage' figures in the *Report on the Settlement of the Land Revenue in the Madras Presidency*. The 'general' price index is the general weighted index from *Index Numbers of Indian Prices 1861-1931* (and annual addenda), summary table I, and the first rice index is from summary table III of the same publication. These series stop in 1941 and have been extended using the Reserve Bank of India indices (see *Banking and Monetary Statistics of India*) of 'general' and 'food' prices respectively. The Tanjavur rice price index is from the *Statistical Atlas of the Madras Presidency*, 1963 edition.

cash-crop markets loomed much larger than the economy of the land tax. Government officers regularly justified the level of the land tax by pointing out that the dues paid to money-lenders far exceeded the dues paid to the government. What the government recognized only hazily was that the advance of 'the money-lender', and all that he represented, was steadily undermining the systems of rural control which they had erected around the business of transferring land revenue.

There were two such systems which were of major importance in different parts of rural Tamilnad. The less important (in geographical extent) was the zamindari settlement which used estate-owning landlords as rent-collecting intermediaries between the government and the village. The more extensive system was the ryotwari settlement in which the chain of government command reached right down to the village and ended there in the persons of village officers. In the nineteenth century, zamindars and the ryotwari village officers were the principal agents of government in rural Tamilnad. In the twentieth they declined towards insignificance.

Zamindars

The principal zamindari estates had evolved from the poligari military settlements of the sixteenth to eighteenth centuries. A large number (though not all) of the estates survived the wars of the eighteenth century, the battles with the British (particularly in 1799-1801), and the adjustment to British rule. In their enthusiasm for a permanently-settled revenue-farming system in the first two decades of the nineteenth century, the British created a number of new estates (*mittas*) in areas which had not previously been settled in great estates. Many of these mittas collapsed within the next twenty years, and since by that time the Government of Madras had become attached to the ryotwari form of tenure, which eliminated such intermediaries between government and the village, the areas were re-settled in this form. However a number of these newly-created mitta estates survived, and from the 1830s to the end of the century the number of casualties among either new or old estates was relatively small.[3] In the early twentieth century, the Madras government still listed 634 estates in the Tamil districts, and these estates covered nineteen per cent of the total area. The estates ranged from the 2,104 square miles held by the raja of Ramnad and inhabited by almost half a million people, to minute estates with only a few dusty acres and no inhabitants at all. In between these extremes, there were estates of all sizes. Most of the 'ancient' estates huddled towards the upper end of the scale and could be counted among the 112 estates which each commanded more than 5,000 acres and 8,000 people, while most of the mittas were included in the 512 estates which were smaller than this. Nearly all the estates were situated on the plain, and here they accounted for rather more than a third of the total area. There was only a handful

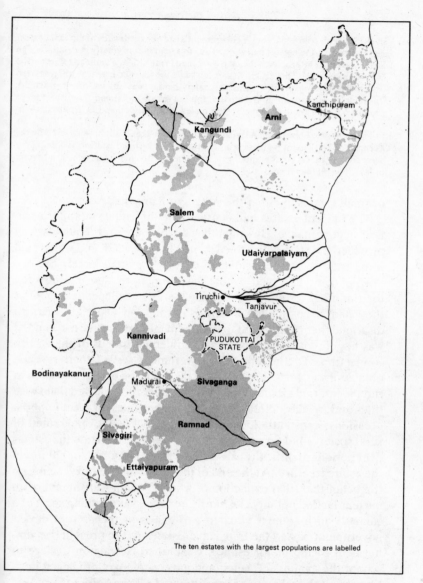

The ten estates with the largest populations are labelled

Map 9   Zamindari and Inam estates in Tamilnad

Note: This is an original map based on data and individual survey maps in Rev 1224
(C) 30 June 1945 in the Tamilnadu Archives. The Government of Madras never had
a proper map of the estates within its province until it finally decided it ought to know
where the estates were in order to abolish them. The survey and mapping carried out

in 1945 revealed how inaccurate government's previous estimates of the exact extent
and position of the estates had been. Thus this map differs greatly in detail, though
little in overall pattern, from the map contained in my article 'Tamilnad estates in the
twentieth century'. That article was writen while the file used here was still restricted
under the thirty-year rule, and the map therein was drawn off fragmentary
information in maps from Gazetteers, the Survey of India, and the district maps
prepared by the Madras Survey office under W.A. Hasted and D. Seshacharlu in
1922.

The map here shows zamindari and mitta estates, that is all those covered by the
Permanent Settlement regulation in 1801, and 'Whole Inam' estates. 'Whole Inams'
were inams (that is lands granted with a discounted revenue liability) which covered
at least one whole village.

of small estates in either the valleys or Kongunad.[4]

The ancient estates had considerable difficulties in adjusting to
British governance. By origin they were military settlements which
provided the state with armed men in time of need, and which paid
some tribute. In the eighteenth century they had largely become
independent, had paid tribute very irregularly and had devoted
their military resources to securing their own independence. After
they had been quelled by British troops in 1801,[5] the British
disarmed them and set out to turn them into revenue farmers and, it
was hoped, 'great landlords' and influential friends of the British
connection. To this end, the government settled their revenue
obligations in perpetuity, allowed them a more or less free hand to
run the internal affairs of their estates, liberally endowed them with
titles and medals, allotted them prominent roles on great imperial
occasions, constantly looked to them to act as the spokesmen of
rural society, and set up the Court of Wards to help tide the estates
over periods of difficulty caused by sickness, minority, or failures in
the estate treasury. At the end of the nineteenth century, acting on
the belief that 'that extinction or wholesale impoverishment of an
ancient landed nobility can hardly be viewed as anything short of a
calamity in a country situated as India is at the present days',[6]
government passed the Impartible Estates Act to prevent dismem-
berment of the major estates, established Newington College to
school the zamindars' heirs, and gave zamindars privileged positions in all the schemes of constitutional reform before the second
world war.

Yet the support of government was far from complete. By the
1820s Madras had become a 'ryotwari province' in which zamindaris
were an aberration, tolerated as long as they relieved the government of the burden of extending the onerous ryotwari adminis-

tration even further. In the short term it was always easier and cheaper for government to patch up the zamindari system rather than replace it, but schemes of wholesale expropriation of the zamindari estates were regularly discussed.[7]

The management of a zamindari estate in the nineteenth and early twentieth centuries revolved around three interdependent strategies: firstly the zamindar had to maintain the appurtenances of traditional lordship, secondly he had to collect the revenue, thirdly he had to maintain a role in the economy of his estate. Each of these strategies was pursued in its own right—the zamindar wanted to be a lord, had to collect the revenue on behalf of government, wanted to keep some grip on the local economy—but also they were crucially interdependent. If the revenue was not delivered to the government then the existence of the estate was in danger. Without the prestige of lordship and the backing of government, the zamindar would not be able to dominate the local economy. Without the prestige of lordship and involvement in the local economy, it would prove difficult to secure funds to pay the government's revenue. However, despite the fact that the zamindar needed to ride all three of these horses, the three began to pull in slightly different directions and gradually it became more and more difficult to straddle them.

It was difficult enough from the beginning. Once the poligars had been defeated, disarmed and incorporated within the British Empire, it was difficult for them to maintain an aura of independent lordship. What, after all, was a military leader without his troops? Many of the more ancient and substantial poligari families reacted by investing heavily in the pomp and circumstance of lordship—mostly through lavish ceremonials to mark occasions in the life of the family and their favoured temples—and by working to ensure that the British overlords continued to grant the zamindars public guarantees of their political importance. Since the British overlords were reluctant to use executive (or even for the most part, legislative) power to emphasize the zamindars' importance, the zamindars were obliged to resort to the courts and to seek judgments which publicly confirmed the status and glamour of their lordship (through suits which guaranteed 'traditional rights' over communal resources, 'traditional roles' in temple ritual and temple control and so on) even when the substance of that lordship had disappeared.[8]

But such a strategy held the seeds of its own downfall. Even if the investments in ceremonial and in legal process did maintain a 'husk of sentiment' surrounding the emptying shell of zamindari power, they were expensive and, in the long run, offensive to the British overlords who saw such activities as horribly misguided; in their eyes, the zamindar's future lay in a role as 'improving landlord' not as a quaint and cantankerous relic of the past.

Revenue collection was not easy. The estates lay mostly in the harsh dry tract, and they had been founded there as part of colonization schemes associated with military expansion. It seems clear that to some extent the continued occupation and exploitation of such a miserable tract *depended on* the exercise of lordly power. Certainly in the early nineteenth century in certain estates which were temporarily taken into direct management by government officials, the population quickly dwindled and cultivation was abruptly reduced until the government was obliged to restore the zamindar and allow him to resuscitate cultivation by the usual means at his disposal. Certainly many of the new mitta estates collapsed in the same period because the upstart estate-holders could not collect revenue from the villages without the reserves of military force which the ancient zamindars had always used.[9]

While the British undermined the zamindars' military power, they did little to replace it with a judicial capability. Until the Estates Land Act of 1908 there was no clear statement of the legal relations between zamindars and their subjects, and it proved particularly difficult to use legal process to collect rents. Legal reckoning in British courts which honoured precedent relied on the production of records. If in the ryotwari areas the government and the courts made scant provision for settling disputes between two parties bearing crumbly bits of cadjan leaf which detailed mutually contradictory rights, in the zamindari tracts they made virtually no provision at all. Most suits about arrears of rent reached no result—because the zamindar could not convince the court that a particular ryot occupied a certain tract of land, was supposed to pay a certain rent, and indeed had not paid it—and those zamindars who did get a decree faced yet a further difficulty: the machinery for enforcing court decrees was bad enough in the tracts of land under direct government (ryotwari) control, but outside these areas it was even worse.[10]

Finally, few estate-owners had established systems of close management. In pre-British days, the poligars ran their territories by policing them, not by attending to administrative detail. Few had elaborate estate bureaucracies which reached down into the village. Thus in the nineteenth century, a search in most zamindari offices would not have revealed any land records or any details of the assessment of rents. Many zamindars and their principal administrative officers had a very hazy idea about the exact location of villages within their estates. Most of the records were kept by the karnams or village accountants and the zamindar's perception of his rights in and dues from the villages often depended on the information which the karnams were prepared to pass on. There were systems for land assessment, but these seem to have been the work of the village karnam and headman, rather than the estate office, for very often they differed radically from village to village and showed no overall pattern throughout the estate.[11]

Under these circumstances it was hardly surprising that the zamindars found it difficult to command an estate revenue adequate to pay the government's tax demand. In the early part of the nineteenth century, when in many cases the British pitched the demand rather high as part of the retribution for the rebellions of 1799-1801, and when prices were depressed, several zamindars had especial difficulty in paying the revenue and even some of the older estates collapsed under the strain. Yet as the century progressed, matters improved. While the government demand rose only slowly (it was not quite permanently settled because the government invented new cesses to add to the original peshkash) prices began to rise rather faster. Moreover, cash-crops began to spread throughout the dry tract and as a result incomes rose and population increased. Between the 1850s and the 1920s, estates generally managed to collect enough revenue to satisfy the government and to maintain some of the more important pretensions of lordship, although expensive litigation and ritual made many zamindars horribly reliant on bankers.

This limited degree of success was made possible by the zamindars' involvement in the local economy. This involvement was peripheral rather than central, but it was nonetheless important. It was not a new departure for the zamindars, but was in many ways only a slight transformation of old roles. The establishment of poligari estates had entailed colonization of new tracts of land as part of a strategy of expanding the Vijayanagar state's resources, and from the start the poligars had played some part in clearing new land, building irrigation works, and ensuring the supply of some agricultural inputs. In the nineteenth century, the zamindar retained direct control over irrigation works[12] and over forest and waste lands[13] which were vital for supplying various inputs to the agricultural economy. Moreover, the zamindars exercised some control over agrarian marketing. The principal markets of the estates had always taken place either in the estate town (and sometimes even in the palace yard) or under the aegis of temples which were, in turn, under the control of the zamindar. This again continued in the nineteenth and early twentieth centuries. Finally, the poligar had always maintained close links with the leading men of the estate villages, whether as part of the machinery of military mobilization and command, or as part of the network of clan and caste hierarchies.[14] This continued as an alliance in which each party helped to sustain the other's economic fortunes: the leading villagers raised the revenues which enabled the estate to exist, while the zamindar allowed the leading villagers sufficient opportunities to exploit estate administration to their own advantages. As already noted, rent collection depended very much on the village officers, and the schemes which the village officers devised to extract rents from within the village were generally outside the zamindar's interest and control. In many cases, the zamindari village officers may have distributed the estate demand equitably. Yet clearly in some villages they could tilt the assessment. 'Rents are not paid regularly by powerful ryots,' noted one observer, 'only small and weak ryots pay regularly.'[15]

It is now commonly noted that 'traditional' lordship in south India revolved around a redistributive role. Lords managed the attributes of ritual status and redistributed these to their subjects in such a way that all were incorporated within the moral community and their respective ranks and rights were well-defined. Lords also managed some material resources in an equivalent matter, and in many respects the cycles of ritual and material redistribution overlapped and intermeshed. The zamindars in the nineteenth century were able to uphold at least some elements of such a redistributive role.

As the nineteenth century gave way to the twentieth, the strains inherent in this system of zamindari management became markedly more difficult to contain. Two factors were especially important in this change. Firstly, the government started to bypass the zamindars, to extend elements of direct control over the villages within the estates, and thus to undermine the 'lordship' of the zamindars in a very public way. This was achieved largely through two pieces of legislation. In the Estates Land Act of 1908, government set out to define the rights and obligations of zamindars and their tenants, and thus to guarantee to the tenant certain privileges and rights vis-à-vis the zamindar. The Act was important as an ideological step, yet because the province's judicial machinery was not equipped to implement the provisions of the Act, and because the zamindars set out to sabotage the Act by litigation, it was less important in practice.[16] The Proprietary Estates Village Services Act of 1894, however, was much more important because it transferred from the zamindar to the government the responsibility to pay and discipline the headmen and karnams of villages inside the estates. The justification for this move was the growing amount of governmental business undertaken by these estate village officers (including collection of education and local board cesses, registration of births and deaths, and recording of agricultural statistics).[17] But the effect was to sever an important link between the zamindar and some of his most important subjects. The zamindars complained bitterly about the Act for the next half-century. In the midst of the troubles of the 1930s, one zamindar characterized the Act as the origin of all his difficulties for through it, he argued, 'Government did in fact shatter the very basis of the administration' of the estates.[18] While these two Acts posed the most direct threats to the zamindar, the increasing use of legislation in general served to undermine zamindari pretensions to autonomous lordship. The increase of representative institutions at the local and provincial level had much the same effect, for they created new channels of political communication between estate society and government.

Secondly, the zamindar's role in the economic life of his territory, and thus his ability to redistribute the material resources of his subjects, was undermined by a shift in the foundations of economic activity. Between the 1890s and the 1920s the cultivation of cotton and groundnut spread rapidly in the dry tract in which the zamindaris were situated. Before long, the leading villagers of the estates found that their most important economic transactions were no longer made at the zamindar's estate office, but at the cash-crop markets. Whereas it had once been easiest to tap the economy of the estate tract by acting as an intermediary between the estate and the village—in other words by serving as an estate village officer—it was now best to serve as an intermediary between the village and the institutions of export marketing. This change of interest was symbolized by a simple geographical shift. The major strands of the market economy were the railways and, largely because of the legal difficulties experienced in building railway tracks across zamindari land, the railways tended to by-pass the estates and the palace-towns. The cash-crop markets serving the estate tracts were usually sited outside the estates themselves. For instance, while a large part of the expansion of cotton cultivation in the far-south took place in the zamindaris of Madurai, Ramnad and Tirunelveli, the main marketing centres were in the non-estate towns of Virudhunagar, Tuticorin, and Tirumangalam. Similarly, the groundnuts grown in the estate of Arni were marketed at Ranipet some way to the north of the estate. In the first quarter of the twentieth century, there was a distinct shift in the pattern of urban growth within the dry tract. Zamindari palace-towns were largely stagnant or in decline while the new rail-heads were growing rapidly.

Some zamindars were aware of the threat posed by this redirection of the economic life of the estates, and some attempted to resist. The raja of Ramnad, for instance, forced his ryots to give 'written undertakings that they would not in future raise chillies or cotton on their lands'.[19] Several zamindars tried to discourage cash-cropping by levying high rates of rent on areas sown with cash-crops.[20] Some zamindars tried to establish some form of control over the new marketing centres. Ramnad was again prominent; he waged a long battle against the managers of the market in the booming cotton town of Rajapalaiyam just beyond the border of his estate, and later tried to gain control over the market by working through the new institutions of local self-government. Other zamindars followed similar tactics.[21]

Many more zamindars, however, responded by allowing their role in the economic life of their territories to atrophy. In particular they neglected their responsibility to maintain tanks and other small irrigation works within their estates. By the early twentieth century, the government was sufficiently worried by the evidence of this neglect to look around for ways to force zamindars to attend to their irrigation works. But clauses inserted in the 1908 Act were not effective and the government did not push through specific and effective legislation on this matter until the critical years of the second world war.[22] Furthermore, in some estates where the zamindar customarily supported a number of village personnel who were crucial to the maintenance of the local economy—messengers, watchmen, irrigation overseers, potters, carpenters, smiths, shepherds—these responsibilities were also allowed lapse.[23]

The results of these two changes in the political and economic coherence of the estates were obvious by the 1920s. 'The tenant has very little to do with the zamindar nowadays', noted one rural politician in the 1920s, 'except to pay his rent. All his relations are with the Government and the Government has taken all the powers of the zamindar; the zamindar has only to pay his peishcush and receive what he gets from the tenant.'[24] In other words, the zamindar had ceased to play such important roles in the life of his peasantry, and fewer people had a vested interest in sustaining cycles of redistribution of material and ritual resources within the estate. Many zamindars had drifted away into an urban lifestyle; many appeared to resign themselves to an inevitable yet glorious decline. Several observers remarked on the demise of a sense of community in the estates. Looking back romantically to the 1870, one such observer noted:

In those days, the zamindars and their tenants were acting something like one family, each sharing the festivities, the joys and the sorrows of the other. Whenever there was a feast or marriage in the tenant's house, the zamindar generally gave timber, gave a feeding and other such things... Subsequently however when the administration changed hands, the tenants began to feel the difficulty of the high rent which was collected without the human touch. The zamindars began to lead a new modern life, their style of living went up, their scale of expenditure increased and therefore they wanted more money. They became friends of the officers they had to entertain now and again.[25]

Although the relations of zamindars and tenants had probably never been so smooth as such nostalgic reminiscences would like to suggest, there was certainly a growth of tension. Ryots perceived the decline in the redistributive activities of the zamindar and resented it. By the 1920s, there was a steady drone of complaint about the deterioration of estate irrigation works, and in several cases the ryots retaliated by refusing to pay their rents. In two estates the ryots reacted to the zamindar's refusal to maintain the irrigation works by running riot and shooting dead some estate employees.[26] There was also a growing dispute between ryots and estate officials over the use of forests. This ran parallel to similar disputes in the government forests, but was conducted with greater bitterness and in some estates ryots and estate officials murdered one another with monotonous regularity.[27] The failure to maintain village functionaries prompted similar disgust. In Ramnad, the zamindar had allowed these duties to lapse from the 1910s, and in the 1930s a government officer noted the resentment this had provoked:

The administration lost every vestige of moral authority with the ryot who were thus presented with a glaring example of systematic disregard of legal obligations by the proprietor in a matter closely bound up with the revenue tenure. This placed the proprietor on a level in the public eye with the worst defaulting ryot. An appreciable body of villagers in each village used to have an interest in preserving the tank, in economically using the water, and sharing the total nanja yield [i.e. the paddy crop] of the village honestly with the proprietor instead of as had now become the custom deceiving the proprietor in every possible way.[28]

In some cases the zamindar's slackening grip on the economic life of his estate, combined with the expenses of litigation and ceremonial grandeur, resulted in a degeneration of his ritual role. Several zamindars failed to maintain their duties to support temples and charitable endowments within their estates. Again this was quickly perceived and resented. Ryots in one estate complained to government that 'the village deities have to go on hunger strike for some days in the month' because of the zamindar's neglect,[29] and in another estate the ryots formed their own fund to maintain the rituals that the zamindar had allowed to lapse.[30] In several estates, the ryots simply withheld rents on the ground that by neglecting his ritual duties the zamindar had foregone his moral right to the income.[31] In the Ramnad estate from the late nineteenth century the zamindar had occasionally sought a way out of his economic troubles by diverting revenue earmarked for temples and trusts. When this device became especially flagrant in the early 1930s, he was taken to court by outraged tenants who accused him of misappropriating 10 lakhs of temple funds, melting down gold and silver offerings so that they might be used as surety for raising loans, and eating off the temples' silverware because he had already pawned his own.[32]

Most of the estates staggered through the first quarter of the century. They were helped by the willingness of bankers to extend loans, and by the willingness of government to lend policemen to put down any serious disturbance and to take the estate under the management of the Court of Wards when the treasury threatened to empty completely. But the depression of the 1930s confounded this precarious accounting and turned the tensions within the estates into serious troubles. The fall in prices halved the monetary income from estate agriculture, and government, zamindar and leading ryots fought to preserve their own personal portion.

The government was in the strongest position and managed to extract virtually the full amount of revenue from the estates throughout the decade (though it had to allow some payments to be delayed). The zamindars were faced with particular difficulties on account of certain government actions. In 1935, the government changed the procedures which a zamindar could use to sell a tenant's land to realize arrears and made it senseless to use the procedure for arrears below Rs 20; this meant that a large number of ryots were now virtually immune from court process.[33] Next in 1936, the Agriculturists Debt Relief Act (see above) contained a provision to scale down arrears of old debts, including arrears of zamindari rent, and many ryots saw this as an incentive to accumulate debts in the hope of similar pieces of legislation in the future.[34] Further, the Congress was installed in the ministry in 1937 and the revenue minister, T. Prakasam, wrote a report which argued that the soil in the estates was the property of the ryot not the zamindar and suggested that all rents should be reduced to the level of 1802.[35] Finally, because so many estates found themselves in financial difficulties at the same time, the government could not offer them all the facilities of the Court of Wards. This was reserved for a few large estates, while all the others were thrown back on their own resources.

The result of economic depression and government neglect was that many zamindars found it impossible to maintain their level of estate income. During the first two years after prices started to fall, both zamindars and ryots treated the depression as an unremarkable short cycle. They drew on their stocks and their resources of credit and waited for prices to recover. But by 1931-2, cash and

Table 28: Sales of land under the Estates Land Act 1926-7 to 1941-2

| 1 | No. of Land Sales | Land sold | | Arrears due | Amount realized by sale | 6 as % of 4 | 6 as % of 5 |
| | | Annual Rental value | Estimated Market value | | | | |
	2	3	4	5	6		
1926-7	16 431	114 150	1 218 237	419 146	305 183	25.1	72.8
1927-8	21 160	159 557	1 404 266	371 118	329 347	23.4	88.7
1928-9	18 141	162 347	1 443 474	476 749	316 533	21.9	66.4
1929-30	19 174	99 374	1 781 240	504 215	342 728	19.2	68.0
1930-1							
1931-2	25 374	237 728	2 378 889	825 736	449 136	18.9	54.4
1932-3	30 478	237 732	2 346 516	1 134 048	818 773	34.9	72.2
1933-4	34 132	255 327	8 986 682	1 012 864	644 526	7.1	63.6
1934-5	14 403	97 520	632 118	453 353	356 253	56.4	78.6
1935-6	11 362	67 808	636 910	382 593	326 561	51.3	85.3
1936-7	18 133	117 164	1 264 207	558 922	430 087	34.0	76.0
1937-8	10 895	69 897	623 087	367 237	323 898	52.0	88.2
1938-9	5 545	30 958	325 229	188 499	180 165	55.4	95.6
1939-40	7 582	47 225	530 548	307 702	270 709	51.0	88.0
1940-1	8 812	65 979	641 042	409 418	368 463	57.5	90.0
1941-2	8 526	48 245	563 255	385 001	342 401	60.8	88.9

Source: *Report on Working of Estates Land Act in Madras Presidency* (Annual) for given years. I have not been able to find the issue for 1930-1. Figures are for Madras Presidency.

credit had become scarce and rent collections dipped. Even in the estates under the Court of Wards administration, where a nil balance was a religious goal, the arrears started to mount up. Two deputations of Salem zamindars begged government to remit, or at least to delay, the demand for peshkash but government was unmoved.[36] Between 1931 and 1934, many zamindars resorted to the courts to try and maintain their income, and the number of suits and applications under the 1908 Act reached a record level. But this device yielded very little. The suits cost a lot in time and lawyers' fees, and often reached no result. Many zamindars found that when they sold up land for arrears, they had to buy in the land themselves and then lease it out again (often to the old tenant) in order to maintain cultivation. In 1933-4, the sales of land realized only 7.1 per cent of the estimated market value. Many estates realized that in litigation they were only throwing good money after bad, and after 1934 the number of suits fell off rapidly. In the Sivaganga estate, the annual outlay on litigation had by 1933-4 risen to the colossal figure of Rs 3 lakhs, but after 1934 the zamindar gave up the fight and allowed 20,000 court decrees covering Rs 15 lakhs of rent arrears to gather dust in the estate office.[37] By the last years of the decade, estate litigation had fallen well below the 'normal' level. The courts could not help the zamindars to collect rent.

Some zamindars looked around for other methods to sustain their declining incomes. In Sivagiri, the zamindar hired gangs to accompany his officials on their forays into the villages. In Bodinayak-kanur the zamindar took to distraining plough cattle. In several Tirunelveli estates the zamindars tried to levy illegal taxes on trees and on irrigation water. Some zamindars had their ryots arrested and thrown into jail for debt, or at least threatened to do so.[38]

Many others petitioned government for assistance. In normal times, the government was reasonably willing to take estates which faced bankruptcy under the administration of the Court of Wards, but in the 1930s there were so many requests for assistance that all but a few of the major estates were refused. Besides which, the government was being hardly more successful at collecting rents in the estates which were already under the aegis of the Court of Wards at the start of the depression. In the Poravipalayam estate, the Court of Wards managed to collect only a little over half the current demand. In the Kudapalli estate, it simply could not oblige the ryots to take leases, which were normally put up to auction, until it agreed to forego cash rents completely and collect some rents in kind. In Marungapuri and Poravipalayam estates, which had both come under the Court in order to clear off a deadweight of old debts, the income from rent collections by 1933-4 was not enough to pay off the interest.[39]

The Court of Wards turned away the Talaivankottai estate in 1933 and allowed it to go into the hands of the receiver with debts that totalled three-and-a-half times the annual income.[40] The Nelkattumseval estate reached the same ratio of debt to income in 1934, Palaiyampatti in 1935 and Papanad in 1936; Devacottah's debts reached twice the level of annual income in 1937, Sivagiri's reached thrice the level in 1938 (after a year in which it collected

only 15.6 per cent of the rent demand) and Doddapanayakkanur's
reached twice the level in the same year. These were all moderately
large estates which over the past century had come to expect
government protection; but this time the government ignored their
petitions (and those of several smaller estates—Sivasamudram,
Palayavanam, Kadavur).[41]

In a large number of the estates the ryots had simply refused to
pay rents when the prices of agricultural commodities fell. If the
zamindar resorted to force, illegal exactions, or the courts, the ryots
replied with organization and protest. In most estates, the zamindar
relied on the leading ryots to act as village officers and to collect the
rents; in the depression, these leading ryots were faced with a
decision either to protect the estate, or to protect their fellow-
villagers and their own pockets. In many cases they chose the latter
option.

In both Sivagiri and Kannivadi estates, the zamindar's attempts
to collect rents by force provoked the foundation of ryot associations which successfully resisted the zamindar. In Sivasamudram
the village officers led a campaign to withhold rents. In Avanam the
association was so strong that the zamindar complained by 1938 that
'a very few of the ryots pay whatever they like or choose' while the
rest of ryots paid nothing at all. In south Tanjavur, where there
were many estates owned by Chettiar grain-traders and where the
rents were still paid in kind, there were pitched battles fought to
control the grain-heap and by the second half of the decade very
little rent was paid in this area.[42]

The largest and most visible protests came in the largest estates.
The Udaiyarpalaiyam estate in Tiruchi (sixth largest in population
and income) put in 4,500 execution petitions for rent arrears in
1930. The ryots responded by demanding remission of rent and
when this was refused they set fire to the zamindar's property and
threatened to murder him.[43] The zamindar then launched 12,000
rent suits (on a rough average, one for each ryot family in the estate)
and the ryot opposition immediately gelled into a formal association. Several village officers supported the association and a
karnam, recently dismissed by the estate, was prominent as an
organizer.[44] The estate's dewan was at a loss:

In the face of such a strong combination coercive processses can have no
effect. Distraints are easily frustrated and properties even if they are seized,
are forcibly rescued.... There is no chance of a successful prosecution for

such offences in view of the combination organised as aforesaid and the difficulty of finding independent witnessses to prove the facts of offences. The village officers are themselves ryots and they are the foremost to default and also to advise the other ryots to refuse payments, though not openly... At times when their presence is necessary they remain indoors and pretend absence.[45]

The proportion of rents collected in Udaiyarpalaiyam fell from sixty-eight per cent in 1936, to forty-three per cent in 1937 and almost nil in 1938.

In the second largest estate, Sivaganga, the usual problems were complicated by a resettlement of rents undertaken in the 1920s. There were two features of this resettlement that provoked special difficulties.First, it commuted most of the rents from kind to cash for the first time, and of course estimated the rate of cash rent from the high level of prices that prevailed in the mid-1920s. Secondly, it was carried out by government officials, who aimed to make an equitable settlement of rents without any concession to the details of relative status and power among the ryot population; that meant, for instance, that those leading ryots who had been most successful in manipulating the rent demand in previous years now faced the largest rise in demand. Even before the prices slumped, the zamindar had not been able to collect the rents under this new settlement; by 1933 the arrears equalled 1½ times the demand, and the annual outlay on litigation had reached 3 lakhs.[46]

The Sivaganga ryots responded with a considerable level of organization. At the village level, the ryots formed *oppandams* or village unions, while above these *oppandams* there appeared a Ryots Association.As in many other estates, this central association was led by estate officials, many of whom had been dismissed from service. The leader in Sivaganga had been dismissed from the estate office for embezzlement, and nine other men who had lost estate jobs because of retrenchment or dismissal acted as his lieutenants. The Association collected Rs 6,000 in subscriptions and invested in a car and a typewriter. However such a formal organization was vulnerable to attack and the zamindar managed to disperse it in 1931.[47] The *oppandams*, however, were a different proposition.

When the estate set out to distrain crops, the villagers cut them in advance and hid them. The estate then tried to prosecute such villagers and had 1,100 criminal cases on its hands. The *oppandams* managed to exclude the estate officials from many villages. One tahsildar on distraint duty was assaulted, and another officer sent to visit the scene of this crime found the village totally deserted except for one woman who threatened personally to kill all of the officer's children if he started breaking into village houses to find something to distrain. Another official was stranded in a village when ryots absconded with the bulls from his cart. The *oppandams* imposed strict discipline on their members and issued fines if members dared to pay their rents.[48] When police opened fire on some ryots in 1934, rent collections competely ceased for several weeks. The estate manager was alarmed by the rise in criminal cases and the rise in violent incidents and concluded: 'It is clear that we cannot hold down an area of 1753 sq.m. by methods of mere force.'[49] The Court of Wards reported:

In some centres, the combination of villagers was so strong that nobody dared to give any information about the lawless activities... the estate collector had not at all exaggerated the strength of the 'oppandams' and the tyranny they exercised by levying fines, burning houses and cutting crops by night to intimidate those who paid rent to the estate or even spoke against the 'oppandams'.[50]

Most of the village establishment, the Court noted, had deserted to the rebel side:

On the one hand they [estate village officers] exaggerated their difficulties and wrote alarming reports about the difficulties of collection, while on the other they slyly connived with the ryots in making any coercive steps and processes in Court infructuous by tampering with the evidence at the very sources... village officers often... are the worst defaulters in the village... the estate hands over the melwaram [zamindar's portion] paddy to them for want of granaries and in a number of cases the melwaram paddy thus entrusted to them has to be recovered from them by civil suit. The moment the estate takes any steps against them they turn hostile to the estate; they even go to the extent of returning the distrained properties handed over to them to the defaulting ryots.[51]

In 1934, the Court of Wards took the first available opportunity to throw the estate back to the zamindar, and he in turn abandoned any idea of maintaining rent collections. The agitation died away but so did the prestige, the solvency, and the future prospects of the estate.[52]

The Ramnad estate was both the largest and the most troubled. Here the zamindar's neglect of his duties regarding temples, forests and irrigation works had been especially glaring, the ryots were particularly interested in cash-crop farming and trade, and the level of mutual antagonism was exceptionally high. The estate had intermittently faced bankruptcy for much of the previous half century, and was now supported by a galaxy of loans (including one from the London money market), the estate administration was a shambles, many villages had been let out on long leases to ease the problems of collection and administration, and the estate had relied so often on legal process to collect rents that it was no longer effective—'The ryots have become habituated to the repeated sales of their holdings for arrears without making any visible difference to themselves.'[53] The extent of the estate's internal decay meant that the troubles of the depression were much less violent than in Sivaganga or Udaiyarpalaiyam. The Maravar villagers managed to exclude estate officials from the villages and collections fell off rapidly. The zamindar got police assistance to aid rent collection, but after this had provoked one or two violent incidents both the zamindar and the senior police officials were unwilling to continue the practice.[54] Rent collections dived downwards from 1931. Meanwhile, over a third of the estate had been let out on long leases and these dues proved almost impossible to collect, partly because the estate's records of these leases were in a hopeless state, and partly because most of the lessees were substantial merchants, lawyers, and bankers who could easily match the zamindar in a court of law. Finally, the estate had long since lost the loyalty of, and control over, its village officers. Thus in the depression, when the first signs of bankruptcy meant that the estate stopped paying salaries, the village officers merely obstructed rent collection work, or embezzled funds on a large scale.[55]

The estate slid into a state of hopeless bankruptcy. By the end of the decade, its debts amounted to roughly Rs 28 lakhs, even after some Rs 12 lakhs of rent arrears had been written off as irrecoverable. The government moved in and began to rejig the administration but the power and authority of the estate had so conclusively dissolved that the ryots continued to refuse rent payments even after the war had begun to inflate the prices of agricultural produce. Ryot associations appeared and conspired 'to defraud the estate of its melvaram dues' and government was again obliged to use the police to attempt to reduce the heavy arrears of rent.[56]

Ryot resistance to rent demands helped to create a movement in favour of abolishing the zamindari estates. The movement was strongest in the Telugu areas, where zamindaris were thicker on the ground and where the violence of the 1930s had been more acute, and it was also supported by a number of urban interests which supported the idea on a number of political and ideological grounds. There were also anti-zamindari meetings in the southern districts regularly from 1931 onwards. Meanwhile the bankruptcies and difficulties of the depression had persuaded many zamindars that their estates should be dissolved and indeed one zamindar put forward a bill to abolish zamindars in 1937. In the prologue to the bill he noted: 'The zamindars themselves have been hard hit during the period of depression and they would also not be unwilling to part with their zamindaris provided reasonable and equitable compensation is paid to them for the loss of their property.'[57] This zamindar was both a relative newcomer to the role and also a merchant. More ancient zamindars probably found that their view of the future was affected rather more by sentiment and rather less by economic calculation, yet by the end of the 1930s, even some ancient zamindars were well-disposed to abolition.[58]

Meanwhile the difficulties of the decade began to affect the government's view of the estates. From 1933, estates were regularly failing to pay their government revenue and when the Ramnad estate's failure became consistent, the default was big enough to make a considerable dent in the government's income. Next, there were all the instances of disorder which entangled the police. And finally there was the unavoidable evidence of the decrepit state of zamindari administrations. Here again Ramnad, which the government reluctantly but inevitably took under the Court of Wards in 1935, provided the most outstanding example. The estate had no list of its own villages. The accounts of holdings and cultivation were, in the government's view, 'on a par with the record of Podu cultivation in the Agency tracts' (that is, shifting cultivation in the jungle).[59] Forty per cent of the land deeds were registered in the names of people who had long ago relinquished any interest in the land, and another forty per cent in the names of people long since placed on the pyre. The legal department was initiating so much litigation each year that it could not afford the court stamps to keep any of it alive long enough to get a judgment. Several villages had declared independence and excluded all estate officials for two decades. Estate officials had no notion of a demand, collection, and balance statement but merely collected what they could and wrote out a 'demand' figure in retrospect. Few officials knew much about rent assessments, and this was not surprising since 'they are expressed in units of pre-British money, which while bearing the same name have different values in modern currency in different parts of the estate; and further they are expressed in three different units of linear measurement [two of which had the same Tamil name]. All of this makes the calculation of revenue demand a mysterious process.'[60] To a government which was currently striving to attune its own rather sluggish administration to the demands of famine, war, and rapid economic development, the discovery that a fifth of its territory was still covered by administrative machinery that was receding into the eighteenth century was rather unnerving. 'Landlords in such economic circumstances', concluded the Madras government, 'can be of little benefit to their estates and it is doubtful if they will provide that conservative element in a society which a landholding class is expected to supply.'[61] The Congress ministry had utterly failed to move towards zamindari abolition between 1937 and 1939, but soon after the ministry had resigned the British wartime administration began thinking how to abolish the estates.[62] The war caused a considerable delay, but this administrative initiative finally resulted in legislation in 1948.

The estates had lost much of their relevance as a political system at the onset of British rule. They had survived because the British had left them a residual political role on the grounds that the survival of the estates eased problems of administration: it was the simplest way to keep some of the most arid areas of the province under cultivation, and to keep some of the most turbulent ones away from a dangerous entanglement with the government's administration. The zamindars retained the cachet of their history, and a function in the economy of the harsh plains tract, which enabled them to continue to play a redistributive role in the honoured manner of local lordship. However, matters were changing rapidly at the turn of the twentieth century. The new administrative aggressiveness of the British undermined the fragile props of zamindari rule, while the advance of cash-cropping pulled the leading ryots away from their involvement in an economy which was dominated by the redistributive activity of the zamindar. Mutual obligations and loyalties quickly decayed. The price-fall of the depression transformed antagonisms into disorders. A dividing line ran through the estates between the zamindar and his leading ryots. The ryots were now in political terms connected directly to the government, and in economic terms connected directly to the market. To them, the estate was redundant; they refused to help it survive, and without them the zamindar was powerless. Some leading ryots continued to extract revenue from the rest of the village, preserved their own customary share from this revenue, and passed less on to the estate; the rate of 'embezzlement' by village officers and other estate servants soared. Some simply refused to obey estate orders, while others set themselves up as defenders of the village against the depredations of the estate; village officers figured prominently in many of the ryots associations which appeared during the decade. By the end of the decade, many estates were bankrupt, while government, ryots, urban politicians and even a number of zamindars were bent on abolition.

Ryotwari village office

'Village office' was a term applied to certain functions undertaken in the countryside on behalf of the government. The most important of these functions related to the calculation and collection of government revenue, and the two most important officers were the headman, whose chief job was to collect the revenue, and the karnam, who maintained the revenue records. A number of watchmen, messengers, and other assistants, known collectively as the 'village menials', assisted the headman and karnam.

These posts—particularly those of the headman and karnam— were vitally important in the politics of rural society. If the village officers were invested with considerable responsibility by government, if they remained relatively unfettered either by government or by their fellow-villagers acting in combination, and if they worked in unison, they could lord it over their fellow villagers and impose their own tax on the surplus production of the village. Their independence and their power clearly differed greatly from period to period and from tract to tract. In brief, the village officers, and particularly the headmen, had always been more important on the plains as compared to the valleys. On the plains, the headman had emerged as sub-agent of poligar colonization, as the chief of the plains village, as a ranking soldier in the poligar militias, and as a collector of revenue. In the valleys by contrast, village headmen had

probably emerged only in post-Vijayanagar times as part of the
state's attempt to extract a greater degree of surplus from these rich
agricultural areas. It seems, however, that by this device the state
did not succeed in splitting the communities of co-sharing superior
landholders (*kaniyatchikarans* or mirasidars) in the valleys. Both
the headman and the karnam, who was vital to the maintenance of
records in this tract, remained as subordinates to the juntos of
mirasidars who dominated the valley villages. Moreover, the events
of the later eighteenth century probably accentuated this contrast
between plains and valleys. The Nawab and other rulers of the
south used armed tax-farmers to extract the maximum revenue
from the valley areas and this policy helped to crush the office of
headman out of existence. Meanwhile, the disorderly fighting on
the plains allowed many village officers to engross lands and to
rewrite the village records before the British arrived. In their early
surveys, the British found several plains villages where the village
officers claimed to hold up to a third of the land on rent-free service
tenure.[63]

In the first half of the nineteenth century, the British settlement
of the rural areas was itself so fragmented and localized that these
local differences remained. However the main result of British
policy in this period was to reduce the power of the plains headmen
and thus to bring the plains more into line with the valleys. The
settlement officers took away much of the land claimed by headmen, then for some years employed a system of village lessees who
rode roughshod over the headmen, and finally resorted to a
ryotwari system which, because it relied entirely on the records held
by the village karnams, built up these men so that they almost
entirely overshadowed the headmen. As a result, the headman's
post in the Kaveri valley had become a 'sinecure' and elsewhere 'in
very many instances the emoluments of office have been frittered
away, or the man is incompetent, and his powers and duties have in
consequence been usurped by the curnum or taken by the taluk
officials'.[64]

Around mid-century, this trend was put sharply into reverse. The
new ryotwari settlement, based on an extensive survey and recording of every field in the province, was a powerful device for
extracting revenue from the countryside but, as one British official
noted, with the degrading of the village headman 'there is no
fulcrum on which to rest the lever'.[65] Thus from about 1860, the

British set out to build up the strength of the village headman. In part this was a natural result of the new revenue survey and settlement which reduced (but by no means effaced) the importance of the karnam's records, and which subsequently led the government to surround the karnam with obligatory examinations and close supervision. The relative decline of the karnam certainly opened up the way for the untrammelled power of the headman, but it was a series of deliberate acts of policy which really built up the headman's post.

The government set out to choose the most respectable and prestigious village families for the headship and to make the post effectively hereditary.[66] Then they cleared away all local rivals to his power by obstructing the karnam and by transferring the duties of village magistrate and village police chief, which had often been held by separate officers, into the headman's hands. Next, as the top levels of the administration expanded in the later years of the century and government business increased, the headman became the sole executor of all new government functions and policies within the village. He acquired new duties under the Arms Act, the excise rules, irrigation laws, salt laws, and electoral rules for local and provincial government.[67]

The new revenue survey certainly limited the village officers' ability to divert revenues intended for government. Some headmen and karnams adjusted slowly to this fact and there was a rash of dismissals for embezzlement in the 1870s when the new surveys were being implemented.[68] But soon village officers came to realize that government had made them the executors of a wide range of rules and laws and it was within their power to impose a tax on the villagers for fulfilling their duties favourably, or even just equitably.

It is enough to catalogue some of the most important of these powers. The village officers controlled the process through which land-deeds were issued for newly-cultivated fields; they conducted the sales of lands for arrears of revenue; they collected the revenue and wrote up the records of revenue payment; they transferred land-deeds at time of sale or inheritance; they decided cases in which one man encroached on another's land or irrigation sources; they vetted applicants who wanted a licence to indulge in the profitable liquor-trade; they could even free land from encumbrances because land sold up for arrears was deemed free of encumbrances (unless someone protested before the sale) and the

officers could easily arrange for such land to be covertly resold to its
original owner at a nominal price. Village officers could of course
use these powers to personal advantage; they could assign themselves the deed for new lands even if someone else had cleared
them; they could buy in land sold up for default at a barely-
publicized sale; they could run a liquor business through a disguised
agent, and so on.[69] Certainly, some village officers ran their own
arrangements within the village with little attention to the government's rules or to the details of government records. Such officers
often paid the entire village revenue out of their own pocket and
then made their own personal settlement within the village. Many
village officers extracted fees for doing their job properly or without
prejudice.[70] Besides, the goverment's rules were so multifarious,
and often so irrelevant, that they were necessarily broken, yet even
so this afforded the opportunity for the village officer to raise a
fee.[71]

Of course there were limits to the headman's freedom of action,
but those imposed by the government were not particularly res-
trictive. The major form of supervision over the village officers was
the jamabandi tour. Each year a senior revenue officer visited three
or four centres in each taluk; the village officers and other interested parties from the surrounding area assembled at these
centres; and the officers and his party then checked the village
accounts and heard any petitions against the village officers'
conduct. The affair was more like a royal progress than a departmental audit, and even in 1883 a senior Madras civilian thought it
'unnecessary and little more than a farce'.[72] The revenue officials'
clerks checked the accounts and inspected the complainants' petitions. The check was of necessity somewhat cursory; few petitioners
would stand out against the village officers and risk their retribution
in the future, and many even of those who did were deflected by the
clerks. In a tract entitled 'The Jamabandi Farce' one landowner
wrote: 'The Revenue Inspector or the clerk glance through the
petitions and hush up those that contain allegation against the
revenue or village officials. On the rest they put short notes and
place them before the Jamabandi officer for normal disposal. It
would be surprising to note that the disposals in most cases would be
nothing but "petition dismissed".'[73] Most Collectors found that
there were few petitioners. 'I have done the jamabandi of over 250
villages,' wrote one, 'and not more than two or three dozen have

appeared before me from the first to the last.' Another noted that he had seen only a handful of petitioners in ten years of jamabandi administration.[74]

Indeed other reports alleged that jamabandi resulted not in a correction of accounts, or a display of patriarchal justice, but an occasion for the village officers to buy their immunity by passing on some of their 'informal taxes' to the government's clerks. A Tanjavur landowner insisted that 'bribery and corruption are the chief outstanding features of this so-called Jamabandi', and detailed the fees which the government clerks levied from the village officials.[75] It was hardly surprising that the village officers complained that the jamabandi party 'sit in the place like a flight of locusts'.[76]

The main restriction on the village officers was, of course, the tolerance of their fellow-villagers. The rate at which the officers could levy their informal taxes depended on both the personal prestige of the village officer, and the degree of wealth and co-operation among other villagers. A clever and prestigious man could use his patronage carefully so that he secured enough friends, intimidated his enemies, and judged carefully just what rate of 'informal taxation' the village could stand. A cohesive and moderately egalitarian village community could limit the power of the village officers through informal sanctions. Some headmen were undermined by their fellow-villagers who either exposed their corruption to government, or withheld their revenue payments and thus made the headman look hopelessly inefficient.[77] Many more headmen, however, seem to have prospered in the second half of the nineteenth century. This was particularly so on the plains where the pre-existing hierarchy of social relations and the concentration of economic power were favourable. In the valleys, many headmen remained subordinated to mirasidari communities, yet increasingly as these communities were breaking down, village headmen also prospered in this tract. The British approved of this. They found that if the village officers were weak, then the systems of both formal and 'informal' taxation would not work; in these cases the revenue would decline and the government would have no means to recover it. Their policy, therefore, was to back the village headman to the greatest possible extent, make him wealthy, and thus·put government in a position to proceed against his personal property if the revenue collections failed. By the early twentieth century, there was a rule of thumb among Collectors that the property of a headman should be worth as much as one revenue instalment of the whole village (there were three or four in a year) or, preferably, worth as much as the entire annual demand of the village. By the early twentieth century, the latter was in the region of 5,000 to 15,000 rupees.[78]

Of course some headmen families did lose their wealth and status because of mismanagement, demographic disaster, or simply bad luck. In this case, the administration would transfer the post to a more likely candidate. In other cases, the headman remained a poor, relatively powerless agent of the village elite. The point is that in some cases the post did create wealth, but more often it underwrote wealth. Government tried to choose men of wealth in the first place, allowed them considerable opportunities to profit from the system, and made the post in most cases hereditary so that families might accumulate wealth and prestige over a long period. The result was that headmen often consciously separated themselves from the mass of villagers. Many paid large sums in land revenue and boasted that they were 'of noble family'. Some emphasized their claim to belong to an extensive village elite by publicly listing their kin relationships with other headmen, with local zamindars and with important men in government service, the co-operative movement or local politics.[79] To be a headman was to be part of the gentry.

While the second half of the nineteenth century saw a significant expansion in the power and prestige of village office, and particularly the village headship, the first half of the twentieth century saw a significant decline. This was not the result of any single administrative act or even the by-product of a constructive policy. Rather it was the result, firstly of the same sort of political and economic forces which undermined the zamindars, and secondly of the failure of the government to reorganize village office to suit the change of circumstances. In brief, the more aggressive government machinery of the twentieth century reached down more firmly into the village and this reduced the independence which the village headman had enjoyed in the looser state of affairs in the nineteenth century. Without this independence, the village headman found it more difficult to impose his own system of taxation on the village and to build up the prestige associated with a relatively autonomous local hegemony. Meanwhile, at the same time, there were many new opportunities to create wealth, from cash-cropping, produce trading, money-lending, professional occupations and even labour migration. It was difficult (but by no means impossible) for the village officer to follow these new avenues of opportunity because they required a form of mobility that was denied to a man who was tied down in the village by his official post. Whereas village office had once been one of the most important ways to amass wealth and prestige in the village, particularly on the plains, there were now many other ways which allowed many people to rival the wealth and prestige of the headman.

The most obvious way in which government pressure hemmed in the headmen concerned the matter of pay. Until the turn of the century, headmen were paid in a variety of different and over-lapping methods. They held some lands on rent-free service te-nures, were allowed to collect certain dues officially from their fellow-villagers, and were also paid a supplement to these amounts by the government. In a series of measures which culminated in 1906, the government took over the duty of paying the headmen. The fees and inam lands were abolished, the yield from these sources was theoretically incorporated in the land revenue, and the government became the sole paymaster. The obvious interpreta-tion of this reform was that the village officers had ceased to be local satraps and had become a lowly component of the government machine. In the case of the karnams, whom government was still endeavouring to bring under strict control and supervision, this was the intended effect. But in the case of the headman, government wished to preserve the illusion that his power and prestige was locally based, for this would make him a more useful instrument of government policy. Thus the headman's pay was styled 'a mere honorarium' rather than a salary.[80]

But this cosmetic touch failed to prevent difficulties in the future. While the headman might gain some local prestige from remaining nominally an independent local head, he would lose prestige if the government publicly paid him less than other local officials. Thus when in 1919 the government decided to raise the pay of the karnams and village menials but made no corresponding change in the headman's pay on the grounds that it was just an honorarium, the headmen were incensed. 'That a talaiyari [watchman] under him should draw more pay than a village munsiff [headman]', warned one politician, 'is a thing which touches his honour and sentiment.'[81] Government was forced to give way and the illusion of the headman's financial independence faded away.

Next, between 1915 and 1925 the government altered the relationship of the headman to his immediate superiors and inferiors. Firstly, they cut back on the number of village menials. While this seemed to the government to be a rational measure of retrenchment, to the headman it was a public reduction of his private army and thus a visible blow to his local prestige.[82] Secondly, the government gave new supervisory and disciplinary powers to the tahsildars who were the headmen's immediate superiors in the revenue hierarchy.[83] Thirdly, they transferred some of the headman's most important revenue duties to members of the provincial services, and introduced new procedures which allowed the revenue staff more opportunities to check up on the village officer's day-to-day administration. The most important of these matters transferred was the control over the sale of property for arrears. The most important of the new procedures was a 'provisional demand statement' which allowed the revenue staff to look over the accounts before the jamabandi camp.[84] Fourthly, the village headman lost his role in local judicial matters. In 1920, government set up new village courts staffed by locally elected magistrates and allowed these courts to rival those of the headman in matters of minor jurisdiction. The rivalry was very fierce, and often the elections to these new courts became violent. Moreover, within a decade ninety-six per cent of the total number of suits submitted to village courts went to the elected courts and only four per cent to the headmen. Even by 1924, one village officer petition complained that 'in the absence of civil and criminal powers, the village munsiffs are practically unable to command any sort of influence in the village.'[85] Finally, the government established a new political institution to rival the headman within the village. These new village panchayats, begun in 1920, were designed as the lowest level in a hierarchy of local-government institutions. They were given authority to raise local taxes and to look after a number of communal amenities. The scheme was somewhat half-hearted, and was not spread throughout the province, but it nevertheless excited a lot of local interest. Ironically, the government had originally intended to give the headmen the ex-officio chairmanship of these panchayats. Yet the Act was passed while the headmen were agitating about the other reductions in their power, and the headmen opposed it because they saw in other parts of the Act (measures to abolish hereditary right to the headship and to reduce the number of headmen's posts) evidence of the government's final attempt to convert them into lowly civil subordinates. Thus the headmen lost this chance to strengthen their own power and to forestall the introduction of a rival source of local authority.[86]

In the early twentieth century the government was bringing into the village a number of permanent and peripatetic officials who qualified the authority and independence of the headman, and sometimes operated as his rival. The head of the new village court, the chairman of the panchayat, and the tahsildar were the most important, but there were also the inspectors of an enlarged and strengthened police force, the elected members of local government boards, and the subordinates of a host of government departments ranging from registration and irrigation to health and education.

From the first world war onwards, the government received a constant stream of petitions detailing the grievances of village officers. These grievances were remarkably consistent, whatever the year or geographic origin of the petitions. The complaints fell into two main categories. The first included complaints about the diminution of their powers and the increase in the level of government supervision. Most of these complaints were directed at the tahsildars and Collectorate staff:

Whenever we are summoned before them [the taluk and divisional staff] we are being treated as hirelings and slaves. We are not even called by our proper names but by the name of the village to which we are officer.... We feel this treatment the most when we are treated with disrespect even before the ryots of our own villages when they assemble during the Jamabandi and humbly submit that this kind of treatment conduces to the loss of our authority and respect in performing our duties in the village.[87]

They wanted the government to retract the tahsildar's power to impose fines on village officers, to stop the revenue staff summoning them to the taluk headquarters, to allow them more opportunities for appeal against punishment, to remove the new procedures introduced into the revenue-collection, to abolish the new courts, and to give the headman the ex-officio chairmanship of the village panchayat. Associated with these demands were a number of others designed to improve the headmen's local status. The most important of these were an increase in pay and a confirmation of the right to hereditary succession, which the government was threatening to rescind from the 1910s onwards.[88]

The second set of complaints concerned the restrictions on the village officers' ability to benefit from new opportunities for profit and power. In the early twentieth century there were several new and spectacular opportunities for profit brought within reach of a substantial landlord. These opportunities included extensive money-lending, investment in the purchase of good land even in quite remote areas, commission agency business in cash-crops, and operation of small processing factories. There were also considerable attractions to a career in law or in local politics. The rate at which men from the upper levels of landed society were drawn into commerce, the professions and politics increased markedly in the opening decades of the twentieth century. However, for a village officer, many of these avenues were blocked. Certain activities were specifically forbidden; these included election to most formal institutions of representative government, and bidding for government contracts (which was one of the most lucrative aspects of local commerce). Other activities were virtually impossible because of the restrictions on a village officer's mobility. Most commercial, professional, and political activities necessitated extensive travelling, and many of the cultivators who successfully followed these avocations became at least temporarily resident in towns. A village officer was strictly forbidden to reside outside his village, and had to humble himself before the tahsildar to get permission for even a short absence. Of course many village officer families managed to share the duties of the hereditary office and the opportunities of new avocations among different members of the family, and many village officers conducted commercial businesses through thinly-disguised agents. But there were many who were inhibited by the regulations, and there were many petitions which complained against this inhibition. Village officers regularly petitioned that the obligation to reside in the village and to ask official permission for leave of absence should be lifted; occasionally they specifically asked that the ban on government contracting be withdrawn; and from the 1920s onwards, the question of the ban on village officers' seeking election to local boards and legislative councils became a major issue in the region's politics. This was a tricky problem because the government still clung to the notion that the village headmen were leaders of local society rather than lowly bureaucrats and thus could not disqualify village officers on the grounds that

they were public servants. In 1915, they laid down that it was
'undesirable' for village officers to join political associations and in
1920 banned karnams, but not headmen, from standing for elections to legislatures and local boards. The position remained
uncertain, despite mounting evidence of the village headmen's
influence over elections and of occasional involvement in party
politics, until in 1934 the government specifically stated that village
headmen must go on leave if they wished to stand for elections.[89]
This provision was so open to manipulation (headmen officially
went on leave but in fact continued to control the post through an
agent) that in 1939 the government ordered that headmen must
resign before offering themselves for election. Although the Congress, as it returned to an electoral strategy after 1934, had
deliberately wooed the village officers and had held out promises
that it would lighten the restrictions on the political (and commercial) activities of the headmen, in fact the Congress ministers in
office from 1937 to 1939 inherited not only power but also many
political assumptions from their British predecessors and consequently refused to honour their promises. As one Congress minister
noted in 1939, the headman was too much of a public servant to be
allowed the privileges of a private citizen:

The village munsiff signs literacy and residence applications of voters in the
village. He is in charge of the preparation of the electoral rolls. If he were to
be a prospective candidate, it would be unfair to other candidates. As an
agent of the government, the village munsiff has many powers. A politician
village munsiff most often abuses his powers and victimises his opponents. It
is an undesirable concentration of power, if the village officer is allowed to
take charge of a Panchayat Court or Board.... I know of many cases of
village munsiff presidents being nothing short of Hitler.[90]

From 1920 onwards, the question of reforming village office was
discussed almost continuously in a desultory fashion within the
Madras Secretariat. The problem was that government was extending a closer and more centralized form of control over the
Madras countryside, and that control was undermining the village
officers' traditional role and making them both less effective and
more truculent. On the one hand, the government still needed the
village officers because they were a cheap form of rural administration, because they were still necessary to carry out new governmental duties (most notably in the business of requisitioning and
distributing foodgrains during the second world war), and because

it would be expensive and laborious to replace them. On the other hand the disgruntlement of the village officers made them a potential fifth column within the administration. They could still exert power within the electorate, and they were vulnerable to the blandishments of the Congress.

However, these debates came to nothing. Only two courses of reform seemed avaiblable for consideration, and both seemed unlikely. The first would be to restore the headmen to their role as prestigious leaders of local society. This was of course impossible on many counts, but most important it would mean reducing or even abolishing their pay so that they no longer appeared to be public servants, and most revenue officials were sure that this would result in an open revolt. The second course was to complete their transformation into members of the centralized bureaucracy, but this would mean the abolition of hereditary right and much besides, and revenue officials were equally sure that this would cause open revolt.[91] Reform seemed impossible, and so the system of village officers was allowed gradually to decay.

This decay took a specific form. The prestige and profits of the post declined, while the duties associated with it increased. The result was that many holders of the village headship went into financial decline, while the newly rich and powerful members of rural society were not anxious to come forward to take the post. As with the zamindars, it was the period of the depression that turned institutional decay into an economic crisis.

Many village officers, just like the majority of landholders relied very heavily on credit, and certain village officers had deployed their official powers to command large amounts of credit. The price-fall of the depression reduced the volume of cash flowing through the village economy and put a tourniquet round the money market. Creditors generally accepted that their debts would have to 'lie fallow' for as long as the economy was depressed since litigious attempts to recover debts would probably be fruitless, and at best could only result in foreclosure on landed property and thus a solidifying of reserves of liquid capital. However, in the case of debts owed by village officials, there was often a political as well as an economic motive behind efforts to recover debts. Rivals and enemies often realized that if they started proceedings against a village officer they could perhaps embarrass him sufficiently for the government to remove him from office. Evidently many village officers suffered in this way. A Tanjavur headman who was arrested on a debt decree in 1931 argued that the proceedings had begun 'out of spite' and 'at the instigation of some of his enemies'. He in fact survived this crisis, but his rivals returned to the attack in 1933, had him arrested on another decree, and subsequently dismissed from his post.[92] Another headman who was brought down in 1933 had twenty acres of land on which he had raised a complicated network of loans amounting to over 3,000 rupees. He argued that 'my financial position is quite sound' and undoubtedly it would have been in normal times; but the depression had restricted his ability to command new credit, reduced the value of land and thus also the ratio of land value to debt, and thereby provided an opportunity for his enemies to portray him as bankrupt.[93] Another Tanjavur headman dismissed in 1938 had land worth nearly Rs 16,000, good connections in government service and the local elite, and a hereditary connection with the headship stretching back over seventy-five years. Yet all his properties were mortgaged and 'interested individuals' managed to persuade the authorities that his liabilities exceeded his assets and thus he was unfit for the head-man's post.[94] Another man dismissed in 1939 had inherited his debts at the same time that he had inherited the village office some twenty-five years before, and had survived without trouble until in the depression his enemies took him to court and had him dismissed.[95]

At the same time, headmen were faced with the problem of collecting a revenue demand which, in real terms, almost doubled in the four years following 1929. Under these circumstances, the village officer was especially aware of the changes which had reduced the status of his office and set up economic and political rivals within the village. As one Collector reported in a survey of the 1930s:

Villagers have come into closer touch with the townsfolk and meek acquiescence has given place to a spirit of self-assertiveness among all classes of society... Besides in the old days when the ryots were less educated and were confined to their own villages, there was a greater respect for authority, and the ryots therefore paid their kist more readily than now. Moreover, land revenue officers in the past employed devices for the speedy collection of revenue which, though highly efficacious, can scarcely be considered appropriate or go unchallenged nowadays. The ryot is now fully aware of his legal rights and the implications of the law, and the land revenue officers dare not (even if they would) resort to these old rough and ready methods.[96]

Those headmen who still paid the revenue from their own resources and then made their own settlement within the village were especially vulnerable when revenue became more difficult to extract and credit was scarce, but it was not only these ambitious headmen who faced difficulties. The result was a rash of defalcations by village headmen. There were numerous cases in which the headman tried to maintain his revenue collections (or at least the appearance) by collecting excess amounts from the less truculent, less powerful, and less intelligent members of the village, or by manufacturing records to show that he had tried using coercive processes or had even sold off land for arrears.[97] If these measures failed, the headman was often sacked for 'slackness in collection'.[98] Some even went so far as to avoid this indignity by committing suicide,[99] while many others collected all they could and made off. In the 1920s the government had uncovered an average of eleven embezzlements on the part of village officers each year, but in the 1930s the number had risen to 152 a year and there were good reasons to suppose that many other cases escaped detection.[100]

It was this investigation into embezzlement that revealed to the government how poor many of its village headmen had become. The Collector of South Arcot, the district with most defalcations per year (twenty-nine), reported:

The majority of the village headmen in this district are poor and depend mainly upon their pay. The worst of them misappropriate Government money.... It is reported that many of the headmen do not keep the Government money separate from their private money and spend from the common fund. The illiteracy of the ryots renders misappropriation easier as most of them do not take care to verify whether the amounts entered in the Kachayats [receipts] given to ryots are brought to the village monetary accounts. Even where misappropriation is detected the more influential of the headmen square up the parties who are illiterate and make it difficult to prove the fact of misappropriation.[101]

Further inquiries in the late 1930s found that a large number of village headmen in Ramnad were 'impoverished', most in South Arcot were 'very poor', and many in Madurai were financially 'dependent on their meagre honorarium'.[102] Similarly in the 1930s, government found that their usual expedient of seizing the property of village officers who embezzled, or simply did not supply the revenue, failed in many cases because the village officer and his family had no property to speak of; as a result they amended the revenue rules so that Collectors could sack village officers who were found to be insolvent.[103]

Indeed throughout the 1930s and the 1940s the government was reminded that its image of the village headman as a local gentleman who performed government services in his spare time (rather like an English J.P.) and took a small honorarium to cover his expenses, had been swept away and replaced by the figure of a harassed bureaucrat surviving on a pitiable salary. It was not simply that the office no longer conveyed the status and the resources which helped a man assume the role of a gentleman, but it was also because the bureaucratic load of the job had increased. This aspect was particularly stressed in the 1940s when wartime administration weighed heavily on the village officers. Indeed, in 1945, the recent increase in workload was listed by the Village Officers Association: 'collection of sales tax, agricultural loans, tobacco tax, entertainments tax, soldiers welfare, recruiting, Grow More Food campaign, checking on smuggling, rationing, co-operative societies, the National war front, reading circles....'[104] The result of this increase in duties was emphasized by another petition:

If the Government still believe that some rich people of villages are carrying out the village administration in their leisure hours... we beg to submit that the idea is more than fifty years old in almost all the cases. The volume of work of a village officer at present is far from capable of being turned out in the leisure hours of a village gentleman.[105]

From the early 1920s, the government had noted a rising trend of resignations among village officers. Many of these were clustered in the years of Gandhian non-co-operative agitation, (1921-2, 1930-1, 1942) when nationalist fervour corroborated a sense of disillusionment with the post, but there was a steady trickle in other years.[106] Moreover, the government found it increasingly difficult to replace these losses. After resignations associated with the Civil Disobedience campaign, the Collector of Salem reported that it was difficult to replace village officers who had resigned, died or retired,[107] and in North Arcot it was reported that many village officers had decided to 'resign their posts and seek employment as vakils' clerks under mittadars [zamindars]...Resignations by karnams are frequent and it is difficult to find respectable residents in the village to replace them.'[108] There had also been intermittent protests at the diminution of the village officers' powers and the increase in his bureaucratic duties, and this disgruntlement finally produced a Madras Presidency Village Officers Association in the early years of the depression, as well as a number of district and local unions and a constant stream of village officer conferences.[109] In 1945-6, these associations threatened to organize a strike and frightened the government into some precipitate concessions.[110]

Moreover, it was a measure of the changing status of village office that matters of pay and perquisites gradually moved to the forefront of village officer protests. In 1920, the headmen had justified their claim to more pay on grounds of the status-differential between themselves and the karnams and menials, but by the late 1930s and the 1940s they were demanding more pay on the grounds that their government 'honorarium', rather than any yield from land or perquisites, was their major source of income.[111] As one Collector noted in 1947: 'Some of the old mirasi families whose heads were really the headmen of the village, have lost their status and their influence and their present representatives hold on to their office merely for the emoluments.'[112] Indeed, in the 1940s the aspirations of the village headmen, as expressed by the demands of the village officer associations underwent a noticeable change. Up to this point they had argued most forcibly for a return of their ancient freedoms and privileges, but in the 1940s they began to argue that they should be recognized as full-time servants of government and be paid and treated accordingly.[113]

In sum, zamindars and village officers had been integral parts of imperial control in nineteenth-century south India. The political backing of the British government enabled the holders of these offices to acquire (or confirm) positions of wealth and status. These reserves of wealth and status helped the British to raise revenue and keep the peace in an essentially remote rural society.

But in the twentieth century both zamindari and village office decayed. New economic opportunities in rural society created pools of wealth which surpassed those controlled by the government and its agents. Gradually, these rival economic systems corroded the hierarchies upon which the institutions of zamindari and village office were based. Meanwhile, the government was gaining a capacity for greater interference and involvement in the control of rural society and, as the institutions of village office and zamindari declined, government hastened the process of decline by setting up new institutions to by-pass those in decay.

The critical point came in the 1930s and 1940s when economic turmoil exposed the hollowness of the zamindars' and village officers' power and status. In the same period government was gradually assuming responsibility for the economic development of rural south India. The institutions which had once appeared to assist imperial control by standing between government and rural society, now seemed to stand in the way of the government's policies. Zamindari estates were administratively awkward because they disrupted the statistical coverage necessary for planning development, because they created legal problems over government plans to develop their resources, and because they provided focal points for debilitating political agitations. Village officers were administratively awkward because they had lost much of their authority, because they had become truculent, and because they were inadequate as an agency for administering policies of rural development.

Thus from the late 1930s the government moved towards abolition of the zamindari estates.[114] There was intermittent discussion during the war, some interim legislation to allow the government to undertake urgent economic measures,[115] an enquiry once hostilities had ended (which showed the extent of the government's ignorance of the estates when the efforts to map the estates—the first such attempts undertaken—showed that the estimates of zamindari area which the government had used for the past half century were inaccurate by twenty per cent),[116] and an Act of abolition in 1948. This Act was motivated less by ideas of social levelling than by a kind of bureaucratic outrage. Indeed, the preamble to the Act was just an outburst of the government's resentment at the obstacles the estates placed in the way of smooth administration. And the zamindars were given sufficient compensation, and allowed to retain sufficient land, so that they continued to stand out clearly from the mass of the population.[117] As for the village officers, the strike-threat in 1946 showed the need to reform village administration, and also provided the opportunity for government (whose Congress ministers had once shown considerable sympathy for the village officers' claims for restored status) to sweep away their powers and pretensions as a reward for such truculence.[118] Government's attempts to deal with the strike became closely associated with schemes to reform village panchayats and increase their powers. Soon after, an Act was passed which transferred many administrative responsibilities—including registration, control of forests, control of wastes and other communal properties—from the village officers and revenue staff to elected village panchayats. The scheme was not comprehensively implemented because there was little effort to spread such panchayats throughout the province, but it provided the basis for later schemes of 'panchayati raj'. The Panchayats Act of 1950 was little different from that of 1946, except for a lot of flag-waving in the preamble about village democracy.[119] In the 1950s, this emergent scheme of village panchayats was linked up with the scheme to establish a hierarchy of administrative institutions to distribute development funds from the central government out into the rural areas and the result was the Panchayati Raj legislation of 1958. As this new scheme of village government emerged between 1946 and 1958, the village officers were reduced to mere functionaries—the headman to the office of tax-gatherer, the karnam to the post of clerk.

The demise of the zamindars and village officers marked the passage of a rural elite and the collapse of a system of rural control. The new leaders of the countryside were marked out by their involvement in agrarian production and commerce rather than by their association with the machinery of revenue collection. The importance of the state in rural society would no longer depend on a role as guarantor of patrimonial power, but as an assistant in the generation of commercial wealth and as an arbiter in disputes over its distribution. In the second third of the twentieth century, the government became aware of these imperatives and began to shift the basis of its administration as rapidly as it could. But there was one aspect of the rural economy in which the government had been heavily involved since the start of the colonial period (and for a long time before). That was irrigation.

IDEOLOGIES OF IRRIGATION

Irrigation water was peculiarly important for agriculture in any region of Tamilnad. Studies of the growth of agricultural output in other regions of India have emphasized that the provision of water has had a much larger impact on agricultural output than any other single factor (fertilizer, seeds, marketing facilities, land reform).[120] Meanwhile the rainfall of Tamilnad is mostly under thirty-five inches a year, well below the level for most of India, and the heat is tropical. Besides, there is no source of irrigation water other than the rain that falls in the region; unlike the Gangetic plain, the south does not have a source like the snows of the Himalayas.[121]

The problem was that the tropical heat meant that plant growth could be especially fast and lush if water was provided, and that the provision of extra water had an extraordinarily marked effect on agricultural productivity. But the heat, the low level of rainfall, the absence of any source such as melting snow ensured that water was scarce. Furthermore, the rainfall was very variable from year to year and place to place, and fell mostly in two short seasons. The short duration of these seasons meant that some form of water storage was necessary for the cultivation of most crops. Only poor millets and groundnut could be grown without any artificial irrigation, and then with a very poor yield and at great risk because of the variability of rainfall from year to year. Over about half of the region (that part to the north and east) folk culture and meteorological record judged that one year in every eight or ten there would not be enough rain for normal cultivation; over the rest, the proportion was one year in five.

These factors meant that irrigation was always enormously important, but also that it would require a large amount of engineering and social organization. Water had to be collected and then distributed, and both these operations had to be performed both on a large scale and on a small scale. The principal form of large-scale irrigation was the river systems, although there were also a few large reservoirs mainly in Chingleput district. Tamilnad's rivers were mostly filled by the rainfall which the monsoon deposited on the Western Ghats, and to a lesser extent on the Eastern Ghats and Tamilnad hills, with some addition from the run-off from the plains themselves. Only the Kaveri had much of a catchment area beyond the boundaries of the province, and although this area lay on the southern Deccan where the rainfall was meagre, the area which drained into the Kaveri was enormous (about 28,000 square miles) and the supplies fairly well-assured. Four other river systems —the Palar-Cheyyar, Ponnaiyar, Vaigai, and Tambraparni-Chittar —were counted as perennial but even they were reduced to a trickle outside the monsoon season.[122] Besides, the slope of the plain to the east of the Tamilnad hills was extremely gentle, and the rivers tended to build up banks of silt where they debouched into the sea;

this meant not only that the rivers were highly seasonal because of the monsoon pattern of rainfall, but also that during the monsoon they were very easily prone to flooding.

Any attempt to use this river water for irrigation would require a form of engineering that would hold up the monsoon rainfall to prevent flooding, distribute it over a wide area and a period of time longer than the monsoon itself, and finally make adequate provision for drainage. Given the importance of irrigation to the prosperity of the region, it is not surprising that we find irrigation works that stretch back virtually as far as the recorded history of human settlement. The Kallanai or Grand Anicut on the Kaveri is traditionally dated to the second century A.D., and the earliest dams on the Tambraparni were probably built in the seventh to ninth centuries.[123] Nor is it surprising to find that these engineering works combined simplicity with an attempt to make the maximum use of the water available. The Grand Anicut system was devised to leave the monsoon floods in the Coleroon channel where they would safely run away into the sea without inflicting damage on the cropping area in the delta to the south; meanwhile the remainder of the water entered the lower Kaveri and its deltaic branches and thus supplied an extremely simple system of flush irrigation. In essence, the water flowed gently across the seventy miles of the delta, running from field to field, occasionally passing in and out of the river branches, and gradually being used up or evaporating before it reached the sea. The water passed through literally thousands of different farms on the way. Cultivation had to be carried on serially—earliest in the west near the Anicut, and latest in the east near the sea. Apart from the Anicut itself, little was needed in the way of engineering, except the occasional bank; the fields themselves acted as water-ducts.

The Tambraparni system was marginally more complex. Here the anicuts diverted the water for irrigation out of the main bed of the river, leaving the flood-excess to flow down towards the sea. The water taken out by the anicuts was then run into a similar series of graded fields, with rather more in the way of tanks and channels to store and direct the water as it flowed down the slope. These tanks and channels meant that the system needed a little more maintenance and regulation than did the Kaveri, but it was still far from complex. Basically both systems required some form of central organization to build and maintain the anicuts, then little more than a machinery for settling disputes between adjacent plots and adjacent villages. Both systems were designed for growing paddy and, since very few crops were as tolerant of waterlogging as paddy, could not be used for growing anything else without substantial additional works of local engineering.

Only a small portion of the region fell within the valleys of the major river systems and could be watered by riverine irrigation. In the other areas, rainfall water had to be collected in tanks, or tapped from natural reservoirs beneath the ground. Both systems had become widely used within Tamilnad and each had its rather special implications for engineering works and social organization.

Collecting water in tanks presented fewer engineering difficulties than tapping water stored beneath the ground and thus this device had been used wherever it was geographically possible. This had mostly been in the eastern part of the plains. Here the soil was not too porous and retained water reasonably well, and the gentle slope of the coastal plain made it easy to form a tank by building a bank or bund across the line of natural drainage. In many parts of the eastern plains, such as the outskirts of the Tondai region and the eastern part of Ramnad district, virtually every possible site was occupied with the characteristic crescent-shaped bund. The construction and administration of tanks presented a very different picture to those of the river systems. Firstly, tanks were much less permanent structures than the riverine anicuts. The tank-bunds were steadily eroded by the rainfall that filled the tank, and by the passage of the very people and animals using the water. Moreover, such a construction was bound to accumulate silt and unless this was removed, the depression behind the bund rapidly filled up. Thus, there were no special difficulties attending the initial construction of tanks, but once built they demanded constant attention. The initial construction required no special technical knowledge, simply an eye for the lie of the land and a lot of humping earth. However after this, the bund had to be constantly maintained and the silt regularly dug out so that tanks were, in effect, constantly being re-built. Secondly, tanks were less efficient and reliable than river systems. They took up potentially cultivable land, they usually relied on very localized catchment and thus were vulnerable to seasonal fortunes, and they lost most of their supply through percolation or evaporation; one estimate put the annual loss through evaporation at seventy-five inches a year. The supply tended to be meagre and variable, and thus the question of distribution was especially vulnerable to dispute. Since several tanks were often connected either in chains along the contours or by channels which helped to supplement the rainfall run-off with the water from streams and rivulets, the question of distribution often became exceptionally complicated. In sum, tanks were relatively easy to found, but they did demand some degree of organization to keep them in good repair and to manage the distribution of their water.[124]

Little is known about this form of organization in pre-British times. From the very start of the British occupation, there were reports that the maintenance of tanks was badly neglected and that some efficient 'traditional' system was in decline. Buchanan talked of the poor state of the tanks in 1800,[125] and similar remarks became a litany for every irrigation commission.[126] It is fairly safe to assume that in pre-British times the maintenance of the tanks was generally one of the responsibilities of the local chieftains of the plains. Certainly many of the tanks were built by these chieftains, particularly during the expansion of the poligari settlement; the ability of these chieftains to colonize the plains and to provide food for their armed followers depended on this form of irrigation.

The peasantry of the plains considered it was the duty of the local overlord to look after the tanks, and this customary assumption was written into the law on zamindari tenure in the British period. Most probably, the tanks were built and repaired by some form of corvée labour. In some villages in the twentieth century, there were still remnants of systems for circulating the duty to repair the tank among the leading cultivating families. In others, there were special inam lands to support specialist irrigation maintenance men. But in most places there were neither such inams nor such rota systems, and it seems probable that the local chieftain looked after the tanks either by impressing labour from the village or by hiring gangs of itinerant professional earth-workers. As to the organization of the distribution of water, again there are surviving examples of local rota systems, in which the leading cultivators all had specific rights to the supply of water and took it in turns to oversee the business of distribution. More often, however, the village had a *nirganti* or irrigation overseer, who was paid out of the chieftain's share of grain at the harvest.[127]

Wells were the most expensive and difficult method of securing irrigation water. They demanded some expertise in engineering, particularly if they were of any depth, and were generally built by the caste of professional masons and earth-workers known as Oddars. They were similarly laborious to keep in repair, and also expensive to use. Whereas water from rivers and tanks was usually distributed by gravity, well-water had to be raised upwards and propelled along. As a result, wells were most common in those regions where other types of irrigation were not possible—particularly in the west of the plains where the rivers were often buried in inaccessible gorges and the soils were so porous that tanks were of no use. The black-soil areas of the far south and, in particular, Kongunad relied heavily on well-irrigation even though in Kongunad the great depth of the water-table and the prevalence of hard old gneissic rocks made it especially difficult and expensive to sink a well. Most wells provided only a meagre if reasonably reliable supply, and this coupled with the difficulties involved in distributing well water over any distance tended to ensure that wells were individually owned and individually built.[128] Thus well-irrigation involved no special problems of social organization and no traditional role for the state.

In sum, all the irrigation works of the region required some administration and maintenance, although it was the smaller tank systems on the plains that required the most. While the construction of the major riverine systems had been a state enterprise, the work of control and maintenance on all the irrigation systems had almost always been decentralized—either to the village itself, or more often to local overlords.

At first, the British took over the system much as they found it, and the decentralized nature of the early British rural administration fitted well over the existing framework of decentralized management of irrigation. Collectors and local revenue officials took a personal interest in the irrigation works of their locality, and this system extended as far as the region's major irrigation system, the Kaveri. Each year in the first quarter of the nineteenth century, the Collector of Tanjavur raised gangs of labourers to build a temporary embankment out of grass, clay, and sand to divert sufficient water into the Kaveri rather than the Coleroon channel and thus ensure the irrigation of the delta.[129] But as the British administration of south India became gradually more centralized, there arose a considerable problem over locating the responsibility for the maintenance of irrigation. The loose management by the

Collector and other revenue officials was evidently inadequate once the increasing duties of the revenue department diverted their attention elsewhere.

The result was a division of responsibility between state and locality which evolved from a series of casual decisions in the early part of the century, and was formalized into codes of rules and regulations towards the end. The state took over the duty of building and maintaining large-scale works, which generally meant riverine systems, and abandoned to the locality both the maintenance of small feeder channels from these works within the village, and the entire management of small-scale works.

The British initially moved into the management of large-scale irrigation systems by setting about repairing the Kaveri works which had deteriorated during the wars of the eighteenth century. This point of entry into a responsibility for irrigation seems to have committed them to the idea of riverine inundation systems suited to paddy cultivation on the model of the Kaveri works. Indeed, throughout the nineteenth and early twentieth centuries the British spent a large part of their fairly slim irrigation budget tinkering with the Kaveri system itself, and much of the rest building similar kinds of systems on the other major rivers. On the Kaveri, they began by repairing the Grand Anicut in 1804, equipped it with sluices to scour away the silt in 1830, built a permanent dam to replace the annual embankments at the Upper Anicut in 1836, built two dams on the Coleroon in 1840, equipped the Upper Anicut with sluices and a regulator and built another dam across the Kaveri in 1845, put falling shutters on the top of the Grand Anicut and built regulators on the Kaveri and Vennar channels in 1886, built another protective breakwater dam above the Grand Anicut in 1924, and finally constructed the Grand Anicut Canal as part of the Kaveri-Mettur project in 1936. These were the major works—and each of these was a considerable and often a pioneering work of irrigation engineering—and some modification of the sluices, regulators or other details was almost continuously in progress.[130]

The British Government of Madras, just as much as the pre-British rulers of the region, was attracted to the Kaveri simply because it was the largest and most reliable of the region's rivers. Because of the greater supply of water in this river as compared to any other local source, any money spent on irrigation works here would have much greater effect than money spent elsewhere.

Similarly, after the Kaveri the other perennial rivers provided the most attractive sites for irrigation works. In 1869 government added another anicut to the seven existing anicuts on the Tambraparni-Chittar system, and between then and the end of the century built works on the Palar-Cheyyar, Ponnaiyar-Gadilam and Vaigai rivers. These systems were all designed for similar use: to irrigate paddy cultivation on an inundation system.[131] From its initial venture into irrigation projects on the Kaveri, the Government of Madras's administration of irrigation was designed to deal with such projects and gradually it became a prisoner of its own design. The government devised a quasi-commercial system to assess whether an irrigation project was worthwhile. The government could charge for the water, and if these charges added up to a respectable return on the capital sunk in the work, then the project was reckoned to be 'productive' and thus worth building. However, the government had a particular way of assessing water-rates and that depended on a calculation of the potential yield of paddy on the irrigated tract. Thus the government would only build an irrigation work if, hypothetically, it would enable a sufficient increase in paddy cultivation to pay the government interest on its outlay. This was a very restricting system of assessment, both because it demanded a 'commercial' return, and because the unit of commercial accounting was effectively limited to paddy.[132] It was these limitations which made the government concentrate its efforts on the Kaveri and other major rivers, and turned the Madras irrigation department into world-leaders in the design and construction of inundation systems. Yet by the end of the century they were running out of sites where they could exercise this expertise. In the 1890s they built several small systems to create patches of paddy cultivation on the upper reaches of some of the larger rivers, and on the lower reaches of some of the lesser streams. After this there were simply no other sites where there was enough water next to a suitably graded tract of cultivation such that an inundation system could be created. Thus to keep up their momentum, the irrigation engineers had to find a new source of water. The swansong of the nineteenth-century Madras irrigation department was the Periyar project, which extended the inundation system on the valley of the river Vaigai by using riverine water which would not normally have entered the region at all. To achieve this, they had to build a large dam across an inaccessible gorge three thousand feet up amidst malarial jungle on the Western Ghats, and bore a tunnel over a mile through the mountain to divert water from a river that would have flowed down into the Arabian Sea.[133]

In the meantime, the state paid very little attention to the small tanks and other small irrigation works which were the main form of water-conservation over most of the region. It was assumed that these could be adequately maintained within the locality, by some form of self-help. Yet as we have noted, irrigation on the plains was probably only rarely maintained by some form of village co-operative system and generally depended on organization by an overlord. Yet, at the establishment of British rule, these overlords had either been crushed out of existence, or reduced to the role of revenue-farmers. In the latter role, they could find little personal interest in the upkeep of irrigation and, except for a few notable exceptions, they simply allowed the tanks, dams and channels within their territory to deteriorate. The government constantly noted this, and also saw that the minor works in ryotwari villages were often in no better state. 'To whatever part of the country we turn,' noted the Public Works Commission of 1852, 'we find the vast majority of tanks, even in a good season, watering far less than they once did, and far less than they could now if kept in proper repair.'[134] Given that the maintenance of many tanks had probably once depended on forced labour, the decline was hardly surprising. With the blithe confidence in statute so characteristic of Indian provincial governments in the nineteenth century, they attempted to remedy this state of affairs by passing laws which would enable cultivators to oblige those responsible to attend to the maintenance of irrigation works. The zamindar's responsibility was written into the general framework of zamindari law, and ryotwari villages were covered by a *kudimaramat* act, which stated in general terms that the cultivators were jointly responsible for the maintenance of local irrigation woɪks. But of course such statutes were only effective if they could be enforced through legal process, and of course the Madras legal system was simply not up to this.[135]

Collectors still organized sporadic repairs of village tanks and channels, but there was no systematic maintenance. Gradually however, the government was edged towards a greater degree of responsibility. An Act in 1857 enabled revenue officials to levy a 'voluntary cess' to finance minor works of repair; this was widely used to help the construction of temporary dams on seasonal rivers,

but was limited in scope because of the need to secure a financial
commitment from many different farmers. The commission that
reported on the great famine of 1877-8, however, spent a lot of its
time commenting on the urgent need for irrigation in the region,
and particularly on the plains. It recommended a reform of the law
on *kudimaramat*, and a concerted scheme to improve the condition
of the tanks. The main result of this was a Tank Restoration
Scheme. Although the Irrigation Commission in 1901-3 fulsomely
approved the Scheme, and urged that it be intensified, it was never
properly equipped with men and funds, was always vulnerable to
government retrenchment, and had already been abolished and
reconstituted twice by 1935.[136] Moreover, given the enormous
number of tanks in the province and the rapid way in which they
deteriorated, the government's skeletal restoration scheme was not
really keeping up with the rate of deterioration. 'As a result', the
government concluded in 1935, 'though more than half a century
has elapsed since tank restoration schemes were first started, a
considerable area has not yet been touched by them, while in parts
of the areas investigated, works still remain to be executed.
Meanwhile the tanks which were repaired some decades ago have
deteriorated.'[137] Government's own figures showed that the area
irrigated by 'minor works', which generally meant tanks, was
steadily diminishing. First-crop irrigation under minor works fell
from 1,284,333 acres in 1891 to 1,152,250 in 1911 and 1,102,660 in
1931. Second-crop figures were rather more steady—448,594,
399,626 and 461,854 acres in the same respective years.[138]

The commission following the 1877-8 famine also recommended
that the government should relax its conditions about the profitability of irrigation projects and set apart Rs 75 lakhs a year for the
construction of 'protective' works. Even so, the criteria for judging
the feasibility of a suggested 'protective' project remained much the
same as for a so-called 'productive' project, only the required return
on capital was lowered (three, four, five or six per cent, depending
on the particular region in which the project was to be located). Not
surprisingly, they failed to spend the entire allotment in most
years.[139] Indeed, few large-scale projects were built after the spate
in the 1890s, except for two further adjustments to the Kaveri
system—one medium-size scheme in Tiruchi district in 1929 and the
huge Kaveri-Mettur project, conceived in the 1920s, built at a cost
of Rs 6½ crores, and beginning operation in 1934. This scheme

entailed a large dam and reservoir near the Mysore border, which held up more of the monsoon flood waters and enabled these to be directed into the southern part of Tanjavur rather than flowing down the Coleroon into the sea. It was hoped that the scheme would create another third of a million acres of flush paddy irrigation in a new deltaic system in south Tanjavur, and also provide better protection for the delta as a whole. Many other projects were suggested, both 'productive' and 'protective', but were rejected. There were two principal reasons for this. The first lay in the logic of the system for assessing irrigation projects. The second lay in the government's increasing confusion in the matter of irrigation law.

The irrigation department had run out of sites suitable for inundation systems geared to flush-paddy cultivation. Moreover, the water-rates had become consolidated with the land revenue and the 'real' level of the land revenue was not keeping pace with inflation so that the chances of devising a system which would yield a suitable 'return' in increased revenue from water-rate were steadily diminishing.[140] In order to get round these difficulties and to provide itself with some work, the irrigation department began to inflate its estimates of the returns from the projects which it submitted. Naturally enough, the schemes once built failed to live up to expectations. The Tholudur scheme in South Arcot yielded less than four per cent on the capital cost and even the prestigious Kaveri-Mettur project had reached a return of only two per cent by the late 1940s. Thus the Board of Revenue soon started to distrust the irrigation department's calculations and to turn away schemes which looked doubtful.[141]

Meanwhile a further reason for the decline in government's revenue from irrigation, and for the government's increasing reluctance to invest in irrigation projects, was the government's own incompetence over irrigation law. The Irrigation Report in 1858, Famine Commission in 1880 and Irrigation Commission in 1901 all noted that Madras was the only province that had failed to define the government's legal rights over irrigation water, but had left the matter to an English easement law which was completely inadequate and to a batch of case law which was quite unfathomable. The problem arose mainly over the rights of zamindars and inamdars. They had legally defined responsibilities for irrigation within their domains, but the government not only had no effective way to coerce them into these responsibilities, but also found that its own powers to control and charge for irrigation facilities that passed through or by zamindari land were in severe doubt. From about the 1880s, zamindars began to discover these facts through the courts, and the government lost successive court actions on its right to charge zamindars and inamdars for the use of water from government channels, and even to regulate and limit the amount of water a zamindar or inamdar took from a government channel that happened to pass by his land. The conclusive court case on this issue, which was known as the Urlam case, was decided against the government in 1917 and the Madras government spent the next twenty years trying unsuccessfully to get the Privy Council to reverse the decision.[142] The problems which this decision created were especially obvious in the administration of the prestigious Periyar project. Between the ambitious engineering feat on the Western Ghats and the area of eastern Madurai district that the redirected water was to irrigate, lay the Cumbum valley which was largely owned by zamindars. The government set aside a certain amount of water to irrigate this valley on the way down, but soon discovered that there was no legal way to monitor or limit the amount of water the Cumbum zamindars siphoned off. Before long, the Cumbum valley was growing noticeably richer but nowhere near so much water was reaching eastern Madurai as had been supposed, and the government's revenue from the scheme was badly reduced. As one of the superintending engineers complained:

These tanks [in Cumbum] and the zamin and inam lands in general have always been the bane of the Executive Engineer in charge. What has happened with regard to them ought to be an object lesson in dealing with new irrigation schemes where such lands exist. The question was badly handled in the Periyar system from the beginning. Up to about 1915 there was even good reason for doubting that water-rate was paid for all the areas actually irrigated in zamin and inam villages. I do not know if it is certain even now that all the area irrigated is accounted for and charged for. It would have paid Government to have bought out all the proprietors [i.e. zamindars] in the beginning. Unless the question is settled it is likely to get worse. Once the courts take a hand in the matter there is no knowing what curious decisions may be given.[143]

The zamindari estates were mostly in the dry areas of the plains, thus this legal difficulty coupled with the bias of the method of project-assessment, meant that the government could not conceive of building irrigation works in those tracts where they were most obviously needed. Meanwhile, there was a long and tedious attempt to pass a bill to define the government's powers over irrigation water. Bills were discussed or drafted in 1915, 1924, 1926, 1930, and 1938 but none was passed. The bills drafted in the 1920s were the most comprehensive but they were killed by the zamindari lobby,[144] and by the time the Congress government returned to the question in 1938 the legal morass had got significantly worse and it was no longer possible to dust off the 1924 draft and bring it into law. In 1938 the committee set up to revise the provincial Famine Code insisted on some new approach to legislation over irrigation, and the Prakasam committee on the zamindari tenure brought out a wealth of evidence about the disastrous state of irrigation works within the zamindaris.[145] As a result, government set about drafting a new bill which would, among other things, enable government to repair irrigation works inside zamindari estates and recover the cost from the zamindar, give the government power to ration the offtake from an irrigation project when water was scarce, and annul the special rights of the zamindars and inamdars. When the government then asked the district Collectors to forward information on any court proceedings in their district that might affect the drafting of the bill, they were immediately inundated with over a thousand pages detailing suits in progress; they quickly abandoned the idea of attempting a comprehensive scheme of legislation for the duration of the war.[146]

After some increase in the irrigated area from the projects of the 1890s, there was in fact a trend of decline from then until the Kaveri-Mettur project began to take effect in the late 1930s. Since, as we have seen, the net sown area also declined, the proportion of the net sown area under irrigation remained at about one-third. This picture of overall stagnation of the scope of irrigation until the mid-1930s disguises very different trends at the level of the separate districts. The major 'productive' projects on the peripheral bits of the Kaveri system caused some considerable rise in the irrigated area of South Arcot and Tiruchi districts. However, in those districts dominated by tank irrigation and by smaller river-cum-tank-systems, there was a clear decline. Chingleput lost nearly a quarter of its irrigated area between the 1910s and the second world war, North Arcot and Tirunelveli also declined badly, while Ramnad which had both tanks and zamindars lost nearly two-fifths of its wet tract in the same period.

By the 1930s, the government was forced to admit that its own

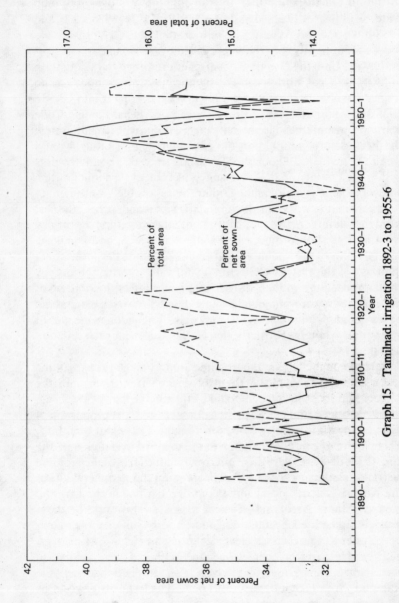

Graph 15 Tamilnad: irrigation 1892-3 to 1955-6

Note: The figures for 1884-5 to 1891-2 have been omitted as they are improbably high and erratic.

Source: *Season and Crop Report.*

accounting system was largely to blame. At first it simply reasoned that the difficulty lay in the low level of the water rates. The government could not devise any more paying projects and thus 'the development of irrigation under Government sources in the province has proceeded to a stage at which the law of diminishing returns has begun to operate'.[147] The result was stagnation:

For some years past irrigation has been more or less at a standstill and new irrigation projects do not appeal to government. The reason is probably that for the majority of schemes to be done storage is necessary and it is almost impossible to design a storage scheme with the water rates in force that will pay a reasonable return on the capital invested. Moreover experience of the Cauvery Mettur Project has not been very happy; the return expected has not been realised and this fact has apparently made Government even more reluctant to undertake new projects.[148]

Meanwhile ten years earlier the Madras Director of Agriculture had suggested the projection of irrigation schemes designed for some crop other than flush paddy. He argued that flush irrigation was very wasteful of water, encouraged a fragile monoculture (which at the time was being badly hit by the fall of paddy prices in the early years of the depression), and had several other malign side-effects. 'On the other hand', he went on, 'there is a very definite demand in the world markets for vegetable oils and for cotton which is capable of spinning 40's warp. We have excellent conditions in Madras for producing both of these commodities, if only we could be guaranteed against failure of crop by a supply of irrigation water...Under such conditions it would be possible to charge an economic rate for the water supplied.'[149] Another sympathetic officer pointed out that the idea of providing irrigation for crops other than paddy had been so conclusively ignored that 'at present practically nothing is known about the quantity of water required for irrigation of dry crops through the agency of a system specially constructed for the purpose'.[150] Of course so-called dry crops were already grown under riverine irrigation systems, but mainly as a second crop, and none of the existing irrigation projects was designed to supply water in the amounts and over the periods required by such crops.

Yet before the second world war, the government made no move to alter its system of irrigation accounting and project assessment so that different sorts of schemes might be built. Meanwhile there was one area where irrigation was expanding and that was the one area where the government was not involved—wells. In 1903 the government had tinkered with a scheme to assist cultivators to sink wells, but had quickly lost interest in the idea.[151] Meanwhile in many parts of the plains, cultivators themselves had invested in wells. This was particularly noticeable in the black-soil areas, especially in Kongunad but also in the far south. This was not new, merely the acceleration of an existing trend. The acreage irrigated by wells in Coimbatore grew from 270,571 in 1891 to 366,443 in 1931 and 395,173 in 1951. Corresponding figures in Salem were 63,349, 76,904 and 114,254 acres, and there were rather less impressive increases in most areas of the plains.[152] Despite the massive expenditure on the Periyar, Kaveri-Mettur and other major irrigation projects, wells were gradually irrigating a larger share of the total irrigated acreage. Around the turn of the century they supplied about a fifth of the total irrigated area and by the second world war this proportion had risen to a quarter.

The increasing investment in wells was clearly associated with the expansion of cropping for the market. In Kongunad in particular, but also to an increasing extent in North Arcot and Madurai, wells were used to irrigate small 'gardens' of extremely intensive cultivation. The crops grown were generally Cambodia cotton, which responded well to a steady secure supply of water, spices, fruit and vegetables, and also some paddy and high-grade millet. From the late 1930s, these gardens also included increasing quantities of sugar-cane. It was a measure of the profitable attractions that between the 1880s and 1940s over 40,000 wells had been sunk in Coimbatore district at an individual cost which was reckoned between Rs 150 and Rs 600 at the start of the period, and rather more than Rs 1,000 by the end.[153] Moreover, towards the end of the period more and more well-owners were also investing in engines to replace the bullock as the motive power to raise the water. By 1945-6, there were 2,048 oil-engines driving well pumps in Tamilnad, with more than half of these in the two districts of Coimbatore and North Arcot.[154] Moreover, once electricity was available, cultivators were quick to adopt this new form of power to raise water. When the government acquired some war-surplus pumps from the Indian Army in 1945, adapted them for irrigation purposes and put them up for sale, it was amazed at the response and at the subsequent demand for permits to import pumps.[155] By the late 1940s, a handful of small entrepreneurs in Kongunad had started up profitable businesses manufacturing electric pumpsets.[156] When the

Government of India planners inspected Kongunad's irrigation in the 1950s, they were astounded by evidence of investment in well irrigation:

The cultivators in this area have developed lift irrigation from wells at considerable cost. The wells are as deep as 150 feet with extra bores of 8″ to 9″ diameter at the bottom for another 200 to 300 feet depth to augment the supply... Enormous expenses have been incurred by the people to secure water for irrigation. Villagers have spent Rs 30,000 to Rs 40,000 on a well... In a village situated three miles from Coimbatore, an open well was constructed at an estimated cost of Rs 1,18,000 involving a lot of cutting and wedging rocks over a period extending almost three generations. And even then the supply of water was hardly sufficient to feed a 5″ pump. In another case, a well has been dug at a cost of about Rs 75,000 and water lifted from a depth of 120 ft and taken through underground pipes to the farm to avoid any wastage of water on the way.[157]

Wells and pumps were expensive and it was reckoned that it was three times more expensive to irrigate from a well rather than a government channel.[158] The expansion of well irrigation was a measure of the demand for water (particularly for highly commercial agriculture), the decline of the tanks, and the failure of government to expand irrigation. From the early 1930s, the same motives that led cultivators to invest in wells also brought about an increasing pressure on the govenment to sort out its own irrigation policy. In 1938, the Tirunelveli District Landholders Association complained that government was neglecting the tanks and had, through the Urlam case, got itself into a ridiculous position on irrigation law; the Association went on to argue: 'In the interests of irrigation in an agricultural country the State should have the paramount power of distribution and control of water-supply not only in ryotwari areas but in zemin and inam areas as well.' It even argued that: 'Necessary legislation should be brought to enable the Provincial Government to exercise effective control over private forests for conservation and development in the interests of irrigation.'[159] In 1947, landholders in central Tanjavur complained that local channels were badly neglected and that it was foolish of government to believe that they should be maintained by local co-operative endeavour: 'many channels remain in bad repairs and the yield is also steadily going down. The State cannot really tolerate this, especially at a time of World Food Crisis like this.'[160] In 1934, a Tirunelveli landholder wrote to *The Hindu* that the system of *kudimaramat* repairs for local irrigation works had been pronounced dead by the 1903 Irrigation Commission, but was still employed by government as the only means to maintain small projects, and 'the result is mutual recrimination between the Government and the ryots and a good deal of heart-burning on the part of the ryots towards a government that does not provide an adequate and suitable remedy for the situation.'[161]

Indeed by the 1930s the situation, particularly with regard to tanks, was so bad and the level of local pressure was so great that the government was gradually obliged to take a larger role in the maintenance of the small irrigation works that served the plains. In a haphazard way government resumed the decentralized system of state supervision that had characterized the traditional pattern of irrigation management. Without any overall decision on policy, the district administration in Tiruchi began to take over the repair of small tanks and channels and levy a cess from the beneficiaries to pay for the work. Before long the system spread to parts of Madurai, Salem, and Chingleput, and in 1933 the matter was discussed and generally approved at a provincial conference of Collectors.[162] Within the next four years the government had informally taken over much of the maintenance of small irrigation and the Joint Secretary to the Government admitted that 'if the numerous requests for Government aid to clear silt from channels is evidence, we have complaints of rapid deterioration'.[163] The fees system begun in Trichinopoly was semi-officially transformed into a system of irrigation panchayats through which local government officials and leading local cultivators got together to plan repairs.

The war, the approach of famine and the national Grow More Food campaign translated some of these tentative advances into a more concerted policy. The Tank Repair scheme, which had again been rescued from retrenchment in 1935, was given a new priority and more funds. Four pieces of ad hoc and temporary legislation were passed to enable government to control irrigation more closely for the duration of the war; in particular the government took powers to control zamindars' use of water, to force zamindars to repair irrigation works within their own estates, and to make zamindars pay for water from government projects. Then in 1944, the government finally initiated a scheme to encourage the sinking of wells, by offering to the needy of the dry districts a subsidy of twenty-five per cent towards the cost of sinking new wells or repairing defunct old wells. The scheme was soon modified to raise the subsidy to fifty per cent and to set a target of 50,000 new wells. By March 1947, they had completed 29,818 new borings and were at work on 32,587 more.[164]

The mid-1940s saw an unusual flurry of government activities in the matter of irrigation. There was not only the wells scheme, but also a concerted scheme begun in 1945 to repair tanks and local irrigation channels, and an effort initiated in 1947 to translate the ad hoc legislation of the war years into a comprehensive irrigation law.[165] The irrigated acreage began to show an upward trend again. In three years following the end of the year, two-fifths of Tamilnad's net sown acreage was irrigated, and this was significantly higher than the third which had been the rough average over the past half century. The figures slumped in the next few years, largely because of disastrous rainfall, but by the mid-1950s had begun a slow but significant rise. Wells were still being subsidised and the government repaired 3,314 of the total of 27,444 tanks in Tamilnad between 1950 and 1958 with the result that the proportion of irrigation supplied by government's riverine projects dropped from thirty-eight to twenty-one per cent in the 1950s while the proportion supplied by tanks rose from thirty-six to forty per cent and by wells from twenty-five to thirty-six per cent.[166] But government's renewed concern for irrigation had been stimulated by one thing—the threat of famine in the 1940s and the need to extend the cultivation of foodcrops. This lent a certain bias to government's plans. The idea, which had been growing through the 1920s and 1930s, to extend irrigation for crops other than paddy on the grounds that this made both commercial and technical sense, now faded into the background. Government was again looking for sites where irrigation could extend the production of paddy, and again this affected the procedure for assessing irrigation projects. In the late 1950s government decided that their employment of riverine water for irrigation was 'exhaustive' and that the 'possibilities for further storage works are insignificant'.[167] Yet no large-scale project had been built since the time, twenty years earlier, when the chief engineer for irrigation had reckoned that there was enough water for another three million acres and many possibilities for storage systems, so long as government stopped concentrating on building irrigation works designed only for flush paddy.[168] Of course the deployment of water from tanks and wells was completely out of the government's control and much of it was used for cash-crops. But the planning of major schemes to provide water for some form of cultivation other than paddy was delayed for at least another decade.

In sum, the government was jolted out of its deteriorating, nineteenth-century scheme for managing irrigation by the demands of war and the threat of famine. The policy of development, in this case, was to a large extent triggered off by a feeling of desperation. This was true not only of irrigation but of the government's general policy towards intervention in the rural economy.

GOVERNMENT, FARM AND FOOD

Even though agriculture was the mainstay of the population, and even though agriculture provided the wealth that government could tax, it was not until the very closing years of colonial rule that the government in Madras (and in India as a whole) came to take a serious interest in agriculture. While in the nineteenth century several Collectors and other officials took a lively interest in the history, art, and religion of their subjects, it is impossible to find a single work on agriculture. Not until Frederick Nicholson emerged in the last decades of the century could Madras pretend to have an agricultural expert. In any official work a chapter flourishing a title about 'the land' would inevitably turn out to be a tedious study of land tenure, with perhaps a bare list of crops grown. The Madras government encouraged, and to some extent supported, some experiments with the cultivation and processing of cotton in mid-century, and a small agricultural college was established in 1876. The enthusiasm of one Governor (Sir William Denison) led to the import of a farrago of English agricultural machinery and to the establishment of an experimental farm where, in the style of the gentleman-amateur, a number of local gentry were allowed to experiment, harmlessly and inconclusively, with these implements and other possible innovations.[169] There were also some private experiments which the government encouraged but these fared little better. One European entrepreneur imported a Whitney gin from America but had to abandon it 'as eight strong men turning the gin could scarcely clean as much daily as ten or twelve feeble old women or children could clean with the churka [a hand-driven mangle arrangement]'.[170]

The government was driven towards a more active interest in agriculture by a series of crises. However each step forward was halting and reluctant. Until very late in the day, the officers assigned to agriculture had little or no special training or experience, and they had to exist as a small minority within a bureaucracy which was committed to norms and practices very different from those of economic development. They had two special disabilities. Firstly, there was little documented knowledge about the peculiar characteristics of tropical and sub-tropical agriculture and, as many of them later found out, knowledge translated from European experience could prove disastrously misleading. Secondly, the agricultural officers were generally trained in the first instance, as were most government officers, in the revenue department. Here they had to learn about agriculture as a way to assess the revenue-paying capacity of the farmer, and it took a long time for the agriculture department to move away from the attitudes and suspicions which this relationship created on both sides.

These facts help to explain both the halting growth of the agriculture department, and the overall policies it pursued. The impetus to the foundation of the department in 1887 was the Great Famine of 1876-8, and the report which followed. Little was done before 1905 when a series of crippling crop diseases (notably on groundnut and sugar-cane) gave the department an urgent task to perform, and until the somewhat lucky discovery of the Cambodia cotton plant indicated a future for crop-breeding work. According to the legend about the discovery of the Cambodia plant, the department had indiscriminately imported a number of cotton plants and was attempting to grow them under rain-fed conditions. The plants were mostly dying when an old farmer passed by (as he will in such legends) and suggested that they give one of them a dose of water. As a result of this gnomic advice, the department found that this plant would flourish under irrigation and the rapid spread of Cambodia cotton on irrigated red-soils had begun. There are several rather different versions of this story. This led to a reorganization of the department, and the creation of the Agricultural College and Research Institute at Coimbatore.[171]

The department, however, had very little money for research. Moreover there was no structure which could bring the department together with other departments interested in developmental work (notably the irrigation department) and this hampered many obvious lines of research and experiment. One notable project which suffered in this way was the idea of a comprehensive soil survey. Without such a record of the particular characteristics—fertility, water requirements, organic composition—of various soils, the agriculture department had little of the basic information on which to work. There were a number of surveys of particular areas made between 1914 and 1928 by various government departments, but to the end of the colonial period the irrigation engineers built new irrigation works with only the haziest idea of the water-requirement of the tract they benefitted, and the agriculture department was still making crashing errors in its attempts to acclimatize strains of crop on soils which turned out to be unsuitable. In 1947 there had still been no comprehensive soil-survey.[172]

Other items of research and propaganda were simply misdirected. For many years the department advocated that paddy fields should be ploughed deep and often, and to this end urged the farmers to replace their wooden ploughs with heavier iron versions. By the 1940s, however, it had discovered that this was bad advice; such deep ploughing was unnecessary and even perhaps damaging to the soil, and certainly shortened the life-expectancy of plough-cattle. Similarly, for many years the department complained about the smallness of plots and the proliferation of the bunds or banks which cut up the land into these small areas and thus prevented the use of any large-scale machinery. By the 1940s, however, they came to realize that on most of the region's territory which was on something of an incline, the harsh climate would soon have eroded the soil if these bunds had not been present. They now turned to advocating more intensive bunding.[173]

But these mistakes did not damage the region's agriculture, largely because the department's propaganda was in the main far too limited to overcome the farmer's attachment to well-worn practices. This was not because the department made no effort to spread its views; it was committed to a policy of dissemination from the very beginning and ran trial plots, demonstration farms, leaflet campaigns, agricultural shows and, later, farmers' journals. But these activities were severely restricted by funds. Most of all, the department had very few officers and it was impossible to establish and maintain the sort of personal contact with the farming population which might have led the officials to understand the intricacies of individual farmers' problems, and led the farmers to trust the officials' proposed solutions.

Lack of funds meant that the department had to concentrate its resources on certain activities. One was cattle-breeding and cattle-diseases, but the most important was testing and multiplying the seed of vigorous strains of the region's most important crops. There were some early attempts at plant-breeding and hybridization, but most of this work consisted in importing known and vigorous strains of crop from different parts of the province, of India and from abroad, and seeing whether they would acclimatize to the conditions in any of the many different areas of the region. This work began on the research station at Coimbatore in 1913, soon developed in a string of research sub-stations in differently endowed tracts, and a policy of testing certain crops on fields hired from individual farmers. The efforts were, until the 1940s, limited to the cash-crops that were exported, although they included rice since this until 1922 was also an export crop.

The department's main successes came in sugar and cotton. After discovering the Cambodia and karunganni plants which provided the basis for twentieth-century expansion of cotton production on the region's red and black soils respectively, they worked hard to produce improved varieties. K1 was simply a more robust version of the original karunganni plant, but the new Cambodias were attuned to special growing condition; Co3 was designed to suit the particularly difficult soil and rainfall regime of the Salem cotton tract, while Co4 was designed to be grown as a summer-crop in a complex rotation mainly on well-irrigated lands. The sugar-cane varieties bred at Coimbatore (Cocanes) were a massive improvement on local varieties (giving up to double the yield) and were soon adopted as better markets and better water-supplies made sugar a boom crop in the 1930s. By the 1940s, ninety per cent of the region's sugar acreage was planted with the new canes, and the Coimbatore varieties had also been widely adopted in other regions of India.

In the case of rice and groundnut, the department was less successful. Experiments with rice began in 1913 and the research stations produced a wealth of new varieties of plant. These were gradually adopted in the 1930s and by the outbreak of the second world war almost a third of the province's acreage was planted with new paddy strains. But these new plants increased yields by only ten to twenty-five per cent, and often required an increased outlay on manure, irrigation, and labour. Thus many farmers found them uneconomic and rejected them after experiment. Groundnut presented formidable technical problems for a shoe-string department. The rate of seed-multiplication in this crop was rather slow, the seeds were bulky, and they were difficult to store because of their susceptibility to damp. Thus after the initial success at the turn of the century in finding the 'Mauritius' strain which avoided the diseases prevalent in the region, the department paid little attention to groundnut until the 1930s. It then produced the AH 25, which had better quality and yield, but this had spread to no more than 300,000 acres by the mid-1940s because of the technical difficulties with seed-multiplication.[174]

It was fully in keeping with the government's general policy of laissez-faire in economic matters that the agricultural department should conceive its role as a support service which experimented with various plants and bits of machinery and gently disseminated the results. But this conception limited the department's interest in agriculture as an economic system. Frederick Nicholson in the 1890s wrote a *Report regarding the possibilites of introducing Land and Agricultural Banks into the Madras Presidency* which was the first attempt to outline the importance of capital in the region's agricultural production, to argue that commercialization of agriculture was creating distortions and difficulties in the supply of capital, and to suggest that the government ought to do something to help. Gilbert Slater, who arrived in India in 1915 to become the Madras University's first professor of economics, took to touring the villages in his vacations and sent off bright students to conduct village surveys which provided a baseline and model for later research.[175] But the government was reluctant to delve into, let alone to intervene in, the workings of the agrarian economy. Nicholson's report on local money-lending and the need for agricultural banks prompted not a scheme of government rural banks but the foundation of the co-operative department in 1905. Nicholson in fact favoured some form of co-operative finance, but the government seized on this solution largely because it was thereby enabled to limit its role to the provision of supportive services, rather than any form of direct intrusion. Co-operative banks were supposed to finance and run themselves and, it was hoped, after initial encouragement from the government, the spread of co-operative financial institutions would be self-sustaining.

Although in fact the co-operative movement required more

government finance and more government personnel over a longer time than was expected, and still limped along somewhat lamely, it was still a suitably limited form of governmental involvement and the idea of 'co-operation' became a panacea which the government applied to all economic problems which swam unavoidably into its view. The government fell into a general framework of interpretation which blamed the 'middleman' for most economic problems, and which found the solution in the replacement of the 'middleman' by a co-operative. As a result, the co-operative department acquired a large number of experimental projects. The poverty of handloom weavers was blamed on the master weavers and yarn merchants, and weavers' co-operatives were prescribed as the cure. Low prices for farm produce were attributed to middlemen's profits, and a number of marketing or 'loan and sale' societies began in the 1920s. The exploitation of urban casual labour led to a move to found co-operative labour unions. Complaints by government servants about urban prices led to consumer co-operatives.[176]

The depression might have jolted the Madras government out of its complacency in matters of agriculture. The Government of India, which was more sensitive than the provincial government in the south to the potential effects of economic distress on the Congress campaign of civil disobedience, attempted to disturb that complacency by sending off a stream of letters and telegrams asking for information on the current economic situation in the province. The Secretariat in Madras duly passed the enquiry on to the individual Collectors. But administrative attitudes and practices were deeply ingrained. Madras was experienced in deflecting enquiries from Delhi which might result in a greater degree of central interference. Collectors were accustomed to believe that if they reported difficulties in their district it would imply that they were incompetent and thus damage their chances of promotion. The chain of enquiry from Delhi through Madras and out into the districts was thus matched by an opposite chain of overwhelming complacency. The first of these Government of India enquiries in mid-1930 did in fact prompt some investigation by the Collectors. Most admitted that the money-market had become exceptionally tight, that consumption of articles like cloth and liquor had almost certainly dropped, and that there were marginally more bankruptcies, foreclosures on mortgages, and court suits about debt.[177] But the Collectors' major barometer of economic distress was the ability to collect revenue; the Government of Madras summing up the opinions of Collectors, told the Government of India that 'the ease with which the land revenue has been collected in spite of a sharp decline of prices in 1928-9 suggests that the ryots have so far not been very seriously hit by the low prices'.[178]

However, the Government of India's requests became regular. A telegram arrived in January 1931 and in response Madras set up an Economic Depression Enquiry Committee which noted that weavers were particularly distressed, that the money-market was exceptionally tight, but that there was little cause for alarm.[179] Following this there was a Government of India enquiry every six months or so and the answers from Madras became a monotonous litany. The stylized, repetitive character of the Collectors' answers suggested that they were based on supposition rather than research. There were, however, two administrative results. The Government of Madras appointed its first Economic Adviser, mainly for the task of preparing the deadening replies to the Government of India. And, after Delhi criticized the figures inserted in the Government of Madras' replies to its enquiries, Madras appointed a Statistical Officer who, after he had told government that its vast effort at statistical collection provided almost no material useful for assessing economic trends, was rather left to his own devices.[180]

There was, however, another source of pressure which through the decade became steadily more important. This came from members of rural society. It was mainly in one area in the Telugu districts of the Madras Presidency that the economic depression clearly and obviously stimulated Civil Disobedience agitation, and government found that it could deal reasonably well with this isolated outbreak by concentrating its powers of repression. Yet there was a more widespread and insistent murmur of complaint that made itself heard in the legislatures and at public meetings. Much of this consisted in complaints against the level of the land revenue, which was not surprising since the real incidence had risen steeply as prices fell. In 1931 and 1932, and again in 1934, there were large numbers of public meetings in rural areas, and numerous petitions to the government.[181] Government responded by suspending, and then remitting, about eight per cent of the revenue demand in each year from 1932 to 1937, but it stressed that this was an act of grace rather than any alteration in the principle of revenue demand (which was fixed in each district for thirty-year periods and was not designed to fluctuate according to price changes within that period).[182] Government was not especially surprised or worried by these campaigns of complaint; after all it was only a slight advance on the drone against the land revenue that emerged constantly from Tanjavur and from other parts of the valley zone. There were, however, other items of complaint that looked politically more disturbing.

From the turn of the century, and more especially from the first world war, there had emerged in India an economic orthodoxy about the nature of empire. It had begun with Ranade, R.C. Dutt and the description of the drain of India's economic resources to the mother-country. It had since been nurtured and embellished, chiefly by the school of economists from Bombay University.[183] It grew into particular importance in the 1920s because it provided a meeting-ground for a peculiarly powerful combination of intellectuals, businessmen, and nationalist politicians. Indian businessmen (particularly those in Bombay during the post-war recession in the cotton industry) found in the theories of the Bombay economists an explanation for many of their difficulties. Since the nub of the economic theory was that in important respects India's economy was run in the interests of Britain rather than of India, the theory held an obvious interest for the nationalists. There were two particularly important strands of the argument. The first was that Indian taxation was set too high, largely to pay for an expensive government machinery and for certain essentially imperial commitments, notably the Indian army. Such high taxation, the argument continued, reduced demand and, because some of the government revenue was spent outside the country, drained away wealth. The second was that India needed tariff protection to achieve industrial growth and that government was not only reluctant to raise protective tariffs, but in fact in the nominal interests of financial security kept the rupee at an artificially high level which made imported goods cheaper and Indian exports less competitive. These arguments occupied many scholarly articles and books in the 1920s, fuelled numerous debates in the All-India Legislative Assembly (where big business had a strong voice) and came to have a clear influence over the annual resolutions of the Congress.

When prices and trade slumped from 1929 it was clear that India (as most other non-European countries) was more severely hit than most western countries in terms both of the extent of the price-fall and of the loss of trade.[184] What is more, while the western economies began (shakily) to recover after 1933, the depression lingered on in India for much of the rest of the decade. Economists, businessmen, and nationalists now argued with special vigour that the particular severity and longevity of the depression in India was to a large extent the result of government policies, some of which served to transfer the impact of the depression from Britain to India. There were renewed attacks on the level of government expenditure, which had risen in real terms in the depression, but the major outburst was reserved for the question of the exchange rate and the government's careful (and thus, it was argued, deflationary) monetary policy. The economist P.S. Narayan Prasad was among many who pointed out that other agricultural countries had suffered less than India and attributed this to the devaluation of their currencies. India in the meantime had compensated for the loss of export value and balanced her payments, not by a devaluation which might have promoted an increase in the volume of goods exported, but by a massive export of gold. 'The consumption of capital has been allowed', Prasad wrote, 'and it should not be surprising at all if this bill, drawn on hope, is likely to be heavily discounted by experience.'[185] Meanwhile, the argument continued, the government had made no use of fiscal tools to promote recovery; indeed the government's restriction of the currency and the parsimonious policies of the Imperial Bank were at the bottom of the tightness in the money-market and the continued downward pressure on prices.

Normally the Government in India relied on a conservative rural interest to counter-balance the essentially urban ideologies of economists, businessmen, and politicians. Yet the conditions of the depression made these same economic arguments increasingly appealing to a rural audience. Indeed government must have been distressingly surprised when the raja of Bobbili, a large landowner from the Telugu districts and a confirmed loyalist (a few months later he became chief minister), entered a minute of dissent into the report of the government's Economic Depression Enquiry Committee in which he criticized the Imperial Bank for its policy of stringency. The Bank had in fact withdrawn finance from rural trading and thus helped to tighten the money-market but, Bobbili argued, a proper central bank responsive to the needs of the country's economy would have attempted to ease the credit situation.[186]

In 1931, the president of the South Indian Chamber of Commerce also pressed government to liberalize the Imperial Bank's credit policies. While this man was clearly the representative of the business community, he also pressed government for several other reforms which would raise agricultural prices and increase trade in agricultural goods. These included remission of land revenue, lower railway freights for rural produce, and more loans to farmers. This advocacy was hardly surprising since the business community in such an overwhelmingly agricultural region depended on rural produce and on rural consumers. Even so, it showed government that there was an ever-broadening area of common ground for businessmen and rural interests to join together in an attack on the government's management of the economy.[187]

In 1933 a conference of Tanjavur landholders coupled their demand for a remission of land revenue with a demand that the relationship between the rupee and sterling be severed since it 'adversely affects the interest of the vast majority of Indian agriculturists'.[188] In 1938, the Tirunelveli District Landholders Association argued that the continued depression of agricultural prices would be overcome only if the government were prepared to manipulate tariffs, railway rates, and the currency with that aim in view.[189] One Tirunelveli landholder had spelt out the details of this argument as early as 1930:

Some of the residents of this village are taking out leases of lands in other parts of the country. This system commenced in or about 1899 and it is growing from year to year from a small begining. The persons who enjoyed such leases were making a net profit of about Rs 3000 a year. For more than a year they have not been making any profit at all. The market price of every agricultural produce has been affected by the exchange policy of Government. If gold currency is adopted in this country, or if the rate of exchange is made to adjust itself to the market value of silver to gold, then this loss of income will not have been brought about. The serious consequence of this policy can easily be gauged when it is remembered that the annual rent paid by these lessees exceeds Rs 1 lakh every year. If a similar loss is caused by act of God, the people will easily bear it with resignation. But there cannot be any justification for the Government of an agricultural country to adopt any policy which will reduce their income in money value.[190]

Throughout the decade, this truculence and increasing ideological awareness was channelled into petitions, sporadic agitations, press campaigns, and legislature debates. Government slowly responded. In May 1933 it compiled another (confidential) report on the effect of the depression and summoned the district Collectors together in conference to discuss remedies.[191] In 1934, it appointed C.R. Srinivasan to investigate the region's rice production and trade, and W.R.S. Sathyanathan to find out what effect the depression had had on rural credit. It also called a provincial economic conference at which prominent citizens could air their views and government could justify its activities. Srinivasan's report detailed how the local rice trade was being undermined by imports from Burma where production was cheaper, and Sathyanathan's report argued that the inability of cultivators to pay off debts had meant that the deadweight of old debts had increased and new credit was hard to find.[192]

Government attempted some piecemeal measures to aid the rice trade—notably lowering railway freight rates so that locally produced rice would reach the markets with a better chance of competing with the cheap sea-imports—but was reluctant to take any more aggressive steps.[193] Indeed, the agriculture department began to build for itself a 'natural' theory of the causes of the depression which was useful because it provided a shield against accusations of the government's responsibility. According to this theory, the depression was an inevitable retribution for the years of rising prices; farmers had done well and now they must do badly. This was the reply offered to the president of the province's Oilseeds Association when he complained that the depression had annihilated the market for groundnuts.[194] The government merely pointed out in response that large profits had been made in the 1920s. This was also the argument that underlay the government's justification of the maintenance of the revenue-demand; rising prices had reduced the incidence and it was just a counter-vailing swing that meant that falling prices would now increase it.[195]

In the hands of the Director of Agriculture this theory extended to an argument about over-production, particularly in the case of paddy. According to him, prices had fallen as a natural consequence of an increase in supply brought about by extensions of acreage and increases in yield. The situation in Madras was aggravated by a similar increase in other countries (notably Burma) where rice could be produced more cheaply and exported to Madras. Too much rice was being produced in Madras and throughout Asia. Although this argument implied that Madras farmers might then profitably switch from paddy to another crop, the Director recognized that this would be difficult because so many of the region's irrigation works were designed specifically for paddy cultivation, and he made no suggestion that government should take any action. On reading his reports, the government concluded: 'There is nothing that the Government can do in this....It is entirely left to the people to take to cultivation of any product they desire.'[196]

The solution to a problem caused by a process of natural over-expansion was clearly a period of natural attrition, and this interpretation was shared by the revenue department. In the last thirty years, noted that department in a memorandum on the effect of the depression on land revenue,

a great deal of money has been invested in land, particularly in wet land, by people who are not cultivating ryots, and who mostly belong to a class which is specially vocal in representing its grievances. The Government consider it inevitable that much of the land brought under cultivation during the period of high prices will go out of cultivation with the fall in prices. This cannot, and indeed should not, be prevented. It is also inevitable that people who invested money in land when its price was high will receive, like other investors all over the world, a much reduced return now that its value has fallen. Land will be relinquished, and land will pass into other hands of debtors unable to meet their obligations. The process may perhaps be checked if Debt Concilation Boards are set up. A private Bill for their constitution is under consideration. But no concession that the Government can grant will stay the course of these economic tendencies.[197]

In fact at the Economic Conference in April 1934 the Chief Secretary stated categorically that 'generally we are not in favour of debt concilation boards' and the move to set them up faltered for the moment.[198] Within a decade of these statements about the over-production of food, the government was to conclude that the region suffered from chronic deficit of foodgrains.

In the second half of the decade, the government moved towards a marginally more active role. After Sathyanathan's report, it finally admitted that it should make some effort to untangle the rural credit market and began a series of debt Acts which was completed after the Congress had come into power in mid-1937. It also entered on the business of regulating produce-marketing in a more deliberate fashion. The Royal Commission on Agriculture in 1928 and the Banking Enquiry in 1930 had both indicated the need for the government to organize the markets for cash-crops, and this had resulted in a piece of enabling legislation (the Madras Commercial Crops Markets Act) in 1933. In the late 1930s, government used this legislation to establish a handful of regulated market-yards in the major centres of trade in cotton, groundnuts and sugar.[199]

Finally, the government set up a committee to review the working of co-operative societies and to suggest ways in which the societies might act as the medium for a greater governmental role in the economy.

Although these moves represented a noticeable shift in governmental attitude, they had effected little real change before the outbreak of war. This was largely a question of scale. The government still devoted very little money to development activities and even the Congress ministry, despite its aspirations, could find little extra money in the government coffers for such purposes. The Government of India provided some assistance with a dole from a surplus of central funds, but this was not enough to launch a serious development plan and much of it was frittered away on khadi schemes and rather ill-defined rural reconstruction projects which, apart from some sinking of wells for drinking water, probably did more for the organizational strength of the lower levels of the Congress party than for the wealth of the region.[200]

The second world war saw a dramatic change in the government's attitude to agriculture and in its role in the economy in general. The causes of this dramatic change were very basic. Britain needed India's help in the war, both as a source of supply and as a base for operations in the eastern theatre. The manipulation of the Indian economy to serve the war effort proved so disruptive that not only did it threaten India's ability to contribute to the war effort, but it caused a famine in Bengal and came close to creating widespread economic distress and political disorder throughout India. The government was obliged to overcome its reluctance to intervene in the economy.

At the start of the war these future developments were in no way anticipated. The Government of India was supremely confident about food supplies and undertook, as one of India's major contributions to the war effort, to feed Indian and British troops in India and to help supply Ceylon, Persia, Aden, the Middle East, and the Arabian Principalities.[201] As grain prices started to rise in 1940, a new Director of Agriculture in Madras pointed out that in 1917-18 wartime conditions had created difficulties in the food market in the province, that at that time Madras was still an exporter of grain, and that Madras was now dangerously dependent on imports and thus perhaps more vulnerable.[202] But his warnings went unnoticed. The Government of India reacted to the inflation of prices with a series of six Price Control Conferences, at which representatives of all the provinces repeatedly stated their belief in laissez-faire and their fear that governmental intervention in the production, marketing and pricing of food would be counter-productive.[203] The Government of Madras appointed a committee to consider price-control. The committee concluded that 'the ramifications of the rice trade are far too complicated' and that little could be done beyond attempts to dissuade traders from forcing up grain prices by speculation. To this end, the government issued licences to all grain-dealers and established Taluk Price Committees to supervise the market. These gatherings of officials and non-officials published lists of local prices which everyone ignored.[204] In March 1942, the Government of India was beginning to take a more sanguine look into the future but their directive to the provincial governments still had a vagueness and pomposity which hardly smacked of intense concern:

I am directed to invite attention to the need that has arisen of increasing the food and fodder supplies of India. The matter has assumed greatly increased importance owing to the exigencies of the war situation. On the one hand more food is needed for meeting India's military commitments; on the other hand transport conditions may produce difficulties in areas which normally import food or fodder from neighbouring provinces or states or from Burma. These considerations, along with the latest trend of prices of food grains in different parts of the country, indicate clearly the necessity not only for an all-India drive for increased production but also for aiming at regional self-sufficiency in food grains and animal fodder so far as this is attainable.[205]

In 1942 India made a net export of grain, the Viceroy and Secretary of State did not discover a problem in food supply until September, and at the end of the year the Viceroy still believed that any concerted government intervention was 'not likely to yield results comparable to the panic they would create'.[206]

But as 1942 turned into 1943, food became the most important issue in Indian government and dominated the correspondence between Delhi and London for the next fifteen months. Prices soared, local shortages developed into famines, and in Bengal in 1943 the worst famine since the 1870s (and possibly the worst in the colonial period) took a death toll that ran into an indeterminate number of millions.[207] Government both in Delhi and in Madras diagnosed the cause as a simple shortage, and the solution as a

larger and better organized supply. The evidence for this diagnosis
was easily available; the Japanese progress towards eastern India
had disrupted India's prime source of imported food (Burma), the
Midnapur cyclone in October 1942 in Bengal and a poor monsoon in
central India had reduced the amount of local production, and this
was just the last straw in a process that had steadily reduced the per
capita availability of grain in India from 437 lbs per annum in 1931-2
to 355 lbs a decade later.[208]

Clearly the interpretation was at least partially right—though
Amartya Sen has suggested that the decrease in the supply of grain
in Bengal in 1943 was nowhere near so great as was thought at the
time[209]—and the solution was unavoidable. Yet a better interpretation, as London and Delhi began to realize in 1943,[210] lay in the
effects of wartime demand on the Indian economy. The British war
effort in India was being financed for the most part by printing
money. Between 1939 and 1945, the supply of money roughly
quintupled. At the same time there was a decrease in the supply of
consumer goods, and little attempt by government to increase taxes
or loan issues to soak up much of the artificially created demand.
The result was a massive inflation of the price of those commodities
which were available in the market—chiefly food and cloth. High
prices, hoarding, and disrupted transportation made it almost
impossible for grain to flow to areas of local shortage.[211] Meanwhile, the sudden and unprecedented shift in the value of money
had a differential effect on the real incomes of various sections of
society. While many merchants, landowners and others who commanded substantial assets could keep ahead of inflation, those at
the bottom end of the labour market and at the fringes of small-scale
production fell rapidly behind. For the latter it became rapidly more
difficult to command grain. In Bengal, where agriculture had been
especially stagnant in recent decades and where much of the
inflationary military spending had been concentrated, the effects
were most disastrous.[212] It would of course have been impossible to
deflate the economy in the short term. In fact by mid-1943, the
government had begun to devise ways to check the growth of money
demand and by the last years of the war these measures had started
to take effect.[213] The government therefore decided that it could
only check the spread of famine and distress by increasing the
supply of foodgrains, and by intervening to ensure that the supply
was distributed in the best possible way.

In the second half of 1942, the Government of India became rather more urgent and precise in urging provincial governments to undertake plans to increase the production of grain. The Madras government set about dissuading farmers from growing certain non-food crops and, in order to overcome farmers' fears that a spurt in production would produce an unsaleable glut of grain, guaranteed to purchase any surplus stocks that might appear.[214] Yet the immediate emphasis was on problems of distribution and price control. After the manifest failure of its price committees, the Madras government in late 1942 set restrictions on the export of grain from the province, tightened up the provisions for licensing grain traders, and ordered the tax department to monitor stocks of grain. A poor harvest in the non-Tamil parts of the province in the winter of 1942-3 caused localized shortages and problems which this sort of machinery could not manage. In early 1943 the Government of Madras began plans to move grain from surplus to deficit areas of the province. At the same time, the Government of India launched a 'Basic Plan' to move grain from surplus to deficit provinces.[215]

Initially government believed that the attempt to direct movements of grain would not involve excessive state intervention. The government intended simply to order the market what to do. But it was a naive intention, and it ignored the fact that the market was already badly distorted by inflationary conditions. The result was that after its initial, timid, interventionist step the government found itself on a slippery slope. Government wished only that the market should function as it 'normally' did, but since the prevailing conditions were so manifestly abnormal, government would only be able to secure its goal if it controlled the market sufficiently to annul the effect of these prevailing conditions. This led to two parallel developments. The first was a steadily increasing involvement in the mechanics of the market. The second was a desperate attempt to secure from outside India sufficient stocks of grain to enable the government to dominate the market.

The initial idea was that the government should direct all movements of grain between provinces and between districts. However, the scheme of inter-provincial movements never got off the ground. The Government of India tried to set up the scheme with very little information and almost no administrative machinery. It relied on the co-operation of the provinces but the provinces felt that this signal of distress meant that it was time they looked after themselves. Delhi sent out fifty-two questionnaires about provinces' production and exports and received only three replies. As a result, the quotas of inter-provincial movements in the 'Basic Plan' were worked out by a Delhi official on the eve of the meeting which drafted the plan. Moreover, Delhi had no way to oblige the supposedly surplus provinces to contribute their quotas.[216]

Thus before long Madras, which was supposed to receive imports under the Plan, had to concentrate on its own resources. It started out with a scheme to move grain between surplus and deficit districts by offering contracts to merchants. The merchants did not co-operate very well, so the government pressed tentatively forward. Under the second scheme, the merchants supplied the capital and took a (regulated) profit from this inter-district movement, but the subordinate government officials did the job of uncovering the stocks of surplus grain in the producing districts. Before long the government found that it had to add a new cadre of Grain Movement Officers to ensure that once the Grain Purchase Officers had found the grain the merchants would move it to the right market according to the terms of their contract. Then came a cadre of Food and Loading Inspectors to check the grain at the rice mills and railway stations, and then Marketing Assistants and Agricultural Development Officers to check the quality at purchase and at retail points. Next the government had to start its own transport services and to build its own storage godowns. Finally, it found it necessary to dispense with the merchants and put up the capital itself. In 1942-3, the Government of Madras supplied none of the capital for the grain-market, but in 1943-4 it put up Rs 82.7 million and by 1946-7 government's commitment had risen to Rs 291.4 million.[217]

So long as the government controlled only a part of the grain supply and part of its distribution, the remainder of the market acted according to the dictates of demand. Prices outside that part of the distribution system supervised by the government continued to spiral, and a considerable quantity of grain poured through the channels of the government distribution system and out onto an expensive black market.[218] It was this that led the government step-by-step to replace the buyers, carriers and suppliers of capital in the grain-market. As this proved to be ultimately ineffective, the Government of India conceived the idea that if it could command a sufficiently large stock of grain from sources outside the country, it could flood this into the market and force prices downwards. The

Viceroy started towards this policy in December 1942 when the first intimations of the coming crisis in Bengal, and the Government of India's forecast that the supply of foodgrains in the coming year would fall a million tons short of the requirement, obliged him to ask London to find him 600,000 tons of wheat. He also mentioned that India would have difficulty in supplying food to Ceylon and the Middle East as had been promised in 1940.[219] This was an abrupt reversal of the role that Britain envisaged India as playing in wartime supply, and Churchill in particular was enraged. London replied to Delhi's letter with an injunction not to abandon the supplies to Ceylon and an excuse that there were no ships available for imports of wheat. In response the Viceroy, Lord Linlithgow, threatened to stop supplying Ceylon and the Middle East after February 1943 and to cut the level of rations supplied to the troops in India.[220] London then offered a quarter of the wheat requested, the Viceroy accepted with thanks and the argument seemed to be over.[221] But in the next few months Bengal starved, the Viceroy asked for half a million tons, an increasingly impatient Cabinet replied with an offer of a little Iraqi barley, and the Viceroy retorted with an ultimatum:

I am bound in terms to warn the Cabinet that the Government of India cannot be responsible for the continuing stability of India now, or for her capacity to serve as a base against Japan next year, unless we have appropriate help in prospect.[222]

An intervention by Auchinleck and the Chiefs of Staff in London persuaded Churchill and the Cabinet to arrange a shipment of another 50,000 tons but the Cabinet took this opportunity to make it plain that the idea of importing a million tons of grain into India every year was wholly unacceptable at any time.[223] But by this time the Indian administration was arranging rationing in Calcutta, the new Viceroy, Lord Wavell, decided that food was the most important task, and the Gregory Committee on Foodgrains which followed from the Bengal famine reported in September 1943 that India needed an import of 1½ million tons to make a scheme of food distribution workable.[224] When London offered only 100,000 tons, Wavell played his trump card. He demanded 1½ million tons to feed the troops in India with the clear implication that if the request was refused, India could not and would not support the war effort. Churchill fumed, ridiculed Wavell's concern, derided his statistics and denied the existence of a shortage.[225] In reply, Wavell wrote:

The fact is the Prime Minister has calculated his war plans without any consideration at all of India's needs: I am afraid that he may be courting a first-class disaster to the Empire, unless we are lucky.[226]

In early 1944, London offered 200,000 tons and Wavell replied that he could no longer supply the troops. Churchill finally gave in and by early 1945 grain was arriving in India at a rate of over a million tons a year.[227]

This was of course too late to ease the problems of distributing food in the middle years of the war. Thus the government was gradually forced to admit that it must intervene, not only in the movement of grain from surplus to deficit areas, but also in the final retailing process. In June 1943, the Madras government set up a system of 'informal rationing' in the major cities. The idea was to supply licensed retailers with stocks of grain equivalent to their custom, but it was soon clear that any such attempts to try to 'manage' a theoretically free-market system were doomed to failure. Strict rationing on a card system began in Madras City in September 1943 and gradually spread until by mid-1946 all the province's inhabitants who according to the government's calculations did not grow all their food requirements themselves were on some form of rationing. To supply this system, the government had had to abandon the scheme of purchasing grain from cultivators and millers in favour of compulsory requisition. In October 1944, the Madras government ordained that all the crop beyond that portion required for seed, revenue, and subsistence could if necessary be compulsorily requisitioned by the government. So far as possible, the government continued to acquire what it needed to supply the deficit areas and the ration shops by purchase, but it now did not hesitate to step in and seize stocks of grain if it felt that supplies were being held up or black-marketed.[228]

At the end of 1944, the Government of India commissioned a review of the food administration. The author, Mr. Butler, found that systems differed widely in different provinces, but recommended government to consider 'the possibility of continuing foodgrains control after the present emergency recedes as a means of stabilizing the economy of the country from the producers' and consumers' point of view by the maintenance of prices at a predetermined level'. The Government of India agreed that 'the eventual aim should be…the accurate assessment and acquisition of the surplus of every holding'.[229] A few months later the enquiry into the Bengal famine also remarked that: 'In our view, a policy of laissez-faire in the matter of food supply and distribution is impossible in the future.'[230]

The Madras government had used procurement largely as a threat, and was reluctant to see it translated into a blunt instrument of policy designed for constant use in the future.[231] But the winter of 1945-6 saw the worst season on record in the province. The south-west monsoon failed badly and by the end of the year stocks of food were very low. The government thought up many rescue plans—including sending farmers and labourers off to newly-liberated Burma to reopen the paddy-tracts—but in the short term it had to settle for a scheme of monopoly procurement. It set out to monopolize the entire trade in grain above the level of the village. The surplus was acquired in the village by the revenue staff, handed over to licensed dealers, stored in the government's set of seventy-nine new godowns, transported by the Civil Supplies Transport Unit's fleet of 212 vehicles, and distributed through ration shops to 42 million people. In 1942, food administration had taken up half the time of one Madras government employee; in 1946 there were 15,000 food officials. In 1942, food administration cost virtually nothing; in 1946-7 it swallowed a quarter of the provincial budget.[232]

Thus by the end of the war, the Government of Madras was managing food supplies in a way that it had considered impolitic, if not impossible, in 1942. A large number of cultivators still sold on the blackmarket, yet in every year after 1942-3 the Madras government handled a larger amount of grain than the volume which in 1934 C.R. Srinivasan had estimated as the total inter-district movement.[233] In the process, as one contemporary observer remarked:

The role of the general administrator has altered with a vengeance. In addition to his other duties, he has now become a monopolist, the only wholesale dealer in the province with full control over all retail dealings, except for small quantities within village boundaries, and was responsible for the conduct of majority of retail grain shops in the province. One of the largest business in the country was being run by a government department staffed by general administrators with the general administrators in the districts as its agencies.[234]

Once government had erected food controls, they would prove difficult to dismantle. Controls had kept India's prices below world prices in the latter years of the war and any form of decontrol would

Table 29: Madras Presidency: food administration 1942-3 to 1948-9

	Cost of food administration Rs lakhs	Losses on state-trading Rs lakhs	Cost + Losses as % of provincial budget	Number of food officials	Rice procured (tons)	Estimated % of total crop less seed	Millets procured (tons)	Estimated % of total crop less seed	Grain import tons	Grain import Rs lakhs
1942-3					721 164	15.6			143	461
1943-4	18.7	140.6	5.3	151	841 419	17.1			397	1162
1944-5	62.9	453.3	12.5	1 443	1 025 216	20.3	27 472	1.3	302	884
1945-6	93.7	−138.2*		10 039	1 313 895	31.1	116 739	6.7	251	568
1946-7	161.8	1 200.7	23.9	5 903	1 498 465	30.6	123 647	7.1		
1947-8	153.3	23.9	3.5	8 263	947 405	22.0	25 258	1.4	487	3008
1948-9	118.7	159.8	5.2	5 852	1 366 735	32.1	76 064	3.8	388	2429

*i.e. a profit

Source: *Measures of Food Control*, 31, 41, 119, 120; Natarajan, *Food and Agriculture*, 41.

have encouraged export smuggling and sent prices up. Decontrol
was tried in 1947-8 and in 1955-6; each time it survived one good
harvest but, at the first sign of a poor yield, prices began to soar (in
eight months in 1947, prices rose 250 per cent), and controls were
reimposed.[235]

While the foodgrain market provided the most spectacular
instance of government's headlong intervention into the agrarian
economy, there were two other, related areas of increasing intrusion. First the government decided that it was perfectly proper to
set out to influence the cropping pattern of the province's farmers.
Again, it was to a large extent goaded into this decision by the
Government of India. In 1941-2, when the international market for
groundnuts had collapsed and the first intimations of a food deficit
had been received, the Government of Madras set out to encourage
farmers to transfer land from groundnuts to millet. In May 1942,
this was joined by a campaign to prevent the cultivation of
short-staple cotton (which had its chief market in Japan) and to
withdraw from betel and plantain cultivation rich delta land that
might be put down to paddy.[236] In the crisis of 1945-6, the
government urged farmers to plant every available acre with food,
and to grow an extra food crop in the summer months where this
was at all feasible.[237]

These latter projects took place under the auspices of the Grow
More Food campaign, which was launched by the Government of
India in the summer of 1942 and which also encompassed the second
area of new government intrusions—a greater role in the provision
of agricultural inputs. This began, like the food story, when
inflation began to push up the prices of certain articles and thus
distort the pattern of distribution. The government then stepped in
to control distribution and, soon concluding that the major causes
of distribution problems lay in the paucity of supplies, set about
plans to increase the availability. The three main items involved
were manures, iron and steel, and seeds. In 1943 the government
started to control the distribution of oilcake, which was the major
source of fertilizer other than animal manure. It first imposed
licences on dealers, then banned exports and set ceiling prices.
When these measures proved ineffective, it took to compulsory
requisition of half the oil-mills' output. Some of the oilcake was sold
through government rural depots and co-operative societies, while
some was distributed free. At the same time, the government

entered on projects to increase the supply of manure. Certain municipalities started schemes to compost town refuse; forest restrictions were eased to allow farmers to collect leaf mould; the government fostered one or two factories to crush bones into bonemeal; and the agricultural department began research on the production and use of fishmeal manure.[238] The price of the iron and steel mostly used for axles and wheel-rims of country-carts soared from 1942 onwards because of the diminution of imports, and in 1944 the government took to distributing iron and steel through its own growing number of rural depots. From 1943, the government also took a small part in distributing seeds, but this became especially important in the crisis of 1945-6 when government agricultural officers distributed packages of seeds, oilcake, and loans in an attempt to ginger up production.[239] The Grow More Food campaign also entailed plans to extend the acreage under cultivation, to introduce more mechanization, and to extend irrigation. The plans were conceived in haste and under great stress in 1942-3, the seasons between 1944 and 1947 were exceptionally unkind and it was clear by the end of the war that the campaign as a whole had had only a marginal effect.[240]

Yet it was far from unimportant. In the five years following 1943, the Madras government spent Rs 5½ crores on the Grow More Food campaign (this figure does not include the expenditure on food procurement and distribution schemes) and this sum dwarfed governmental expenditure on agriculture in previous years. The agriculture department had been enlarged and galvanized into action, Grow More Food propaganda had reached most corners of the province, and the schemes that distributed seeds, loans and fertilizers mainly through local agricultural societies had created in the space of two years 1,456 societies with 42,000 members.[241] There was thus a rudimentary organization for development that had not existed prior to the war. Moreover, the mistakes and failures of the campaign led to rather more concerted thinking about agricultural planning.

Indeed, little more than a year after the Grow More Food campaign had begun as a wartime measure, the Government of India concluded that it would have to continue beyond the war, and sent a senior agriculture official to Madras to find out information needed for centrally-planned schemes.[242] This visiting official announced that the Government of India would provide financial help for schemes to extend cultivation and irrigation, and to supply seed and manure. Then in June 1944 the Government of India distributed a short 'Unofficial Note' in which it contemplated a ten-year plan costing Rs 1,000 crores with the aim of increasing India's agricultural production by fifty per cent.[243] In October the Government of Madras called a conference of all officials involved in agricultural work to assess the experience of the past two years. The conference concluded that recent schemes had often been badly thought out and too quickly implemented and that in future there must be more planning in general and more stringent government controls of particular items like stocks of manure.[244] Following this, the Government of Madras began to think about re-organizing the agriculture department. The Government of India commissioned a *Report on the Technological Possibilities of Agricultural Development in India* and this prompted the Director of Agriculture in Madras to write a commentary on the Report about the special conditions of the south.[245] In November 1946 the Government of India announced that it had revised and rationalized its intentions about agricultural planning and now intended to achieve an extra three million tons of food through a five-year plan. Madras was to contribute an extra 6½ lakh tons of rice to this total and the provincial government completed its draft of the Madras component of the first agricultural five-year-plan in early 1947.[246] The Government had moved remarkably quickly away from the tentative dabbling in agricultural economics which had characterised the 1930s.

As the government moved from the desperation of the Grow More Food campaign to the ambition of the first five-year-plan, it made several startling discoveries about the task that lay ahead. The first was that the amount of knowledge and organization that the Department of Agriculture had achieved in over half a century of existence was entirely inadequate for any effective attempt at state intervention. Madras's remarkable new Director of Agriculture, B. Viswanath, thought that the work on the research stations had been badly planned and barely co-ordinated. Despite so many years of experiment, he concluded,

We do not know the particular deficiences of soils, the plant foods taken out by crops, plant foods supplied by manures and the response of crops in increased yield. We are not yet in a position to say with any degree of certainty, the amount of manure or fertiliser or water that can be applied to a given crop in a given locality. This is so because the studies on soils and manures in relation to crop growth have been of an isolated character and lack co-ordination necessary for attaining greater fertiliser and manure efficiency in terms of crop yields.

Furthermore, he added, 'we have been endeavouring to solve the cattle problem for over forty years, talking of pastures and grazing grounds, without achieving very much in that direction'.[247] The department had successfully produced and disseminated some high yielding varieties of seed, but owing to the fact that such seeds used up nutrients in the soil at a rapid rate and that there was no attempt during the dissemination of these seeds to ensure that they were used in conjunction with increased supplies of manure, the yields rapidly fell off and farmers were naturally discouraged. The Madras Board of Revenue added that it would not be possible for the government to attempt any form of agricultural planning on the basis of its current level of knowledge about the economic resources and systems of the province:

The present methods [of government surveillance] do not give enough accurate and up-to-date information to enable the planning authorities to see precisely what can be done, and what should be done, to arrange schemes in the proper order of preference; and to work out the most economic and effective investment of the funds provided by the Government …The Board considers that, in economic affairs and planning, partial views tend to be false views … Government… will probably do more harm than good by its intervention unless it is provided with a complete (or nearly complete) and very carefully analysed statement of the facts. Such a statement cannot be obtained from administrative departments engaged in handling urgent matters of detail, nor from private students with limited resources.[248]

These views pointed to the need for a substantial overhaul in the whole structure of government, but most particularly to a re-organization of the agricultural department which was clearly suffering from the strains of rapid expansion during the war. One of the department's major tasks in the latter part of the war was the scheme to distribute oilcake manures, and the working of the scheme exemplified the department's difficulties; the end links in the chain of distribution were 'poorly paid temporary store-keepers' and their tendency to small-scale corruption tended to undermine the point of the scheme and the image of the agricultural department. As one of Viswanath's lieutenants noted: 'This work was new to the Department and sufficient experienced staff was not available to handle such large quantities of commodities under Trading Schemes. All of a sudden, heavy responsibility was thrown on the staff. The same period synchronised with the period of rapid and large expansion of the activities of the Department in several directions. Most of the Agricultural Demonstrators are inexperienced probationers fresh from the College and they were saddled with this and several other urgent items of work.'[249] In the first five-year-plan, Madras planned to add a thousand personnel to the agriculture department.[250]

The second discovery was the extent of the agrarian problem. In 1944, S.Y. Krishnaswami as Special Development Officer was detailed to calculate the province's deficit in the supply of food-grains.[251] Working on the assumption that virtually no millets entered into trade beyond the village, he set out to calculate how much rice the province's population needed after the millet was consumed. He took a daily adult ration as 24 oz of rice or 28 oz of millet, and reduced the population figure by a quarter to take account of the lower levels of consumption by children. On this basis, Krishnaswami reckoned that the supply of foodgrains in the early 1940s fell short by some 2,000,000 tons. 'This deficit' he concluded, 'is a rather startling figure'.[252]

It was indeed. In recent years, officials in Madras had considered as a rule of thumb that with the fall-off of Burma imports the province had to find an extra 300,000 to 400,000 tons each year;[253] and even at the height of the crisis brought on by the poor monsoon of 1945-6, the government was talking only of an extra deficit of 100,000 tons on top of that.[254] Krishnaswami's methods of calculation were open to criticism on points of details, but other attempts at calculating the deficit came to similarly gloomy results. B. Natarajan, who became Economic Adviser to the Government of Madras after the war, calculated the availability of food grains at various levels of per capita requirement. He found that there had been less than 19 oz a head regularly since the late 1930s and less than 18 oz a head since 1945-6.[255] The Foodgrain Policy Committee of 1942 had used some rather shaky statistics on the distribution of millet- and rice-eaters to reach the conclusion that, with the collapse of imports, the Madras Presidency lacked 13,000 tons of millet and 257,000 tons of rice. Moreover, its attempt to break these figures down by district showed that the Tamil portion of the Presidency was particularly badly off; it lacked 80,000 tons of rice and 269,000

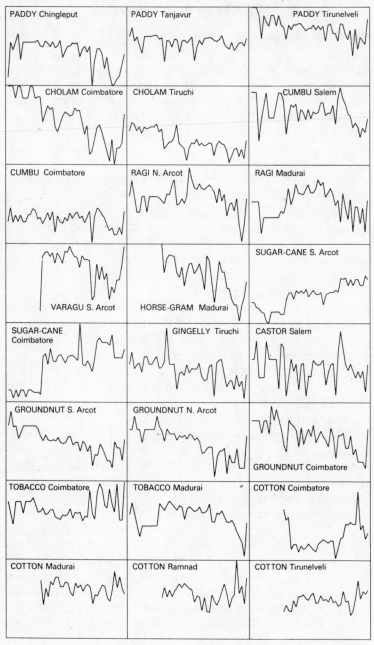

Graph 16   Crop-yields per acre in selected districts, 1904-5 to 1953-4

Note: The official yield data was taken from the *Season and Crop Report of Madras Presidency* and *Agricultural Statistics of British India*. There is no attempt to separate yields on irrigated and unirrigated areas; the yield shown represents the total out-turn divided by the total acreage. Each plot shows the years from 1904-5 to 1953-4 with the two years for which data were not available (1942-3 and 1943-4) omitted and the graph closed up. In six of the plots the data for the first thirteen years were defective and therefore discarded. From 1916-17 onwards the official data were used without modification. In that year the Board of Revenue realised that districts always reported a yield that was less than 'normal', and thus thereafter the Board multiplied up the district report by a factor which, if applied to the data from 1904-5 to 1915-16, would have made the reports (from each crop in each district) average the 'normal' yield. (See BP 136 5 June 1917.) I have treated the data for the years up to 1915-16 in the same way. This has not been entirely successful – see the leap in many of the plots about a quarter of the way through – and accounts for the discarding of the early figures on cotton, varagu and horse-gram. The ranges represented on the full length of the x axis of each plot are as follows, in tons per acre:
paddy, 0.3-1.0; cholam, 0.18-0.46; cumbu, 0.12-0.37; ragi, 0.35-0.62; varagu, 0.25-0.59; horse-gram, 0.57-1.0; sugar-cane, 2.0-4.0; gingelly, 0.1-0.2; castor, 0.13-0.23; groundnut, 0.3-0.6; tobacco, 0.3-0.64; cotton, 0.023-0.067.

tons of millet (or 197,000 and 275,000 tons respectively, if Madras City is included).[256]

The third discovery was that this difficulty over food supply arose not simply because agriculture was failing to expand in line with population, nor even because it was stagnant. Rather in certain important ways agriculture seemed actually to be in decline. One important cause of the decline in foodgrains was a fall in the acreage under millet which contemporary observers attributed to the transference of land to cash-cropping (yet as we have suggested this argument must be extended). The other major cause was a decline in yields per acre. The evidence for this was a little startling, not least because the Madras agriculture department counted the discovery and dissemination of higher yielding varieties of paddy (which now covered two-thirds of the paddy acreage according to departmental estimates) as one of its greatest successes. Of course there was a possibility of statistical error. Yield figures were notoriously little better than guesswork. One important source of possible error was the gradual inclusion of the zamindari areas within the ambit of statistical collection. The zamindaris were undoubtedly poorer on average than the ryotwari tract and thus the inclusion of zamindari statistics could by itself have depressed the estimates. But there are good reasons to suppose that this factor had only a limited effect. Firstly, the zamindaris accounted for less than

Crop and district	1904-5 to 1953-4				1918-19 to 1953-4			
	Average yield	Signi-ficance	R^2	Rate	Average yield	Signi-ficance	R^2	Rate
PADDY								
Chingleput	0.594	0.0001	0.323	−0.8	0.570	0.0001	0.484	−1.5
Tanjavur	0.692	n.s.			0.678	n.s.		
Tirunelveli	0.817	0.0001	0.427	−0.5	0.784	0.006	0.183	−0.4
CHOLAM								
Coimbatore	0.346	0.0001	0.742	−1.4	0.309	0.0001	0.456	−1.3
Tiruchi	0.265	0.0001	0.591	−0.8	0.246	0.009	0.161	−0.4
CUMBU								
Salem	0.289	0.008	0.121	−0.3	0.281	n.s.		
Coimbatore	0.197	n.s.			0.194	n.s.		
RAGI								
North Arcot	0.508	n.s.			0.510	0.001	0.248	−0.5
Madurai	0.488	n.s.			0.503	0.0001	0.347	−0.5
VARAGU								
South Arcot		inadequate data			0.495	0.0001	0.355	−0.8
HORSE GRAM								
Madurai		inadequate data			0.817	0.0001	0.476	−0.8
SUGAR-CANE								
South Arcot	2.699	0.0001	0.725	+0.7	2.868	0.0001	0.537	+0.5
Coimbatore	2.920	n.s.			3.213	n.s.		
GROUNDNUT								
South Arcot	0.450	0.0001	0.668	−0.6	0.429	0.0001	0.361	−0.5
North Arcot	0.448	0.0001	0.650	−0.7	0.427	0.0001	0.537	−0.9
Coimbatore	0.475	0.0001	0.490	−0.6	0.455	0.0003	0.315	−0.6
GINGELLY								
Tiruchi	0.141	0.0001	0.329	−0.5	0.138	0.001	0.268	−0.6
CASTOR								
Salem	0.175	n.s.			0.171	n.s.		
TOBACCO								
Coimbatore	0.522	n.s.			0.520	0.004	0.199	+0.5
Madurai	0.484	n.s.			0.490	0.0001	0.591	−0.8
COTTON								
Coimbatore		inadequate data			0.036	0.005	0.189	+0.9
Madurai		inadequate data			0.051	n.s.		
Ramnad		inadequate data			0.048	n.s.		
Tirunelveli		inadequate data			0.045	n.s.		

Note: I could not find data for the years 1942-3 and 1943-4 and these have simply been omitted from all the calculations. 'Average yield' shows the mean yield over the years shown in tons per acre. 'R^2' and 'Significance' show the regression coefficient and its associated t statistic of a simple linear regression of yield against time. The

'Rate' of change was found by dividing the slope of the regression line by the mean yield, and it represents the annual percentage change in yield. The regression exercise was also tried in the log-linear form. In no case did this either alter the significance, change the regression coefficient by more than ±0.5, or alter the rate of change by more than 0.1.

The Government of Madras changed its techniques for recording yield data between 1916 and 1918, and it is necessary to manipulate the earlier data in order to make it compatible with the figures from 1917-18 onwards. In those cases labelled 'inadequate data', this manipulation produced ridiculous results. Even in the other cases, the earlier figures are extremely doubtful, and the right-hand set of calculations are more useful than the left-hand set. The data on cotton was particularly bad in the early years because government found it difficult to monitor the rapid advances in yield associated with the adoption of the karunganni and Cambodia cotton plants. The yields were almost certainly increasing in these years.

The table covers all the major growing areas of the major crops.

a fifth of total area. Secondly, they were mostly included within the statistical net by the first world war and the decline in yields was visible after that. Indeed the pre-war yield statistics were dubious on many counts, but the government tightened up its procedures in 1916-17 and thereafter the data are a bit more credible. The trends in yields of grain crops, as noted in chapter 3, were steady or rising until the late 1920s or early 1930s and then declined to a trough in the years of bad rainfall in the late 1940s. The patterns among commercial crops were more variable. In the case of both cotton and sugar, the graphs of yields show a distinct upward trend but with a rather 'stepped' shape. Cotton yields leapt upwards in the early years of the century with the spread of Cambodia and karunganni, and again in the late 1940s and early '50s with the spread of seed-selection schemes. In the interim, however, there was a slack period, with definite signs of decline in the wake of the depression in the mid-1930s. Sugar-cane yields leapt upwards in the late 1930s with the spread of new varieties of cane, but had also gone through a slough in the mid-1930s. Groundnut, meanwhile, had also turned downwards from the mid-1930s and had not recovered. In North Arcot the yield dropped by almost fifty per cent, and in South Arcot and Coimbatore there were also clear trends of decline. The trend in the yield of most crops was distinctly downward.

Even after the reforms in statistical practice in 1916-17, these figures may still not be very reliable. Yet all arguments which tried to attribute declining yields to statistical illusion would have to deal with two important findings. Firstly, from 1942 onwards the

Government of Madras conducted a series of crop-cutting experiments with the precise aim of checking its current system of
yield estimates. The most thorough of these tests, conducted in
1944-5 with 954 separate experiments, showed several local vagaries but came out with an overall error of only 2.3 per cent. The
smallness of this error surprised even the government.[257] Secondly,
there was evidence of declining yields even on the government's
research stations:

In regard to millets, a definite decline in yield per acre is seen both on the
large scale and on the demonstration plots run by the department. Decline
in yields and quality is noticeable even on the research stations where
conditions of cultivation are at their best. The yield of paddy at Aduturai,
Coimbatore, Pattambi and Palur show definite decline. K1 cotton at
Koilpatti shows decline in quality and there is a general complaint about
deterioration in the quality of H1 cotton. These have to be investigated.[258]

Moreover, the department was beginning to understand the reasons. 'The decline in dry areas', it noted 'is traceable, weather and
season apart, to slow surface erosion by which surface soil is
removed.' Next, a close inspection of statistics on paddy showed a
close correlation between expansion of acreage and decline of
yields which suggested that water was being spread too thinly or that
labour was being badly managed. Next there had been little
expansion of riverine irrigation in recent years, and probably some
decline of tanks and other small irrigation works. Next, B. Viswanath reckoned that farmers tended to manure cash-crops rather
than millets. Finally, government's research and propaganda work
had largely ignored the millet crops. Except for some small
experiments in Kongunad, the department had made no attempt to
develop better strains of millet until a crash programme was
launched under the Grow More Food campaign in 1943-4. Meanwhile, the yields of millet grown on research-plots had been diving
downwards—from 1,865 lbs per acre in the early 1930s to 1,700 lbs
in the late 1930s and 1,300 lbs in the early 1940s in the case of
irrigated cholam, with corresponding figures of 1,618, 666 and 600
lbs for the rain-fed crop.[259]

The fourth discovery was that one of the most important reasons
for the decline, and consequently one of the most important
constraints on future growth, was the fertility of the soil itself. For
many years the government had monitored acreage, contributed to
irrigation, and attempted to develop seeds, but only in the war had

it begun to take a serious interest in manure. The extent of the problem now seemed staggering. In the main rice-growing area of the Kaveri delta, tests showed that eighty-seven per cent of the soils were deficient in nitrogen and eighty per cent deficient in phosphate and this was a major cause of the comparatively low yields.[260] Moreover, while the department thought it understood the way in which nitrogen performed in the cycle of paddy-cultivation, it had little idea how phosphates were fixed in the soil and used up in the process of plant-growth. Furthermore, the deficiency of phosphates was the result of a long-term decline and it required a reasonably extended solution. The land would need at least five years of treatment with phosphatic fertilizer before any recovery in yield would result, and this fact would clearly make it difficult to convince a farmer to make the necessary outlay.[261] S.Y. Krishnaswami estimated how much nitrogen, phosphates, and potash the province needed to maintain the fertility of the land at a stable level, and then calculated the quantities of these elements that were available in the manures and fertilizers used in the province. Even with the spectacular assumption that virtually all the available resources were in fact used, the resources covered only one third of the requirement.[262]

Although the government made no historical analysis of the problem, it seems clear how the soil had become so drained. It is known that soil nutrients can build up reasonably quickly in tropical conditions because of the chemical properties of monsoon rain and the rotting power of tropical heat. Moreover because of certain geological properties the soils of south India were reasonably rapidly replaced despite constant leaching and erosion by wind and rain. Thus so long as the land was not used too intensively, careful rotation and frequent fallowing was probably enough to maintain the level of fertility.[263] Yet in the past century, the usage had become more constant, old rotations had been discarded in the quest for cash-crop profits, and new crops and new strains of seed which made heavier demands on the soil had come into use. At the same time, manurial practices appear to have remained unchanged, or if anything to have deteriorated. Cattle manure was still the single most important source of fertilizer, and provided four-fifths of the total in the 1940s. It seems certain that because of the difficulties over grazing, the number of cattle and other animals was falling. By the 1940s, it was reckoned that the total resources of cattle manure would supply only 1/25th of the acreage under paddy, let alone other crops.[264] The decline went largely uncorrected for several reasons. Firstly it was slow and cumulative and thus easy to neglect. Secondly, so long as those making the decisions about the use of resources were making increasing profits from cash-crops, they neglected to notice that others were getting steadily less to eat. Thirdly, so long as the expansion into the virgin deltas of southeast Asia was producing more and more food with relatively low inputs, it made sense for south India to cover its growing deficit through imports. Thus until the 1940s, south India virtually ignored its most accessible source of extra fertilizer. The oilcake that was produced when oils were pressed from oilseeds was particularly useful on rain-fed crops and could also be used in paddy production. While the acreage under groundnuts grew rapidly from the late nineteenth century, the use of groundnut cake hardly increased. Evidence collected by the Royal Commission on Agriculture in the 1920s showed that it was little used. Partly, of course, this was because the groundnuts were largely exported uncrushed. Yet even when the seeds were crushed and oilcake was produced in the province, a large portion of the oilcake was sold off for export and used as a fertilizer overseas. As late as 1938-9, 127,000 tons of oilcakes were exported from the province.[265]

Meanwhile, there were few alternative sources of fertilizer. The Department of Agriculture favoured green manure crops, did numerous experiments on their utility, and trumpeted their benefits. But such crops could not seem economic so long as they occupied land on which the farmer had to pay revenue. They enjoyed little popularity before the government finally allowed as part of the Grow More Food compaign that land sown with green manure crops should not be taxed. Parrys began manufacturing artificial fertilizers around the turn of the century, the business expanded after the first world war, and imports of chemical fertilizer increased through the 1930s. In the second half of that decade Madras imported an annual average of 42,640 tons, which accounted for more than half the all-India total of fertilizer imports. But again popularity was limited, and indeed Parrys found that the usage of fertilizer waned after an initial enthusiasm. They attributed this to the fact that, at the current state of the art, fertilizers were effective in the long term only if they were used in conjuction with bulky organic manures. After experiment farmers who could not secure

enough organic manure discovered that their investment in fertilizers was not worthwhile. Manure remained the limiting factor.[266]

The fifth and final discovery was that the dimensions of the
agrarian problem and the complexity of the solution demanded
both a considerable degree of state involvement and a rigorously
co-ordinated approach to planning. When in April 1945 B. Viswanath was asked to draw up a plan to re-organize the agricultural
department, his reply consisted not of a plan for bureaucratic
rearrangements but of an essay on the process of agricultural
development. The Grow More Food campaign had been comparatively ineffective, he argued, because there had been no
attempt to fit it in with the existing agrarian economy. The notable
successes in breeding high-yielding strains of crops had come to
nothing because the attention had been so firmly on a good *yield*
that they had ignored the resistance to drought and disease, and
they had not ensured that farmers used the new seeds in conjunction
with appropriate amounts of water and fertilizer. Meanwhile,
although there had been this research on yields and some sporadic
experiments with soils and manures, the pests and diseases which
took away a remarkable proportion of the crop had barely attracted
the department's attention. Moreover, although agriculture in the
region was so notably prey to the climate, there had been little
research about rainfall regimes, the tolerance of crops to variations
in rainfall and related matters. Farmers still relied on astrology to
predict the rainfall, and Viswanath thought that this might form a
good starting point for research; the department should hire 'a
reputed almanac calculator who is a scholar in Hindu Astronomy
and a modern mathematician with a sound knowledge of astronomy
and planetary movements'.[267]

This suggestion was evidence of Viswanath's wish to use as the
starting point of the department's work, not some ideal picture of a
scientific agriculture, but the prevailing pattern of cultivation. They
needed to understand the logic and science of traditional practices
before they could understand how to improve them. But at the same
time, he was aware that if agriculture was to provide the province's
food and most of its wealth, it would require research and planned
application of improvements that could only be undertaken by the
state. As he concluded: 'The days of individualism are gone. Either
the farmers should organize themselves or the State should organize
them and teach them ways and means of obtaining a decent and

secure living.' And he set out a programme: research on new strains of crop, their adaptability, drought-resistance, and yield; research on the use of water and manure to make optimum use of resources; research on pests and diseases; the establishment of machinery through which the state could supply co-ordinated packages of improved inputs (good seeds, requisite amounts of fertilizer and pesticide, advice on irrigation and cultivation practice) and the necessary finance.[268]

In fact the first five-year-plan returned somewhat to the desperate and disorganized approach which had characterized the Grow More Food campaign.[269] Yet Viswanath had laid out the strategy of the green revolution. He also realized it would take twenty years. It would take a long time to build up the state's machinery, to acquire the necessary basis of research knowledge, to develop and multiply the seeds.

THE STATE AND THE STATE OF THE ECONOMY

After the first world war, the government was edged gradually towards a more active role in the region's economy, and in the region's rural economy in particular. Two principal developments drove the government forward—firstly the agrarian crisis, and secondly the increasing importance and fragile character of the urban economy. The government's attitude to the internal economy passed through three definite stages which roughly coincided with the three decades of the 1920s, 1930s and 1940s. In the 1920s, it took note of the growing series of problems but relied strongly on the hope that they would simply go away. This was a period which found the government investigating the workings of the economy with a degree of interest which it had not shown since the early years of colonial rule. There were four major all-India commissions of enquiry—the Indian Industrial Commission, Banking Enquiry, and Royal Commissions on Agriculture and Labour respectively—and countless provincial and departmental surveys into handlooms, other handicrafts industries, co-operatives, forests, cattle breeds and many other topics. It was also a period when the findings of these enquiries seemed to convince the government that the economy was so complex that it was best left alone. The government's standard solution to particularly intractable problems was the formation of co-operatives, a device which was supposed to provide a solution without directly involving the machinery of government. At the same time and in the same spirit, the government was forced to admit that its systems of rural conrol—the zamindars and ryotwari village office—were growing less efficient, indeed troublesome, but believed that any attempt to reform or replace these systems would be prohibitively expensive and prohibitively disruptive. Finally, too, the government was obliged to recognize that the expansion of industry in wartime was also throwing up new problems. The collapse of the post-war boom saw the first disputes involving organized labour in Madras. But for the moment this was something which could be safely countered by strengthening the urban police force and ridiculing the politicians involved in trade unionism.

The 1930s imposed a change in attitude. The ostrich-eye view of the 1920s had depended on the argument that the market was the best regulator of the economy, but in the 1930s the market seemed to be the origin of economic problems. The government thus moved towards a role as the overseer of the market. Where the market seemed to have broken down, or to be working in an odd way, this simply required the government to provide some institutional or legislative support. The government thus began to equip itself to monitor the state of the market in a more continuous fashion than hitherto. It commissioned enquiries (such as that by Srinivasan on the paddy trade) which explained how the market worked, set up the new posts of Economic Adviser and Statistical Officer, and gave its agriculture, industry, and co-operative departments the responsibility for keeping a closer watch on the fluctuations of the economy. One of the standard responses to evidence of economic disorder was still the co-operatives and the government encouraged the spread of loan-and-sale and other forms of marketing society in areas where the unregulated machinery of commercial transactions seemed to have broken down. But the government now went farther than this. It was prepared to make adjustments to revenue tariffs and railway rates to preserve existing patterns of trade which were threatened by outside influences. It was also prepared to set up local committees to police the cash-crop markets which fell into a particularly disorderly state during the decade. It also intervened when the market for capital seemed to be cracking up and tried to untie the knots in the rural credit network by setting up machinery for debt conciliation and slightly extending the scope of rural co-operative banking. Finally, it was also ready to intervene in the market for industrial labour and help to settle disputes between mill-owners and their workforce. For the moment these interventions extended little farther than providing an institutional machinery for settling such disputes. Similarly during this decade, the government grew increasingly sceptical about the future prospects of its two systems of rural control. The zamindaris seemed to be moving rapidly towards economic and political disaster. The village officers threatened to become a fifth column within the government's own rural administration. The government began to debate reforms of zamindari and village office but without any trace of enthusiasm.

The aftermath of the depression and the advent of war quickly rendered obsolete such tentative steps to cosset the market principle. To prosecute the war, the government demanded a greater degree of efficiency from the economy, but the initial strains of wartime exposed all the critical features of the economy's development. A sense of desperation precipitated a revolution in the government's attitude to the economy. The government now had to re-direct, or even take over, many of the functions of the market. It became the main purveyor of food. It entered into the trade in agricultural inputs both as producer, wholesaler, and retailer. It organized the production and distribution of the principal item of mass consumption besides foodstuffs—textiles. Furthermore, it had to accept the idea that controlling the market meant structuring production. It began to take on the responsibility for deciding and directing the future of the region's agriculture, which meant not only a renewed interest in irrigation, but also attempts to channel resources into the production of specific crops and a whole programme of research and development. The government also began to organize the textile industry, by sharing out the market between handlooms and mills and then policing this division. But controlling production meant controlling producers and that involved the government in the sociology of the rural and urban economies. It began trying to regulate the relationships between capitalist and worker and between landowner and labourer. These latter interventions, however, were restricted to some of the most sensitive portions of the economy. In the textile industry, the government tried to keep the peace between mill-owner and mill-employee, and in the Kaveri delta it tried to regulate the disputes of mirasidars and their subordinates. To complete this irruption into the business of social engineering, the government finally swept away the institutions of zamindari and village office. Zamindars were abolished, while village officers lingered on in a much reduced role.

The fact that the government was taking a much more creative part in the economy made its view of the economy and its future particularly important. Unfortunately there is no statement of this view which is not obscured under layers of colonial complacency, or distorted by the fervour of nationalism and the smooth talk of 'development'. There is, however, some discernible eloquence in the actions of government. The advance of state intervention in the economy was founded on a fear of public disorder and a despairing realization of the extent of agrarian decline. The government's initial aim was to stop the trend of deterioration and to repair some of the damage already done. Its actions were designed to preserve and conserve. Principally it was committed to preserving the urban economy, however fragile it might be. That meant pampering the insecure textile mills, preventing the attrition of petty industries such as the handloom, and securing the urban food supply. Governmental action was limited by the very weakness of the economy. The government could not risk precipitating any major structural change in the economy for this might turn economic crisis into economic and political disaster. It could not allow the mills to ride roughshod over their handloom competitors and thus create both an untrammelled market and a source of proletarian labour at the same time. The strains of transition were too risky. Similarly it could not allow the mirasidars of the central Kaveri to rationalize their systems of production to such an extent that they dispensed with excess supplies of labour. That again was too risky for it was not at all clear where the surplus labour could be absorbed. Such policies committed the government not only to constrain the protests of the disadvantaged and thus to combat strikes and rural disorder, but to limit the ambitions of the privileged, and thus to constrain mirasidar and mill-owner. It was a politics of desperate compromise rather than a politics of optimistic vision.

Conclusion

The recent historiography of colonialism and post-colonialism has repeatedly stressed the extent to which western-oriented trade, assisted by imperial or neo-imperial state systems, has moulded the societies and economies of the non-western world. But this view, however correct in outline, has a somewhat flat, two-dimensional appearance. In order to invest the picture with some depth, we must add another dimension: the extent to which local society helped to shape the colonial state and to channel the colonial economy. The survivals and legacies of the pre-colonial period have also helped to build the post-colonial world. Missionaries, utilitarians and now neo-Marxists have been attracted to the delusion that there was a theoretical tabula rasa in the non-western world.

Tamilnad contains one of India's oldest and most complex civilizations. Its two thousand years of recorded history, and particularly the last five hundred before the imposition of colonial rule, do not convey an impression of a static 'traditional society' but rather of rapid economic change, social evolution, and political experiment. These changes are most conveniently viewed through two interlinked processes: the gradual and imperfect interpenetration of two different economic and social systems within the region, and the increasingly complex history of warfare and state formation. Although reasonably well marked off from neighbouring territories, Tamilnad was by no means unified in any political or economic sense before the coming of colonial rule. There were two principal regions (each internally fragmented) with different geographies and different social histories. The economy of the valleys was based on irrigation and the cultivation of rice; the economic security which these facilities offered had attracted a dense population. The society of the tract was marked by a strict division, underwritten by religion and the state, between those who controlled the land and those who worked it. This agrarian society had been influenced by the expansion in its midst of an urbane culture centred on the religious and royal capitals. The polities of the tract were petty princedoms which guaranteed the rights of the agrarian elite, contributed to continued prosperity by patronizing irrigation and extending foreign trade, and defended valley civilization against any intruder. The economy of the plains, by contrast, was based originally on hunting and herding, but had gradually though imperfectly been transformed through a long history of cultural contact, diplomatic alliance, and military colonization from the valleys. The social structure of the plains represented a fusion of the quasi-tribal customs of the early inhabitants with the military organization of local chieftains and military colonists. The result was a complex hierarchical system based on units of lineage and clan at the bottom, modulated by considerations based on length of residence, comparative military might, and adopted valley-based cultural values in the middle ranges, and topped out by a local military governance which drew its authority both from the spear and the state.

From the late medieval period onwards, Tamilnad's fragmented political system of small valley principalities and numerous plains chiefs crumbled away as a result of the accelerating tempo of local warfare (prince against prince and tract against tract) and the threat of invasion from the north. By the eighteenth century, the princes and chiefs had virtually been replaced by warlord states, mostly run by northern invaders. This political evolution had engendered a parallel change in the economy. Firstly, the demands of warfare had given rise to systems of state extraction based on centralized taxation organized by state appointees. In the valleys, the land-controllers had lost their untrammelled dominance and their military protection, and now had to bargain away resources and prestige in order to retain the vestiges of privilege. The economy of the valleys had become the commissary of the military state. In the plains, meanwhile, the growing demand for resources had pushed forward arable cultivation and other forms of petty production, and had persuaded the tract's sparse and mobile population to settle down, grow crops, and increase. Secondly, there had been a consequent rise in both internal and external trade. The two tracts were increasingly inter-dependent. The warlord capitals created pools of commercial demand. The states encouraged overseas trade as a means to raise additional revenue, and the front-runners of Europe's expanding maritime trade were only too anxious to assist.

Against the background of this historical evolution, the establishment of British colonial rule—a military power interested in fiscal extraction and overseas commerce—does not appear as a sharp break with the past. Moreover just as the Deccani warriors of the late medieval period had looked on the south as a source of supplies, so the Company Government required no more of Madras than a steady supply of food, tax revenue and articles of trade. In no other part of India was there such a large element of continuity with the recent past. The rulers of Madras could draw on the legacy of the past to construct an administrative apparatus which for its achievement of the limited aims of peace and a good treasury balance was the envy of the other provinces of British India. After a little experimentation and a lot of talk the Madras government adopted a system of taxation which employed zamindars, tahsildars and village officers and which differed little in overall shape from those used by its predecessors. Any innovations in judicial convention and bureaucratic practice were adjustments made in the interests of efficiency rather than structural change. Under this regime, the economy of rural Tamilnad continued along its set course of expansion based on the extension of arable agriculture and the growth of internal and external trade. As colonial trade expanded in the wake of the progress of the colonial flag, it tapped a production system which had evolved to supply the princes and warriors of the pre-colonial period.

In the nineteenth century, agriculture was extended under the impetus of a growing population and an increasing demand for agricultural produce among new industries and newly rich consumers in the industrializing west. This latter demand was, however, casual rather than insistent. There were understretched agricultural regimes all over the world and many of these were more conveniently placed or more open to direct European transformation (by, for instance, plantation systems) than that of southern India. Yet the Tamilnad countryside responded to the demand because the colonial state provided the minimum facilities (roads, ports and, later, railways) and because the dominant of the countryside saw opportunities for profit. The systems of social organization which had been forged as part of the post-medieval state systems were easily adapted to production for the overseas market. Those who controlled land in the valleys and, more especially, those who controlled labour in the plains, found it relatively easy to direct cultivation to meet this new source of demand. With only minimal interference by the state, little intrusion by foreign capital beyond the ports, and little complaint from the ranks of rural labour, there was no reason for those interested in the market to overhaul the local systems of production just because the market was different and larger than before. In the valleys, production was still based on state irrigation works, managed by a legally and culturally defined elite of land-controllers, and carried out by subsistence labourers who bargained away their economic freedom for a relatively secure diet. Production continued to increase so long as the state provided more irrigation water, and demographic increase (or migration) provided more labour. There was also a slow but significant increase in the intensity with which the land was utilized, achieved largely by the application of increased amounts of unfree or poorly rewarded labour. In the plains, meanwhile, arable cultivation extended rapidly on a modified form of the pattern of military colonization. In this tract, agricultural extension required considerable capital investment in the form of local irrigation works, and soil improvement; such 'investment' amounted principally to a mobilization of labour on an unusual scale. The dominating figures in local society used their command over labour to push out cultivation into many areas which would not have merited attention were it not for overseas demand. Here the rapidity and extent of change—from a backward, partially pastoral tract to a supplier of world commodity markets—threatened to overwhelm the local hierarchy. Land was relatively freely available until the early twentieth century, capital was increasingly accessible until the depression, and every family had its own store of labour power. Gradually the dominant figures in the economy of this tract came to control not so much land or even labour, but rather merely labour's product. So far as international commerce was concerned, the tract remained remote and unreliable, and it was thus still relatively easy for a minority of dominant figures to stand across the slim, tentative avenues which led from the foreign markets, through the port, to the local market-town and out into the village. At each staging post along these avenues, the outsiders subcontracted the risks of closer and deeper involvement. By acting as the last and vital links in the chains of commercial access, by controlling the supply of scarce resources of water, fertilizer and capital, and by manipulating a residual grip over the labour of others, the dominant class of the plains continued to stand out well above their neighbours. In both the valleys and the plains, the leaders of local society used established patterns of hierarchy and clientage—supplemented wherever necessary by cash or by force—to realize the produce demanded in the market.

In one section of the plains, the inheritance from the past and the adaptation to the present were rather different. Kongunad was a frontier province. At the start of the nineteenth century it was fairly thinly populated with pioneer farmers. The land was still fresh, and cultivation in this particularly dry tract was expensive but rewarding. Under the impetus of peace and marketing opportunities, the frontier in Kongunad moved rapidly forwards. Here the farmers invested heavily in irrigation (wells) and in soil improvement, attracted the necessary extra labour by modified systems of wage payment rather than 'traditional' forms of clientage and, like any capitalist or semi-capitalist enterprise, responded quickly to changes in market demand. The costs of cultivation in this tract made a close association with the market inevitable; a close association with the market dictated a more nakedly commercial organization of production.

By the early twentieth century, everywhere except Kongunad, the limits of expansion by these methods were rapidly approaching. Appropriate land was running scarce, and reserves of other important inputs—water, fertilizer, and labour (given current methods of deployment)—even more so. The countryside now had to cope with the consequences of rapid expansion. In the plains, the natural fertility of hitherto under-exploited land had been rapidly used up and there were limited but significant signs of soil exhaustion and soil erosion. In the valleys, there were growing difficulties about the supply and distribution of water. In both tracts, yields began to fall. The approaching crisis elicited very different reactions from the inhabitants of the two tracts. The people of the valleys looked beyond their usual horizons for a new frontier. The labourers and bankers found it in the expanding plantation tracts and rice deltas of southeast Asia. The dominant mirasidari families sought the assistance of government as educator, employer and patron. The agrarian economy of the valleys was allowed to grind to a halt. In the plains, however, the powerful drew on their reserves of social and economic authority to save themselves at the expense of others. In essence, the dominant groups began trying to discard the surplus of labourers who were not necessary to the production of commercial profit. They combated the problems of exhaustion and erosion by increasing the practice of fallowing and by concentrating scarce productive resources on the most rewarding lands and on the commercially most rewarding crops. The stagnation of the valleys and the distortion of the plains conspired to decrease production of food both absolutely and, of course, per capita. To some extent the resulting deficit could be made good by imports, but there was undoubtedly a decline in the availability of food. This had two subsequent effects. Firstly, it increased the basic insecurity of those at the bottom of the economic heap, and widened the real gap between rich and poor, powerful and powerless. Secondly, it restricted the possibility of any further transformation of agriculture. Even with the quickly expanding imports of rice from southeast Asia, it was not possible to rely on a commercial market for grain. Even the most commercial tract, Kongunad, was heavily weighted down by the need to maintain production for local subsistence.

So far as the Tamilnad countryside was concerned, the depression of the 1930s was not simply a dramatic drop of price and demand. Rather it signalled on the one hand the beginning of the end for the colonial economy, and on the other the collapse of the rural pillars supporting the colonial state. There was much irony in this coincidence, for it had been the growth of commercial production and trade under the prompting of colonial demand which had gradually undermined the rural pillars of the colonial state; commercial management had gradually superseded revenue management as the generator of local wealth and power, and the systems of local despotism which underpinned the colonial state in the countryside could not stand such qualification. By the early twentieth century, the systems of zamindari estates and ryotwari village office were in such disarray that they crumbled away in the atmosphere of heightened social and economic tension of the 1930s and 1940s. Meanwhile at the same time much of the machinery of colonial trade, which had been the original agent of this political decay, also came apart in the depression. When overseas demand slackened dramatically, it was soon discovered how fragile was the structure of internal trade and local finance which had been overlaid on the agrarian economy to service the export business. The financial institutions which had grown up in the past half-century and which performed the signal service of linking the external system of trade to the internal system of production, were revealed as brittle and insecure. They rested on no basis firmer than an optimistic view of the future, and they crumpled when that optimism could not be sustained. Other institutions along the channels of colonial trading also faltered; commission agencies were put out of business, village traders starved of funds, entrepôt towns stopped in their tracks.

The new systems of marketing and finance which emerged out of the depression period functioned very differently from those of the earlier period. While crop exports were increasing on a long-term trend, the wealth accumulated in agrarian commerce was either exported, hoarded, or re-invested in the rural economy. It is impossible to estimate how much was used in each of these three ways, but it is undoubtedly true that many of the profits of commerce were eventually spent in the countryside, both in order to maintain production and in efforts to increase control over production; local elites would buy carts and minor processing plants to increase their hold over trade, hire more labour to advance their prestige and their production at the same time, redistribute the wealth within the local community by purchasing local services, and spend in many other ways which increased local status, respect, and social power. In the aftermath of the depression, however, a greater portion of the wealth accumulated in agrarian commerce was siphoned off to the region's urban economy. Rationalized systems of marketing and concentrated control over liquid capital began to displace the graded chains of rural finance and marketing. The adverse shift in the terms of trade between rural and urban goods helped to discourage reinvestment in the agrarian economy and to transfer wealth from countryside to town.

The consequent rise in urban demand and in the availability of venture capital provided the stimulus for urban growth. The rising urban entrepreneurs were generally survivors from the wreck of the colonial trading system. In the towns of the plains, the mercantile groups which had mediated between the export houses and the villages now moved towards small-scale industrial enterprises. In Kongunad, where it had been members of the rural rich who had entered into agrarian commerce in the pre-depression period, the same figures now extended their interests further into the towns. In the valleys, where so many of the bankers who financed local trade had withdrawn or migrated, the response was more muted. These merchant entrepreneurs and agrarian capitalists of the plains and Kongunad chose to set up mills and factories which required relatively small amounts of fixed capital, and which produced consumer goods for the local market. In some cases the articles produced were traditionally in demand in the region (cloth), and in other cases the demand had been created by foreign imports (white sugar, matches) which were now more expensive in real terms as well as hindered by protective tariffs or the disorder of international trade in depression and war.

Industrialization against a background of agrarian decline was, however, subject to severe limitations. Beyond a certain point of expansion, the market was immovably slack. In part this was simply due to poverty and in part it was a consequence of the unreconstructed condition of rural society and the continuation of established patterns of consumption. Rural wealth was concentrated in the hands of a few who habitually spent more on local goods and artisanal services than on urban produce. Thus for the most part the towns of the region could not sustain growth as new industrial centres. Indeed the towns continued to depend not so much on the dynamo of an emergent industrial capitalism as on the extractive might of the state. The salaries of government servants and the expenditure on government contracts remained one of the most important sources of urban demand. By the 1940s, government's limited ventures into social welfare—notably food rationing and the handloom support schemes—were helping to redistribute resources into the towns and to attract the casualties of declining agriculture. The towns which grew up under these conditions were filled with service industries and artisan workshops. Such enterprises supplied the most secure market, achieved the best return per unit of investment, and made the most exploitative use of the labour available. The handloom, tanning, beedi-rolling, and other petty industries which expanded from the period of the first world war onwards were part of the logic of declining agriculture. The countryside exported its spare labouring capacity to the towns where it could be used to produce cheap goods for the local market and for the export trade. Agrarian decline transformed urban growth. The countryside remade the town in its own image.

There were, however, exponents and advocates of capitalist principles who argued that the only agency which could break the vicious circle of stagnation was the power of the state. Such advocates were found scattered through the length and breadth of the region's economy. In the agriculture of the valleys, commercial farmers wanted state assistance in their bid to rationalize labour usage; they wished to discard existing systems of attached labour and use the market principle of wage labouring to cut labour costs and management difficulties. In the textile towns the mill-owners wanted the state to abet their efforts to push the costs of labour down to the level which the glutted labour market would tolerate. On the plains, the dominant farmers wanted the state to provide the inputs of water and fertilizer which would push out the frontier of commercial agriculture. In the metropolis, even expatriate entrepreneurs argued that the state must plan the allocation of scarce industrial resources, and must take a hand in providing the capital-goods industries and infrastructural services which were a necessary foundation for industrial growth.

The state, however, was not keen to act as the handmaid of private accumulation. The colonial state was too weak, embattled and unsure of its bases of support to contemplate with equanimity the social turmoil which would attend any attempt to transform such a society into the semblance of an industrializing community. By the second world war the colonial state had been driven towards a much enlarged role in economic management not by the prospects for a prosperous future but by the consequences of a miserable past. The state merely wanted to forestall disaster. It carved out for itself a conservationist role, and attempted to freeze the economy at its present stage of agrarian decline and unresolved urban development. On the one hand the state lent assistance to the pioneers of the new economy, such as the mill-owners and the commercial farmers, but on the other hand it also tried to preserve the practices and practitioners of the old ways—the handlooms, and the tied labour systems of valley agriculture. And it tried to police and mitigate the conflict between the two. The state dictated market-sharing arrangements to the mill and handloom components of the textile industry, and tried to lay down rules about the usage of different sorts of labour in valley agriculture.

For most of the colonial period, the most visible and audible figures in the Tamilnad countryside were the valley mirasidars. The British had had good reasons to invest them with particular importance. The valley mirasidars grew the stocks of food necessary for the towns and for the army. They sent their sons to government schools and into government service. They quickly learnt the techniques of colonial politics and bribed, petitioned, pleaded, and agitated their way into the lobbies of the imperial government. As a result they were allowed to retain many of their 'ancient' privileges for much of the nineteenth century. By the early twentieth century, however, the centre of political gravity in the Tamilnad countryside was rapidly shifting away from the valley mirasidars towards the dominant figures of the plains. The stagnation of valley agriculture as a whole, the declining fortunes of mirasidars as individuals, and the rising irritant of pannaiyal labour agitation, steadily undermined the platform of their political prominence. Meanwhile the cash-crop farming and the processing, factory, and artisan industries of the plains were emerging as the major sources of wealth in Tamil society. The leading men of the petty-producing society of the plains—the commercially-minded landholders, local bankers and traders, handloom-capitalists, and nascent urban entrepreneurs—provided the muscle of all of the region's successive political movements. In the Justice party of the 1920s and early 1930s they were junior partners of the zamindari 'gentry' and the commercial elite of Madras City. In the Congress from the late 1930s to the early 1960s they ran in uneasy harness with urban professionals. But in the mid-1930s, they had already begun to flex their independent political muscles when they prompted the Backward Classes Move-ment, a pressure group which united some of the major cultivating groups of the plains (drawn from the Kallar-Maravar-Agamu-daiyan, Padaiyichi, and Gounder caste groups) with some of the prominent mercantile and industrial communities of small-town society (Sengundar weavers, Asari artisans, Chetty bankers and traders). From the late 1940s a similar alliance would emerge as the dominant force of the Dravidian movement. Since Independence, whatever the political colouring of the party in power, the logic of universal suffrage in a society still so internally fragmented and so economically stratified has ensured that to a large extent the government must reflect the political mentality of the petty pro-ducers in its largest constituent region—the plains.

Tamilnad's role in Independent India was a natural evolution from the political and economic developments of the later colonial period. Tamilnad was not to play a leading role in the development of a new industrial society in the independent country. Most of the heavy industries located in Tamilnad in the 1950s and 1960s were casual offshoots of north India's industrial complex. Meanwhile Tamilnad's role was to consume the manufactures largely made in the north, and to export in return supplies of food and labour. Professional men from Tamilnad migrated to the offices of Delhi and the other major cities. Tamil labourers moved into the chawls of Bombay and other manufacturing centres. In good years, Tamilnad contributed grain to government's procurement and rationing grid. Tamilnad's political leaders were truculent but finally willing agents in the formulation of this particular role for the southern state. Tamilnad remained relatively prosperous compared to other regions, and much less turbulent socially and politically than states such as Bombay, Bihar, West Bengal and Haryana.

The administration of rural Tamilnad was adjusted to clear away the detritus of the colonial era and to bring the machinery into line with political realities. The colonial systems of rural control were dismantled and replaced with systems more suited to the task in hand. The zamindaris were swept away in 1948. The importance of the ryotwari village officers declined through the 1950s as the government set up new agencies in the countryside in the scheme known loosely as panchayati raj. The new elective bodies in the countryside attracted the rural elite of farmers and traders heavily interested in production for the market.[1] Whereas the schemes of zamindari estates and ryotwari village office had operated by allowing the rural agents of government to control the flow of resources from the village to the state, panchayati raj enabled the local agents to derive power and perhaps profit from some control over the flow of resources back from the central state to the countryside. In both cases, the state purchased its security and its freedom at a considerable cost.

The state then used the local machinery established in the wartime economy and both supplemented and improved under panchayati raj to channel investment and expertise back into the countryside in order to roll back an internal frontier for agricultural expansion. The state's function in agricultural growth had been acknowledged during the second world war, and much of the activity which evolved as the 'green revolution' had been prefigured in Viswanath's rural development plans of 1946. In the plains and in Kongunad, government recognized the necessity for investing in irrigation works which were not designed solely or even mainly for flush paddy cultivation. At first government mostly helped individual farmers to rebuild tanks and provided finance and expertise for sinking wells; but by the late 1960s it also began to build river-based irrigation systems (such as the PDP project) which were designed to extend the acreage and improve the yields of 'dry' crops such as cotton and millets. In the valleys, the government gradually put together the packages of seeds, fertilizers and credit which gave a new lease of life to the involuted agriculture and exhausted soils. Subsidies, the provision of inputs, and artificially high prices for grain provided a new stimulus for rural trade and credit.[2] The agrarian economy began to pick itself up from the slough of the slump and wartime dislocations. By the mid-1970s, urban wealth was again being recycled into agriculture by private agency as well as by the state. In Kongunad, where the leaders of rural society had built up an urban economy in the 1930s and '40s, townsmen now returned to the countryside to invest in the production of valuable crops such as cotton and sugar.

The towns now stood over the countryside in more imposing fashion than before. The colonial trading economy was superseded by the planned foreign-exchange policies of Independent India; the urban sector of Tamilnad and the rest of India replaced the remote markets of the west as the destination of the countryside's surplus produce; the distributive channels of the new network of administration flowed down through the towns on their way to the countryside; urban banks and urban-based co-operatives harboured the finance necessary for agricultural growth; and, as a consequence of all these forces, the centres of political gravity were found in the towns. The urban population itself expanded as a by-product of the aggrandisement of the post-colonial state. Processing, artisanal and service industries dominated the towns. Coimbatore and its satellite towns continued to expand into a second generation of intermediate goods factories—pumps, textile machinery, light engineering—but it was an isolated ripple in an otherwise calm lake.

The state's attempts to promote Tamilnad's agriculture reflected a specific set of constraints and priorities. The estate recognized that the last century of agrarian history had shown that there was little hope of progress on the basis of the current state of agrarian organization. As T.W. Schultz pointed out in the mid-1960s, the decision of small-scale agricultural producers not to invest in agricultural growth was often quite logical and rational from their point of view.[3] The region's agriculture had drifted up a cul-de-sac of small-scale production and it would be difficult if not impossible to turn it round and seek an exit. The strategy of the post-colonial state was to attempt to change the scale of agricultural operations, not by destroying the small producers, but by incorporating them within a wider framework established by the state.[4] Whereas the colonial economy had overlaid a system of extraction over the rural economy, the post-colonial state now overlaid a system (or systems) of productive organization. Since one signal aim of this strategy was to avoid doing too much damage to the existing patterns of local rural organization, naturally the strategy differed slightly in the three different regions of plains, valleys, and Kongunad. In each case the state schemes provided a scale of agricultural management which was not possible within local society and which was supposed to be necessary to agricultural growth. In the plains this entailed a new role for the state as the builder and manager of irrigation. State schemes of riverine irrigation and well and tank subsidies superseded the very local and fragmented methods for managing irrigation. In the valleys, where the state had always been the provider of irrigation water, the state's organization of agriculture now extended into marketing and the provision of various inputs. Firstly from 1942 onwards the state moved in to shore up and then to take over the systems for marketing paddy. Although thereafter government involvement in the grain trade waxed and waned, some form of government control of marketing in the valleys has remained. Secondly, the state became increasingly involved in the provision of credit, seeds and fertilizer in the intensive development programmes which were best suited to the valley farmer. As provider of inputs and marketing skills, the state has taken over the role traditionally played by the mirasidar in valley society and carried it out on a much larger scale. In Kongunad (and to a lesser extent elsewhere) the principal innovation in agrarian organization has been the sugar factory. Sugar has replaced cotton as the booming crop of the region. The sugar factory effectively managed production over a large catchment area by making contracts with individual landholders in which the factory supplied inputs of seed, credit, and fertilizer and secured the produce. The factory then also organized the wage labour for the harvest on the scale of the whole catchment area; plots were planted and harvested in sequence so that the factory might have a reasonably steady flow of cane. The effective unit of organization was not the owner-cultivator holding, but the sugar factory and its catchment area.[5]

The fact that this new era of state management saw new systems overlaid on old practices, rather than any attempt to undermine existing forms of local organization, has contributed to the continuity of prevailing patterns of rural society. In the plains the wells and riverine irrigation systems have mostly been accessible to the larger farmers. They have increased such farmers' productivity and labour demand so much that they continue to dominate systems of local redistribution in which small farmers bargain their surplus labour for the surplus produce of their larger neighbours. In Kongunad, the sugar factories are often co-operatives or joint-stock companies. In either case they tend to be promoted by the region's entrepreneurial rural elite. They represent a new attempt, in association with the state, to extend commercial agriculture. They provide the capital, the state supplies much of the expertise, and the smaller landholders and the landless are paid reasonably well for the services of their labour. In the valleys, it is now reasonably clear that the packages of new inputs have been useful and accessible mainly to the larger farmers and resulting differentials in productivity between large and small operators have helped to underline the basic dual stratification of valley society.[6] Moreover here the state has actively resisted any attempt by the valley farmers to transform systems of labour usage. A series of Acts beginning with the Tanjavur Pannaiyal Protection Act of 1952 and the Tamil Nadu Cultivating Tenants Protection Act of 1955 has attempted with some success to preserve the pannai and waram systems of labour usage. They have attempted to halt the drift towards annual tenancy contracts by granting the waramdar some fixity of tenure, and to halt the drift towards larger scale usage of labour gangs by providing something of a 'closed shop' for pannaiyals. The valleys' history of sullen labour relations, punctuated by occasional but inconsequential outbreaks of violence, has continued into the 1970s. The heirs to the chieftain of the plains, the mirasidar of the valleys, and the pioneer farmer of Kongunad, still stalk the Tamilnad countryside.

Bibliography

1. Government files   2. Government reports
3. Government annuals   4. Private papers
5. Books, articles and dissertations

1 GOVERNMENT FILES

(a) National Archives of India, New Delhi
Education, Health and Lands Department
Home Department
Judicial Department

(b) Tamilnadu Archives, Madras
Proceedings of the Board of Revenue
Proceedings of the Court of Wards
Development Department
Home Department
Judicial Department
Local Self Government Department
Public Department
Public Works and Labour Department
Revenue Department

2 GOVERNMENT REPORTS

(a) Great Britain
Report of the Indian Irrigation Commission 1901-3: Part II, Provincial.
Parliamentary Papers, 1904, Cd. 185.
Royal Commission on Agriculture in India. Volume III, Evidence taken in Madras (London, 1927).
Royal Commission on Labour in India. Evidence volume III, Madras and Coorg (London, 1931).
India (Food Situation 1943). Speech by the Food Member of the Governor-General's Council and other papers. Parliamentary Papers, 1942-3, Cmd. 6479.

(b) Government of India
Indian Famine Commission 1898, Appendices volume II: Evidence taken

before the Indian Famine Commission (Calcutta, 1898).

Evidence taken before the Reforms Committee (Franchise) (Calcutta, 1919).

Report of the Indian Cotton Committee 1919 (Calcutta, 1919).

Minutes of Evidence taken before the Indian Cotton Committee (Calcutta, 1920).

Report of the Indian Sugar Committee (Simla, 1921).

Report of the Indian Taxation Enquiry Committee (Delhi, 1925).

General Report on Eight Investigations into the Finance and Marketing of Cultivators' Cotton 1925-8 (Bombay, n.d.).

Report of the Indian Central Banking Enquiry (Calcutta, 1931).

Index Numbers of Indian Prices, 1861-1931 (Delhi, 1933) and annual addenda.

Report of the Indian Tariff Board on the Sugar Industry (Delhi, 1938).

Imperial Council of Agricultural Research, *Report on the Cost of Production of Crops in the Principal Sugarcane and Cotton Tracts in India: Volume IV, Madras* (Delhi, 1938); *Supplementary Volume IV, Madras* (Delhi, 1940).

Report of the Foodgrains Policy Committee (Delhi, 1943).

Technological Possibilities of Agricultural Development in India by W. Burns (Lahore, 1944).

Famine Enquiry Commission Final Report (Madras, 1945).

Foodgrains Policy Committee, Interim Report 1948 (Delhi, 1948).

All-India Rural Credit Survey. Volume I, The Survey Report, Part I (Rural Families). (Bombay, 1956).

Committee on Plan Projects, *Report on Minor Irrigation Works in Madras State* (Madras, 1959).

(c) Government of Burma

Report of the Land and Agriculture Committee (Rangoon, 1938).

(d) Government of Madras

i. Selections from the Records

Mr Hyde's Report on the Introduction of a Ryotwari Settlement into the South Arcot Collectorate and the Correspondence relating thereto (Cuddalore, 1904).

Report of Commissioner Mr Dent on the Disturbances in the South Arcot District in 1841 and the Government Order thereon (Cuddalore, 1868).

LIII. *Papers relating to the General Revenue Survey of the Madras Presidency* (Madras, 1858).

LXXIV. *Papers relating to the General Revenue Survey of the Madras Presidency* (Madras, 1863).

Collection of papers relating to the Settlement of Tinnevelly by Mr Puckle, 1872-9 (Madras, n.d.).

Proposals for a new settlement of the Land Revenue in Five Taluks of Coimbatore, by H.F. Clogstoun (1875) (Madras, n.d.).

LXV. *Papers relating to the Survey and Settlement of the Salem District* (Madras, 1879).

N.S. XI. *A Collection of Papers relating to the Value of Land in the Early Years of the Nineteenth Century* (Madras, 1916).

Papers relating to Zamindaries, Mittahs etc. in Tinnevelly District (Madras, 1934).

N.S. I. *A Collection of Papers relating to the Inam Settlement in the Madras Presidency* (Madras, 1948).

ii. Reports etc.

Report of the Commissioners for the Investigation of Alleged Cases of Torture in the Madras Presidency (Madras, 1855).

Memorandum on Mirasi Tenure by W. H. Bayley (Madras, 1856).

Correspondence relating to the Revision Proposed in the Village Revenue Establishments of the Madras Presidency. Part I (Madras, 1867).

List of Fairs and Festivals occurring within the limits of the Madras Presidency by J. L. Ranking (Madras, 1868).

Report on the Revision of the Revenue Establishments in the Madras Presidency by J. H. Garstin (Madras, 1883).

A Manual of Madras Administration by C. D. McLean (Madras, 1885).

Report of the Agricultural Committee (Madras, 1889).

A Statistical Atlas of the Madras Presidency (Madras, 1895; other issues in 1906, 1913, 1924, 1936, 1949, 1963).

Report regarding the Possibilities of introducing Land and Agricultural Banks into the Madras Presidency by F. A. Nicholson (Madras, 1895-7).

Report on the Famine in the Madras Presidency during 1896 and 1897 (Madras, 1898).

Statement of the Police Committee on the Administration of the District Police in the Madras Presidency (Madras, 1902).

Revised Form of Village Accounts (Madras, 1910).

Village Officers' Manual (Madras, 1913).

The Madras Court of Wards Manual (Madras, 1913).

Report of the Forest Committee (Madras) (Madras, 1913).

Report of the Madras Survey and Land Records Committee (Madras, 1915).

Handbook of Commercial Information, Madras by M. E. Couchman (Madras, 1916).

Madras Criminal Tribes Manual (Madras, 1924).

A Notebook of Agricultural Facts and Figures compiled by R. C. Wood (Madras, 1928).

Report on the Survey of Cottage Industries in the Madras Presidency by D. Narayana Rao (Madras, 1929).

Madras Provincial Banking Enquiry Committee. Volume I, Report; Volumes II, III, Written evidence; Volumes IV, V, VI, Oral evidence (Madras, 1930).

Revised Form of Village Accounts (Madras, 1930).

The Civil Disobedience Movement 1930-1 (n.p., n.d.).

Village Officers' and Ryots' Manual (Madras, 1931).

Report of the Rice Production and Trade in the Madras Presidency by C. R. Srinivasan (Madras, 1934).

Scheme of Road Development for the Madras Presidency by A. Vipan (Madras, 1935).

Report on Agricultural Indebtedness by W. R. S. Sathyanathan (Madras, 1935).

Report of the Madras Estates Land Act Committee. Part I (Main Report); Part II (Area studies); Appendices to the Report; Reprints of documents; Memoranda submitted to the committee, Part I (Landholders), Part II (Tenants), Part III (Other); Part III (Price levels and graphs); Oral Evidence Parts I–IV; Irrigation Reports from Zamindars; Report from Collectors; Landholders Statements, Parts I–IV. (Madras, 1938).

Madras Labour, July 1937—October 1938 (Madras, 1938).

A Note on the Economic Resources of the Province of Madras and Possibilities of their Development by L.B. Green (Madras, 1939).

Report of the Economist for Enquiry into Rural Indebtedness, 1946 by B.V. Narayanaswamy Naidu (Madras, 1946).

Award of Industrial Tribunal on the Conditions of Labour in the Textile Industry in the Madras Presidency, chairman M. Venkataramaiya (Madras, 1947).

Five-year Plan for Food Production in Madras Province, 1947/8–1951/2: schemes relating to the Agriculture Department (Madras, 1947).

Report of the Court of Enquiry into Labour Conditions in the Handloom Industry by B.V. Narayanaswamy Naidu (Madras, 1948).

A Survey of Procurement and Rationing of Food in the Madras State compiled by I.R. Jones (Pudukottai, 1951).

Report of the Special Officer on Land Tenures in the Ryotwari Areas of the Madras Province by N. Raghavendra Rao (Madras, 1951).

Report of the Committee on Agricultural Production (chairman, M. Bhaktavatsalam) (Madras, 1959).

iii. Manuals and Gazetteers

Cox, A. F., *A Manual of the North Arcot District in the Presidency of Madras* (Madras, 1881).

Crole, C. S., *A Chingleput District Manual* (Madras, 1879).

Francis, W., *Madura District Gazetteer*, I (Madras, 1906).

Francis, W., *Gazetteer of the South Arcot District* (Madras, 1906).

Garstin, J. H., *Manual of the South Arcot District* (Madras, 1878).

Le Fanu, H., *A Manual of the Salem District in the Presidency of Madras* (Madras, 1883).

Moore, L., *A Manual of the Trichinopoly District in the Presidency of Madras* (Madras, 1887).

Nelson, J. H., *The Madura Country: a manual* (Madras, 1868).

Nicholson, F. A., *Manual of the Coimbatore District in the Presidency of Madras* (Madras, 1887).

Pate, H. R., *Tinnevelly District Gazetteer*, I (Madras, 1917).

Stuart, H. A., *Coimbatore District Manual* (Madras, 1898).

Venkasami Row, T., *A Manual of the District of Tanjore in the Madras Presidency* (Madras, 1883).

(e) Census of India

Census of India 1881. Madras. (Madras, 1882-3).
Census of India 1891. Volumes XIII to XV. (Madras, 1893).
Census of India 1901. Volumes XIV to XVI. (Madras, 1902).
Census of India 1911. Volume XII. (Madras, 1912).
Census of India 1921. Volume XIII. (Madras, 1922).
Census of India 1931. Volume XIV. (Madras, 1932).
Census of India 1941. Volume II. (Delhi, 1942).
Census of India 1951. Volume III. (Madras, 1953).
Census of India 1961. Volume IX. (Madras, 1965).

3 GOVERNMENT ANNUALS

Report on the Administration of the Akbari Department of the Madras Presidency.
Agricultural Statistics of British India.
Administration Report of the Agriculture Department of the Madras Presidency.
Banking and Monetary Statistics of India.
Statistical Tables relating to Banks in India.
Annual Report on the Working of the Madras Co-operative Credit Societies Act.
Report on the Working of the Estates Land Act in the Madras Presidency.
Report on the Administration of the Estates under the Court of Wards in the Madras Presidency.
Report on the Working of the Factories Act in the Madras Presidency.
Report on the Working of the Forest Department in the Madras Presidency.
All-India Income Tax Report.
Report on the Administration of the Income Tax in the Madras Presidency.
Report on the Working of the Department of Industry in the Madras Presidency.
Accounts relating to the Inland (Rail and River Borne) Trade of India.
Joint-stock Companies in British India and in the Indian States of Mysore etc.
Report on the Administration of Civil Justice in the Presidency of Madras.
Report on the Settlement of the Land Revenue in the Madras Presidency.
Report on the Administration of the Police Department in the Madras Presidency.
Report on Public Instruction in the Madras Presidency.
Report on the Administration of the Public Works Department in the Madras Presidency.
Report on the Administration of the Registration Department of the Madras Presidency.
Annual Statement of the Sea-Borne Trade of British India.
Annual Statement of the Sea-Borne Trade of the Madras Presidency.
Season and Crop Report of the Madras Presidency.
Review of the Sugar Industry of India.
Trade Statistics of the United Kingdom.
The Villagers' Calendar.

4 PRIVATE PAPERS

(a) Kept in the library of the Nehru Memorial Museum, New Delhi
C. Ramalinga Reddy
P. Shanmugham Chetty
T. R. Venkatarama Sastri

(b) Kept in the archive of the Centre of South Asian Studies, Cambridge
W. W. Georgeson
J. T. and J. P. L. Gwynn
T. I. S Mackay
C. Masterman
R. Tottenham
S. Wadsworth

(c) Kept in the National Archives of India, New Delhi
P. S. Sivaswami Aiyer

5 BOOKS, ARTICLES AND DISSERTATIONS

Adas, M., 'Immigrant Asians and the economic impact of European imperialism: the role of the South Indian Chettiars in British Burma', *JAS*, XXXIII, 3 (1974).

——, *The Burma Delta: economic development and social change on an Asian rice frontier, 1852-1941* (Madison, 1974).

Adicéam, E., *La Géographie de l'irrigation dans le Tamilnad* (Paris, 1966).

Agricultural Economics Research Centre, University of Madras, village surveys series: no. 30, Kaliyanapuram (1956–7); no. 40, Rajagambiran (1957–8); no. 42, Sengipatti (1956–7); no. 47, Upattur (1958); no. 48, Vadamalaipuram (1958–9); no. 49, Arilikottai (1958); no. 58, Keeranathan (1964).

'Agricultural Development in Tamilnadu', mimeo (Madras, 1976).

Measures of Food Control, Procurement and Controlled Distribution of Food and their Effects on the Agrarian Economy (Madras, n.d.).

Alavi, H., 'Peasant classes and primordial loyalties', *Journal of Peasant Studies*, I, 1 (1973).

Anandan, M., 'Rice crop in the Tanjore delta', *MAJ*, XXVII, 7 (1939).

Andrus, J. R., *Burmese Economic Life* (Oxford, 1947).

Appadorai, A., 'The committee system of village administration in Cola time—an interpretation' in *Dr S. Krishnaswami Aiyangar Commemoration Volume* (Madras, 1936).

Appadurai, A., 'Right and left hand castes in South India', *IESHR*, XI, 2-3 (1974).

Appadurai, A., 'Kings, sects, and temples in South India 1300-1700 A.D.', *IESHR*, XIV, 1 (1977).

Arasaratnam, S., *Indians in Malaysia and Singapore* (Oxford, 1970).

——, 'Indian commercial groups and European traders 1600–1800: changing relationships in southeastern India', *South Asia* (new series) I, 2 (1978).

Arbuthnot, A.J., *Sir Thomas Munro: selections from his minutes and other official notes* (London, 1881).

Arnold, D., 'Labour relations in a south Indian sugar factory 1937–9', *Social Scientist*, VI, 5 (1977).

——, 'Dacoity and rural crime in Madras, 1860–1940', *Journal of Peasant Studies*, VI (1978–9).

——, 'Looting, grain riots and government policy in south India 1918', *Past and Present*, 84 (1979).

Arokiaswami, M., 'Adigaman of Tagadur: his origin', *JIH*, XXXII (1954).

——, 'The origin of the Vellalas', *JIH*, XXXIII (1955).

——, *The Kongu Country* (Madras, 1956).

——, 'The Mudaliars of Taramangalam', *Quarterly Journal of the Mythic Society*, XLVII (1956–7).

——, 'Democratic experiments in ancient south India', *JIH*, XXXV (1957).

Arrowsmith, A., *Atlas of South India from Cape Comorin to the River Kistnah* (Madras, 1822).

Arunachalam, P., 'Vetci: or the first stage of war during the Sangam period', *Proceedings of the Second International Conference Seminar of Tamil Studies* ed. R. E. Asher (Madras, 1971), II.

Aykroyd, W. R., *The Conquest of Famine* (London, 1974).

Bagchi, A. K., *Private Investment in India 1900-1939* (Cambridge, 1972).

Baker, C. J., 'Tamilnad estates in the twentieth century', *IESHR*, XIII, 1 (1975).

——, 'Madras headmen', *Economy and Society: essays in Indian economic and social history* ed. K. N. Chaudhuri and C. J. Dewey (Delhi, 1979).

——, 'Economic reorganization and the slump in south and southeast Asia', *Comparative Studies in Society and History*, 23, 3 (July 1981).

Balasubramaniyam, 'The problem of Tinnies cotton and its solution', *Indian Cotton Growing Review*, V, 4 (1951).

Baldaeus, P., *A True Description of the East-Indian Coasts of Malabar and Coromandel as also of the Isle of Ceylon* incorporated in *A Collection of Voyages and Travels* comp. A. Churchill (London, 1704), III.

Baliga, B. S., *Compendium on History of Handloom Industry in Madras* (Madras, 1960).

——, *Studies in Madras Administration* (2 vols., Madras, 1960).

Banaji J., 'Chayanov, Kautsky, Lenin: considerations towards a synthesis', *Economic and Political Weekly* 2 Oct. 1976.

——, 'Summary of selected parts of Kautsky's "The Agrarian Question" ', *Economy and Society*, V, 1 (1976).

——, 'Capitalist domination and the small peasantry: Deccan districts in the late nineteenth century', *Economic and Political Weekly*, special number, August 1977.

Bastampillai, B., 'The Indian Tamil immigrant labourer and constitutional reform in Ceylon: a brief survey', *Proceedings of the Second International Conference Seminar of Tamil Studies* ed. R. E. Asher (Madras, 1971), II.

Bayley, W. H., and Hudleston, W., *Papers on Mirasi Right* (Madras, 1892).

Beaglehole, T. H., *Thomas Munro and the Development of Administrative Policy in Madras 1792–1818: the origins of the Munro System* (Cambridge, 1966).

Beck, B. E. F., *Peasant Society in Konku: a study of right and left subcastes in South India* (Vancouver, 1972).

Berna, J. J., *Industrial Entrepreneurship in Madras State* (New York, 1960).

Bernstein, H., 'African peasantries: a theoretical framework', *Journal of Peasant Studies*, VI, 4 (1979).

Beteille, A., *Caste, Class, and Power: changing patterns of stratification in a Tanjore village* (Berkeley and Los Angeles, 1965).

Bhaduri, A., 'A study of agricultural backwardness under semi-feudalism', *Economic Journal*, March 1973.

——, 'The evolution of land relations in eastern India under British rule', *IESHR*, XIII, 1 (1976).

Bhogendranath, N. C., *Development of the Textile Industry in Madras (up to 1950)* (Madras, 1957).

The House of Binny (Madras, 1969).

Blackburn, S. H., 'The Kallars: a Tamil "Criminal Tribe" reconsidered', *South Asia*, (new series) I, 1 (1978).

Blagden, C.O., *The Mackenzie Collection* (London, 1916).

Blyn, G., *Agricultural Trends in India, 1891–1947: output, availability, and productivity* (Philadelphia, 1966).

Bokhari, S. A. R., 'Carnatic under the Nawabs as revealed through "Sayeed Nama" of Juswant Rai', M. Litt. thesis, Madras University, 1965.

Boserup, E., *The Conditions of Agricultural Growth* (London, 1965).

Brown, Hilton, *Parry's of Madras: a story of British enterprise in India* (Madras, 1954).

Buchanan, F., *A Journey from Madras through the Countries of Mysore, Canara and Malabar* (London, 1807).

Byres, T., 'Land reform, industrialization and the marketed surplus in India: an essay on the power of rural bias', *Agrarian Reform and Agrarian Reformism: studies of Peru, Chile, China and India* ed. D.Lehmann (London, 1974).

Caldwell, R., *The Tinnevelly Shanars: a sketch of their religion and their social condition and characteristics, as a caste* (Madras, 1949).

——, *A Political and General History of the Tinnevelly District of the Presidency of Madras from the earliest period to its cession to the English Government in A.D. 1801* (Madras, 1881).

The Travels of the Abbé Carré in India and the Near East 1672 to 1674 trans. Lady Fawcett, ed. Sir Charles Fawcett, Volume II (London, 1947).

Cassen, R. H., *India: Population, Economy, Society* (New York, 1978).

Chakravarti, N. R., *The Indian Minority in Burma: the rise and decline of an immigrant community* (Oxford, 1971).

Chandrasekharan, K. S., 'The physical geography of the Tanjore district', *JMGA*, XII, 2 (1937).

Chatterton, A., 'The weaving competitions in Madras', *Indian Textile Journal*, IX.

Chaudhuri, B. B., 'Growth of commercial agriculture and its impact on the peasant economy', *IESHR*, VII, 1 and 2 (1970).

Chayanov, A.V., *The Theory of Peasant Economy* ed. by D. Thorner, R. E. F. Smith, and B. Kerblay (Irwin, 1961).

Cheng Siok Hwa, 'Indian labour in the rice industry of pre-war Burma', *Proceedings of the Second International Conference Seminar of Tamil Studies*, ed. R. E. Asher (Madras, 1971), II.

Couteur, J., *Letters chiefly from India containing an Account of the Military Transactions* (London, 1790).

Cronin, V., *A Pearl to India: the life of Roberto de Nobili* (London, 1858).

Dalal and Co., *Textile Industry of South India* (fifth issue, Madras, 1954).

Das Gupta, A., *Malabar in Asian Trade, 1740–1800* (Cambridge, 1967).

Davis, K., *The Population of India and Pakistan* (Princeton, 1951).

Derrett, J. D. M., *The Hoysalas: a medieval Indian royal family* (Oxford, 1957).

Desai, B. A., and Thingalaya, N. K., 'Irrigation factor and yield variability in rice-growing districts in India', *Indian Journal of Agricultural Economics*, XX, 3.

Dirks, N. B., 'Political authority and structural change in early south Indian history', *IESHR*, XIII, 1 (1976).

——, 'The structure and meaning of political relations in a south Indian little kingdom', Humanities Working Paper 14, California Institute of Technology, 1978.

Djurfeldt, G., and Lindberg, S., *Behind Poverty: the social formation in a Tamil village* (London, 1975).

Dubois, J. A., *Hindu Manners, Customs and Ceremonies* trans. and ed. H. K. Beauchamp (Oxford, 2nd ed., 1899).

Dumont, L., *Une Sous-Caste de l'Inde du Sud: organisation sociale et religion des Pramalai Kallar* (Paris and The Hague, 1957).

——, 'Distribution of some Maravar sub-castes', *Anthropology on the March* ed. L. K. Balaratnam (Madras, 1963).

Dupuis, J., *Madras et le Nord du Coromandel: étude des conditions de la vie Indienne dans un cadre géographique* (Paris, 1960).

Duraisami, S.V., 'Low prices and the plight of the lowly ryots', *MAJ*, XXII, 14 (1934).

——, 'Marketing of cultivators' cotton at Tirupur, Madras Presidency', *MAJ*, XXIV, 2 (1936).

Dutt, R. C., *The Economic History of India* (reprint: Delhi, 1976).

Dykes, J. W. B., *Salem, an Indian Collectorate* (London, 1853).

Epstein, T. S., 'Productive efficiency and customary systems of rewards in rural south India', *Themes in Economic Anthropology* ed. R. Firth (London, 1967).

Farmer, B. H., *Agricultural Colonisation in India since Independence* (London, 1974).

——, (ed.), *Green Revolution? Technology and change in rice-growing areas of Tamil Nadu and Sri Lanka* (London, 1977).

Firminger, W. K., *The Fifth Report from the Select Committee of the House of Commons on the Affairs of the East India Company. Volume I,*

Introduction and Text of the Report (Calcutta, 1917).

Foster-Carter, A., 'The modes of production controversy', *New Left Review*, 107 (1978).

Foulkes, G. F. F., *Local Autonomy* (2 vols., Madras, 1937-8).

Frank, A. G., *Capitalism and Underdevelopment in Latin America* (New York and London, 1967).

——, *Latin America: underdevelopment and revolution* (New York and London, 1969).

Frykenberg, R. E., ' "Company Circari" in the Carnatic, *c.* 1779–1859: the inner logic of political systems in India', *Realm and Region in Traditional India* ed. R. G. Fox (Delhi, 1977).

Fullarton, W., *Narrative of Military Transactions* (London, 1784).

Gandhi, M. P. (ed.), *Indian Cotton Textile Industry Centenary Volume 1851–1950* (Bombay, 1951).

Ganesamurti, N., 'Economic survey of a south Indian village—Perumanallur', *MAJ*, XXIII, 7 (1935).

Geertz, C., *Agricultural Involution: the process of ecological change in Indonesia* (Berkeley, Los Angeles and London, 1974).

Geoghegan, J., *Note on Emigration from India* (Calcutta, 1873).

Gleig, G. R., *Life and Correspondence of Major-General Sir Thomas Munro* (London, 1830).

Glick, C. E., 'The changing position of two Tamil groups in western Malaya', *Proceedings of the Second International Conference Seminar of Tamil Studies* ed. R. E. Asher (Madras, 1971), II.

Gopal, M. H., *Tipu Sultan's Mysore: an economic study* (Bombay, 1971).

Gopalakrishnan, K. S., 'Evolution of settlements in Cauvery delta', *Indian Geographical Journal*, XLVIII, 2 (1973).

Gopalan, K. S., 'A note on the agricultural geography of the environs of Tanjore', *JMGA*, XII, 2 (1937).

Gopalratnam, P., 'Rural studies: Madathupalaiyam village, Coimbatore district', *MAJ* XIX, 12 (1931).

Gorwala, A. D., *The Role of the Administrator, Past, Present and Future* (Poona, 1952).

Gough, E. K., 'Brahman kinship in a Tanjore village', *American Anthropologist*, LVIII (1956).

——, 'Caste in a Tanjore village', *Aspects of Caste in South India, Ceylon and Northeast Pakistan* (Cambridge, 1960).

Govinda Row, B., 'Some aspects of economic controls in India during the war', *IJE*, XXIV (1943-4).

Gowda, M. S. L., *Indian Economic Census: economic planning, special volume* (Madras, 1936).

Griffiths, P., *A History of the Inchcape Group* (London, 1977).

Grist, D. H., *Rice* (London, 5th ed., 1975).

Gurney, J. D., 'The debts of the Nawab of Arcot 1763–1776', D.Phil. thesis, Oxford University, 1968.

Hall, K. R., 'Price making and market hierarchy in early medieval south India', *IESHR*, XIV, 2 (1975).

Hanumantha Rao, C. H., *Agricultural Production Functions, Costs and*

Returns in India (London, 1965).

Hardgrave, R. L., *The Nadars of Tamilnad: the political culture of a community in change* (Berkeley and Los Angeles, 1969).

Harkness, H., 'Account of the Province of Ramnad, southern peninsula of India. Compiled from the "Mackenzie Collection", and edited by the Secretary of the Royal Asiatic Society', *Journal of the Royal Asiatic Society*, III (1836).

Harriss, J., 'The mode of production controversy: themes and problems of the debate', Madras Institute of Development Studies Working Paper No. 6.

——, *Capitalism and Peasant Farming: a study of agricultural change and agrarian structure in northern Tamil Nadu* (University of East Anglia monographs in development studies no. 3, 1979).

Hasan, M., *History of Tipu Sultan* (Calcutta, 2nd ed., 1971).

Haswell, M. R., *Economics of Development in Village India* (London, 1967).

Hjejle, B., 'Slavery and agricultural bondage in the nineteenth century', *Scandinavian Economic History Review*, XV, 1 and 2 (1967).

Hoole, E., *Madras, Mysore and the South of India or a personal narrative of a mission to these countries from 1820 to 1828* (London, 2nd ed., 1844).

Hudson, D., 'Siva, Minakshi, Visnu—reflections on a popular myth in Madurai', *IESHR*, XIV, 1 (1977).

Hurd III, J., and Young, K. C., 'The supply and demand for railroad services in India 1882–1939', *Papers presented to the 5th European Conference on Modern South Asian Studies* (mimeo, Leiden, 1976).

Hussein, Syed Sha Ali, *Co-operative Land Mortgage Banks in Madras* (Madras, n.d.).

Ingram, J. C., *Economic change in Thailand 1850–1970* (Stanford, 1971).

Irschick, E. F., *Politics and Social Conflict in South India: the non-Brahman movement and Tamil separatism 1916–29* (Berkeley and Los Angeles, 1969).

Ito, Shoji, 'A note on the "business combine" in India—with special reference to the Nattukottai Chettiars', *The Developing Economies*, II, 3 (1966).

Jain, R.K., *South Indians on the Plantation Frontier in Malaya* (New Haven and London, 1970).

Jayaraman, R., 'Indian emigration to Ceylon: some aspects of the historical and social background of the emigrants', *IESHR*, IV, 4 (1967).

Kadhirvel, S., *A History of the Maravas* (Madurai, 1977).

Kailasapathy, K., *Tamil Heroic Poetry* (Oxford, 1968).

Kanakasabhai, V., *The Tamils Eighteen Hundred Years Ago* (Tirunelveli, 2nd ed., 1956).

Kannayya, A., 'The cultivation of Cambodia cotton in the central districts', *MAJ*, XXVII, 8 (1939).

Karashima, Noboru, 'Nayaks as leaseholders of temple lands', *Journal of the Economic and Social History of the Orient*, XIX (1976).

Kaufmann, S. B., 'Popular Christianity, caste and Hindu society in south India 1800–1915: a study of Travancore and Tirunelveli', Ph.D. thesis,

Cambridge University, 1980.

Kautsky, K., *Die Agrarfrage* (Stuttgart, 1899).

Kessinger, T. G., *Vilyatpur 1848–1968: social and economic change in a north Indian village* (Berkeley, Los Angeles and London, 1974).

Kindleberger, C. P., *The World in Depression 1929–39* (Stanford, 1973).

Knight, H., *Food Administration in India 1939–47* (Stanford, 1954).

Kondapi, C., *Indians Overseas 1838–1949* (Delhi, 1951).

Krishna Ayyar, P. V., 'Co-operation in agriculture with special reference to sugarcane crop in Coimbatore district', *MAJ*, XXVIII, 2 (1940).

Krishnamurthi, R., 'India through slump and recovery, 1929–37: being a study of the trade cycle in relation to India', M.Litt thesis, Madras University, 1940.

Krishnamurthi, Iyer, M., 'Irrigation in Trichinopoly', *JMGA*, VII, 3 (1933–4).

Krishnamurti, E.R. (ed.), *Madras Stock Exchange Silver Jubilee Souvenir 1937–62* (Madras, 1962).

Krishnan, V., 'Fairs, festivals and shandies in Trichinopoly district', *JMGA*, VII, 3 (1933–4).

——, 'Trade centres of Tinnevelly district', *JMGA* XV, 3 (1940).

——, *Indigenous Banking in South India* (Bombay, 1959).

Krishnan, V. S., 'The Tambraparni ryot: a study of the rural economy of the Tinnevelly district', Gokhale prize essay, Madras University, 1931.

Krishnaswami, A., *The Tamil Country under Vijayanagar* (Annamalainagar, 1964).

Krishnaswami, S. Y., *Rural Problems in Madras: monograph* (Madras, 1947).

——, 'Major irrigation works of ancient Tamilnad', *Proceedings of the First International Conference Seminar of Tamil Studies* (Kuala Lumpur, 1966), I.

Krishnaswami, T. B., *In Old Salem* (Madras, 1933).

Kirshnaswami Aiyangar, S., *South India and her Muhammedan Invaders* (Madras, 1921).

Kumar, D., *Land and Caste in South India: agricultural labour in the Madras Presidency during the nineteenth century* (Cambridge, 1965).

——, 'Landownership and inequality in Madras Presidency, 1853–54 to 1946–47', *IESHR*, XII, 3 (1975).

Kuttilingam Pillai, I.S. , 'A plea for a protective duty on rice', *MAJ*, XXVII, 5 (1940–1).

Laclau, E., 'Feudalism and capitalism in Latin America', *New Left Review*, 67 (1971).

Lanessan, J. L. de, *L'Indo-Chine Francaise* (Paris, 1889).

League of Nations, *World Production and Prices, 1925–34* (Geneva, 1935).

——, *World Production and Prices, 1937–8* (Geneva, 1938).

——, *Industrialization and Foreign Trade* (Geneva, 1945).

Lee, C. H., 'The effects of the depression on the primary-producing countries', *Journal of Contemporary History*, IV (1969).

Lenin, V. I., *The Development of Capitalism in Russia* (Moscow, 1956).

Lewis, W. A., *Economic Survey, 1919–1939* (London, 1949).

——, *Aspects of Tropical Trade 1883–1965* (Stockholm, 1969).

Little, K. W., 'Alambady cattle', *JMGA*, XI, 2 (1936).

Ludden, D., 'Agrarian organization in Tinnevelly district: 800–1900 A.D.', Ph.D. thesis, University of Pennsylvania, 1978.

——, 'Ecological zones and the cultural economy of irrigation in Tamilnadu', *South Asia* (new series) I, 1 (1978).

McAlpin, M., 'Railroads, prices and peasant rationality: India, 1860–1920', *Journal of Economic History*, XXXIV, 3 (1974).

McEvedy, C., and Jones, R., *Atlas of World Population History* (Harmondsworth, 1978).

Mackenzie, A.T., *History of the Periyar Project* (Madras, 1899).

Mahadevan, R., 'The development of modern entrepreneurship in the Chettiar community of Tamilnadu, 1900–1930', *Indian History Congress*, proceedings of the 34th session (Chandigarh, 1973).

Mahalingam, T.V., 'The Pasupatas in south India', *JIH*, XXVII (1949).

——, 'The Banas in south Indian history', *JIH*, XXIX (1951).

——, *South Indian Polity* (Madras, 2nd ed., 1967).

——, *Kancipuram in Early South Indian History* (Madras, 1969).

——, *Administration and Social Life under Vijayanagar: Part II, Social Life* (Madras, 2nd ed., 1975).

Maizels, A., *Industrial Growth and World Trade* (Cambridge, 1963).

Maloney, C., 'Archaeology in south India: accomplishments and prospects', *Essays on South India*, ed. B. Stein (Hawaii, 1975).

Mansergh, N. (ed.), *The Transfer of Power 1942–7: Volume III* (London, 1971); *Volume IV* (London, 1972).

Maraimalai Adigal, *Velalar Nakarikam* [Tamil–Vellala civilization] (Madras, 1927).

Marx, K., *Capital* volume I (London, 1974); volume III (London, 1969).

——, *Grundrisse* trans. M. Nicolaus (London, 1973).

Matthen, C. P., *I Have Borne Much* (Madras, 1931).

Mencher, J. P., *Agriculture and Social Structure in Tamilnadu: past origins, present transformations, future prospects* (Durham, 1978).

Menon, Saraswathi, 'Historical development of Thanjavur kisan movement: interplay of class and caste factors', *Economic and Political Weekly*, annual number, Feb. 1979.

Meyer, E., 'Impact de la dépression des années 1930 sur l'économie et la société rurale de Sri Lanka', *Purusartha* (Paris, 1975).

Minakshi, C., *Administration and Social Life under the Pallavas* (Madras, 1938).

Mudaliar, C.Y., *The Secular State and Religious Institutions in India: a study of the administration of Hindu public religious trusts in Madras* (Wiesbaden, 1974).

Mukherjee, N., *The Ryotwari System in Madras* (Calcutta, 1962).

——, and Frykenberg, R.E., 'The ryotwari system and social organization in the Madras Presidency', *Land Control and Social Structure in Indian History*, ed. Frykenberg (Madison, 1969).

Mukerji, K., *Levels of Economic Activity and Public Expenditure in India* (London, 1962).

Murton, B.J., 'Key people in the countryside: decision makers in interior Tamilnadu in the late eighteenth century', *IESHR*, X, 2 (1973).

——, 'Some propositions on the spread of village settlement in interior Tamil Nadu before 1750 A.D., *Indian Geographical Journal*, XXXVIII, 2 (1973).

Myers, R. H., *The Chinese Peasant Economy: agricultural development in Hopei and Shantung, 1890–1949* (Harvard, 1970).

Nadarajan, M., 'The Nattukottai Chettiar community and south-east Asia', *Proceedings of the First International Conference Seminar of Tamil Studies* (Kuala Lumpur, 1968), I.

Nagaswamy, R., 'South Indian temple—as an employer', *IESHR*, II, 4 (1965).

——, 'Hero stones of Tamilnadu', *Indian Historical Review*, LI (1973).

Nanjudan, S., *Indians in Malayan Economy* (Delhi, 1950).

Narain, D., *Impact of Price Movements on Areas under Selected Crops in India 1900–1939* (Cambridge, 1965).

Narasimhan, V.S., 'Agricultural labour in the southern taluks of Coimbatore district', M.Litt. thesis, Madras University 1959.

Narayanaswamy Naidu, B.V., *Groundnut* (Annamalainagar, n.d.).

——, *The Co-operative Movement in the Madras Presidency* (Annamalainagar, 1933).

——, 'Nidhis or loan societies of Madras', *IJE*, XVIII (1937–8).

——, and Hariharan, S., *Groundnut: marketing and other allied problems* (Annamalainagar, 1941).

——, and Thiruvengadathan, S., *The Madras General Sales Tax Act: a study* (Annamalainagar, 1940).

——, and Vaidyanathan, P., *The Madras Agriculturists' Relief Act—a study* (Annamalainagar, 1939).

——, and Venkataraman, V., *The Problem of Rural Indebtedness* (Annamalainagar, 1935).

Natarajan, B., *Food and Agriculture in Madras State* (Madras, 1953).

Natarajan, K. A., 'Industrial economics: industrial development of Madras (Tamil Nadu) with special reference to institutional infrastructure', M.Litt. thesis, Madras university, 1973.

Natarajan, M. S., 'A study of the capital market of Madras Presidency with special reference to its evolution and indigenous institutions', Ph.D. thesis, Madras University, 1934.

——, *The Capital Market of the Madras Presidency with special reference to its evolution and indigenous institutions* (Calcutta, 1936).

Nelson, J. H., *A View of the Hindu Law as administered by the High Court of Judicature at Madras* (London, 1877).

——, *A Prospectus of the Scientific Study of the Hindu Law* (London, 1881).

——, *Indian Usage and Judge-made Law in Madras* (London, 1887).

Nilakanta Sastri, K. A., *The Pandyan Kingdom from the earliest times to the sixteenth century* (London, 1929).

——, *The Colas* (Madras, 2nd ed., 1955).

——, and Venkataramanayya, N., *Further Sources of Vijayanagar History: volume I* (Madras, 1946).

Norton, J. B., *The Administration of Justice in Southern India* (Madras, 1853).

Nye, P. H., and Greenland, D. J., *The Soil under Shifting Cultivation* (Farnham Royal, 1960).

The Life of the Icelander Jon Olaffson: volume II, Travels 1618–1679 (London, 1931).

Oxaal, I., Barnett, T., and Booth, D. (eds.), *Beyond the Sociology of Development: economy and society in Latin America and Africa* (London, 1975).

Pandian, T. B., *The Slaves of the Soil in Southern India* (Madras, 1893).

Patnaik, U., 'Development of capitalism in agriculture', *Social Scientist*, I (1972).

——, 'Neo-populism and Marxism: the Chayanovian view of the agrarian question and its fundamental fallacy', *Journal of Peasant Studies*, VI, 4 (1979).

Paul, M.S., 'The commercial geography of Udayarpalaiyam taluk', *JMGA*, VII, 3 (1932).

Pearse, A. S., *The Cotton Industry of India* (Manchester, 1930).

Phillips, J. T., *An Account of the Religion, Manners and Learning of Malabar in the East Indies in several letters written by some of the most learned men of that country to the Danish missionaries* (London, 1717).

Pillay, K.K., 'Aryan influence in Tamilaham during the Sangam epoch', *Proceedings of the First International Conference Seminar of Tamil Studies* (Kuala Lumpur, 1966), I.

——, *A Social History of the Tamils* (2 vols., Madras, 2nd ed., 1975).

Playne, S., *Southern India; its history, peoples, commerce and industrial resources* (London, 1914–15).

Poduval, R. N., *Finance of the Government of India since 1935* (Delhi, 1951).

Ponniah, J. S., 'Underneath the cloth', *IJE*, XIII (1932–3).

——, 'The Broach of South India', *The Indian Commerce*, I, 3 (1933).

——, 'The kapas market at Dindigul: a study in the local factors that influence prices', *MAJ*, XXII, 11 (1934).

——, 'Cotton and cotton marketing in the Tinnevelly district', *JMGA*, XV, 2 (1940).

——, 'Production and marketing of raw cotton in the Madras Presidency,' D. Litt. thesis, Madras University, 1944.

Popkin, S. L., *The Rational Peasant: the political economy of rural society in Vietnam* (Berkeley, Los Angeles, and London, 1979).

Post, K. W. J., ' "Peasantization" and rural political movements in West Africa', *Archives Européenes de Sociologie*, XII, 1 (1972).

Prest, A. R., *War Economies of Primary Producting Countries* (Cambridge, 1948).

Price, P., 'The royal model and merchant aims in nineteenth-century south India' and ' "Contempt for my authority": Raja, temple and government in nineteenth-century Ramnad and Sivaganga', unpublished papers, 1977-8.

Radha Bai, C., 'An economic study of the cinematograph industry in the

Madras Presidency', M.Litt. thesis, Madras University, n.d.

Raghavan, V., *The Great Integrators: the saint-singers of India* (Delhi, 1966).

Rajah, M. C., *The Oppressed Hindus* (Madras, n.d.).

Rajamanickam, A. S., 'The crops of the Trichinopoly district', *JMGA*, VII, 3 (1933–4).

Rajayyan, K., *South Indian Rebellion: the first war of independence 1800–1801* (Mysore, 1971).

——, *Rise and Fall of the Poligars of Tamilnadu* (Madras, 1974).

Ramachandra Chettiar, C. M., 'The geographical limits of Kongu Nadu at various epochs', *JMGA*, V (1930).

——, 'The geographical distribution of crime and civil litigation in south India', *JMGA*, XII, 2 (1937).

Ramachandra Sastri, E., *History of the Criminal Tribes in the Madras Presidency* (Madras, 1929).

Ramachandran, C. E., 'Tamil society in the seventeenth century', Ph.D. thesis, Madras University, 1974.

Ramakrishnan, K. C., 'Finance and forced sale of produce', *MAJ*, XVIII, 3 (1920).

——, 'The agricultural geography of the Coimbatore district', *JMGA*, V, 2 (1930–1).

——, 'A model of intensive cultivation in the Cauvery valley', *JMGA*, VII, 3 (1933–4).

——, 'Debt legislation and rural credit in Madras', *IJE*, XIX (1938–9).

Ramakrishnan, K.T., 'Joint-stock banking in India', Ph.D. thesis, Madras University, 1949.

Ramamurthy, K., 'Some aspects of the regional geography of Tamilnad', M.Litt. thesis, Madras, 1945.

Ramaswamy Tatachar, D., *The Vanamamalai Temple and Mutt* (Tinnevelly, 1937).

Ranga, N. G., *Economic Organization of Indian Villages: Volume I, Deltaic Village* (Bezwada, 1926); *Volume II* (Bombay, 1929).

——, 'The cotton mill industry of the Madras Presidency', *IJE*, II (1930-1).

——, *Agricultural Indebtedness and Remedial Measures* (Tenali, 1931).

Rangacharya, V., 'The geographical data of the Sangam works', *JMGA*, III, 2 (1928).

Ranganathachari, N., 'Marketing of cotton in Coimbatore district', M.Sc. thesis, Madras University, 1958.

Rangaswami Saraswati, A., 'Political maxims of the Emperor-poet Krishnadeva Raya', *JIH*, IV (1925–6).

Ranson, C. W., *City in Transition* (Madras, 1938).

Rao, P. R. K., 'Rainfall of Madras State', *Memoirs of the Indian Meteorological Service*, XXX (1953).

Rau, C. H., 'The banking caste of southern India', *Indian Review*, VIII, 8 (1907).

Ray, P. K., *Indian's Foreign Trade since 1870* (London, 1934).

Ray, R. K., 'The crisis of Bengal agriculture 1870–1927—the dynamics of immobility', *IESHR*, X, 3 (1973).

——, and Ray, R., 'The dynamics of continuity in rural Bengal, a study of quasi-stable equilibrium in underdeveloped societies in a changing world', *IESHR*, X, 2 (1973).

Raychaudhuri, T., *Jan Company in Coromandel 1605–90* (Sgravenhage, 1962).

Reinhart, G., *Volkart Brothers: in commemoration of the seventy-fifth anniversary of the foundation* (Winterthur, 1926).

Rey, P.-P, *Les Alliances de classes* (Paris, 1973).

Richards, F. J., 'Cross-cousin marriage in south India', *Man*, XCVII, (1914).

Robequain, C., *The Economic Development of French Indochina* (London, 1944).

Roxborough, I., 'Dependency theory in the sociology of development: some theoretical problems', *West African Journal of Sociology and Political Science*, I, 2 (1976).

Rowe, J. W. F., *Primary Commodities in International Trade* (Cambridge, 1965).

Sandhu, K. S., *Indians in Malaya: some aspects of their immigration and settlement 1786–1957* (Cambridge, 1969).

Sankaranarayana, D., 'Industries and occupations of Tinnevelly district', *JMGA*, XV, 3 (1940).

Sarada Raju, A., *Economic Conditions in the Madras Presidency 1800–1850* (Madras, 1941).

Saraswathi, S., *The Madras Panchayats System: volume I, a historical survey* (Delhi, 1972).

Sarveswara Rao, B., *The Economic and Social Effects of Zamindari Abolition in Andhra* (Waltair, 1963).

Sathyanatha Aiyar, R., *History of the Nayaks of Madura* (Madras, 1924).

Sau, Ranjit, 'A theory of rent and agrarian relations', *Economic and Political Weekly*, review of agriculture, June 1979.

Sauliere, A., 'The revolt of the southern Nayaks', *JIH*, XLV (1966).

Sayana, V. V., *The Agrarian Problems of Madras Province* (Madras, 1949).

Schultz, T. W., *Transforming Traditional Agriculture* (Yale, 1964).

Scott, J. C., *The Moral Economy of the Peasant: rebellion and subsistence in southeast Asia* (Yale, 1976).

Sen, A. K., 'Starvation and exchange entitlements: a general approach and its application to the great Bengal famine', *Cambridge Journal of Economics*, I (1977).

Sen, Bhowani, *Evolution of Agrarian Relations in India* (Delhi, 1962).

Seshadri, P. S., 'South Indian village studies: a preparatory study of "Villur" village no. 119 in Tirumangalam taluk, Madura district, Madras province', *MAJ*, XXIII (1935).

Sewell, R., *A Forgotten Empire (Vijayanagar): a contribution to the history of India* (London, 1900).

Shiva Rao, B., *The Industrial Worker in India* (London, 1939).

Simha, S. L. N., *History of the Reserve Bank of India (1935–51)* (Bombay, 1970).

Sinha, N. C., and Khera, P. N., *Indian War Economy (supply, industry and finance)* (Calcutta, 1962).

Sivagnanam, Ma. Po, *Enathu Porattam* [Tamil—my life's struggle] (Madras, 1974).

Sivashanmugham Pillai, J., *Legislative Protection for the Cultivating Tenant and Labourer* (Madras, 1947).

Sivaswamy, K. G., *Farm Tenancy under Ryotwari Holdings in Madras: and principles of legislation* (n.p., 1941).

——, *Caste and Standard of Living versus Farms, Rents and Wages* (Madras, 1947).

Slater, G., *Some South Indian Villages* (Oxford, 1918).

——, *Southern India: its political and economic problems* (London, 1936).

Soundara Rajan, K. V., 'Determinant factors in the early history of Tamilnad', *JIH*, XLV (1967).

Sovani, N. V. (ed.), *Reports of the Commodity Prices Board* (Bombay, 1948).

——, *Economic Relations of India with South East Asia and the Far East* (Delhi, 1949).

Spate, O. H. K., Learmonth, A. T. A., and Farmer, B. H., *India, Pakistan and Ceylon* (London, 3rd ed., 1967).

Spencer, G. W., 'Religious networks and royal influence in eleventh century south India', *Journal of the Economic and Social History of the Orient*, XII, 1 (1969).

——, 'Royal initiative under Rajaraja I', *IESHR*, VII, 4 (1970).

——, 'The politics of plunder: the Cholas in eleventh-century Ceylon', *JAS*, XXV, 3 (1976).

Srinivas, M. N. (ed.), *India's Villages* (Bombay, 1955).

Srinivas, P. R. (ed.), *Indian Finance Yearbook 1935* (Calcutta, 1935).

Srinivasa Iyengar, C. R., 'Rice culture in the Madras Presidency', *MAJ*, XXXII, 11 and 12 (1944).

Srinivasa Iyengar, P. T., 'Geographical control of early Kongu history', *JMGA*, V (1930).

Srinivasa Raghavaiyangar, S., *Memorandum on the Progress of the Madras Presidency during the Last Forty Years of British Administration* (Madras, 1893).

Srinivasachari, C. S., *A History of the City of Madras* (Madras, 1939).

Sri Raman, P., 'Resuscitation of rural credit societies in Madras', *IJE*, XXII (1941–2).

Stein, B., 'The economic function of a medieval south Indian temple', *JAS*, XIX, 2 (1960).

——, 'Coromandel trade in medieval India', *Merchants and Scholars: essays in the history of exploration and trade* ed. J. Parker (Minneapolis, 1965).

——, 'Brahman and peasant in early south Indian history', *Adyar Library Bulletin*, XXXI–XXXII (1967–8).

——, 'Social mobility and medieval south Indian Hindu sects', *Social Mobility in the Caste System in India: an interdisciplinary symposium* ed. J. Silverberg (Paris, 1968).

——, 'Integration of the agrarian system of south India', *Land Control and Social Structure in Indian History* ed. R. E. Frykenberg (Madison, 1969).

——, 'The segmentary state in south Indian history', *Realm and Region in Traditional India* ed. R.G. Fox (Delhi, 1977).

——, 'Circulation and historical geography of Tamil country', *JAS*, XXXVII, 1 (1977).

——, 'Temples in Tamil country, 1300–1750 A.D.', *IESHR*, XIV, 1 (1977).

Stokes, E.T., *The Peasant and the Raj: studies in agrarian society and peasant rebellion in colonial India* (Cambridge, 1978).

Subbarayalu, Y., 'The political geography of the Chola country from A.D., 800 to 1300 as gleaned from epigraphy and literature', M.Litt. thesis, Madras University, 1969.

Subrahmanya Aiyer, K. V., *Historical Sketches of Ancient Dekhan* volume I (Madras, 1917); volume II (Coimbatore, 1967); volume III (Coimbatore, 1969).

Subrahmanyam, N., 'Communication-lines and town-sites of Coimbatore', *JMGA*, V, 3 (1930).

——, 'Seasonal control of rural life and activities in the Conjeeveram region', *JMGA*, XVII, 2 (1942).

Subrahmanyam, V., 'Some aspects of the chemistry of swamp soils', *Current Science*, V, 25 (1937).

Sundara Reddy, R.V., 'Sugar industry of Madras', *MAJ*, XXVII, 8 (1939).

Swaminathan, K. D., 'The horse-traders of Malaimandalam', *JIH*, XXXII (1954).

Tambiah, S. J., *World Conqueror and World Renouncer: a study of Buddhism and polity in Thailand against a historical background* (Cambridge, 1976).

Tavernier, J. B., *Travels in India* trans. V. Ball, ed. W. Croske (London, 1925).

Taylor, W., *A Catalogue Raisonnée of Oriental Manuscripts in the Government Library* (Madras, 1862).

Thani Nayagam, X. S., 'Tamil migration to Guadeloupe and Martinique 1855–83', *Proceedings of the Second International Conference Seminar of Tamil Studies* ed. R. E. Asher (Madras, 1971).

Thomas, P.J., *The Problem of Rural Indebtedness* (Madras, 1934).

——, *War-Time Prices* (Oxford, 1943).

——, *Some South Indian Villages: a re-survey* (Madras, 1940).

——, and Sundarama Sastry, N., *Commodity Prices in South India 1918–38* (Madras, 1940).

Thorner, D., 'Marx on India and the Asiatic mode of production', *Contributions to Indian Sociology*, IX (1966).

Thurston, E., *Castes and Tribes of Southern India* (7 vols, Madras, 1909).

Timoshenko, V. P., *World Agriculture and the Depression* (Michigan, 1933).

Tomlinson, B. R., *The Political Economy of the Raj 1914–1947: the economics of decolonization in India* (London, 1979).

Trench, V., *Lord Willingdon in India* (Bombay, 1934).

Triantis, S. G., *Cyclical Changes in Trade Balances of Countries Exporting Primary Products 1927–33* (Toronto, 1967).

Vaidyanatha Aiyar, A., *A Memorandum on the Ryotwari Landholders in Madras* (Madras, 1933).

Vasantha Devi, M. N., 'Some aspects of the agricultural geography of south India', M.Litt. thesis, Madras, 1963.

Venguswamy, V., *Congress in Office* (Bombay, 1940).

Venkata Raman, K. R., 'A note on the Kalabhras', *JIH*, XXXIV (1956).

Venkatarama Aiyar, K. R., 'Agricultural indebtedness', *MAJ*, XXIII (1935).

——, 'Medieval trade, craft and merchant guilds in south India', *JIH*, XXV (1947).

Venkataraman, K. S., *The Handloom Industry in South India* (Madras, 1940).

Venkataramana Iyengar, C. V., 'The mill industry in Coimbatore', *JMGA*, V (1930–1).

Venkatarangaiya, M., *The Freedom Struggle in Andhra Pradesh (Andhra)*, volume III (Hyderabad, 1965).

The Vijayanagar Empire as seen by Domingo Paes and Fernao Nuniz (Delhi, 1977).

Vridhagirisan, V., 'The Kadavarayars', *JIH*, XVI (1937).

Ward, B. S., *Geographical and Statistical Memoir of the Provinces of Madura and Dindigul* (Madura, 1895).

Washbrook, D. A., 'Country politics: Madras 1880 to 1930', *MAS*, VII, 3 (1973).

——, *The Emergence of Provincial Politics: the Madras Presidency 1870–1920* (Cambridge, 1976).

Wee, H. van der, *The Great Depression Revisited* (The Hague, 1972).

Wheeler, J. T., *Handbook to the Cotton Cultivation in the Madras Presidency* (Madras, 1862).

——, *Madras in Olden Times: being a history of the Presidency* (Madras, 1882).

Whitehead, H., *Village Gods of South India* (Calcutta, 1921).

Wickizer, V. D., and Bennett, M. K., *The Rice Economy of Monsoon Asia* (Stanford, 1941).

Wijetunga, W. M. K., 'South Indian corporate commercial organizations in south and southeast Asia', *Proceedings of the First International Conference Seminar of Tamil Studies* (Kuala Lumpur, 1966), I.

Zacharias, C. W. B., *Madras Agriculture* (Madras, 1950).

Notes

Preface

1 *UN Demographic Yearbook 1952* (New York, 1952), table 1. The countries with larger populations were China, USSR, USA, Japan, Indonesia, Pakistan, UK, West Germany, Italy and France. At this time Nigeria was attributed a population smaller than that of Tamilnad (around 25 million), but the estimate of Nigeria's population was revised steadily upwards in subsequent years and it is probable that in 1950 it was at least 30 million.

2 A.V. Chayanov, *The Theory of Peasant Economy* ed. D. Thorner, R. E. F. Smith and B. Kerblay (Irwin, 1961). Two notable books which have used Chayanovian ideas to explain Asian rural history are R.H. Myers, *The Chinese Peasant Economy: agricultural development in Hopei and Shantung, 1890–1949* (Harvard, 1970) and T.G. Kessinger, *Vilyatpur 1848–1968: social and economic change in a north Indian village* (Berkeley, Los Angeles and London, 1974). Both were criticized for allowing the theory to run away with the data. For a fascinating argument about the modern perversion of Chayanov's work see J. Banaji, 'Chayanov, Kautsky, Lenin: considerations towards a synthesis', *Economic and Political Weekly* 2 Oct. 1976, 1594–1607.

3 See especially J. C. Scott, *The Moral Economy of the Peasant: rebellion and subsistence in southeast Asia* (Yale, 1976); and a critique which accepts the whole style of analysis, S. L. Popkin, *The Rational Peasant: the political economy of rural society in Vietnam* (Berkeley, Los Angeles and London, 1979).

4 See H. Alavi, 'Peasant classes and primordial loyalties', *Journal of Peasant Studies*, I,1 (1973).

5 Here we are concerned with the general import of writings on dependency and underdevelopment and we do not need to investigate the many different and often conflicting schools. See I. Oxaal, T. Barnett, and D. Booth (eds.), *Beyond the Sociology of Development: economy and society in Latin America and Africa* (London, 1975); I. Roxborough, 'Dependency theory in the sociology of development: some theoretical problems', *West African Journal of Sociology and Political Science*, I, 2 (1976).

6 The principal contributors to the debate were Utsa Patnaik, Paresh Chatto-padhyay and Jairus Banaji. Ashok Rudra has, I understand, collected the papers together in a publication in Delhi. Aidan Foster-Carter reviews some of the literature in 'The modes of production controversy', *New Left Review*, 107

(1978). John Harriss and Hamza Alavi are also planning to collect the papers in a publication. I am grateful to John Harriss for allowing me to see his paper 'The mode of production controversy: themes and problems of the debate', Madras Institute of Development Studies Working Paper No. 6.

7 Much of this literature has been published in the *Journal of Peasant Studies* with outriders in the *Economic and Political Weekly*, *Economy and Society*, and the *Journal of Contemporary Asia*.

8 V. I. Lenin, *The Development of Capitalism in Russia* (Moscow, 1956).

9 K. Kautsky, *Die Agrarfrage* (Stuttgart, 1899); J. Banaji, 'Summary of selected parts of Kautsky's "The Agrarian Question" ', *Economy and Society*, V, 1 (1976). Kautsky's formulations have become especially important for both Banaji and Patnaik in the aftermath of the mode of production debate. See U. Patnaik, 'Neo-populism and Marxism: the Chayanovian view of the agrarian question and its fundamental fallacy', *Journal of Peasant Studies*, VI, 4 (1979).

10 J. Banaji, 'Capitalist domination and the small peasantry: Deccan districts in the late nineteenth century', *Economic and Political Weekly*, special number, Aug. 1977, 1375-1404.

11 Especially *Capital*, Volume I (London, 1974), parts iii, vii and viii; and Volume III (London, 1969), parts iv and vi.

12 H. Bernstein, 'African peasantries: a theoretical framework', *Journal of Peasant Studies*, VI, 4 (1979); for a rather different view see K. W. J. Post, ' "Peasantization" and rural political movements in West Africa', *Archives Européennes de Sociologie*, XII, 1 (1972).

13 A. G. Frank, *Capitalism and Underdevelopment in Latin America* (New York and London, 1967); A. G. Frank, *Latin America: underdevelopment and revolution* (New York and London, 1969); E. Laclau, 'Feudalism and capitalism in Latin America', *New Left Review*, No. 67 (1971).

14 Especially in *Grundrisse*, trans. M. Nicolaus (London, 1973); see also D. Thorner, 'Marx on India and the Asiatic mode of production', *Contributions to Indian Sociology*, IX (1966).

15 Banaji, 'Capitalist domination'.

16 B. Stein, 'The segmentary state in south Indian history', in *Realm and Region in Traditional India* ed. R. G. Fox (Delhi, 1977); the contributors to this volume discuss other theories of Asian political organization including the 'galactic polity' from S. J. Tambiah, *World Conqueror and World Renouncer: a study of Buddhism and polity in Thailand against a historical background* (Cambridge, 1976).

17 This form of polity would of course be considerably modified in conquest states such as that of the Moghuls. This difference may account for many contrasts in the development of northern and southern India in the pre-colonial period.

18 It is possible that southern India (and indeed perhaps India as a whole) had a rather different demographic history from that of Europe, without the 'long swings' whose phasing has recently been used to explain some of the more dramatic social changes of medieval Europe. Southern India certainly had famines and disasters in the similar period, but it seems likely that the region normally had a very high birth rate to match the very high death rate expected from warfare, disease, and disaster. A population curve sustained by a very high birth and death rates would be less susceptible to short-term, localized shocks,

and was therefore probably smoother than the contemporary curve in Europe. This is, of course, very speculative. As C. McEvedy and R. Jones note, comparing the smooth curve of India's population history to the notched curve of China: 'Happy is the graph that has no history'. *Atlas of World Population History* (Harmondsworth, 1978).

19 P.-P. Rey, *Les Alliances de classes* (Paris, 1973).

20 This is not meant to suggest that there were no large landholdings. Indeed there were, but the characteristic unit of production was a small farm.

21 The great exception was wells.

22 The 'Tamilnad' of this book does not include two districts of the modern state of Tamil Nadu : Kanyakumari (which formed part of Travancore during British rule), and The Nilgiris (which was and is a hill region). Map 2 shows the relationship of 'Tamilnad' to the British province of the Madras Presidency.

Chapter 1

1 C. Maloney, 'Archaeology in south India: accomplishments and prospects' in B. Stein (ed.), *Essays on South India* (Hawaii, 1975).

2 P. R. K. Rao, 'Rainfall of Madras State', *Memoirs of the Indian Meteorological Service*, XXX (1953).

3 On irrigation see: E. Adicéam, *La Géographie de l'irrigation dans le Tamilnad* (Paris, 1966); J. Dupuis, *Madras et le Nord du Coromandel: étude des conditions de la vie indienne dans un cadre géographique* (Paris, 1960); O. H. K. Spate, A. T. A. Learmonth and B. H. Farmer, *India, Pakistan and Ceylon* (London, 3rd. ed., 1967); and the various volumes of the Madras District Gazetteers.

4 V. Rangacharya, 'The geographical data of the Sangam works', *JMGA*, III, 2 (1928); V. Kanakasabhai, *The Tamils Eighteen Hundred Years Ago* (Tirunelveli, 2nd ed., 1956); C. Maloney, 'Archaeology in south India'; S.Y. Krishnaswami, 'Major irrigation works of ancient Tamilnad' and K. K. Pillay, 'Aryan influence in Tamilaham during the Sangam epoch' in *Proceedings of the First International Conference Seminar of Tamil Studies*, vol. I (Kuala Lumpur, 1966); K.V. Soundara Rajan, 'Determinant factors in the early history of Tamilnad', *JIH*, XLV (1967).

5 P. Arunachalam, 'Vetci: or the first stage of war during the Sangam period', *Proceedings of the Second International Conference Seminar of Tamil Studies*, ed. R. E. Asher (Madras, 1971), II.

6 K. Kailasapathy, *Tamil Heroic Poetry* (Oxford, 1968), 241.

7 Ibid., 11, 249, 253, 260.

8 K. K. Pillay, 'Aryan influence in Tamilaham'; K. K. Pillay, *A Social History of the Tamils* vol. I (Madras, 2nd ed., 1975), especially chs. 8, 9, 10, 11.

9 B. Stein, 'Brahman and peasant in early south Indian history', *Adyar Library Bulletin*, XXXI–XXXII (1967–8).

10 N. B. Dirks, 'Political authority and structural change in early south Indian history', *IESHR*, XIII, 1 (1976).

11 Krishnaswami, 'Major irrigation systems of ancient Tamilnad'.

12 T. Venkasami Row, *A Manual of the District of Tanjore in the Madras Presidency* (Madras, 1883), 180; K.V. Subrahmanya Aiyer, *Historical Sketches*

of Ancient Dekhan, vol. II (Coimbatore, 1967), especially 55–6; K. S. Gopal-krishnan, 'Evolution of settlements in Cauvery delta', *Indian Geographical Journal*, XLVIII, 2 (1973).

13 E. Thurston, *Castes and Tribes of Southern India* (Madras, 1909), VII, 361ff; Maraimalai Adigal, *Velalar Nakarikam* [Tamil-Vellala civilization] (Madras, 1923); T. V. Mahalingam, *Kancipuram in Early South Indian History* (Madras, 1969), 11ff; M. Arokiaswami, 'The origin of the Vellalas', *JIH*, XXXIII (1955).

14 Stein, 'Brahman and peasant', 255; K. R. Venkata Raman, 'A note on the Kalabhras', *JIH*, XXXIV (1956).

15 D. Ludden, 'Agrarian organization in Tinnevelly district: 800-1900 A.D.', Ph.D. thesis, Pennsylvania, 1978, III; C. Minakshi, *Administration and Social Life under the Pallavas* (Madras, 1938); Y. Subbarayalu, 'The political geography of the Chola country from A.D. 800 to 1300 as gleaned from epigraphy and literature', M. Litt. thesis, Madras, 1969; K. A. Nilakanta Sastri, *The Colas* (Madras, 2nd ed., 1975 reprint); B. Stein, 'Integration of the agrarian system of south India' in R. E. Frykenberg (ed.), *Land Control and Social Structure in Indian History* (Madison, 1969).

16 Subbarayalu, especially 56–63.

17 Ibid.; Ludden, 'Agrarian organization', III; M. Arokiaswami, 'Democratic experiments in ancient south India', *JIH*, XXXV (1957); A. Appadorai, 'The committee system of village administration in Cola time—an interpretation', in *Dr S. Krishnaswami Aiyangar Commemoration Volume* (Madras, 1936); K.R. Hall, 'Price-making and market hierarchy in early medieval south India', *IESHR*, XIV, 2 (1975); B. Stein, 'Circulation and historical geography of Tamil country', *JAS*, XXXVII, 1 (1977).

18 Ludden, 'Agrarian organization', V.

19 Kailasapathy, *passim*; R. Nagaswamy, 'Hero stones of Tamilnadu', *Indian Historical Review*, LI (1973).

20 T.V. Mahalingam, *South Indian Polity* (Madras, 2nd ed., 1967), VI; Nilakanta Sastri, *Colas*, 454–7.

21 M. Arokiaswami, *The Kongu Country* (Madras, 1956); M. Arokiaswami, 'Adigaman of Tagadur: his origin', *JIH*, XXXII (1954); M. Arokiaswami, 'The Mudaliars of Taramangalam', *Quarterly Journal of the Mythic Society*, XXXXVII (1956–7); T.V. Mahalingam, 'The Banas in south Indian history', *JIH*, XXIX (1951); V. Vridhagirisan, 'The Kadavarayars', *JIH*, XVI (1937); S. Krishna-swami Aiyangar, *South India and her Muhammedan Invaders* (Madras, 1921), especially 14–40.

22 Arokiaswami, *Kongu Country*; P.T. Srinivasa Iyengar, 'Geographical control of early Kongu history', *JMGA*, V (1930); C.M. Ramachandra Chettiar, 'The geographical limits of Kongu Nadu at various epochs', *JMGA*, V (1930); B.J. Murton, 'Some propositions on the spread of village settlement in interior Tamil Nadu before 1750 A.D.' *Indian Geographical Journal*, XXXVIII, 2 (1973).

23 V. Raghavan, *The Great Integrators: the saint-singers of India* (Delhi, 1966).

24 See for example, D. Ramaswamy Tatachar, *The Vanamamalai Temple and Mutt* (Tinnevelly, 1937).

25 T.V. Mahalingam, 'The Pasupatas in south India', *JIH*, XXVII (1949); B. Stein, 'Social mobility and medieval south Indian Hindu sects' in J. Silverberg (ed.),

Social Mobility in the Caste System in India: an interdisciplinary symposium (Paris, 1968).

26 Stein, 'Brahman and peasant'.

27 G.W. Spencer, 'Religious networks and royal influence in eleventh century south India', *Journal of the Economic and Social History of the Orient*, XII, 1 (1969); G.W. Spencer, 'Royal initiative under Rajaraja I', *IESHR*, VII, 4 (1970); B. Stein, 'The economic function of a medieval south Indian temple', *JAS*, XIX, 2 (1960); R. Nagaswamy, 'South Indian temple — as an employer', *IESHR*, II, 4 (1965); Dirks, 'Political authority and structural change'.

28 B. Stein, 'The segmentary state in south Indian history' in R. G. Fox (ed.), *Realm and Region in Traditional India* (Delhi, 1977).

29 W. M. K. Wijetunga, 'South Indian corporate commercial organizations in south and southeast Asia', *Proceedings of the First International Conference Seminar of Tamil Studies*, I; K. R. Venkatarama Ayyar, 'Medieval trade, craft and merchant guilds in south India', *JIH*, XXV (1947); B. Stein, 'Coromandel trade in medieval India' in J. Parker (ed.), *Merchants and Scholars: essays in the history of exploration and trade* (Minneapolis, 1965); K. D. Swaminathan, 'The horse-traders of Malaimandalam', *JIH*, XXXII (1954); G. W. Spencer, 'The politics of plunder: the Cholas in eleventh-century Ceylon', *JAS*, XXXV, 3 (1976).

30 Krishnaswami Aiyangar, *South India and her Muhammedan Invaders*, 1–70; Nilakanta Sastri, *Colas*, ch. XVI.

31 Nagaswamy, 'Hero stones of Tamilnadu'; Arunachalam, 'Vetci'.

32 The legacy of this is lugubriously recorded in H. Whitehead, *Village Gods of South India* (Calcutta, 1921).

33 Mahalingam, 'The Banas'; Mahalingam, *Kancipuram*; Vridhagirisan, 'Kada-varayars'; Nilakanta Sastri, *Colas*, 372–5; Krishnaswamy Aiyangar, *South India and her Muhammedan Invaders*, 35–41; A. Krishnaswami, *The Tamil Country under Vijayanagar* (Annamalainagar, 1964), 8–13; J.D.M. Derrett, *The Hoy-salas: a medieval Indian royal family* (Oxford, 1957), 6–7.

34 Amir Khusru, cited in Krishnaswami Aiyangar, *South India and her Muham-medan Invaders*, 83.

35 Ibid.

36 Ibid.; R. Sewell, *A Forgotten Empire (Vijayanagar): a contribution to the history of India* (London, 1900); K. A. Nilakanta Sastri and N. Venkataramanayya, *Further Sources of Vijayanagara History*, vol. I (Madras, 1946).

37 Mahalingam, *South Indian Polity*, 255–66; Nilakanta Sastri, *Colas*, 454–7; Krishnaswami Aiyangar, *South India and her Muhammedan Invaders*, es-pecially 70–1; Swaminathan, 'Horse-traders of Malaimandalam'; Nilakanta Sastri and Venkataramanayya, *Further Sources*, I, 90ff., 299.

38 Derrett, *Hoysalas*, especially 182–9.

39 Sewell, especially 72, 122, 150, 207; Nilakanta Sastri and Venkataramanayya, *Further Sources*, I, 197.

40 Nilakanta Sastri and Venkataramanayya, *Further Sources, passim*; Sewell, 130-50, 167; Krishnaswami, *Tamil Country*, 177ff.; R. Sathyanatha Aiyar, *History of the Nayaks of Madura* (Madras, 1924); N. B. Dirks, 'The structure and meaning of political relations in a south Indian little kingdom', Humanities Working Paper 14, California Institute of Technology, 1978.

41 Krishnaswami, *Tamil Country*, 99–104.

42 T. V. Mahalingam, *Administration and Social Life under Vijayanagar: Part II, Social Life* (Madras, 2nd ed., 1975), 76–112.

43 A. Appadurai, 'Kings, sects, and temples in south India 1350–1700 A.D.', *IESHR*, XIV, 1 (1977)—an issue of *IESHR* reprinted as B. Stein (ed.), *South Indian Temples: an analytical reconsideration* (Delhi, 1978).

44 B. Stein, 'Temples in Tamil country, 1300–1750 A.D.' in ibid; C. E. Rama-chandran, 'Tamil society in the seventeenth century', Ph.D. thesis, Madras, 1974, 244–7.

45 D. Hudson, 'Siva, Minaksi, Visnu — reflections on a popular myth in Madurai' in Stein, *South Indian Temples*.

46 Appadurai, 'Kings, sects, and temples'.

47 A. Rangaswami Saraswati, 'Political maxims of the Emperor-poet Krishnadeva Raya', *JIH*, IV (1925–6), 72.

48 For example, L. Dumont, *Une Sous-Caste de l'Inde du Sud: organisation sociale et religion des Pramalai Kallar* (Paris and The Hague, 1957).

49 Much of this comes from an imaginative reading of the passages on Kallar, Maravar, Agamudaiyan, Padaiyichi in Thurston, *Tribes and Castes*; see also S. H. Blackburn, 'The Kallars: A Tamil "Criminal Tribe" reconsidered', *South Asia*, (New Series) I, 1 (1978).

50 Fernao Nuniz, whose chronicle is reproduced in Sewell, and in *The Vijayanagar Empire as seen by Domingo Paes and Fernao Nuniz* (Delhi, 1977).

51 Blackburn, 'The Kallars', especially 44.

52 See Dumont, *Une Sous-Caste*; B. E. F. Beck, *Peasant Society in Konku: a study of right and left subcastes in south India* (Vancouver, 1972).

53 Dirks, 'The structure and meaning'.

54 For example: Beck, *Peasant Society*, 41-2 on the Kongunad pattagars; F. Buchanan, *A Journey from Madras through the Countries of Mysore, Canara and Malabar* (London, 1807), II, 327 on the Anamalai poligars; T.B. Krishna-swami, *In Old Salem* (Madras, 1933), 107-8; H. Le Fanu, *A Manual of the Salem District in the Presidency of Madras* (Madras, 1883), I, 47-8; see also W. Taylor, *A Catalogue Raisonnée of Oriental Manuscripts in the Government Library* (Madras, 1862) and C.O. Blagden, *The Mackenzie Collection* (London, 1916).

55 K. Rajayyan, *Rise and Fall of the Poligars of Tamilnadu* (Madras, 1974); S. Kadhirvel, *A History of the Maravas* (Madurai, 1977); Dirks, 'Structure and meaning'.

56 See the relevant entries in Thurston, *Castes and Tribes*.

57 My card index resolutely refuses to yield up the reference to this quotation.

58 Thurston, *Castes and Tribes*, relevant entries; E. Ramachandra Sastri, *History of the Criminal Tribes in the Madras Presidency* (Madras, 1929); R. Caldwell, *A Political and General History of the District of Tinnevelly in the Presidency of Madras from the earliest period to its cession to the English Government in A.D. 1801* (Madras, 1881), especially 103–10.

59 N. Karashima, 'Nayaks as leaseholders of temple lands', *Journal of the Economic and Social History of the Orient*, XIX (1976); Krishnaswami, *Tamil Country*, 73–104.

60 Mahalingam, *Administration and Social Life*, II, 213–36; K. A. Nilakanta Sastri,

The Pandyan Kingdom from the earliest times to the sixteenth century (London, 1929), 219–21, 235.

61 Ramachandran, 'Tamil society in the seventeenth century', 178–9; A. Sauliere, 'The revolt of the southern Nayaks', *JIH*, XLV (1966); Ludden, 'Agrarian organization', IV; J. H. Garstin, *Manual of the South Arcot District* (Madras, 1878), 223–5.

62 Ramachandran, 'Tamil society in the seventeenth century', 40–67.

63 Sathyanatha Aiyar; Sauliere, 'Revolt of the southern Nayaks'.

64 Stein, 'Temples in Tamil country'.

65 V. Cronin, *A Pearl to India: the life of Roberto de Nobili* (London, 1958), especially 36–8; F. A. Nicholson, *Manual of the Coimbatore District in the Presidency of Madras* (Madras, 1887), 89–90; Tavernier, I, especially 216; *The Travels of the Abbé Carré in India and the Near East 1672 to 1674*, trans. Lady Fawcett, ed. Sir Charles Fawcett, vol. II (London, 1947), especially 583; P. Baldaeus, *A True Description of the East-Indian Coasts of Malabar and Coromandel as also of the Isle of Ceylon* in *A Collection Of Voyages and Travels* ed. A. Churchill (London, 1704), III, especially 650–1; J. T. Phillips, *An Account of the Religion, Manners, and Learning of the Peoples of Malabar in the East Indies in several letters written by some of the most learned men of that country to the Danish missionaries* (London).

66 Ramachandran, 'Tamil society in the seventeenth century', 199–200.

67 This is the overriding impression from Buchanan.

68 On kaval see Rajayyan, *Rise and Fall of the Poligars*; Kadhirvel; Caldwell, *History of the District of Tinnevelly*, 103; Blackburn, 'The Kallars'; J. H. Nelson, *The Madura Country* (Madras, 1868).

69 M. Hasan, *History of Tipu Sultan* (Calcutta, 2nd ed., 1971); Le Fanu, I, 50 ff.; W. K. Firminger (ed.), *The Fifth Report from the Select Committee of the House of Commons on the Affairs of the East India Company. Volume I, Introduction and text of the Report* (Calcutta, 1917), 191–4.

70 Dumont, *Une Sous-Caste*, 20–3; L. Dumont, 'Distribution of some Maravar sub-castes' in L. K. Bala Ratnam (ed.) *Anthropology on the March* (Madras, 1963); Blackburn, 'The Kallars'; Garstin, *Manual of the South Arcot District*, 179; Venkasami Row, 406–7.

71 Ludden, 'Agrarian organization', IV develops this argument in much more detail.

72 T. Raychaudhuri, *Jan Company in Coromandel 1605–90* (S. Gravenhage, 1962); Baldaeus, especially 650–2.

73 Ramachandran, 'Tamil society in the seventeenth century', 80–88.

74 Mahalingam, *Administration and Social Life*, II, 133–67.

75 A. Das Gupta, *Malabar in Asian Trade, 1740–1800* (Cambridge, 1967).

76 See retrospective comments in Buchanan, II, 180, 186.

77 *The Life of the Icelander Jon Olaffson Volume II Travels 1618–1679* (London, 1931), 125.

78 S. A. R. Bokhari, 'Carnatic under the Nawabs as revealed through "Sayeed Nama" of Juswant Rai' M. Litt. thesis, Madras, 1965, 90–1.

79 Hasan, *Tipu Sultan*, 335 ff.; M. H. Gopal, *Tipu Sultan's Mysore: an economic study* (Bombay, 1971), especially 18–22.

80 Hasan, *Tipu Sultan*; Nicholson, *Manual of Coimbatore District*, 340-1.

81 K. Rajayyan, *South Indian Rebellion: the first war of independence 1800-1801* (Mysore, 1971).

82 For administration in the Company territories see Garstin, *Manual of the South Arcot District*, 218-25.

83 Buchanan, II, 215-16.

84 See A. J. Arbuthnot, *Sir Thomas Munro: selections from his minutes and other official notes* (London, 1881).

85 J. T. Wheeler, *Madras in Olden Times: being a history of the Presidency* (Madras, 1882).

86 J.D. Gurney, 'The debts of the Nawab of Arcot 1763–1776', D.Phil. thesis, Oxford, 1968; S.A.R. Bokhari, 'Carnatic under the Nawabs as revealed through "Sayeed Nama" of Juswant Rai', M.Litt. thesis, Madras, 1965.

87 M. Hasan, *History of Tipu Sultan* (Calcutta, 3rd ed., 1971); M. H. Gopal, *Tipu Sultan's Mysore: an economic study* (Bombay, 1971).

88 K. Rajayyan, *Rise and Fall of the Poligars of Tamilnadu* (Madras, 1974); K. Rajayyan, *South Indian Rebellion: the first war of independence 1800–1801* (Mysore, 1971); B. S. Ward, *Geographical and Statistical Memoir of the Provinces of Madura and Dindigul* (Madura, 1895).

89 T. H. Beaglehole, *Thomas Munro and the Development of Administrative Policy in Madras 1792–1818: the origins of the Munro system* (Cambridge, 1966); N. Mukherjee, *The Ryotwari System in Madras* (Calcutta, 1962).

90 J. W. B. Dykes, *Salem, an Indian Collectorate* (London, 1853), 168–220; B. S. Baliga, 'Acquisition of estates and their conversion into ryotwari tenure' in *Studies in Madras Administration* vol. I (Madras, 1960); see also the chapters on land revenue in the Madras district gazetteers, especially: C. S. Crole, *A Chingleput District Manual* (Madras, 1879); H. Le Fanu, *A Manual of the Salem District in the Presidency of Madras* (Madras, 1883); H. R. Pate, *Tinnevelly District Gazetteer* (Madras, 1917); J. H. Nelson, *The Madura Country* (Madras, 1868); T. Venkasami Row, *A Manual of the District of Tanjore in the Madras Presidency* (Madras, 1883).

91 Dykes, 180–96; Le Fanu, I, 310–41; Baliga, 'Acquisition of estates.

92 C. J. Baker, 'Tamilnad estates in the twentieth century', *IESHR*, XIII, 1 (1975).

93 R. E. Frykenberg, "Company Circari" in the Carnatic c.1779–1859: the inner logic of political systems in India', in R. G. Fox (ed.), *Realm and Region in Traditional India* (Delhi, 1977); Selections from old records of South Arcot: *Mr Hyde's Report on the Introduction of a Ryotwari Settlement into the South Arcot Collectorate and the Correspondence relating thereto* (Cuddalore, 1904).

94 Dykes; Le Fanu, I.

95 For the ideological debates see Mukherjee, *Ryotwari System*; Beaglehole; G.R. Gleig, *Life and Correspondence of Major-General Sir Thomas Munro* (London, 1830); A.J. Arbuthnot, *Sir Thomas Munro: selections from his minutes and other official notes* (London, 1881).

96 Rev 951 14 May 1855, reproduced in Selections LIII: *Papers relating to the General Revenue Survey of the Madras Presidency* (Madras, 1858); see also Frykenberg, "Company Circari"; N. Mukherjee and R. E. Frykenberg, 'The ryotwari system and social organization in the Madras Presidency', in Frykenberg (ed.), *Land Control and Social Structure in Indian History* (Madison, 1969).

97 See for example B.J. Murton, 'Key people in the countryside: decision makers in interior Tamilnadu in the late eighteenth century', *IESHR*, X, 2 (1973); W.K. Firminger (ed.), *The Fifth Report from the Select Committee of the House of Commons on the Affairs of the East India Company, volume I, Introduction and text of the Report* (Calcutta, 1917), 268–81.

98 Venkasami Row, 400–12; Firminger, 197, 217, 244; Selections: *Memorandum on Mirasi Tenure*, by W. H. Bayley (Madras, 1856); D. Ludden, 'Agrarian organization in Tinnevelly district: 1800–1900 A.D.' Ph.D. thesis, Pennsylvania, 1978.

99 See for example the Director of Revenue Settlement, dated 5 Nov. 1857 and 28 July 1858, and other papers in *General Revenue Survey* (1858); Selections LXV: *Papers relating to the Survey and Settlement of the Salem District* (Madras, 1879).

100 Selections (New Series) I: *A Collection of Papers relating to the Inam Settlement in the Madras Presidency* (Madras, 1948); *Correspondence relating to the Revision Proposed in the Village Revenue Establishments to the Madras Presidency. Part I.* (Madras, 1867); Rev 664 5 May 1925; GOM: *Report on the Revision of the Revenue Establishments of the Madras Presidency* by J. H. Garstin (Madras, 1883).

101 Ludden 'Agrarian organization'; *Mr. Hyde's Report*; Selections from the Records of the South Arcot District: *Report of Commissioner Mr. Dent on the Disturbances in the District in 1841 and the Government Order thereon* (Cuddalore, 1868); Venkasami Row, 415–19; Rev 3118 7 Dec. 1938.

102 *Mr. Hyde's Report*, 9.

103 Selections: *Collection of papers relating to the Settlement of Tinnevelly District, by Mr. Puckle, 1872–9* (Madras, n.d.).

104 G. Beardsley dated 23 Nov 1858 in Selections LXXIV: *Papers relating to the General Revenue Survey of the Madras Presidency* (Madras, 1863), 641. *Report of Commissioner Mr. Dent.*

105 See especially *Memorandum on Mirasi Tenure*; W. H. Bayley and W. Hudleston, *Papers on Mirasi Right* (Madras, 1892).

106 Rev 1537 (C) 25 Aug. 1922, Tanjore resettlement report, 5–7.

107 Notes on payment of revenue in kind in Rev 3118 7 Dec. 1938.

108 Ludden, 'Agrarian organization', VI; *Settlement of Tinnevelly District, by Mr. Puckle*, 33–4.

109 J. B. Norton, *The Administration of Justice in Southern India* (Madras, 1853).

110 D. A. Washbrook, *The Emergence of Provincial Politics: the Madras Presidency 1870–1920* (Cambridge, 1976), ch. 2.

111 Norton, *Administration of Justice*; J. H. Nelson, *Indian Usage and Judge-made Law in Madras* (London, 1887); J. H. Nelson, *A Prospectus of the Scientific Study of the Hindu Law* (London, 1881); J. H. Nelson, *A View of the Hindu Law as administered by the High Court of Judicature at Madras* (London, 1877).

112 Washbrook, *Emergence of Provincial Politics*, ch. 3.

113 Selections: *Papers relating to Zamindaries, Mittahs etc. in Tinnevelly District* (Madras, 1934).

114 *Collection of Papers relating to the Inam Settlement.*

115 *General Revenue Survey* (1858).

116 See *Report on the administration of civil justice in the Presidency of Madras* (annual).

117 GOM: *Statement of the Police Committee on the Administration of the District Police in the Madras Presidency* (Madras, 1902).

118 Chandra Y. Mudaliar, *The Secular State and Religious Institutions in India: a study of the administration of Hindu public religious trusts in Madras* (Wiesbaden, 1974).

119 *Collection of Papers relating to the Inam Settlement.*

120 *MELAC*, I, 79-81.

121 Mukherjee, *Ryotwari System*: for the discussions on the prospects of reform see *General Revenue Survey* (1858) and (1863).

122 J. T. Gwynn 5 Feb. 1908, Gwynn papers Box III no. 239, SAS Archive.

123 Home (Jud) 2550 15 Nov. 1911.

124 *Collection of Papers relating to the Inam Settlement*, 26-9.

125 *MELAC*, I, 79-84.

126 For one of the first examples of the implementation of the revised ryotwari settlement see *Papers relating to the Survey and Settlement of the Salem District.*

127 Rev 2435 26 June 1918.

128 Rev 1537(C) 25 Aug. 1927, Tanjore resettlement report.

129 Ludden, 'Agrarian organisation', VI.

130 C. J. Baker, 'Madras headmen', in K. N. Chaudhuri and C. J. Dewey (eds.), *Economy and Society: essays in Indian economic and social history* (Delhi, 1979).

131 *Papers relating to Zamindaries, Mittahs etc. in Tinnevelly District*; Dykes, 210.

132 On the need to compel cultivation see for instance F. Buchanan, *A Journey from Madras through the Countries of Mysore, Canara and Malabar* (London, 1807), III, 433.

133 GOM: *Report of the Commissioners for the Investigation of Alleged Cases of Torture in the Madras Presidency* (Madras, 1855).

134 GOM: *Report of the Madras Survey and Land Records Committee* (Madras, 1915).

135 Ibid., I, 25.

136 V. Mahadeva Ayyar, Ibid., II, 125.

137 BP 834 12 Apr. 1926; BP 1510 7 July 1926; BP 850 15 Apr. 1926.

138 Norton, *Administration of Justice*; 'The Zillah Courts were established for the protection of the people, but in consequence of the facility with which forged Bonds are established by the evidence of false witnesses as genuine, the Courts, instead of being a protector, are a source of oppression to the people.' Petition reproduced in *Report of Commissioner Mr. Dent*, 35.

139 G.F.F. Foulkes: *Local Autonomy* (Madras, 1937-8), I, 131.

140 *Survey and Land Records Committee*, I, 30-1.

141 C. Chakravarti Ayyangar, *MPBC*, II, 249.

142 A.F.G. Moscardi, *Survey and Land Records Committee*, II, 124.

143 There are many examples of this in the statements of evidence in *Madras Survey and Land Records Committee*, II; and in the memoirs of Madras Collectors and other revenue servants, for example J. P. L. Gwynn, C. Masterman, R. Totterham, S. Wadsworth, SAS Archive.

144 A.F.G. Moscardi, *Survey and Land Records Committee*, II, 124.

145 Among many references in the evidence volumes of the *MPBC* see II, 94, 302, 337, 524; III, 366; BP 1510 7 July 1926; BP 834 12 Apr. 1926.

146 For example Rev 1537 (C) 25 Aug. 1922, Tanjore resettlement report, 22-6.
147 See example in Norton, *Administration of Justice*, and Nelson, *A View of the Hindu Law*.
148 Cotton and Sullivan, 6 Mar. 1843, BP vol. 1849, pp. 3393-4, quoted in Ludden, 'Agrarian organization', VIII.
149 A. Sarada Raju, *Economic Conditions in the Madras Presidency 1800–1850* (Madras, 1841), 123-8; Ludden, 'Agrarian organization', VIII; GB: *Report of the Indian Irrigation Commission 1901–3: Part II Provincial*, Parliamentary Papers 1904 Cd. 1851.
150 S. Srinivasa Raghavaiyangar, *Memorandum on the Progress of the Madras Presidency during the last Forty Years of British Administration* (Madras, 1893), 47-8.
151 Ludden, 'Agrarian organization', VIII.
152 Sarada Raju, 124-5.
153 Madras Public Works Commission, 1852, quoted in Srinivasa Raghavaiyangar, 33.
154 Buchanan, especially I, 7 and II, 164, 180-1, 261.
155 J. T. Wheeler, *Handbook to the Cotton Cultivation in the Madras Presidency* (Madras, 1862); F. A. Nicholson, *Manual of the Coimbatore District in the Presidency of Madras* (Madras, 1887), 181-2, 188; Srinivasa Raghavaiyangar, 32-5, 62; Ludden, 'Agrarian organization', VIII.
156 Srinivasa Raghavaiyangar, 62.
157 Ibid.
158 J-B. Tavernier, *Travels in India*, trans. V. Ball, ed. W. Croske (London, 1925), I, 216.
159 W. Fullarton, *Narrative of Military Transactions* (London, 1784); J. Couteur, *Letters chiefly from India containing an Account of the Military Transactions* (London, 1790).
160 Buchanan, *passim*.
161 E. Hoole, *Madras, Mysore and the south of India or A Personal Narrative of a Mission to these Countries from 1820 to 1828* (London, 2nd ed., 1844), especially 53, 135, 151, 293, 299.
162 Le Fanu, I, 230-8.
163 A Arrowsmith, *Atlas of South India from Cape Comorin to the River Kistnah* (London, 1822).
164 *Papers relating to the Survey and Settlement of the Salem District*, 62-3.
165 Nicholson, *Manual of the Coimbatore District*, 179-82, 295.
166 *General Revenue Survey* (1863), especially H. Newell dated 28 July 1855, 25.
167 H. Harkness, 'Account of the Province of Ramnad, Southern Peninsula of India. Compiled from the "Mackenzie Collection", and edited by the Secretary to the Royal Asiatic Society', *Journal of the Royal Asiatic Society*, III (1836).
168 *Settlement of Tinnevelly District, by Mr Puckle*.
169 *See Report on the Settlement of the Land Revenue in the Madras Presidency* (annual).
170 Ludden, 'Agrarian organization', VIII.
171 The sociology is mostly culled from the 'population' chapters of the District Gazetteers and from E. Thurston, *Castes and Tribes of Southern India* (Madras, 1909).

172 Sarada Raju, 187–8.

173 R.L. Hardgrave, *The Nadars of Tamilnad: the political culture of a community in change* (Berkeley and Los Angeles, 1969).

174 S.B. Kaufmann, 'Popular Christianity, caste and Hindu society in south India 1800–1915: a study of Travancore and Tirunelveli', Ph.D. thesis, Cambridge, 1980, ch. 3.

175 Population figures are conveniently collected in D. Kumar, *Land and Caste in South India: agricultural labour in the Madras Presidency during the nineteenth century* (Cambridge, 1965), 120–3.

176 H. St. A. Goodrich dated 1869–70 in *Papers relating to the Survey and Settlement of the Salem District*, 231.

177 For example, Selections: *Proposals for a new settlement of the Land Revenue in Five Taluks of Coimbatore*, by Mr H. F. Clogstoun (1875) (Madras, n.d.); *Settlement of Tinnevelly District, by Mr. Puckle*, 8–9; GOM: *Report of the Agricultural Committee* (Madras, 1889), 63–5.

178 Kumar, *Land and Caste*, ch. 7.

179 Selections (new series) XI: *A Collection of Papers relating to the Value of Land in the Early Years of the Nineteenth Century* (Madras, 1916), especially G.W. Saunders dated 31 Mar. 1826.

180 Kumar, *Land and Caste*, 142; H.A. Stuart, *Coimbatore District Manual* (Madras, 1898), 324.

181 B.S. Ward, *Geographical and Statistical Memoir of the Provinces of Madura and Dindigul* (Madura, 1895), III, 5-11; Nelson, *Indian usage, 175-6;* L. Moore, *A Manual of the Trichinopoly District in the Presidency of Madras* (Madras, 1878), 265; Venkasami Row, 445–55.

182 D. Arnold, 'Dacoity and rural crime in Madras, 1860–1940', *Journal of Peasant Studies*, VI (1978–9).

183 W. Francis, *Madura District Gazetteer* vol. I (Madras, 1906), 92.

184 S. H. Blackburn, 'The Kallars: A Tamil "Criminal Tribe" reconsidered', *South Asia* (New series), I 1 (1978); E. Ramachandra Sastri, *History of the Criminal Tribes in the Madras Presidency* (Madras, 1929); GOM: *Madras Criminal Tribes Manual* (Madras, 1924).

185 This is not quite the same view as that presented in Hardgrave.

186 See D. Ludden, 'Ecological zones and the cultural economy of irrigation in southern Tamilnadu', *South Asia* (new series) I, 1 (1978).

187 W. H. Bayley and W. Hudleston, *Papers on Mirasi Right* (Madras, 1892)

188 F. J. Richards, 'Cross-cousin marriage in south India', *Man*, XCVII (1914); E. K. Gough, 'Brahman kinship in a Tanjore village', *American Anthropologist*, LVIII (1956).

189 Stein, 'Brahman and peasant'; Ludden, 'Agrarian organization', IV.

190 Dumont, *Une Sous-Caste*; Blackburn, 'The Kallars'; Thurston, *Castes and Tribes*, III, 62.

191 *Census of India 1891* Vol. XIII, Madras, I, 232

192 Thurston, *Castes and Tribes*, III, 63.

193 Buchanan, I, 32.

194 B.J. Murton, 'Some propositions on the spread of village settlement'.

195 Beck, *Peasant Society*; Dumont, *Une Sous-Caste*.

196 For a modern survival of the pattern see T.S. Epstein, 'Productive efficiency and

customary systems of rewards in rural south India', in R. Firth (ed.), *Themes in Economic Anthropology* (London, 1967).

197 A. Appadurai, 'Right and left hand castes in south India', *IESHR*, XI, 2-3 (1974) assembles the many references to the right-left division.

198 Srinivasa Iyengar, 'Geographical control of early Kongu history'; Ramachandra Chettiar, 'The geographical limits of Kongu Nadu'; N. Subrahmanyam, 'Communication-lines and town-sites of Coimbatore', *JMGA*, V, 3 (1930).

199 Beck, *Peasant Society*.

200 C. M. Ramachandra Chettiar, 'The geographical distribution of crime and civil litigation in south India', *JMGA*, XII, 2 (1937).

201 Beck, *Peasant Society*.

Chapter 2

1 S. Srinivasa Raghavaiyangar, *Memorandum on the Progress of the Madras Presidency during the Last Forty Years of British Administration* (Madras, 1893), 66-72; A. Sarada Raju, *Economic Conditions in the Madras Presidency 1800–1850* (Madras, 1941), 204-7, 301.

2 Srinivasa Raghavaiyangar, 58; GOM: *Report of the Agricultural Committee* (Madras, 1889), Nicholson's appendix.

3 See S. Playne, *Southern India: its history, peoples, commerce and industrial resources* (London, 1914–15); H. Brown, *Parry's of Madras: a story of British enterprise in India* (Madras, 1954).

4 See C.J. Baker, 'Economic reorganization'.

5 M. Adas, *The Burma Delta: economic development and social change on an Asian rice frontier, 1852–1941* (Madison, 1974), 22; J. C. Ingram, *Economic Change in Thailand 1850–1970* (Stanford, 1971), 8; C. Robequain, *The Economic Development of French Indochina* (London, 1944), 220.

6 J. Geoghegan, *Note on Emigration from India* (Calcutta, 1873).

7 K. S. Sandhu, *Indians in Malaya: some aspects of their immigration and settlement 1786–1957* (Cambridge, 1969); C. E. Glick, 'The changing position of two Tamil groups in western Malaya', in *Proceedings of the Second International Conference Seminar of Tamil Studies* ed. R. E. Asher, vol. II (Madras, 1971); R. K. Jain, *South Indians on the Plantation Frontier in Malaya* (New Haven and London, 1970); S. Arasaratnam, *Indians in Malaysia and Singapore* (Oxford, 1970).

8 B. Eastampillai, 'The Indian Tamil immigrant labourer and constitutional reforms in Ceylon: a brief survey', in Asher, *Proceedings*; E. Meyer, 'Impact de la dépression des années 1930 sur l'économie et la société rurale de Sri Lanka', *Purusartha* (Paris, 1975); R. Jayaraman, 'Indian emigration to Ceylon; some aspects of the historical and social background of the emigrants', *IESHR*, IV, 4 (1967).

9 Adas, *Burma Delta*; N. R. Chakravarti, *The Indian Minority in Burma: the rise and decline of an immigrant community* (Oxford, 1971); J. R. Andrus, *Burmese Economic Life* (Oxford, 1947), 23–34; Cheng Siok Hwa, 'Indian labour in the rice industry of pre-war Burma' in Asher, *Proceedings*; N.V. Sovani, *Economic Relations of India with South East Asia and the Far East* (Delhi, 1949), 37–45.

10 Arasaratnam, *Indians in Malaysia and Singapore*.

11 M. Adas, 'Immigrant Asians and the economic impact of European imperialism: the role of the south Indian Chettiars in British Burma', *JAS*, XXXIII, 3 (1974); A. Savarinatha Pillai, 'Monograph on Nattukottai Chettis' Banking Business', *MPBC*, III, 1170–1217; M. Nadarajan, 'The Nattukottai Chettiar community and south-east Asia' in *Proceedings of the First International Conference Seminar of Tamil Studies* vol. I (Kuala Lumpur, 1968).

12 Sovani, *Economic Relations*, 40–1.

13 Jayaraman, 'Indian emigration to Ceylon', 336.

14 Sandhu, 289, summing up information from *The Hindu* 7 Apr. 1946, C. Kondapil, *Indians Overseas, 1838–1949* (Delhi, 1951), 301, and S. Nanjudan, *Indians in Malayan Economy* (Delhi, 1950), 36.

15 Adas, 'Immigrant Asians'; Andrus, 75–6. The Chettiars also spread into French Indochina see J. L. de Lanessan, *L'Indo-Chine française* (Paris, 1889), 502–3.

16 Government of Burma: *Report of the Land and Agriculture Committee* (Rangoon, 1938), II, 39 and III, 77.

17 Sandhu, 262, 275.

18 Ibid., 291.

19 Andrus, 182.

20 See for instance, K. Mukherji, *Levels of Economic Activity and Public Expenditure in India* (London, 1962).

21 J. W. F. Rowe, *Primary Commodities in International Trade* (Cambridge, 1965).

22 League of Nations, *World Production and Prices, 1925–34* (Geneva, 1935) and *World Production and Prices, 1937–8* (Geneva, 1938)

23 GOM: *Report of the Rice Production and Trade in the Madras Presidency* by C. R. Srinivasan (Madras, 1934). There is a copy in Dvt 322 2 Mar. 1935.

24 Rowe; W.A. Lewis, *Aspects of Tropical Trade 1883–1965* (Stockholm, 1969); W.A. Lewis, *Economic Survey, 1919–39* (London, 1949).

25 The following discussion draws heavily on the work of Tom Tomlinson, see especially, B. R. Tomlinson, *The Political Economy of the Raj 1914–1947: the economics of decolonization in India* (London, 1979).

26 See *Royal Commission on Labour in India. Evidence Vol. III, Madras and Coorg* (London, 1931).

27 Rev(Spl) 593(C) 23 Oct. 1918; D. Arnold, 'Looting, grain riots and government policy in south India 1918', *Past and Present*, No. 84, (1979)

28 A. Maizels, *Industrial Growth and World Trade* (Cambridge, 1963), 79–81.

29 Ibid.; C.P. Kindleberger, *The World in Depression 1929–39* (Stanford, 1973); C. H. Lee, 'The effects of the depression on primary producing countries', *Journal of Contemporary History* IV (1969); V. P. Timoshenko, *World Agriculture and the Depression* (Michigan, 1933); League of Nations, *World Production and Prices 1925–34*.

30 Lewis, *Economic Survey*.

31 Kindleberger; H. van der Wee (ed.), *The Great Depression Revisited* (The Hague, 1972).

32 League of Nations, *World Production and Prices 1925–34*, 66; *World Production and Prices, 1938–9*, appendix I, 88.

33 V. D. Wickizer and M. K. Bennett, *The Rice Economy of Monsoon Asia* (Stanford, 1941), 85–100, 320–9.

34 S. G. Triantis, *Cyclical Changes in Trade Balances of Countries Exporting Primary Products 1927–33* (Toronto, 1967); Timoshenko; Rowe.
35 Kindleberger, chs. 3, 8.
36 Maizels, 80.
37 League of Nations, *World Production and Prices, 1925–34*, 37–8.
38 League of Nations, *Industrialization and Foreign Trade* (Geneva, 1945).
39 Timoshenko; Lewis, *Aspects of Tropical Trade*.
40 Lewis, *Economic Survey*.
41 Maizels, 81, 86–110.
42 League of Nations, *Industrialization and Foreign Trade*.
43 Tomlinson, *Political Economy*, 8–29.
44 League of Nations, *World Production and Prices 1925–34*.
45 *Srinivasan Report*.
46 Tomlinson, *Political Economy*, 83–8.
47 Ibid., 35–9; R. Krishnamurthi, 'India through slump and recovery, 1929–37; being a study of the trade cycle in relation to India', M.Litt. thesis, Madras, 1940.
48 A lot of the yield from gold sales was invested in securities; see *All India Income Tax Report, 1934–5*.
49 N. C. Sinha and P. N. Khera, *Indian War Economy (Supply, Industry and Finance)* (Calcutta, 1962).
50 R. N. Poduval, *Finance of the Government of India since 1935* (Delhi, 1951), 119–20.
51 A. R. Prest, *War Economies of Primary Producing Countries* (Cambridge, 1948).
52 Baker, 'Economic reorganization'.

Chapter 3

1 These rates were calculated from figures in *Census of India 1951* Volume III Madras and Coorg, Part II-A, Table A-II; and *Census of India 1961*, Volume IX Madras, Part II-A, Table A-I.
2 The growth of the urban population is considered in chapter 5.
3 K. Davis, *The Population of India and Pakistan* (Princeton, 1951).
4 R. H. Cassen, *India: Population, Economy, Society* (New York, 1978), especially 78–94.
5 *Census of India 1911*, Vol. XII Madras, Part II, Table XV–A.
6 *Season and Crop Report* for 1910–11.
7 According to ibid., 30 per cent of net sown area was irrigated in 1910–11.
8 B. J. Murton, 'Some propositions on the spread of village settlement in interior Tamil Nadu before 1750 A.D.', *Indian Geographical Journal*, XXXVIII, 2 (1973).
9 E. Adicéam, *La Géographie de l'Irrigation dans le Tamilnad* (Paris, 1966); M.N. Vasantha Devi, 'Some aspects of the agricultural geography of south India', M.Litt thesis, Madras, 1963; K. Ramamurthy, 'Some aspects of the regional geography of Tamilnad', M.Litt thesis, Madras, 1945; See also the various district Gazetteers, the several editions of the *Statistical Atlas of the Madras Presidency*, and issues of the JMGA.

10 N. B. Dirks, 'The structure and meaning of political relations in a south Indian little kingdom, Humanities working paper no. 14, October 1978, California Institute of Technology.

11 F. Buchanan, *A Journey from Madras through the Countries of Mysore, Canara and Malabar* (London, 1807), II, 198 and III, 458–60.

12 Rev 1892 23 Sept. 1934, South Salem resettlement report, 15.

13 Rev 3165 1 Nov. 1913, North Arcot resettlement report, 13.

14 BP 834 12 Apr. 1926.

15 F. A. Nicholson, *Manual of the Coimbatore district in the Presidency of Madras* (Madras, 1887), 295.

16 *The Madras Court of Wards Manual* (Madras, 1913), 140–3; Dvt 1126 15 Sept. 1933; Rev 3034 24 Aug. 1918; *Report of the Forest Committee (Madras)* (Madras, 1913).

17 S. Y. Krishnaswami, *Rural Problems in Madras: Monograph* (Madras, 1947), 78–107; Adicéam; *Report of the Indian Irrigation Commission 1901–3* GB: Parliamentary papers, 1904, Pt. II.

18 Adicéam, 222.

19 GOM: *A Notebook of Agricultural Facts and Figures*, compiled by R.C. Wood (Madras, 1928), 117–23.

20 Imperial Council of Agricultural Research, *Report on the cost of production of crops in the principal sugarcane and cotton tracts in India, vol. IV, Madras* (Delhi, 1938), and *supplementary vol. IV, Madras* (Delhi, 1940); Dvt 3244 18 Aug. 1945; V. V. Sayana, *The Agrarian Problems of Madras Province* (Madras, 1949), 220–2; M. S. L. Gowda, *Indian Economic Census: economic planning, special volume* (Madras, 1936), 104–12.

21 Nicholson, *Manual of the Coimbatore District*, 480.

22 R. Sivarama Ayyar, *MPBC*, IV, 396.

23 G. Slater, *Some South Indian Villages* (Oxford, 1918), 29, 35 (Vadamalai-puram).

24 Figures on livestock come from appendix IV in each district entry in *A Statistical Atlas of the Madras Presidency* (Madras, 1924).

25 *Manual of the Court of Wards*, 142.

26 *Report of the Forest Committee*; Rev 3034 24 Aug. 1918; Selections LXV, *Papers relating to the Survey and Settlement of the Salem District* (Madras, 1879), 8–10.

27 For a good survey of local labour systems see K. G. Sivaswamy, *Caste and Standard of Living versus Farms, Rents and Wages* (Madras, 1947).

28 GOM: *Report on the Famine in the Madras Presidency during 1896 and 1897* (Madras, 1898), I, 48 and II, 139.

29 T. S. Epstein, 'Productive efficiency and customary systems of rewards in rural south India', in R. Firth (ed.), *Themes in Economic Anthropology* (London, 1967).

30 D. A. Washbrook, 'Country politics: Madras 1880 to 1930', *MAS*, VII, 3 (1973).

31 S. Srinivasa Raghavaiyangar, *Memorandum on the Progress of the Madras Presidency during the last Forty Years of British Administration* (Madras, 1893).

32 B. V. Narayanaswamy Naidu, *Groundnut* (Annamalainagar, n.d.); Sayana, 24-5.

33 H. Brown, *Parry's of Madras: a story of British enterprise in India* (Madras,

1954), 35–6; W. Francis, *Gazetteer of the South Arcot District* vol. I (Madras, 1906), 124.

34 A. Kannayya, 'The cultivation of Cambodia cotton in the central districts', *MAJ*, XXVII, 8 (1939); GOI: *Report of the Indian Cotton Committee 1919* (Calcutta, 1919), 121; G. Slater, *Southern India: its political and economic problem* (London, 1936), 113–14.

35 Slater, *Southern India*, 112–13; *Annual Report of the Indian Central Cotton Committee* for 1921–2, 36; GOI: Indian Central Cotton Committee, *Minutes of Evidence taken before the Indian Central Cotton Committee* (Calcutta, 1920), II, ii, 142.

36 Selections LXV, *Papers relating to the Survey and Settlement of the Salem District*, 62–3.

37 Rev 2026 5 Sept. 1916.

38 Rev 3165 1 Nov. 1913.

39 Selections LXV, *Papers relating to the Survey and Settlement of the Salem District*; and figures from the *Season and Crop* reports.

40 I have lost the reference to the first world war scheme, but the similar scheme in the second world war is in Rev 2095 23 Oct. 1944.

41 Nicholson, *Manual of the Coimbatore district*, 295.

42 Slater, *Some South Indian Villages*, 18–21 (Mallur), 48 (Vadamalaipuram); R. Sivarama Ayyar, *MPBC*, II, 1328.

43 M.S. Paul, 'The commercial geography of Udayarpalaiyam taluk', *JMGA*, VII, 3 (1932), 189.

44 *Season and Crop* for 1928–9, 3; Rev 1044 22 Apr. 1938, North Salem resettlement report, 30.

45 H. C. Sampson in Indian Cotton Committee, *Evidence*, II, ii, 19; on the possibilities of 'minimal' cultivation of cotton see V. Ramaswami Mudaliar and R. Balasubramaniyam, 'The problem of Tinnies cotton and its solution', *The Indian Cotton Growing Review*, V. 4 (1951).

46 Slater, *Some South Indian Villages*, 33 (Vadamalaipuram).

47 *Season and Crop* for 1928–9, 4.

48 T. S. Sabapathi Pillai, *MPBC*, III, 776.

49 S. P. Rajamanicka Pandaram, *MPBC*, II, 32.

50 P. S. Seshadri, 'South Indian village studies: a preparatory study of "Villur" village no. 119 in Tirumangalam taluk, Madura district, Madras province', *MAJ*, XXIII (1935), 141.

51 Slater, *Some South Indian Villages*, 33 (Vadamalaipuram).

52 Ibid.; P. J. Thomas and K. C. Ramakrishnan, *Some South Indian Villages: a re-survey* (Madras, 1940), 9–11.

53 Thomas and Ramakrishnan, 9–11; survey of Peykulam, *MPBC*, V, 35; W. S. Subramania Ayyar, *MPBC*, II, 210; BP 1213 10 Sept. 1947; Rev 1357(C) 8 Apr. 1918; K. G. Sivaswamy, *Farm Tenancies under Ryotwari Holdings in Madras: history and principles of legislation* (n.p., 1941).

54 For example, survey of Peykulam, *MPBC*, V, 34 ff.

55 See Rev 1357(C) 8 Apr. 1918 for the apotheosis of this argument.

56 For example, Buchanan, II, 313, 320.

57 F. A. Nicholson, *Report regarding the possibilities of introducing Agricultural Banks into the Madras Presidency* (Madras, 1895–7), I, 233.

58 For example, M. M. Ramachandra Bhupathi, *MPBC*, III, 1016; N. G. Ranga, *MPBC*, III, 738–59; Nicholson, *Agricultural Banks*, I, 230; M.G. Vasudevayya, *MPBC*, III, 183.

59 This idea belongs to David Washbrook.

60 The evidence volumes of the *MPBC* contain countless references.

61 N. M. Ramachandra Bhupathi, *MPBC*, III, 1016.

62 Nicholson, *Agricultural Banks*, I, 235.

63 Sivaswamy, *Caste and Standard of Living*, 17.

64 Nicholson, *Agricultural Banks*, I, 232–3.

65 P. Duraisami, *MPBC*, II, 557; see also *MPBC*, III, 664.

66 R. Sivarama Ayyar, *MPBC*, II, 324–5; S. Mathuranayagam Pillai, *MPBC*, 112; Rev 1892 23 Sept. 1924, South Salem resettlement report, 26.

67 *Report of the Forest Committee*: S. Cox in S. Playne, *Southern India: its history, peoples, commerce and industrial resources* (London, 1914–15), 717–20.

68 *Report of the Forest Committee*, I, 3.

69 Ibid., I, 3.

70 A deputy tahsildar, who cited the need to get wood for cremation as an emotive example, B. Suryanarayana, Ibid, II, 276–7.

71 See *Report on the Working of the Forest Department in the Madras Presidency* (annual).

72 Dvt 1575 29 Oct. 1931.

73 Rev 3034 24 Aug. 1918; Dvt 710 5 Mar. 1936.

74 Dvt 1126 15 Sept. 1933.

75 *Report of the Forest Committee*, I, 6–8; II, *passim*.

76 Rev 3165 1 Nov. 1913, North Arcot resettlement report, 29.

77 *Report of the Forest Committee*, II, *passim*.

78 Dvt 922 1 May 1930; Dvt 1876 11 Oct. 1930; Dvt 1126 15 Sept. 1933; Dvt 1537 22 Oct. 1931; Dvt 1575 29 Oct. 1931.

79 C. K. Ramaswami Gounder 1 Dec. 1937, in Dvt 2038 19 Aug. 1938.

80 *Report of the Forest Committee*, II, 291–2, 300–2, 395.

81 K. Ramaswami Ayyar in ibid., II, 329.

82 Statistics on 'fodder crops' are especially fallible because of the crop known as 'fodder cholam'; this is almost certainly sometimes reported as 'cholam' (an edible grain) and sometimes as 'fodder crop'.

83 Krishnaswami, *Rural Problems*, 223–4.

84 *Report of the Forest Committee*, I, 8.

85 Ibid., I, 7.

86 Ibid., I, 7.

87 Nicholson, *Manual of the Coimbatore District*, 245; *Manual of the Court of Wards*, 140–3; V.C. Rangaswami, *MPBC*, IV, 614–15.

88 V.C. Rangaswami, *MPBC*, IV, 614–15.

89 Rev 1044 22 Apr. 1938.

90 This judgement is based on evidence in: Survey of Peykulam, *MPBC*, V, 36–8; Thomas and Ramakrishnan, 16 (Vadamalaipuram); P. S. Seshadri, 'South Indian village studies', 232–3; AERC surveys of Vadamalaipuram (48), Rajagambiran (40), Sengipatti (42), Upattur (47), Arilikottai (49), Vadagareddipatti (54).

91 BP 1213 10 Sept. 1947; Sivaswamy, *Caste and Standard of Living*.

92 The livestock censuses were published separately and reproduced in the appendices to the various editions of *A Statistical Atlas of the Madras Presidency*.

93 *Report on the Working of the Forest Department in the Madras Presidency* (annual).

94 BP 1213 10 Sept. 1947; BP 3422 22 Nov. 1932.

95 *MELAC*, II, 168-9, 181; IV, 238; CoW 26-P 22 Nov. 1940; Rev 3105 (C) 5 Dec. 1938.

96 Petition from Udaiyarpalaiyam taluk in Dvt 2138 29 Nov. 1930.

97 Rev 1892 23 Sept. 1934.

98 This exercise compares figures in BP 1213 10 Sept. 1947 and figures in Rev 1357 (C) Apr. 1918.

99 G. Blyn, *Agricultural Trends in India, 1891–1947: output, availability, and productivity* (Pennsylvania, 1966), appendix 3A, 253–311.

100 BP 237-M 4 Aug. 1942; Krishnaswami, *Rural Problems*, 140; J. S. Ponniah, 'Production and marketing of raw cotton in the Madras Presidency', D.Litt. thesis, Madras, 1944, II, 77–98.

101 P. J. Thomas, *The Problem of Rural Indebtedness* (Madras, 1934); R. S. Vaidyanatha Aiyar, *A Memorandum on the Ryotwari Landholders in Madras* (Madras, 1933); B. V. Narayanaswamy Naidu and V. Venkataraman, *The Problem of Rural Indebtedness* (Annamalainagar, 1935); GOM: *Report on Agricultural Indebtedness* by W. R. S. Sathyanathan (Madras, 1935).

102 Thomas and Ramakrishnan, 31–2 (Vadamalaipuram); see also Ponniah, 'Production and marketing', II, 25 on finance in the southern cotton tracts.

103 AERC (40) Rajagambiran.

104 AERC (48) Vadamalaipuram; see also the surveys of Vadamalaipuram in Slater, *Some South Indian Villages* and Thomas and Ramakrishnan.

105 AERC (42) Sengipatti.

106 This impression is culled from the data on land transfers in the AERC surveys.

107 AERC (49) Arilikottai; AERC (40) Rajagambiran; AERC (54) Vadagareddipatti.

108 *Census of India 1951*, vol. III Madras and Coorg, Pt. IIA, Tables B-I and B-III.

109 N. Subrahmanyam, 'Seasonal control of rural life and activities in the Conjeeveram region', *JMGA*, XVII, 2 (1942); V. S. Krishnan, 'The Tambraparni Ryot: a study of the rural economy of the Tinnevelly district', Gokhale Prize Essay, 1931 (in Madras University library); M. Krishnamurthi Iyer, 'Irrigation in Trichinopoly', *JMGA*, VII, 3 (1933–4); A. S. Rajamanickam, 'The crops of the Trichinopoly district', *JMGA*, VII, 3 (1933–4); K. C. Ramakrishnan, 'A model of intensive cultivation in the Cauvery valley', *JMGA*, VII, 3 (1933–4); K. S. Gopalan, 'A note on the agricultural geography of the environs on Tanjore', *JMGA*, XII, 2 (1937).

110 See the chapters on agriculture in the various district *Gazetteers*; Vasantha Devi, 'Some aspects of the agricultural geography of south India'.

111 There are many good, personal descriptions of rice cultivation in GB: *Royal Commission on Agriculture in India, Volume III, Evidence taken in Madras* (London, 1927); D.H. Grist, *Rice* (London, 5th ed., 1975).

112 BP 1213 10 Sept. 1947.

113 Slater, *Some South Indian Villages*, 59 (Gangaikondan).

114 BP 1213 10 Sept. 1947; K. Balakrishna Ayyar, *MPBC*, III, 904-6; T. Venkasami Row, *A Manual of the District of Tanjore in the Madras* (Madras, 1883), 380-1; Rev 1890 3 Sept. 1946.

115 BP 1213 10 Sept. 1947; and see examples of waram contracts in Rev 1357(C) 8 Apr. 1918.

116 BP 1213 10 Sept. 1947.

117 'The big porakkudi is in a much better position, being absolute owner of his own cattle and often employing pannaiyals. He is a real middleman, not a contract labourer.' Rev 1537(C) 25 Aug. 1922.

118 For the addresses of the big estates see the preliminary survey for a putative agricultural income tax in Rev 924(C) 5 May 1945.

119 BP 1213 10 Sept. 1947.

120 Dvt 385 (C) 13 Feb 1937.

121 Slater, *Some South Indian Villages*, 68 (Eruvellipet).

122 Section on Tanjore in the reports on debt slavery in Dvt 385 (C) 13 Feb. 1937.

123 Rev 1537 (C) 25 Aug. 1922.

124 Ibid.; BP 1213 10 Sept. 1947; Sivaswamy, *Caste and Standard of Living*.

125 See the surveys of Dusi, Gangaikondan and Eruvellipet in Slater, *Some South Indian Villages*; surveys of Chittampatti and Kodikulam in *MPBC*, V.

126 D. Kumar, *Land and Caste in South India: agricultural labour in the Madras Presidency during the nineteenth century* (Cambridge, 1965); B. Hjejle, 'Slavery and agricultural bondage in the nineteenth century', *Scandinavian Economic History Review*, XV, 1 and 2 (1967).

127 Kumar, *Land and Caste*, 144-67.

128 GOM: *Report of the Agricultural Committee* (Madras, 1889), 63, 91.

129 M. Adas, *The Burma Delta: economic development and social change on an Asian rice frontier, 1852–1941* (Madison, 1974), 58; C. Robequain, *The Economic Development of French Indochina* (London, 1944); J. C. Ingram, *Economic change in Thailand, 1850-1970* (Stanford, 1971).

130 Dvt 1312 26 Oct. 1933.

131 *Report of the Forest Committee*, II, *passim*.

132 BP 92 11 July 1934; Rev 1537(C) 25 Aug. 1922.

133 V. Subrahmanyam, 'Some aspects of the chemistry of swamp soils', *Current Science*, V, 25 (1937).

134 Venkasami Row, 348–9; K. S. Chandrasekharan, 'The physical geography of the Tanjore district', *JMGA*, XII, 2 (1937), 119; M. Anandan, 'Rice crop in the Tanjore delta', *MAJ*, XXVII, 7 (1939)

135 On a trend from 1884–5 to 1955–6, in each year an extra 0.0121 of the total area of the Tanjore district was double-cropped, an extra 0.068 in South Arcot, an extra 0.069 in Chingleput, 0.047 in North Arcot, and 0.030 in Madurai. In Tirunelveli and Ramnad, however, there was a decline (0.029 and 0.016).

136 *Srinivasan Report*; Slater, *Some South Indian Villages*, 87(Dusi); Chandrasekharan, 'The physical geography of the Tanjore district'; BP 619 14 Mar. 1923; Rev 1537(C) 25 Aug. 1922.

137 Blyn, *Agricultural Trends in India*.

138 B. Viswanath in Dvt 910 3 Mar. 1947.

139 Selections LXV, *Papers relating to the Survey and Settlement of the Salem District*; Rev 3118 7 Dec. 1938; Rev 1357(C) 25 Aug. 1922.

140 Rev 1537 (C) 25 Aug. 1922.

141 For example, BP 619 14 Mar. 1923.

142 Rev 1590 10 Aug. 1934; BP 71 15 Jan. 1945; Rev 314 15 Feb. 1934.

143 See the statistics in *Report on Public Instruction in the Madras Presidency* (annual).

144 T.N. Kalidoss, *MPBC*, II, 142.

145 See for example the description by K. Balakrishna Ayyar, *MPBC*, III, 908.

146 D.N. Strathie, *MPBC*, III, 1241.

147 Krishnan, 'Tambraparni ryot', 25; see also ibid., 74.

148 On migration see K. S. Sandhu, *Indians in Malaya: some aspects of their immigration and settlement (1786–1957)* (Cambridge, 1969); N. R. Chakravarti, *The Indian Minority in Burma: the rise and decline of an immigrant community* (Oxford, 1971); X. S. Thani Nayagam, 'Tamil migration to Guadeloupe and Martinique 1853–83', C. E. Glick, 'The changing position of two Tamil groups in West Malaya', Cheng Siok Hwa, 'Indian labour in the rice industry of pre-war Burma', in *Proceedings of the Second International Conference Seminar of Tamil Studies* ed. R. E. Asher (Madras, 1971), II; N. V. Sovani, *Economic Relations of India with South East Asia and the Far East* (Delhi, 1949), 37–47); J. Geoghegan, *Note on Emigration from India* (Calcutta, 1873); *Census of India 1951* vol. III Madras and Coorg, Pt. I, 25–6; S. Arasaratnam, *Indians in Malaysia and Singapore* (London, 1970); J. R. Andrus, *Burmese Economic Life* (Oxford, 1947), 23–5; E. Meyer, 'Impact de la dépression des années 1930 sur l'économie et la société rurale de Sri Lanka', *Purusartha* (Paris, 1975); R. Jayaraman, 'Indian emigration to Ceylon: some aspects of the historical and social background of the emigrants', *IESHR*, IV, 4 (1967).

149 Letter from J. T. Gwynn written in Radhapuram between April and September 1910, Gwynn papers, Box III, SAS Archive.

150 Slater, *Some South Indian Villages*, 82; Thomas and Ramakrishnan, 118.

151 Slater, *Some South Indian Villages*, 8 (Eruvellipet).

152 Seshadri, 'South Indian village studies', 141–2.

153 Slater, *Some South Indian Villages*, 73–4 (Gangaikondan).

154 Rev 1537 (C) 25 Aug. 1922.

155 See the references in footnote 148.

156 Estimates of remittance in Dvt 2064 9 May 1947, and Andrus.

157 Rev 1357 (C) 1918.

158 Rev 1537(C) 25 Aug. 1922.

159 Slater, *Some South Indian Villages*, 86 (Dusi).

160 Thomas and Ramakrishnan, 188.

161 Ibid., 153 (Eruvellipet).

162 Ibid., 121-2 (Pallakurichi); Slater, *Some South Indian Villages*, 78

163 Slater, *Some South Indian Villages*, 57 (Gangaikondan); Thomas and Ramakrishnan, 71.

164 Surveys of Kodikulam and Chittampatti, *MPBC*, V.

165 For example see G. Djurfeldt and S. Lindberg, *Behind Poverty: the social formation in a Tamil village* (London, 1975).

166 Krishnan, 'Tambraparni ryot', 22.

167 Tanjore Collector 22 Nov. 1936 in Dvt 385(C) 13 Feb. 1937.

168 Dated 20 Dec. 1938 in Dvt 859 27 May 1936.

169 Tanjore Collector 15 Mar. 1934 in Dvt 859 27 May 1936.

170 Dvt 859 27 May 1936; Dvt 946 7 Apr. 1938; PWL 462-L 23 Feb. 1933; for an individual history of mirasidari obstruction and governmental helplessness see PWL 2055-L 14 July 1930.

171 Letter dated 26 Jan. 1933 in Dvt 859 27 May 1936.

172 T. B. Pandian, *The Slaves of the Soil in Southern India* (Madras, 1893), 26–9.

173 Sivaswamy, *Caste and Standard of Living*, 23.

174 Rev 2435 26 June 1918; Dvt 859 27 May 1936.

175 G. R. Hilson 6 May 1930 in Dvt 1299 28 June 1930.

176 Ibid.; BP 1662 28 May 1931; Rev 2046 8 Nov. 1930; *Season and Crop* for 1932–3, 6; Rev 989(C) 5 June 1933; Dvt 1312 26 Oct. 1933.

177 Vaidyanatha Aiyar, *A Memorandum*; Dvt 587 20 Apr. 1931; Dvt 1439 2 Oct. 1931; Dvt 1312 26 Oct. 1933; Rev 73 P 10 Jan. 1934; Rev 1959 16 Sept. 1931.

178 Tanjore Collector 18 May 1933, in Rev 989 (C) 5 June 1933.

179 For example, Thomas and Ramakrishnan, 116 (Gangaikondan).

180 M. P. Ramalinga Mudaliar, *MPBC*, II, 387.

181 I. S. Kuttilingam Pillai, 'A plea for a protective duty on rice', *MAJ*, XXVIII, 5 (1940–1), 163–4.

182 BP 71 15 Jan 1945; PWL 584–I 8 Mar. 1934.

183 Sandhu, 182–5, 310–17; *Census of India 1951*, Vol. II, Pt.I, 25–6; Andrus, 29, 34, 688; Jayaraman, 'Indian emigration to Ceylon'.

184 Dvt 2064 9 May 1947.

185 M. K. Vellodi, 6 Jan. 1934 in PWL 584–I 8 Mar. 1934.

186 Rev 989(C) 5 June 1933.

187 R. Sivarama Ayyar, *MPBC*, V, 397.

188 Slater, *Some South Indian Villages*, 81.

189 Thomas and Ramakrishnan, 146.

190 J. L. S. Brown, 11 Oct. 1940 in BP 463 13 Feb. 1941.

191 GOM: *Report of the Economist for Enquiry into Rural Indebtedness, 1946* by B. V. Narayanaswamy Naidu (Madras, 1946), 39; Shoji Ito, 'A note on the "business combine" in India—with special reference to the Nattukottai Chettiars', *The Developing Economies*, II, 3 (1966)LJ; *Measures of Food Control, Procurement and Controlled Distribution of Food and their Effects on the Agrarian Economy* prepared by the Agricultural Economics Research Centre, University of Madras (Madras, n.d.)

192 Figures are from Slater, *Some South Indian Villages*; Thomas and Ramakrishnan; and M. R. Haswell, *Economics of Development in Village India* (London, 1967).

193 K. Gough in M. N. Srinivas (ed.), *India's Villages* (Bombay, 1955), 100–1.

194 A. Béteille, *Caste, Class, and Power: changing patterns of stratification in a Tanjore village* (Berkeley and Los Angeles, 1965), 195–6.

195 AERC (30).

196 R. Sivarama Ayyar, *MPBC*, II, 335.

197 Ramakrishnan, 'A model of intensive cultivation'.

198 Krishnan, 'Tambraparni ryot'.

199 Ibid., 54.

200 Sivaswamy, *Caste and Standard of Living*, 28.

201 Ibid., 27.

202 T.S. Sabapathi Pillai, *MPBC*, III, 776.

203 BP 386-M 9 Sept. 1942; BP 237-M 4 Aug. 1942.

204 Rev 2870 27 Nov. 1947.

205 Landholders' petition dated 12 Sept. 1947 in Rev 2299 30 Sept. 1947.

206 K. Rama Varma Raja dated 2 Sept 1947 in Ibid.

207 Rev 2870 27 Nov. 1947.

208 Rev 2014 7 Nov. 1945.

209 Sivaswamy, *Caste and Standard of Living*, 13.

210 GOM: *Scheme of Road Development for the Madras Presidency*, by A. Vipan (Madras, 1935).

211 For example Home 4030(C) 24 July 1939.

212 Rev 2014 7 Nov. 1945.

213 Tanjore Collector 17 Aug. 1945 in ibid.

214 Tanjore Collector 20 Mar. 1946 in ibid.

215 M. Anantanarayanan, 13 June 1946, in Dvt 4685 23 Dec. 1946.

216 K. Bhashyam 2 Aug. 1946 in Ibid. On the Tanjavur agitations see Saraswathi Menon, 'Historical development of Thanjavur Kisan Movement: interplay of class and caste factors', *Economic and Political Weekly*, Annual number, Feb. 1979.

217 AERC (30) Kaliyanapuram.

218 See Béteille, *Caste, Class, and Power*; E. K. Gough, 'Caste in a Tanjore village' in E. R. Leach (ed.), *Aspects of Caste in South India, Ceylon and Northeast Pakistan* (Cambridge, 1960); J. P. Mencher, *Agriculture and Social Structure in Tamilnadu: past origins, present transformations, future prospects* (Durham, 1978).

219 Nicholson, *Manual of the Coimbatore District*, 184–5.

220 Buchanan, II, 275–6, 286, 308, 316, 331–2.

221 Ibid., II, 255, 315, 319–20; III, 454.

222 Nicholson, *Manual of the Coimbatore District*, 184–5, 204, 216–32, 491–2; Sarada Raju, 116–17; Adiceam, 222.

223 Nicholson, *Manual of the Coimbatore District*, 491–2.

224 Ibid., 394.

225 BP 2866 9 Sept. 1937; Rev 322 23 Sept. 1934.

226 Nicholson, *Manual of the Coimbatore District*, 444–5.

227 Krishnaswami, *Rural Problems in Madras*, 189–90; K. W. Little, 'Alambady cattle', *JMGA*, XI, 2 (1936), 127–9; K. C. Ramakrishnan, 'The agricultural geography of the Coimbatore district', *JMGA*, V, 2 (1930–1) Nicholson, *Manual of the Coimbatore District*, 480.

228 Nicholson, *Manual of the Coimbatore District*, 445.

229 Ibid., 179–83; H. Le Fanu, *A Manual of the Salem District in the Presidency of Madras* (Madras, 1883); J. W. B. Dykes, *Salem: an Indian Collectorate* (London, 1853).

230 Nicholson, *Manual of the Coimbtore District*, 216–32.

231 B. E. F. Beck, *Peasant Society in Konku: a study of right and left subcastes in South India* (Vancouver, 1972), dates the decline of Gounder caste headmen to the early twentieth century.

232 J. T. Wheeler, *Handbook to the Cotton Cultivation in the Madras Presidency* (Madras, 1862)

233 Ibid., 250; Nicholson, *Manual of the Coimbatore District*, 232.

234 Ponniah, 'Production and marketing', II, 47–50; A. Kannayya, 'The cultivation of Cambodia cotton'; Sir Clement Simpson in *Evidence taken before the Indian Cotton Committee*, II, ii, 22; P. Gopalratnam, 'Rural studies: Madathupalaiyam village, Coimbatore district', *MAJ*, XIX, 12 (1931).

235 Narayanaswamy Naidu, *Groundnut*; Ramakrishnan, 'Agricultural geography', 103.

236 BP 1213 10 Sept. 1947.

237 N. Ganesamurti, 'Economic survey of a south Indian village—Perumanallur', *MAJ*, XXIII, 7 (1935), especially 274; Gopalratnam, 'Rural studies: Madathupalaiyam'; Rev 1892 23 Sept. 1934, South Salem resettlement report, 18; Dvt 2038 19 Aug. 1938; Dvt 1575 29 Oct. 1931; BP 1213 10 Sept. 1947.

238 Nicholson, *Manual of the Coimbatore District*, 179–80, 271–2.

239 The official wage censuses, though of doubtful value, appear to confirm this; see PWL 1933-L 2 Sept. 1927; PWL 1586-L 28 July 1932.

240 Sivaswamy, *Caste and Standard of Living*, 11–12; Gopalratnam, 'Rural studies: Madathupalaiyam', 523.

241 Ganesamurti, 'Economic survey—Perumanallur'.

242 See statements of evidence in GB: *Royal Commission on Labour in India. Evidence Vol. III Madras and Coorg* (London, 1931).

243 Dvt 2241 9 Sept 1938 (the 1936 wage census); BP 632 3 Mar. 1939.

244 V. S. Narasimhan, 'Agricultural labour in the southern taluks of Coimbatore district', M.Litt thesis, Madras, 1959, 52–78.

245 AERC (58) Keeranathan; average worked out from 10 other AERC surveys.

246 BP 1213 10 Sept. 1947; Rev 1357(C) 8 Apr. 1918.

247 Nicholson, *Manual of the Coimbatore District*, 300–1.

248 The other districts: Chingleput, 1.59 crores; South Arcot 2.71; North Arcot 2.14; Tanjavur 4.06; Madurai 3.52; Ramnad, 3.26; Tirunelveli, 4.51; Tiruchi, 2.64; Salem 2.58; in the data it is impossible to separate transfers of agricultural land from transfers in houses and other forms of immoveable property; *Report on the administration of the Registration Department of the Madras Presidency* for 1925.

249 R. S. Subrahmanya Ayyar, *MPBC*, II, 468–9.

250 T. A. Ramalingam Chettiar, *MPBC*, IV, 427.

251 N. G. Ranga, *MPBC*, III, 741, 747.

252 C. M. Ramachandra Chettiar, 'The geographical distribution of crime and civil litigation in south India', *JMGA*, XII, 2 (1937), 75.

253 Ibid., 72.

254 Nicholson, Manual of the Coimbatore District, 268.

255 BP 1213 10 Sept. 1947.

256 Ibid.

257 Ganesamurti, 'Economic survey—Perumanallur', 273.

258 BP 1249 16 Apr. 1928.

259 Krishnaswami, *Rural Problems in Madras*, 139–40; P. V. Krishna Ayyar, 'Co-operation in agriculture with special reference to sugarcane crop in Coimbatore district', *MAJ*, XXVIII, 2 (1940); Ponniah, 'Production and marketing', II, 163–70.

260 AERC (58) Keeranathan.

261 Dvt 2138 29 Nov. 1930; Dvt 1575 29 Oct. 1931.

262 C. G. Nataraja Mudaliar, *MPBC*, III, 727.

263 AERC (58) Keeranathan; see also Beck, *Peasant Society*.

264 R. C. Dutt, *The Economic History of India* (reprint, Delhi, 1976).

265 M. McAlpin, 'Railroads, prices and peasant rationality: India, 1860–1920', *Journal of Economic History*, XXXIV, 3 (1974).

266 D. Narain, *Impact of Price Movements on Areas under Selected Crops in India 1900–1939* (Cambridge, 1965); C.H. Hanumantha Rao, *Agricultural Production Functions, Costs and Returns in India* (London, 1965).

267 P. H. Nye and D. J. Greenland, *The Soil under Shifting Cultivation* (Farnham Royal, 1960).

268 It is possible that changes in the category 'fallow' were caused by re-definition of areas described as 'waste', 'forest', or 'not available for cultivation'. This possibility was tested using correlation and regression procedures (on district-level data). The results tended to discount this possibility.

269 BP 2866 9 Sept. 1937.

270 R. Sivarama Ayyar, *MPBC*, II, 344; survey of Kambliampatti, *MPBC*, V.

271 Blyn, *Agricultural Trends in India*, appendix 3A, 253–311, for the district-war calculations see below table 30.

272 Survey of Kambliampatti, *MPBC*, V, 46.

273 Haswell, 40.

274 The following table shows Pearson zero-order correlation coefficients of fallows with the acreage under paddy, dry grains and pulses, oilseeds, cotton, and other non-food crops (mainly sugar, spices, fruit, vegetables and tobacco) over the period 1884–5 to 1955–6 (from 1915–16 to 1955–6 in the case of Ramnad) for each of the Tamil districts. To smooth out differences caused by slight changes in district boundaries all acreages were expressed as a proportion of the total area of the district. The table lists only those coefficients significant at the .001 level.

	Correlation of fallows with				
	Paddy	Dry grains	Oilseeds	Cotton	Other non-food
Chingleput	−.7297				
N. Arcot			.5252		
S. Arcot	.7884	−.8105	.7190		−.5451
Salem		−.4078	.5775	.4480	.6074
Coimbatore	.3984	−.7471	.4522	.4135	.6865
Tanjavur	−.5208	.4463		.5897	−.4642
Tiruchi				.4893	−.4968
Madurai		−.6657			.5410
Ramnad	−.6666	−.8888		−.8385	−.3973
Tirunelveli		−.7549	−.4137		
Tamilnad	.3605	−8707	.7315	.5166	

The table shows that fallows tended to vary inversely with dry grains in the plains, and with paddy in the valleys; and to vary directly with cotton and oilseeds (mainly groundnut) in the plains. Further investigation with higher-order correlations (controlling for irrigation, price, and the collinear effects of other crops) and linear regressions tended to confirm these relationships.

275 GOM: *Report of the Rice Production and Trade in the Madras Presidency* by C. R. Srinivasan (Madras, 1934), copy in Dvt 322 2 Mar. 1935.

Chapter 4

1 There are some estimates of the proportion of agricultural produce which was exported; they range, on an all-India basis, between 10 and 30 per cent. See for instance GOI: *Report of the Indian Central Banking Enquiry* (Calcutta, 1931), para. 266; K. Mukerji, *Levels of Economic Activity and Public Expenditure in India* (London, 1962).

2 For the definition of 'rural produce' and for some of the figures on which this calculation is based, see table 4.

3 See section on 'land use and food supply' in chapter 3.

4 D. Ludden, 'Agrarian organization in Tinnevelly district, 800–1900 A.D.', Ph. D. thesis, University of Pennsylvania, 1978, ch. VII.

5 This is an assumption based on a lack of evidence. Nowadays there is considerable trade in dry grains, over quite long distances, in the plain tracts. But British officials constantly asserted that there was little or no trade in dry grains over any significant distance.

6 V. Krishnan, 'Trade centres of Tinnevelly district', *JMGA*, XV, 3 (1940), 276.

7 V. Krishnan, 'Fairs, festivals and shandies in Trichinopoly district', *JMGA*, VII, 3 (1933–4); GOM, *List of Fairs and Festivals occuring within the limits of the Madras Presidency* by J. L. Ranking (Madras, 1868); cattle fairs were listed in GOM, *The Villagers' Calender* (an annual publication of the agriculture department).

8 GOM, *Report of the Rice Production and Trade in the Madras Presidency* by C.R. Srinivasan (Madras, 1934) [Hereafter *Srinivasan Report*], copy in Dvt 322 2 Mar. 1935, 29–30.

9 R. S. Vaidyanatha Ayyar, *MPBC*, II, 77.

10 The following discussion is based on *Srinivasan Report*; Dvt 560 26 Apr. 1934; C. R. Srinivasa Iyengar, 'Rice culture in the Madras Presidency', *MAJ*, XXXII, 11 and 12 (1944).

11 E. Adicéam, *La Géographie de l'irrigation dans le Tamilnad* (Paris, 1966); M. N. Vasantha Devi, 'Some aspects of the agricultural geography of south India', M.Litt. thesis Madras, 1963; K. Ramamurthy, 'Some aspects of the regional geography of Tamilnad', M.Litt. thesis, Madras, 1945.

12 *Srinivasan Report*, 36–7, 71.

13 GOI: *Indian Famine Commission 1898, Appendices Vol. II, Evidence taken before the Indian Famine Commission* (Calcutta, 1898), especially evidence of Abdur Rahim Ahmed and S. P. V. Karuppa Chetty, 70–2.

14 This account is based on 'Report of the Joint Registrar of Co-operative Societies on marketing facilities for Tanjore rice' in Dvt 1247 12 Oct. 1933; Rev 354 19 Feb. 1929; *Srinivasan Report*, 56–9; R. S. Vaidyanatha Ayyar, *MPBC*, II, 77; V. Krishnan, 'The Tambraparni Ryot: a study of the rural economy of the Tinnevelly district', Gokhale Prize essay (in Madras University library), 1931, 50–2.

15 *Srinivasan Report*, 37.
16 Krishnan, 'Tampraparni Ryot'.
17 N.C. Thomas, *MPBC*, III, 886.
18 *Srinivasan Report*, 61–2.
19 Among many references see K. Balakrishna Ayyar, *MPBC*, III, 904–8; R. Sundaram Ayyar, *MPBC*, II, 522; T. N. Kalidoss, *MPBC*, II, 137; W. S. Subrahmanya Ayyar, *MPBC*, II, 210–12; M. Devadason, *MPBC*, II, 277–9.
20 See the figures in *A Statistical Atlas of the Madras Presidency* (Madras, 1924).
21 *Srinivasan Report*; Dvt 1312 26 Oct. 1933; Dvt 1247 12 Oct. 1933; Dvt 560 26 Apr. 1934.
22. There was also a demand for Tamilnad rice on the West Coast.
23 *Srinivasan Report*, 11–12.
24 Ibid., 20–1.
25 K. S. Srinivasa Ayyar, *MPBC* II, 364; K. Balakrishna Ayyar, *MPBC*, III, 904-8; K. S. Venkatarama Iyer, *MPBC*, II, 20; K. Viswanathan, *MPBC*, II, 124; Krishnan, 'Tambraparni Ryot', 41–3.
26 R. Subbiah Mudaliar, *MPBC*, II, 549; Rev 1537(C) 25 Aug. 1922, Tanjore resettlement report, 17.
27 R. Sivarama Ayyar, *MPBC*, II, 337–8.
28 Rev(Spl) 593(JC) 23 Oct. 1918; Home(Jud) 334 10 Feb. 1919; Home(Jud) 2673 2 Dec. 1918; Home(Jud) 15 Nov. 1918.
29 Krishnan, 'Tambraparni ryot', 50–1; K. G. Sivaswamy, *MPBC*, II, 424.
30 *Srinivasan Report*, 57; K. S. Seshachela Ayyar, *MPBC*, II, 428.
31 D. A. Washbrook, 'Country politics: Madras 1880 to 1930', *MAS*, VII, 3 (1973).
32 Srinivasa Iyengar, 'Rice culture in the Madras Presidency'.
33 M. Adas, *The Burma Delta: economic development and social change on an Asian rice frontier 1852–1941* (Wisconsin, 1974), 22,58; J. C. Ingram, *Economic Change in Thailand 1850–1970* (Stanford, 1971), 220; C. Robequain, *The Economic Development of French Indochina* (London, 1944), 220; V. D. Wickizer and M. K. Bennett, *The Rice Economy of Monsoon Asia* (Stanford, 1941), 320–3.
34 Dvt 1312 26 Oct. 1933.
35 *Srinivasan Report*, 20–1; Dvt 560 26 Apr. 1934; Dvt 1312 26 Oct. 1933.
36 Rev(Spl) 593(C) 23 Oct. 1918.
37 I. S. Kutttalingam Pillai, 'A plea for a protective duty on rice', *MAJ*, XXVIII, 5(1940), 161.
38 R. Subbiah Mudaliar, *MPBC*, II, 549; Dvt 560 26 Apr. 1934.
39 Dvt 1312 16 Oct. 1933.
40 Wickizer and Bennett, 85–100; Rev 948 11 May 1934; Rev 775 23 Apr. 1934; N. V. Sovani, *Economic Relations of India with South East Asia and the Far East* (Delhi, 1949), 53–6.
41 Rev 775 23 Apr. 1934; Dvt 1312 26 Oct. 1933; Dvt 322 2 Mar. 1935.
42 *Measures of Food Control, Procurement and Controlled Distribution of Food and their Effects on the Agrarian Economy*, prepared by the Agricultural Economics Research Centre, University of Madras(Madras, n.d), 45.
43 Dvt 1247 12 Oct. 1933; Dvt 56 26 Apr. 1934, especially note by the Deputy Director of Agriculture (Coimbatore).
44 Dvt 1312 26 Oct. 1933.

45 See for example Dvt 587 20 Apr. 1931; Dvt 1439 2 Oct. 1931; Dvt 1312 26 Oct. 1933; *The Hindu* 3 Mar. 1933.

46 Kuttilingam Pillai, 'A plea'; Dvt 322 2 Mar. 1935; Dvt 1247 12 Oct. 1933 especially note by Deputy Director of Agriculture dated 16 June 1933.

47 *Season and Crop Report of the Madras Presidency* for 1934–5 and 1935–6.

48 *Measures of Food Control*; Dvt 228 6 Feb 1941; Dvt 734 9 Apr. 1941; Dvt 138 23 Jan. 1941.

49 K.S. Srinivasa Ayyar, *MPBC*, II, 364.

50 N. Thiruvengadatha Iyengar in *The Hindu* 3 Mar. 1933.

51 *Srinivasan Report*, 62–3.

52 Dvt 1247 12 Oct. 1933.

53 Y. Ranganayakulu, *MPBC*, IV, 200–5; K. Ramiah, 'The economics of Tanjore paddy growing', *MAJ*, XIX, 3(1931).

54 Dvt 1247 12 Oct. 1933.

55 *Srinivasan Report*, 71.

56 Ibid., 71.

57 Dvt 228 6 Feb. 1941; *Measures of Food Control*.

58 S. Playne, *Southern India: its history, peoples, commerce and industrial resources* (London, 1914–15), 182; H. Brown, *Parry's of Madras: a story of British enterprise in India* (Madras, 1954), 235–6; G. Reinhart, *Volkart Brothers: in commemmoration of the seventy-fifth anniversary of the foundation* (Winterthur, 1926).

59 Ludden, 'Agrarian organisation', ch. VIII; J. T. Wheeler, *Handbook to the Cotton Cultivation in the Madras Presidency* (Madras, 1862).

60 J. S. Pooniah, 'Production and marketing of raw cotton in the Madras Presidency', D. Litt. thesis, Madras, 1944 I, iv. The pagination in Ponniah's thesis is rather esoteric; references here to the first volume cite only the chapter (e.g. I, vi) while references to the second volume cite the page (e.g II, 45). Also, Reinhart, *passim*; H. R. Pate, *Tinnevelly District Gazeteer*, vol. I (Madras, 1917), 212–15; GOM: *A Manual of Madras Administration* by C. D. Mclean (Madras, 1885), 501–4.

61 K. C. Ramakrishnan, 'Finance and forced sale of produce', *MAJ*, XVIII, 3 (1920).

62 Wheeler, 126–9; Reinhart, *passim*; W. Francis, *Gazetteer of the South Arcot District* vol. I (Madras, 1906), 124.

63 B.V. Narayanaswamy Naidu, *Groundnut* (Annamalainagar, n.d.), 41–7; A.C. Venkataswami Nayudu, *MPBC*, IV, 353; O.N. Ramaswami Ayyar, *MPBC*, IV, 630–1.

64 Ponniah, 'Production and marketing', I, vii; B. M. Middleton, in GOI, *Indian Cotton Committee; Minutes of Evidence taken before the Indian Cotton Committee*, V, ii, 500.

65 J. S. Ponniah, 'Cotton and cotton marketing in the Tinnevelly district', *JMGA*, XV, 2 (1940).

66 R. Caldwell; *The Tinnevelly Shanars: a sketch of their religion and their social condition and characteristics, as a caste* (Madras, 1849), 48.

67 R. L. Hardgrave, *The Nadars of Tamilnad: the political culture of a community in change* (Berkeley and Los Angeles, 1969), 95–129.

68 J. S. Ponniah, 'The Broach of south India', *The Indian Commerce*, I, 3 (1933).

69 Ponniah, 'Production and marketing', I, vii.
70 Narayanaswamy Naidu, *Groundnut*, 41–3; A.R. Venkataswami Nayudu, *MPBC*, IV, 353; Ponniah, 'Production and marketing', II, 25–38; a general impression from *Minutes of Evidence taken before the Indian Cotton Committee*, II.
71 M. M. Ramachandra Bhupati, *MPBC*, II, 1017.
72 J.S. Ponniah, 'The kapas market at Dindigul: a study in the local factors that influence prices', *MAJ*, XXII, 11 (1934), 394–7; survey of Peykulam village, *MPBC*, IV; B. M. Middleton in *Minutes of Evidence taken before the Indian Cotton Committee*, V, ii, 50; Ponniah, 'Production and marketing', I, vii and II, 121–2; M. K. Pattabhiram, *MPBC*, II, 355–6; C. Dorairaj, *MPBC*, II, 617.
73 Naryanaswamy Naidu, *Groundnut*, 2–3, 41–3; K. S. Seshachela Ayyar, *MPBC*, II, 426–8.
74 This estimate is based on the evidence of witnesses before the *MPBC*, see for instance II, 326–8.
75 Rev 2026 5 Sept. 1916, South Arcot resettlement report; Rev 3165 1 Nov. 1913, North Arcot resettlement report; BP 92 11 July 1934, Salem resettlement report.
76 GOI: *Index Numbers of Indian Prices 1861–1931* (Delhi, 1933) and annual addenda.
77 N. Subrahmanya Ayyar, *IIC Evidence*, III, 174–6; G. Slater, *Some South Indian Villages* (Oxford, 1918), 3 (Eruvellipet).
78 B.V. Narayanaswamy Naidu and S. Thiruvengadathan, *The Madras General Sales Tax Act: a study* (Annamalainagar, 1940), 65–7.
79 O. N. Ramaswami Ayyar, *MPBC*, IV, 630–1.
80 K. G. Sivaswamy, *MPBC*, II, 424.
81 Vithaldas Anandji Sait, *MPBC*, IV, 521.
82 Report of South Arcot Groundnut Committee for 1944, in Dvt 2236 9 June 1945.
83 P. J. Thomas and K. C. Ramakrishnan, *Some South Indian Villages: a re-survey* (Madras, 1940), 171 (Eruvellipet).
84 S. P. Rajamanicka Pandaram, *MPBC*, II, 31; T. N. Ramanathan, *MPBC*, II, 479.
85 Ponniah, 'Production and marketing', I, iv.
86 Slater, *Villages*, 115; Ponniah, 'Production and marketing', I, viii; Ponniah, 'Cotton and cotton markets in the Tinnevelly district', 148.
87 Ponniah, 'Production and marketing', I, vii.
88 Ibid., I, viii.
89 Ibid., I, vii.
90 A. R. A. S. Doraisami Nadar, *MPBC*, IV, 364; M. C. Muthukumaraswami Pillai, *MPBC*, IV, 371; Sir Clement Simpson in *Minutes of Evidence taken before the Indian Cotton Committee*, V, ii, 22.
91 Indian Central Cotton Committee, *General Report on eight investigations into the finance and marketing of cultivators' cotton 1925–8* (Bombay, n.d.), especially 16, 21, 24; Ponniah, 'Production and marketing', I, vii and I, iii, appendix.
92 J. S. Ponniah, 'Underneath the cloth', *IJE*, XIII (1932–3) 1.
93 Ponniah, 'The Broach of south India', 70.

94 Brown, *Parry's*, 236; Dvt 365 10 Mar. 1931.

95 P. S. Seshadri, 'South Indian village studies: a preparatory study of 'Villar' village no. 119 in Tirumangalam taluk, Madura district, Madras province' *MAJ*, XXIII, 4 (1935), 187; S. V. Duraisami, 'Low prices and the plight of the lowly ryots' *MAJ*, XXII, 4 (1934).

96 Dvt 365 10 Mar. 1931; Dvt 2236 9 June 1945; Narayanaswami Naidu, *Groundnut*, passim.

97 For instance the towns of Tindivanam, Tirukkoilur and Vriddhachalam.

98 Thomas and Ramakrishnan, 171 (Eruvellipet).

99 Brown, *Parry's*, 236.

100 Narayanaswamy Naidu, *Groundnut*, 41–5; Narayanaswamy Naidu and Thiruvengadathan, 60; K. S. Venkatarama Ayyar, *MPBC*, IV, 334.

101 Dvt 2236 9 June 1945.

102 Narayanaswamy Naidu, *Groundnut*, 64–70.

103 Rev 1892 23 Sept. 1934, South Salem resettlement report, 18–19.

104 Rev 1034 22 Apr. 1938, North Salem resettlement report, 28.

105 Ponniah, 'Production and marketing', I, vii.

106 Ibid.

107 Ponniah, 'Cotton and cotton marketing in the Tinnevelly district', 148.

108 Ponniah, 'Producting and marketing', I, vii and II, 34–8.

109 Ponniah, 'The Broach of south India', 70.

110 Ponniah, 'Production and marketing', I, viii.

111 Ponniah, 'Production and marketing', II, 25, 38, 42; A. R. A. S. Doraisami Nadar, *MPBC*, IV, 360; Isaac Nadar, *MPBC*, IV, 383–93.

112 Ponniah, 'The Broach of south India', 70; Hardgrave, 150–1.

113 PWL 2093–L 25 Sept. 1933; PWL 398–L 16 Feb. 1933; PWL 2424–L 12 Nov. 1935; PWL 1141–L 27 May 1932.

114 Pub(Gen) 1810(C) 9 Nov. 1936; Pub(Gen) 1242(C) 9 July 1937; Pub(Gen) 2135 9 Nov. 1937; Home 2030 1 Sept. 1936.

115 F. A. Nicholson, *Manual of the Coimbatore District* (Madras, 1887), 250, 467, 519.

116 GOI: *Report of the Indian Cotton Committee 1919* (Calcutta, 1919), 121; G. Slater, *Southern India: Its political and economic problems* (London, 1936), 113–14.

117 Ponniah, 'Production and marketing', II, 97–8.

118 Ibid., I, iv.

119 Ibid., I, iv; Vithaldas Anandji Sait, *MPBC*, IV, 514–19; P. Gopalratnam, 'Rural studies: Madathupalaiyam village, Coimbatore district' *MAJ*, XIX, 12 (1931), 524.

120 Ponniah, 'Production and marketing', I, iv.

121 Ibid., I, iv and vi; S. V. Duraisami, 'Marketing of cultivators' cotton at Tirupur, Madras Presidency', *MAJ*, XXIV, 2 (1936); N. Ranganathachari' 'Marketing of cotton in Coimbatore district', M.Sc. thesis, Madras, 1958.

122 Rev 1000 11 May 1932; Ponniah, 'Production and marketing', II, 45–7.

123 A. Kannayya, 'The cultivation of Cambodia cotton in the central districts', MAJ, XXVII, 8 (1939), 278.

124 *Report of the Indian Cotton Committee 1919*.

125 F. J. Stanes in *Minutes of Evidence taken before the Indian Cotton Committee*, V, ii, 64–6; Duraisami, 'Marketing of cultivators' cotton', 68–9.

126 Ponniah, 'Production and marketing', I, vi; Duraisami, 'Marketing of culti-
     vators' cotton', 71.
127 Ponniah, 'Production and marketing', I, iv.
128 Ranganathachari, 'Marketing of cotton'; Duraisami, 'Marketing of cultivators'
     'cotton'.
129 Ponniah, 'Production and marketing', II, 38.
130 C. V. Venkatarama Iyengar, *MPBC*, IV, 457.
131 Ponniah, 'Production and marketing', I, vi and II, 38; Vithaldas Anandji Sait,
     MPBC, IV, 518–21; Duraisami, 'Marketing of cultivators' cotton', 66-9; Dvt
     2356 19 June 1945.
132 Ponniah, 'Production and marketing', I, iv and II, 37–41.
133 Ibid., I, iv and II, 168–70; T. A. Ramanathan Chettiar, *MPBC*, IV, 419–25.
134 Duraisami, 'Marketing of cultivators' cotton'; Dvt 2356 19 June 1945.
135 Ranganathachari, 'Marketing of cotton', 45–7.
136 Figures from *Annual Report of the Indian Central Cotton Committee.*
137 Ibid.
138 Ponniah, 'Protection and marketing', I, iv.
139 S. Y. Krishnaswami, *Rural Problems in Madras: Monograph* (Madras, 1947), 329.
140 J. Hurd III and K. C. Young, 'The supply and demand for railroad services in
     India 1882–1939' in *Papers Presented to the Fifth European Conference on
     Modern South Asian Studies*, mimeo, Leiden, 1976.
141 Rev 1892 23 Sept 1934.
142 S. Arasaratnam, 'Indian commercial groups and European traders 1600–1800:
     changing relationships in southeastern India', *South Asia* (new series) I, 2
     (1978).
143 F. Buchanan, *A Journey from Madras through the Countries of Mysore, Canara
     and Malabar* (London, 1807), II, 261 and III, 433, 465.
144 D. Balaji Rao, *MPBC*, II, 271–2; P. Thyagaraja Chetty, *IIC Evidence*, III, 59;
     W.B. Hunter, *IIC Evidence*, III, 275.
145 D. Balaji Rao, *MPBC*, IV, 149.
146 Vidya Sagar Pandya, *IIC Evidence*, III, 257–62; P. Thyagaraja Chetty, *IIC
     Evidence*, III, 59; V. C. Rangaswami, *MPBC*, II, 541; M. S. Natarajan, *The
     Capital Market of the Madras Presidency with Special Reference to its Evolution
     and Indigenous Institutions* (Calcutta, 1936), 16–32.
147 W. S. Subramania Aiyar, *MPBC*, II, 215.
148 Nicholson, *Manual of the Coimbatore District*, 264.
149 N.P. Krishna Ayyangar, *MPBC*, II, 169.
150 K. Balakrishna Ayyar, *MPBC*, III, 908.
151 Ibid.
152 N. G. Ranga, *Economic Organisation of Indian Villages, Volume I, Deltaic
     Village* (Bezwada, 1926), 37.
153 V. S. Seshachela Ayyar, *MPBC*, II, 426.
154 F. A. Nicholson, *Report regarding the possibilities of introducing agricultural
     banks into the Madras Presidency* (Madras, 1895-7).
155 M. S. Natarajan, *The Capital Market*; V. Krishnan, *Indigenous Banking in
     South India* (Bombay, 1959).
156 G. F. F. Foulkes, *Local Autonomy* (Madras, n.d. (probably 1937)), II, 81.
157 V. C. Rangaswami, *MPBC*, II, 541

158 M. Subbiah Mudaliar, *MPBC*, II, 545; Waljee Kanjee, *MPBC*, IV, 210.
159 M. Nadarajan, 'The Nattukottai Chetty community and south-east Asia' in *Proceedings of the First International Conference Seminar on Tamil Studies* (Kuala Lumpur, 1968), I, 252–3; C. H. Rau, 'The banking caste of southern India', *Indian Review*, VIII, 8 (1907), 593.
160 C. H. Rau, 'The banking caste'; K. Ramanathan Chettiar, *MPBC*, IV, 158–65; O. R. M. M. S. M. Sevaga Chettiar, *MPBC*, IV, 243–59; A. Savarinatha Pillai, 'Monograph of Nattukottai Chetties' banking business', *MPBC*, III, 1170–1217; A. Savarinatha Pillai, *MPBC*, 337–45; Memorandum of Nattukottai Nagarathars' Association, *MPBC*, III, 1105–9; Wadsworth papers, SAS Archive, 268–70.
161 A. Savarinatha Pillai, *MPBC*, III, 1174, quoting P.R. Sundara Ayyar in *The Indian Review*, January 1906.
162 M. Adas, 'Immigrant Asians and the economic impact of European imperialism: the role of the south Indian Chettiars in British Burma', *JAS*, XXXIII, 3 (1974).
163 O. R. M. M. S. M. Sevaga Chettiar, *MPBC*, IV, 243; M. Ramanathan Chettiar, *MPBC*, IV, 160–3.
164 A. Savarinatha Pillai, *MPBC*, IV, 339.
165 A. Savarinatha Pillai, *MPBC*, III, 1172–4.
166 Ibid.
167 Krishnan, *Indigenous Banking*, 37–8.
168 Natarajan, *The Capital Market*, 52.
169 A. Savarinatha Pillai, *MPBC*, III, 1174–5.
170 Ibid., 1176; L.K. Tulsiram, *MPBC*, IV, 302–5.
171 G. Palaniappa Mudaliar and V. Gopalakrishna Chettiar, *MPBC*, IV, 292–3.
172 O. R. M. M. S. M. Sevaga Chettiar, *MPBC*, IV, 243–6.
173 D. Sankaranarayana, 'Industries and occupations of Tinnevelly district', *JMGA*, XV, 3 (1940), 267; Krishnan, *Indigenous Banking*, 13–20; *MPBC*, II, 75–6; S. N. Subba Ayyar, *MPBC*, IV, 276–89.
174 S. N. Subba Ayyar, *MPBC*, IV, 276–89.
175 Survey of Madura town, *MPBC*, V, 351–68; Waljee Kanjee, *MPBC*, IV, 355–65.
176 A. Savarinatha Pillai, *MPBC*, III, 1175; Natarajan, *The Capital Market*; Krishnan, *Indigenous Banking*.
177 Slater, *Southern India*, 110; *IIC Evidence*, III, 91.
178 K. Viswanathan, *MPBC*, II, 124.
179 V. Gopalakrishna Chettiar, *MPBC*, IV, 292–3; M. C. Muthukumaraswami Pillai, *MPBC*, IV, 366–9; A. R. A. S. Doraisami Nadar, *MPBC*, IV, 355–65; S. Venkataswami Chetty, *MPBC*, IV, 231–40.
180 V. Gopalakrishna Chettiar, *MPBC*, IV, 292–3.
181 S. Venkataswami Chetty, *MPBC*, IV, 231.
182 A. R. A. S. Doraisami Nadar, *MPBC*, IV, 356–7.
183 M. C. Muthukumaraswami Pillai, *MPBC*, IV, 366.
184 Ibid., 366–7.
185 Survey of Madura town, *MPBC*, V, 351–68.
186 Figures in *Report on the Administration of the Registration Department of the Madras Department*; it is probable that only mortgage loans from *professional* moneylenders were registered.

187 *IIC Evidence*, III, 55.

188 Ibid., 51.

189 W. S. Subramania Ayyar, *MPBC*, II, 207.

190 Waljee Kanjee, *MPBC*, IV, 207–15; Krishnan, *Indigenous Banking*, passim; L. K. Tulsiram, *MPBC*, IV, 302–4; Lila Ram Narain Doss and Pahalajani, *MPBC*, IV, 262–7; S. Venkataswami Chetty, *MPBC*, IV, 233–4; Seth Naraindas Radhakishenda Lulla, *MPBC*, IV, 493–501.

191 Natarajan, *The Capital Market*, 50–3, 58.

192 Chit funds are described in Natarajan, *The Capital Market*; Krishnan, *Indigenous Banking*; *MPBC*, I (Report), 33–4; C. D. Nayagam, *MPBC*, IV, 350–2.

193 R. Sivarama Ayyar, *MPBC*, IV, 394.

194 Nicholson, *Agricultural banks*, 242–4.

195 C. W. B. Zacharias, *Madras Agriculture* (Madras, 1950), 195; Natarajan, *The Capital Market*, 123–9; N. Giriya Chettiar, *IIC Evidence*, III, 446–7; B. V. Narayanaswamy Naidu, 'Nidhis or loan societies of Madras', *IJE*, XVIII (1937–8), 569–79; T. A. Ramanathan Chettiar, *MPBC*, IV, 426, 444; B. Muthukumaraswami Mudaliar, *MPBC*, IV, 480–1.

196 G. V. Ganesa Ayyar, *MPBC*, IV, 309–10.

197 Natarajan, *The Capital Market*, 50–8, 135; Narayanaswamy Naidu, 'Nidhis'.

198 M. S. Natarajan, 'A study of the capital market of Madras Presidency, with special reference to its evolution and indigenous institutions' Ph. D. thesis, Madras, 1934, 129.

199 T. A. Ramanathan Chettiar, *MPBC*, III 426, 444.

200 B. Muthukumaraswami Mudaliar, *MPBC*, IV, 481.

201 Natarajan, 'A study of the capital market', 163–6.

202 G. V. Ganesa Ayyar, *MPBC*, IV, 312–14; C.V. Venkatarama Iyengar, *MPBC*, IV, 453–5; Narayanaswamy Naidu, 'Nidhis'.

203 G. V. Ganesa Ayyar, *MPBC*, IV, 310, 317.

204 Narayanaswamy Naidu, 'Nidhis', 574.

205 C. V. Venkatarama Iyengar, *MPBC*, IV, 457–60; L. W. Thompson, *MPBC*, IV, 502.

206 *Joint-stock companies in British India and in the Indian States of Mysore*, etc. (annual)

207 D. R. Balaji Rao, *MPBC*, II, 271–2 and IV 143–51; Vidya Sagar Pandya, *IIC Evidence*, III, 260; Natarajan, *The Capital Market*, 16–20; C. S. Srinivasachari, *A History of the City of Madras* (Madras, 1939), 316. Two other substantial joint-stock banks in the Madras Presidency, the Nedungadi Bank and Canara Bank, had their headquarters and most of their business on the West Coast.

208 Natarajan, 'A study of the capital market', 93.

209 Isaac Nadar, *MPBC*, IV, 399.

210 Y. Ranganayakulu, *MPBC*, IV, 198.

211 Krishnan, *Indigenous Banking*, 47.

212 Report of the Economic Depression Enquiry Committee, in BP 1662 28,May 1931, 28.

213 Ibid., 28–9.

214 T. S. Sabapathi Pillai, *MPBC*, III, 777.

215 GOM: *Report on Agricultural Indebtedness*, by W. R. S. Sathyanathan (Madras, 1935), 44; Rev 989(C) 5 June 1933; B. V. Narayanaswamy Naidu and V.

Venkataraman, *The Problem of Rural Indebtedness* (Annamalainagar, 1935), 4.

216 *Report on Agricultural Indebtedness (1935)*, 16–17.

217 M. C. Muthukumaraswami Pillai, *MPBC*, IV, 367.

218 L. K. Tulsiram, *MPBC* IV, 303.

219 O. R. M. M. S. M. Sevaga Chettiar, *MPBC*, IV, 254; Slater, *Southern India*, 110.

220 A. Savarinatha Pillai, *MPBC*, IV, 345; S. Mathuranayagam Pillai, *MPBC*, II, 110.

221 A. Savarinatha Pillai, *MPBC*, IV, 344.

222 V. Krishnan, *Indigenous Banking*, 86; A. Savarinatha Pillai, *MPBC*, IV, 1178.

223 A. Savarinatha Pillai, *MPBC*, IV, 1176, 1184.

224 G. Balasubrahmanyam, *MPBC*, II, 423; see also D. R. Balaji Rao, *MPBC*, IV, 158–9, 165; M. Balasubrahmanyam, *MPBC*, II, 423.

225 O. R. M. M. S. M. Sevaga Chettiar, *MPBC*, IV, 254.

226 Krishnan, *Indigenous Banking*, 15, 86.

227 The 1941 *Census* had no details on mother tongues.

228 C. V. Venkatarama Iyengar, *MPBC*, IV, 460; L. W. Thompson, *MPBC*, IV, 502.

229 T. A. Ramanathan Chettiar, *MPBC*, IV, 444.

230 G. V. Ganesa Ayyar, *MPBC*, II, 128.

231 Zacharias, *Madras Agriculture*, 110; Narayanaswamy Naidu, 'Nidhis'; K. T. Ramakrishnan, 'Joint-stock banking in India', Ph.D. thesis, Madras, 1949, 77–87.

232 For instance, R. Sivarama Ayyar, *MPBC*, IV, 401–2.

233 Rev 948 11 May 1934; Rev 989(C) 5 June 1933; Rev 282 5 Feb. 1932; Rev 360 25 Feb. 1933.

234 N. G. Ranga, *Agricultural Indebtedness and Remedial Measures* (Tenali, 1931); Narayanaswamy Naidu and V. Venkataraman, *The Problem of Rural Indebtedness*; P. J. Thomas, *The Problem of Rural Indebtedness* (Madras, 1934); R. S. Vaidyanatha Aiyar, *A Memorandum on the Ryotwari Landholders in Madras* (Madras, 1933); K. S. Venkatarama Aiyar, 'Agricultural indebtedness', *MAJ*, XXIII (1935); *The Indian Commerce*, I, 2 (1933), 33–6; see also *The Mirasidar*, a journal published for a short time in the 1930s, a few copies of which are decaying in the attic of the Madras University library.

235 BP 4185 22 Nov. 1934.

236 BP 391 2 Feb. 1934.

237 BP 3616 23 Nov. 1937; BP 3926 21 Dec. 1937; BP 533 21 Feb. 1939.

238 BP 3926 21 Dec. 1937.

239 V. V. Sayana, *The Agrarian Problems of Madras Province* (Madras, 1949), 163–6; B. V. Narayanaswamy Naidu and P. Vaidyanathan, *The Madras Agriculturists' Relief act—A Study* (Annamalainagar, 1939).

240 Krishnaswamy, *Rural Problems*, 371–5; Sayana, 163; Narayanaswamy Naidu and Venkataraman, *Rural Indebtedness*, 52.

241 Krishnaswamy, *Rural Problems*, 373–4; Sayana, 163–6; Narayanaswamy Naidu and Venkataraman, *Rural Indebtedness*, 53.

242 Narayanaswamy Naidu and Vaidyanathan, *Madras Agriculturists' Relief Act*, 23.

243 Ibid.

244 BP 622–S 5 Mar. 1942.

245 Board of Revenue resolution dated 27 Feb. 1942 in Ibid.

246 K. C. Ramakrishnan, 'Debt legislation and rural credit in Madras', *IJE*, XIX (1938–9), 644.

247 Nicholson, *Agricultural banks*, 237–41.

248 *MPBC*, I (*Report*), 54, 76.

249 Zacharias, *Madras Agriculture*, 160–9.

250 Thomas, *Rural Indebtedness*; GOM, *Report on Agricultural Indebtedness*.

251 Narayanaswamy Naidu and Venkataraman, *Rural Indebtedness*, especially 35–7.

252 Zacharias, *Madras Agriculture*, 110–11, 159–63.

253 Ibid., 165–7; Narayanaswamy Naidu and Venkataraman, *Rural Indebtedness*, 35–42.

254 Narayanaswamy Naidu and Venkataraman, *Rural Indebtedness*, 44–7.

255 GOI: *All India Rural Credit Survey. Volume I, The Survey Report, Part I (Rural Families)* (Bombay, 1956), 180–1.

256 W. Subramanai Ayyar, *MPBC*, II, 207.

257 T. N. Krishnaswami, *MPBC* III, 723.

258 K. T. Ramakrishnan, 'Joint-stock banking in India', 87, 195.

259 B. R. Tomlinson, *The Political Economy of the Raj 1914–47: the economics of decolonization in India* (London, 1979), 36–7.

260 *The Indian Commerce*, I, 2 (1933), 33–6.

261 *Report on the Administration of the Income Tax in the Madras Presidency* for 1934–5.

262 G. Balasubrahmanyam, *MPBC*, II, 423.

263 K. C. Ramakrishnan, 'Debt legislation and rural credit in Madras', 644.

264 See the correspondence about buying land in Mambalam in the early 1930s in the R. K. Shanmugham Chetty papers, Nehru Memorial Museum, New Delhi.

265 Figures from *Joint-stock companies in British India and in the Indian States of Mysore etc.* (annual); see also *Report on the working of the Department of Industries in the Madras Presidency* (annual).

266 See for example: South Arcot Electricity Distribution Company, *The Hindu* 14 Oct. 1933; Vizagapatam Electrical Supply Company, *The Hindu* 4 Sept. 1933; Karaikal Electrical Supply Company, *The Hindu* 27 Oct. 1934; Cuddapah Electrical Company, *The Hindu* 15 Oct. 1935; East Ramnad Electrical Supply Company, *The Hindu* 9 Jan. 1937.

267 See for example: Carnatic Investment Trust, *The Hindu* 18 Jan. 1937; Jai Bharat Insurance Company, *The Hindu* 7 Feb. 1931; Madras People's Bank, *The Hindu* 12 Dec. 1933; Bank of Hindustan, *The Hindu* 23 Dec. 1933; Indo-Carnatic Bank, *The Hindu* 17 Nov. 1934; South India Fire and General Insurance, *Justice*, 23 Mar. 1931.

268 Indian Steel Rolling Mills, *The Hindu* 10 Apr. 1934; Hindustan Tobacco, *The Hindu* 12 Oct. 1935; Vizag Sugars, *The Hindu* 5 Oct. 1935; Movie Co., *The Hindu* 6 Oct. 1933; Madras Pictures, *The Hindu* 6 May 1936; Star of the East Films, *The Hindu* 11 Nov. 1932.

269 Madras Sugars, *The Hindu* 3 Dec. 1934.

270 Srimati Sugar Mills, *The Hindu* 2 Feb. 1937.

271 East Ramnad Electrical Supply Company, *The Hindu* 9 Jan. 1937.

272 Madras Pictures, *The Hindu* 6 May 1936.

273 National Movietone, *The Hindu* 4 Apr. 1935.

274 *Report on the working of the Department of Industries in the Madras Presidency* for 1933–4, 14.

275 Natarajan, *The Capital Market*, 17; S. Narayanaswamy, 'History of Madras Stock Exchange' in E. R. Krishnamurti (ed.), *Madras Stock Exchange Silver Jubilee Souvenir 1937–1962* (Madras, 1962), 33–5.

276 Dvt 1518 13 June 1939.

277 B. V. Sri Hari Rao Naidu, Registrar of Joint-stock Companies, 13 Dec. 1938, in ibid.

278 Note from Madras Stock Exchange dated 25 Feb. 1939 in ibid.

279 *Madras Mail* 22 Oct. 1938.

280 Dvt 1518 13 June 1939.

281 H. M. Hood and K. Devasikhamani in GB: *Royal Commission on Agriculture in India, Vol. III, Evidence taken in Madras Presidency* (London, 1927), 647. Dr P. Subbarayan in ibid., 549; B. Sitarama Raju, *MPBC*, II, 47; K.S. Seshachela Iyer, *MPBC*, II, 428.

282 Thomas and Ramakrishnan, *Resurvey*, 113 (Gangaikondan).

283 B. V. Naryanaswamy Naidu, *The Co-operative Movement in the Madras Presidency* (Annamalainagar, 1933); *Annual Report on the Working of the Madras Co-operative Credit Societies Act.*

284 *MPBC*, I (*Report*), 81–2.

285 Figures from *Annual Report on the Working of the Madras Co-operative Credit Societies Act*; P. Sri Raman, 'Resuscitation of rural credit societies in Madras', *IJE*, XXII (1941–2).

286 Zacharias, *Madras Agriculture*, 218.

287 P. V. Krishna Ayyar, 'Co-operation in agriculture with special reference to sugarcane crops in Coimbatore district', *MAJ*, XXVIII, 12 (1940).

288 Syed Sha Ali Hussain, *Co-operative Land Mortgage Banks in Madras* (Madras, n.d. (probably 1941)).

289 *Statistical Tables relating to Banks in India, 1925* (Calcutta, 1927), 12–18.

290 *MPBC*, I (*Report*), 28; Natarajan, 'A study of the capital market', 93.

291 Vidya Sagar Pandya to T. R. Venkatarama Sastri 9 Aug. 1938, Venkatarama Sastri papers, Nehru Memorial Museum, New Delhi; Natarajan, *The Capital Market*, 17.

292 Figures from *Report on the Working of the Department of Industries in the Madras Presidency* (annual).

293 *The Hindu* 8 Feb. 1933, 23 Mar. 1934, 17 Nov. 1934.

294 Reserve Bank of India, *Banking and Monetary Statistics of India* (Bombay, 1954), especially Statement 29, 357–61.

295 K. T. Ramakrishnan, 'Joint-stock banking in India', 87–95.

296 For instance, Jai Bharat Insurance Company, *The Hindu* 7 Feb. 1931; South India Fire and General Insurance, *Justice* 23 Mar. 1931.

297 C. P. Matthen, *I Have Borne Much* (Madras, 1931); S. L. N. Simha, *History of the Reserve Bank of India (1935–51)* (Bombay, 1970), 183–6.

298 Vidya Sagar Pandya to T. R. Venkatarama Sastri 28 Aug. 1938, Venkatarama Sastri papers, Nehru Memorial Museum, New Delhi.

299 Dvt 1518 13 June 1939.

300 Vidya Sagar Pandya to T.R. Venkatarama Sastri, 9 Aug. 1938, 25 Aug. 1938, 17 Jan. 1939, 31 Jan. 1939; Venkatarama Sastri to Pandya 26 Jan. 1939; Venkata-

rama Sastri papers, Nehru Memorial Museum, New Delhi.

301 Reserve Bank of India, *Banking and Commercial Statistics 1954*, Table 22, 279–81.

302 *Report of the Forest Committee (Madras)* (Madras, 1913).

303 D. Kumar, *Land and Caste in South India: agricultural labour in the Madras Presidency* (Cambridge, 1965), 142; the later range is estimated from several statements in the evidence volumes of the *MPBC*.

304 Rev 1892 23 Sept. 1934, South Salem resettlement report, 12; Rev 1044 22 Apr. 1938, North Salem resettlement report, 38–9; H. Le Fanu, *A Manual of the Salem District in the Presidency of Madras* (Madras, 1883).

305 T. A. Ramanathan Chettiar, *MPBC*, IV, 445; BP 194 19 Jan. 1928; V. Mahadevan Aiyar in GOM: *Madras Survey and Land Records Committee* (Madras, 1919), II, 125.

306 *Madras Survey and Land Records Committee*, I, 20.

307 GOI: *Report of Civil Justice Committee 1924–5*, extensively quoted in G.F.F. Foulkes, *Local Autonomy* (Madras, 1937–8), I.

308 Government admitted that most of its own statistics on land were meaningless, but went on collecting them regardless. See *Madras Survey and Land Records Committee*, I.

309 D. Kumar, 'Landownership and inequality in Madras Presidency 1853–54 to 1946–47', *ESHR*, XII, 3 (1975).

310 These shaky estimates were derived by comparing, at taluk and district level, evidence on occupations (cultivator, labourer etc.) with patta statistics, data on estimated size of electorates based on property-owning franchises in GOI: *Evidence taken before the Reforms Committee (Franchise)* (Calcutta, 1919), II,vii, data from an unfinished pilot survey of assessees for a potential agricultural income tax in Rev 924(C) 5 May 1945 and BP 1494 3 Oct. 1945, and evidence from the village surveys compiled by G. F. F. Foulkes, Gilbert Slater, Thomas and Ramakrishnan, the Agricultural Economics Research Council of Madras University, various students publishing in the *Madras Agricultural Journal*, and the *MPBC*, V.

311 J. A. Dubois, *Hindu Manners, Customs and Ceremonies*, trans. and ed. H. K. Beauchamp (Oxford, 2nd ed., 1899), 87 ff.

312 K. S. Seshachela Ayyar, *MPBC*, II, 426.

313 T. A. Ramanathan Chettiar, *MPBC*, IV, 445.

314 K. S. Srinivasa Ayyar, *MPBC*, II, 366.

315 O. R. M. M. S. M. Sevaga Chettiar, *MPBC*, IV, 243; Memorandum of Nattukottai Nagarathars' Association, *MPBC*, III, 1107–8.

316 See exchange between M. Ramanathan Chettiar and H. M. Hood in *MPBC*, IV, 163–5.

317 *Madras Survey and Land Records Committee*, I, 20, 25; II, 43, 45, 69–70, 131; BP 288 28 Jan. 1939; Rev 2735 2 Dec 1916; S. Wadsworth, 'Lo, the poor Indian, 126, SAS Archive; Tottenham manuscript, 17, SAS Archive.

318 P. S. Sundara Ayyar, *MPBC*, II, 94.

319 *MPBC*, II, 302.

320 *MPBC*, II, 94, 302, 337, 366; IV, 366, 407, 544.

321 R. Sivarama Ayyar, *MPBC*, IV, 407.

322 Dvt 859 27 May 1936; Rev 2435 26 June 1918; GOM: *Village Officers' Manual*

(Madras, 1913), 38; GOM: *Village Officers' and Ryots' Manual* (Madras, 1931), 52–3; T. B. Pandian, *The Slaves of the Soil in Southern India* (Madras, 1893), 26–9; M. C. Rajah, *The Oppressed Hindus* (Madras, n.d. (around 1925)), 10–12.

323 N. Marjoribanks, Collector of South Arcot, 31 Oct. 1917 in Rev 2435 26 June 1918.

324 Compare the 1913 and 1931 editions of the *Village Officers' Manual*.

325 Hopetoun Stokes 12 Sept. 1933 in Dvt 859 27 May 1936.

326 W. K. Firminger (ed), *The Fifth Report from the Select Committee of the House of Commons on the Affairs of the East India Company, dated 28th July 1912, Volume I* (Calcutta, 1917), 191, 194–200.

327 Foulkes, *Local Autonomy*, 62.

328 For a good description see R. Sivarama Ayyar, *MPBC*, II, 335; Rev 1357(C) 8 Apr. 1918.

329 K. G. Sivaswami, *Farm Tenancy under Ryotwari Holdings in Madras: history and principles of legislation* (n.p., 1946); Rev 1357(C) 8 Apr. 1918.

330 Report of special officer on land tenure, in BP 1213 10 Sept. 1947.

331 Rev 2735 2 Dec. 1916, preliminary draft of resettlement of the Periyar tract, 18.

332 J. Sivashanmugham Pillai, *Legislative Protection for the Cultivating Tenant and Labourer* (Madras, 1947), 3; BP 851(S) 29 Mar 1942.

333 Shoji Ito, 'A note on the "business combine" in India — with special reference to the Nattukottai Chettiars', *The Developing Economies*, II, 3 (1966); M. Nadarajan, 'The Nattukottai Chettiar community and south-east Asia', in *Proceedings of the First International Conference Seminar of Tamil Studies*.

334 Nicholson, *Manual of the Coimbatore District*, 94–5, 179–83, 295, 300–1.

335 T. A. Ramanathan Chettiar, *MPBC*, IV, 427; N. G. Ranga, *MPBC*, III, 738–41, 747; R. S. Subrahmanya Ayyar, *MPBC*, II, 468–71; Survey of Kambliampatti village, *MPBC*, V.

336 *Evidence taken before the Reforms Committee (Franchise)*, II, vii, 472–565.

337 Worked out from data in BP 1494 3 Oct. 1945.

Chapter 5

1 On Parry's and Binny's see Hilton Brown, *Parry's of Madras: a story of British enterprise in India* (Madras, 1954); S. Playne, *South India: Its history, peoples, commerce and industrial resources* (London, 1914–15), 139, 164; Sir Percival Griffiths, *A History of the Inchcape Group* (London, 1977), 38–49; *The House of Binny* (Madras, 1969).

2 See Playne, 133–85

3 J. B. Norton, *The Administration of Justice in Southern India* (Madras, 1853), 100.

4 Playne, 636–716; GOM: *Handbook of Commercial Information, Madras* by M. E. Couchman (Madras, 1916); C. Abdul Hakim in *IIC Evidence*, III, 130–6.

5 See Playne, 636–716; J. Dupuis, *Madras et le Nord du Coromandel: étude des conditions de la vie indienne dans un cadre géographique* (Paris, 1960).

6 A. Sarada Raju, *Economic Conditions in the Madras Presidency 1800–1850* (Madras, 1941), 204–7.

7 N. C. Bhogendranath, *Development of the Textile Industry in Madras (up to 1950)* (Madras, 1957), 9–10.

8 Griffiths, 44.
9 Playne, 481–2.
10 Ibid., 413–14; Bhogendranath, 9–13; F. Stanes in *IIC Evidence*, III, 449–53.
11 Bhogendranath, 12–13.
12 Ibid., 15.
13 Ibid., 16–19.
14 Vidya Sagar Pandya in *IIC Evidence*, III, 257.
15 R. Mahadevan, 'The development of modern enterpreneurship in the Chettiar community of Tamilnadu, 1900–1930', *Indian History Congress*, III, Proceedings of 34th session (Chandigarh, 1973), 134–5; C. V. Venkataramana Iyengar, 'The mill industry in Coimbatore', *JMGA*, V (1930–1).
16 Griffiths, 49.
17 Bhogendranath, 25–8.
18 J. S. Ponniah, 'Production and marketing of raw cotton in the Madras Presidency', D.Litt. thesis, Madras, 1944, II, 101–4.
19 Bhogendranath, 32.
20 A. S. Pearse, *The Cotton Industry of India* (Manchester, 1930).
21 Bhogendranath, 34.
22 Mahadevan, 'The development of modern entrepreneurship', 136–7.
23 *The Hindu*, jubilee supplement, 17 Jan. 1971.
24 I am enormously indebted to R. Sunderraj for information on the Coimbatore mill industry.
25 See 'company III', Bhogendranath, 178, 186.
26 Bhogendranath, 27–34; Venkataramana Iyengar, 'The mill industry', 116.
27 Information from R. Sunderraj.
28 Mahadevan, 'The development of modern entrepreneurship', 136–7; Bhogendranath, 61; N. G. Ranga, 'The cotton mill industry of the Madras Presidency', *IJE*, 11(1930–1).
29 A. K. Bagchi, *Private Investment in India 1900–1939* (Cambridge, 1972), 237–47.
30 O. H. K. Spate, A. T. A. Learmonth and B. H. Farmer, *India, Pakistan and Ceylon* (London, 3rd ed., 1967), 755–7; P. S. Lokanathan in *JMGA*, XI (1936–7), 209.
31 Harveys also extended their Papanasam mill, and north Indian capital was invested in some predominantly Tamilian enterprises; see for example the prospectus of the Tiruchi mill in *The Hindu* 4 May 1936.
32 Information on mill construction comes from several sources (which do not quite agree): Bhogendranath, 65–7; M. P. Gandhi (ed.), *Indian Cotton Textile Industry Centenary Volume 1851–1950* (Bombay, 1951), appendix; Ponniah, 'Production and marketing' I, appendices I and II to chapter vi, and appendix I to chapter vii; Dalal and Co., *Textile Industry of South India*, fifth issue (Madras, 1954); Dvt 2287(C) 19 Sept. 1939.
33 Venkataramana Iyengar, 'The mill industry', 118.
34 Bhogendranath, 64–74.
35 See the prospectus of the Rajapalaiyam mill, *The Hindu* 18 May 1936; two other mills, Janakiram and Shri Shanmugham, were floated in the 1930s and began operations during the war.
36 Dvt 2287(C) 19 Sept. 1939.
37 Dvt 869 19 July 1933; Dvt 2287(C) 19 Sept. 1939.

38 Dvt 2287(C) Sept. 1939

39 The Commissioner of Labour, dated 3 Aug. 1939, in Dvt 2287(C) 19 Sept. 1939.

40 P. D. Asher, dated 3 Aug. 1939 in Dvt 2287(C) 19 Sept. 1939.

41 S. L. N. Simha, *History of the Reserve Bank of India* (1935–51) (Bombay, 1970), 183–8; correspondence between Vidya Sagar Pandya and T. R. Venkataramana Sastri Aug. 1938 to Jan. 1939 in the T. R. Venkataramana Sastri papers, Nehru Memorial Museum, New Delhi. Dvt 2287(C) 19 Sept. 1939.

42 Dvt 2287(C) 19 Sept. 1939; Dvt 2059 23 Aug. 1938.

43 Bhogendranath, 165.

44 Dvt 2287(C) 19 Sept. 1939.

45 Dvt 2287(C) 19 Sept. 1939; Bhogendranath, 68; tables of receipts of Indian cotton at the mills in *Annual Report of the Indian Central Cotton Committee*.

46 Dvt 2059 23 Aug. 1938; Dvt 989 11 Apr. 1938; Dvt 1693 4 Sept. 1930; Dvt 2532 12 Oct. 1938.

47 Pearse, 105–13; B. Shiva Rao, *The Industrial Worker in India* (London, 1939), 121.

48 PWL 854-L 7 Apr. 1934.

49 Dvt 2059 23 Aug. 1938; Dvt 869 19 July 1933; Dvt 989 11 Apr. 1938; PWL 66-L 8 Jan. 1936.

50 PWL 1490-L 19 May 1930.

51 GOM: *Madras Labour, July 1937—October 1938* (Madras, 1938); Dvt 2352 19 Oct. 1937.

52 K. A. Natarajan, 'Industrial economics: industrial development of Madras (Tamil Nadu) with special reference to institutional infrastructure', M. Litt. thesis, Madras, 1973, 140–8; Dvt 989 11 Apr. 1938; Dvt 2711 6 Dec. 1937.

53 Dvt 2059 23 Aug. 1938.

54 Dvt 2059 23 Aug. 1938; Dvt 2532 12 Oct. 1938; Dvt 2792 8 Nov. 1938; Dvt 208 24 Jan. 1939.

55 Dvt 2971 8 Dec. 1939.

56 Dvt 2287(C) 19 Sept. 1939, especially notes by D. N. Strathie dated 3 Aug. 1939 and by L. B. Green dated 14 Aug. 1939; Dvt 2059 23 Aug. 1938, especially note by Strathie dated 16 July 1938.

57 Dvt 2971 8 Dec. 1939; Dvt 2287(C) 19 Sept. 1939; Dvt 2059 23 Aug. 1938.

58 Bhogendranath, 75–86.

59 GOM: *Award of industrial tribunal on the conditions of labour in the textile industry in the Madras Presidency*, chairman M. Venkataramaiya (Madras, 1947), 8–10; Bhogendranath, 77–8, 97–9.

60 Bhogendranath, 107–17.

61 Bhogendranath, 78–82.

62 Karimuthu Thiyagaraja Chettiar in *Indian Textile Journal*, October 1948, 102.

63 Dvt 4637 18 Dec. 1946.

64 Dvt 3189 20 Aug. 1946; Dvt 2610 5 July 1946; Dvt 2416 20 June 1946; Dvt 3840 9 Oct. 1946.

65 Dvt 2648 8 July 1946.

66 Dalal and Co., *Textile Industry*; Gandhi, *Textile industry*, appendix.

67 Bhogendranath, 175–92.

68 *The Hindu*, jubilee supplement, 17 Jan. 1971.

69 I am grateful to R. Sunderraj for information on the Naidu families; see also J. J.

Berna, *Industrial Entrepreneurship in Madras State* (New York, 1960), especially 65–8.

70 Berna, 26–7, 76.

71 Bhogendranath, 75–86; B. S. Baliga, *Compendium on History of Handloom Industry in Madras* (Madras, 1960), 65–73.

72 Dvt 3189 20 Aug. 1946; GOM: *Award of industrial tribunal*; Bhogendranath, 258–9.

73 Ibid., 258–9.

74 See the initial discussions in Dvt 840 2 March 1945, and S. Y. Krishnaswami's 'Note for textiles sub-committee of the Post-War Reconstruction Department' dated 5 Dec. 1944 in Dvt 840 2 Mar. 1945.

75 Note from B. W. Batchelor in Dvt 840 2 Mar. 1945.

76 B. V. Narayanaswamy Naidu and S. Hariharan, *Groundnut: marketing and other allied problems* (Annamalainagar, 1941), 59.

77 Dvt 2236 9 June 1945.

78 R. L. Hardgrave, *The Nadars of Tamilnad: the political culture of a community in change* (Berkeley and Los Angeles, 1969), 150–1.

79 GOI: *Report of the Indian Sugar Committee* (Simla, 1921); GOI: *Report of the Indian Tariff Board on the Sugar Industry* (Delhi, 1938); GOI: ICAR, *Report on the cost of production of crops in the principal sugarcane and cotton tracts in India* (Delhi, 1938), vol. IV and supplementary vol. IV.

80 Brown, *Parry's*, 163–5, 201–2, 218–19, 242, 273–4.

81 R. V. Sundara Reddy, 'Sugar industry in Madras', *MAJ*, XXVII, 8 (1939); D. Sankaranarayanan, 'Industries and occupations of Tinnevelly district', *JMGA*, XV, 3 (1940), 269–70; *Review of Sugar Industry of India* (annual).

82 Brown, *Parry's*, 284.

83 *Indian Finance Yearbook* (1935), 237–9; GOI: *Report of the Indian Tariff Board on the Sugar Industry*, 13–18.

84 See prospectuses in *The Hindu* 11 Oct 1934, 3 Dec. 1934, 2 Feb. 1937; Sundara Reddy, 'Sugar industry'.

85 GOI: *Report of the Indian Tariff Board on the Sugar Industry*, 18–35.

86 *Review of Sugar Industry of India* from 1934–5 to 1937–8.

87 Ibid.

88 GOI: *Report of the Indian Tariff Board on the Sugar Industry*; Sundara Reddy, 'Sugar industry'.

89 Brown, *Parry's*, 297–301; there was also a history of labour unrest and govenment intervention parallel to that in the cotton industry, see for instance D. Arnold, 'Labour relations in a south Indian sugar factory', *Social Scientist*, VI, 5 (1977).

90 This statistical exercise was repeated using slightly different criteria for 'growth' and 'stagnation' and dividing up the years from 1891 to 1961 into slightly different time-periods. Although the details were different, the general conclusions about the intermittent character of town growth, and about the geographical distribution of growth and stagnation in different periods, remained.

91 *Census of India 1891*, xiv Madras, table xvii; *Census of India 1951* III Madras and Coorg, Pt. II-a, tables B-I and B-III.

92 Berna, especially 27.

93 See the following prospectuses: Star of the East Films, *The Hindu* 11 Nov. 1932; Movie Co., *The Hindu* 6 Oct. 1933; Madras Pictures, *The Hindu* 6 May 1936; C. A. Radha Bai, 'An economic study of the cinematograph industry in the Madras presidency', M.Litt. thesis, Madras, n.d., especially 50–3; *Financia Expertus*, II, 1(January 1937).

94 The figures refer to 'Madras State', which included the districts of Malabar, South Kanara and the Nilgiris besides the Tamil districts. *Report on the working of the Factories Act in Madras State in 1955* (Madras, 1956).

95 Dvt 2058 21 Aug.1939.

96 Pitty Thyagaraja Chetty in *IIC Evidence*, III, 54.

97 K. S. Venkataraman, *The Handloom Industry in South India* (Madras, 1940), 35–6.

98 L. K. Tulsiram in *MPBC*, IV, 299.

99 Pitty Thyagaraja Chetty in *IIC Evidence*, III, 54; A. Chatterton, 'The weaving competitions in Madras', *Indian Textile Journal*, IX; Dvt 2058 21 Aug 1939.

100 Baliga,*Compendium*, 11–13, 18.

101 BP 937 11 Apr. 1942.

102 Dvt 2106 4 Sept.1940.

103 Dvt 447 2 Mar.1942

104 N. Giriya Chettiar in *IIC Evidence*, III, 447; D.M. Amalsad, note on 'Handloom Weaving' in Dvt 806 3 Apr. 1937.

105 Ma. Po. Sivagnanam, *Enathu Porattam*[Tamil–My life's struggle] (Madras, 1974), 31–4.

106 'Survey of cotton handloom industry in Madras Presidency' by the Co-oporative department in Dvt 2058 21 Aug. 1939.

107 Dvt 2058 21 Aug.1939.

108 GOM: *Report on the Survey of Cottage Industries in the Madras Presidency* by D. Narayana Rao (Madras, 1929), 33 [hereafter, *Cottage Industries*].

109 R. Sivarama Ayyar in *MPBC*, IV, 398; Dvt 806 3 Apr. 1937.

110 N.Giriya Chettiar in *IIC Evidence*, III, 445.

111 See Baliga, *Compendium*; Venkataraman, *Handloom Industry*.

112 Dvt 2058 21 Aug. 1939.

113 For regional surveys see Dvt 2058 21 Aug. 1939; *Cottage Industries*; Dvt 618 14 Mar. 1940; Dvt 447 2 Mar. 1942; GOM: *Report of the Court of Enquiry into Labour Conditions in the Handloom Industry* by B. V. Narayanaswamy Naidu (Madras, 1948).

114 Fortnightly report for the second half of July 1930, Home Political file 18 vii of 1930, National Archives of India, New Delhi; Pub Gen 1251(C) 18 Sept. 1930.

115 Ibid.

116 GOM: *The Civil Disobedience Movement 1930–1* (n.p., n.d.), 139.

117 Ibid.; Pub Gen 1251 (C) 18 Sept. 1930.

118 BP 4256 26 Nov. 1934.

119 Dvt 806 3 Apr. 1937; Dvt 1519 20 June 1938

120 Dvt 618 14 Mar.1930.

121 BP 937 11 Apr. 1942.

122 Rev 1320 16 June 1942; BP 484 18 Feb. 1942.

123 Rev 1982 7 Sept. 1942; Rev 1809 17 Aug. 1942; Dvt 447 2 Mar. 1942; Rev 2723 4 Dec. 1942.

124 Dvt 447 2 Mar. 1942.
125 Bagchi, *Private Investment*, 240–1; Dvt 1730 12 Sept. 1930.
126 BP 284 18 Feb. 1942.
127 Dvt 1218 12 Sept. 1932.
128 Dvt 2287(C) 19 Sept. 1939; Dvt 950 4 Apr. 1939; Dvt 2106 4 Sept. 1930.
129 Pitty Thyagaraja Chetty in *IIC Evidence*, III, 55.
130 L. K. Tulsiram in *MPBC*, IV, 296–7.
131 Ibid., 297.
132 Dvt 447 2 Mar. 1942; Dvt 806 3 Apr. 1937; Dvt 2966 29 Nov. 1938.
133 Venkataraman, *Handloom Industry*, 69.
134 GOM: *Report of the Court of Enquiry into Labour Conditions in the Handloom Industry*.
135 For example Dvt 447 2 Mar. 1942; Dvt 618 14 Mar. 1940; Dvt 2058 21 Aug. 1939.
136 Rev 2723 4 Dec. 1942; Rev 1982 7 Sept. 1942.
137 BP 484 18 Feb. 1942; BP 937 11 Apr. 1942.
138 Dvt 447 2 Mar. 1942.
139 Director of Industries, dated 19 Dec. 1936 in Dvt 806 3 Apr. 1937.
140 Dvt 1730 12 Sept. 1930.
141 BP 937 11 Apr. 1942; Dvt 447 2 Mar. 1942.
142 Baliga, *Compendium*, 11–18.
143 Baliga, *Compendium*, contains a thorough survey of official interest in the handloom industry.
144 Baliga, *Compendium*, 25–6.
145 *Cottage Industries*.
146 Dvt 1730 12 Sept. 1930.
147 Dvt 1218 12 Sept. 1932.
148 Baliga, *Compendium*, 38–46; Dvt 950 4 Apr. 1939.
149 Dvt 806 3 Apr. 1937; Dvt 2966 29 Nov. 1938; Dvt 1519 20 June 1938; Dvt 2058 21 Aug. 1939.
150 D. H. Amalsad, 'Note on protection of Hand Spinning and Handloom Weaving Industries', dated 27 Aug. 1938 in Dvt 2106 4 Sept. 1940.
151 Dvt 2058 21 Aug. 1939.
152 Baliga, *Compendium*, 52.
153 Dvt 447 2 Mar. 1942.
154 BP 937 11 Apr. 1942.
155 Rev 1320 16 June 1942.
156 Rev 2723 4 Dec. 1942; Rev 1982 7 Sept. 1942; Rev 1809 17 Aug. 1942.
157 BP 937 11 Apr. 1942.
158 Note dated 6 Feb. 1942 in Rev 1809 17 Aug. 1942.
159 Baliga, *Compendium*, 60–81.
160 Ibid., 81–5.
161 Ibid., 102.
162 Ibid., 83.
163 Ibid., 85.
164 See *Cottage Industries*.
165 C. Abdul Hakim in *IIC Evidence*, III, 134.
166 M. Devadason in *MPBC*, II, 280.
167 C. M. Kothari and Mohammed Ismail Sahib in *MPBC*, IV, 656–65.

168 *Cottage Industries*, preliminary report on Tanjore and South Arcot, 37–9.
169 C. M. Kothari and Mohammed Ismail Sahib in *MPBC*, IV, 665.
170 M. Devadason in *MPBC*, II, 280.
171 *Cottage Industries*, preliminary report on Tanjore and South Arcot, 37–8.
172 Dvt 2296 26 Sept. 1940.
173 GB: *Royal Commission on Labour in India* (London, 1931), Evidence vol. III, Pt. 1, 322–3.
174 C. W. Ranson, *City in Transition* (Madras, 1938), 74.
175 Dupuis, 519.
176 I refer to the TVS group.
177 These observations about imports are based on table 5.

Chapter 6

1 See B. R. Tomlinson, *The Political Economy of the Raj 1914–1947: the economics of decolonization in India* (London, 1979).
2 Sir John Rees in GB, 5 Parliamentary Dabates (Commons), CXVI (1919), 2379, quoted in E. F. Irschick, *Politics and Social Conflict in South India: the non-Brahman movement and Tamil separatism* (Berkeley and Los Angeles, 1969), 210.
3 B. S. Baliga, 'Acquisition of estates and their conversion into ryotwari tenure', *Studies in Madras Administration* (Madras, 1960), I, 46–108; J. W. B. Dykes, *Salem, an Indian Collectorate* (London, 1853), 190–216; H. Le Fanu, *A Manual of the Salem District in the Presidency of Madras* (Madras, 1887), I, 283–320.
4 See C. J. Baker, 'Tamilnad estates in the twentieth century', *IESHR*, XIII, 1, 1–44.
5 K. Rajayyan, *South Indian Rebellion: the first war of independence 1800–1801* (Mysore, 1971); K. Rajayyan, *Rise and Fall of the Poligars of Tamilnadu* (Madras, 1974).
6 Rev 645–6 24 Sept. 1895.
7 Baliga, 'Acquisition of estates'.
8 Pamela Price, 'The royal model and merchant aims in nineteenth-century south India', and ' "Contempt for my authority": Raja, temple and government in nineteenth-century Ramnad and Sivagangai', unpublished papers 1977–8.
9 Selections: *Papers relating to Zamindaries, Mittahs etc. in Tinnevelly District* (Madras, 1934); W. K. Firminger, *The Fifth Report from the Select Committee of the House of Commons on the Affairs of the East Company. Volume I, Introduction and Text of the Report* (Calcutta, 1917), 281.
10 *MELAC*, Oral evidence III, 18 and IV, 194–5, 198; G. F. F. Foulkes, *Local Autonomy* (Madras, 1937–8), II, 102–33.
11 See for example the descriptions of estate administration in CoW 1041 13 Oct. 1938; CoW 739 1 Aug. 1938; CoW 187 17 Feb. 1938; Rev 946(C) 7 May 1937.
12 *MELAC*, Irrigation Reports from Zamindars.
13 *MELAC*, Oral evidence II, 168–9 and IV, 269.
14 N. Dirks, 'The structure and meaning of political relations in a south Indian little kingdom', Humanities Working Paper 14, California Institute of Technology, 1978.

15 BP 746 7 Mar. 1933; Rev 989(8-S) 1 May 1936; CoW 72 22 Mar. 1935; CoW 900 25 May 1944; CoW 699 2 Dec. 1941; V. V. Sayana, *The Agrarian Problems of Madras Province* (Madras, 1949), 110; *MELAC*, Oral evidence III, 187.

16 See the annual *Report on the Working of the Estates Land Act in the Madras Presidency*; Foulkes, I, 102–33.

17 Home Judicial File 1–2 of 1922, National Archives of India, New Delhi; Rev 664 5 May 1925.

18 Rev 989(8-S) 1 May 1936.

19 *MELAC*, Memoranda Pt. II, 113.

20 *MELAC*, Oral evidence II, 112, 172; Landholders statements Pt. III, 2–3.

21 LSG 1984 7 Sept. 1923; LSG 811 9 May 1922.

22 *MELAC*, Irrigation Reports from Zamindars.

23 Rev 989(8-S) 1 May 1936; CoW 602 12 June 1937; CoW 42 11 Jan. 1940.

24 GB: *Royal Commission on Agriculture in India. Evidence volume III, Madras and Coorg* (London, 1931), 360.

25 *MELAC*, Oral evidence II, 125.

26 *MELAC*, Memoranda Pt. II, 171–2; Oral evidence, IV, 233, 269.

27 *MELAC*, Memoranda Pt. II, 168–9; Oral evidence, IV, 269.

28 Rev 989(8-S) 1 May 1936; CoW 602 12 June 1937; CoW 42 11 Jan. 1940.

29 *MELAC*, Oral evidence II, 167.

30 CoW 182 18 May 1941.

31 Rev 409 26 Feb. 1929.

32 Printed memorial signed by P. S. Subramania Aiyar and D. Venkatapathi Aiyar dated 22 Feb. 1933 in P. S. Sivaswami Aiyar papers, National Archives of India, New Delhi.

33 BP 126 30 Sept. 1935; CoW 695 12 Oct. 1936.

34 B. V. Narayanaswamy Naidu and P. Vaidyanathan, *The Madras Agriculturists' Relief Act—a study* (Annamalainagar, 1939); BP 2713 25 Sept. 1939.

35 *MELAC*, Pt. I (Main Report).

36 BP 751 4 Mar. 1931; BP 546 17 Feb. 1932; for further details on estates' financial difficulties see Baker, 'Tamilnad estates'.

37 Rev 122 20 Jan. 1933; CoW 35 30 Jan. 1934; CoW 679 27 Nov. 1941; CoW 653 15 Nov. 1941.

38 *MELAC*, Memoranda Pt. II, 106, 168, 181, 187; Oral evidence II, 188–9; Oral evidence IV, 228–9, 236–7; Rev 3105(C) 5 Dec. 1938; BP 2506 28 July 1934; BP 129 28 Sept. 1936.

39 CoW 1 29 Jan. 1934; CoW 2 24 Jan. 1935.

40 Rev 1475(C) 23 July 1937.

41 Rev 946(C) 7 May 1937; Rev 2819(C) 26 Nov. 1935; Rev 394(C) 22 Feb. 1936; Rev 2705 15 Dec. 1936; Rev 1952(C) 4 Sept. 1936; Rev 2268 6 Nov. 1937; Rev 1759(C) 27 Aug. 1937; Rev 3105(C) 5 Dec. 1938; Rev 2699(C) 16 Oct. 1939; Rev 563 10 Mar. 1941; BP 4204 4 Dec. 1936; BP 889 28 Mar. 1939; CoW 7 4 Jan. 1934; CoW 155 23 Feb. 1939; CoW 26 22 Nov. 1940; CoW 118 12 Mar. 1941.

42 BP 129 28 Sept. 1936; BP 114 4 Oct. 1941; Rev 946(C) 7 May 1937; *MELAC*, Landholders statements Pt. III, 1–2.

43 Rev 946(C) 7 May 1937.

44 BP 93 29 Sept. 1933; BP 126 30 Sept. 1935; BP 129 28 Sept. 1936.

45 *MELAC*, Oral evidence III, 230.

46 Rev 409 26 Feb. 1929; Rev 1071(C) 31 May 1929; Rev 122 20 Jan. 1933; CoW 35 30 Jan. 1934.

47 Rev 1071(C) 31 May 1929; CoW 31 9 Dec. 1931.

48 CoW 31 15 Dec. 1932.

49 Rev 1071(C) 31 May 1929; Rev 122 20 Jan. 1933; CoW 31 9 Dec. 1931.

50 CoW 31 15 Dec. 1932.

51 CoW 31 9 Dec. 1931; Rev 435–6 23 Feb. 1932.

52 CoW 679 27 Nov. 1941; CoW 653 15 Nov. 1941.

53 Rev 2906(C) 6 Dec. 1935; CoW 332 6 Dec. 1935; BP 246 3 Feb. 1925; Rev 621(C) 10 May 1926.

54 Rev 2253(C) 13 Dec. 1933.

55 Rev 2239(C) 23 Sept. 1935; Rev 2906(C) 6 Dec. 1935; Rev 989(8-S) 1 May 1936; CoW 332 6 Dec. 1935; CoW 35 17 Jan. 1936; CoW 144 20 Feb. 1939.

56 CoW 528 28 Sept. 1942; CoW 30 Nov. 1942. See also CoW 19 22 Oct. 1937; CoW 858 12 Dec. 1936; CoW 18 18 Oct. 1940; CoW 938 21 Sept. 1937; CoW 2 25 Jan. 1939; CoW 687 15 Oct. 1940.

57 BP 3707 1 Dec. 1937.

58 I am grateful to David Ludden, who interviewed the Ettaiyapuram family, for this information.

59 CoW 858 12 Dec. 1936; CoW 215 23 Feb. 1937.

60 CoW 330 5 Dec. 1935. See also *MELAC*, Memoranda Pt. II, 113; Oral evidence II, 112, 172; Landholders' statements Pt. III, 2–3.

61 Rev 2526(C) 18 Oct. 1940.

62 Ibid.; Rev 1432(C) 27 Mar. 1943; Rev 2513 6 Nov. 1942; Rev 2214 2 Oct. 1942; BP 790-M 4 Dec. 1942.

63 GOM: *Report on the Revision of the Revenue Establishments in the Madras Presidency* by J. H. Garstin (Madras, 1883); *Correspondence relating to the Revision Proposed in the Village Revenue Establishments of the Madras Presidency*, Part I (Madras, 1867); GOM Selections: *Mr Hyde's Report on the Introduction of a Ryotwari Settlement into the South Arcot Collectorate and the Correspondence relating thereto* (Cuddalore, 1904); Firminger, 196–7; T. Venkasami Row, *A Manual of the District of Tanjore in the Madras Presidency*, 415–17.

64 *Correspondence relating to the Revision Proposed in the Village Revenue Establishments*, I, introduction by Charles Pelley, iii–iv.

65 C. S. Hearn in ibid., 301–2.

66 Charles Pelley in ibid.

67 GOM: Selections LIII, *Papers relating to the General Revenue Survey of the Madras Presidency* (Madras, 1858), especially 17; *Village Officers' Manual* (Madras, 1913).

68 *Report on the Revision of the Revenue Establishments*, 4.

69 See *Village Officers' Manual*, especially 38; Rev 2435 26 June 1918; Rev 3068 20 Nov. 1939; Dvt 859 27 May 1936; Dvt 859 27 May 1936; BP 265 24 Jan. 1928; BP 265 24 Jan. 1928; BP 1254 10 May 1927; BP 2421 13 Aug. 1930; *MPBC*, II, 94.

70 Collector of Chingleput 1 June 1938 in BP 288 28 Jan. 1939.

71 Note by Revenue Divisional Officer 30 May 1926 in Rev 1006 23 June. 1926.

72 *Report on the Revision of the Revenue Establishments*, 14–15.

73 Petition of M. S. V. Murthi 5 Apr. 1938 in BP 2000 20 July 1938.

74 See Collectors' letters in Rev 8 2 Jan. 1914; see also papers of Sir Richard Tottenham and S. Wadsworth, 'Lo, the poor Indian', especially 126, both in SAS Archive.

75 Petition of K. Krishnamurti 7 May 1938 in BP 2000 20 July 1938.

76 V. K. Ramanujachariar speaking in the Madras Legislative Council quoted in Rev 8 2 Jan. 1914

77 See for example petition of O. M. Subramania Pillai 30 Aug. 1938 in Rev 1687 8 July 1939; petition of V. Kethiripal Pillai 24 Aug. 1931 in BP 3583 12 Nov. 1931.

78 For example BP 1947 10 June 1936.

79 BP 451 8 Feb. 1930; BP 2187 2 July 1936; Rev 64 10 Jan. 1939; see also BP 1254 10 May 1927; BP 336 30 Jan. 1933; BP 716 3 Mar. 1933; BP 2837 19 Oct. 1933; BP 1947 10 Jan. 1936; Rev 1662 5 July 1939.

80 See the history of the village service cess in Rev 664 5 May 1925; note by Revenue department 23 Apr. 1926 in Rev 1006 23 June 1926.

81 Rev 1958 14 Aug. 1920; T. N. Ramakrishna Reddy to C. R. Reddy 5 Aug. 1920 in C. R. Reddy papers file 52, Nehru Memorial Museum, New Delhi.

82 M. Venkatarangaiya, *The Freedom Struggle in Andhra Pradesh (Andhra)* volume II (Hyderabad, 1965), 263–5.

83 *Sudarsini* 1 Jan. 1918, Madras Native Newspaper Reports.

84 Rev 1958 14 Aug. 1920; Rev 2742 23 Nov. 1928; Rev 157 27 Jan. 1944; Dvt 859 27 May 1936; BP 64 13 Aug. 1929; BP 988 31 Mar. 1932.

85 BP 1994 26 Aug. 1924; BP 2123 12 Aug. 1930.

86 Rev 1958 14 Aug. 1920.

87 Petition from Salem branch of the Tamilnad Village Officers' Association 7 Dec. 1945 in Rev 256 7 Feb. 1946.

88 Rev 2747 23 Nov. 1928; Rev 1489 4 Aug. 1930; Rev 2331 14 Oct. 1941; Rev 1323 3 July 1929; Rev 446 13 Feb. 1940; Rev 2095 18 Sept. 1942; Rev 157 27 Jan. 1944; BP 163 2 Feb. 1944.

89 BP 19 7 Feb. 1934; Rev 833 6 June 1925; Rev 8(C) 4 Jan. 1938; Rev 2214 28 Aug. 1939.

90 Note by Bezwada Gopala Reddi 20 Mar. 1929 in Rev 2214 28 Aug. 1939; for fuller treatment of the politics of village office see C. J. Baker, 'Madras headmen', *Economy and Society: essays in Indian economic and social history*, ed. K. N. Chaudhuri and C. J. Dewey (Delhi, 1979).

91 Rev 337 28 Dec. 1938; Rev 1006 23 June 1926; BP 2910 18 Oct. 1938; BP 2549 9 Aug. 1937; BP 572 16 Mar. 1925.

92 BP 2837 19 Oct. 1933.

93 Ibid.

94 Rev 64 10 Jan. 1939.

95 Rev 63 10 Jan. 1939.

96 S. Ahmed Ali 31 May 1940 in BP 463 13 Feb. 1941; see also BP 288 28 Jan. 1939.

97 BP 2331 14 Aug. 1932; BP 716 3 Mar. 1933; BP 1387 16 May 1933; BP 2837 19 Oct. 1933; BP 1771 8 May 1935; Rev 2773 26 Oct. 1938.

98 For example Rev 295 1 Feb. 1938.

99 For example Rev 1131 20 May 1938.

100 BP 1523 7 June 1941.

101 Ibid.

102 BP 2910 18 Oct. 1939; BP 2549 9 Aug. 1937.

103 BP 3009 31 Aug. 1936; BP 6-S 6 Feb. 1942.

104 L. M. Parasivam Pillai, president of the Tamilnad Village Officers' Association, 12 July 1945 in Rev 1164 18 June 1945.

105 Petition from Mayavaram village officers 10 Aug. 1945 in Rev 1834 9 Oct. 1945.

106 For example Pub 818 31 May 1932; Rev 587(C) 3 Mar. 1938.

107 Collector of Salem 24 Feb. 138 in BP 988 31 Mar. 1932.

108 Board of Revenue note 13 July 1927 in Rev 2647 17 Dec. 1927.

109 On village officers' organizations see especially BP 446 13 Feb. 1940; Rev 1323 3 July 1929; Rev 1489 4 Aug. 1930.

110 Rev 256 7 Feb. 1946; Rev 843 20 Apr. 1946; Rev 1207 5 June 1946.

111 For example Rev 33 13 Jan. 1943; Rev 2095 18 Sept. 1942; Rev 157 27 Jan. 1944; BP 163 2 Feb. 1944.

112 B. Madhavanam Nayudu, Collector of Ramnad, 8 Apr. 1947 in BP 1069 8 Aug. 1947.

113 See especially memorandum from the.Tamilnad Village Officers' Association 9 May 1945 and memorandum from Mayavaram taluk village officers in Rev 1834 9 Oct. 1945.

114 Rev 2526(C) 18 Oct. 1940.

115 Rev 1432(C) 27 Mar. 1943.

116 Rev 1224(C) 30 June 1945; see also Rev 251(C) 7 Feb. 1945; Rev 1260(C) 7 July 1945; Rev 1849(C) 2 Aug. 1947.

117 Rev 1833(C) 1 Aug. 1947; Rev 2280 29 Sept. 1947; Rev 2810(C) 25 Nov. 1947; B. Sarveswara Rao, *The Economic and Social Effects of Zamindari Abolition in Andhra* (Waltair, 1963).

118 Rev 311 6 Feb. 1947; Rev 256 7 Feb. 1946.

119 S. Saraswathi, *The Madras Panchayats System: volume I, a historical survey* (Delhi, 1972).

120 B. A. Desai and N. K. Thingalaya, 'Irrigation factor and yield variability in rice-growing districts in India', *Indian Journal of Agricultural Economics*, XX, 3, 63–5.

121 The basic sources on irrigation are: E. Adicéam, *La Géographie de l'irrigation dans le Tamilnad* (Paris, 1966); J. Dupuis, *Madras et le Nord du Coromandel: étude des conditions de la vie indienne dans un cadre géographique* (Paris, 1960); S. Y. Krishnaswami, *Rural Problems in Madras: monograph* (Madras, 1947); O. H. K. Spate, A. T. A. Learmonth and B. H. Farmer, *India, Pakistan and Ceylon* (London, 3rd ed., 1967); the work of David Ludden; and the district gazetteers.

122 Also some small ghat streams in Tirunelveli.

123 Venkasami Row; D. Ludden, 'Agrarian organization in Tinnevelly district: 800–1900 A.D.', Ph.D. thesis, University of Pennsylvania, 1978.

124 Spate, Learmonth and Farmer, 775–8; Adicéam, 301–55.

125 F. Buchanan, *A Journey from Madras through the Countries of Mysore, Canara and Malabar* (London, 1807).

126 For example GB: *Report of the Indian Irrigation Commission 1901–3: Part II, Provincial*. Parliamentary Papers, 1904, Cd. 185, especially 114–15; A. Sarada Raju, *Economic Conditions in the Madras Presidency 1800–1850* (Madras, 1941), 116–28.

127 For example PWL 1568-I 26 July 1932; Adicéam, 354.

128 Adicéam, 202–96; there were some jointly-owned wells, particularly in Tirunelveli.

129 'Note on the irrigation works on the Kaveri river', Tamilnadu Public Works
Department note, 1978.

130 Ibid.; Adicéam, 393; *Report of the Public Works Department in the Madras
Presidency*, annual.

131 Ludden, 'Agrarian organization'; Adicéam; *Indian Irrigation Commission
1901–3*.

132 Krishnaswami, *Rural Problems*, 78–81, 96–103.

133 A. T. Mackenzie, *History of the Periyar Project* (Madras, 1899); PWL 3249-I 17
Nov. 1930.

134 *Public Works Commission 1852*, 110, quoted in Sarada Raju, 128.

135 Rev 247 7 Feb. 1934; BP 646 6 Mar. 1942.

136 *Indian Irrigation Commission 1901–3*; Krishnaswami, *Rural Problems*, 89–95.

137 GOI Finance department note 15 Feb. 1935 in PWL 904-I 8 Apr. 1935.

138 Figures from the *Statistical Atlas of the Madras Presidency*, various editions;
Madurai and Ramnad districts omitted because the data do not distinguish
between major and minor works.

139 Krishnaswami, *Rural Problems*, 78–81.

140 GOI: *Report of the Indian Taxation Enquiry Committee* (Delhi, 1925), I, 103–7;
see for example the fate of the Pattagar of Palaiyakottai's scheme in Rev 630 28
Mar. 1944.

141 Krishnaswami, *Rural Problems*, 96–103; *Report of the Public Works Department in the Madras Presidency* for 1948–9, Part II-A (Irrigation), 9–10; Rev 2231
1 Nov. 1937.

142 Rev 2145 13 Sept. 1947; Rev 1355(C) 20 June 1942.

143 M. O'Brien, note on Mr Hall's report, 21 June 1930, in PWL 3249-I 17 Nov.
1930, copy in J. P. L. Gwynn papers, Box II, SAS Archive.

144 V. Trench, *Lord Willingdon in India* (Bombay, 1934), 135–49.

145 *MELAC*, Irrigation reports from Zamindars; Rev 1355(C) 20 June 1942.

146 Rev 2145 13 Sept. 1947.

147 Board of Revenue note 5 Apr. 1940 in Rev 1355(C) 20 June 1942.

148 Chief engineer for irrigation in ibid.

149 PWL 3249-I 17 Nov. 1930.

150 J. F. Hall's report on the Periyar project in ibid.

151 Krishnaswami, *Rural Problems*, 94–6.

152 *A Statistical Atlas of the Madras Presidency*, various editions.

153 Adicéam, 202 ff.; F. A. Nicholson, *Manual of the Coimbatore District in the
Presidency of Madras* (Madras, 1887), 394.

154 BP 1213 10 Sept. 1947.

155 GOM: *Report of the Committee on Agriculture Production* (1959), 30–8;
Agriculture Economics Research Centre, *Agricultural Development in Tamilnadu* (mimeo, Madras, 1976), II, 71.

156 J. J. Berna, *Industrial Entrepreneurship in Madras State* (New York, 1960),
especially 44–8.

157 GOI, Committee on Plan Projects: *Report on Minor Irrigation Works in Madras
State* (Madras, 1959), 7.

158 Adicéam, 282.

159 Rev 2217 31 Aug. 1938.

160 Mirasidars of Tirukkarugavu, received 21 Jan. 1947, in Rev 2145 13 Sept. 1947.

161 A. S. Kuppuswami Iyer in *The Hindu* 6 Jan. 1934.

162 Rev 247 7 Feb. 1934; PWL 904-I 8 Apr. 1935.

163 Note dated 1 Feb. 1938 in BP 646 6 Mar. 1942.

164 Rev 522 3 Mar. 1947.

165 Ibid.

166 GOM: *Report of the Committee on Agricultural Production (chairman, M. Bhaktavatsalam)* (Madras, 1959), 18–19, 28.

167 *Report on Minor Irrigation Works*, 2.

168 PWL 3249-I 17 Nov. 1930.

169 Krishnaswami, *Rural Problems*, 108.

170 J. T. Wheeler, *Handbook to the Cotton Cultivation in the Madras Presidency* (Madras, 1862), 33.

171 Krishnaswami, *Rural Problems*, 109–12.

172 Ibid., 113–14; B.H. Farmer, *Agricultural Colonisation in India since Independence* (London, 1974), 139 ff.; BP 1030 11 July 1945.

173 Krishnaswami, *Rural Problems*, 126–35.

174 Ibid., 135–44.

175 See G. Slater, *Some South Indian Villages* (Oxford, 1918) and *Southern India: its political and economic problems* (London, 1936).

176 *Annual Report on the Working of the Madras Co-operative Credit Societies Act*; B. V. Narayanaswamy Naidu, *The Co-operative Movement in the Madras Presidency* (Annamalainagar, 1933).

177 Rev 765 1 Apr. 1931.

178 GOM revenue secretary to GOI chief secretary 28 Oct. 1930 in BP 3315 10 Nov. 1930; see also BP 2880 4 Oct. 1930.

179 BP 1662 28 May 1931.

180 Rev 1752–3 14 Aug. 1931; Rev 227–8 30 Jan. 1932; Rev 1687–8 9 Aug. 1932; Rev 1293 24 July 1933; Rev 2552–3 22 Dec. 1932; Rev 9 3 Jan. 1933.

181 For example Rev 1959 16 Sept. 1931; Rev 314 15 Feb. 1934; Rev 73 10 Jan. 1934.

182 Rev 2627 16 Dec. 1937.

183 The development of these theories can be traced in the issues of the *Indian Journal of Economics*.

184 See for example articles in the 1932–3 volume of *IJE*.

185 P. S. Narayana Prasad, 'World depression in India', *IJE*, XVI (1935–6), 121–44.

186 *Report of the Economic Depression Enquiry Committee*, 25, copy in BP 1662 28 May 1931.

187 Rev 2066 1 Oct. 1931; Dvt 365 10 Mar. 1931.

188 A. Srinivasa Iyengar forwarding resolutions of Mannargudi Landholders' Association 26 Nov. 1933 in Rev 314 13 Feb. 1934.

189 Tirunelveli District Landholders' Association 4 July 1938 in Rev 2217 31 Aug. 1938.

190 R. Sivarama Ayyar, *MPBC*, II, 335.

191 Rev 989(C) 5 June 1933; Rev 948 11 May 1934.

192 GOM: *Report of the Rice Production and Trade in the Madras Presidency* by C. R. Srinivasan (Madras, 1934), copy in Dvt 322 2 Mar. 1935.

193 Rev 775 23 Apr. 1934; Dvt 1312 26 Oct. 1933; Dvt 1247 12 Oct. 1933; Dvt 560 26 Apr. 1934.

194 Dvt 365 10 Mar. 1931.

195 See especially Rev 41(C) 6 Jan. 1934.

196 Dvt 2046 8 Nov. 1930; Dvt 1299 28 June 1930.

197 Rev 41(C) 6 Jan. 1934.

198 Rev 948 11 May 1934.

199 Krishnaswami, *Rural Problems*, 328–31.

200 N. S. Venguswamy, *Congress in Office* (Bombay, 1940).

201 'The Indian demand for imported foodgrains', memo by L. S. Amery, sent on 8 Jan. 1943, in N. Mansergh (ed.), *The Transfer of Power 1942–7*, Volume III (London, 1971), 473–8.

202 BP 858-M 17 Dec. 1941.

203 GB: *India (Food Situation 1943). Speech by the Food Member of the Governor-General's Council and other papers.* Parliamentary Papers, 1942–3, Cmd. 6479, 4–9.

204 Dvt 4524 16 Nov. 1945.

205 J. D. Tyson 10 Mar. 1942 in BP 851-S 29 Mar. 1942.

206 Lord Linlithgow to L. S. Amery 26 Dec. 1942 in *Transfer of Power*, III, 224.

207 A. K. Sen, 'Starvation and exchange entitlements: a general approach and its application to the great Bengal famine', *Cambridge Journal of Economics*, I (1977); W. R. Aykroyd, *The Conquest of Famine* (London, 1974).

208 H. Knight, *Food Administration in India 1939–47* (Stanford, 1954); GOM: *A Survey of Procurement and Rationing of Food in the Madras State* compiled by I. R. Jones (Pudukottai, 1951).

209 Sen, 'Starvation and exchange entitlements'.

210 War Cabinet 4 Aug. 1943, *Transfer of Power*, IV, 155.

211 A. R. Prest, *War Economies of Primary Producing Countries* (Cambridge, 1948), 28–87.

212 Sen, 'Starvation and exchange entitlements'; G. Blyn, *Agricultural Trends in India, 1891–1947: output, availibility and productivity* (Philadelphia, 1966).

213 Prest, *War Economies*, 62–5.

214 BP 386-M 9 Sept. 1942; BP 97-M 22 June 1942; BP 289-M 15 Aug. 1942; BP 237-M 4 Aug. 1942.

215 Agricultural Economics Research Centre, University of Madras, *Measures of Food Control, Procurement and Controlled Distribution of Food and their Effects on the Agrarian Economy* (Madras, n.d.); Krishnaswami, *Rural Problems*; B. Natarajan, *Food and Agriculture in Madras State* (Madras, 1953).

216 *India (Food Situation 1943)*; *Measures of Food Control*, 25–30.

217 B. Govinda Row, 'Some aspects of economic controls in India during the war', *IJE*, XXIV (1943–4), 314–22; *Measures of Food Control*; Dvt 4524 16 Nov. 1945; Dvt 2589 3 July 1946; Dvt 631 14 Feb. 1945.

218 GOI food department memorandum 1 Sept. 1943 in *Transfer of Power*, V, 196–200.

219 Linlithgow to Amery 30 Nov. 1942 and 3 Dec. 1942 in *Transfer of Power*, III, 326, 333; GOI food department to Secretary of State 9 Dec. 1942 in ibid., 358.

220 Secretary of State to GOI food department 15 Dec. 1942 in *Transfer of Power*, III, 372–3.

221 Amery to Linlithgow 16 Jan. 1943 in *Transfeer of Power*, III, 514–15.
222 GOI food department to Secretary of State 15 July 1943, Amery to Linlithgow 26 July 1943, Linlithgow to Amery 13 Aug. 1943, *Transfer of Power*, IV, 75, 115, 169.
223 Memorandum by chiefs of staff 17 Sept. 1943 in *Transfer of Power*, IV, 270–3; War Cabinet 24 Sept. 1943 in ibid., 319.
224 GOI: *Report of the Foodgrains Policy Committee* (Delhi, 1943); GOI food department to Secretary of State 22 Dec. 1943 in *Transfer of Power*, IV, 445.
225 GOI food department to Secretary of State 21 Dec. 1943 and Wavell to Amery 25 Feb. 1944 in *Transfer of Power*, IV, 558–60.
226 War cabinet Feb. 1944, and Wavell to Amery 25 Feb. 1944 in *Transfer of Power*, IV, 700–8, 758.
227 Wavell to Amery 23 Mar. 1944 and 29 Mar. 1944, War Cabinet on Indian foodgrains 6 and 28 Apr. 1944, Amery to Wavell 12 Feb. 1945 and 11 July 1945 in *Transfer of Power*, IV, 828–30, 844, 862–5, 937–8 and V, 602, 1229.
228 *Measures of Food Control*; *A Survey of Procurement and Rationing.*
229 GOI food department 8 Dec. 1944 in Dvt 631 14 Feb. 1945.
230 GOI: *Famine Enquiry Commission Final Report* (Madras, 1945), 59.
231 Dvt 631 14 Feb. 1945.
232 Natarajan, *Food and Agriculture*, 19, 39, 41; *Measures of Food Control*, 31, 120; Dvt 4524 16 Nov. 1945; Dvt 2589 3 July 1946; Dvt 2461 25 June 1945.
233 *Srinivasan Report*, 97–100.
234 A. D. Gorwala, *The Role of the Administrator, Past, Present and Future* (Poona, 1952).
235 Natarajan, *Food and Agriculture*, 29 ff.; GOI: *Foodgrains Policy Committee, Interim Report 1948* (Delhi, 1948); *A Survey of Procurement and Rationing.*
236 BP 386-M 9 Sept 1942; BP 97-M 22 June 1942; BP 289-M 15 Aug. 1942; BP 237-M 4 Aug. 1942; BP 117-M 26 June 1942.
237 Rev 238 6 Feb. 1945; Dvt 409 1 Feb. 1947.
238 Dvt 229 21 Jan. 1947; Rev 1396 8 July 1944.
239 Rev 238 6 Feb. 1945; BP 1030 11 July 1945; Dvt 229 21 Jan. 1947; Krishnaswami, *Rural Problems*, 143–4.
240 Krishnaswami, *Rural Problems*; Natarajan, *Food and Agriculture*; C. W. B. Zacharias, *Madras Agriculture* (Madras, 1950).
241 BP 1030 11 July 1945.
242 Note of discussion with D. D. Sethi, the GOI's director of agricultural education (food), 17 Sept. 1943 in Rev 1396 8 July 1944.
243 Rev 238 6 Feb. 1945.
244 BP 1030 11 July 1945.
245 GOI: *Technological Possibilities of Agricultural Development in India* by W. Burns (Lahore, 1944); BP 1030 11 July 1945.
246 Dvt 2535–6 9 June 1947 contains GOM: *Five-year plan for food production in Madas Province 1947/8–1951/2; schemes relating to the agriculture department.*
247 BP 1030 11 July 1945.
248 Board of Revenue note 3 Jan. 1945 in Rev 238 6 Feb. 1945.
249 N. Raghavendra Rao, joint director of agriculture, 10 May 1945 in Dvt 229 21 Jan. 1946.
250 996 to be accurate; Dvt 2535–6 9 June 1947.

251 'A note on the agricultural deficiencies of the Maras Province' by S. Y. Krishnaswami in BP 1373 2 Aug. 1944, reworked in Krishnaswami, *Rural Problems*, chapter 6.

252 Krishnaswami, *Rural Problems*, 161.

253 Dvt 228 6 Feb. 1941; Dvt 734 9 Apr. 1941.

254 Dvt 4524 16 Nov. 1945.

255 Natarajan, *Food and Agriculture*.

256 Ibid., 144–16.

257 Dvt 910 3 Mar. 1947.

258 B. Viswanath in Dvt 910 3 Mar. 1947.

259 Ibid.

260 Dvt 229 21 Jan. 1947.

261 Dvt 910 3 Mar. 1947.

262 Krishnaswami, *Rural Problems*, 114–21.

263 P. H. Nye and D. J. Greenland, *The Soil under Shifting Cultivation* (Farnham Royal, 1960).

264 Krishnaswami, *Rural Problems*, 114–21; Dvt 229 21 Jan. 1947.

265 Dvt 229 21 Jan. 1947.

266 Ibid.; Dvt 1311 31 Mar. 1945.

267 BP 1030 11 July 1945.

268 Ibid.

269 Dvt 2535–6 9 June 1947.

. Conclusion

1 J. P. Mencher, *Agriculture and Social Transformation in Tamilnadu: past origins, present transformations, future prospects* (Durham, 1978), especially 271–2.

2 B. H. Farmer (ed.), *Green Revolution? Technology and change in rice-growing areas of Tamil Nadu and Sri Lanka* (London, 1977).

3 T. W. Schultz, *Transforming Traditional Agriculture* (Yale, 1964).

4 See, for instance Mencher, and J. H. Harriss, *Capitalism and Peasant Farming: a study of agricultural change and agrarian structure in northern Tamil Nadu* (University of East Anglia monographs in development studies no. 3, 1979).

5 Agricultural economists in Tamil Nadu have taken a keen interest in extending the form of organization of production represented by the sugar factory to other crops, even paddy.

6 See especially Farmer, *Green Revolution*.

Index